Chinese Syntax in a Cross-Linguistic Perspective

OXFORD STUDIES IN COMPARATIVE SYNTAX
Richard Kayne, General Editor

Chinese Syntax in a Cross-Linguistic Perspective

EDITED BY AUDREY LI

ANDREW SIMPSON

and

WEI-TIEN DYLAN TSAI

OXFORD
UNIVERSITY PRESS

OXFORD
UNIVERSITY PRESS

Oxford University Press is a department of the University of Oxford.
It furthers the University's objective of excellence in research, scholarship,
and education by publishing worldwide.

Oxford New York
Auckland Cape Town Dar es Salaam Hong Kong Karachi
Kuala Lumpur Madrid Melbourne Mexico City Nairobi
New Delhi Shanghai Taipei Toronto

With offices in
Argentina Austria Brazil Chile Czech Republic France Greece
Guatemala Hungary Italy Japan Poland Portugal Singapore
South Korea Switzerland Thailand Turkey Ukraine Vietnam

Oxford is a registered trade mark of Oxford University Press
in the UK and certain other countries.

Published in the United States of America by
Oxford University Press
198 Madison Avenue, New York, NY 10016

Library of Congress Cataloging-in-Publication Data
Chinese Syntax in a Cross-linguistic Perspective / edited by Audrey Li,
  Andrew Simpson, and Wei-Tien Dylan Tsai.
    p. cm.
  Summary: "Chinese Syntax in a Cross-linguistic Perspective collects twelve new papers
  that explore the syntax of Chinese in comparison with other languages"— Provided by publisher.
  Includes bibliographical references and index.
  ISBN 978–0–19–994567–2 (paperback) — ISBN 978–0–19–994565–8 (hardcover) —
  ISBN (invalid) 978–0–19–994566–5 (ebook) 1. Chinese language—Syntax.
2. Chinese language—Grammar, Comparative. 3. Chinese language—Comparison.
4. Chinese language—Foreign elements. 5. Chinese language—Influence on foreign languages.
6. Comparative linguistics. I. Li, Yen-hui Audrey, 1954– editor. II. Simpson, Andrew, 1962– editor.
III. Tsai, Wei-Tien Dylan, 1964– editor.
  PL1241.C4858 2014
  495.15—dc23
                    2014018513

Essays in honor of Professor C.-T. James Huang

Contents

Preface

Chinese linguistics is a field that is well established and growing significantly through-out Asia, North America, and Europe, as interest in China and the Chinese language continues to develop at a fast rate. While there are very many research papers and books that regularly analyze Chinese in isolation, there is much less published research on the cross-linguistic comparison of Chinese with other languages, showing how the analysis of Chinese can inform our understanding of syntactic phenomena in other languages, and how insights gained in the study of other languages can in turn shed interesting new light on patterns in Chinese. This multi-authored, new volume, *Chinese Syntax in a Cross-Linguistic Perspective,* attempts to broaden this line of comparative inquiry, con-necting studies of Chinese with work currently being carried out on other languages. The sixteen chapters all make significant contributions to analyses of aspects of the syntax of Chinese in direct comparison with that of non-Sinitic languages. Each chap-ter in the volume compares a specific major phenomenon in Chinese syntax with at least one other language, in many cases with other languages of Asia, but also with those of Europe, North America, and Africa. The volume presents fresh perspectives on major syntactic issues in Chinese and what the study of Chinese can offer linguists working on other, genetically unrelated languages.

The volume also serves as a Festschrift dedicated to commemorating the work of Professor James Huang of Harvard University as he reaches the age of 65. For over three decades, Jim Huang has been the most influential of generative linguists active in the study of Chinese, consistently demonstrating how aspects of the structure of Chi-nese reveal broader properties of Universal Grammar. Since his seminal MIT disserta-tion in 1982, his works have inspired countless linguists working in the field of Chinese linguistics and generative grammar, and it is safe to say that without his pioneering re-search first paving the way and then leading the development of the study of Chinese theoretical syntax, such a field would not exist in the rich way we presently know it. Jim Huang's major role in the growth of generative Chinese linguistics has been continually present not only in the form of concrete research and influential publications, but also in more intangible contributions to the field, which are equally enduring. His genuine compassion, strong support, and kind, generous encouragement to everyone seeking his advice have cultivated generations of dedicated linguists passionate about generative linguistic research. When the editors solicited the help of some of the most well-known linguists working in the field of Chinese syntax to create this special volume, along with

several other prominent linguists whose work also connects to Chinese, it was consequently not surprising that the response was overwhelmingly positive and enthusiastic.
The resulting list of contributors to the volume represents scholars from across different
regions and fields, and is an impressive testimony to the great appreciation broadly felt
for such a trail-blazing giant.

Jim has impacted linguistic research in important ways since the 1980s, and he is
still producing highly influential works. His latest significant work, *Syntactic Analyticity
and Parametric Theory*, has already generated great excitement in the field and extensive
reference to the work, even when circulated as an unpublished manuscript. The editors
thought that it would be most fitting for the present volume to be headlined by this
bold and provocative new work, as a way to highlight Jim's continuing productivity and
enduring influence. As Jim has never refused to help anyone asking him for a favor, he
kindly consented to the request from the editors to include this work in the volume, to
the great delight of all the other contributors.

The volume opens with Jim's most recent work, followed by 15 additional chapters.
These are divided into three thematic sections, on (a) the Nominal domain, (b) the
Predicate domain, and (c) the C-domain. In addition to chapters on synchronic, adult
syntax, the volume also includes a chapter on Chinese diachronic syntax in a comparative perspective, and one on the acquisition of syntax in Chinese, in comparison with
that of other languages. We believe that the collection is an interesting cross-section
of work currently being carried out on the syntax of Chinese in a cross-linguistic perspective and offers up a very grateful tribute to Jim's lifelong, tremendously productive
engagement in the field.

Contributors

MICHAEL BARRIE Department of English, Sogang University

LISA LAI-SHEN CHENG Department of Linguistics, Leiden University

GENNARO CHIERCHIA Department of Linguistics, Harvard University

FRANCESCA DEL GOBBO Department of Linguistics, University of California, Irvine

SHENGLI FENG Department of Chinese Language and Literature, Chinese University of Hong Kong

YANG GU Department of Linguistics and Modern Languages, Chinese University of Hong Kong

JIE GUO National Research Centre for Foreign Language Education, Beijing Foreign Studies University

C.-T. JAMES HUANG Department of Linguistics, Harvard University

L. JULIE JIANG Department of East Asian Languages and Literatures, University of Hawaii

AUDREY LI Department of Linguistics and East Asian Languages and Cultures, University of Southern California

WEI-WEN ROGER LIAO Academia Sinica, Taipei, Taiwan

JO-WANG LIN Department of Foreign Languages and Literatures, National Chiao Tung University, Tsinchu, Taiwan

KEIKO MURASUGI Department of British and American Studies, Nanzan University

MASAO OCHI Graduate School of Language and Culture, Osaka University

MAMORU SAITO Department of Anthropology and Philosophy, Nanzan University

ANDREW SIMPSON Department of Linguistics, University of Southern California

RINT SYBESMA Department of Chinese Studies, Leiden University

SZE-WING TANG Department of Chinese Language and Literature, Institute of Chinese Studies, The Chinese University of Hong Kong

WEI-TIEN DYLAN TSAI Graduate Institute of Linguistics, National Tsing Hua University

YUYUN IRIS WANG Department of East Asian Languages and Cultures, University of Southern California

ALEXANDER WILLIAMS Department of Linguistics, University of Maryland

Chinese Syntax in a Cross-Linguistic Perspective

1

On Syntactic Analyticity and Parametric Theory

C.-T. JAMES HUANG

1. Introduction

Modern linguistic theory considers language a product of nature and nurture: the particular grammar of any individual is a 'linguistic phenotype' that has grown from a 'linguistic genotype' with the nurture of after-birth experience. In the Principles and Parameters (P&P) framework of generative grammar, the linguistic genotype—termed Universal Grammar (UG)—consists of a finite set of principles and a limited number of open parameters whose values are yet to be set by the nurturing effect of the child's primary linguistic data (PLD). Thus each attained grammar (say, G_E and G_C for English and Chinese) is a linguistic phenotype that results when all the parameters have been set in conformity with the PLD. Language variation is thus a function of parametric variation. Nature enables the growth of grammar, at the same time setting the limits of variation.

Studies of language variation, both from the generative tradition and from earlier descriptive approaches, have shown that languages do not vary at random, but within bounds and in patterns. Edward Sapir (1921: 120–121) wrote almost a century ago:

> [I]t must be obvious to anyone . . . that there is such a thing as a basic plan, a certain cut, to each language. This type or plan or structural "genius" of the language is something much more fundamental, much more pervasive, than any single feature of it that we can mention. . . . All languages differ from one another but certain ones differ far more than others. This is tantamount to saying that it is possible to group them into morphological types.

The fact that languages differ in ways that allow them to be classified into one type or another is the basis of much research on linguistic typology. As an early example, Sapir proposed classifying languages as analytic, synthetic, or polysynthetic (1921: 127–128):

> An analytic language is one that either does not combine concepts into single words at all (Chinese) or does so economically (English, French). . . .

In a synthetic language (Latin, Arabic, Finnish) the concepts cluster more thickly, the words are more richly chambered, . . . The three terms are purely quantitative—and relative, that is, a language may be 'analytic' from one standpoint, 'synthetic' from another, ...

Greenberg's (1963) seminal work capitalized on the fact that languages typically exhibit *correlating* differences, and it has inspired numerous important other studies in linguistic typology. Many or most of his findings have been offered as descriptive generalizations that obtain "overwhelmingly beyond chance frequency." Together, the aggregation of correlating differences enables one to talk about languages types.

In generative grammar, much work has sought to derive (and explain) similar generalizations within parametric theory under the P&P framework. Differently from the descriptive approaches, the parametric approach seeks to derive the correlating differences as consequences of setting a parameter to a certain value, rather than listing the correlations as observed. For example, it has been well known since Greenberg's work that while VO languages use prepositional phrases, OV languages employ postpositional phrases, in the overwhelming majority of cases. Within P&P, an early Head Directionality parameter (of X-bar theory) was proposed (Stowell 1981, Huang 1982, etc.) that provides for an open choice of head-initial or head-final for an XP, to be determined by the PLD. The correlation between verb-object order and the preposition-postposition choice *follows* from a general application of the head parameter, as a default consequence of setting the parameter as head-final or head-initial, respectively. The widely discussed Pro Drop parameter was formulated, in the work of Rizzi (1982), to derive a cluster of cross-linguistic differences (null subject, free inversion, and long subject-extraction) otherwise thought to be completely independent and unrelated. Another early parameter—concerning word order, (non-) configurationality, radical pronoun drop, etc.—was proposed by Hale (1983) and developed in Jelinek (1984), and found its way into parts of Baker's (1996) Polysynthesis Parameter, which characterizes a range of language types depending on the extent to which arguments are directly linked to verbal morphology. Still another early example was Huang's (1982) *Wh*-movement Parameter, which distinguishes *wh*-in-situ languages from *wh*-movement languages by 'derivational timing': movement takes place either overtly (in Syntax) or covertly (in Logical Form, LF), and was shown to derive a number of similarities and differences with respect to certain grammatical constraints among different language types.

These parameters are 'macro-parameters' in the sense that they derive large-scale clusters of cross-linguistic differences, greatly reducing the number of possible choices available to the child acquiring a language. More recent research, however, has shifted considerable attention to research on micro-variations and 'micro-parameters,' following the suggestion of Borer (1984) and Chomsky (1995) that all parameters should be attributed to, and stated in terms of, variations in the nature of relevant lexical items and functional heads. This restriction in the expressive power of parametric theory is motivated by considerations of empirical adequacy and theoretical parsimony, the latter ever more important for current works in the Minimalist Program (Chomsky 2005, et seq.). One area where the traditional macro-parameters have proven empirically inadequate is their inability to make finer distinctions among languages or to accommodate certain counterexamples observed in less 'well-behaved' languages. As a famous simple case in point, both English and French are verb-initial (and prepositional), but a head-initial setting of the Head Parameter does not account for the fact that while the finite verb precedes negation and certain adverbs in French, it must follow them in English. Following the insights of Pollock (1989) and Emonds (1978) Chomsky (1991) [1995 Chapter 2] attributes the variation to a micro-parameter in the derivational timing of V-to-T movement, based on the nature of the tense (or agreement) element T, informally put as follows: In French, the T element is of such a nature that it triggers overt V-to-T movement, whereas in English, T is of such a nature that V-to-T movement is delayed until LF.

The rise of micro-parametric theory raises the question about the status of macro-parameters and the usefulness of macro-parametric research, an important topic of discussion on the current scene, involving several important contenders (Kayne 2005–2013; Gianollo et al. 2008; Baker 2008; Holmberg 2010; and Roberts and Holmberg 2010, among others). An important issue is whether micro-parameters are able to capture the significant, sometimes large-scale, correlations of parametric differences among languages that the macro-parameters were designed to capture. While some micro-parameters may derive correlating properties, others may have very little effect beyond the original facts that motivate their postulation. Though the jury is still out, it is fair to say that while most (or even all) actual variations may be characterized as micro-variations, there also exist large-scale macro-parametric patterns of variation that must be captured somehow.

The goal of this chapter is threefold. First, on a descriptive level, I will review a fairly large number of distinguishing properties of Chinese syntax, with special focus on Modern Mandarin (as compared to English), Old Chinese (as compared to Modern Mandarin), and some Modern Chinese dialects (in mutual comparison). It will be shown that these properties cluster—in that they either jointly occur in one language or are jointly absent in another, in a way that bears witness to the fact that languages differ in ways that allow them to remain in 'a certain cut.' These properties jointly place the varieties of Chinese on a continuum of relative analyticity in the sense of Sapir (1921): Modern Mandarin as a highly analytic language, Old Chinese as a language of significant synthesis, and the modern dialects as representing varying stages of development toward mild synthesis. Some of these contrasting properties have been observed in the literature in isolation or as independent contrasting properties, but their clustering in each language under discussion, once pointed out, provides a clear case for the existence of macro-parameters—of a 'mega-parameter,' in fact. Second, I will show that, in spite of their clustering, the contrasting properties in one language as opposed to another can each be accounted for as a point of micro-variation, attributed to the nature of a particular triggering or non-triggering head, following some version of Minimalist syntactic theory—for example, the Probe-Goal system of Chomsky (2000, et seq.). It will be seen that while some contrasting properties of Modern Chinese readily lend themselves to description in terms of high analyticity, some other properties heretofore described in other terms can be reduced to the same property as well, thus dispensing with some of the macro-parameters proposed in the earlier literature. Third, it will also be shown that the parametric approach to synchronic variation is readily applicable to diachronic change (as amply demonstrated by such works as Roberts and Roussou 2003, and Roberts 2007), and that the Probe-Goal system, with the notion of relative 'strengths' of triggering heads, offers an interesting link to insights from much research on grammaticalization. These points will be laid out in the following sections, and will be summarized in the conclusion.

2. Analyticity of Modern Chinese Syntax

We start by reviewing some salient typological properties of the major lexical categories in Modern Mandarin.

2.1. VERBS AND VERB PHRASES

One prominent feature of Chinese grammar that has attracted considerable attention in recent studies is its extensive use of light verbs (see T.-H. J. Lin 2001, 2014 for extensive discussions). Compare the examples in English and Chinese in (1–2):

(1) a. John telephoned.

 b. John telephoned his sister.

(2) a. Zhangsan **da**-le   dianhua.
 Zhangsan hit-Perf telephone

 b. Zhangsan **da**-le   dianhua   gei meimei.
 Zhangsan hit-Perf telephone to sister

 c. *Zhangsan dianhua-le.
 Zhangsan telephone-Perf

 d. *Zhangsan dianhua-le   meimei.
 Zhangsan telephone-Perf sister

While in English the noun *telephone* may be denominalized and used as a verb, its counterpart *dianhua* in Chinese cannot. For the verbal usage, the noun occurs as an object of a light verb, *da* (literally 'hit,' but with only the elementary semantics of 'do'). Similarly, while the following nouns may be used directly as verbs in English: *fish, sneeze, snore, yawn,* etc., in Chinese a light verb in the form of *da* is required:

(3) *da yu* 'to fish'; *da penti* 'to sneeze'; *da hu* 'to snore'; *da haqian* 'to yawn'; *da you* 'to get oil'; *da shui* 'to fetch water'; *da deng* 'to use a lamp'; *da maoxian* 'to knit (do the yarn)'; *da majiang* 'to do (play) mahjong'; *da zi* 'to type (do the characters)'; *da lie* 'to go hunting'.

These examples illustrate Chinese as a language of high analyticity, in the traditional typological scheme that dates back to Sapir (1921). In comparison with Modern Chinese, English is relatively synthetic. And Old Chinese (OC) bears more resemblance to English in this respect. In spite of its nonexistence in any OC corpus, the following sentence would be considered grammatical by anyone with some proficiency in Classical Chinese:

(4) Wu Wang dian   Yue Wang, yue...
     Wu King phone Yue King, saying
     'King Wu telephoned (or telegrammed) King Yue, saying that....'

Actual examples include *yu* 'fish, to fish,' *shi* 'food, to eat (cf. feed),' *fan* 'rice, to eat rice,' and many more (see below for more details). At the other extreme are polysynthetic languages like Inuktitut and Mohawk:

(5) Inuktitut:
     tavvakiqutiqarpiit
     'Do you have any tobacco for sale?'

(6) Mohawk (from Baker 1996)
     Washakoty'tawitsherahetkvhta'se'.
     'He made the thing that one puts on one's body ugly for her.'

while other languages would be situated at various intermediate positions in the continuum:

(7) Isolating··· Analytic...................... Synthetic ... Polysynthetic
     Modern Chinese ... English ... Italian / Romance...... Inuktitut /
                       Old Chinese   Mohawk

In addition to the light verb construction, Chinese abounds in the use of what has come to be known as the 'pseudo noun incorporation' (PNI) construction (after Massam 2001).[1] The PNI refers to the use of verb-object *phrases* denoting actions that are otherwise expressed by simplex verbs in a more synthetic language. In one variety, such examples seem to spell out the typical (or 'cognate') verb of a noun:

(8) *bu yu* catch-fish 'to fish'; *zhuo yu* catch-fish 'to fish'; *bo pi* remove-skin 'to peel';
     zuo meng make-dream 'to dream'; *kai wanxiao* make-joke 'to joke'; etc.[2]

---

[1] In other works, this construction has been known as the 'anti-passive' construction. The constructions are said to involve 'pseudo incorporation' (in Massam 2001) because, in spite of their phrasal status, they correspond to simplex denominal or intransitive verbs which are, in the prevalent syntactic literature (Baker 1988; Hale and Keyser 1993 and subsequent works), considered to be derived via noun incorporation in the more synthetic languages (from English to Mohawk). The semantics of a PNI construction exhibits the characteristics of a lexical word or compound, with the object NP being morphologically bare and referentially non-denoting.

[2] That the Chinese expressions are *phrases* rather than words is clearly evidenced by the position of the aspectual suffix *–le* and intervening adverbial expressions:

(i)   ta   zhuo-le   san   tian yu.
      s/he catch-Perf three day fish
      'He/she fished for 3 days.'

(ii) ta   nian-le   liangge zhongtou (de) shu
      s/he read-Perf two   hours   (of) book
      'He/she read for two hours.'

That is, incorporation in English results in a lexical category, while pseudo-incorporation or the use of a light verb results in a phrasal category.

In another variety, a PNI construction spells out the typical (or cognate) object of a verb:

(9)   *chi fan* eat-rice 'to eat'; *he jiu* drink-wine 'to drink'; *kan shu* read-books 'to read'; *chang ge* sing-song 'to sing'; *tiao wu* jump-dance 'to dance'; etc.

In both cases, what is important is that while English regularly employs simplex de-nominal or intransitivized verbs, Chinese must resort to the phrasal strategy of a verb-object phrase, or PNI.

Another property that sets Chinese apart from English concerns the phenomenon of 'coercion' (Pustejovsky 1995), illustrated by the grammaticality of (10a) with an intended meaning of (10b) or (10c).

(10)   a.   John began a book.

b.   John began reading/writing/editing a book.

c.   John began to read/write/edit a book.

As pointed out by Lin and Liu (2005), this type of 'coercion' does not occur in Chinese:

(11)   a.   *Zhangsan kaishi yi-ben shu.
Zhangsan begin one-Cl book

b.   Zhangsan kaishi kan/xie/bian   yi-ben shu.
Zhangsan begin read/write/edit one-Cl book
'Zhangsan began to read/write/edit a book.'

The verb *begin* appears to be able to 'eat up' (i.e., synthesizes with) a prototypical complement of the verb in English, but its Chinese counterpart *kaishi* does not have this property.

We find a parallel contrast in the expression of causative events or accomplishments as well. English abounds in simplex predicates that express completed events or accomplishments, whereas Chinese typically resorts to complex expressions such as (a) verb-result compounds, (b) resultative phrases, or (c) periphrastic caus-ative constructions.Chinese simplex verbs are typically not accomplishments. The following three-way contrast among Modern Chinese, English, and Italian exem-plifies the continuum indicated in (7): whereas English readily admits the synthetic 'enter, exit' and the analytic 'come in, go out,' Chinese requires the analytic strategy and Italian strongly favors the synthetic strategy:

(12)   English   Modern Chinese   Italian
enter, come in   jin lai 'come in', *ru   entrare, ??venire dentro
exit, go out   chu-qu 'go out', *chu   uscire, ??andare fuori

Similarly, while English has many verbs that exhibit the unaccusative-causative al-ternation, in Chinese the corresponding simplex verbs are typically unaccusative. A causative reading would require compounding with a light verb or an appropriate action verb, as in (14c–d), respectively.

(13) a. The window broke.

 b. John broke the window.

(14) a. chuangzi po-le.
       window break-Perf
       'The window broke.'

 b. *Zhangsan po-le   chuangzi.
      Zhangsan break-Perf window

 c. Zhangsan da-po/nong-po/gao-po-le   chuangzi.
      Zhangsan hit-break/make-break/make-break-Perf window
      'Zhangsan broke the window.'

 d. Zhangsan ti-po/tui-po/ya-po/qiao-po-le   chuangzi.
      Zhangsan kick-break/push-break/crush-break/knock-break-Perf window
      'Zhangsan kicked/pushed/crushed/knocked the window broken.'

Furthermore, while action verbs in English may often describe accomplishments and telic (bounded) events, Chinese action verbs are purely activity-denoting and atelic. A famous contrast was pointed out by Tai (1984) between English *kill* and Chinese *sha*. The latter, often inaccurately translated as 'kill,' actually does not strongly imply death, hence (16) is not contradictory as (15) is.

(15) #John killed Bill several times, but Bill did not die.

(16) Zhangsan sha-le   Lisi haoji ci,   dan Lisi dou mei si.
      Zhangsan kill-Perf Lisi several time, but Lisi all not die.

Another contrast obtains with 'incremental theme' verbs (Dowty 1979) like *write* and *eat*. Specifically, with a definite object, *write* has a telic reading (hence compatible with a phrase like 'in 30 minutes'), while its Chinese counterpart *xie* does not. A telic reading for *xie* would require compounding with a result-denoting state (as in (19)):

(17) John wrote the letter in 30 minutes.

(18) *Zhangsan zai 30 fenzhong nei, jiu xie-le   nei-feng xin.
       Zhangsan at 30 minute   in   then write-Perf that-Cl letter

(19) Zhangsan zai 30 fenzhong nei, jiu xie-wan-le   nei-feng xin.
      Zhangsan at 30 minute   in   then write-finish-Perf that-Cl letter
      'Zhangsan finished writing the letter in 30 minutes.'

In other words, while English action verbs may be telic or atelic, Chinese action verbs are atelic by themselves, though they may be telicized by means of compounding or phrasal combination.[3] More generally, of Vendler's (1967) verb types, Chinese has the three elementary types only—state, achievement, and activity—but not accomplishment.

---

[3] The verb *xie* 'write' can be telicized with a quantified object:

(i) ta 30 fenzhong nei, jiu xie-le   wu-feng xin.
     he 30 minute   in, then write-le 5-Cl   letter
     'He wrote 5 letters in 30 minutes.'

We have now seen that Chinese verbs exhibit a high degree of simplicity or 'purity' in several ways, with the following prominent properties:

(20) a. the light verb construction

  b. pseudo noun incorporation

  c. compounds or phrasal accomplishments

  d. verbal atelicity, and

  e. absence of verbal coercion

That these properties all *cluster* within the same language is worth noting, indicating that they represent special cases of a more general character of the language. Indeed, it would be completely surprising if Chinese were, say, rich in light verbs but poor in pseudo noun incorporation, or rich in both light verbs and verbal coercion.

2.2. NOUNS AND OTHER CATEGORIES

It is significant that the same high degree of analyticity is fully observed in the nominal domain as well. This is manifested in at least two major ways, in the requirement of (a) a classifier in the context of a numeral quantifier, and (b) a localizer in the context of location-denoting DP. Consider first the classifier requirement:

(21) *yi ben shu* 'one Cl book'; *liang zhi bi* 'two Cl pen'; *wu pi ma* 'five Cl horse'; *ershi-wu ge xuesheng* '25 Cl student'; etc.

At an elementary level we can see that what is expressed by a single count noun *book* in English is expressed in Chinese by a phrasal sequence of *ben + book*. This situation is not unlike the contrast between English simple verbs like *phone* and the corresponding light-verb constructions in Chinese. Hence the classifier *ben* may be termed a 'light noun' in the same sense that *da* is a light verb. The parallel is further exhibited by the selectional restriction between a light noun or verb and its complement. Thus, for example, *ben* selects *shu* 'book' but not *xuesheng* 'student.' Similarly, light verbs with the elementary semantics of DO, CAUSE, and BECOME, etc., differ on the types of complement root VPs they select.[4]

The classifier requirement on a noun in Chinese has another parallel in the verbal domain. It has been suggested (Krifka 1987; Chierchia 1998) that nouns in general have only elementary denotations, that is, they denote kinds but not individuals (or units of matters).[5] To denote individual units or members and be counted, they each need to be individuated (or atomized) with the help of a classifier. This is not unlike

---

[4] As early as his (1948), Y.-R. Chao already referred to classifiers as 'auxiliary nouns.' One might as well consider the light verbs as auxiliary verbs (in the sense that they take VP complements). Tang (1990) was the first to argue that classifiers should head a noun phrase within Abney's DP system. In particular, in parallel to the CP-TP-VP layers on the 'clausal spine,' we have DP-ClP-NP in the 'nominal spine.' These assumptions about nominal (and clausal) structures are much in the spirit of these earlier works.

[5] Krifka (1995) specifically proposes that all Chinese nouns denote kinds as their elementary meanings. The requirement of an individual classifier is often likened to the obligatory use of a measure word in association with a mass noun, e.g., *a *(cup of) water*, and so all Chinese nouns are likened to mass nouns in their extensions (Chierchia 1998), which leads to the prediction that

the fact that Chinese action verbs, as noted above, are atelic and do not denote accomplishments. To be telic, such verbs as *chi* 'eat' require quantified objects (such as 'three apples,' as in note 3 above) or must be complemented by a result (as in *chi-wan* 'eat-finish'). Thus, atelic verbs are a kind of 'mass verbs,' just as mass nouns might as well be termed a kind of 'atelic nouns.'

Now consider the requirement of a localizer, as when a DP occurs with a location-selecting verb or preposition. Whereas English *arrive at, go to, come from,* and others directly take DPs as their objects, the corresponding objects in Chinese require the presence of localizers like *bian* 'side,' *nar* 'there,' *li* 'inside,' *shang* 'top':

(22) a. They went to John.

 b. This idea came from John.

 c. Bill stood at the table.

(23) a. tamen qu-le   Zhangsan-*(nali).
    they   went-to Zhangsan-there

 b. zhe-ge zhuyi shi cong Zhangsan-*(nar) lai   de.
    this-Cl idea   be from Zhangsan-there come Prt

 c. Lisi zhan   zai zhuozi-*(pang/shang/xia/hou/qian).
    Lisi stand at table-side/top/under/back/front

Again we may think of localizers as a kind of 'light nouns,' whose presence enables noun phrases to denote locations, much as classifiers enable noun phrases to denote individual atoms of a kind.

We have seen that in both the verbal and nominal domains, Modern Chinese exhibits a consistent pattern of high analyticity over a range of related constructions. Similar observations may be made of other lexical categories as well, such as prepositions and adjectives. By comparison with certain English prepositions, such as *beside, above, in,* etc., Chinese employs a discontinuous (hence analytic) strategy with a pure preposition *zai* 'at,' followed by a corresponding localizer or location noun: *zai . . . pang,* 'at X's side' *zai . . . shang* 'at XP's top,' and the like. As for adjectives, it has been suggested that a gradable adjective in English includes an implicit degree morpheme, *pos,* that turns the adjective into a degree-denoting predicate (Kennedy 2007), while the marker *hen* in Mandarin is the overt realization of that morpheme, or an aspectual marker for a gradable adjective (Dong 2005)—hence an auxiliary, or light adjective. Thus, in addition to the list in (20), we have:

(24) a. numeral classifier for count nouns

 b. localizer for locational nouns

 c. discontinuous prepositions

 d. overt positive degree marker

numeral classifier languages cannot have plural markings. This further assimilation of all nouns to mass nouns has turned out to be controversial (Cheng and Sybesma 1999; Kim 2011; among many others). The real generalization may simply be that Chinese count nouns are number-neutral, whereas English bare count nouns denote singular atoms. Mass nouns universally, on the other hand, are number-irrelevant since they denote entities that are cumulative and homogeneous, unless atomized with appropriate measure words.

It is useful to note that, while these distinguishing properties of Chinese are well known, they have, in the main, been mentioned as if they are independent, unrelated features of the language. Given the above discussion, it should not be surprising that these properties should jointly occur, also together with those in (20) in Chinese, but are jointly absent in English. The clustering of these properties makes it clear that Modern Chinese is consistently more analytic than English, with respect to the structure of every lexical category.[6]

3. Capturing Analyticity Syntactically

How do we capture the range of properties that systematically distinguish Chinese from a (relatively) more synthetic language? Within the classical P&P framework, we might simply propose a 'analytic-synthetic' parameter, so that Chinese is [+analytic], and another language may be [-analytic]. Such an approach, however, would be at odds with the requirements of a more restricted, hence more explanatory theory of linguistic variation, and is not acceptable in most current versions of parametric theory. In line with recent thinking and consistent with the Lexical Parameterization Hypothesis of Borer (1984) and Chomsky (1995), I assume that the parametric differences may be attributed to the nature of a number of semi-lexical, light categories that are part of the makeup of full lexical items. Along the general spirit of a checking-theoretic framework (e.g., the 'Probe-Goal system' of Chomsky 2000, 2001), let's assume that grammatical operations are driven by the need to license, or remedy, certain 'imperfections' that have appeared on such defective items. A defective category may contain formal grammatical features F that are not fully interpretable (semantically or phonetically) and therefore require licensing in some way by other items. An F feature may be 'strong' (or affixal) or 'weak.' A [+strong] feature F marks a strongly defective head that requires licensing by overt head movement (Move), while a [-strong] feature may be licensed simply under an appropriate matching configuration (Agree), or allow the movement to 'procrastinate' until LF, where it takes place covertly (as in Chomsky 1991). In addition, a defective head may (or may not) contain the feature [+EPP], requiring an appropriate phrase XP to move to its Spec position. Languages may differ as to whether certain lexical items have acquired such features of imperfection, and if so, whether the features are [+strong], [+EPP], or not.

There is some intuitive appeal to the idea that grammatical operations are driven by the presence of defective elements. Borrowing (and adapting) an analogy from J. Uriagereka (1998) and Lasnik (2003), we may say that a lexical item becomes defective when it is infected with a virus. If the situation is serious (e.g., +strong, or +EPP),

---

[6] Not all languages exhibit consistent analyticity or synthesis across all categories. For example, while many other analytic languages of Asia have both light verbs and classifiers, many analytic languages of Africa (Ewe, Yoruba, etc.) make heavy use of light verbs and pseudo-incorporation, but not of classifiers of the kind familiar from Chinese. As has been noted by Sapir, analyticity is quantitative and relative, but not absolute. In this case, Chinese is 'better behaved' than Yoruba in cross-categorial analyticity, much as Japanese is better behaved than German with respect to cross-categorial head-finalness.

remedy is immediately needed on site (head-movement) or in the immediate neighborhood (movement to Spec), to cure the relevant ailments. If the situation is not as serious, then remedy may be given at a distance (Agree) or delayed until LF (covert movement). The system seems to go well in capturing certain insights from research on grammaticalization, as Roberts and Roussou (2003) and Roberts (2007) have shown.

Turning to the English-Chinese contrasts at hand, let's assume the theory of lexical decomposition as in Hale and Keyser (1993, 2002) and much other work,[7] where a simplex verb like *phone* (or *fish, sneeze,* etc.) in English has the complex structure in (25a) with a light verb that has the elementary semantics of 'do' but is phonetically null, and is derived by noun incorporation, as depicted in (25b):

(25) a.

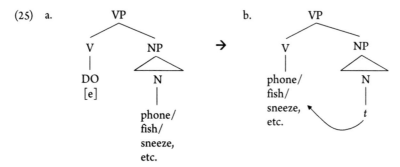

Adopting the 'Probe-Goal' checking system, the strongly affixal DO needs to be licensed. As such, it probes its search domain and identifies a lexical noun like *phone, fish, sneeze,* etc., as its goal, incorporating it to the position under V, thus forming a verb by noun-incorporation.

The corresponding expressions in Chinese would each have a similar underlying structure, except that the light verb is phonetically non-null, thus blocking noun incorporation. In particular, the light verb is phonetically independent, thus at least not an affix, and not [+strong] in the relevant sense. Therefore it does not trigger movement of the nouns *dianhua, yu,* or *penti.* It is reasonable to consider the light verb *da* a defective lexical category, hence formal (and 'uninterpretable' in some extended sense), as it has lost its original lexical meaning of 'hit.' However, since it is not an affix, it at most triggers Agree, but not Move.

(26) a.

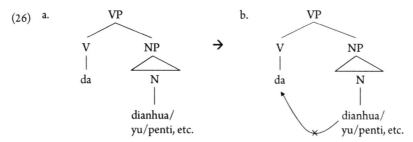

[7] The theory of lexical decomposition has its early origin in McCawley (1968), and was revived in Baker (1988), Larson (1988), and Huang (1988). It is widely adopted today in various versions of syntactic theory. Much of the syntax reflects the semantic insights of Davidson (1967), revived in Dowty (1979), Parsons (1990), and more recent semantic works.

Movement under noun incorporation thus gives rise to some degree of syntheticity in English, whereas non-movement (or covert movement) retains full analyticity for Chinese.

As an alternative to the overt light verb *da*, Chinese may employ a proto-typical (or cognate) verb like *bu* or *zhuo* 'catch' (for object *yu* 'fish') or *chi* 'eat' (for object *fan* 'rice'), and so on. The result is a pseudo-incorporation construction. Again, as in fact proposed by Baker (2011), one may assume that pseudo-incorporation does involve true incorporation, but only covertly.

The contrast between English and Chinese with respect to causative accomplishments may be characterized in a similar way. Each causative accomplishment is underlyingly a complex structure headed by a causative light verb. The English causative light verb CAUSE, being phonetically null and a [+strong] affix, triggers verb movement, resulting in a synthetic causative verb:

(27)   [$_{VP}$ CAUSE [$_{VP}$ (the window) break ...]]   →   break (the window)

The Chinese instantiation of CAUSE is an overt light verb like *da*, *nong*, or *gao*, which blocks verb movement and results in compounding as in (14c). As an alternative to the light verb, an appropriate action verb like *ti* 'kick,' *tui* 'push,' *ya* 'press,' and *qiao* 'knock' may be used, as in (14d), and this accounts for the widespread occurrence of resultative verb compounds.

The other contrasting properties observed above can be accounted for in similar ways. With respect to the nominal domain, for example, we may assume that, in all languages, count nouns are derived from a structure with an individuating functional head (see Borer 2005). In English, the divider head is phonetically null and triggers movement, as in (28), while in Chinese we have an overt individuating head in the form of an overt classifier, which blocks movement:

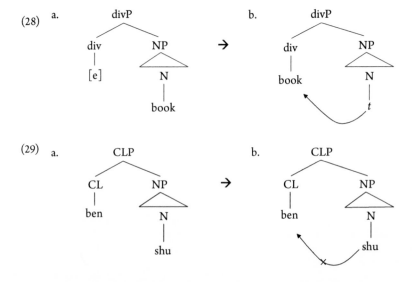

In the same way, we may assume that a location-denoting DP is embedded under a Localizer Phrase, whose head is filled by the null category PLACE (or SIDE, FRONT, etc.) that triggers movement in English, but by an overt localizer like *limian, pangbian, qian,* etc., in Chinese (Kayne 2005 et seq.; Huang 2010).

In each of these cases, we see that head movement results in synthesis, whereas non-movement preserves lexical analyticity. The latter makes Chinese a 'Davidsonian language par excellence' in the sense that it fully spells out each component of a decomposed predicate, as assumed in much work on the semantics of events.

4. Analyticity in Functional Syntax

There are many other properties of Chinese syntax that can now be seen as special parts of a bigger picture. In this section I claim that a number of such properties can be attributed to the analytic properties of clausal functional categories—in the region of T and C.

The first concerns *wh*-questions: in English *wh*-phrases move to Spec of CP, but in Chinese they stay in situ. Movement brings a *wh*-phrase to (the Spec of) a relevant interrogative C category, while non-movement keeps the two items apart. Thus the in-situ versus movement contrast is simply another instance of the analytic-synthetic difference:

(30) $[_{CP} C_{[+Q]} [_{TP}$ he bought what$]]$ (movement: synthetic)

(31) $[_{CP} [_{IP}$ ta mai-le shenme$] C_{[+Q]}]$ (in situ: analytic)
            he bought what

Cheng (1991) argues plausibly that the in-situ strategy in Chinese is related to the existence of an overt question particle (such as *ne*) in the position of Q. While the null C in English is [+strong] and triggers auxiliary inversion (*What did you buy*), the (sometimes lexical) C in Chinese is non-suffixal, thus [-strong] and does not trigger movement to C. As for phrasal movement of the *wh*-phrases, this is due to the [EPP] feature. A functional head F^0 is [+EPP] if it is of such nature as to require its Spec position to be filled by a certain XP in its domain. In English, C with [+EPP] requires its Spec to be filled by a *wh*-phrase, hence triggering overt *wh*-movement; in Chinese, the [-strong] C is [-EPP], hence keeping the *wh*-phrase in situ (or delaying the movement to LF, as in Huang 1982).

There is another way to relate the English-Chinese differences to the analytic-synthetic parameter, drawing upon an insight from Tsai (1994). Tsai shows that English *wh*-phrases are lexically complete with their quantificational forces. Thus just as *somewhat, somehow, somewhere, whatever, whoever,* and *wherever* are unambiguous with their quantificational force because they each contain an existential or universal operator (*some-* and *-ever*), so are *who, what, where,* etc., unambiguous (with interrogative force) because, he proposes, these items contain an (invisible) interrogative operator each as part of their *lexical* makeup. Each of these items then is lexically a combination of a noun stem and a quantificational operator. On the other hand, it has been well known that Chinese *wh*-phrases are 'indeterminate' (a term first due to S.-Y. Kuroda) with respect to their quantificational forces: a *wh*-word like *shei* could be interpreted as an existential, universal or interrogative quantifier, depending on the type of external operator that binds it. In particular, a *wh*-phrase is interrogative in Chinese only in the environment of a c-commanding question operator (or the particle *ne*), universal in the environment of *dou*, and existential in a *non-veridical* environment (see Li 1992, 1998; cf. Giannakidou 2002). While an English interrogative phrase is a continuous (hence synthetic) *wh*-phrase by itself, a Chinese interrogative is a discontinuous (hence analytic) phrase of the form *OP* (or *ne*) . . . *wh-phrase*. An English interrogative word is formed in the lexicon, but a Chinese interrogative 'word' is not formed until syntax. This difference, in the derivational timing of a *wh*-word (lexicon vs. syntax), directly gives rise to a difference in the derivational timing of *wh*-movement (overt in syntax vs. covert in LF).[8]

A similar picture obtains with expressions like *who the hell, what the Dickens,* and *why on earth* and their Chinese counterparts. Pesetsky (1987), who dubbed these 'aggressively non-d-linked *wh*-phrases,' observes that (a) they must occur as a single continuous phrase, and (b) they must occur in Spec, CP (even though normal simplex *wh*-phrases may stay in situ in multiple *wh*-questions):

(32)   What the hell are you doing?   Why on earth are you still here?!

(33)   *What are you doing the hell?   *Why are you still here on earth?!

(34)   *Who saw what the hell?   (cf. Who saw what?)

The corresponding expressions in Chinese involve, unsurprisingly, a discontinuous (hence analytic) strategy, with the adverbial *daodi* occurring with an interrogative element in its c-command domain, as first observed by Kuo (1996):[9]

(35)   Zhangsan daodi yao   shenme shihou cai   lai?
        Zhangsan daodi want what   time   then come
        'When the hell will Zhangsan eventually come?'

(36)   Ni daodi mingtian qu-bu-qu?
        you daodi tomorrow go-not-go
        'Do you want to go tomorrow or not?' (Make up your mind, for God's sake!)

Huang and Ochi (2004) offered a unifying analysis for *daodi* in Chinese, *wh-the-hell* in English, and corresponding *ittai* in Japanese. They proposed that questions involving

---

[8] The same can be said of the universal *wh-ever* words (*whoever, whatever, wherever,* etc.), which do move overtly, though not *some-wh* words (*somewhat, somewhere, somehow,* etc.). In this respect, though, we find a parallel situation in Chinese, in that the *wh*-words must occur or move to the left of its licenser *dou* to obtain the universal reading, though the existential *wh*-phrase is simply licensed in situ, in an affective or non-veridical context.

[9] The expression *daodi*, with its literal meaning 'reach-bottom,' conveys an attitude of impatience or annoyance (i.e., let's get to the bottom of the damn question, quick!), much as the *wh-the-hell* expressions in English.

these expressions involve a functional projection in the upper TP region (in the spirit of Cinque 1999) representing speaker attitude, called Attitude Phrase (AttP), which contains the attitudinal adverbial *daodi, the hell, on earth*, etc., c-commanding an interrogative phrase. In English, Att^0 contains a formal feature that is [+strong] and overtly attracts a *wh*-phrase to it, forming a *wh-the-hell* constituent at the Spec, AttP. Subsequent movement triggered by the [+strong] feature of C moves the phrase to Spec, CP. On the other hand, in Chinese (and Japanese), the [-strong] nature of Att^0 requires only an Agree relation, thus the *daodi . . . wh*-phase remains discontinuous—with the movement procrastinated to LF. Again, we can see this difference as another instance of the synthetic-analytic difference.

As for Pesetsky's second observation (i.e., that *what the hell*, etc., may not be left in situ even in a multiple question (34)), Huang and Ochi argued that this follows as a consequence that the *wh*-phrase has the status of an adjunct, having moved to AttP and assembled with *the hell, on earth*, and the like. As already independently observed (Huang 1982), in English multiple questions, adjunct *wh*-phrases cannot stay in situ:[10]

(37) *What did you buy why?   (cf. Why did you buy what?)

(38) *Which car did you fix how?   (cf. How did you fix which car?)

Several other examples of a similar synthetic-analytic contrast find themselves in the existence (or not) of negative quantifiers like *nobody*, the reciprocal NP *each other*, and what Safir and Stowell (1988) dub 'binominal-*each*' constructions. In English such expressions exist as single constituents, along with a discontinuous option:

(39) a. John did not see anybody.

     b. John saw nobody.

(40) a. They each criticized the other(s).

     b. They criticized each other.

(41) a. They each ate three apples.

     b. They ate three apples each.

But in Chinese, only the discontinuous (analytic) forms are acceptable in the corresponding examples.

(42) a. Zhangsan mei you   kanjian renhe ren.
        Zhangsan not have see   any   person
        'Zhangsan has not seen anybody.'

     b. *Zhangsan kanjian-le meiyou ren
        Zhangsan see-Perf   no   person

---

[10] In Huang (1982) and subsequent developments (e.g., Lasnik and Saito 1984, a.o.), the trace of an adjunct created in LF would not be properly governed, in violation of the ECP. Kuo (1996) showed that the distribution and interpretation of *daodi* questions exhibit clear Subjacency, CED (and ECP) effects. Huang and Ochi (2004) argue that this follows from LF movement of the *daodi+wh*-phrase as an adjunct.

(43)   a.   tamen ge   piping-le   duifang.
            they   each criticize-Perf other
            'They each criticized the other(s).'

       b.   *tamen piping-le   bici.
            they   criticize-Perf each-other

(44)   a.   tamen ge   chi-le   san-ge pingguo.
            they   each eat-Perf 3-Cl   apple
            'They each ate three apples.'

       b.   *tamen chi-le   ge   san-ge   pingguo.
            they   eat-Perf each three-Cl apple

It has been argued that, in some languages, negative quantifiers like *nobody* are syntactically derived from a combination of *not + anybody* under adjacency, when the two items are brought together by some syntactic operations. The most interesting case comes from Norwegian (and other Scandinavian languages), in the analysis of Christensen (1986), who observes that the expression *ingen bøker* 'no books' in Norwegian may occur after a finite verb in the main clause, but not in the embedded clause:

(45)   a.   Arne kjøpte ingen bøker
            Arne bought no   books
            'Arne bought no books.'

       b.   *Jon beklager at   Arne kjøpte ingen bøker.
            John regrets   that Arne bought no   books.

Furthermore, in the presence of an auxiliary, *ingen bøker* cannot occur postverbally even in the main clause:

(46)   a.   *Jon har kjøpt   **ingen bøker**.
            Jon has bought no   books
            'Jon has bought no books.'

       b.   Jon har **ikke** kjøpt   **noen bøker**.
            John has not   bought any   books
            'John has not bought any books.'

The ungrammatical examples can be corrected by using a discontinuous strategy of the form *ikke . . . neon bøker* 'not . . . any books' as in (47), or by placing *ingen bøker* before the verb as in (48):

(47)   Arne ikke kjøpte noen bøker.
       Arne not bought any   books
       'Arne did not buy any books.'

(48)   Jon har **ingen bøker** kjøpt.
       John has no   books bought
       'Jon has no books bought.'

Christensen (1986) argues that this state of affairs follows if one assumes that all instances of grammatical *ingen bøker* 'no books' are derived from an underlying *ikke ... neon bøker* string by a local rule that contracts *ikke-neon* 'not any' to *ingen* 'no,' when the two elements occur adjacent to each other. Thus the underlying structure for (45a) has the form of (47), where *ikke* 'not' is separated from *noen bøker* 'any books' by the verb *kjøpte*. Adjacency may be obtained for (47), however, if the main verb *kjøpte* vacates itself by moving to C (by V-T-C movement), thereby enabling the contraction rule to apply. After the subject *Arne* is moved the Spec, CP, the grammatical (45a) is obtained. The '*not-any* → *no*' rule cannot apply if the clause is embedded as in (45b), however. In this case, T-to-C is blocked by the complementizer *at* 'that,' so the verb *kjøpte* continues to intervene between *ikke* and *noen*, blocking contraction. The ungrammaticality of (46a) also follows because, from its underlying structure in (46b), it is the auxiliary *har* that undergoes V-T-C but not the main verb, and so the adjacency requirement is not met. Finally, this situation can be remedied if the object *noen bøker* in (46b) is pre-posed before *kjøpt*, yielding *Jon har ikke noen bøker kjøpt* 'John has not any books bought,' making contraction possible again, with the result shown in (48).

Given the above account, it is easy to see why Chinese does not allow a postverbal expression like *meiyou ren* 'nobody' as in (42b). Since Chinese does not have V-T or T-C movement, a verb cannot vacate itself from between *meiyou* 'not' and *renhe ren* 'anyone' in (42a).[11] Thus, a significant difference between Norwegian and Chinese with respect to postverbal negative quantifiers can be seen as a case of the synthetic-analytic parameter, formally attributable to a difference in the nature of a functional head (+ or – strong) that gives rise to V-second in one language but not the other.

As for English, the distribution of negative quantifiers is quite free. This can be due to the fact that additional movement operations (extended XP movements) are allowed (as in the analysis of Kayne 1998), or one could assume that the type of synthesis (in LF) as permitted in Norwegian has been further reanalyzed in English, so that its products are now available directly from the English lexicon. In this particular aspect then, we can see a ranking of relative syntheticity from English > Norwegian > Chinese on a continuum.

A similar view may apply to the reciprocal and binominal expressions. Assuming Kayne's general approach, (40b) can be derived from something like (40a) by a series of movements: from *each criticized other* to *each other criticized* by pre-posing *other*, and to *criticized each other* by VP (remnant) movement, etc., eventually yielding (40b).[12] The binominal construction can be derived in a minimally different fashion: *each ate three apples* → *three apples each ate* → *ate three apples each*. As for Chinese, given the non-triggering nature of *ge* 'each,' these expressions are not available.

---

[11] A second strategy involving object pre-posing is available, and it can be said that Chinese does have 'nobody' in preverbal positions. (Cf. Huang 2003 for discussion.)

[12] Earlier treatments (e.g., Chomsky 1973, following earlier work by Ray Dougherty) employ *each*-lowering to derive (44b). In the interpretative framework, Heim, Lasnik, and May (1991) propose an *each*-raising rule to derive various interpretations associated with the reciprocal construction. The crucial difference is simply that the related operations are not triggered in Chinese.

We have seen that a number of differences between English and Chinese may be traced to a parametric difference in the nature of clausal functional heads, T and C, in whether they trigger head movements and/or XP-movements. A highly analytic language is one whose T and C are not strongly defective (and dependent), and thus do not trigger movement. That Chinese does not move from V to T is clear from the following two facts. First, like English and unlike French, the main verb does not precede adverbs or negation.

(49)   Zhangsan changchang kan   dianying.
       Zhangsan often   watch movie
       'Zhangsan often goes to the movies.'

(50)   Zhangsan bu xihuan Lisi de piping.
       Zhangsan not like   Lisi de criticism
       'Zhangsan does not like Lisi's criticism.'

Second, while English moves an auxiliary to T (as in (51)), Chinese does not even allow auxiliaries to move:

(51)   a.   John cannot come to visit you.

       b.   John has not read about this news.

(52)   a.   Zhangsan bu neng lai   kan ni.   (* ... neng bu ...)
            Zhangsan not can   come see you

       b.   Zhangsan meiyou   niandao zhe-ze   xinwen.   (* ... you mei ...)
            Zhangsan not-have read   this-CL news

The lack of V-to-T (and therefore also of T-to-C) movement thus basically keeps the lexical and functional heads in their base positions. This, plus the (general) lack of XP movement to Spec, CP, leads to what might be termed 'Kaynean word order par excellence' for a typical Chinese sentence:

(53)   Chinese canonical word order
       Subject—Adjunct—Verb—Complement

That is, the surface word order basically corresponds to the relative height (in terms of asymmetric c-command) among the components, in reverse to their order of (external) Merge, as Kayne (1994) would have it. This result also gives rise to what Huang (1982, 1984) referred to as the Postverbal Structure Constraint (PSC), which provides that the verb may be followed by at most one constituent (object or complement) per clause, requiring all other elements to occur preverbally—a sort of 'backward Verb-Second' requirement, counting from the end.[13]

---

[13] As amusingly suggested by a participant in my 1996 seminar at the Girona Summer Institute of Linguistics. There is no requirement that the verb must be followed by something, of course (e.g., as in the case of an intransitive sentence). Note that the PSC as originally proposed, while useful as a point of departure for much discussion, had theoretical and empirical problems that now disappear when it's seen as a consequence of Kayne's LCA and the hypothesis that Chinese has V-to-V and V-to-v, but no v-to-T movement.

Thus, what seems to be a completely independent property of word order (Kaynean word order, or the PSC in earlier work) can now be seen as a special case of high analyticity.

Before we conclude this section, it is worthwhile to point out that, although Chinese has no V-to-T or T-to-C movement, it does allow V-to-V and V-to-v movement. V-to-V movement would be required given the widely assumed Larsonian analysis of dative, double-object, and other constructions involving triadic predicates (Larson 1988):

(54)   Zhangsan [VP song-le   [VP Lisi [V' tV liang-ben xiaoshuo]]]

       Zhangsan   give-Perf   Lisi   two-CL   novel

Even with non-triadic predicates, V-movement out of VP is possible, as illustrated in the following cases (I shall assume this is V-to-v, since the requisite movement is not for lexical but for grammatical—e.g., Case-theoretic—reasons):

(55)   Zhangsan [vP chi-le   [VP Lisi [V' tv yi-wan   mian]]]
       Zhangsan   eat-Perf   Lisi   one-bowl noodle
       'Zhangsan ate a bowl of noodles of Lisi.'

(56)   Zhangsan [vP kai-le   [VP Lisi [V' tv yi-ge   wanxiao]]]
       Zhangsan   poke-Perf   Lisi   one-CL joke
       'Zhangsan made fun of Lisi once.'

(57)   Zhangsan [vP tan-le   [VP [V' [V' liang-ci tv gangqin]]]]
       Zhangsan   play-Perf   twice   piano
       'Zhangsan played the piano twice.'

In (55)–(56) the verb moves above an applicative object ('outer object'), and in (57) it moves above a low adjunct, an 'incidentive' adverb, which is underlyingly above the verbal head.[14] In addition to deriving the correct order of constituents, one independent piece of evidence for movement comes from coordinate constructions like the following:

(58)   Zhangsan chi-le   Lisi yi-wan   mian,   Wangwu liang-pan shuijiao.
       Zhangsan eat-Perf Lisi one-bowl noodle Wangwu two-dish dumpling
       'Zhangsan ate a bowl of noodles of Lisi, and two dishes of dumplings of Wangwu.

(59)   Zhangsan tan-le   liang-ci gangqin, san-ci jita.
       Zhangsan play-Perf twice   piano   thrice guitar
       'Zhangsan played the piano twice and the guitar three times.'

The familiar coordination test implies that *Lisi yi-wan mian* 'Lisi a bowl of noodles' and *liang-ci gangqin* 'two-time piano' are each a syntactic constituent, but such

---

[14] See Soh (1998) for more discussion of vP-internal head movement.

constituents yield no coherent meanings. The problem disappears, however, if verb-movement is postulated. For example, assume that *tan* 'play' undergoes across-the-board (ATB) movement out of two conjoined VPs:[15]

(60)   Zhangsan [$_{vP}$ tan-le [$_{VP}$ liang-ci t$_v$ gangqin], [san-ci t$_v$ jita]].

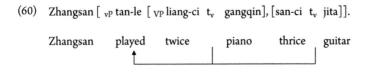

| Zhangsan | played | twice | piano | thrice | guitar |

Examples (57) and (59)–(60) show that V may move across a low incidentive adjunct, but recall from (49)–(50) that it cannot cross a higher adjunct like 'often' or negation; thus movement cannot proceed as high as T.

In short, we conclude that Chinese has V-to-V and V-to-v, but no v-to-T or T-to-C movement.[16] In general, the distance of movement along the clausal spine corresponds to the extent of grammaticalization of a given functional category—the more grammaticalized, the higher the movement, and the higher degree of synthesis. (See Roberts and Roussou 2003 for related insightful discussion.)

Now we are in a position to consider yet another parametric difference between English and Chinese, concerning the distribution of gapping. It was observed early on by Sanders and Tai (1972) that, different from English, Chinese does not allow (canonical) gapping:

(61)   John eats rice, and Bill spaghetti.

(62)   *Zhangsan chi fan, Lisi mian.
        Zhangsan eat rice Lisi noodles

The question is why English and Chinese should differ precisely this way and not, say, the other way around.[17] This question was never seriously addressed for a long time. Tang (2001) argues for an interesting answer on the basis of Johnson's (1994) theory of gapping (cf. also Johnson 2009), according to which the verb moves across the board out of a conjoined vP, into a functional head μ in the IP region (between T and v):

(63)   [$_{TP}$ [$_{\mu P}$ eats [$_{vP}$ [$_{vP}$ John t$_v$ rice], and [$_{vP}$ Bill t$_v$ spaghetti]]]

---

[15]The same ATB movement also derives corresponding sentences in English like *He put the book on the table and the pencil on the chair.*

[16] Recall that, although V-movement may cross a low incidentive adjunct (like '3 times'), a question arises concerning the verb's position when suffixed with aspect markers like *-le, -zhe, -guo*. Since these aspectual categories are semantically higher in position than manner adverbs like *xiaoxindi* 'carefully' or means adverbs like *yong daozi* 'with a knife,' and yet the verb+aspect combination occurs syntactically lower than these adverbs, I shall assume that Chinese aspectual suffixes only trigger Agree in Syntax but undergo Aspect Hopping in PF (keeping with the familiar treatment of Tense in English) or covert movement in LF.

[17] Sanders and Tai (1972) proposed to account for the difference by an immediate dominance condition that applies to Chinese but not to English. This begs the same question, of course.

The derivation yields (61) after *John* moves to Spec, TP. Note the striking similarity between the ATB movement structure for gapping as in (63) and the ATB movement structure for (58)–(59) as depicted in (60). The crucial difference is that the ATB movement in (58)–(60) is V-to-v out of a conjoined VP, whereas the ATB movement in (61) and (63) is v-to-μ out of a conjoined vP. While (63) is a structure for 'canonical gapping' in the TP domain, (61) is a structure for 'short gapping' in the vP domain. The question is now why 'short gapping' is possible in both Chinese and English (see note 15), but 'canonical gapping' is possible only in English. The answer is straightforward, according to Tang (2001): because Chinese has only V-to-v movement, while English has both V-to-v and (limited) v-to-I movement.[18]

Summarizing this section, we have seen that a number of syntactic properties form a cluster that distinguishes Chinese from English (and other languages):

(64) a. *wh*-in-situ

b. discontinuous *wh-the-hell* construction

c. absence of negative quantifiers

d. absence of reciprocal pronouns

e. absence of bi-nominal *each*

f. Kaynean word order par excellence (or 'V2 counting backward')

g. absence of canonical gapping

Some of these properties have heretofore been observed or treated as independent properties, but given the analyses noted above, their clustering is immediately explained, with each of them reflecting the same analytic nature of functional heads on the clausal spine in Chinese.

Given the properties we have reviewed, as summarized for lexical categories in (20) and (24) and for clausal functional categories in (64), and given the Uriagereka-Lasnik metaphor of a virus, Modern Chinese might as well be termed a 'healthy' language, as compared to the less analytic ones.

5. Analyticity in Argument Structure

Languages may differ on how conceptual structures are represented and formed morphologically and syntactically, and how functional categories affect or constrain grammatical operations. They may also differ in how information in the lexicon interacts with syntax—in how argument structure is projected to syntax or manipulated by grammar. Here again, we see a number of parametric differences that may be profitably seen as reflecting the analytic/synthetic divide.

One difference bears some resemblance to the distribution of *nobody, each other,* etc., as discussed above: in each case, an (adverbial) *not* or *each* at a clausal level may

---

[18] Cf. Paul (1999), who argues for the existence of some limited cases of gapping in Mandarin, and for potential verb-raising beyond the vP.

(or may not) serve an adjectival role in a nominal structure. The following pair in English is another such case:

(65)   a.   Jennifer types fast, Dorothy drives fast, etc.

      b.   Jennifer is a fast typist, Dorothy is a fast driver, etc.

Lin and Liu (2005) observes that a sentence corresponding to (65b) in Chinese must express 'fast' as an adverb, but not as an adjective:

(66)   Zhangsan shi yi-ge   (da zi) da-de hen kuai de daziyuan
      Zhangsan be one-Cl (type) type very fast De typist
      'Zhangsan is a typist who types fast.'

(67)   *Zhangsan shi yi-ge   hen kuai de daziyuan
      Zhangsan be one-Cl very fast De typist

Similarly, whereas (68) in English may refer to a person who is beautiful but may not sing very well or a person with average appearance who sings beautifully, a corresponding sentence in Chinese is not ambiguous.

(68)   Jennifer is a beautiful singer.

For the two readings, *piaoliang* 'beautiful' must occur in construction with a noun or with a verb, respectively:

(69)   Amei shi yi-ge   hen piaoliang de geshou.
      Amei be one-Cl very beautiful De singer
      'Amei is a singer who is beautiful.'

(70)   Amei shi yi-ge   chang-de hen piaoliang de geshou
      Amei be one-Cl sing   very beautifully De singer
      'Amei is a singer who sings beautifully.'

These English examples illustrate sub-lexical modification into parts of a noun. 'Fast' modifies the *drive* part of *driver*, and *beautiful* modifies the *sing* part of *singer*, to the exclusion of the head suffix *-er*. Larson (1998) proposes that ambiguities arise in English because certain nouns may contain a Davidsonian event place in their argument structure. Thus *singer* is taken to denote an event-individual pair $\langle e, x \rangle$ such that Singing (e) and Agent (e, x), and the ambiguity arises because *beautiful* may be predicated of e or of x.

Another way to state the English-Chinese contrast is to relate it to Chierchia's (1998) Nominal Mapping Hypothesis, according to which nouns in Chinese denote kinds and are of type $\langle e \rangle$, whereas English nouns denote predicates of type $\langle e,t \rangle$. The elementary, static, semantic type $\langle e \rangle$ can be modified by an adjective that describes the quality of an individual, but the dynamic type $\langle e,t \rangle$ could have a component open to modification by the event modifier. If so, it is no surprise that a language that requires a numeral classifier is also a language that does not allow sub-lexical modification.

The phenomenon illustrated is part of a larger picture and rich topic that goes well beyond the scope of our concern, but the relevant point here is that Chinese contrasts with English in the way described, not the other way around. This difference is in line with what we have seen elsewhere with respect to the relative complexity of lexical items.[19]

As we saw in section 2, the lack of simplex accomplishment verbs is compensated for by the richness of resultative compounds and phrasal resultative constructions. English also abounds in phrasal resultatives, though its resultative compounds are somewhat limited (to verb-particle constructions like *turn on, pick up*, etc.). One well-known property of English resultatives is the Direct Object Requirement (DOR), originally due to Simpson (1983) and made famous by Sybesma (1992, 1998) and Levin and Rappaport (1995), which provides that the result clause of such a construction must be predicated on an object in the main clause:

(71) a.   John$_i$ hammered the metal flat$_i$.

  b.   *John$_i$ hammered the metal tired$_i$.

Apparent predication on the subject is possible only with a passive, inchoative, or unaccusative sentence, where the subject binds an object trace:

(72) a.   The metal$_i$ was hammered t_i flat$_i$.

  b.   The garage door$_i$ rumbles t_i open$_i$.

  c.   The river$_i$ froze t_i solid$_i$.

The DOR rules out resultatives with an unergative verb like *cry* or *run*, and explains the need for a 'dummy reflexive' in such cases:

(73) a.   *John cried silly.

  b.   *Bill ran exhausted.

(74) a.   John cried himself silly.

  b.   Bill ran himself exhausted.

A (by now) well-known problem from Chinese is that unergative resultatives are perfectly fine without a dummy reflexive, in apparent violation of the DOR:

(75) a.   Zhangsan ku-de hen lei.
      Zhangsan cry-De very tired
      'Zhangsan cried [himself] exhausted.'

  b.   Lisi pao-de manshen dahan.
      Lisi ran-De full-body big-sweat
      'Lisi ran [himself] sweating all over the body.'

[19] Many (possibly related) examples in English also do not find their Chinese counterparts, including *An occasional woman in America speaks Finnish; Let's have a quick cup of coffee*; etc., though it is not clear how it can be accommodated by an event place in the semantic structure of objectual nouns like *woman* and *coffee*.

Another peculiar fact is that a resultative with an unergative or transitive main verb may be causativized:

(76)   a.   zhe-jian shi   ku-de Zhangsan yanjing dou hong le
            this-CL thing cry-De Zhangsan eyes   all red   Perf/FP
            'This thing caused Zhangsan to cry [himself] red-eyed.'
            (Lit.: *This thing cried Zhangsan red-eyed.)

       b.   baozhi   kan-de Lisi touhunyanhua.
            newspaper   read-De Lisi dizzy
            'The newspaper caused Lisi to read [himself] dizzy.'
            (Lit.: *The newspaper read Lisi dizzy.)

But this is totally impossible in English, as the literal translations above show. Only unaccusatives or inchoatives can be causativized:

(77)   a.   The door rumbled open.

       b.   John rumbled the door open.

(78)   a.   John got angry.

       b.   He got John angry.

So why does Chinese allow unergative resultatives, and the causativization of unergative resultatives, but English allows neither?

Huang (2006a) proposed that these questions have a single answer: the examples (75) are actually *not* unergative, but unaccusative/inchoative resultatives. As such, they do obey the DOR as other unaccusatives do in (72b–c). And as unaccusatives, they can be causativized as in (76). In support of this proposal, crucial reference is made to the verbal clitic -*de*, which literally means 'get,' which (just as English *get*) may alternate between 'become' and 'cause' meanings, as just illustrated in (78). That is, in both (75a–b), -*de* heads the main verb with its inchoative meaning, but is itself phonologically supported by an unergative verb expressing the manner or source of the change: Zhangsan *got* (= *de*) exhausted from crying in (75a), and got profusely sweating from running in (75b). And when a causative component is added on top of the inchoative component, movement of verb-*de* will cross the experiencer *Zhangsan*, producing the causatives in (76a–b). So, Chinese does not violate the DOR with an unergative resultative, nor can it causativize an unergative resultative.

The question boils down to why English resultatives cannot be analyzed in the same way. The answer again turns to the synthetic-analytic difference between the two languages. In English, what corresponds to *de* in Chinese would be a null light verb, BECOME or CAUSE, which, due to its [+strong] nature, attracts a verb that agrees with it in thematic properties. Thus the lower component may only host an unaccusative or inchoative verb, and only such a verb would be the input for causativization. The movement may occur in lexical structure in the sense of Hale and Keyser (1993), or overt syntactic movement triggered by strong features. In Chinese, on the other hand, it is only the phonological defectiveness of -*de* that triggers movement. Movement of this type may be delayed to the PF component, again a type of derivational timing that characterizes relative analyticity, as we have seen above and elsewhere.[20]

A very similar type of apparent unaccusative use of unergatives can be observed below:

(79) a. xiao niao gei fei le
          small bird give fly Perf
          'The little bird flew away.'

      b. xiao gou gei pao le
          small dog give run Perf
          'The puppy ran away.'

Shen and Sybesma (2010) studied a type of passive-like construction involving *gei* 'give' taking an intransitive VP as its complement (the so-called '*give*-passive') and observed that the complement VP must be unaccusative, not unergative or transitive. In examples (79), however, the verbs 'fly' and 'run' are unergative in their normal meanings, but they are allowed. The key to the problem is that these verbs are translated as 'fly away' and 'run away,' as shown. That is, in these examples the verbs actually express the manner of a covert unaccusative verb as its head (i.e., a silent DIAO 'get off' or ZOU 'get away,' as in *fei-diao, pao-zou*). Again, this state of affairs comes about in Chinese because the silent head accounts for its syntactic and semantic status, requiring phonetic support only in PF.

In both the resultatives and the so-called '*give*-passives,' the point is that the existence of some apparent counter-examples to the DOR or the unaccusative requirement found in Chinese does not warrant the conclusion that the DOR or even the Unaccusative Hypothesis does not apply in Chinese. What we have seen is that the violations are only apparent, and it is the analytic nature of the non-triggering heads that give rise to the appearance of violations.

This way of thinking is in line with the theory of light verb syntax proposed in Lin (2001, see also Lin 2014) in the account of apparent 'unselectiveness' of the subject or object in Chinese, as illustrated in (80):

(80) kai   che; kai gaosu gonglu; kai   zuobian; kai   wanshang; kai   haowan
      drive car drive super highway drive left-side drive night   drive fun
      'drive a car; drive [on] the freeway; drive [on] the left side; drive [at] night; drive [for] fun.'

(81) chi fan; chi fanguan; chi kuaizi;   qie rou; qie zhe-ba dao; etc.
      eat rice eat restaurant eat chopsticks cut meat cut this-CL knife
      'eat rice; eat [at the] restaurant; eat [with] chopsticks; cut the meat; cut [with] this knife; etc.'

Note that in each case above, a transitive verb may, instead of a selected theme argument, take one of a range of non-arguments as its object, resulting in apparent

---

[20] The same applies to the compounds, with the assumption that there is a null DE 'get' with inchoative-causative alternation, to which the overt verb is attached as an adjunct, in PF. In English, movement into null GET in overt syntax requires Agree in relevant theta-features, thus preventing an unergative verb from filling the position of an inchoative GET.

syntax-semantics mismatches (as if someone eats a restaurant, cuts a knife, etc.). The 'object' would otherwise normally be introduced with a prepositional phrase, as given in the English translation. English does not enjoy this type of freedom from the normal requirements of selection. Lin's proposal is that the difference arises from a difference in the relative analyticity of argument structure. In particular, a predicate like *put* in English is lexically associated with an argument structure like <Agent, Theme, Location> (perhaps having acquired this 'virus' as a result of operations of lexical syntax in the sense of Hale and Keyser 1993). The formal features associated with the predicate make it necessary for it to move and be placed in a proper fixed location in the syntactic tree, given Baker's (1988) Uniformity of Theta-Assignment Hypothesis (UTAH). In Chinese, however, a predicate enters the computation without a full argument structure, thus exhibiting considerable freedom in its syntactic positioning, sometimes moving into the position of a silent light verb that takes an adjunct as its object:

(82)   Zhangsan YONG zhe-ba dao   qie

      Zhangsan use   this-CL knife cut

In order for Lin's theory to hold, one difference in the nature of the light verb must also play a role. In particular, while in English a covert light verb must contain formal features that trigger movement of a root verb under feature-agreement, in Chinese a covert light verb must not contain [+strong] features that trigger agreement-based movement. As a result, movement occurs in PF—importantly—for pure reasons of phonology, with no semantic consequences.

We have seen in this section, then, that Chinese exhibits a high degree of simplicity in argument structure, both within nouns and verbs, accounting for a number of differential properties with respect to sub-lexical adjectival modification, apparent unexpected behaviors of the resultative construction, apparent unaccusative use of unergative verbs, and apparent freedom from selection requirements.

More generally, we have seen that Modern Mandarin displays high analyticity at almost every level of grammar: lexical structure, functional structure, and argument structure, leading (among other things) to its explicit Davidsonian syntax and canonical Kaynean word orders, on the one hand, and a range of apparent syntax-semantics mismatches, on the other.[21] Some of the properties we have reviewed may have been observed before, but are often presented as independent, unrelated phenomena, but given the analyses proposed here, they can all be seen as special cases of a larger picture, and their clustering is thereby explained. This full range of properties distinguishes Modern Mandarin not only from English and other non-Sinitic languages, putting it near one extreme of the analytic-synthetic continuum. In fact, this range of properties also distinguishes Modern Mandarin from Old Chinese quite sharply, as we shall now see.

---

[21] This last characterization is somewhat paradoxical. This arises from the fact that in addition to the overt, fully lexical categories, Modern Chinese has also developed the use of affixal and/or silent light verbs. But these categories are without formal features that trigger agreement-based movement, and they only require phonetic licensing at PF.

6. Old Chinese Typological Properties

In contrast to Modern Chinese, Old Chinese (Archaic Chinese, 500 B.C. to 200 A.D.) exhibits a full array of properties that make it a relatively synthetic language. Indeed, it will be seen that Old Chinese behaved more like Modern English, in the relevant typological properties we have reviewed.

6.1. LEXICAL CATEGORIES

At the lexical level, the following properties put OC in sharp contrast with Modern Chinese.

(83)   Old Chinese (OC) lexical categories

    a.   denominal verbs: no need for light verbs

    b.   true incorporation: no pseudo incorporation

    c.   simplex causatives: no compounds or phrasal accomplishments

    d.   countable nouns: no need for numeral classifiers

    e.   nouns qua locations: no need for localizers

Many words in OC exhibit polysemy between a nominal and verbal meaning, a case of denominalizaton on a par with English *telephone,* but not Mandarin *da dianhua* (recall also (4) above).

(84)   a.   魚   *yu*   'fish, to fish'

    b.   食   *shi*   'food, to eat'

    c.   衣   *yi*   'clothing, to get clothed'

    d.   飯   *fan*   'rice, to have rice'

    e.   歌   *ge*   'song, to sing'

    f.   王   *wang*   'king, to be a king'

In each case, the verbal usage may be derived via noun-incorporation into a light verb with the elementary meaning of DO, thus making pseudo-incorporation unnecessary—no examples like *bu yu* 'catch fish' or *chi fan* 'eat rice' that are found in Modern Mandarin.

OC also abounds in examples of causativization, with simplex verbs exhibiting alternations between causative and non-causative readings:

(85)   a.   破   po   'break (both inchoative and causative uses)'

    b.   小   xiao   'small, belittle (= make small)'[22]

---

[22] Many causatives also have both a physical and 'mental' sense. The causative verb *xiao* could mean 'to make x small' or 'to consider x to be small' (the latter expressing a mental causation, also termed 'putative' use, i.e., 'to claim x to be small'). Other well-known examples include 好 *hao* (with the stative 'good' and the putative 'consider x to be good' = 'like x'), and 賢 *xian* (alternating between 'able, virtuous' and 'consider x to be virtuous = value x for x's abilities and virtues'). See K. Mei (2003) and Feng (2005).

    c. 受/授 shou 'receive, bestow (= cause to receive)'

    d. 假 jia 'borrow, lend (= cause to borrow)'

These alternations indicate the existence of verb movement into a light verb CAUSE. Some causative verbs in OC start out as nouns, which first denominalize and then causativize, much as English *food* > *feed (on)* > *feed (someone)*. Some examples from the Classical texts:

(86)   君子問人之寒, 則衣之; 問人之饑, 則食之; 稱人之美, 則爵之。《禮記‧表記》
        junzi   wen ren-zhi han, ze yi   zhi; wen ren-zhi ji,   ze   shi
        gentleman ask person's cold, then clothe him; ask person's hunger, then feed
        zhi; cheng ren-zhi mei,   ze   jue   zhi.   (*Liji, Biaoji*)
        him; praise person's virtues, then nobility him

    'When a gentleman wonders about one's being cold, he will clothe him; when he wonders about one's hunger, he will feed him; and as he praises one's virtues, he will make him a member of the noble class.'

(87)   諸母漂, 有一母見信飢, 飯信。　《史記:淮陰侯列傳》、
        zhu   mu   piao you yi mu   jian Xin ji,   fan Xin   (*Shiji*)
        various women wash, have one woman see Xin hungry, rice Xin

    'Various women were washing clothes [by the river]. One woman saw Xin being hungry, so she riced Xin [= fed him with rice].'

Mei (1989, 2008a, 2008b, 2012, and references cited therein) has postulated a denominative prefix and a causative prefix in OC (and earlier), both reconstructed in the form of **s-*. In the terms of the Probe-Goal system, we can take the **s-* as an affixal light verb with the elementary meaning of DO or CAUSE (or CONSIDER, see note 22). Due to their highly affixal (hence [+strong]) nature, **s-*$_{DO}$ triggers denominalization by noun-incorporation, and **s-*$_{CAUSE}$ triggers causativization by verb-movement:

(88)

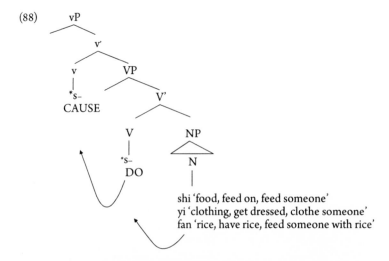

    shi 'food, feed on, feed someone'
    yi 'clothing, get dressed, clothe someone'
    fan 'rice, have rice, feed someone with rice'

Note that the availability of denominalized verbs in OC means the general absence of overt light verb constructions as widely used in Modern Chinese—this is property (83a). The general absence of 'phrasal verbs' involving pseudo noun-incorporation also follows, given that simplex verbs may be formed by genuine noun-incorporation—property (83b). And, the availability of making a lexical causative verb by incorporating a non-causative with the causative affix *s-* also makes it unnecessary to resort to complex expressions of accomplishment like resultative compounds or phrases—property (83c). Indeed, it is pointed out in Mei (1991 and references) that the resultative compounds and phrases that are so productive in Modern Mandarin were not fully established until late Middle Chinese.[23] As a result, as far as the verbal domain is concerned, OC was robustly synthetic.[24]

The same is true of the nominal domain. It has been pointed out (Peyraube 1996, 2003) that classifiers were not required for numerated count nouns in OC, nor any localizers for nouns denoting locations. These can be seen from the two familiar passages from *Lunyu* (Confucian Analects):

(89)　三人行, 必有我師焉。
　　　san　ren　　xing, bi　　you　wo shi　　yan
　　　three person walk　must have　my teacher there
　　　'When three people get together, there must be a teacher of mine there.'

(90)　八佾舞於庭。是可忍也，孰不可忍也?
　　　Bayi wu　　yu ting, shi　ke　ren　　　ye, shu　bu　ke　ren　　　ye
　　　8x8　dance at hall　this can tolerate Prt, what not kan tolerate Prt
　　　'To have the 8x8 court dance performed in [his own] hall! If this can be tolerated, what [else] cannot be tolerated?'

These examples may be taken to show that, like their verbal counterparts, the nouns in OC were also incorporated into their covert 'light noun' heads—an abstract Div^0 head above the root NP, or the light noun PLACE or Loc head. (On the latter, see Huang 2010 for more details.) As far as the lexical categories are concerned, then, OC was consistently synthetic.

---

[23] The rise of the resultative compound was triggered by the loss of the *s-* prefix from the causative verbs, and a subsequent initial-devoicing, causing opacity of the causative-inchoative distinction in the child's primary linguistic data, which in turn led to a reanalysis that treats all verbs as non-causative, hence atelic. See Mei (1991), Huang (1995), Wei (2003) and Feng (2014) for discussion.

[24] A question may arise as to why the availability of denominal verbs and simplex causatives implies the absence (or infrequent occurrence) of the light verb construction, pseudo-incorporation, and compound and phrasal accomplishments. A plausible explanation is the notion of 'synthetic blocking' (see Poser 1992; Kiparsky 2005; Embick 2007). If a language has *kill* as a synthetic accomplishment verb, one would not resort to a (less economical) analytic or periphrastic version such as *John caused him to become not alive.* The latter is perhaps fully grammatical still, but is simply 'shelved,' unless there is a special reason that calls for the use of the analytic form. This must be the case in OC, at least as far as the causatives are concerned. Periphrastic expressions involving such verbs as *shi* and *ling* (both meaning 'cause') are easily attestable in the classical texts and can safely be assumed to be available in the oral language of the time.

6.2. CLAUSES

At the clausal level, OC exhibits several word order differences from Modern Chinese (MnC). The best known is that *wh*-objects are fronted to a preverbal position after the subject:

(91)   沛公安在?《史記·項羽本紀》
       Peigong an   zai?   (*Shiji.Xiangyu*)
       Peigong where be-at
       'Where is Lord Pei?'

(92)   吾谁欺, 欺天乎?《论语·子罕》
       wu shei qi,   qi   tian   hu?   (*Lunyu.Zihan*)
       I   who deceive, deceive heaven Q
       'Who do I deceive; do I deceive Heaven?'

When an object is relativized, the relative pronoun *suo* appears in the preverbal position as well. There are two versions of object relatives: depending on whether the subject carries nominative or genitive case, as in (93)–(94), respectively:[25]

(93)   魚我所欲也; 熊掌亦我所欲也。《孟子》
       yu wo suo yu ye; xiongzhang yi   wo suo yu ye   (*Mencius*)
       fish I what like FP, bear-palm also I what want FP
       'Fish is what I desire; a bear's palm is also what I desire.'

(94)   是聰耳之所不能聽也, 明目之所不能見也, 辨士之所不能言也。(荀子. 儒效)
       shi cong-er zhi suo bu neng ting ye, ming-mu zhi suo bu neng jian ye,
       this sharp-ear Gen what not can hear Prt, bright-eye Gen what not can see Prt
       bianshi zhi suo bu neng yan   ye
       debater Gen what not can express Prt   (*Xunzi.Ruxiao*)
       'This is what even a sharp ear cannot hear, what even a keen eye cannot see. [and] what even an eloquent debater cannot express.'

Certain constituents get pre-posed when they bear the focus, for example when they occur with *wei* 'be' or 'only':

(95)   率師以來, 唯敵是求。《左傳·宣公十二年》
       shuai shi   yilai, wei di   shi   qiu   (*Zuozhuan.Xuan 12*)
       lead   troop since only enemy Dem seek
       'Since leading the troops, no one but the enemies [have I been] running after.'

---

[25] In Huang (2008), the alternation between (93) and (94) is identified as a case of Nominative-Genitive conversion phenomenon well known from the syntax of Altaic languages (the so-called *ga-no* conversion in Japanese, and genitive subjects in Turkish, etc.). Although the *suo*-relatives have remained in Modern Chinese (but with an overt or null head, unlike the OC examples here, which are free relatives), genitive subjects are not allowed any more: **ta de suo ai de ren* 'the person that he-Gen suo loves.' Parallel to this development was the loss of the gerundive construction. Huang (2008) hypothesizes that the genitive subjects arose from the presence of a nominal feature incorporated into the CP. Subsequent detachment of the nominal feature from the CP in Modern Chinese, as part of the development toward analyticity, led to the loss of genitive subjects.

Or when they serve as contrastive topics, as pointed out by Aldridge (2012):

(96) 楚國方城以為城，漢水以為池。 《左傳・僖公四年》
     Chu guo Fangcheng yi wei cheng, Han Shui yi wei chi   (*Zuozhuan. Xi 4*)
     Chu state Fangcheng use be wall   Han River use be moat
     'The Chu used Mt. Fangcheng as their castle wall and the River Han as their moat.'

Pronominal objects are cliticized before the verb in the domain of negation:

(97) 昔君之惠也，寡人未之敢忘。《国语・晋语》
     xi   jun   zhi hui   ye, guaren wei zhi gan wang   (*Guoyu.Jinyu*)
     past prince's favor FP, I   not it dare forget
     'The favor of the prince in the past, I dare not forget it.'

Sometimes pre-posed objects trigger 'clitic doubling,' as already shown in (95) above with the demonstrative *shi*, and in (98) below with *zhi*:

(98) 宋何罪之有？ 《墨子・公输》
     Song he   zui   zhi you   (*Mozi.Gongshu*)
     Song what sin/crime it have
     'What sin/crime does Song have?'

These word order properties indicate that the clausal structure of OC includes an active functional category that hosts the relevant preverbal materials. In particular, there exists a functional category FP whose head F^0 possesses the relevant features that trigger movement. The [+EPP] feature triggers movement of an operator (a *wh*-phrase, a focused *only*-phrase, or the relative pronoun *suo*) to the Spec of FP, and the [+strong] affixal feature makes F^0 a comfortable home for a cliticized pronoun:[26]

(99)

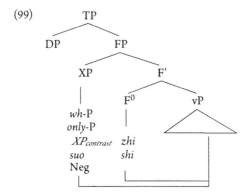

---

[26] I shall leave aside the exact details of the analysis, especially concerning the position of the relative pronoun *suo* and the negative morpheme *bu* and its related cousins *wu, wei, mo*, etc., and the preposed object pronoun under it. *Suo* originated as a place word with [+operator] feature but was generalized for the relativization of other categories (a situation also attested in other languages,

There is another well-known difference in word order between OC and MnC with respect to the occurrence of postverbal clausal adjuncts. Examples like the following are typical:

(100)   萬乘之國，被圍於趙。《史記.魯仲連》
         wan sheng zhi guo,   bei wei   yu   Zhao   (*Shiji.Luzhonglian*)
         10K carriage Gen nation, get surround by/at Zhao
         'A nation of 10 thousand carriages got surrounded by/in Zhao.'

In the following clips from *Mencius*, the adjunct phrase *yi yang* 'with a sheep' has the choice of preceding or following the VP. According to some, the choice is not entirely free, but motivated by considerations of focus (cf. Liu 1958; Lu 1982):

(101)   a.   何可廢也？ 以羊易之！《孟子.梁惠王》
           he ke fei   ye yi yang yi   zhi   (*Mengzi.Lianghuiwang*)
           how can abolish Prt with sheep replace it
           'How can we abolish [the sacrifice]? Replace it with a sheep!'

      b.   我非愛其財而易之以羊也。《孟子.梁惠王》
           wo fei ai   qi cai   er yi   zhi yi   yang ye
           I   not love its wealth and replace it   with sheep Prt
           'It's not because I love [to save] the wealth that I replaced it with a sheep.'

Although traditional descriptions generally treat the positional alternation in terms of adjunct preposing or postposing, Huang (2006b) suggested a different analysis in the spirit of Kayne (1994), assuming that postverbal adjuncts arise from the fronting of VPs. This allows us to assimilate the structure of sentences with postverbal adjuncts to a structure akin to (99), and would have the virtue of explaining the clustering of several word-order properties of OC: the same language that allows postverbal adjuncts by VP fronting also allows several cases of DP fronting, *and* the joint disappearance of these processes in Modern Chinese.[27] Aldridge (2013) adopts the proposed existence of a VP-fronting process in OC for the alternation shown in (101a–b)—as well as its loss in MnC—but she argues (a) that the process does not apply to produce true postverbal adjuncts as in (100), and (b) that the structure of (101b) does not involve a postverbal adjunct PP, but an applicative construction. In

including Swiss German and Modern Greek; see Huang 2010) and was aptly analyzed as a relative pronoun in Ma (1898); Ting (2010) argues that it has the property of a climbing clitic. As for the negative operator, the literature includes various claims: that it is a Spec, or a head, or an adjunct. I tentatively assume that it can be base-generated in Spec of the FP. I also assume that the movement of the interrogative *wh*-phrase, the *only*-phrase, and the relative pronoun is A-bar movement, and this explains the possibility of 'clitic doubling' by a resumptive pronoun (at least in the case of *wh*- and *only*-phrase movement). See Aldridge (2012), and Feng (1996) for more detailed discussions.

   [27] If the alternation in (101) is motivated by focus (as asserted by Liu 1958), note that the focus in this case is not on the fronted VP, but what is left behind. The VP fronting may well be a strategy to highlight an information focus as opposed to identification focus (in the sense of Kiss 1998), i.e., by vacating the non-focalized VP out of the focus position.

particular, *yi yang* in (101), translated above as 'with a sheep' is in fact not a PP, but involves a (semi-lexical) applicative verb *yi* (more appropriately translated as 'use') merged above the VP complement, which (optionally) moves. In her analysis, (101b) has the following relevant structure:[28]

(102) ... [[$_{VP}$ yi   zhi]$_j$ [$_{v'}$ yi$_i$ [yang [$_{APPL'}$ t$_i$ [$_{VP}$ t$_j$]]]]]...

        replace it ⬆   use   sheep |

Aldridge also argues, with Djamouri et al. (2013), that postverbal adjuncts like the *yu* PP in (100) should be base-generated with a verb that moves higher up across the object.[29] Regardless of the details of the correct analysis, we see that OC may be characterized as having an appropriate functional element that triggers some EPP movement, or head-movement but that is not available in MnC.

Still another difference that distinguishes OC from MnC, first brought to light by Wu (2002), concerns the existence of canonical gapping. We saw above, in connection with (61)–(64), that MnC does not allow canonical gapping because it has only V-to-V and V-to-v movement, but no v-to-I or I-to-C movement. Interestingly, Wu (2002) shows that canonical gapping is allowed in OC (see also K. Mei 2003):

(103)   為客治飯而自∅藜藿。《淮南子·說林》
       wei ke   zhi fan er   zi __ lihuo   (*Huainanzi.Shuolin*)
       for guest cook rice and self   grass
       'For guests cook rice, but for onself [cook] grass.'

He (2008) provides further examples, including the following, arguing plausibly that in OC, the verb moves out of vP into the IP region.

(104)   上醫醫國，其次∅疾人。《國語·晉語八》
       shangyi   yi   guo,   qici jiren
       best-doctor cure nation, next patient
       'The first-rate doctor cures a state; the next-level doctor a patient.'

This is not surprising, given other established cases of movement into the Focus Phrase. Note that, if correct, this provides fascinating evidence for the Johnson-Tang

---

[28] An argument Aldridge adduces in support of the VP-movement analysis is that it correctly predicts that *wh*-movement of *sheep* is possible only if VP-movement has not taken place—as in (101a), but impossible if it has—as in (101b) or (102). A similar contrast could be observed in English: 'Which sheep (did you) use *t* to replace the cow?' vs. *Which sheep$_i$ [to replace the cow] (did you) use *t*$_i$? VP-movement of *to replace the cow* bleeds *wh*-movement of *which sheep*.

[29] Since (the relevant) postverbal adjuncts are not possible in MnC, the verb must have moved higher in OC than in MnC. There is some doubt about the movement when the object is non-referential and presumably occurs lower than an adjunct, and so a smaller-scale VP movement might still be involved in deriving postverbal adjuncts.

analysis of gapping, and strengthens our point that an otherwise unrelated difference in the distribution of gapping is reducible to a case of micro-variation in relative
analyticity.

6.3. THE MACRO-HISTORY OF CHINESE SYNTAX

Summarizing, Old Chinese and Modern Chinese (MnC) differ systematically over
a range of constructions on the analytic-synthetic continuum, at both the level of
lexical categories and the level of clausal functional categories, and in these respects,
OC behaves more like English than it does MnC. With respect to the lexical categories, MnC exhibits properties of a "Davidsonian language par excellence," while OC
exhibits considerable polysemy through derivational synthesis. And at the clausal
level, whereas a canonical Kaynean word order typifies the internal constituents of
the clause in MnC, considerable departure from the canonical order occurs in OC.
We also see that the difference in the degree of analyticity can be characterized in
each case within the Probe-Goal system on the basis of the nature of a probing head:
a head with [+EPP] or a [+strong] affixal feature leads to movement and synthesis,
while [-EPP] and a [-strong] head preserves analyticity by leaving elements in situ.
While each case of the variation may be described in terms of a micro-parameter associated with a particular probing head, the clustering of parametric values across
the board gives rise to the picture of a macro-parameter, the analytic-synthetic
macro-parameter.

These differences reflect a macro-parametric *change* in the history of Chinese
syntax, as has been pointed out in other recent works (K. Mei 2003; Wei 2003; Feng
2005; Huang 2006b; Xu 2006; and Hu 2005, 2008). More specifically: Old Chinese
(dating from 500 B.C. to 200 A.D.) was fairly synthetic as described, but the language
underwent a gradual change from the late Han toward analyticity, peaking around
the Tang-Song dynasties (roughly from 200 to 1000 A.D.),[30] after which a new cycle
of development has developed toward mild synthesis in varying degrees in various
dialects, resulting in the major dialect groups of Modern Chinese.[31]

Thus both synchronic variation (such as between Chinese and English) and diachronic change (such as between Old and a later stage of Chinese) may be characterized in parametric terms. They are often two sides of the same coin, especially among
dialects and related languages of the same family. In particular, while synchronic

---

[30] In his 歸田錄 *Guitian Lu* the Northern Song scholar Ouyang Xiu (1007–1072) laments the
excessive use of *da*, even among supposedly respectable scholars of his time, as an example of language corruption, citing such examples as *da yu* 'to fish,' *da shui* 'to fetch water,' *da fan* 'to fetch rice,'
da san 'to hold up an umbrella,' *da nian* 'to paste (paper),' *da liang* 'to measure,' *da che* 'to build a
vehicle,' etc., aptly illustrating the widespread use of the light verb construction as evidence of high
analyticity.

[31] This cycle of change is commonly observed, both in macro-patterns for a language and on
micro-scales for particular linguistic units—the most famous being the "Jespersen's cycle" concerning English negation, which is replicated in many other languages. See Gelderen (2011 and
references therein) for extensive treatment of this topic from the perspective of Minimalist parametric theory.

variation results from variation in parameter setting (defined in terms of [interpretable], [strong], [EPP], etc.), diachronic change results from parametric change or resetting (i.e., reanalysis in the terms of grammaticalization research) that gives rise to (often multiple) new consequences. (See Roberts and Roussou 2003; Roberts 2007; and references therein for relevant discussion.)

In the next section, we turn to some parametric variation among Chinese dialects. We shall see that some of the cross-dialectal differences can again be seen as differences on the analytic-synthetic continuum, again describable in terms of the presence or absence of triggering heads in the vocabulary of the Probe-Goal checking system.

7. Parametric Variation among Chinese Dialects

I shall highlight three micro-parametric differences among three varieties of Modern Chinese: Mandarin, Cantonese, and Taiwanese Southern Min (TSM).

7.1. BARE CLASSIFIER PHRASES

A cross-dialectal variation that has attracted considerable recent attention concerns the distribution of a 'bare classifier phrase,' a numeral-classifier phrase where the numeral 'one' is missing. In Mandarin, an unstressed *yi* 'one' may drop, giving rise to a 'bare classifier phrase' (BCP) like *ben shu* 'Cl book' with the meaning of *yi ben shu* 'a book':

(105)   wo xiang mai [e] ben shu   song-gei ta
         I   want buy   Cl book give-to him
         'I would like to buy a book to give to him.'

(106)   ta ba [e] ge hao   pengyou gei dezui le
         ta BA   Cl good friend   give offend Perf/FP.
         'He got a good friend offended.'

In Mandarin, a BCP is allowed only in the environment of a governing verb or preposition as in (105)–(106), but prohibited from the subject position:

(107)   *[e] ben shu   bei tou   le
              Cl book get steal Perf/FP
         'Intended: A book got stolen.'

(108)   *[e] ge hao   pengyou zou le.
              Cl good friend   left Perf/FP
         'Intended: A good friend left.'

Cantonese, by contrast, allows a BCP in both subject and object positions, as observed in Cheng and Sybesma (1999: 511).[32]

---

[32] The BCP in Cantonese may have either definite or indefinite interpretation, with the definite interpretation being required in the subject position, as in (110a).

(109) ngo soeng maai bun syu (lei taai).
       I   want buy Cl book come read
       'I want to buy a book (to read).'

(110) a. zek gau zungji sek juk.
           Cl dog like eat meat
           'The dog likes to eat meat.'

       b. ngo zungji tong zek gau waan.
           I   like with Cl dog play
           'I like to play with a/the dog.'

TSM presents a still different picture: it does not allow any BCP at all.

(111) a. *goa xiunnbe boe *(chit) pun chheh lai   khoann.
           I   want   buy (one) Cl book come read
           'I would like to buy a book to read.'

       b. *i ka *(chit) pun chheh phangkinn khi a.
           he BA one Cl book lose   away FP
           'He lost a book.'

       c. *(chit) chia kau-a tsau-tshutkhi a.
           one Cl dog run-out-away FP
           'A dog ran away.'

These differences are summarized below:

(112) The distribution of a BCP in Chinese dialects

       a. Mandarin: *(subject) V/P ᵒᵏ(object)

       b. Cantonese: ᵒᵏ(subject) V/P ᵒᵏ(object)

       c. TSM: *(subject) V/P *(object)

How do we understand this pattern of distribution from a parametric point of view? I suggest that this reflects a ranking of relative analyticity among the three dialects: Cantonese > Mandarin > TSM, with Cantonese having progressed furthermost in acquiring some degree of synthesis, while TSM has remained most analytic.[33] First consider the difference between Cantonese and Mandarin. Building on Li (1998), assume that the BCP arises from the deletion of unstressed *yi* 'one,' which results in an empty category [$_{one}$ e] subject to the head-government requirement of the Empty Category Principle (ECP). Thus (105)–(106) are well-formed with the [e] governed by a verb or preposition, but (107)–(108) are ill-formed because the [e] is not properly governed. This explains the subject-object asymmetry as observed.[34] As for the

---

[33] See Cheng and Sybesma (2005) and Tang (2006) for further discussion of the phenomenon in Wu and Xiang dialects. See also Jiang (2012) for arguments in favor of the traditional 'one'-deletion analysis.

[34] An alternative is to follow Tsai (2001), who attributes the pattern to Diesing's (1992) Mapping Hypothesis, requiring that materials in the IP domain be mapped to specific readings, and that a bare classifier phrase (BCP) can only be interpreted as non-specific. The validity of this claim

Cantonese pattern, we assume following Simpson (2005) that here, the empty numeral position [e] is filled by the classifier that raises into it on its way to D⁰. Once the empty numeral and D positions are filled, the head-government requirement becomes irrelevant, and a BCP may occur in both subject and object positions. The Cantonese-Mandarin contrast thus boils down to one in the possibility of Cl-Num-D movement. We propose that this situation comes about because of a difference in the nature of the empty numeral *one*, as follows:

(113) The null numeral 'one' micro-parameter:

    a.   In Mandarin, $[_{one}\ e]$ is [-strong], triggering Agree with Cl.

    b.   In Cantonese, $[_{one}\ e]$ is [+strong], triggering Move of Cl.

    c.   In TSM, $[_{Num}\ one]$ is lexical and hence [-strong].

Since Cl does not move to $[_{one}\ e]$ in Mandarin, a subject-object asymmetry is observed, given the head-government requirement of the ECP.[35] In Cantonese, movement of Cl not only fills the $[_{one}\ e]$ position but also opens up the possibility of further moving up to fill an otherwise empty D, as shown below:

(114)

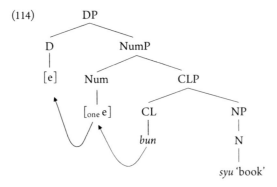

Following Li (1998), Simpson (2005) and also Longobardi (1994), we assume that a DP receives a definite interpretation if D⁰ is lexically filled with a Cl. This explains why Cantonese allows a BCP with definite reference to occur in both subject and object positions.[36]

    As for TSM, the non-affixal $[_{Num}\ one]$ is also [-strong] and triggers only Agree with Cl, but exhibits no subject-object asymmetry since it is not an empty category.

---

is now less clear in view of Jiang's (2012) recent finding that a BCP in Mandarin can in fact be specific, a point also attested in (106), where the BCP is governed by the preposition *ba*, which generally implies specificity for its indefinite object.

    [35] Unless it is immediately preceded by a demonstrative, which may serve as its head-governor: *zhe-ben shu* 'this-Cl book', *na-ben shu* 'that-Cl book', etc. A demonstrative phrase is freely allowed in a subject position. See note 37 below for more details.

    [36] We assume that Cl-to-D movement is optional, since a BCP in Cantonese may also have indefinite reference, when it does not occur in subject position. In Mandarin, since there is no Cl-to-Num movement, the Cl never has a chance to fill the D position, so only the indefinite reading is available.

This establishes the TSM > Mandarin > Cantonese order in a hierarchy of relative analyticity.[37]

In this respect, then, the difference between Mandarin and Cantonese with respect to Cl-to-Num raising is parallel to the well-known difference between English and French with respect to V-to-I raising (Emonds 1978, Pollock 1989):

(115) a. John often kisses Mary.

     b. *John kisses often Mary.

(116) a. *Jean souvent embrasse Marie

          Jean often   kisses   Marie

     b. Jean embrasse souvent Marie

          Jean kisses   often   Marie

In the treatment of Chomsky (1995), French T^0 is [+strong] and triggers overt V-to-I movement over an adverb like 'often,' whereas the [-strong] T^0 in English triggers Agree but no overt Move. Movement of V-to-I is delayed until LF, where it applies covertly. In the same manner, we can say that Cl-to-Num (and to D) movement occurs overtly in Cantonese, but covertly in Mandarin.

Lasnik (1995) proposes an alternative way to derive the French-English difference: while French has overt V-to-I movement (hence the pattern in (116)), English has affix-hopping in PF (hence the pattern in (115)). A parallel way to state the Cantonese-Mandarin difference could be that while Cantonese has a base-generated null Num, which triggers overt Cl-movement, Mandarin creates the null Num later, by deleting an unstressed *yi* 'one' in PF. In both cases, the more synthetic languages employ overt movement, while the more analytic ones do not.

Regardless of which alternative is followed, the differences in derivational timing correctly characterize English and Mandarin Chinese as being more analytic than French and Cantonese, respectively.

7.2. VERB-OBJECT WORD ORDER

These dialects also exhibit a pattern of variation in word order that can be similarly described in terms of a V-movement parameter. Liu (2002) has shown that Chinese dialects may be divided according to whether they are "strongly, mildly, or weakly

---

[37] The deletion/omission of 'one' is also allowed immediately following a demonstrative in Mandarin (*zhe ben shu* 'this book,' *na ben shu* 'that book') and Cantonese (*ni bun syu* 'this book,' *go bun syu* 'that book'). This is expected, assuming that the empty 'one' is governed by the demonstrative. In TSM, as expected, the corresponding forms are ill-formed: *che pun chheh* for 'this book' and *he pun chheh* for 'that book.' Although forms like *chit pun chheh* and *hit pun chheh* are grammatical in TSM, these are derived from the contraction of 'this+one' and 'that+one,' respectively, but not from any deletion of 'one':

(i)   chit pun chheh = che + chit pun chheh 'this+one Cl book'

(ii) hit pun chheh = he + chit pun chheh 'that+one Cl book'

    A parallel pattern also optionally obtains in Mandarin, as in *zhei ben shu, nei ben shu*, with *zhei* =*zhe* +*yi*, and *nei* =*na* + *yi*.

VO-type" languages, and Cantonese, Mandarin, and TSM are a member of each respective type. More specifically: (a) Cantonese is almost strictly SVO, with the verb preceding the object even when the object is definite or focalized; (b) Mandarin allows SVO or SOV order (preferring the latter for focalized objects); and (c) TSM strongly favors the SOV order. These are illustrated by examples (117)–(119):

(117)   a.   ngo m   jungyi bun syu   (Cantonese)
             I   not like   Cl book
             'I don't like this book.'

        b.   ??ngo bun syu m   jungyi
             I   Cl book not like

(118)   a.   wo bu xihuan zhe ben shu   (Mandarin)
             I   not like   this Cl book
             'I don't like this book.'

        b.   wo zhe ben shu   bu xihuan
             I   this Cl book not like
             'I don't like this book.'

(119)   a.   ??goa khuann bou chit pun chheh   (TSM)
             I   read   not this Cl Book
             'I can't read this book.'

        b.   goa chit pun chheh khuann bou
             I   this Cl book   read   not
             'I can't read this book.'

We can characterize these differences in terms of whether V-movement across a definite object (in Spec of VP) is obligatory, optional or blocked—a pattern that again reflects their relative analyticity.

7.3. OTHER VARIATIONS IN V-MOVEMENT

There are several other correlated variations among these dialects. Lamarre (2008) reports on a parametric difference in the choice between two forms expressing 'he went to Beijing':

(120)   a.   ta dao   Beijing qu le
             he toward Beijing go Perf/FP
             'He went to Beijing.'

        b.   ta qu Beijing le.
             he go Beijing Perf/FP
             '= (120a)'

Option (b) represents the synthetic form and option (a) the analytic form. The synthetic form is obtained when a light null predicate replaces *dao* and triggers movement of *qu*. Lamarre notes that while Mandarin allows both options (a) and (b), Cantonese requires option (b), while an earlier stage of Mandarin (of the Ming-Qing period, 1368–1911 A.D.) allows only option (a). A ranking of relative analyticity obtains among these dialects, then: Ming-Qing Mandarin > Modern Mandarin > Cantonese.

A difference between Mandarin and TSM with respect to causative incorporation is observed in Cheng et al. (1997). The following contrast is representative:

(121)   a.   na   ping   jiu   hai   zan laoda   he-zui   le. (Mandarin)
             that bottle wine cause our big-brother drint-drunk FP
             'That bottle of wine caused our Big Brother to get drunk (from drinking it).'

        b.   na   ping   jiu   he-zui-le   zan laoda   (Mandarin)
             that bottle wine drink-drunk-Perf our big-brother
             'That bottle of wine got our Big Brother drunk (from drinking it).'

(122)   a.   hit   kuan   chiu hai   lan laotua-e   lim-tsui   a.   (TSM)
             that bottle wine cause our big-brother drink-drunk FP
             '= (121a)'

        b.   *hit   kuan   chiu lim-tsui   lan laotuo-e a.   (TSM)
              that bottle wine drink-drunk our big-brother
             'Intended: = (121b)'

The Mandarin synthetic option (121b) is formed when a null light verb in place of *hai* 'cause' attracts the main verb *he-zui* 'drink-drunk.' But the same process is unavailable in TSM as shown in (122b).

Finally, Tang (2006) shows that the above patterns of variation correspond to the distribution of aspectual suffixes among these dialects. In particular, while Mandarin aspectual suffixes are limited to the durative *zhe,* the perfective *le,* and the experiential *guo,* Cantonese allows higher-level elements to occur after aspectual suffixes (e.g., *sai* 'all,' *tak* 'only,' and *ngaang* 'should,' suggesting that the verb (or VP) has moved to a higher position than in Mandarin. On the other hand, TSM aspects are expressed by lexical auxiliaries preceding the verb, rather than as suffixes. Thus, corresponding to Mandarin perfective and durative aspectual suffixes -*le* and -*zhe,* TSM resorts to the lexical auxiliaries *wu* 'have' and *ti* 'be at':

(123)   ta   chang-le/zhe   ge   (Mandarin)
        he sing-Perf/Dur song
        'He has sung / is singing songs.'

(124)   i   u/ti   chhiunn kua.   (TSM)
        He have/be-at sing   song
        'He has sung / is singing songs.'

This means that while Mandarin and Cantonese have [-strong] suffixes that trigger Agree and covert V-movement (or Affix-Hopping in PF), TSM has lexical auxiliaries that are subject to neither process.

In short, we have seen that the analytic-synthetic opposition can be used to describe systematic and correlating differences among dialects, as it does for the description of large-scale typological variation and change. In the case of Chinese dialects, we see a number of correlating differences (with respect to classifier-phrase structure, verb-object order, causative incorporation, distribution of aspectual elements, etc.) jointly point to a systematic difference in relative analyticity among TSM, Mandarin, and Cantonese.

8. Summary and Conclusion

In the preceding sections I have juxtaposed a number of salient syntactic properties of Modern Chinese and showed that, together and in comparison with English, they characterize Modern Chinese as a language of high analyticity at multiple levels—with respect to lexical structure, clausal functional structure, and argument structure. By contrast, we saw that Old Chinese differed consistently from Modern Chinese in displaying a range of properties that make it a language of considerable synthesis. OC and MnC mark two important stages in the long history of Chinese syntax, during which the language developed from considerable synthesis to high analyticity, peaking at Late Middle Chinese, before gradually acquiring some features of mild synthesis again, as seen among the modern dialects.

We saw that the typological features exhibit remarkable consistency, across different categories and different domains of grammar. Their joint occurrence in one language and joint absence in another point to the existence of macro-variations and macro-parameters. In each case of our observation, however, it was shown that each distinguishing property could be characterized by a micro-parameter defined over the nature of some lexical or functional items. We saw that the general features of a checking system, couched in a P&P framework, shed light on the nature of synchronic variation and diachronic change. In the latter case, the parametric treatment of grammatical change accords well with grammaticalization research and captures some of its important insights, as has been shown in recent generative literature on historical syntax.

This picture, with observed macro-variation patterns that are, nevertheless, described in micro-parametric terms, brings us back to a question mentioned at the beginning, on the status of macro-parameters in current linguistic theory. As Baker (2008) argues, important generalizations would be lost in "a world of micro-parameters" if nothing is done to explain the clustering of correlating parametric values that have been observed, both herein and elsewhere in the literature. For example, if the 16 properties mentioned above of Modern Mandarin (summarized in (20), (24) and (64)) were each derived from an independent micro-parameter, there could be as many as 65,536 (2 to the 16th power) dialects realizing all the logical possibilities, but the overwhelming majority of these logical possibilities are clearly not realized. How do we explain this fact?

To be sure, at least in our case, the answer is not to give up the micro-parametric approach and return to a macro- or mega-parameter like [α analytic] or [β synthetic]. For one thing, the postulation of such parameters goes against the spirit of minimalist research and has to be abandoned in view of mounting evidence for the minimal size of UG. For another, a parameter like [α analytic] is too crude to capture the finer details of variation, including the fact that the analytic-synthetic opposition is a continuum, and a language is either more analytic or less so than another, but not in absolute terms. And, the extent of property-clustering may vary from language to language: not all languages exhibit consistent analyticity or synthesis across all categories (see note 6). In fact, a given property could be subject to lexical variation within a given language or dialect as well.[38]

There are other considerations relevant to a full discussion on the tension between micro- and macro-parameters, but I will leave this with a reference to a plausible answer in recent works that suggest an independent mechanism for deriving macro-parametric effects from micro-parameters—in particular the recent proposal in Roberts and Holmberg (2010) that macro-parameters exist as "aggregates of micro-parameters acting in concert" as a result of children's conservative learning strategy. Very simply put, the macro-parameters-as-aggregates hypothesis assumes that children will generalize the value of a fixed micro-parameter concerning one lexical or functional category to a similar parameter concerning other categories. If a given formal property for a given light verb has its value set at [+strong], then the same value setting is assumed for light nouns, light adjectives, and light prepositions as well, and conversely a [-strong] setting for a given category will be generalized to other categories, unless evidence to the contrary is encountered, in which case a departure from the default will result. This would be sufficient to explain the correlation of properties that give rise to macro-parameters as observed without having to postulate macro-parameters as irreducible primitives. Future research will be needed to determine how far this hypothesis can go, for all apparent cases of macro-variation, both here and in other languages.

Acknowledgments

This chapter is based on a good number of lectures I have given over the last several years, in colloquia, lecture series, and conference presentations at various locations, including Rutgers University, University of Toronto, Sophia University, University of Chicago, Nankai University (IACL-12), Hunan University, Chinese University of Hong Kong (GLOW-in-Asia 7), Academia Sinica, Peking University, Beijing Language and Culture University, Tsing Hua University, National Taiwan Normal University, and the 2005 Summer Linguistic Institute held at MIT-Harvard. My heartfelt thanks go to the many people—students, friends, and colleagues, too many to mention without inadvertently leaving out some—for their generous comments that have helped shape the current version of this paper. This work was supported in part by National Science Council (Taiwan) #NSC102-2811-H-001-017.

---

[38] As illustrated by some of the examples of inter-dialectal variation discussed earlier. Another case in point is the existence in Mandarin of certain verb-object combinations that differ in their degree of analyticity: among the so-called V-O compounds, *bo-pi* 'peel' is a phrase (hence a case of pseudo-incorporation), *chu-ban* 'publish' is a word (hence a case of noun-incorporation), while *dan-xin* 'worry' has an intermediate status and can be used in either way (see Huang 1984).

References

Aldridge, Edith. 2012. Focus and Archaic Chinese word order. *Proceedings of NACCL-22 and IACL-18*, ed. Louis Liu and Lauren Eby, 84–101. NACCL Proceedings Online, http://chinalinks.osu.edu/naccl/naccl-22/NACCL-22_Proceedings.htm.

Aldridge, Edith. 2013. PPs and applicatives in Late Archaic Chinese. *Studies in Chinese Linguistics* 33, 139–164.

Baker, Mark. 1988. *Noun Incorporation*. Chicago: Chicago University Press.

Baker, Mark. 1996. *The Polysynthesis Parameter*. Oxford: Oxford University Press.

Baker, Mark. 2008. The macroparameter in a microparametric world. In *The Limits of Syntactic Variation*, ed. T. Biberauer, 351–374. Amsterdam: John Benjamins.

Baker, Mark. 2011. On the syntax of surface adjacency: The case of pseudo noun incorporation. Paper presented at the Workshop on Syntax-Semantics Interfaces. Academia Sinica, Taipei.

Borer, Hagit. 1984. *Parametric Syntax: Case Studies in Semitic and Romance Languages*. Dordrecht: Foris Publications.

Borer, Hagit. 2005. *In Name Only*. Structuring Sense, Vol. I. Oxford: Oxford University Press.

Chao, Yuen-Ren. 1948. *Mandarin Primer*. Cambridge, MA: Harvard University Press.

Cheng, Lisa Lai-Shen. 1991. *The Typology of Wh-Questions*. Doctoral dissertation, MIT.

Cheng, Lisa L.-S., C.-T. James Huang, Y.-H. Audrey Li, and C.-C. Jane Tang. 1997. Causative compounds across Chinese dialects: A study of Cantonese, Mandarin and Taiwanese. *Chinese Languages and Linguistics* 4, 199–224.

Cheng, Lisa L.-S., and Rint Sybesma. 1999. Bare and not-so-bare nouns and the structure of NP. *Linguistic Inquiry* 30, 509–542.

Cheng, Lisa L.-S., and Rint Sybesma. 2005. Classifiers in four varieties of Chinese. In *Handbook of Comparative Syntax*, ed. Guglielmo Cinque and Richard S. Kayne, 259–292. Oxford: Oxford University Press.

Chierchia, Gennaro. 1998. Plurality of mass nouns and the notion 'semantic parameter'. In *Events in Grammar*, ed. Susan Rothstein, 53–103. Dordrecht: Springer.

Chomsky, Noam. 1973. Conditions on transformations. In *A festschrift for Morris Halle*, ed. Stephen Anderson and Paul Kiparsky, 232–286. New York: Holt, Rinehart & Winston.

Chomsky, Noam. 1991. Some notes on economy of derivation and representation. In *Principles and Parameters in Comparative Grammar*, ed. Robert Freidin. Cambridge, MA: MIT Press. [Also reprinted as Chapter 2 of Chomsky 1995.]

Chomsky, Noam. 1995. *The Minimalist Program*. Cambridge, MA: MIT Press.

Chomsky, Noam. 2000. Minimalist inquiries: The framework. In *Step by Step: Essays on Minimalist Syntax in Honor of Howard Lasnik*, ed. Roger Martin, David Michaels, and Juan Uriagereka, 89–155. Cambridge, MA: MIT Press.

Chomsky, Noam. 2001. Derivation by Phase. In *Ken Hale. A Life in Language*, ed. Michael Kenstowicz, 1–52. Cambridge, MA: MIT Press.

Chomsky, Noam. 2005. Three factors in language design. *Linguistic Inquiry* 36, 1–22.

Christensen, Kirsti-Koch. 1986. Norwegian *ingen*: A case of post-syntactic lexicalization. In *Scandinavian Syntax*, ed. Ö. Dahl and A. Holmberg. Stockholm: Institutionen för lingvistik, Stockholms universitet.

Cinque, Guglielmo. 1999. *Adverbs and Functional Heads*. Oxford: Oxford University Press.

Davidson, Donald. 1967. The logical form of action sentences. In *The Logic of Decision and Action*, ed. N. Rescher, 81–95. Pittsburgh: University of Pittsburgh Press.

Diesing, Molly. 1992. *Indefinites*. Cambridge, MA: MIT Press.

Djamouri, Redouane, Waltraud Paul, and John Whitman. 2013. Syntactic change in Chinese and the argument-adjunct asymmetry. In *Breaking Down the Barriers*: Studies in Chinese Linguistics and Beyond, ed. Guangshun Cao, Hilary Chappell, Redouane Djamouri and Thekla Wiebusch, 577–594. Taipei: Institute of Linguistics, Academia Sinia.

Dong, Hongyuan. 2005. *Gradable Adjectives in Chinese and Degree Morphemes*. Ms., Cornell University.

Dowty, David. 1979. *Word Meaning and Montague Grammar*. Dordrecht: Springer.

Embick, David. 2007. Blocking effects and analytic/synthetic alternations. *Natural Language & Linguistic Theory* 25, 1–37.

Emonds, Joseph. 1978. The verbal complex V'-V in French. *Linguistic Inquiry* 9, 151–175.

Feng, Shengli. 1996. Prosodically constrained syntactic changes in early Archaic Chinese. *Journal of East Asian Linguistics* 5, 323–371.

Feng, Shengli. 2005. Qingdongci yiwei yu gujin Hanyu de dongbin guanxi [Light-verb movement and verb-object relation in Modern and Classical Chinese]. *Yuyan Kexue [Linguistic Sciences]* 1, 3–16.

Feng, Shengli. 2014. Historical syntax of Chinese. In *The Handbook of Chinese linguistics*, ed. C.-T. James Huang, Y.-H. Audrey Li, and Andrew Simpson, 537–575 Malden, MA: Wiley-Blackwell Publishers.

Gelderen, Elly van. 2011. *The Linguistic Cycle: Language Change and the Language Faculty*. Oxford and New York: Oxford University Press.

Giannakidou, Anastasia. 2002. Licensing and sensitivity in polarity items: From downward entailment to (non-)veridicality. *Proceedings of CLS 39*. Chicago: Chicago Linguistic Circle.

Gianollo, Chiara, Cristina Guardiano, and Giuseppe Longobardi. 2008. Three fundamental issues in parametric linguistics. In *The Limits of Syntactic Variation*, ed. Theresa Biberauer, 109–142. Amsterdam: John Benjamins.

Greenberg, Joseph H. 1963. Some universals of grammar with particular reference to the order of meaningful elements. In *Universals of Grammar*, ed. Joseph H. Greenberg, 73–113. Cambridge, MA: MIT Press.

Hale, Kenneth. 1983. Warlpiri and the grammar of non-configurational languages. *Natural Language & Linguistic Theory* 1, 5–47.

Hale, Kenneth, and Samuel J. Keyser. 1993. On argument structure and the lexical expression of syntactic relations. In *The View from Building 20: Essays in Honor of Sylvain Bromberger*, ed. K. Hale and S. J. Keyser, 53–109. Cambridge, MA: MIT Press.

Hale, Kenneth, and Samuel J. Keyser. 2002. *Prolegomenon to a theory of argument structure*. Cambridge, MA: MIT Press.

He, Chuansheng. 2008. *Verb Movement in Archaic Chinese*. Ms., Hong Kong Polytechnic University.

Heim, Irene, Howard Lasnik, and Robert May. 1991. Reciprocity and plurality. *Linguistic Inquiry* 22, 63–101.

Holmberg, Anders. 2010. Parameters in minimalist theory: The case of Scandinavian. *Theoretical Linguistics* 36, 1–48.

Hu, Chirui. 2005. Cong yinhan dao chengxian I [From covert to overt I]. *Yuyanxue Luncong* 31, 1–22.

Hu, Chirui. 2008. Cong yinhan dao chengxian II [From covert to overt II]. *Yuyanxue Luncong* 38, 99–127.

Huang, C.-T. James. 1982 [1998]. *Logical Relations in Chinese and the Theory of Grammar*. Doctoral dissertation, MIT. (Published in 1998 by Garland Publishing.)

Huang, C.-T. James. 1984. Phrase structure, lexical integrity, and Chinese compounds. *Journal of the Chinese Language Teachers Association* 19, 53–78.

Huang, C.-T. James. 1988. *Wo pao de kuai* and Chinese phrase structure. *Language* 64, 274–311.

Huang, C.-T. James. 1995. Historical syntax meets phrase structure theory, paper presented at IACL-4, University of Wisconsin at Madison, 1995.

Huang, C.-T. James. 1997. On lexical structure and syntactic projection. *Chinese Languages and Linguistics* 3, 45–89.

Huang, C.-T. James. 2003. The distribution of negative NPs and some typological correlates. In *Functional Structure(S), Form and Interpretation*, ed. Y.-H. Audrey Li and Andrew Simpson, 262–280. New York: Routledge, 2003.

Huang, C.-T. James. 2005. Syntactic analyticity: The other end of the parameter. Lecture notes, 2005 LSA Linguistic Institute, Harvard University and MIT.

Huang, C.-T. James. 2006a. Resultatives and unaccusatives: A parametric view. *Bulletin of the Chinese Linguistic Society of Japan* 253, 1–43.

Huang, C.-T. James. 2006b. The macro-history of Chinese syntax and the theory of change. Paper presented at the Workshop on Chinese Linguistics, University of Chicago.

Huang, C.-T. James. 2008. Variation and change in parametric theory: Three questions concerning the syntax and history of suo sentences. Keynote speech, at The Past Meets the Present: A Dialogue Between Historical Linguistics and Theoretical Linguistics, Academia Sinica, July 2008.

Huang, C.-T. James. 2010. Lexical decomposition, silent categories, and the localizer phrase. *Yuyanxue Luncong* 39, 86–122.

Huang, C.-T. James. 2013. Variations in non-canonical passives. In *Non-canonical Passives*, ed. Artemis Alexiadou and Florian Schaefer, 95–114. Amsterdam: John Benjamins.

Huang, C.-T. James, and Masao Ochi. 2004. Syntax of the hell. In *Proceedings of NELS-34*, 279–294

Jelinek, Eloise. 1984. Empty categories, case and configurationality. *Natural Language and Linguistic Theory* 2, 39–76.

Jiang, L. Julie. 2012. *Nominal Structure and Language Variation*. Doctoral dissertation, Harvard University.

Johnson, Kyle B. 1994. *Bridging the Gap*. Ms., University of Massachusetts, Amherst.

Johnson, Kyle. 2009. Gapping is not (VP-)ellipsis. *Linguistic Inquiry* 40, 289–328.

Kayne, Richard. 1994. *The Antisymmetry of Syntax*. Cambridge, MA: MIT Press.

Kayne, Richard. 1998. Overt vs. covert movement. *Syntax* 1, 128–191.

Kayne, Richard. 2005. *Movement and Silence*. Oxford: Oxford University Press.

Kayne, Richard. 2013. Comparative syntax. *Lingua* 130, 132–151.

Kennedy, Chris. 2007. *Vagueness and Grammar: The Semantics of Relative and Absolute Gradable Adjectives*. Ms., University of Chicago.

Kim, Young-Wha, ed. 2011. *Plurality in Classifier Languages*. Seoul: Hankook Munhwasa Publishing.

Kiparsky, Paul. 2005. Blocking and periphrasis in inflectional paradigms. *Yearbook of Morphology* 2005, 113–135.

Kiss, Katalin. 1998. Identificational focus versus information focus. *Language* 74, 245–273.

Krifka, Manfred. 1987. Common nouns: A contrastive analysis of Chinese and English. In *The Generic Book*, ed. Gregory Carlson and F. Jeffry Pelletier, 398–411. Chicago: University of Chicago Press.

Krifka, Manfred. 1995. Common nouns: A contrastive analysis of Chinese and English. In *The generic book*, ed. Gregory Carlson and Francis Pelletier, 398–411. Chicago: University of Chicago Press.

Kuo, Chin-Man. 1996. *The Interaction Between daodi and Wh-Phrases in Mandarin Chinese*. Ms., University of Southern California.

Lamarre, Christine. 2008. *Divergent Evolution of Directionals in Two Non-Standard Varieties of Sinitic*. Paper presented at the symposium The Past Meets the Present, Academia Sinica.

Larson, Richard. 1988. On the double object construction. *Linguistic Inquiry* 19, 335–391.

Larson, Richard. 1998. Events and modification in nominals. In *SALT VIII*, ed. D. Strolovitch and A. Lawson, 145–168. Ithaca, NY: Cornell University.

Lasnik, Howard. 1995. Verbal morphology: Syntactic Structures meets the Minimalist Program. In *Evolution and Revolution in Linguistic Theory: Essays in Honor of Carlos Otero*, ed. H. Campos and P. Kempchinsky, 251–275. Washington, D.C.: Georgetown University Press.

Lasnik, Howard. 1999. On feature strength: Three minimalist approaches to overt movement. *Linguistic Inquiry* 30, 197–217.

Lasnik, Howard. 2003. *Minimalist Investigations in Linguistic Theory*. New York: Routledge.

Lasnik, Howard, and Mamoru Saito. 1984. On the nature of proper government. *Linguistic Inquiry* 15, 235–289.

Levin, Beth, and Malka Rappaport Hovav. 1995. *Unaccusativity: At the Syntax-Lexical Semantics Interface*. Cambridge, MA: MIT Press.

Li, Y.-H. Audrey. 1992. Indefinite *wh* in Chinese. *Journal of East Asian Linguistics* 1, 125–156.

Li, Y.-H. Audrey. 1998. Determiner phrases and number phrases. *Linguistic Inquiry* 29, 693–702.

Lin, T.-H. Jonah. 2001. *Light Verb Syntax and the Theory of Phrase Structure*. Doctoral dissertation, University of California, Irvine.

Lin, T.-H. Jonah. 2014. Light verbs. In *The Handbook of Chinese Linguistics*, ed. C.-T. James Huang, Y.-H. Audrey Li, and Andrew Simpson, 73–99. Malden, MA: Wiley-Blackwell Publishers.

Lin, T.-H. Jonah, and C.-Y. Cecilia Liu. 2005. Coercion, event structure and syntax. *Nanzan Linguistics* 2, 9–31.

Lin, Jo-Wang. 1998. On existential polarity *wh*-phrases in Chinese. *Journal of East Asian Linguistics* 7, 219–255.

Liu, Danqing. 2002. Hanyu fangyan de yuxu leixing bijiao [A comparative study of word order types among Chinese dialects]. In *Cong yuyi leixing dao leixing bijiao* [*From Semantic Types to Typological Comparison*], ed. Youwei Shi, 222–244. Beijing: Beijing Language and Culture University Press.

Longobardi, Giuseppe. 1994. Reference and proper names: A theory of N-movement in syntax and logical form. *Linguistic Inquiry* 25, 609–665.

Liu, Jingnong. 1958. *Hanyu wenyan yufa* [*Grammar of Classical Chinese*]. Taipei: Chung-Hua Shuju.

Lu, Guo-Yao. 1982. Mengzi *yi yang yi zhi, yi zhi yi yang* liangzhong jiegou leixing de duibi yanjiu [A study of the contrast between *yi yang yi zhi* and *yi zhi yi yang* in the Mencius]. In *Xianqin Hanyu yanjiu* [*Studies on Pre-Qin Chinese*], ed. Cheng Xiangqing, 272–290. Jinan: Shandong Educational Press.

Ma, Jianzhong. 1898. *Ma shi wentong* [*Ma's Grammar*]. Beijing: Commercial Press.

Massam, Diane. 2001. Pseudo noun incorporation in Niuean. *Natural Language & Linguistic Theory* 19, 153–197.

McCawley, James D. 1968. Lexical insertion in a transformational grammar without deep structure. *Proceedings of CLS 4*: 71--80. Chicago: Chicago Linguistic Society.

Mei, Kuang. 2003. Yingjie yige kaozhengxue he yuyanxue jiehe de hanyuyufashi y anjiu de xin jumian [Anticipating a new horizon of the historical syntax of Chinese incorporating philology and linguistics]. In *Gujin tongsai: Hanyu de lishi yu fazhan* (*Historical Development of Chinese Language*), ed. Dah-An Ho, 23–47. Taipei: Institute of Linguistics, Academia Sinica.

Mei, Tsu-lin. 1989. The causative and denominative functions of the *s- prefix in Old Chinese. In *Proceedings of the 2nd International Conference on Sinology*, 33–51. Taipei: Academia Sinica.

Mei, Tsu-Lin. 1991. Cong han dai de *dong-sha* he *dong-si* lai kan dongbu jiegou de fazhang [On the historical development of the 'verb-result complement' construction based on V-*kill* and V-*die* in the Han Dynasty]. *Yuyanxue Luncong* [Essays on Linguistics] 16, 112–136.

Mei, Tsu-Lin. 2008a. Jiaguwen li de jige fufuyin shengmu [Some consonant cluster in oracle bone inscriptions]. *Zhongguo Yuwen* 3, 195–207. (In Chinese)

Mei, Tsu-Lin. 2008b. Shanggu Hanyu dongci zhuo-qing bieyi de laiyuan [The origin of voicing alternation in Old Chinese verbs]. *Minzu Yuwen* 3, 3–20. (In Chinese)

Mei, Tsu-lin. 2012. The causative *s- and nominalizing *-s in Old Chinese and related matters in Proto-Sino-Tibetan. *Language and Linguistics* 13, 1–28.

Parsons, Terence. 1990. *Events in the semantics of English*. Cambridge, MA: MIT Press.

Paul, Waltraud. 1999. Verb gapping in Chinese: A case of verb raising. *Lingua* 107, 207–226.

Peyraube, Alain. 1996. Recent issues in Chinese historical syntax. In *New Horizons in Chinese Linguistics*, ed. C.-T. James Huang and Y.-H. Audrey Li, 161–214. Dordrecht: Springer.

Peyraube, Alain. 2003. On the history of place words and localizers in Chinese: A cognitive approach. In *Functional Structure(S), Form and Interpretation*, ed. Y.-H. Audrey Li and Andrew Simpson, 180–198. London: Routledge-Curzon.

Pesetsky, David. 1987. Wh-in-situ: Movement and unselective binding. In *The Representation of (In)Definiteness*, ed. Eric Reuland and Alice ter Meulen, 98–129. Cambridge, MA: MIT Press.

Pollock, Jean-Yves. 1989. Verb movement, Universal Grammar, and the structure of IP. *Linguistic Inquiry* 20, 365–424.

Poser, William. 1992. Blocking of phrasal constructions by lexical items. In *Lexical Matters*, ed. Ivan Sag and Anna Szabolsci, 111–130. Stanford, CA: CSLI Publications.

Pustejovsky, James. 1995. *The Generative Lexicon*. Cambridge, MA: MIT Press.

Rizzi, Luigi. 1982. *Issues in Italian Syntax*. Dordrecht: Foris Publications.

Roberts, Ian. 2007. *Diachronic Syntax*. Oxford: Oxford University Press.

Roberts, Ian, and Anders Holmberg. 2010. Introduction: Parameters in minimalist theory. In *Parametric Variation: Null Subjects in Minimalist Theory*, ed. Theresa Biberauer, Anders Holmberg, Ian Roberts, and Michelle Sheehan, 1–57. Cambridge: Cambridge University Press.

Roberts, Ian and Anna Roussou. 2003. *Syntactic Change: A Minimalist Approach to Grammaticalization*. Cambridge: Cambridge University Press.

Safir, Ken, and Tim Stowell. 1988. Binominal *each*. In *Proceedings of NELS 28*, 426–450.

Sanders, Gerald, and James H-Y. Tai. 1972. Immediate dominance and identity deletion. *Foundations of Language* 8, 161–198.

Sapir, Edward. 1921. *Language: An Introduction to the Study of Speech*. New York: Harcourt Brace Jovanovich.

Shen, Yang, and Rint Sybesma. 2010. Jufa jiegou biaoji *gei* yu dongci jiegou de yansheng guanxi [On the marker *gei* and its relation to the derivation of VP structure]. *Zhongguo Yuwen*. 3, 222–237.

Simpson, Andrew. 2005. Classifiers and DP Structure in Southeast Asia. In *The Oxford Handbook of Comparative Syntax*, ed. Guglielmo Cinque and Richard Kayne, 806–838. Oxford: Oxford University Press.

Simpson, Jane. 1983. Resultatives. In *Papers in Lexical-Functional Grammar*, ed. L. Levin et al., 143–157. Bloomington: Indiana University Linguistics Club.

Soh, Hooi Ling. 1998. *Object Scrambling in Chinese*. Doctoral dissertation, MIT.

Stowell, Tim. 1981. *Origins of Phrase Structure*. Doctoral dissertation, MIT.

Sybesma, Rint. 1992. *Causatives and Accomplishments: The Case of Chinese ba*. Doctoral dissertation, Leiden University.

Sybesma, Rint. 1998. *The Mandarin VP*. Dordrecht: Springer.

Tai, James H.-Y. 1984. Verbs and times in Chinese: Vendler's four categories. In *Papers from the Parasession on Lexical Semantics*, ed. David Testen, Veena Mishra, and Joseph Drogo, 289–296. Chicago: Chicago Linguistic Society.

Tang, C.-C. Jane. 1990. *Phrase Structure in Chinese and the Extended X-Bar Theory*. Doctoral dissertation, Cornell University.

Tang, Sze-Wing. 2001. The (non-)existence of gapping in Chinese and its implications for the theory of gapping. *Journal of East Asian Linguistics* 10, 201–224.

Tang, Sze-Wing. 2006. Hanyu fangyan shoushi huatiju leixing de canshu fenxi [A parametric analysis of the typology of theme topics in Chinese dialects]. *Yuyan Kexue* [*Linguistic Sciences*] 5, 3–11.

Ting, Jen. 2010. On the climbing of the particle *suo* in Mandarin Chinese and its implications for the theory of clitic placement. *The Linguistic Review* 27, 449–483.

Tsai, W.-T. Dylan. 1994. *On Economizing A-Bar Dependencies*. Doctoral dissertation, MIT.

Tsai, W.-T. Dylan. 2001. On subject specificity and theory of syntax-semantics interface. *Journal of East Asian Linguistics* 10, 129–168.

Uriagereka, Juan. 1998. *Rhyme and Reason*. Cambridge, MA: MIT Press.

Vendler, Zeno. 1967. *Linguistics in Philosophy*. Ithaca, NY: Cornell University Press.

Wei, Pei-Chuan. 2003. Shanggu Hanyu dao zhonggu Hanyu yufa de zhongyao fazhan [Important developments from Archaic to Middle Chinese grammar]. In *Gujin Tongsai: Hanyu de lishi yu fazhan* [*History and Development of Chinese Language*], ed. Dah-An Ho, 75–106. Taipei: Academia Sinica.

Wu, Hsiao-hung Iris. 2002. On Ellipsis and Gapping in Mandarin Chinese. MA thesis, National Tsing Hua University.

Xu, Dan. 2006. *Typological Change in Chinese Syntax*. Oxford: Oxford University Press.

Part One

THE NOMINAL DOMAIN

2

A Parametric Analysis of Nominal Arguments in Classifier Languages

L. JULIE JIANG

1. Introduction

An important property of Romance and Germanic languages is that they have overt morphological exponents of grammatical number. For example, in English, whether or not we are referring *one book* or *many* will determine the form of the noun we use: *book* versus *books*. Additionally, numerals in these languages combine directly with nouns: *one book* versus *two books*. Nevertheless, not all languages are like Romance and Germanic languages: most Sino-Tibetan languages, such as Mandarin and most other East Asian languages, do not express grammatical number, and more important, do not allow numerals to combine directly with nouns. For example, in (1), a 'measure word' or 'classifier' is required to connect a noun with a numeral regardless of whether the noun is conceptually count or mass. In this chapter, we refer to languages with a typically extensive inventory of 'measure words' or 'classifiers' that must be used in combining a numeral with any noun as *classifier languages* (ClLs in short).[1]

(1) a. *san   xuesheng   a'. *san   ge   xuesheng* (Mandarin)
         three student   three $Cl_{individual}$ student
                                    'three students'

     b *yi   shui   b'. *yi   sheng shui*
        one water   one Cl_{liter} water
                                    'one liter of water'

In addition to obligatorily requiring classifiers when counting nouns with numerals, ClLs at least share two more properties. First, they freely allow an indefinite use of numeral-classifier phrases, as illustrated with one example from Mandarin (2a) and one from Yi, a Sino-Tibetan ClL (2b).[2]

---

[1] See Jiang (2012) for a more refined definition of 'classifier languages.'

[2] Some ClLs allow a definite interpretation of the numeral-classifier phrase in addition to the indefinite interpretation, such as Bangla (Dayal 2010; Jiang 2012) and Vietnamese (Nguyen 2004).

(2)   a.   wo mai le   *san   zhang zhuozi*   (Mandarin)
           I   buy Asp three Cl   desk
           'I bought three desks.'

      b.   *nga zhuop-zyr sɔ   ma vy lo.*   (Yi)
           I   desk   three Cl bought
           'I bought three desks.'

Second, all ClLs freely allow bare arguments. So far, no known ClLs disallow bare nouns to freely appear in argument position regardless of whether or not they possess overt articles. In Mandarin, for example, its bare nouns receive a kind interpretation when occurring with a kind level predicate (e.g., Krifka 1995) (3i); they receive a generic reading in generic sentences (e.g., Cheng and Sybesma 1999; Yang 2001) (3ii); in episodic sentences, they can receive either a definite or an existential reading in both subject and object position (e.g., Yang 2001) (3iii).

(3)   Mandarin Bare nouns
      (i)   bare nouns with kind level predicates
            xiong jue-zhong   le.
            bear   vanish-king Asp
            'The bear is extinct.'   (Krifka 1995)

      (ii) bare nouns in generic sentences
            gou   hen   *jiling.*
            dog   very   smart
            a. Dogs are intelligent.'

            b. 'The dog(s) is/are intelligent.'   (Yang 2001)

      (iii) bare nouns   in   episodic sentences
            a.   *waimian gou zai   jiao.*
                 outside   dog Prog   bark
              i. 'Outside, dogs are barking.'

              ii. 'Outside, the dog(s) are/is barking.'   (Yang 2001)

            b.   *fangjian li   zuo zhe yi   ge nansheng yi ge nüsheng,*
                 room   inside sit Prog one Cl boy   one Cl girl
                 nansheng kan-qi-lai   hen   nianqing.
                 boy   look   very young
                 'There is a boy and a girl sitting in the room; the boy looks very young.'

Besides the above three main universal properties that ClLs share, there are properties that are also typical of them but in a variable manner. They concern different ways in which classifier system may be realized. The first property along which ClLs may vary is whether or not numeral-less classifier phrases (a.k.a., *bare ClPs* in the literature) are freely allowed, as exemplified in (4a) and (4b). This is a dimension along which ClLs vary significantly (e.g., see Cheng and Sybesma 1999; 2005; Simpson 2005).

(4)   a.   *zek gau zungji sek juk.*   (Cantonese)
           Cl dog like eat meat
           'The dog likes to eat meat.'

b. *__jia gau__ be   lim   zhui.*   (Southern Min)
   Cl dog want drink water
   Intended: 'The dog wants to drink water.'   (Cheng and Sybesma 1999; 2005)

The second variable property of ClLs lies in the existence of an overt definite determiner. The majority of ClLs lack overt determiners like 'the' or 'a,' although they do, of course, have demonstratives like 'that' and 'this' (5). Nevertheless, a small number of ClLs do have overt determiners, such as Yi (e.g., Jiang and Hu 2010; Jiang 2012) (6).

(5)   a   __zhe ge ren__   b.   __liang ge ren__   c.   __zhe liang ge ren__   d.   __zhe ren__   (Mandarin)
         this Cl man   two Cl man   this two Cl man   this man
         'this man'   'two men'   'these two men'   'this man'

(6)   a.   __tsho ma su__   b.   __tsho tsh1 ma__   c.   __tsho nyip ma__   d.   __tsho tsh1 nyip ma__   (Yi)
          man Cl the   man this Cl   man two Cl   Man this two Cl
          'the man'   'this man'   'two men'   'these two men'

      e.   __tsho nyip ma su__   f.   __*tsho su__
           man two Cl the   man the
           'the two men'

In this chapter, I aim to explain the above language universals and variation in ClLs. More generally, I consider how the facts from ClLs inform us about nominal argument formation. This chapter is organized as follows. Section 2 presents previously established data on bare ClPs and reviews two analyses of bare ClPs. In Section 3, I propose an analysis of numeral-classifier phrases in ClLs that explains their universal properties and derives their variable properties. Section 4 presents consequences that follow from the proposed analysis, discusses predictions that my analysis makes about other types of ClLs, and points out directions for typological investigation in the future. Section 5 summarizes and concludes.

2. Established Data on Bare ClPs and Two Previous Analyses

In this section, I will present previously established data on bare ClPs in four SVO ClLs and four SOV ClLs and review two analyses of bare ClPs. The four ClLs with the SVO word order to be examined are Cantonese, Mandarin, Southern Min, and Wu (Fuyang dialect). Cantonese freely allows bare ClPs [Cl-NP] to appear in both subject and object position. When Cantonese bare ClPs appear in object position, they can either be definite or indefinite (nonspecific), as shown in (7a) and (7b); they only receive a definite interpretation when occurring in subject position (7c) (e.g., see Cheng and Sybesma 1999).

(7)   a.   *ngo zungji tong __zek gau__ waan.*   (Cantonese)
           I   like   with Cl dog play
           'I like to play with the dog.' Not: 'I like to play with a dog/ dogs.'

b. *ngo soeng maai <u>bun syu</u>   (lei   taai).*
   I   want buy   Cl book come read
   'I want to buy a book (to read).'

c. <u>zek gau</u> *zungji sek juk*
   Cl   dog like   eat meat
   'The dog likes to eat meat.'
   Not: 'Dogs like to eat meat.'/ 'A dog likes to eat meat.'   (Cheng and Sybesma 1999)

Mandarin allows bare ClPs in a rather limited distribution, with an indefinite reading only, as illustrated in (8a) and (8b) (see Lü 1944; Chao 1968; Li 1997; Cheng and
Sybesma 1999; among many others).

(8) a. *wo xiang   mai <u>ben shu</u>*   (Mandarin)
       I   would-like buy Cl book
       'I would like to buy a book.'

   b. **<u>zhi gou</u> yao   guo   malu.*
      Cl dog want cross road
      Intended: 'A dog wants to cross the road.'   (Cheng and Sybesma 1999)

The contrast between (8a) and (8c) shows that Mandarin exhibits a subject-object
asymmetry with respect to the position in which bare ClPs can appear. However, it is
not the case that Mandarin bare ClPs are freely allowed in the postverbal position. Lü
(1944: 170–171) has examined and described a series of contexts in which Mandarin
bare ClPs are disallowed. One of these contexts can be characterized along the following lines: Mandarin bare ClPs can never occur in a coordination structure after the first
conjunct in a listing situation where there are multiple nominals, as illustrated in (9).

(9) *ta mai le   (yi) jian yifu,   *(yi)* **ben shu,** *he *(yi)* **zhang CD.**   (Mandarin)
    he buy Asp one Cl clothes,   one Cl book, and one Cl   CD.
    'He bought a piece of clothes, a book, and a CD.'

Differing from Cantonese and Mandarin, Southern Min does not allow bare ClPs
at all; their classifiers can never appear with a noun without the occurrence of a numeral, as shown in (10) (e.g., Cheng and Sybesma 2005).

(10) A **ua siuN bue <u>bun zhu</u>*   (Southern Min)
        I   want buy Cl book
        Intended: 'I would like to buy a book.'

   b. **<u>jia gau</u> be   lim   zhui*
      Cl dog want drink water
      Intended: 'The dog wants to drink water.'   (Cheng and Sybesma 2005)

In Wu (Fuyang dialect),[3] bare ClPs can appear in either preverbal positions (subject and shifted object positions) or postverbal positions (base-generated object

---

[3] This Wu (Fuyang dialect) is different from the Wu (Wenzhou dialect) discussed in Cheng
and Sybesma (2005). Wu-Fuyang dialect belongs to the Taihu Lake clusters of the Northern Wu
dialect. It is spoken in the Fuyang city, in the northwest of Zhejiang province and to the southwest
of Shanghai, with about 600,000 speakers (c.f. X. Li 2011).

positions) (e.g., X. Li 2011). Preverbal bare ClPs in Wu (Fuyang) have a definite interpretation, as shown in (11a) and (11b), and postverbal bare ClPs have an indefinite interpretation, as shown in (11c).

(11) a. *tsəʔ giu sʔ-n̠iɔ die.*   (Wu:Fuyang)
        Cl dog die   Part
        'The dog died.'

    b. *ŋɤ saŋ gə yoʔ   bu tsʰotsʔ ma le   uælæ die.*
        I   last Cl month Cl car   buy Perf back Part
        'I went to buy the car last month.'

    c. *ŋɤ maʔ le   bu tsʰotsʔ. n   tsʰæ-tsʰa-kʰan zʔ goʐ   tsoʔ ?*
        I   buy Perf Cl car.   you guess be   what car
        'I bought a car. Can you guess what car it is?   (X. Li 2011)

Turning to ClLs with the SOV word order, some SOV ClLs do not allow bare ClPs at all, such as Japanese or Korean, as illustrated in (12) and (13), respectively.

(12) a. **kodomo ri-ga   benkyoo shite-iru*   (Japanese)
        child   Cl -Nom study   do-be
        Intended reading: 'One/The child is studying.'

    b. **John-wa   hong satsu-o   katta*
        John-Top book Cl   -Acc bought
        Intended reading: 'John bought a book.'

(13) a. **soi   mali-ka   swuley-lul kkul-ko iss-ta*   (Korean)
        cow Cl -Nom cart-Acc   pull-Del Prog-Decl
        Intended reading: 'The/One cow is pulling a cart.'

    b. **na-nun haksayng myeng-ul po-ass-ta*
        I-Top   student Cl-Acc see-Past-Decl
        Intended reading: 'I saw one/the student.' (Jiang 2012)

Other SOV ClLs do freely allows bare ClPs; Bangla and Yi are cases in point. Bangla freely allows bare ClPs in the order [NP-Cl] but not [Cl-NP]; its bare ClPs only receive a definite interpretation (14) (Dayal 2010, 2011b, 2012).

(14) a. **ta boi*   b. *boi   ta*   (Bangla)
        Cl book   book Cl
                 'the book'   (Dayal 2011b)

Compared with bare ClPs in other ClLs, Yi bare ClPs behave quite differently in that although they are freely allowed in both subject and object positions, they *only* receive an *indefinite* interpretation (15).

(15) a. *tsho   ma dza dzu ndʐɔ*   (Yi)   [indefinite]
        person Cl rice eat Progressive
        'A person is having meal.'

    b. *tshi mu   ma ʂɯ   bo o*   [indefinite]
        he   horse Cl look-for go SFP
        'He went to look for a horse.'

c. *si-hni ma* sini *sse-vo ma* i go   nyi, #*si-hni ma* dʑi   ndʐa.   [*definite]
    girl   Cl and boy   Cl house sit, girl   Cl very beautiful
    Intended: 'A girl and a boy are sitting in the room; the girl is very pretty.'

d. *a-nyie ma* a-hie   yo   yie.   [generic]
    cat   Cl mouse catch should
    'A cat should catch mice.'

e. **ko-lo   ma* gi   o.   [*kind]
    dinosaur Cl extinct SFP
    Intended: 'Dinosaurs are extinct.'   (Jiang 2012)

In episodic sentences, Yi bare ClPs can freely appear in both subject and object positions, receiving an indefinite interpretation only (15a, b), and cannot be used anaphorically (15c). In generic sentences, Yi bare ClPs receive a generic interpretation (15d). Yi bare ClPs cannot occur with kind level predicates (15e).

To summarize the data that I have shown above, in SVO languages, Min disallows bare ClPs, Mandarin allows bare ClPs in object position only, with an indefinite interpretation, Wu (Fuyang) allows definite bare ClPs in subject position and indefinite bare ClPs in object position, and Cantonese allows definite bare ClPs in both subject and object positions and indefinite bare ClPs in object position only. In SOV languages, neither Japanese nor Korean allows bare ClPs, but Bangla and Yi freely allow bare ClPs in both subject and object positions. In Bangla, bare ClPs only receive a definite interpretation, whereas bare ClPs in Yi only receive an indefinite interpretation.

In the rest of this section, I will briefly review two analyses of bare ClPs proposed by Cheng and Sybesma (1999, 2005) and Simpson (2005), respectively. Cheng and Sybesma (1999) propose that classifiers are like determiners in Romance and Germanic languages, which turn predicates to arguments and yield the definite interpretation (comparable to an iota operator 'ι' in the semantics). Their argument for this proposal is based on the fact that bare ClPs [Cl-NP] in Cantonese can freely occur in argument positions with a definite interpretation. In their analysis, all definites (bare ClPs and bare nouns) and generics have the structure in which a Cl is filled either by the ι operator (realized as an overt classifier) or a moved noun, as in illustrated in (16a). As for indefinite nominals (i.e., numeral-taking ClPs, bare ClPs, and bare nouns), Cheng and Sybesma propose that they all have the structure in (16b), in which Num and Cl may be left empty and the head of NumP can undo the definiteness introduced by the head of ClP.

(16)   a. Definites and generics   b. Indefinites

                ClP (≈DP)   NumP

           Cl   NP   Num   ClP
                     |
                     N   Cl   NP
                                                               |
                                                               N

Cheng and Sybesma explain the interpretational and distributional differences of bare ClPs phrases among the four Chinese dialects, Cantonese, Mandarin, Southern Min, and Wu, by adopting some assumptions in Longobardi (1994). In particular, they make the following two assumptions: (i) when the Cl position is filled (by a classifier or a moved noun), the ClP receives either a definite or a generic interpretation and is not limited to lexically governed positions, and (ii) when the phrase above NP contains an empty head, it receives an indefinite interpretation, and the empty head must be lexically governed. According to Cheng and Sybesma, Cantonese differs from Mandarin and Min in whether or not it is possible to have an overt classifier without a numeral and whether or not definiteness is expressed by a segmental operator ι in Cl in the form of a full-fledged classifier. Min differs from Cantonese and Mandarin in that Min cannot have empty numerals, whereas other ClLs can. However, their analysis has the following problems. First, as pointed out by Simpson (2005), it is problematic to assume that classifiers correspond to the definite article since definite articles are always higher than Numeral Phrases in the structure (e.g., *the three boys* in English). Second, semantically, the head of ClP might not be the locus of definiteness since, for instance, bare ClPs are also freely allowed in Yi but only receive an indefinite interpretation. Third, the government-based account would predict that indefinite bare ClPs in Yi cannot appear in subject position but only object position, similar to those in Cantonese; however, it is not the case (e.g., see (15)).

Simpson (2005) argues against the view that Cls correspond to the definite article, as in Cheng and Sybesma (1999, 2005), and proposes a head movement account for bare ClPs based on Longobardi's (1994) DP hypothesis. Longobardi's DP hypothesis has several important components. The first one is that an empty D head leads to a default existential interpretation; second, an empty head must be lexically governed (as a result of ECP constraints); third, if the D head is filled, the DP receives a definite interpretation. Simpson analyzes definite bare ClPs in Cantonese as a result of the Cl-to-Num-to D movement, as shown in (17).

(17)

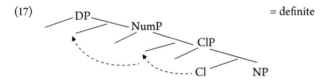

= definite

When the head of ClP undergoes Cl-to-Num-to-D movement, the D head position is filled, and the whole bare ClP receives a definite interpretation—this is the case for the definite bare ClPs in Cantonese. When no movement occurs from Cl to D, the D head position remains unfilled, and the DP receives a default existential reading, as illustrated in (18).

(18)

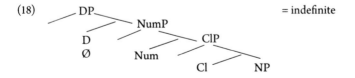

= indefinite

Syntactically, when the D head is not filled, the distribution of the DP is restricted to lexically governed position (due to the ECP constraint).

Simpson's analysis can explain why indefinite bare ClPs can only occur in object positions but not subject positions in the three languages: Mandarin, Cantonese, and Wu (Fuyang); it also can explain language variation with respect to different semantic interpretations of bare ClPs in these languages while keeping a universal structure—DPs for all nominal arguments. However, there are some problems for this DP hypothesis-based analysis as well. First, like the analysis in Cheng and Sybesma (1999, 2005), the government-based account cannot explain why the indefinite bare ClP can freely appear in both subject and object position in Yi. Second, if we assume head movement from Cl to D position for definite readings in Cantonese, we should expect that bare nouns in this language might also undergo N-to-D movement to receive a definite interpretation in the same way as its bare ClPs. However, it is not the case. Unlike bare ClPs, which can freely receive a definite interpretation, bare nouns in Cantonese do not freely allow a definite reading (see Cheng and Sybesma 2005; Wu and Bodomo 2009; Simpson et al. 2011 for discussions on Cantonese bare nouns).

In the next section, I will present an analysis of nominal arguments in ClLs that explains the universal properties that ClLs share and derives in a parametric manner their variable properties.

3. An Alternative Account for the Universal Properties and Variable Properties in ClLs

3.1. WHAT CLLS HAVE IN COMMON

In this section, I will show the analysis of the semantics and structure of numeral-classifier phrases adopted in this chapter. First, I adopt the analysis that nouns in ClLs are kind-referring (e.g., see Krifka 1995; Chierchia 1998; Yang 2001; Dayal 2011b; X. Li 2011; Jiang 2012). Second, I adopt the analysis that classifiers are relations between numerals and kinds (e.g., see Krifka 1995; Jiang 2012). In other words, classifiers can be viewed as 'transitive'; they have two semantic arguments: the noun and the numeral. The semantics of classifiers is to turn a kind-referring noun into a property, measure/check *atoms* in this set, and relate a numeral with the atomized noun (19ia) (see Jiang 2012 for details). Third, I adopt the analysis that numerals are phrasal in the syntax (e.g., Selkirk 1977; Li 1999; Haegeman and Guéron 1999; Borer 2005; Ionin and Matushansky 2006; Di Sciullo 2012; among others) and are ambiguous in the Universal Lexicon (e.g., Jiang 2012; Dayal 2012). In particular, I adopt the analysis of numerals in Jiang (2012), which is based on the analysis of indefinites in terms of choice functions, as in Reinhart (1997), Winter (1997), and Kratzer (1998). In these works, indefinites are assumed to involve a function variable in their semantics that assigns an individual to the restriction of the predicate (c.f. Winter 1997: 409); this function is a choice function that is subject to existential closure. The existential quantification associated with the choice function is assumed to apply at any scope site (see Winter 1997: 409–411 for details). This choice function analysis of indefinites has an advantage in explaining their long-distance scope behaviors. Jiang (2012) attributes the choice function variable to numerals as part of their lexical semantics and argues that each numeral of type <<e,t>, <e,t>> has a lexically predictable alternant of type <<e,t>, e>, formed via a lexical rule, as shown in (19ib).

Regarding the structure of numeral-classifier phrases, I adopt the analysis proposed in Li (1997) and Cheng and Sybesma (1999), as illustrated in (19ii).

(19)   Semantics and Structure of Numeral-Classifier Phrases
   i.   Semantics of bare nouns, classifiers, and numerals
      a. $Cl_{individual} = \lambda k \lambda n\, [n(AT(^{\cup}k))]$
            $= \lambda k \lambda n f_{\exists}\, (n(AT(^{\cup}k)))$
      b. Lexical rule of ambiguous numerals
            $Numeral_{<<e,t>, <e,t>>} = \lambda P[n(P)]$
            If $\alpha \in Num_{<<e,t>, <e,t>>}$, then $\lambda P\, f\exists\, (\alpha\, (P)) \in Num_{<<e,t>, e>}$

         f is a choice function and is subject to existential closure ($f\exists$) at arbitrarily chosen scope sites

   ii. Structure of Num-CIPs

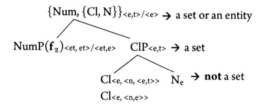

$\{Num, \{Cl, N\}\}_{<e,t>/<e>}$ → a set or an entity

$NumP(\mathbf{f_{\exists}})_{<et, et>/<et,e>}$ $ClP_{<e,t>}$ → a set

$Cl_{<e, <n, <e,t>>}$ N_e → **not** a set
$Cl_{<e, <n,e>>}$

In (19ii), I represent the structure of numeral-taking CIPs in the framework of *bare phrase structure* as in Chomsky (1994 et seq.).[4] According to this framework, the basic structure-building operation that comes 'free' (in that it is required in some form for any recursive system) is *Merge*. Merge can be viewed as a function that takes two elements, say α and β, and creates a new one consisting of the two; the simplest element constructed from α and β is the unordered set {α, β} (see Chomsky 2004: 108).[5]

Let us look at a concrete example from Mandarin to see how the analysis above works. In (20a), the numeral-classifier phrase *san ge ren* 'three Cl man' has the semantics and structure in (20b) and (20c), respectively.

(20) a. *san*   *ge*   *ren*   (Mandarin)
          three $Cl_{individual}$ man
          'three men'

---

[4] Although I have adopted the framework of *bare phrase structure* (Chomsky 1994, 1995 et seq.) to illustrate the structure of numeral-classifier phrases, not much would change if I adopted standard X-bar theory.

[5] When *Merge* maps two elements α and β into a set of the two {α, β}, some mechanism has to be put in place to determine which of the two elements should be the head of the phrase. Perhaps this can be done by type theory or some feature-based theory; this is a general concern, and the reader should feel free to adopt his or her preferred analysis.

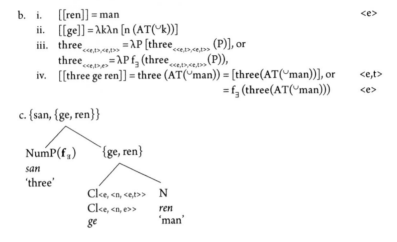

b. i.   [[ren]] = man $<e>$
    ii. [[ge]] = λkλn [n (AT($^∪$k))]
    iii. three$_{<<e,t>,<e,t>>}$ = λP [three$_{<<e,t>,<e,t>>}$ (P)], or
         three$_{<<e,t>,e>}$ = λP f$_∃$ (three$_{<<e,t>,<e,t>>}$(P)),
    iv. [[three ge ren]] = three (AT($^∪$man)) = [three(AT($^∪$man))], or $<e,t>$
                                                = f$_∃$ (three(AT($^∪$man))) $<e>$

c. {san, {ge, ren}}

    NumP(f$_∃$)   {ge, ren}
    san
    'three'
                    Cl$_{<e, <n, <e,t>>}$ N
                    Cl$_{<e, <n, e>>}$ ren
                    ge   'man'

In (20b), *AT* means *atomicity checking* and is the function of individual classifiers like *ge*. It can be understood as a relation between numerals and atomized noun denotation. Specifically, *AT* turns the kind-referring noun *ren* 'man' into sets containing singular *atoms* and relates numeral *san* 'three' with the atomized noun (20biv).[6] 'Atoms' can be simply defined in the traditional way: as definite singular count nouns (e.g., *the desk, the concept*), which are relevant only to the plural domain but not to the mass domain (e.g., Link, 1983).[7] In (20c), the classifier *ge* first merges with the noun *ren* 'man,' forming a set {ge, ren}; this set *obligatorily* merges with a numeral *san* 'three,' forming {san, {ge, ren}}, as required by the semantics of classifiers (e.g., (19ia)).

As we will see, the above analysis of the semantics and structure of numeral-classifier phrases has very promising consequences—it naturally explains the three universal properties of ClLs shown in section 1. First, it justifies the status of classifiers in ClLs. Since bare nouns in ClLs are kind-referring (i.e., entities; see Carlson, 1977b for reasons why kinds are entities), they cannot combine directly with numerals (i.e., numerals need to combine with sets containing atoms/groups). Therefore, it is reasonable to conjecture that some function becomes necessary in such languages to connect numerals with kind-referring nouns. Classifiers provide such a function, that is, they make a noun denotation atomic/countable and relate numerals with atomized noun denotation. This provides a natural role for classifiers and addresses the issue of why classifiers are obligatory with numerals in ClLs (e.g., (1)). Second, the

---

[6] Crucially, this analysis of individual classifiers in (20), that they take a kind-referring noun and a numeral, can apply to all other types of classifiers as well; thus, it provides a uniform analysis of classifiers in Mandarin (see Jiang 2012 for details).

[7] Or, assuming that the mass domain and the plural domain both contain atoms and only differ in whether they contain minimal stable atoms (i.e., in the mass domain (e.g., *water*), one cannot define the minimal stable atoms; however, atoms can be well defined in the plural domain (e.g., *apples*; Chierchia 2010), the atoms checked by individual classifiers can be defined as the minimal stable ones, and these atoms are still populated by the denotations of definite singular count nouns, as in the traditional view. The proposed atomic checking by individual classifiers is compatible with both views of atoms.

analysis in (19) explains the universal indefinite interpretation of numeral-classifier phrases in ClLs (e.g., (2)). The choice function variable in the lexical semantics of each numeral allows numeral-containing phrases across languages to have an indefinite interpretation. Third, the analysis in (20) correctly predicts that an obligatory ClL in which nouns cannot occur bare as arguments should not exist. Given that bare nouns in ClLs are always argumental, we should expect that any ClL always allows bare nouns to merge directly with verbs and occur freely in argument position.

In the following sub-section, I will propose a parametric analysis of language variation in ClLs with respect to bare ClPs and articles.

3.2. PARAMETERS OF ClLS

The language variation in ClLs, as I propose, can be reduced to two parameters: (i) some ClLs have a process that derives *bare* ClPs in an unrestricted manner, perhaps via a lexical 'intransitivization' process (INTR) for classifiers, but some others don't; (ii) some ClLs have a lexical D in their grammar, while some others don't. These two parameters may be linked in certain ways, and I remain agnostic as to how they could be related. Regarding these two parameters, the second one [±D] is quite straightforward, but the first one $[\pm Cl_{Intr}]$ requires some elaboration, which I will provide below.

As shown above, numeral-containing classifier phrases uniformly exist in classifier languages, including those that freely allow bare ClPs like Cantonese and Yi. Compared with the cross-linguistic behavior of numeral-classifier phrases, it is important to acknowledge that the bare ClP/numeral-less ClP is only a *variable* property of classifier languages, rather than a universal property of them. Such a variable property is attested in some ClLs like Cantonese, Bangla, and Yi (e.g., (7), (14), (15)), but it is not the property of other ClLs such as Min, Japanese, and Korean (e.g., (10), (12), (13)). The variable property (i.e., bare ClP) should be regarded as a special sub-variety of Num-ClPs: ClLs uniformly allow numeral-classifier phrases, but they do not always allow numeral-less classifier phrases. However, if some ClLs freely permit bare classifier phrases, they must also allow Num-ClPs. That is to say, we should not expect to find a classifier language that has only numeral-less ClPs but not Num-ClPs.

With regard to how to account for bare ClPs, it is important to point out that any successful analysis of classifiers has to deal with both the cross-linguistic property of classifiers and their variable property. It has to explain what makes all classifier languages uniformly allow numeral-classifier phrases and why only some ClLs allow numeral-less ClPs. As shown in (20), the universal use of classifiers is the 'transitive' one, that is, classifiers have two semantics arguments and obligatorily require a noun and a numeral in their lexical semantics in order to complete a *numeral-taking* classifier phrase {n, {Cl, NP}}. To derive *numeral-less* bare ClPs {Cl, NP} (a variable property attested only in *some* ClLs), a certain operation becomes necessary to 'remove' one of the two arguments (i.e., the numeral) from the classifiers. Next, I consider two such processes. These two processes are respectively employed by ClLs which allow bare ClPs in a restricted way and by ClLs that freely allow bare ClPs. I use Mandarin and Yi to illustrate the two processes.

As we have seen in (8) and (9), Mandarin allows bare ClPs in a rather limited distribution (e.g., in a position immediately following a verbal element); [8] this can be the result of a process that applies in a *restricted* form, perhaps via a PF one-deletion rule along the lines first pursued in Lü (1944) (and elaborated in Chao 1968; Li 1997; Borer 2005; Huang 2009; Jiang 2012; Li and Feng 2013; among others).[9] What this one-deletion analysis implies is that bare ClPs in Mandarin are *not* really bare in the syntax, that is, they have the structure {one, {Cl, NP}}, and eliding *one* during the process of externalization simply results in a prima facie bare form of the ClPs {~~one~~, {Cl, NP}}. Semantically, eliding *one* either leads to a long-distance choice function (CF) reading or a GQ reading. As for the semantic difference between the prima facie bare ClPs {~~one~~, {Cl, NP}}and NC {one, {Cl, NP}}, it lies in that the former cannot be used in contrastive or focused environments where the information conveyed by the numeral *one* is stressed/important (e.g., Lü 1944; Li and Bisang 2011).[10] This difference can be viewed as the semantic condition for eliding *one*. Except for this difference, Mandarin numeral-less ClPs and numeral-taking ClPs do share two main interpretations: the narrow scope existential reading (i.e., the GQ reading) (e.g., Cheng and Sybesma 1999; Li and Bisang 2011; Jiang, 2012) and the long-distance scope reading (i.e., the choice function reading) (e.g., Jiang, 2012). This *one*-deletion analysis of Mandarin bare ClPs is illustrated in (21).

(21)   One-deletion, deriving bare ClPs (applied in a restricted way)

    a.   *mei   ge youke dou bei   (yi) ge nühai-r huyou   mai le   yi   bu shouji.*
        every Cl vistor all Pass one Cl girl   hoodwink buy Asp one Cl cell-phone
        'Every tourist was hoodwinked to buy a phone by a girl.'[a girl > ∀], [∀ > a girl]
                                                   (Jiang 2012)

---

[8] An example of bare ClPs in a position immediately following a stressed nominal element is given in (1a) below. In addition, Mandarin bare ClPs seem to have a restriction on the types of verbal elements preceding them (1b).

(1)   a.   *zhe/mei   (yi) ge ren*   b.   *wo jiao   guo   *(yi) ge nongmin,*
         this every one Cl person   I   teach Asp   one Cl farmer
         'this person'/ 'every person'   Intended: 'I (have) taught a farmer.'

[9] Both Cheng and Sybesma (1999) and Li and Bisang (2011) provide arguments against the one-deletion view of Mandarin bare ClPs first proposed in Lü (1944), but see Li (1997), Borer (2005), Huang (2009), and Jiang (2012) for arguments in favor of the one-deletion approach.

[10] Two examples to illustrate the difference between numeral-less ClPs and numeral-taking ClPs in Mandarin are given in (4) in which the numeral *one* cannot be omitted.

(2)   a.   *you   *(yi) ge xuesheng, wu ge chefu.*
        have   one Cl student   five Cl carter
        'There is a student and five carters'   (Lü 1944: 167, with slight modification)

    b.   *wo hua   le   *(yi) ge xiaoshi chifan*
        I   spend Perf   one Cl hour   eat-meal
        'I spent one hour eating a meal.'   (Li & Bisang 2012: 345, ex (18))

This difference has a straightforward explanation, namely that in contrastive/focused environment, contrastive/focal stress is required; however, null elements are destressed.

b. Syntax   c. PF

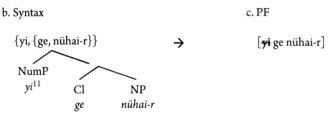

    d.   Semantic condition for eliding *yi* 'one': when the numeral *one* information is not important/stressed/focused.

    e.   Interrelations of bare ClPs: [~~one~~ Cl N] = [*one* Cl N]

        i. [[~~one~~ Cl N]] = $\lambda P \exists f [P (f (\lambda x\ one\ ((^\cup k)(x)))]$ elided *one* → GQ reading

       ii. [[~~one~~ Cl N]] = $f_3(\lambda x[one\ (AT\ ((^\cup k))(x)])$ elided *one* → CF reading

The above *one*-deletion analysis also logically explains why Mandarin bare ClPs {Cl, NP} can only be interpreted as singular and not as 'two,' 'three,' or 'some': as it is 'one' that is deleted from [*one* Cl-N], the [Cl-N] phrase can only be interpreted as singular. With regard to the distribution of bare ClPs in Mandarin (e.g., (8) and (9)), this could be viewed as the result of either certain phonological restrictions (e.g., Lü 1944, Jiang 2012; Li and Feng, 2013) or certain syntactic restrictions such as government (e.g., Cheng and Sybesma 1999; Huang 2009; Li and Bisang 2012).

Turning to Yi, this language allows *unrestricted* bare ClPs (i.e., bare ClPs can appear in any argument position) (e.g., (15)); this could due to a process that derives them in an unrestricted manner, perhaps via a *lexical* 'intransitivization' process (Intr) for classifiers (22).[12]

(22)   Lexical Rule *INTR*, deriving bare ClPs (applied in unrestricted way)

    a. $Cl = \lambda P \lambda n\ [n(AT((^\cup k))]$ or $= \lambda P \lambda n f_3(n(AT((^\cup k)))$

    b.   if $a \in$ Cl, $\lambda k \lambda x\ Cl\ (one)\ (^\cup k)(x) \in$ Cl$_{Intr}$

    c.   Cl$_{Intr}$ $= \lambda P \lambda x\ Cl_{Intr}\ (one)(\ (^\cup k)(x) = \lambda k \lambda x\ [one(AT((^\cup k))(x)]$

    d.   ClP$_{<e,t>/<e>}$

                            Intr

    NumP   ClP   →   e.   Cl$_{Intr}$P $= \lambda x\ [one(AT((^\cup k))] <e,t>$

    n

       NP   Cl   NP   Cl$_{Intr}$

The lexical rule in (22) removes one of the semantic arguments, that is, the numeral *n*, from the classifiers, yielding 'intransitive' classifiers. INTR is to be considered as a parameter [±Cl$_{Intr}$], which a language may or may not have. The lexical

---

[11] One can assume that the numeral *one* in bare ClPs is either realized in a phonetically null form (i.e., [*one*$_{null}$ Cl N]) or is deleted in the phonology after narrow syntax; the difference between these two does not make a difference for the purpose of the current discussion.

[12] It might be appealing to propose another analysis for bare ClPs in Yi: unlike Mandarin, Yi allows *one*-deletion everywhere given that `one' is sandwiched between N and CL in Yi, that is, what comes immediately before the nominal in Yi does not matter, because that element is not adjacent to the numeral 'one.' However, such an analysis, although also potentially applicable to Bangla, will not apply to other ClLs like Cantonese in which numerals precede both N and Cl and bare ClPs are also freely allowed.

rule accounts for the variable property of ClLs, explaining why some languages permit bare ClPs (e.g., Yi, Cantonese, Bangla, and Wu) and others don't (e.g., Min, Japanese, Korean).

After an intransitivized classifier merges with a noun, the structure in (22e) creates property-denoting nominals. In order to achieve the freely argumental use of the classifier-noun phrase {Cl, NP} in Yi (e.g., (15)), this property-denoting nominal can be turned into arguments via whatever device available in this language. Next, I illustrate one of the ways to argumentizing bare ClPs {Cl, NP} in Yi.

The overt definite determiner *su* can first turn {Cl, NP} into arguments with a definite interpretation. In addition to overt operations like lexical determiners, {Cl, NP} can also be turned into arguments via a covert argumentizing operation. Such an operation is not hard to justify: we can assume either a covert D in the syntax (e.g., Borer 2005), or a type-shifting operation in the semantics (e.g., Dayal 2004, 2011a), or a combination of the two (e.g., Chierchia 1998). Both the operation in the syntax and the operation in the semantics are *covert* argumentizing operations, which I refer to as ARG. The two operations are shown in (23).

(23)   a. Syntactic Projection   **or**   b. Semantic Type-Shifting

DP_{null} $\mathbf{ARG}\,(ClP_{<e,\,t>})$

$$D \qquad ClP_{<e,\,t>}$$
$$\mathbf{ARG}$$

After ARG turns property-denoting bare ClPs into arguments, we need a theory to derive the meanings of argumental bare ClPs in Yi (e.g., kinds, definite, indefinite), and various theories are available here, for example, a Chierchia-Dayal style account.

When an argumentizing operations applies to properties, in theory it can turn them into arguments with either a kind ($\cap$), definite (ι), or indefinite interpretation ($f_\exists$). Regarding these three meanings shifted via *covert* operations, Chierchia (1998) and Dayal (2004) have argued that they should be ranked in the way $\{\cap, \iota\} > f_\exists$ (24).

(24)   *Ranking of Meaning* (ranking of the three covert argumentizing operations)
       $\{\cap, \iota\} > f_\exists$ (Chierchia 1998, as revised by Dayal (2004))

The main motivation for the ranking in (24) comes from empirical evidence of the distribution of bare arguments in Hindi and Russian. In particular, Dayal (2004) observes that in languages without overt determiners like Russian and Hindi, their bare arguments can receive a kind interpretation, a definite interpretation, or a narrow scope existential reading, but *never* an indefinite interpretation. The availability of the kind and the definite interpretation of bare arguments and the unavailability of the indefinite reading of bare arguments in these languages suggest that the meaning of kinds and that of definiteness should have the same ranking and should rank higher than the meaning of indefiniteness. In (25), I illustrate how this account of bare ClPs works with two Yi examples.

(25)   Argumentizing bare ClP {Cl, NP} in Yi

    a.   *ke ma ngo xi   la*   b.   *ke ma su ngo xi   la.*

       dog Cl we bite come   dog Cl the we bite come

       'A dog came to bite us'   'The dog came to bite us.'

    c. $[[\text{ke}]]$ = dog $\langle e\rangle$

    d. $[[\text{ma}]] = \lambda k\lambda x\,[\text{one}(\text{AT}((^{\cup}k))(x)]$ $\langle e, \langle e,t\rangle\rangle$

    e. $[[\text{ke ma}]] = \lambda x\,[\text{one}(\text{AT}((^{\cup}k))]$ $\langle e,t\rangle$

    f. $[[\text{ke ma su}]] = \iota\lambda x\,[\text{one}(\text{AT}((^{\cup}k))]$ $\langle e\rangle$

    g.   If {ke, ma} is argumentized covertly via ARG, it can only be indefinite since:

       i.   ARGι {ke, ma} = blocked by the presence of *su*

       ii.   ARG∩ {ke, ma} = undefined for singular properties

       iii. ARG f∃ {ke, ma} = indefinite

In (25f), the overt definite determiner *su* can turn {Cl, NP} into arguments with a definite interpretation. In addition to overt operations like lexical determiners, {Cl, NP} can also be turned into arguments covertly via ARG (e.g., (23)). In principle, ARG could turn Yi {Cl, NP} into arguments with a definite or a kind interpretation due to the Ranking of Meanings in (24). Nevertheless, these two covert options (i.e., ARGι and ARG∩) are unavailable for the following reasons. First, the presence of an overt definite article *su* in Yi blocks the possibility of turning Yi bare ClPs covertly into arguments with a definite reading (e.g., *Blocking Principle*; see Chierchia, 1998) (25gi). Second, turning {Cl, NP} to kinds is undefined because the semantics of singularity of {Cl, NP} (e.g., (25e)) clashes with the conceptual notion of a kind that corresponds to the plurality of all instances of the property (see Dayal, 1992; Chierchia, 1998) (25gii). Accordingly, the only possibility left, according to the Ranking of Meanings, is to turn {Cl, NP} covertly into arguments with an indefinite reading via ARGf∃ (25giii). This indeed is what happens in Yi: its bare ClPs are indefinite only (e.g., (15)).

As we can see, the proposed analysis reduces language variation among these ClLs to two main parameters: $[\pm\text{Cl}_{\text{Intr}}]$ in the lexicon and $[\pm\text{D}]$ in the syntax. As for the third parameter of phonological one-deletion [± *one*-deletion] in the process of externalization (e.g., PF), it is only relevant to ClLs like Mandarin that do not have intransitivized classifiers but do allow bare ClPs in a restricted manner. In the rest of this section, I am going to show two immediate consequences of the proposed analysis.

The first immediate consequence of the proposed analysis is that it can explain the semantic interpretation and syntactic distribution of bare nouns, numeral-classifier phrases, and bare ClPs in other ClLs in a systematic and coherent way. Take Cantonese, for example. Cantonese freely allows definite bare ClPs, allows indefinite ClPs in postverbal position and does not have overt articles; according to the proposed analysis, it is a ClL with the following parametric setting $[+\text{Cl}_{\text{Intr}}, -\text{D}, +one\text{-deletion}]$. First, Cantonese bare nouns and numeral-classifier phrases are expected to behave similarly to those in Mandarin and the rest of other ClLs.[13] Note that in ClLs *with* Ds, numeral-classifier phrases and numeral-less ClPs have the option to shift to definites via the definite D, as in Yi. However, in ClLs *without* D like Cantonese, this option is not

---

[13] See Simpson et al. (2011) and Jiang (2012) for the reasons that Cantonese bare nouns generally do not receive a definite interpretation.

available. Second, since Cantonese has the intransitivization rule of classifiers, its bare ClPs should appear freely in argument position and should receive a definite interpretation despite the absence of D (due to the Rank of Meanings in (24)). Regarding Wu (Fuyang), it should have the same parametric setting $[+Cl_{Intr}, -D, +one\text{-deletion}]$ as Cantonese since it also freely allows bare ClPs in argument position. However, different from Cantonese, the semantic interpretation of Fuyang bare ClPs is restricted and is sensitive to certain syntactic positions (e.g., (11)). Here, I suggest that the restricted interpretations of Fuyang bare ClPs is a result of requirements in the clausal domain (e.g., focus, topic) rather than a result of internal structure of the classifier phrase.

It is worth pointing out that Chierchia (1998) speculates that since ClLs do not need determiners to argumentize their nouns because nouns are kind-denoting (i.e., argumental), they will never develop lexical determiners like the in English because of economy considerations. Nevertheless, this speculation is incorrect and the line of reasoning is also questionable. As we saw, Yi does have a lexical determiner, su. This fact is indeed expected, contra Chierchia's (1998) speculation: if some higher nominal projections above the bare noun, namely bare ClPs and numeral-classifier phrases, are of a predicative type ($<e, t>$), lexical determiners become relevant and may well develop to turn them into arguments.[14] Hence, the second immediate consequence of the proposed analysis is that if a ClL develops a determiner, it will be able to apply only at the level of numeral-classifier phrases, which is property-denoting, but not at the level of bare nouns, which is kind-denoting, by type theoretic considerations. If an intermediate projection between numeral-classifier phrases and bare nouns that is of type $<e,t>$, namely bare ClPs, is available, determiners can apply at this level as well. This is precisely what happens in Yi, as repeated in (26) and illustrated in (27).

(26) a. <u>*tsho   nyip ma*</u> b. <u>*tsho   nyip ma su*</u> c. <u>*tsho   ma*</u> d. <u>*tsho   ma su*</u>
       person two Cl   person two Cl SU   person Cl   person Cl Su
       'two persons'   'the two persons'   'a person'   'the person'

(27) Yi numeral-ClPs, bare nouns, and bare ClPs: *D only applies to* bare ClPs and above[15]
      a. Numeral$<<e,t>,<e,t>>$ = $\lambda P\,[n\,(P)]$ or $<<e,t>,<e,t>>$
                              = $\lambda P f_{\exists}\,(n\,(P))$ $<<e,t>,e>$

---

[14] Although Chierchia (1998) appeals to an economy condition to rule out the presence of Ds in ClLs, such an appeal is too weak since no mention is made regarding the nature of the economy condition that is supposed to be employed. At most, it can be seen as a loose appeal to economy conditions because if it were true, ClLs would have only one way to express definiteness, through bare nouns, and any other way of marking definiteness, say via type-shifting operations, would have to be regarded as uneconomic.

[15] The structure of numeral-classifier phrases in (27i) does not directly account for the linear order [N-Num-Cl] in Yi. In the proposed structure, a classifier is in the head-final position. The motivation is that Yi is a head-final language both in the clausal domain and in the nominal domain, that is, the definite D *su* appears in the head-final position within the nominal domain (25). The headedness in Yi suggests that classifiers should also appear in the head position following nouns. In addition, I assume in (27i) that numerals left-adjoin to ClPs in Yi. As a consequence, numerals and classifiers are not adjacent to form a Num+Cl sequence because nouns separate these elements. In order to obtain the surface Num+Cl sequence, two options are available. One is that after the structure in (27i) is sent to PF, some rearrangement takes place there, which establishes the observed linear order. The other option is that the noun undergoes movement to a higher position to give rise to the Num+Cl sequence.

b. $[[tsho]]$ = person $<e>$

c. $[[ma]] = \lambda k\lambda n[n \ (AT(^{\cup}k))]$ *or* $<e, <n,<e,t>>>$
    $= \lambda k[one \ (AT(^{\cup}k))]$ $<e, <e,t>>$

d. $[[tsho \ nyip \ ma]]$ = two $(AT \ (^{\cup}person))$ *or* $<e,t>$
    $= f_{\exists}(two(AT(^{\cup}person))$ $<e>$

e. $[[tsho \ ma]]$ = one $(AT(^{\cup}person))$ $<e,t>$

f. $[[tsho \ nyip \ ma \ su]] = \iota\lambda x \, [two \ (AT \ (^{\cup}person))]$ $<e>$

g. $[[tsho \ ma \ su]] = \iota\lambda x \, [one \ (AT(^{\cup}person))]$ $<e>$

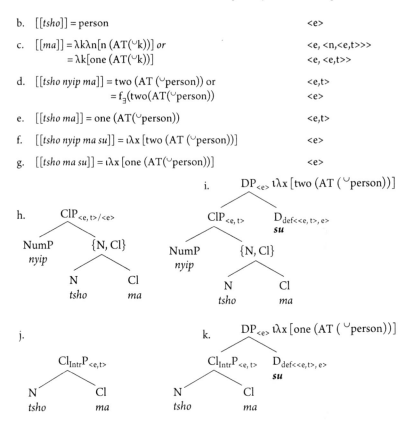

In addition to the two consequences above, a series of further consequences are expected to follow from the proposed analysis, which I will address in Section 4.

4. Further Consequences and Future Vistas

4.1. GENERIC INTERPRETATION OF BARE ClPS

So far, our discussion of bare ClPs mainly surrounds the definite and indefinite interpretations; we have seen that the proposed analysis can correctly predict the interpretation of the bare ClP in a ClL. A further consequence of the proposed analysis is that it predicts that bare ClPs may receive generic interpretation in generic sentences. The reason is straightforward: as argued in Krifka et al. (1995), the genericity in generic sentences does not come from the noun phrase but rather from an operator *Gen*, which quantifies over situations as well as objects. Semantically, the *Gen* operator can be viewed as a universal quantifier ($\forall$) quantifying over situations/possible worlds (e.g., see Kratzer 1981; Chierchia 1995). Syntactically, this Gen operator needs to be located in a *structurally high enough* position to quantify over both the external argument and the internal argument. Accordingly, *Gen* should be introduced at a position above *v*P (assuming the VP-internal Subject Hypothesis; see, e.g., Koopman and Sportiche 1991). Here we may simply assume that the *Gen* operator merges with IP since the structural details of this do not make much difference for the purposes of the current discussion (or see Chierchia, 1995 for the assumption that Gen merges with AspP). Because of the property-denoting nature of bare ClPs, when bare ClPs appear in generic sentences, they can be quantified over by the *Gen* operator, receiving a generic interpretation. This prediction is borne out by examples from Yi and Zhuang, a Tai language with an obligatory classifier system. In Yi, bare ClPs can receive a generic interpretation in generic sentences in addition to the indefinite interpretation in episodic sentences; relevant examples are repeated in (28). In Zhuang, bare ClPs are also freely allowed; they receive a definite interpretation in episodic sentences and a generic interpretation in generic sentences, as illustrated in (29) (e.g., Sio and Sybesma 2008; Liu 2010).

(28) a. *tsho̠   ma̠ dza dzu ndz̠ɔ.*   (Yi)   [indefinite]
          person Cl rice eat Progressive
          'A person is having meal.'

      b. *a-nyie ma a-hie yo   yie.*   [generic]
          cat   Cl mouse catch should
          'A cat should catch mice.'   (Jiang 2012)

(29) a. *ko:ŋ¹ ha:k⁸ ʔeu¹ te¹ pai¹ ham⁸ nai⁴*   (Zhuang)   [definite]
          Cl   officer ask him go   night this
          'The officer asked him to go there tonight.'

      b. *tu⁰ be⁴   saµ¹ iu²   tu⁰ mou¹*   [generic]
          Cl sheep clean more than Cl pig
          Sheep are cleaner than pigs.'   (Liu 2010)

4.2. TYPOLOGICAL INVESTIGATION FOR THE FUTURE

As we have seen in Section 3, the two parameters $[\pm D, \pm Cl_{INTR}]$ have captured three basic types of ClLs. The first type lacks the functional category D in the syntax as well as the lexical intransitivization rule of classifiers (i.e., $[-D, -Cl_{INTR}]$ ClLs); this type of ClL is represented by Mandarin, Min, Japanese, and Korean, in which unrestricted bare ClPs are not admitted (30i). The second type of ClL that was discussed has both the functional category D and the lexical intransitivization rule of classifiers (i.e., $[+D, +Cl_{INTR}]$ ClLs), as represented by Yi and Bangla (30ii).[16] In this type of ClL, bare ClPs are freely allowed in argument position, and Ds are only detected at the numeral-classifier phrase level and the bare ClP level (if allowed). The third type of ClL that does not have Ds but has the lexical rule of classifiers, that is, $[-D, +Cl_{INTR}]$ is instantiated by Cantonese and Wu (Fuyang) (30iii). This type of ClL also freely allows bare ClPs in argument position, and the bare ClPs can receive a definite interpretation despite the absence of D (due to the Rank of Meanings in (24)). Since nothing in the theory predicts a one-to-one correspondence between the presence of D and the lexical rule of classifiers, the proposed analysis predicts that one more type of ClL should be attested: one has D but lacks the lexical rule of classifiers, i.e., $[+D, -Cl_{INTR}]$ (30iv).

---

[16] See Dayal (2010, 2011b, 2012); and Jiang (2012) for arguments for the DP analysis of Bangla nominal arguments.

(30)   Predicting ClLs with $[\pm D, \pm Cl_{INTR}]$

	ClLs	D	Cl_{INTR}
(i)	Mandarin, Southern Min, Japanese, Korean	–	–
(ii)	Yi, Bangla	+	+
(iii)	Cantonese, Wu (Fuyang)	–	+
(iv)	?	+	–

ClLs that have the functional category D but lack the intransitivization rule of classifiers, that is, $[-Cl_{INTR}, +D]$ ClLs (30iv), are expected to have four main properties. First, they have no unrestricted bare ClPs by virtue of lacking the lexical intransitivization rule of classifiers. Second, their bare nouns should denote kinds and behave similarly to those in Mandarin and the rest of ClLs. Third, their numeral-classifier phrases should also behave similarly to those in Mandarin and the rest of ClLs. Fourth, since the only type of property-denoting nominals is numeral-classifier phrases, D should be detected only at this level, turning numeral-classifier phrases into arguments with a definite interpretation. I find that Thai matches the properties in (30iv) (see also Jiang, 2012).[17]

In addition, Mandarin allows *one*-deletion to apply to its numeral-classifier phrases in a restricted manner during the process of externalization in the PF. In principle, there could be ClLs similar to Mandarin in having the $[-D, -Cl_{INTR}]$ setting but different from it in disallowing *one*-deletion. We have seen that Southern Min/Korean/Japanese instantiates this type (i.e., their bare ClPs are simply banned (10), (12), (13)). The proposed analysis of language variation, thus, has rich consequences for the typology of nominal argument, as will be summarized in the following.

(31)   Updated Typology of nominal arguments

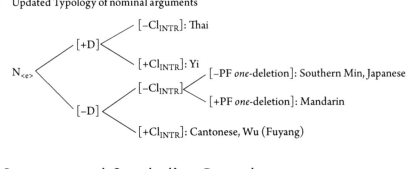

5. Summary and Concluding Remarks

In this chapter, I showed three universal properties and two variable properties of nominal arguments in ClLs. I presented an account for these language universals and variation that is free from the empirical problems of previous analyses. The proposed account is based on three core analyses of bare nouns, classifiers, and numerals: (i) bare nouns in ClLs are kind-referring, (ii) classifiers are relations between numerals

---

[17] Relevant Thai examples can be found in Jenks (2011) and Jiang (2012).

and kinds, and (iii) numerals are phrasal in the syntax and ambiguous in the Universal Lexicon. These analyses, as we have seen, explain the universal properties of nominals in ClLs. I proposed a parametric analysis that reduces language variation in ClLs to two main parameters: $[\pm Cl_{Intr}]$ in the lexicon and $[\pm D]$ in the syntax. As for the third parameter of phonological one-deletion $[\pm$ *one*-deletion$]$ in the process of externalization, it is only relevant to ClLs like Mandarin, Southern Min, and Japanese/Korean, which do not have intransitivized classifiers.

It was shown that a series of further consequences followed naturally from the proposed analysis of language variation. First, this analysis explains language variation regarding bare ClPs across ClLs in a systematic and coherent manner. Second, the proposed analysis predicts that if a ClL develops a determiner, it will be able to apply only at the level of numeral-classifier phrases, which is property-denoting, but not at the level of bare nouns, which is kind-denoting, by type theoretic considerations. If an intermediate projection between numeral-classifier phrases and bare nouns that is of type <e,t>, namely bare ClPs, is available, determiners can apply at this level as well. Third, the proposed analysis correctly predicts the existence of generic ClPs in a principled way. Last but not least, I speculated that the proposed two main parameters, i.e., $[\pm Cl_{INTR}]$ and $[\pm$ lexical D$]$ predict further ClL types that are indeed attested.

References

Borer, Hagit. 2005. *Structuring Sense, Volume 1: In Name Only*. Oxford: Oxford University Press.

Carlson, Greg N. 1977a. A unified analysis of the English bare plurals. *Linguistics and Philosophy* 1: 413–456.

Carlson, Greg N. 1977b. *Reference to Kinds in English*. Doctoral dissertation, University of Massachusetts, Amherst.

Chao, Yuen Ren. 1968. *A Grammar of Spoken Chinese*. Berkeley: University of California Press.

Cheng, Lai-Shen Lisa, and Rint Sybesma. 1999. Bare and not-so-bare nouns and the structure of NP. *Linguistic Inquiry* 30(4), 509–542.

Cheng, Lai-Shen Lisa and Rint Sybesma. 2005. Classifiers in four varieties of Chinese. In *The Oxford Handbook of Comparative Syntax*, ed. Guglielmo Cinque and Richard Kayne, 259–292. New York: Oxford University Press.

Chierchia, Gennaro. 1995. Individual-level predicates as inherent generics. In *The Generic Book*, ed.Gregory N. Carlson and Francis Pelletier, 176–223. Chicago: University of Chicago Press.

Chierchia, Gennaro. 1998. Reference to kinds across languages. *Natural Language Semantics* 6, 339–405.

Chierchia, Gennaro. 2010. Mass nouns, vagueness and semantic variation. *Synthese* 174, 99–149.

Chomsky, Noam. 1995. *The Minimalist Program*. Cambridge, MA: MIT Press.

Dayal, Veneeta. 1992. The singular-plural distinction in Hindi generics. *Proceedings of SALT II*, *OSU Working Papers in Linguistics* 40, 39–58.

Dayal, Veneeta. 2004. Number marking and (in)definiteness in kind terms. *Linguistics and Philosophy* 27(4), 393–450.

Dayal, Veneeta. 2010. *Bangla Classifiers: Mediating Between Kinds and Objects*. Presented at the Conference on Bantu, Chinese and Romance DPs. University of Leiden.

Dayal, Veneeta. 2011a. *Bare Noun Phrases*. In *Semantics: An International Handbook of Natural Language Meaning*, ed. Maeinborn, von Heusinger, and Portner, 33(2), 1088–1109. Berlin: de Gruyter.

Dayal, Veneeta. 2011b. *Bangla Classifiers: Mediating Between Kinds and Objects*. Paper presented at International Workshop on Syntax-Semantics Interface. Institute of Linguistics, Academia Sinica, Taiwan.

Dayal, Veneeta. 2012. Bangla classifiers: Mediating between kinds and objects. *Italian Journal of Linguistics*. 24(2), 195–-226.

Di Sciullo, Anna Maria. 2012. *Asymmetry in Complex Numerals*. Talk given at Harvard University.

Haegeman, Liliane, and Jacqueline Guéron. 1999. *English Grammar: A Generative Perspective*. Oxford: Blackwell.

Huang C.-T. James. 2009. *Variation and Change in Parametric Theory: An East Asian Perspective*. Harvard-MIT handout.

Jenks, Peter. 2011. *The Hidden Structure of Thai Noun Phrases*. Doctoral dissertation, Harvard University.

Jiang, L. Julie, and Suhua Hu. 2010. *An Overt Determiner in a Classifier Language*. Presented at GLOW-in-Asia VIII, Beijing, China. (Published in 2011 in *Universals and Variation: Proceedings of GLOW-in-Asia VIII 2010*, ed. Mingge Gao. Beijing: Beijing Language and Culture University Press.)

Jiang, L. Julie. 2012. *Nominal Arguments and Language Variation*. Doctoral dissertation, Harvard University.

Koopman, Hilda, and Dominique Sportiche. 1991. The position of subjects. *Lingua* 85(2/3), 211–-258.

Krifka, Manfred. 1995. Common nouns: A contrastive analysis of Chinese and English. In *The Generic Book*, ed. Gregory Carlson and Francis Pelletier, 398–411. Chicago: University of Chicago Press.

Krifka, Manfred, Francis Jeffry Pelletier, Gregory N. Carlson, Alice ter Meulen, Godehard Link, and Gennaro Chierchia. 1995. Genericity: An introduction. In *The Generic Book*, ed. Gregory N. Carlson and Francis J. Pelletier, 1–124. Chicago: University of Chicago Press.

Kratzer, Angelika. 1981. The notional category of modality. In *Words, Worlds, and Contexts*, ed. H. J. Eikmeyer and H. Rieser, 38–74. New York: de Gruyter.

Li, Charles, N., and Sandra, A. Thompson. 1976. Subject and topic: A new typology of language. In *Subject and Topic*, ed. Charles N. Li., 458–489. New York: Academic Press.

Li, Xu-Ping. 2011. *On the Semantics of Classifiers in Chinese*. Doctoral dissertation, Bar Ilan University and University of Mainz.

Li, Xuping, and Walter Bisang. 2012. Classifiers in Sinitic languages: From individuation to definiteness-marking. *Lingua* 22, 335–355.

Li, Yen-hui Audrey. 1997. *Structures and Interpretations of Nominal Expressions*. Ms., University of Southern California, Los Angeles.

Li, Yen-hui Audrey. 1998. Argument determiner phrases and number phrases. *Linguistic Inquiry* 29(4), 693–702.

Li, Yen-hui Audrey, and Shengli Feng.. 2013. Beijinghua 'yi' zi shenglüe de yunlü tiaojian [The licensing conditions for the deletion of 'one' in Mandarin]. Ms., University of Southern California and Chinese University of Hong Kong.

Link, Godhard. 1983. The logical analysis of plurals and mass terms: A lattice-theoretical approach. In *Meaning, Use and Interpretation of Language*, ed. R. Bauerle, C. Schwartze, and A. von Stechow, 302–323. Berlin: de Gruyter.

Liu, Danqing. 2010. *Yuyan Kucun Leixing Xue [Linguistic Inventory Typology]*. Presented at International Symposium for Comparative and Typological Research on Languages of China, Hong Kong.

Longobardi, Giuseppe. 1994. Reference and proper names: A theory of N-movement in syntax and logical form. *Linguistic Inquiry* 25, 609–665.

Lü, Shuxiang. 1944. 'Ge' zi de yingyong fanwei, fulun danweici qian 'yi' zi de tuoluo. [On the usages of GE and the dropping of the numeral yi before classifiers]. *Zhongguo wenhua huikan 4*. [Reprinted in 1984 in *Hanyu yufa lunwenji*, ed. Lü, Shuxiang, 145–174. Beijing: Commercial Press. Nguyen, Tuong Hung. 2004. *The Structure of the Vietnamese Noun Phrase*. Doctoral dissertation, Boston University.

Reinhart, Tanya. 1997. Quantifier scope: How labor is divided between QR and choice functions. *Linguistics and Philosophy* 20, 335–397.

Selkirk, Elisabeth. 1977. Some remarks on noun phrase structure. In *Formal Syntax*, ed. P. W. Culicover, T. Wasow, and A. Akmajian, 285–316. London: Academic Press.

Sio, Joanna, and Rint Sybesma. 2008. The nominal phrases in Northern Zhuang: A descriptive study. *Bulletin of Chinese Linguistics* 3(1), 175–225.

Simpson, Andrew. 2005. Classifiers and DP structure in Southeast Asian languages. In *The Oxford Handbook of Comparative Syntax*, eds. Guglielmo Cinque and Richard Kayne, 806–838. Oxford: Oxford University Press.

Simpson, Andrew, Hooi Ling Soh, Giang Le, and Hiroki Nomoto. 2011. Bare classifiers and definiteness: a cross-linguistic investigation. *Studies in Language* 35(1), 168–193.

Winter, Yoad. 1997, Choice functions and the scopal semantics of indefinites. *Linguistics and Philosophy* 20, 399–467.

Wu, Yicheng, and Adams Bodomo. 2009. Classifiers ≠ determiners. *Linguistic Inquiry* 40, 487–503.

Yang, Rong. 2001. *Common Nouns, Classifiers, and Quantification in Chinese*. Doctoral dissertation, Rutgers University.

3

Appositives in Mandarin Chinese and Cross-Linguistically

FRANCESCA DEL GOBBO

1. Background

A well-known distinction in the literature on relative clauses is the one between restrictive and appositive (or non-restrictive) relative clauses (see De Vries 2006, 2002, for an overview). Those two types of relative clauses are characterized by specific syntactic and semantics features, the most important of which states that while a restrictive relative clause further 'restricts' the reference of the nominal it modifies, an appositive relative clauses does not, as it simply adds information about that nominal:

(1) the man that I like   (restrictive)

(2) Jeff, whom I like   (appositive)

In (1) above, the relative clause *that I like* further restricts the reference of the nominal *the man*; in (2), the appositive relative clause specifies that I like Jeff, but the content of the relative is not necessary in order to individuate the individual referred to by the proper name, hence the appositive provides additional information.

A recent focus on these constructions has brought to light the fact that we are not facing a homogeneous set. For example, Potts (2002) distinguishes between what he calls *as*-parentheticals and *which*-appositives:

(3) a. Americans should get cheap oil, as the whole world knows.

    b. Americans should get cheap oil, which the whole world knows.

(adapted from Potts 2002)

Potts (2005) brings those two types of appositives under the same umbrella when he claims that, together with other constructions, they trigger conventional implicatures. Specifically, he studies both supplements and expressives. And among the supplemental expressions, he includes *as*-parentheticals, appositive relative clauses, appositive nominals, as well as parenthetical adverbs:

(4) a.   Ames was, as the press reported, a successful spy.

     b.   Ames, who stole from the FBI, is now behind bars.

     c.   Ames, the former spy, is now behind bars.

     d.   Cleverly, Beck started his descent.

     e.   Luckily, Beck survived the descent.

Stowell (2005) brings to our attention the following construction, which he calls a parenthetical restrictive relative:

(5) The guy next door (that I sold my car to) was arrested today. (Stowell 2005)

Finally, Cinque (2006, 2007), on the basis of evidence from Italian, distinguishes between 'integrated' and 'non-integrated' appositive relative clauses.

Against this background, my goal in this chapter[*] is to lay out a theory for a typology of appositive relative clauses. I identify three types of appositive relative clauses: non-integrated, semi-integrated and (fully)-integrated and account for their behavior by introducing two parameters (one linked to the presence or absence of the intonational break and one linked to the relative pronoun).

2. The Empirical Domain

I investigate three sets of languages, whose appositive relative clauses are distinguished by whether they are prenominal or not, whether they are introduced by a relative pronoun or not, and whether there is an intonational break.

In the first set of languages, the appositive relative is prenominal, there is no relative pronoun, and the relative clause is not set off intonationally from the matrix sentence that contains it. Two languages where appositive relatives behave this way are Chinese and Japanese, illustrated respectively in (6) and (7):

(6) [$_{CP}$ Xianglai jiu   bu   ai   du   shu de] Xiaoming xianzai ye   kaishi du
         always   then   not   love study book de Xiaoming now   also begin study
     qi   shu   lai   le
     begin book come ASP
     'Xiaoming, who does not love to study, now also has begun to study.'
                                                          (adapted from Lin 2003)

[*] A preliminary version of this paper was presented at WECOL at UC Davis in 2009 and at the LSA in San Francisco in 2008, as well as at Audrey Li's seminar on Comparative Syntax of East Asian Languages, at USC in 2011. I thank the audiences there, and in particular John Hawkins, Christopher Potts and Ivan Sag. For discussing with me some of the issues raised in the paper, I also would like to thank Brian Agbayani, Ivano Caponigro, Carlo Geraci, Gennaro Chierchia, Naomi Harada, Terri Griffith, Audrey Li, Jon Sprouse and Bernard Tranel. Special thanks also go to my consultant for Mandarin Chinese, Grace Kuo and to the reviewers Dylan Tsai and Masao Ochi for their insightful comments.

(7) [$_{CP}$ Shuuron-o   kaite i-ru   Iwasaki-san]-ga   sono
      master's.thesis-ACC write be-PRES Mr. Iwasaki-NOM the
      gakkai-de   happyo   shi-ta.
      conference-at presentation do-PAST
      'Mr. Iwasaki, who is writing a master's thesis, presented a paper at the conference.'
                                                                 (adapted from Yuasa 2005)

The second set of languages is characterized by appositive relative clauses that are set off intonationally from the matrix. Within the set, it is possible to further distinguish those relative clauses that are introduced by the complementizer (what Cinque 2006, 2007, calls the 'integrated' appositive relative clauses), from the ones that are introduced by a relative pronoun (these are called by Cinque 2006, 2007, the 'non-integrated' appositive relative clauses). Among the languages that are characterized by these types of appositive relatives, we find Italian (exs. (8), (10)) and French (exs. (9), (11)) (Cinque 1982, 2007):

(8) Inviterò   anche Giorgio, [$_{CP}$ che abita qui vicino].
      (I) will.invite also   Giorgio   that lives here close
      'I will invite also Giorgio, who lives nearby.'   (adapted from Cinque 2007)

(9) Ma soeur, [$_{CP}$ que le magistrat avait convoquée pour le lendemain], . . .
      my sister   that the magistrate had summoned for the next.day
      'My sister, whom the magistrate had summoned for the next day, . . .'
                                                                 (adapted from Cinque 1982)

(10) Inviterò   anche Giorgio, [$_{CP}$ il   quale abita qui vicino].
        (I) will.invite also   Giorgio,   the which lives here close
        'I will invite also Giorgio, who lives nearby.'   (adapted from Cinque 2007)

(11) Ma soeur, [$_{CP}$ laquelle   le magistrat avait convoquée pour le   lendemain], . . .
        my sister   the.which the magistrate had   summoned for the next.day
        'My sister, whom the magistrate had summoned for the next day, . . .'
                                                                 (adapted from Cinque 1982)

The third set of languages is represented by English and Romanian (Cinque 2007). In these languages, appositive relatives need to be introduced by a relative pronoun (*modulo* the different type discussed by Stowell 2005) and to be set off intonationally from the matrix:

(12) Ion, [$_{CP}$ pe care   nu uita   sa-l   inviti   la nunta!],
        Ion   Acc which not forget.Imp Subj-him invite.2.Sg at wedding
        te-a   cautat ieri.
        you-has sought yesterday
        'Ion, who do not forget to invite to the wedding!, looked for you yesterday.'
                                                       (adapted from Cinque 2007, citing Grosu 2005)

(13) Ames, [$_{CP}$ who was a successful spy], is now behind bars.   (adapted from Potts 2005)

Appositives in these languages behave in a substantially different way with respect to, among other phenomena: illocutionary independence from the matrix; the ability to take split antecedents; the categorial nature of the antecedent; and binding phenomena.

2.1. ILLOCUTIONARY INDEPENDENCE

English and Romanian allow appositive relative clauses to be illocutionary independent from the matrix:

(14)   There is then our father, by whom will we ever be forgiven for what we have done?

(Cinque 2006)

(15)   It may clear up, in which case would you mind hanging the washing out?

(Huddleston and Pullum 2002)

(16)   I want to talk to that man, who who the hell is he anyway?   (Andrews 1975)

In Chinese, this is not allowed; the appositive relative clause cannot be an interrogative clause:

(17)   a.   *[Hui bu hui yuanliang women de] Zhangsan juedui   bu hui zheme   zuo.
             able not able forgive   us   DE Z.S.   absolute not able this way do

        b.   *[Hui yuanliang women ma de] Zhangsan juedui   bu hui zheme   zuo.
             able forgive   us   Q DE Z.S.   absolute not able this way do
             Int. 'Zhangsan, who will ever forgive us, would have never behaved this way.'

In the previous example, two different strategies for question-formation have been used. In (17a), the auxiliary is followed by its negated copy, and in (17b), the question particle *ma* is added. None of the examples results in grammaticality. Notice, though, that it may be misleading to take the examples in (17) to show that a relative clause cannot be interrogative in Mandarin Chinese. This is because final particles such as *ma* (in example (17b)) are a root phenomenon, and are never allowed in embedded clauses; in other words, yes-no questions with *ma* in Mandarin Chinese are restricted to matrix clauses. As for A-not-A questions (the form used in (17a)), we know that they appear both in direct and indirect questions, as shown in the following examples from Huang, Li, and Li (2009):

(18)   Zhangsan bu xiaode ni   lai   bu lai.
        Zhangsan not know you come not come
        'Zhangsan does not know whether you will come or not.'

(19)   Ni juede ta hui bu hui lai   ne?
        you think he can not can come Q
        'Do you think he will come or not?'

But Huang, Li, and Li (2009) report that if the A-not-A is embedded in an island such as a relative clause, the direct question reading is unavailable:

(20)   *Ni bijiao xihuan lai   bu lai   de   na-yi   ge ren   (ne)?
        you more like   come not come Mod that-one CL person Q
        Int.: 'Do you prefer the person that will come or the one who will not?'

The sentence in (20) is ungrammatical because in order to get the wide scope reading, the A-not-A form should undergo movement at LF, and in (20) this is blocked by the ECP. In order to embed the A-not-A form inside an island, Huang, Li, and Li (2009) claim that an indirect-question interpretation is required, as when the island clauses are selected by appropriate verbs or nouns:

(21) [Ta lai   bu lai]   yidiar dou mei guanxi (*ne?)
     he come not come at.all all no matter Q
     'Whether s/he comes or not does not matter at all.'

(22) Wo xiang taolun [ta lai   bu lai   de wenti]   (*ne?)
     I   want discuss [he come not come Mod question] Q

The problem with our example in (17a), repeated below, is that the A-not-A form cannot take wide scope, and that it is not selected by an appropriate verb or noun:

(17) a. *[Hui bu hui yuanliang women de] Zhangsan juedui   bu hui zheme   zuo
        able not able forgive   us   Mod Z.S.   absolute not able this way do

But notice that if we embed *wh*-words inside appositive relative clauses in Chinese, we either get an indefinite reading or the sentence results in ungrammaticality. Here is an example where the *wh*-word is inside the relative clause and it can only have the interpretation of an indefinite:[1]

(23) Ni na-ge [shenme shihou zou-diu] de baba juedui bu hui zheme   zuo.
     you that-CL what   time   walk-lost Mod father absolute not able this.way do
     'That father of yours, who got lost sometime ago, would never do something like this.'

In the following two examples, instead, the addition of the *wh*-word inside the relative clause renders the sentence ungrammatical:

(24) *Wo xuan le dedao le duoshao piao de Zhangsan
      I   choose Asp obtain Asp how.many tickets Mod Zhangsan
      Int.: 'I chose Zhangsan, who received how many votes?'

(25) *Wo xihuan qu nail de Zhangsan
      I   like   go where Mod Zhangsan
      Int.: 'I like Zhangsan, who went where?'

The examples that more strongly show that an appositive relative clause in Mandarin Chinese cannot be interrogative are the ones in (23) through (25). We know that the

---

[1] As noted by Dylan Tsai, it's unlikely that the *wh*-expression involved in (23) is an indefinite, since there is no intensional context to license polarity interpretations. Rather, the construction in (23) may be related to the so-called *wh*-placeholder construal in Chinese, which typically appear within the scope of a definite determiner such as *nage* in (i):

(i) nage   shei dique lai-guo   zheli
    that.CL who indeed come-Exp here
    'That whatshisname indeed came here before.'

wh-word can have scope over the matrix clause or only over the embedded clause, as the following examples from Huang, Li, and Li (2009) illustrate:

(26) Zhangsan yiwei Lisi mai le   shenme?
      Zhangsan thinks Lisi buy Asp what
      'What does Zhangsan think Lisi bought?'

(27) Zhangsan xiang-zhidao Lisi mai le   shenme
      Zhangsan wonder   Lisi buy Asp what
      'Zhangsan wonders what Lisi bought.'

If an appositive relative clause in Mandarin Chinese could be interpreted as interrogative, then in the sentences (23) through (25) the *wh*-word should be able to take scope over the relative clause, but we saw that this is not possible. I therefore conclude that the evidence here provided shows that appositive relative clauses in Mandarin Chinese cannot be interrogatives, differing therefore in a crucial way from appositives in Romanian and English.

Italian behaves differently, depending on whether the appositive is introduced by the complementizer or by the relative pronoun. If introduced by the complementizer, Italian appositive relatives behave like the Chinese ones in not allowing an illocution that is different from the one of the matrix. If introduced by the relative pronoun, they behave like appositive relatives in English and Romanian, allowing the appositive to have an illocution that is different from the one of the matrix clause:

(28) *Tuo padre, [che potrà   mai perdonarci per quello che abbiamo fatto?],
       your father that will-be-able ever forgive-us for that   that have   done
       non si   sarebbe   mai comportato così.
       not himself would-be ever behaved   this-way   (Cinque 2006)

(29) Tuo padre, [il quale potrà   mai perdonarci per quello che abbiamo fatto?],
      your father the which will-be-able ever forgive-us for that that have   done
      non si   sarebbe   mai comportato così.
      not himself would-be ever behaved   this-way
      'Your father, by whom will we ever be forgiven for what we have done?, would have never
      behaved like that.'   (Cinque 2006)

2.2. SPLIT ANTECEDENTS

In English and Romanian, appositive relatives allow split antecedents:

(30) Kim bought Sandy a book$_j$, and Sam bought her a pen$_j$, [which$_{i+j}$ they gave her for
      Christmas.]   (Arnold 2004)

(31) The Queen serves muffins$_j$, and Prince Charles serves scones$_j$, [which$_{i+j}$/*that they buy at
      Harrods.]   (Arnold 2005)

(32) ?Dacă Ion$_i$ n-o mai iubeşte pe Maria$_j$, [care copii$_{i+j}$ de altfel nu s-au iubit niciodată cu
      adevărat],...
      If I. is no longer in love with M., which young people in any event never really loved each
      other,...   (Cinque 2007)

In Chinese, this is not possible:

(33)   *[Op$_{i+j}$ bu xihuan Xiaoyu de] Zhangsan$_i$ jinlai le, Lisi$_j$ zou Le
               not like   X.   DE Z.S.   enter LE Lisi exit LE

Notice that in Chinese it is perfectly fine to allow split antecedents in a different context, like the following one:

(34)   Zhangsan$_i$ jinlai le, Lisi$_j$ zou le. Tamen$_{i+j}$ bu xihuan Xiaoyu.
        Zhangsan enter LE Lisi left LE they   not like   Xiaoyu
        'Zhangsan entered, Lisi left. They don't like Xiaoyu.'

It is simply impossible to allow split antecedents with relative clauses, even if they are appositive. So, in (33), the operator inside the relative clause can only refer to the individual denoted by the 'head' of the relative, that is, Zhangsan, and it cannot in addition refer to the individual denoted by the subject of the second sentence, that is, Lisi.

It is important to observe that there can be different types of split antecedent constructions. Take the following Italian example from Cinque (2008). In this example, the two antecedents have different theta roles:

(35)   a.   Se Carlo$_i$ non amava più   Anna$_j$, i   quali$_{i,j}$ d' altra parte non si
             If Carlo not love   any-longer Anna   the which of other side   not Recipr.
             erano mai voluti   veramente bene, una ragione c'era.
             were ever wanted really   well   a   reason there was
             'If C. was no longer in love with Anna, who at any rate never really loved each
             other, there was a reason.'

Relative clauses with split antecedents were first noticed by Ross and Perlmutter (1970). The following examples are from Zhang (2007):

(36)   a.   Mary met a man$_i$ and John met a woman$_j$ who$_{i\&j}$ knew each other$_{i\&j}$ well.

       b.   A man$_i$ came in and a woman$_j$ left who$_{i\&j}$ knew each other well.

       c.   The house has a room$_i$ and the shop has a cellar$_j$ which$_{i\&j}$ are joined by a small under-
            ground passageway

Zhang (2007) claims that the two antecedents of relative clauses with split antecedents are originally two conjuncts of a coordinate nominal. She proposes that each has undergone a sideward movement, involving a move from the original working site to a new one. The two nominals take part in the construction of a coordinate clausal complex. In the old working site, a complex nominal is constructed, in which the relative clause takes the remnant coordinate nominal as its antecedent. Finally, the complex nominal adjoins to the coordinate clausal complex. Crucially, the construction that Zhang (2007) studies has a number of restrictions, the most important of which is that the two antecedents need to share the same theta-role. More in general, in order for sentences with split antecedents to be grammatical, they have to be parallel, in a sense that I will not make precise here (for details, see Zhang 2007, section 5). What is relevant for us is that it is the other type of split antecedent relative that is not allowed in Mandarin Chinese. We have seen that in Italian it is grammatical for an appositive relative clause to have two split antecedents, even when they do not share the same theta-role. Under these conditions, similar examples in Mandarin Chinese turn out to be ungrammatical. Let me start with two sentences in a piece of discourse:

(37) a. Ruguo Zhangsan bu ai   Mali le, jiu   yinggai you yi-ge   liyou.
          if   Zhangsan not love Mary Asp then must   have one-CL reason
          'If Zhangsan doesn't love Mary any longer, there must have been a reason.'

      b. Shishi-shang tamen conglai mei-you zhenzheng de   ai   guo duifang.
          reality-on   they ever   not-have really   Mod love Asp the.other
          'At any rate, they never really loved each other.'

If we try to convey what expressed in the two sentences in (37) using a simple sentence and a relative clause—as we did with the Italian example in (35)—the outcome is ungrammatical:

(38) *Ruguo [conglai mei-you zhenzheng de   ai   guo duifang de]   Zhangsan
       if   even   not-have really   Mod love Asp the.other Mod   ZS
       bu ai Mali le, jiu   yinggai you yi-ge   liyou
       not love M. Asp then must   have one-CL reason

(39) *Ruguo Zhangsan bu ai   [conglai mei-you zhenzheng de   ai   guo duifang de]
       if   Zhangsan not love ever   not-have really   Mod love Asp the.other Mod
       Mali le, jiu   yinggai you yi-ge   liyou.
       Mary Asp then must   have one-CL reason.

The sentences in (38) and (39) above are ungrammatical, in the intended reading of 'If Zhangsan doesn't any longer love Mary, who at any rate never really loved each other, there must be a reason.' The ungrammaticality of the sentences in (38) and (39) shows that appositive relative clauses in Mandarin Chinese are not able to take split antecedents, when these do not share the same theta-role.

Italian again shows a split. Appositives introduced by the complementizer behave like the Chinese ones, in not allowing split antecedents, while those introduced by the relative pronoun behave like the English and Romanian ones in allowing the pronoun inside the reference to pick up its reference from two antecedents:

(40) *Se Carlo$_i$ non amava più   Anna$_j$, [che$_{i,j}$ d'altra parte non si   erano mai
       if Carlo not loved any.longer Anna   that of other side not each.other were ever
       voluti   veramente bene], una ragione c'era.
       wanted   really   well a   reason there was
       'If Carlo was no longer in love with Anna, who at any rate never really loved each other, there was a reason.'   (adapted from Cinque 2007)

(41) Se Carlo$_i$ non amava più   Anna$_j$, [i   quali$_{i,j}$ d' altra parte non si
      if Carlo not loved any.longer Anna   the which of other side not each.other
      erano mai voluti   veramente bene], una ragione c'era
      were ever wanted really   well a   reason there was
      'If Carlo was no longer in love with Anna, who at any rate never really loved each other, there was a reason.'   (adapted from Cinque 2007)

2.3. THE CATEGORIAL NATURE OF THE ANTECEDENT

In English, appositives can modify a wide array of antecedents (CPs, APs, VPs, etc.).

(42)   a.   Mary was [$_{AP}$ intelligent], [$_{CP}$ which John never was]. (Demirdache 1991)

        b.   Joe [$_{VP}$ debated in high school], [$_{CP}$ which Chuck did too]. (Thompson 1971)

        c.   They talked [$_{PP}$ from twelve to one o'clock], [$_{CP}$ which is a long time.] (De Vries 2002)

        d.   [$_{IP}$ Fairly hasn't arrived yet], [$_{CP}$ which bothers Green]. (modified from Sells 1985 a)

In Chinese, appositives can only modify nominals:

(43)   a.   Zhangsan hen congming. Lisi conglai jiu bu congming.
             Zhangsan very smart   Lisi ever   just not smart
             'Zhangsan is intelligent. Lisi never has been.'

        b.   *Zhangsan hen [$_{CP}$ Lisi conglai jiu bu de] [$_{AP}$ congming].
             Zhangsan very   Lisi ever   just not DE   smart
             Int.: 'Zhangsan is smart, which Lisi never was.'

(44)   a.   Zhangsan zai gaozhong   zuo-guo bianlun. Lisi conglai meiyou zuo-guo.
             Zhangsan in high-school do-GUO debate. Lisi ever   not-have do-GUO
             'Zhangsan debated in high school, which Lisi never did.'

        b.   *Zhangsan [$_{CP}$ Lisi conglai meiyou zuo-guo de] [$_{VP}$ zai gaozhong   zuo bianlun]
             Zhangsan   Lisi ever   not-have do-GUO DE   in high-school do debate

(45)   a.   Wo [$_{PP}$ cong 1992 dao 1993] zai Beijing Yuyan   Xueyuan xuexi Hanyu.
             I   from 1992 to 1993 in Beijing Language Institute study Chinese
             Shijian tai duan-le.
             period too short-LE
             'From 1992 till 1993 I studied Chinese at the Language Institute in Beijing. It was
             too short (a period of time).'

        b.   *Wo [$_{CP}$ tai duan-le de] [$_{PP}$ cong 1992 dao 1993 zai Beijing Yuyan
             I   too short-LE DE   from 1992 to   1993 in Beijing Language
             Xueyuan] xuexi Hanyu.
             Institute study Chinese

(46)   a.   Zhangsan hai meiyou lai.   Zhe-jian shi shi   Lisi hen shengqi.
             Zhangsan yet not   arrived this-CL fact make Lisi very mad
             'Zhangsan hasn't arrived yet. This bothers Lisi a lot.'

        b.   *[$_{CP}$ Shi   Lisi hen shengqi de] [$_{CP}$ Zhangsan hai meiyou lai].
             make Lisi very mad   DE   Zhangsan yet not   arrive

Italian again shows a split. The appositive relative clauses introduced by the complementizer behave like the ones in Chinese, that is, they can only modify nominals.
On the contrary, those appositive relative clauses introduced by the relative pronoun
behave like the ones in English: they can modify a vast array of antecedents:

(47) a. [$_{IP}$ Carlo lavora troppo poco]. [$_{CP}$ La qual cosa verrà   certamente notata.]
           Carlo works too   little   the which thing will.be certainly   noticed
           'Carlo works too little, which will certainly be noticed.'

      b. [$_{IP}$ Carlo lavora troppo poco]. *[$_{CP}$Che verrà   certamente notato.]
           Carlo works too   little   that will.be certainly   noticed
           'Carlo works too little, *that will certainly be noticed.'   (adapted from Cinque 1988)

(48) a. Maria è [$_{AP}$ suscettibile]. [$_{CP}$ La qual cosa sua sorella di certo non è.]
           Mary is   touchy   the which thing her sister certainly not be
           'Maria is touchy, which her sister certainly is not.'

      b. Maria è [$_{AP}$ suscettibile]. *[$_{CP}$ Che sua sorella di certo non è.]
           'Mary is   touchy,   *that   her sister   surely is   not.'
                                                        (adapted from Cinque 2007)

2.4. BINDING

When we consider binding phenomena, the situation we have been delineating so far
no longer holds. We would expect the Italian appositive relatives introduced by the
complementizer to behave à la par with the Chinese ones, but this surprisingly does
not happen. Binding of a pronoun inside the appositive by a quantified nominal in the
matrix is not allowed in Italian, regardless of whether the appositive is introduced by
the relative pronoun or by the complementizer. In other words, both types of appositives in Italian behave like appositives in English and Romanian:

(49) *[Nessuno studente]$_i$ può dimenticare la   professoressa Niu, [che/la quale tanto
       no   student   can forget   the professor   Niu that/the which so-much
       lo$_i$ ha aiutato].
       him has helped

(50) *[Every Christian]$_i$ forgives John, who harms him$_i$. (Safir 1986)

In Chinese, instead, binding from the matrix into the appositive is allowed:

(51) [Mei yi-ge   xuesheng]$_i$ dou wang-bu-liao na   yi-ge   [$_{RC}$ bangzhu-guo ta$_i$ de]
       every one-CL student   all forget-not-can that one-CL   help-GUO   him DE
       Niu laoshi
       Niu prof.
       *'No student can forget Prof. Niu, who helped him.'

To summarize, we find that Chinese appositive relative clauses cannot be illocutionary independent of the matrix clause, they cannot have split antecedents, they can
only modify nominals (type NP or DP), and they do allow a quantified nominal in the
matrix to bind a pronoun in the appositive. I classify them as 'integrated' appositive
relative clauses, following the terminology established in Cinque (2006, 2007). In
Italian, appositive relative clauses introduced by the complementizer differ minimally
from the 'integrated' appositives of Chinese, insofar as they do not allow binding. Because in all other respects they do behave like the 'integrated' ones, I classify them

as 'semi-integrated' appositive relative clauses. The other type of appositive relative in Italian, the one that is introduced by the relative pronoun, behaves diametrically different from the 'integrated' type: it does allow illocutionary independence, it can have split antecedents, it can modify 'heads' of different categories, and finally, it does not allow binding. Along with the English and Romanian appositive relative clauses, it belongs to the class of the 'non-integrated' appositives (Cinque 2006, 2007). The empirical facts are summarized in the table in (52).

(52)

	illocutionary independence	split antecedents	categorial nature of antecedent	Binding
Chinese (integrated)	no	no	nominal	yes
Italian (semi-integrated)	no	no	nominal	no
Italian (non-integrated)	yes	yes	CP, AP, VP, etc.	no
English (non-integrated)	yes	yes	CP, AP, VP, etc.	no

I conclude that there are more types of appositives than originally thought by Cinque (2006, 2007). More specifically, I emphasize that the binding facts force us to take into consideration establishing a third category of appositives, what I have called the 'semi-integrated' one. In the following section, I provide an account to explain the variation just observed.

3. Proposal

My proposal is based on three core elements. First, I assume that the syntax of appositive relative clauses (henceforth, ARCs) involves some form of coordination structure (as in Li 2008; Cinque 2007; Rebuschi 2005; Frascarelli and Puglielli 2005). Second, I provide a semantics for ARCs crucially built on the idea that the relative pronoun is E-type (Demirdache 1991; Sells 1985a, b; Del Gobbo 2003a and following work). Finally, I claim that it is the syntax of prenominal relative clauses that prevents them from licensing overt relative pronouns.

I also propose two parameters to account for the variation described in section 2 of this chapter. The first parameter takes the role of the intonational break in ARCs very seriously, and in this I am very close to Potts' (2005) approach:

(53)　Intonational break
　　　If there is an intonational break, the ARCs type-shifts from at issue content to conventional implicature content (CI; Potts 2005).

Potts (2005) agrees with Grice (1975) that conventional implicatures are a conventionally triggered commitment of the speaker, while being logically independent of what it is said (the 'at issue content'). But differently from Grice, Potts (2005) maintains that CIs are not triggered by lexical items such as *but* and *therefore*; they are instead triggered by supplements (and among these, ARCs) and expressives. According to Potts (2005), CIs have the following properties:

(54) a. They contribute to the meaning of the utterance in a conventional way, i.e. they are not cancellable.

   b. They are not part of the central, at issue, content of the utterance, though they may take part of the at-issue content as arguments.

   c. They never take narrow scope with respect to operators in the at-issue content.

   d. They are generally speaker-oriented.

To illustrate, the following example shows how the CI is not cancellable:

(55) a. Edna, a fearless leader, started the descent.

   b. #Edna is not a fearless leader. (Potts 2005)

The following examples show that CIs are not presupposed. In general, as Potts (2005) acknowledges, CIs are used to introduce new information, often to clarify and contextualize the at-issue context around them. Because of this, if their content is backgrounded, the result is infelicity due to redundancy. This is illustrated in example (56), in which the initial sentence sets up a context for the appositive-containing sentence (56a) as well as for the sentence in (56b), which contains a factive predicate *know*:

(56) Lance Armstrong survived cancer.

   a. *When reporters interview Lance, who is a cancer survivor, he often talks about the disease.

   b. And most riders know that Lance Armstrong is a cancer survivor.

The example in (56b) is felicitous. The initial sentence satisfies the presuppositional requirements of *know* by placing into the common ground the content of the complement to *know*. In contrast, when the appositive content in (56a) finds an antecedent, the appositive is infelicitous due to redundancy.

The example in (57) shows how the CIs can never take narrow scope:

(57) *No reporter$_i$ believed that, as he$_i$ wrote, Ames is a spy. (Potts 2005)

The second parameter focuses on the presence versus absence of the relative pronoun:

(58) Presence of the relative pronoun
   If the pronoun is present and it is an E-type one, the ARC is a proposition (type t). If the pronoun is absent or it is not an E-type one, the ARC is a predicate (type <e,t>).

Let's now focus more on the details of the proposal, by spelling out how each component works and how the whole system accounts for the empirical variation we observe.

For the syntax of ARCs, I follow Rebushi's (2005) insight: we need an analysis of restrictive relative clauses that is consistent with Antisymmetry and at the same time is amenable to semantic direct compositionality. Rebushi (2005) hypothesizes that since nominal modification is property conjunction at the semantic level, maybe it is its counterpart (some type of coordination) at the syntactic level, too. He therefore proposes that a functional projection ConjunctionP mediates between the nominal modified by the restrictive relative clause and the relative clause itself, as illustrated in the following tree diagram:

(59)

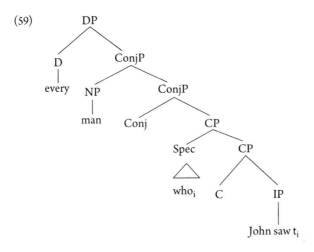

For a subset of the appositive relative clauses, and specifically for non-integrated and semi-integrated appositives, I propose that instead of a Conjunction Phrase (ConjP), there is a Comma Projection that mediates between the 'head' of the relative and the relative itself. Notice that the category Comma is also contemplated by Potts (2005) in his system, but here, differently from what he proposes, I claim that the intonational break is a terminal node that projects its own maximal category. This is very much in accordance with de Vries' (2007) notion of Specifying Coordination, that is, &:P. Notice that both in the case of the restrictive relative clauses and in the case of the appositive relative clauses, the two elements conjoined (either by ConjP or by CommaP) are not of the same syntactic type. Following de Vries (2007), we need to assume that we are dealing with an instance of unbalanced coordinate structure, whose existence needs to be assumed for independent empirical reasons:

(60)   You can depend on [_DP_ my assistant] and [_CP_ that he will be on time].   (Progovac 1998)

Moreover, there is the question of the external visibility of the Conjunctive Phrase. Given that no lexical head subcategorizes for a sheer ConjP, the complement phrase must also be identified as a DP, an NP, or a PP. We therefore need a mechanism allowing the categorial features of one of the conjuncts to percolate to the Conjunction's maximal projection. Rebushi (2005) observes that the configuration we need is justified by Johannessen's (1998) theory, according to which it is the element that occupies the specifier position in the ConjP that transmits its relevant features to

Conj, (under Spec-head Agreement), whence they percolate to ConjP (the maximal projection). Thus, in (59), the resulting fully specified phrase will be a [+Conj,+N]P.

Non-integrated appositives, that is, English, Romanian, and Italian *il quale*-appositives, have therefore the following structure:

(61)

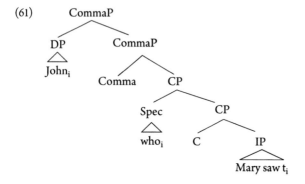

In (61), the 'head' of the relative clause is in the Specifier position of the Comma Phrase projected by the intonational break. The actual appositive relative clause is in the complement position of the Comma Phrase. Following Del Gobbo (2007), I claim that the relative pronoun in the appositive relative clause, *who* in (61), is an E-type pronoun. It is necessarily coindexed with its antecedent, the 'head' of the relative. Following Heim (1990), this means that at LF it is a copy of the antecedent.

For the semantics of both non-integrated and semi-integrated appositive relative clauses, I assume Potts' (2005) distinction between the at-issue and the CI dimensions at the level of composition, but not truth-conditionally. Potts (2005) observes that, in terms of truth conditions, the following two sentences are alike:

(62)   Chuck, who killed a coworker, is in prison.

(63)   Chuck killed a coworker and Chuck is in prison.

It has, in fact, been previously proposed (Sells 1985b; Demirdache 1991) that appositives are like independent sentences, in other words, "assertions-to-follow." In this sense, Del Gobbo (2003a) observes that uttering the relatives in the examples (64)–(67) is equivalent to uttering the pieces of discourse in (68)–(72):

(64)   John, who was late, came to the party with Mary.

(65)   The new professor, who was late, came to the party with Mary.

(66)   They invited a student from UCLA, who arrived late.

(67)   *Every/*No ... professor, who was late/busy, came to the party with Mary.

(68)   John came to the party with Mary. He was late.

(69)   The new professor came to the party with Mary. He was late.

(70)   They invited a student from UCLA. He arrived late.

(71)   *Every/*No professor came to the party with Mary. He was late/busy.

Because of the above facts, Potts (2005) proposes to distinguish the at-issue content from the CI content type-theoretically, that is, in the meaning language. He proposes the existence of both basic at-issue types and basic CI types:

(72)   a. e^a t^a -> basic at issue types

        b. e^c t^c -> basic CI types

Crucially, Potts (2005) claims that CIs bear an asymmetric relationship to at-issue meanings: they apply to at-issue meanings to produce CI meanings.

     In the LF component, I propose, following Potts (2005), that the category Comma causes a type-shift from at issue content to CI content:

(73)   COMMA ~> $\lambda f \, \lambda x. f(x){:}<< e^a, t^a >, < e^a, t^c >>$

At PF, the category Comma isolates its complement intonationally.
For the syntactic structure in (61), we get to the LF in (74):

(74)

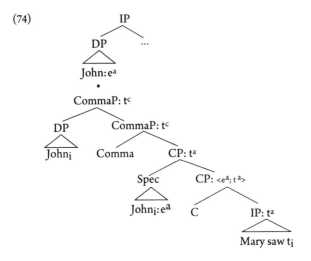

Following Potts (2005), • is a metalogical device, used to separate independent formulae. Let's concentrate on the lower portion of the structure in (74), specifically on the CommaP. The proper name *John,* which occupies the spec position of CP, is a copy of the proper name *John* in the spec of CommaP, by virtue of the fact that it is an E-type pronoun.[2] As a relative pronoun, it originates in the object position of the IP and moves to the Spec of CP, by predicate abstraction. Since the relative pronoun is E-type, it is contentful and not vacuous, and specifically it combines with its sister CP and yields a higher CP of type t^a. This CP of type t^a is then shifted to type t^c by the head Comma. In other words, it is the intonational break that causes the shift from the at-issue dimension to the CI dimension. In (74), the head of the relative *John* is not computed semantically with the relative itself, but with the matrix IP.

---

[2] For an explanation as to why we need an E-type vs. a simple referential pronoun, we refer the reader to Del Gobbo (2003) as well as Sells (1985b) and Demirdache (1991).

This proposals explains why in non-integrated ARCs (i.e., in appositives in English and Romanian, and in Italian *il quale*-appositives and French *lequel*-appositives), split antecedents are allowed, why they can be illocutionary independent of the matrix, and why they can modify any syntactic category. These three empirical facts are all due to the presence of the E-type pronoun. I provide an explanation in what follows.

We know that split antecedents are allowed with pronouns, but not with operators. Ross and Perlmutter (1970) first observed that some relative clauses can have split antecedents, as in the following example:

(75)   A man entered the room and a woman went out who were quite similar.

(Ross and Perlmutter 1970)

Notice that, although not explicitly addressed in the literature, this type of relative clause cannot be introduced by a complementizer (and hence contain an operator):

(76)   *A man entered the room and a woman went out that were quite similar.

On the other hand, a relative pronoun can refer to a split antecedent just like a referential pronoun can:

(77)   A man entered the room and a woman went out. They were quite similar.

Thus, for reasons that as far as I know are still unclear, it is not possible to have split antecedents if, instead of a relative pronoun, the relative clause is headed by an operator or, in different terms, by a nominal deleted at PF because it is identical to the head of the relative.

The presence of the E-type pronoun changes the type of the relative clause from a predicate to a proposition, thereby allowing it to be illocutionary independent of the matrix (something that simple predicates are not able to do). Finally, we know that E-type pronouns can pick up the reference of any syntactic category (Sells 1985a, b; Potts 2002), while properties and propositions are not relativized in the absence of an E-type relative pronoun that can pick up their denotation. Specifically, Sells (1985a) claims that in *which*-relatives, properties and propositions are individuals in the semantic interpretation, and Potts (2000) treats *which*-appositives traces as individual-denoting (i.e., nominalized propositions). We can infer from this that the relative pronouns *which* in English and *il quale* in Italian are able to denote nominalized properties or propositions, but operators (in our raising structures, the raised element denoted by identity with the 'head') are not able to function the same way. We therefore conclude that it is the presence of an E-type pronoun within non-integrated ARCs that allows this type of appositives to be able to modify any kind of syntactic phrase. We also explain the binding facts by assuming with Potts (2005) that the intonational break triggers the type-shift to the CI dimension, thereby blocking binding of any element of the matrix clause into the appositive (Potts 2005). In other words, variables in these appositives are not bound by quantifiers in the matrix clause because the two elements are in two different dimensions.

The analysis of semi-integrated ARCs differs minimally from the one proposed for the non-integrated ones, but in a crucial way. In semi-integrated appositives, the element that raises from within the IP to Spec of CP is a DP that is identical and coindexed to the DP head of the relative. This allows it to delete both in the PF and LF component. As a result of this, that is, because of the absence of a contentful E-type pronoun, the appositive relative clause maintains its status as a property, and it doesn't switch to a proposition status. The Comma node is still responsible for type-shifting from the at-issue dimension to the CI one, and at the level of CommaP, the property $<e^a, t^c>$ is computed with the DP *Gianni* by functional application, yielding a final denotation for the appositive relative as a proposition of type t^c, as it was in the case of the non-integrated appositive relative clauses.

(78)

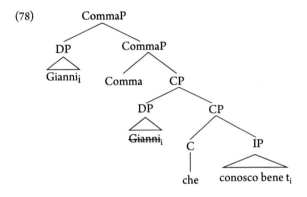

(79)

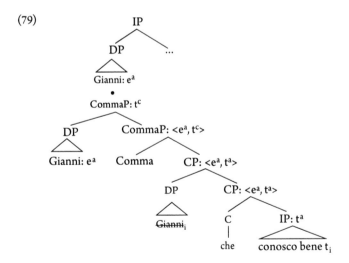

This analysis accounts for all of the properties of semi-integrated appositive relative clauses. Specifically, since no E-type pronoun is present, we explain why split antecedents are not allowed. The appositive cannot be illocutionary independent because it denotes a property and not a proposition. Finally, the absence of the contentful E-type pronoun explains why with this kind of appositive the only modifiable syntactic phrases are DPs. This is because, as we mentioned before, only E-type relative pronouns are able to denote nominalized properties or propositions. In the semi-integrated appositive relative, the raised element denoted by identity with the 'head' is not able to function the same way. This analysis also explains why the semi-integrated ARCs are identical to the non-integrated ones in their blocking of binding from the matrix clause. Regardless of their denotation (property in the case of semi-integrated relatives, and proposition in the case of non-integrated ones), both kinds of ARCs are shifted by the intonational break to the CI dimension. For semi-integrated ARCs as well, then, binding from higher up in the matrix is blocked, because variables and potential binders are in two different dimensions.

Fully integrated appositives, which are found in Chinese and Japanese, are characterized by completely different syntax and semantics. Following recent work by Li (2008) and Rebushi (2005), I take the modifying particle *de* in Chinese to be a special kind of conjunction (with no categorial features):

(80)

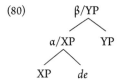

According to Li (2008), *de* doesn't contribute to the categorial feature of the modifier; it is the modified element that determines the category of α. When two α are conjoined, each α is a constituent. It follows that *de* is a head that subcategorizes for two phrases (much like verbs taking double complements), but it doesn't contribute a categorial feature to the dominating category. In this sense, *de* is similar to *and* in English, but the two conjunctions have different constituent structures: *and* forms a unit with the phrase following it, while *de* forms a unit with the modifying phrase.

The structure for the relative clause in Chinese is exemplified below. Within the relative clause, we have movement of *Zhangsan* from inside IP to adjoin to CP. The 'internal head' deletes because it is identical and coindexed with the 'external head.' Since the 'external head' is adjoined to CP, it cannot c-command CP and anything that CP dominates. It follows from this that the 'internal head' cannot be a relative pronoun, as it would not be c-commanded, as it has to, by the 'external head.'

(81)

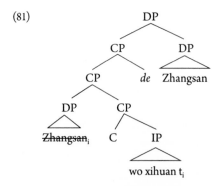

Since it cannot be a relative pronoun, the 'internal head' also cannot be an E-type pronoun, forcing the relative CP to be semantically a property, and not a proposition.

(82)

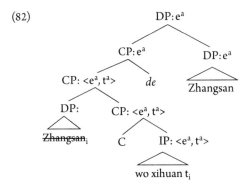

Following Huang (2006), I assume that the conjunction *de* type-shifts the relative from <e,t> to e, allowing it to be computed with the proper name (type e). The question that arises then is: How are the two elements of type e able to combine with each other? Huang (2006) reasons that if the modification relation is a predication relation (following Heim and Kratzer 1998), then conjunction is required by definition. This means that the two conjuncts ought to be of identical type for lambda abstraction. This condition has to be met first, and in Chinese the two elements, modifier and modifiee, are identical with respect to their type. But they are of a lower type, that is, type e. Huang (2006) assumes that type-lifting applies to the two conjuncts, after which both of them are raised to property type, that is, type <e,t>.

In fully integrated appositives (as in the Chinese ones), the absence of the relative E-type pronoun explains why they cannot have split antecedents, why they cannot be illocutionary independent, and why they can only modify nominals. The absence of the intonational break explains the binding phenomena: the appositive is always in the scope of the matrix, as both are in the at-issue dimension, and there is no Comma available to trigger the shift to the CI dimension.

4. Appositives in Japanese

Among the languages whose relative clauses behave similarly to Chinese, we find Japanese. In Japanese, as in Chinese, relative clauses are prenominal, they are not separated from the modified 'head' by an intonational break, and they are not introduced by a relative pronoun. Given that they share these features with relative clauses in Chinese, it is worthwhile to investigate whether appositive relative clauses in Japanese also show the same behavior with respect to illocutionary independence, the possibility to have split antecedents, binding, and the categorial nature of the antecedent.

As we have seen for Chinese, in Japanese as well the appositive relative clause cannot have an illocutionary force that is independent of and different from the matrix one. Specifically, the appositive modifying Taroo in the following example cannot be interrogative (*ka* is the interrogative typing particle in Japanese):

(83)   *[Wareware-o kessite   yurusa-nai dearoo ka] Taroo-wa
       we-Acc   never   forgive-Neg may   Q   Taro-Top
       kono yoo-ni-wa si-nakat-ta   daroo.
       this way-in-Top do-Neg-Past may
       Int. 'Taro, who will ever forgive us, would have never behaved this way.'

The second empirical domain to test involves split antecedents. Recall that in English the following sentences are grammatical:

(84)   The Queen serves muffins$_i$, and Prince Charles serves scones$_j$, which$_{i+j}$ they buy at Harrods.

(85)   A man$_i$ entered the room and a woman$_j$ went out, who$_{i+j}$ were quite similar.

When native speakers of Japanese are asked to provide sentences similar to the two examples above, they necessarily come up with two independent conjoined sentences:

(86)   Erizabesu Zyoo-wa mafin$_i$-o   dasi-te,   Tyaaruzu kootaisi-wa sukoon$_j$-o
       Elisabeth queen-Top muffin-Acc serve-ing Charles prince-Top scone-Acc
       dasu-ga, (sorera-o) karera-wa Harozzu-de ka-u.
       serve-C they$_{i+j}$-Acc they-Top Harrods.-at buy-Pres.
       'Queen Elizabeth serves muffins and Prince Charles serves scones, they buy them at Harrod's.'

In the previous example, *ga*, glossed as 'C,' is a declarative conjunctive marker, simply connecting two sentences without establishing any particular causal relation between the two propositions. Notice that the pronominal object is optional. The following examples show similar results: we can only convey the desired meaning by constructing two independent sentences. The only difference from the previous example (86) is that in the following one (87) the pronominal subject is required:

(87)   Taroo$_i$-wa heya-ni hair-i,   Hanako$_j$-wa heya-o   de-ta-ga,
       Taro$_i$-Top room-in enter-ing, Hanako$_j$-Top room-Acc leave-Past-C
       karera$_{i+j}$-wa totemo ni-te   i-ta.
       they-Top   quite   resemble-ing be-Past
       'Taro entered the room and Hanako left the room, they are quite similar.'

When we attempt to use the relative clause to modify both nominal phrases, that is, trying to establish the split antecedency, we run into ungrammaticality, or at best, we can allow the relative clause to modify only one of the two potential antecedents:

(88)   *[Op$_{i+j}$ Hanako-o   kirat-te i-ru]   Taroo$_i$-ga hait-te ki-ta   ga,
              Hanako-Acc hate-ing be-Pres Taro-Nom enter-ing come-Past though
       Ziroo$_j$-wa de-te   it-ta.
       Jiro-Top   leave-ing go-Past

The only interpretation available for example (88) is that the person who hates Hanako is Taro (alone), that is, the split antecedent interpretation is impossible.

Another trademark feature of an appositive relative clause is the categorial nature of the antecedent. We know that in English, for example, non-integrated relative clauses can modify a variety of antecedents, including VPs, AdjPs, and entire sentences. In the following example, the appositive relative clause modifies the adjective *smart*:

(89)   Mary was smart, which John never was.

In Japanese, once again, a literal translation of the example above is ungrammatical. The only way to convey the same meaning is by using two independent sentences conjoined by a conjunctive particle:

(90)   Hanako-wa   kasikokat-ta ga, Taroo-wa soo-de nakat-ta.
       Hanako-Top smart-Past   C Taro-Top so-P   Neg-Past
       'Hanako was smart, which Taro never was.'

Finally, we know that it is not possible for a higher quantified noun phrase to bind inside an appositive relative clause in English:

(91)   *Every Christian$_i$ forgives John, who harms him$_i$.

In Japanese, instead, we find that instances of binding of the type described are grammatical, as they are in Chinese. In analyzing the following example, we need to keep in mind that according to Hoji (1991), the referential property of pronominals in Japanese is not quite the same as in English. Hoji (1991) claims that epithets, like 'the bastard,' *soitu*, in the following example, should be used as bound pronominals. Fukui (1984) claims instead that *zibun*, 'himself,' can be used as a bound pronominal. Therefore, in the following example, both possibilities are tested, and in both cases, the example is grammatical, confirming the availability for appositive relative clauses in Japanese to contain elements bound from the higher portion of the sentence:

(92)   Dono gakusei$_i$-mo [{zibun/soitu}$_i$-o hihansu-ru]   Yamada-sensei-ni
       which student-all   self/bastard/-Acc criticize-Pres Yamada-professor-to
       kansyasi-te   i-ru.
       appreciate-ing be-Pres
       Lit.: 'Every student$_i$ is appreciating to Prof. Yamada, who criticizes the bastard$_i$.'

The evidence we have allows us to conclude that, with respect to the availability of appositive relative clauses, Japanese behaves quite similarly to Chinese. There are nevertheless some interesting differences between Japanese and Chinese relative clauses, which force us to propose a slightly different syntax.[3] In particular, it has been

[3] Notice that in this chapter I won't discuss the differences or similarities between appositive relative clauses in Japanese, and another Japanese relative clause construction, i.e., the Internally Headed Relative Clause (IHRC). As correctly pointed out by Masao Ochi in his review, an IHRC doesn't need to be restrictive; according to Shimoyama (1999), it involves E-type anaphora; as observed initially by Kuroda (1975/1976), it allows split antecedents; it cannot be illocutionary independent of the matrix; its antecedent is restricted to a nominal element, and binding into it from the matrix is possible (Shimoyama 1999). According to Shimoyama (1999), despite some similarities, ARCs and IHRCs in Japanese cannot be equated completely. I agree with Masao Ochi that it is worthwhile to investigate them against the findings described in this chapter, but I will have to leave this task for a future research project, one that hopefully will have a wider comparative scope.

observed by various linguists that Japanese relative clauses show no island effects, hence they are not generated through movement (the gap inside the relative is *pro*). Given that Japanese relative clauses are not licensed syntactically, both Fukui and Takano (1999) and Takeda (1999) claim that Japanese relative clauses are licensed 'semantically,' through an 'aboutness' relationship. Takeda (1999) follows Chierchia (1998) and argues that the availability of semantic operations such as type-shifting vary from language to language, depending on the morphological/syntactic inventory of the lexicon of a given language. Specifically, Japanese lacks the functional categories (C, T, D; Fukui 1986, 1988, 1995) that are present in English. As a consequence, part of the semantic operations that are originally universal is restricted in English, and less so in Japanese.

The lack of syntactic licensing explains the unavailability of a relative pronoun: given that the relative is adjoined to the 'head,' the 'head' cannot c-command inside of it. Fukui and Takano (1999) also propose that the relative clause in Japanese is TP and not CP. Following Diesing (1990) in spirit, they adopt the following principle:

(93)   A functional category is present in the structure only when it is necessary.

Japanese relative clauses do not need to project up to the CP level, because they are not licensed syntactically, in other words they are not introduced by a null operator or a relative pronoun (Takeda 1999). In addition, according to Fukui (1986, 1988), Japanese also lacks the functional category D. Takeda (1999) provides evidence for the claim that Japanese lacks null determiners and that bare nominals in Japanese are simple NPs. Taking all of the properties of Japanese relative clauses into consideration, I propose the following syntax:

(94)

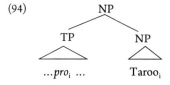

In the structure illustrated in (94), the relative TP is adjoined to the 'head' of the relative, *Taroo*. There is no movement, the relative is licensed through an 'aboutness' relationship, and the surface gap in the relative is occupied by a small *pro* (Takeda 1999). As for its semantics, Takeda (1999) acknowledges that in calculating the meaning for the restrictive relative illustrated in the tree diagram in (95), we encounter a type mismatch. The semantic types of the TP and the NP in question are a proposition and a property, and they cannot be combined by functional application. Takeda (1999) proposes to resort to the lambda abstraction operation, which instead of being triggered by movement, applies over the small *pro*, converting the proposition into a predicate of type <e,t>. This enables us to combine the TP and the 'head' noun by the predicate modification rule, yielding an additional predicate. Finally, Takeda (1999) allows type-shifting to apply to the obtained predicate, yielding the denotation of an individual, hence type e. Takeda (1999) takes for granted that this type-shifting process is universally available across languages, unless blocked.[4]

(95)

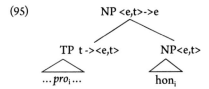

We can adopt Takeda's (1999) analysis of restrictive relative clauses and adapt it to appositive ones in Japanese. Take the following example, from Takeda (1999):

(96) John-ga   kyonen e   otozureta New York
      John-NOM last   year visited   New York
      'New York, which John visited last year, . . .'

The main difference is in the fact that the modified noun is a proper name instead of a common noun. According to Takeda (1999), given that the proper name is an NP, it is still a predicate, hence of type <e,t>. This is not an unreasonable assumption, given that we can interpret proper names as predicates true of just one individual (Quine 1939). The semantic calculation then proceeds exactly as outlined for the case of the common noun, and it is illustrated in the following example:

(97)

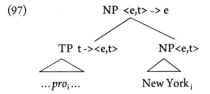

This proposal allows us to explain the characteristics of Japanese appositive relative clauses as described. More specifically:

1. Split antecedents are not allowed because there is no relative pronoun;
2. 'Heads' of other syntactic categories cannot occur because of the absence of the relative E-type pronoun;
3. Binding is allowed because of the absence of the intonational break;
4. The TP cannot be illocutionary independent, because it type-shifts to <et>.

[4] Extending Chierchia's (1998) Blocking Principle, Takeda (1999) proposes the following:

(i)   Generalized Blocking Principle:

   If a language has a certain functional category in its lexicon, the free application of the semantic operation that has the same function as that syntactic category is blocked in that language.
   What underlies the preceding principle is the hypothesis, defended by Takeda (1999), that the applicability of semantic operations can vary across languages. Specifically, given that Japanese lacks a functional C within relative clauses, lambda abstraction can occur freely.

5. Conclusion

Our empirical investigation has led to the following findings:

1. Chinese and Japanese appositive relative clauses are not illocutionary independent, they do not allow split antecedents, the antecedent can only be nominal, and they allow binding, hence they belong to the class of fully integrated appositives;
2. English appositive relative clauses are diametrically different from the integrated ones, insofar as they can be illocutionary independent, allow split antecedents, have antecedents of different categorial nature, and do not allow binding. I classify them as non-integrated appositives.
3. Italian has two types of appositives. The semi-integrated ones share with the integrated ones the following features: they are not illocutionary independent, they do not allow split antecedents, and their antecedents can only be nominal; but differently from the integrated appositives of Chinese and Japanese, these semi-integrated appositives do not allow binding. The second type behaves just like the English ones, and hence are classified as non-integrated.

This is summarized in the table in (98).

(98)

	illocutionary independence	split antecedents	categorial nature of antecedent	binding
???	yes	yes	CP, AP, VP, etc.	yes
Japanese (fully integrated)	no	no	nominal	yes
Chinese (fully integrated)	no	no	nominal	yes
Italian (semi-integrated)	no	no	nominal	no
Italian (non-integrated)	yes	yes	CP, AP, VP, etc.	no
English (non-integrated)	yes	yes	CP, AP, VP, etc.	no

The empirical data is accounted for by a theory that is based on three core elements:

1. The syntax of appositive relative clauses involves a coordination structure;
2. The non-integrated appositives' relative pronoun is E-type;
3. The syntax of prenominal appositive relative clauses prevents them from licensing an overt relative pronoun, and therefore an E-type pronoun. The lack of this pronoun is crucial in establishing their status of fully integrated appositives.

Also crucial to the proposal is the claim that the intonational break type-shifts the content of the appositive from being at-issue content, to being conventional implicature content. Only content that stays at-issue can be bound over.

The empirical data analyzed and the account proposed leave us with an interesting fine-grained typology of appositives, thereby confirming the recent trend in research on appositives, pointing to the conclusion that we are dealing with a more variegated set of constructions than previously thought. What is even more interesting is that the conclusions reached with this study leave us with precise directions to investigate, whether that is enriching the data set of the languages investigated to confirm or disconfirm the findings here established, or determining what other possible types of appositive relative clause there could be. To give an example, we may wonder if there could be a language with appositive relative clauses with E-type relative pronouns but no intonational break, as hinted at in the table in (98).

Finally, a more detailed study of the parameters that are responsible for the typology of appositive relative clauses, paired with an investigation on a higher number of languages, would shed light on a crucial question for parametric theory, specifically whether parameters are implicational or not (see Longobardi, Gianollo, and C. Guardiano, 2008).

References

Andrews, Avery Delano, III, 1975. *Studies in The Syntax of Relative and Comparative Clauses.* Doctoral dissertation, MIT.

Arnold, D. 2004. Non-restrictive relative clauses in construction based HPSG. In *Proceedings of the HPSG04 Conference*, ed. S. Muller., 27–47. Stanford, CA: CSLI Publications.

Chierchia, G. 1998. Reference to kinds across languages. *Natural Language Semantics 6*, 339–405.

Cinque, G. 1982. On the theory of relative clauses and markedness. *The Linguistic Review* 1, 247–294.

Cinque, G. 1988. La frase relativa. In *Grande grammatica italiana di consultazione*, Vol 1, ed. L. Renzi, 443–503. Bologna: Il Mulino.

Cinque, G. 2005. A note on verb/object order and head/relative clause order. In *Grammar and Beyond. Essays in honour of Lars Hellan*, ed. M. Vulchanova and T. A. Åfarli, 69–89. Oslo: Novus Press.

Cinque, G. 2006. Two types of appositives. *University of Venice Working Papers in Linguistics 16*, 7–56.

Cinque, G. 2007. Two types of nonrestrictive relatives. *Proceedings of the Colloque de Syntaxe et Sémantique de Paris* (2008).

Del Gobbo, F. 2001. Appositives schmappositives in Chinese. In *UCI Working Papers in Linguistics 7*, ed. M. Irie and H. Ono, 1–25.

Del Gobbo, F. 2002. Appositives and Chinese relative clauses. In *CLS 38: The Main Session. Papers from the 38th Meeting of the Chicago Linguistic Society*, Vol. 1, ed. M. Andronis, E. Debenport, A. Pycha, and K. Yoshimura, 175–190. Chicago: Chicago Linguistic Society.

Del Gobbo, F. 2003a. *Appositives at the Interface.* Doctoral dissertation, University of California, Irvine.

Del Gobbo, F. 2003b. Appositives and quantification. In *Proceedings of the 26th Annual Penn Linguistics Colloquium.* Vol. 9.1, ed. E. Kaiser and S. Arunachalam, 73–88. University of Pennsylvania Working Papers in Linguistics.

Del Gobbo, F. 2004. On prenominal relative clauses and appositive adjectives. In *WCCFL 23 Proceedings*, ed. B. Schmeiser, V. Chand, A. Kelleherm, and A. Rodriguez, 182–194. Somerville, MA: Cascadilla Press.

Del Gobbo, F. 2005. Chinese relative clauses: Restrictive, descriptive or appositive? In *Contributions to the XXX Incontro di Grammatica Generativa*, ed. L. Brugè, G. Giusti, N. Munaro, W. Schweikert, and G. Turano, 287–305. Venezia: Cafoscarina.

Del Gobbo, F. 2007. On the syntax and semantics of appositive relative clauses. In *Parentheticals*, ed. N. Dehè and Y. Kavalova, 173–201. Linguistik Aktuell/Linguistics Today Series. Amsterdam: John Benjamins.

Demirdache, H. 1991. *Resumptive Chains in Restrictive Relatives, Appositives and Dislocation Structures*. Doctoral dissertation, Massachusetts Institute of Technology.

Frascarelli, M., and A. Puglielli. 2005. A comparative analysis of restrictive and appositive relative clauses in Cushitic languages. In *Contributions to the XXX Incontro di Grammatica Generativa*, ed. L. Brugè, G. Giusti, N. Munaro, W. Schweikert, and G. Turano, 307–333. Venezia: Cafoscarina.

Fukui, N. 1984. *Studies on Japanese Anaphora I: The Adjunct Subject Hypothesis and 'Zibun.'* Ms., Massachusetts Institute of Technology.

Fukui, N. 1986. *A Theory of Category Projection and Its Applications*. Doctoral dissertation, Massachusetts Institute of Technology.

Fukui, N. 1988. Deriving the differences between English and Japanese: A case study in parametric syntax. *English Linguistics* 5, 249–270.

Fukui, N. 1995. The Principles-and-Parameters approach: A comparative syntax of English and Japanese. In *Approaches to Language Typology*, ed. Masayoshi Shibatani and Theodora Bynon, 327–371. Oxford: Oxford University Press.

Fukui, N., and Y. Takano. 1999. Nominal structure: An extension of the symmetry principle. In *The Derivation of VO and OV (LA 31)*, ed. P. Svenonious, 219–254. Amsterdam: John Benjamins.

Grice, H. P. 1975. Logic and conversation. In *Syntax and Semantics*, Vol. 3: *Speech Acts*, ed. P. Cole, and J. Morgan, 41–58. New York: Academic Press.

Grosu, A. 2005. *Relative Clause Constructions and Unbounded Dependencies*. Ms., Tel Aviv University (http://www.linguist.jussieu.fr/~mardale/GROSU_RELATIVE_SEPT2005.doc).

Heim, I. 1990. E-type pronouns and donkey anaphora. *Linguistics and Philosophy* 13, 137–177.

Heim, I., and A. Kratzer. 1998. *Semantics in Generative Grammar*. Malden, MA: Blackwell.

Hoji, H. 1991. KARE. In *Interdisciplinary Approaches to Language: Essays in Honor of Prof. S.-Y. Kuroda*, ed. Carol Georgopoulos and Roberta Ishihara, 287–304. Dordrecht: Reidel.

Huang, C.-T. J., A. Li, and Y. Li. 2009. *The Syntax of Chinese*. Cambridge: Cambridge University Press.

Huang, Shi-Zhe. 2006. Adjectives and nominal modification in Chinese. *Journal of East Asian Linguistics* 15, 343–369.

Huddleston, R. D., and G. K. Pullum. 2002. *The Cambridge Grammar of the English Language*. Cambridge: Cambridge University Press.

Johannessen, J. B. 1998. *Coordination*. Oxford: Oxford University Press.

Kayne, R. S. 1994. *The Antisymmetry of Syntax*. Cambridge, MA: MIT Press.

Keenan, E. L. 1985. Relative clauses. In *Language Typology and Syntactic Description*. Vol. II: *Complex Constructions*, ed. T. Shopen, 141–170. Cambridge: Cambridge University Press.

Kuroda, S.-Y. 1975–1976. Pivot-independent relativization in Japanese II. *Papers in Japanese Linguistics* 4, 85–96. Reprinted in Kuroda (1992).

Kuroda, S.-Y. 1992. *Japanese Syntax and Semantics: Collected Papers*. Dordrecht: Kluwer.

Li, A. 2008. Theories of phrase structures and DE as a head. *Contemporary Linguistics* 2, 97–108.

Lin, J. 2003. On restrictive and non-restrictive relative clauses in Mandarin Chinese. *Tsinghua Journal of Chinese Studies*, New Series, 33(1), 199–240.

Longobardi, G., C. Gianollo, and C. Guardiano. 2008 Three fundamental issues in parametric linguistics. In *The Limits of Syntactic Variation*, ed. T. Biberauer. 109–142. Philadelphia/Amsterdam: John Benjamins.

Potts, C. 2002. The lexical semantics of parenthetical-*as* and appositive-*which*. *Syntax* 5, 55–88.

Potts, C. 2005. *The Logic of Conventional Implicatures*. Oxford: Oxford University Press.

Progovac, L. 1998. Structure for coordination. Parts I and II. *Glot International* 3(7), 3–6; 3(8), 3–9.

Quine, W. v. O. 1939. Designation and existence. *Journal of Philosophy* 36, 701–709.

Rebushi, G. 2005. Generalizing the antisymmetric analysis of coordination to nominal modification. *Lingua* 115, 445–459.

Ross, J. R., and D. M. Perlmutter. 1970. Relative clauses with split antecedents. *Linguistic Inquiry* 1, 350.

Safir, K. 1986. Relative clauses in a theory of binding and levels. *Linguistic Inquiry* 17, 663–689.

Sells, P. 1985a. Anaphora and the nature of semantic representation. Ms., CSLI, Stanford, CA.

Sells, P. 1985b. Restrictive and non-restrictive modification. *CSLI Report* No. 85-28. Stanford, CA: CSLI Publications.

Shimoyama, J. 1999. Internally headed relative clauses in Japanese and E-type anaphora. *Journal of East Asian Linguistics* 8, 147–182.

Stowell, T. 2005. Appositive and parenthetical relative clauses. In *Organizing Grammar*, ed. H. Broekhuis, N. Corver, R. Huybregts, U. Kleinhenz, and J. Koster, 608–617. Mouton de Gruyter, Berlin.

Takeda, K. 1999. *Multiple Headed Structures*. Doctoral dissertation, University of California, Irvine.

Thompson, S. A. 1971. The deep structure of relative clauses. In *Studies in Linguistic Semantics*, ed. C. Fillmore and D. T. Langendoen, 79–96. New York: Holt, Rinehart and Winston.

Vries, M. de 2002. *The Syntax of Relativization*. Doctoral dissertation, Netherlands Graduate School of Linguistics.

Vries, M. de 2006. The syntax of appositive relativization: On specifying coordination, false free relatives, and promotion. *Linguistic Inquiry* 37, 229—270.

Vries, M. de 2007. Invisible constituents? Parentheticals as b-merged adverbial phrases. In *Parentheticals*, ed. N. Dehé and Y. Kavalova, 203–234. Linguistik Aktuell/Linguistics Today Series. Amsterdam: John Benjamins.

Yuasa, E. 2005. Independence in subordinate clauses: Analysis of nonrestrictive relative clauses in English and Japanese. In *Polymorphous Linguistics: Jim McCawley's Legacy*, ed. S. S. Mufwene, E. J. Francis, R. S. Wheeler, 135–160. Cambridge, MA: MIT Press.

Zhang, N. 2007. The syntactic derivations of split antecedent relative clause constructions. *Taiwan Journal of Linguistics* 5, 19–47.

4

Restricting Non-restrictive Relatives in Mandarin Chinese

JO-WANG LIN AND WEI-TIEN DYLAN TSAI

1. Introduction

Typologically speaking, adjectival expressions like relative clauses rarely precede a demonstrative in a prenominal position (cf. Greenberg 1963; Cinque 2005). The word order, nevertheless, is commonly observed among Chinese dialects. In fact, the division between restrictive and non-restrictive relative clauses in Chinese has long been a controversial issue. More specifically, Mandarin relative clauses, marked by the particle *de*, may show up in two positions within the noun phrase, either before the demonstrative-numeral-classifier sequence (DNC) or after the DNC, as shown in (1). We will refer to the pre-DNC relative as RC_1 and the post-DNC relative as RC_2:

(1) (RC_1) Demonstrative Numeral Classifier (RC_2) Noun

Chao (1968) takes the two positions of relative clauses as indicating two different interpretations, that is, RC_1 is restrictive but RC_2 is descriptive (non-restrictive), as illustrated in (2a, b) respectively:[1]

(2) a. [dai   yanjing de] nei-wei xiansheng shi shei?
         wear glasses DE that-Cl mister   be who
         'Who is the gentleman who is wearing glasses (not the one who is not wearing glasses)?

      b. nei-wei [dai   yanjing de] xiansheng shi shei?
          that-Cl wear glasses DE mister   be who
          'Who is the gentleman (who incidentally is) wearing glasses?'

The above distinction between restrictive and descriptive relatives has received a lot of discussion in the literature. For instance, Huang (1982) and Constant (2011a, b) accept his view on positions and interpretations. On the other hand, while

---

[1] Chao's use of the term "descriptive" is often taken to be equivalent to non-restrictive or appositive. Note also that Chao does not exclude the possibility that RC_2 can be restrictive when it is stressed.

maintaining that positions are correlated with interpretations, Lü (1999) and Tsai (1994) take RC_1 to be non-restrictive and RC_2 restrictive, based on an (in)definiteness asymmetry between RC_1 of (3a) and RC_2 of (3b):

(3) a. *zuotian   si-le   [conglai bu xizao de] san-ge   ren.
         yesterday die-Prf ever   not bathe DE three-Cl person
         'Yesterday three people who never bathed died.'

    b. zuotian   si-le   san-ge   [conglai bu xizao de] ren.
         yesterday die-Prf three-Cl ever   not bathe DE person
         'Yesterday three people who never bathed died.'

Still, some others such as Zhang (2001), Del Gobbo (2003, 2004, 2005), and Shi (2010) claim that all Chinese relatives, be it RC_1 or RC_2, can only be interpreted as restrictive relatives.

In contrast to RC_1 and RC_2, relative clauses modifying a proper name or pronoun (abbreviated as RMP hereafter) have received less attention in the literature. However, such relatives seem to be very good candidates where the non-restrictive interpretation of a relative clause should be found. Indeed, Lin (2003) argues that both RC_1 and RC_2 are restrictive but the non-restrictive interpretation is possible when an individual-level relative modifies a proper name or pronoun as illustrated by (4):

(4) [hen ai   chi niupai   de] Laowang jintian que dian-le   yupai.
     very love eat beef-steak DE Laowang today but order-Asp fish-steak
     '(To our surprise), Laowang, who loves eating beef steak very much, ordered fish steak today.'

Del Gobbo (2010) accepts Lin's position but claims that such non-restrictives are "integrated non-restrictive" relatives in the sense of Cinque (2006, 2008). On the other hand, Shi (2010) maintains that all RMPs, including those modifying a proper name, are restrictive.

The goal of this chapter is to examine the restrictive/non-restrictive debate from both the syntactic and semantic perspectives, while discussing what would be the possible cause for such a perplexing debate in a cross-linguistic context. Our presentation is organized as follows: In section 2, we give an overview of complicated issues associated with all sorts of syntactic and semantic construals of RMPs. Sections 3 and 4 then point out difficulties encountered in previous analyses, concluding that RMPs behave more in line with so-called "integrated non-restrictive" relatives in Italian. In section 5, we argue that there is a conceptual connection between RC_1 and a special class of secondary predicates observed in Huang (1987). Based on cross-linguistic evidence for the semantics of proper names from languages such as Portugese, Modern Greek, Hungarian, Syrian Arabic, Russian, and so on, section 6 offers a novel account for the restrictive/non-restrictive paradox of construing modifiers of proper names or pronouns. In section 7, we discuss cross-linguistic variations on non-restrictive relatives, and conclude this article with section 8.

2. Review of the Status of RMPs

When a relative clause modifies a proper name or pronoun, intuitively it should be construed as non-restrictive, because the denotation of a proper name is independent of any modifier. Reasonable though the intuition is, this assumption has been challenged by some linguists. In particular, Del Gobbo (2003) shows that RMPs manifest syntactic properties of restrictive relatives and Shi (2010) argues that all RMPs are semantically restrictive. In this section, we will review the literature's discussion of this issue.

2.1. SYNTACTIC ARGUMENTS

2.1.1. Review of Del Gobbo (2003)

In line with her analysis of RC_1 and RC_2, Del Gobbo (2003) argues that even RMPs are restrictive and provides syntactic arguments for this position on the basis of the binding theory.

According to Safir (1986), a pronoun inside a non-restrictive relative cannot be bound by a quantifier from outside the relative. Del Gobbo (2003) shows that Mandarin RMPs allow binding from outside the relative, as shown in (5). Therefore, according to her, Mandarin relatives anchored to an entity-denoting name must be restrictive rather than non-restrictive.

(5) [mei yi ge xuesheng]$_i$ dou xihuan shi ta$_i$ daoshi de Huang laoshi.
    every one Cl student   Distr like   be he advisor DE Huang teacher
    'Every student$_i$ likes professor Huang, who is his$_i$ advisor.' (Del Gobbo 2003: 144)

For this argument, Constant (2011a) comments that (5) is actually an example of what Fox (2000) refers to as telescoping "illusory binding." He shows that English non-restrictives allow the same kind of telescoping binding.[2] To leave aside whether or not (5) involves the telescoping phenomenon, our own intuition is that (5), if not ungrammatical, is a very unnatural sentence, contrary to Del Gobbo's judgment.

Constant (2011a), following Potts (2003) and Fox (2000), argues that to control for telescoping, a downward entailing quantifier should be used. Once such a quantifier is used, it becomes impossible to bind a pronoun or anaphor contained inside a relative that modifies an entity-denoting name. Consider the contrast between (6a, b) taken from Constant (2011a: 20). The ungrammaticality of (6b) shows that unlike the restrictive relative in (6a), a Mandarin RMP does not allow binding from outside.

(6) a. ban-li   mei-you nusheng$_i$ yuanyi he   [bi   ziji$_i$ ai   de] ren   tanlianai.
        class-Loc not-have girl   willing with compare self short Rel person go.out
        'No girl$_i$ in class is willing to go out with a person shorter than herself$_i$.'

---

[2] His example is (i) (Constant 2011a: 19)

(i)   [Each contestant]$_i$ was asked ten questions about [his]$_i$ wife, who had to sit behind the scenes and couldn't help [him]$_i$.

b. *ban-li   mei-you   nusheng$_i$ yuanyi he [bi   ziji$_i$ ai   de]
    class-Loc not-have   girl   willing with compare self short DE
    Lisi   tanlianai.
    Lisi   go.out
    Intended: 'No girl$_i$ in class is willing to go out with Lisi, who is shorter than herself$_i$.'

Thus, Safir's binding test does not successfully prove that RMPs are not non-restrictive. Note also that when a downward-entailing subject is replaced by a proper name, binding from outside becomes possible, as will be shown in the next paragraph.

Del Gobbo's (2003, 2005) other related argument is based on Giorgi's (1984) observation that the long-distance anaphor *proprio* 'self' in Italian can be bound by the head of the relative or the matrix subject if it is inside a restrictive relative, but it can only be bound by the head of the relative if it is inside a non-restrictive relative.

(7) Gianni$_i$ pensa che Mario$_j$, che t$_j$ ama la   propria$_{j/*i}$ moglie, sia intelligente.
     Gianni thinks that Mario   that loves the own   wife   is smart
     'Gianni thinks that Mario, who loves his own wife, is smart.'

Del Gobbo argues that the Chinese long distance anaphor *ziji* 'self' can be bound by both the head of the relative and the matrix subject when the relative modifies a proper name. We agree with her on this point, though her example is better replaced with a more natural one such as (8). (8a) shows that the long distance anaphor *ziji* is bound by the head of the relative and (8b) shows that it is bound by the matrix subject.

(8) a. Wo renwei xianglai jiu zhi ai   ziji$_i$ de Xiaolizi$_i$ shi gai
         I   think always JIU only love self DE Xiaolizi be should
         fanxingfanxing.
         self.exam
         'I think Xiaolizi, who always only loves himself, should really do self-examination.'

     b. Liu jiangjun$_i$ bu   xiangxin yizhi gen   zai ziji$_i$ shenbian de Xiaolizi
         Liu general   not   believe always follow at self around   DE Xiaolizi
         hui beipan   ta.
         will betray   him
         'General Liu does not believe that Xiaolizi, who always stays around him, would betray him.'

The possibility of long distance binding in (8b) contrasts with the impossibility of long distance binding in (6). A contradictory result thus arises. This contradiction has a reasonable explanation when Huang and Liu's (2001) analysis of Chinese *ziji* 'self' is taken into account. They argue that Chinese *ziji* is ambiguous between a pure anaphor and a pragmatic logophor. The former is subject to Condition A, which requires that the anaphor be locally bound, while the latter can be long distance bound by the matrix subject or the speaker. Following Sells (1987), Huang and Liu (2001) assume that "a logophor refers to a person whose (a) speech or thought, (b) attitude or state of consciousness, and/or (c) point of view, or perspective, is being reported." This person may be the speaker or an internal protagonist denoted by the matrix subject. Given this definition of logophors, the contrast between (6) and (8b) can be explained as follows. The long distance binding in (8b) is expected because *ziji* in (8b) is a logophor whose thought is reported. In contrast to (8b), the matrix subject *mei-you nusheng* 'no girl' is not an individual-denoting NP to which a thought or attitude can be ascribed. Therefore, a logophoric construal of *ziji* in (6) is impossible.

The implication of the above logophoric account for the contrast between (6) and (8b) is that it is not safe to use the anaphor *ziji* as a test of restrictiveness or non-restrictiveness. Long distance binding of *ziji* belongs to the domain of logophoric study, and therefore no clear conclusion can be reached from it with respect to the distinction between restrictiveness and non-restrictiveness.

Del Gobbo's third test is to use root-level adverbs, which are only compatible with non-restrictive relatives but not with restrictive ones. She argues that root-level adverbs such as *shunbianshuo* 'incidentally' do not occur in relatives modifying individual-denoting names. However, Constant (2011a) argues that the Chinese expression *shunbianshuo* patterns more closely with English injections like 'by the way' than with true root-level adverbs such as *frankly* or *incidentally*. He thinks that *guji* 'reckon' and *bacheng* '80 percent' are more like true root-level adverbs and cites the following example to support the claim that relatives modifying individual-denoting names do not resist root-level adverbs:

(9) wo   zui   xihuan de   Zhongguo shiren   you Li Bai,   Du Fu,
     I   most like   DE   China   poet   have Li Bai   Du Fu
     hai you   [guji   ni   mei   kan-guo de] Xu Zhimo.
     also have reckon you have.not   read-Exp DE   Xu Zhimo
     'My favorite Chinese poets are Li Bai, Du Fu, and also Xu Zhimo, who
     you probably haven't read.'

Unfortunately, *guji* 'reckon' and *bacheng* '80 percent' are not good candidates of root-level adverbs. *Guji* 'reckon' is more like a verb. Its subject is normally the first person subject *wo* 'I,' which can be deleted due to pro-drop. So in (9) *wo* 'I' can be added before *guji* without affecting the meaning and grammaticality. Moreover, if *guji* is placed after the subject *ni* 'you,' the sentence becomes ungrammatical.

As for *bacheng* '80 percent,' this adverb may have a speaker-oriented interpretation, but such an interpretation is compatible with restrictive relative clauses as well, as shown by (10):

(10) Zhangsan tiao-le   (nei)-jian ta   laopo bacheng   bu hui xihuan de yifu.
     Zhangsan pick.out-Asp that-Cl   his wife 80.percent not will like   DE clothes
     'Zhangsan picked out the/a dress which his wife probably will not like.'

So if *guji* in the relative clause in (9) is replaced by *bacheng*, it still cannot be concluded that the relative clause must be non-restrictive.

A significant implication of (10) is that in Chinese adverbs conveying the speaker's cognitive or epistemic attitude toward a proposition do not need to surface at the root clause. The adverb *hen buxing* 'very unfortunately' is similar. It can occur not only in a relative modifying an individual-denoting name but also in a restrictive relative. This fact makes the test of root-level adverbs not reliable.

From the above discussion, we can say that Del Gobbo's (2003) binding tests and root-level adverb test are not conclusive evidence for the lack of non-restrictive relatives in Chinese.

2.1.2. Review of Del Gobbo (2010)

Interestingly, in Del Gobbo (2010), she slightly changes her viewpoint. Contra her position in a series of articles that all Chinese relatives are restrictives, Del Gobbo (2010) accepts Lin's (2003) position that RMPs can be non-restrictive. However, even for such non-restrictives, she argues that they are not like the familiar English non-restrictives but are "integrated non-restrictives" in the sense of Cinque (2008). Cinque (2008) observes that Italian has two types of non-restrictive relatives. The integrated ones are introduced by *che/cui*, as illustrated by the following examples:

(11)   a.   Inviterò anche Giorgio, **che/*cui** abita qui vicino.
            I will invite also G., **that/ who** lives nearby.

       b.   Inviterò anche Giorgio, [PP **di cui**] /***che** avete certamente sentito parlare.
            I will invite also G., of whom/that you have certainly heard.

This type of non-restrictives is virtually identical to restrictive constructions. The other type is "non-integrated non-restrictives," which are introduced by *il quale*, as shown in (12):

(12)   a.   Inviterò anche Giorgio, **il quale** abita lì vicino.
            I will invite also G., who lives nearby.

       b.   Inviterò anche Giorgio, [PP **del quale**] /***che** avete certamente sentito parlare.
            I will invite also G., of whom/that you have certainly heard.

The second type is essentially similar to the familiar English non-restrictives. These two types of non-restrictives display different syntactic properties. Del Gobbo (2010) applies Cinque's tests to differentiate these two types of non-restrictives to Chinese RMPs, arguing that they belong to the type of integrated non-restrictives. The following are the three arguments that Del Gobbo (2010) uses to support her position.

First, Italian non-integrated non-restrictives may have independent illocutionary force, but integrated non-restrictives may not. According to Del Gobbo, Chinese RMPs pattern with the latter because it is not possible to have an interrogative non-restrictive relative with the matrix clause remaining declarative, as shown by (13):

(13) *Wo xuan   le   dedao le   duoshao piao   de Zhangsan.
     I   choose Asp obtain Asp how.many tickets DE Zhangsan
     'I chose Zhangsan, who received how many votes?' (Del Gobbo 2010: 405)

Second, non-integrated non-restrictives can have split antecedents, but integrated ones may not. Del Gobbo shows that Chinese RMPs do not allow split antecedents, as illustrated in (14):

(14) *OP_i+_j bu xihuan Xiaoyu de Zhangsan$_i$ jinlai le,   Lisi$_j$ zou le.
        not like   Xiaoyu DE Zhangsan enter Asp Lisi exit Asp
                             (Del Gobbo 2010: 406)

Third, non-integrated non-restrictives allow antecedents of different categories such as DP, AP, PP, and so on, but integrated non-restrictives can only take a DP as their antecedent. Chinese relatives are also like integrated non-restrictives in this respect.

We agree with Del Gobbo on the above discussion. Chinese RMPs are like the Italian integrated *che/cui* non-restrictives rather than the non-integrated *il quale* non-restrictives. As mentioned, according to Cinque (2008), the integrated non-restrictives are virtually identical to the restrictive constructions. Thus, if Del Gobbo is correct, this means that RMPs are syntactically more like restrictive constructions than non-restrictive constructions.

3. Semantic Considerations

In the previous section, we saw that Chinese RMPs display some properties similar to the so-called "integrated non-restrictives" in Italian, which are syntactically more like restrictive constructions than non-restrictive ones. An interesting question to ask then is whether RMPs also display semantic properties similar to those of restrictive constructions. Potts's (2005) discussion of English non-restrictive relatives is a good starting point to examine this issue. In what follows, we will summarize his discussion and compare Mandarin RMPs with English non-restrictive relatives.

Potts (2005) takes non-restrictive relatives as "supplementing" expressions, which contribute conventional implicature (CI) along a separate dimension of semantic composition. He lists a range of defining properties for CIs as given in (15), adapted from Constant (2011b):

(15) Properties of Conventional Implicature Meaning (Potts 2003: 147–155; 2005: 111–115)

    a.   anti-backgrouding: can't repeat backgrounded information (or is redundant)

    b.   independence: at-issue meaning can be calculated independently from CI meaning

    c.   undeniability: can't be denied or questioned with epistemic riders

    d.   non-restrictiveness: can't be used to restrict

    e.   scopelessness: always interpreted with widest scope, regardless of embedding

Consider the property of anti-backgrounding first. McCawley (1981:117) observes that a non-restrictive relative cannot be naturally repeated in a question-answer pair:

(16) Appositives Resist Repetition (McCawley 1981)
    Q: Does John, who speaks French, often go to France for work?
    A: a.   Yes, John often goes to France for work.
       b.   ??Yes, John, who speaks French, often goes to France for work.

Del Gobbo (2003) uses this restriction as a test to show that Chinese RMPs are not non-restrictive relatives in that an RMP which appears in a question can be repeated in the answer, as shown by (17):

(17)   Q: xihuan yinyue de Zhangsan changchang qu yinyuehui ma?
        like   music DE Zhangsan often   go concert   Q
        'Does music-liking Zhangsan often go to concerts?'

       A: dui, xihuan yinyue de Zhangsan changchag qu yinyuehui.
        right like   music DE Zhangsan often   go concert
        'Yes, music-liking Zhangsan often goes to concerts.'

For the above argument, Constant (2011a) says that Del Gobbo does not make it clear whether the proper name *Zhangsan* in (17) denotes an individual or a property and that his consultants accept the dialogue only if there are a number of *Zhangsans* in the context. In addition, he points out that if the proper name *Zhangsan* in (17) is replaced with the popular author *Wang Xiaobo*, the repetition of the relative clause becomes distinctly unnatural.

On the other hand, we find that in many other non-question answer contexts, repetition of an RMP leads to an unnatural sentence due to redundancy. For example, the unnaturalness of the discourse in (18) is particularly striking when (18) is compared with (19), where the head noun modified by the relative is not a proper name but a common noun. This indicates that the content of an RMP cannot be something that is already familiar in discourse.

(18)   Zhang   xiaojie hen   ai   piaoliang #Hen ai   piaoliang de Zhang xiaojie
       Zhang   Miss   very love beautiful   very love beautiful DE Zhang Miss
       mai-le   xuduo yifu.
       buy-Asp many clothes
       'Miss Zhang loves being beautiful very much. #Miss Zhang, who loves being beautiful
       very much, bought many clothes.'

(19)   Women   ban   shang you   xie   xuesheng hen   ai   piaoliang.
       our   class   in   have   some   student   very   love beautiful
       (You   xie   bu   ai.)   Hen   ai   piaoliang de naxie
       have   some   not   love   very   love   beautiful DE those
       xuesheng shang ke   dou bu zhuanxin.
       student attend class   all not attentive
       'In our class some students love being beautiful very much. (Some don't.) Those
       students who love being beautiful are not attentive in class.'

Fang's (2008) study of Chinese relatives points to the same conclusion. According to her, when a relative clause modifies a pronoun (as in (20)) or a proper name (as in (21)), it cannot be anaphoric or part of the common ground knowledge but must convey new information. In this respect, Mandarin RMPs are like English non-restrictive relatives in that both display what Potts (2003, 2005) calls the "anti-backgrounding effect."

(20)   cong xiao   jiu   xihuan gezhong huahua caocao de ta   rujin zhongyu neng
        since child then like   various flower grass DE she now finally can
        han   hua   cao da   jiaodao le
        with flower grass have   dealings Asp
        'She, who has liked various flowers and grass since childhood, now can finally have
        dealings with flowers and grass.'

(21)   jin   nian sishi liu sui de Laoli zai shichang li   zuo le si   nian
        this year forty six old DE Laoli in market   inside do Asp four year
        dazhaxie   shengyi.
        hairy-crab business
        'Laoli, who is 46 years old this year, did hairy crab business for four years.'

At first glance, property (b) seems to be valid, too, because taking away a Mandarin relative modifying a proper name normally does not affect the rest of the sentence.
However, this is not always true. Consider example (4), reproduced below:

(4)   hen ai   chi niupai   de Laowang jintian que dian-le   yupai
        very love eat beef-steak DE Laowang today but order-Asp fish-steak
        '(To our surprise), Laowang, who loves eating beef steak very much, ordered fish steak
        today.'

(4) contains a functional word *que* in the matrix clause, which expresses an adver-
sative relation between two propositions. In (4), the two propositions in opposition
are: the proposition that Laowang loves eating beef steak and the proposition that he
ordered fish steak today. Both propositions are required arguments of the functional
word *que*. This is confirmed by the fact that deletion of the relative clause *hen ai chi
niupai de* 'who loves eating beef steak' in (4) makes the sentence incomplete, as is
shown by (22), which contrasts with (23).

(22)   ⁇ Laowang   jintian que dian-le   yupai.
          Laowang   today but order-Asp fish-steak
        'Laowang ordered fish steak today.'

(23)   Laowang hen ai   chi niupai,   jintian que dian-le   yupai.
        Laowang very love eat beef.steak today but order-Asp fish.steak
        'Laowang loves eating beef steak very much, but today he ordered a fish steak.'

Examples (4) and (23) clearly show that the meaning of an RMP is not always sup-
plementary and cannot be calculated at a dimension completely independent of the
meaning of the matrix clause.

    Property (c) and property (e) can be discussed together. In most cases, it seems
that RMPs cannot be denied or questioned. For example, in (24) and (25), the truth
of the proposition that Wang Daming has fled abroad is entailed, even though they
are embedded under the scope of a negation or question.

(24)   tao qu guowai de Wang Daming bei zhuadao le bu shi zhen de.
        flee go abroad DE Wang Daming Pass get.caught Asp not be true DE
        'It is not true that Wang Daming, who has fled abroad, has been caught.'

(25)   tao qu guowai de Wang Daming bei zhuadao le ma?
        flee go abroad DE Wang Daming Pass get.caught Asp Q
        'Is it the case that Wang Daming, who has fled abroad, has been caught?'

In (24), the negative matrix predicate *bu shi zhen de* 'is not true' only negates the proposition that Wang Daming has been caught but not the proposition that Wang Daming has fled abroad. Similarly, (25) only questions whether Wang Daming has been caught, but not whether Wang Daming has fled abroad. In both cases, the speaker is committed to the truth of the RMP.

However, unlike English non-restrictives, when an RMP is embedded to an attitude verb, its scope can be restricted to the embedded clause, as is illustrated by (26), provided to us by Hsiu-Chen Liao (personal communication).

(26)   Scenario: The information file that the judge possesses indicates that Wang Daming has
            fled to America.
        faguan renwei yao zhuadao tao qu guowai de Wang Daming bu tai keneng,
        judge   think want catch   flee go abroad DE Wang Daming not too possible,
        dan qishi wo zhidao ta yizhi duo zai taiwan, yinggai hen you xiwang zhuadao
        but in.fact I   know he always hide in Taiwan should very have hope   catch
        Intended: 'The judge thinks that Wang Daming has fled abroad and to catch him is not
            possible, but in fact I know he has been hiding in Taiwan. There should be a
            high possibility to catch him.'

We don't know what makes attitude verbs more special than negation and question, but example (26) clearly has an interpretation, confirmed by many speakers, that the content denoted by the relative *tao qu guowai de* 'who has fled to America' can be embedded under the matrix subject's, that is, the judge's, beliefs, thus falsifying both property (c) and (e). This interpretation indicates that an RMP does not have to have the widest scope, and hence does not commit the speaker to its truth.

The last property to consider is property (d). In English, a non-restrictive relative is not used to restrict the head noun to which they are anchored. Is this also true of Mandarin RMPs? Based on semantic considerations, Shi (2010) argues that Mandarin relatives, including RMPs, are always restrictive. In what follows we will briefly discuss his argument.

Contra Lin's (2003) claim that proper names can only be modified by relatives denoting permanent properties, Shi (2010) cites examples to prove that stage-level relatives may modify a proper name or pronoun as well, as illustrated in (27):

(27)   zheng zai jingzuo yundong   de Zhou Botong turan   da jiao
        right Prog sit-in stage.a.demonstration DE Zhou Botong suddenly big scream
        yi sheng, tiao-le   qilai
        one voice jump-Asp   up.come
        'Zhou Botung, who was sitting in to stage a demonstration, suddenly screamed loudly
        and jumped up.' (Shi 2010: 327)

Moreover, he claims that both individual-level and stage-level relatives are restrictive. He uses the following examples to support the restrictive interpretation of RMPs:

(28)   nimen hui kandao pao de geng kuai de Liuxiang.
        you   will see   run De more fast DE Liuxiang
        'You will see a Liuxiang who runs faster.'

(29)   puopuo   yan li de Guorong shi ge you xianhui
        mother-in-law eye in DE Guorong be Cl both virtuous-and-intelligent
        you nenggan de hao   xifu.
        and capable DE good daughter-in-law
        'The Guorong in the eyes of the mother-in-law is a good daughter-in-law who is virtuous
        and intelligent and capable.'

According to Shi, though there is only one individual referred to as *Liuxiang* in the
real world, the timeline can divide him into different stages, that is, the past *Liuxiang,*
the current *Liuxiang,* and the future *Liuxiang.* In (28), the future *Liuxiang* who has a
property of running faster (than before) is contrastive to the past *Liuxiang,* who has
a property of running less fast. Therefore, the relative clause *pao de geng kuai de* 'who
will run faster' in (28) should be analyzed as restrictive in that it helps pick out which
stage of *Liuxiang* the speaker is referring to. On this analysis, the denotation of the
proper name *Liuxiang* is not so much an individual as a property.

Likewise, Shi says that different people may have different images of the same individual, and those different images may cognitively constitute a non-singleton set
which a relative clause may further restrict to a smaller subset. The relative clause in
(29) is therefore restrictive rather than non-restrictive, despite the superficial unique
reference of the proper name.

Shi's (2010) analysis of (28) and (29) is reasonable, especially when we understand it within Carlson's (1977) framework. According to Carlson, there are three
subdomains of ontological entities in the world: stages, objects, and kinds. Stages are
"time-space slices" of individuals; objects are the most familiar things like *Obama* or
this book; kinds are individuals themselves such as the species whales or lions. Stages
are realizations of individuals at different times and/or spaces. On this analysis, the
denotation of a proper name can be a set of stages realizing the individual referred to
by the proper name, and the relative modifying it can indeed be construed as restricting that set of stages.

The above result is in fact not surprising, given that English proper names can also
denote properties and can be modified by a relative clause. In such cases, the definite article *the* must be used as in the example *the John that I knew.* Unlike English,
Chinese does not have articles. Therefore, there is no definite article in the Chinese
examples (28) and (29).

Now what is important is the question of whether Mandarin RMPs are always restrictive in the sense of Shi (2010). In what follows, we briefly comment on this claim.
First consider the following example:

(30)   qinfen   de Zhongguo ren.
        industrious DE Chinese   people
        i. 'All the Chinese people, who are industrious, . . .'
        ii. 'Chinese people who are industrious . . . (Some Chinese people are not industrious)

(30) is ambiguous between two readings. On one reading—the totality reading, all the Chinese people are entailed to be industrious. The other reading does not have the totality entailment but instead implies that some Chinese people are not industrious. This is the familiar restrictive versus non-restrictive contrast.

The restrictive reading of (30) is not a problem when *zhongguo ren* is treated as a common noun that denotes a set of Chinese people, that is, stages realizing the kind individual denoted by *zhongguo ren*. On this interpretation, the denotation of the relative clause *qinfen de* 'who are industrious' intersects with the denotation of the common noun it modifies, as is usual.

The totality reading is more challenging. On this reading, the relative clause is not predicated of the stages realizing the kind individual denoted by *zhongguo ren*, but is predicated of the kind individual itself. In this sense, the totality reading is not a restrictive one because no stages except the individual itself are involved.

The only possibility for Shi's analysis to maintain the restrictive interpretation of (30) is to say that there are many different cognitive images for Chinese people as a whole, namely, a non-singleton set consisting of Chinese people with the image of being industrious, Chinese people with the image of being conservative, and so on and so forth. We are not sure how plausible this analysis is, but intuitively there exists a distinction between Shi's examples (28), (29), and our example (30). Namely, while there is a strong intuition about the contrastive interpretation of (28) and (29), we do not have the same contrastive intuition for the totality reading of (30). For example, when hearing (30), we do not feel that we are contrasting industrious Chinese people with clever Chinese people or whatever. In fact, this seems to be generally the case when the relative clause is an individual-level property such as (31–33):

(31)   you-zhe   yi   tou   wuliu toufa de   Liu xiaojie qishi   shi wei moter.
       have-Asp one head dark   hair   DE   Liu Miss   in.fact be Cl model
       'Miss Liu, who has dark black hair, is in fact a model.'

(32)   juyou   hei   ren   xietong de   Obama dangxuan meiguo   di   sishisiren
       possess black people blood   DE   Obama elected   America the forty.fourth
       zongtong.
       president
       'Obama, who has black blood, was elected the 44th president.'

(33)   shii nüren   de   women juede shi nanren de   nimen dei   zou.
       be   women DE we   think be   man   DE   you   should leave
       'We women think that you men should leave.' (Hu 2008: 50)

(31) has two readings. On one reading, the context has a number of Miss Lius. In this context, the relative clause in (31) is restrictive and contrastive between the property of having dark black hair and the property of not having dark black hair. However, (31) can also be true in a context that contains only one Miss Liu. In such a context, we do not feel that we are contrasting or need to contrast the property of having dark black hair with some other property that Miss Liu might have. (32) is similar. In this example, we are not contrasting the Obama who has black blood with the Obama who doesn't have black blood. Nor does it seem that we are contrasting Obama's property of being a black with his other properties. Instead, it seems that the property of being

a black is used to indicate a contrast between being a black and winning the election. (33) is even more interesting. On the one hand, the world is such that once you are born a male or female, that property won't change. So the relative clauses in (33) can't invoke a contrastive set of individuals between *we women* and *we non-women* or between *you men* and *you non-men*. On the other hand, (33) can be true in a situation in which the only permanent property that we or you share in common is womanhood or manhood. In this context, there is no way to claim that the relative clause is restrictive. We conclude that (31–33) provide very robust evidence that RMPs can have the non-restrictive interpretation, contrary to what Shi (2010) claims.

The implication of the above discussion is this. It is reasonable to say that stage-level relatives modifying a proper name or pronoun can be analyzed as restrictive as Shi (2010) proposes under the assumption that individuals consist of stages as proposed in Carlson (1977). In contrast, when the relative clause modifying a proper name or pronoun is an individual-level relative, it is difficult to obtain the restrictive interpretation in many contexts. Such relatives do not seem to restrict the references of proper names or pronouns and must be non-restrictive in some sense. Given that non-restrictive interpretations are possible after all for individual-level relatives, such interpretations should in principle be available for stage-level relatives as well. We suspect that this interpretation is intuitively blurred simply because restrictive interpretations are easily available for stage-level relatives.

4. Interim Summary

To sum up, we have reviewed some syntactic and semantic properties of Mandarin RMPs. It seems that they have more properties of restrictive relatives than those of non-restrictive relatives, as is summarized in (34):

(34) Properties of RMPs similar to those of English non-restrictives:

    a.   anti-backgrounding effect

    b.   resistance of pronominal binding from outside (not reliable test)

(35) Properties of RMPs that are not similar to those of English non-restrictives:

    a.   not allowing split antecedents

    b.   not allowing non-DP anchors

    c.   not having independent illocutionary force

    d.   not always independent of the matrix clause in terms of meaning

    e.   not necessarily speaker-oriented or having widest scope

    f.   deniable (under scope of attitude verbs)

This result is somewhat surprising. On the one hand, we admit that RMPs can be non-restrictive, in particular those RMPs denoting individual-level properties. On the other hand, RMPs display syntactic and semantic properties that are more like those of restrictive relatives. The contradiction in question reveals that Chinese RMPs are indeed not of the same type as those of English non-restrictive relatives, which are semantically and syntactically independent of the matrix clause. The properties listed in (34) and (35) strongly suggest that though RMPs are semantically non-restrictive, they are syntactically part of the DP to which they adjoin and form an integrated structure with the remaining constituents of the sentence. This explains why they are not semantically independent of the other constituents of the sentence and can scope under attitude verbs. In other words, we syntactically restrict the semantically non-restrictive relatives to possess certain aspects of meaning composition that restrictive relatives share in common. In this sense, Del Gobbo's (2010) extension of Cinque's "integrated non-restrictives" to Chinese RMPs seems to be on the right track.

5. The Syntax of Mandarin Relatives

5.1. *DE*-CONSTRUCTIONS REVISITED

In terms of syntax, there is also evidence showing that Chinese relative clauses behave in line with Italian integrated non-restrictives like (36):

(36)   Giorgio, che francamente non si sarebbemai dovuto comportare così
       'Giorgio, who (lit. that) frankly should never have behaved like that'

For one thing, both RC$_1$ and RC$_2$ in Chinese allow a speech act adverbial such as *laoshishuo* 'frankly speaking' (cf. Thorne 1972; Emonds 1979; Cinque 2008), as evidenced by the following examples:

(37)   wo mei   zema nage [**laoshishuo**   biaoxian hen cha de] xuesheng.
       I   have.not scold that frankly-speaking perform very poor DE student
       'I did not scold that student, who, frankly speaking, performed very poorly.'

(38)   wo mei   zema [**laoshishuo**   biaoxian hen cha de] nage xuesheng.
       I   have.not scold frankly-speaking perform very poor DE that student
       'I did not scold that student, who, frankly speaking, performed very poorly.'

The same observation applies to cases with a speaker-oriented evidential adverb such as *xianran* 'obviously':

(39)   wo mei   zema nage [**xianran**   biaoxian hen cha de] xuesheng.
       I   have.not scold that obviously perform very poor DE student
       'I did not scold that student, who obviously performed very poorly.'

(40)   wo mei   zema [**xianran**   biaoxian hen cha de] nage xuesheng.
       I   have.not scold obviously perform very poor DE that student
       'I did not scold that student, who obviously performed very poorly.'

For another, just like their Italian counterpart in (41), Chinese parasitic gaps may occur in both post- and pre-demonstrative relatives in (42) and (43). This suggests that an operator-variable dependency rather than an E-type construal is involved (cf. Cinque 2008):

(41)   La sola persona che quelli che conoscono bene non possono non ammirareè Gianni.
    'The only person that those that know well cannot but admire is Gianni.'

(42)   nage [wo [yi   jian   *e*] jiu xihuan   de] xuesheng
    that   I   once meet   then like   DE student
    'the student who I like once meeting.'

(43)   [wo [yi   jian   *e*] jiu   xihuan de] nage xuesheng
    I   once meet   then like   DE that student
    'the student who I like once meeting.'

Although for most part we agree with Del Gobbo that Chinese RMPs are integrated non-restrictives, we disagree with her syntactic derivation of RMPs based on the following considerations: Typology-wise, Del Gobbo (2010) attributes the lack of relative pronouns in Chinese to the failure of cyclic c-command in licensing prenominal relativization. This move results in unnecessary complications on the syntactic side. The real reason, in our opinion, is simply that Chinese nominal *wh*'s are variables (cf. Cheng 1991; Li 1992; Tsai 1994; Lin 1996), and cannot function as relative operators. Our analysis thus predicts that we should be able to spot relative usages of genuine *wh*-adverbs in Chinese. This is indeed the case with *weishenme* 'why' and *zenyang* 'how' in (44a, b) (see also Ning 1993; Huang, Li, and Li 2009): In contrast to their nominal counterparts, these *wh*-adverbs can clearly be construed as relative rather than interrogative:

(44)   a.   [[xiaozhang **weishenme** yao qinzi   chuxi] de yuanyin]
        chancellor why   will in.person attend DE reason
    he   Akiu you henda   de guanxi.
    with Akiu have very.big DE relation
    'The reason why the chancellor will attend in person has a lot to do with Akiu.'

    b.   dajia   dou dui   [[xiaozhang **zenyang** chufa   zuobi]   de fangshi]
        people all   about   chancellor how   punish cheating DE way
    gandao   haoqi.
    feel   curious
    'People all feel curious about the way how the chancellor will punish cheating.'

Furthermore, contra Del Gobbo (2010), we are against the idea of treating *de* as a complementizer, one crucial reason being that *de*-construals within nominal projections do not form a homogeneous group (cf. Tsai 2011): on the one hand, relative *de* of RC_2 works exactly like adjectival *de* in licensing topicalization and ellipsis, as evidenced by the parallel between (45a, b) and (46a, b):

(45)   a.   **qunzi**$_k$, Zhaoma mai-le   yi-jian hong **de** e_k.   (topicalization)
        skirt   Zhaoma buy-Prf one-Cl red   DE
    '(As for) skirts, Zhaoma bought a red one.'

    b. Zhaoma mai-le yi-jian hong **de qunzi**,   (ellipsis)
        Zhaoma buy-Prf one-Cl red   DE skirt
        ye   mai-le yi-jian lan   **de** ~~qunzi~~.
        also   buy-Prf one-Cl blue DE skirt
        'Zhaoma bought a red skirt, and also bought a blue one.'

(46) a. **qunzi**$_k$, Zhaoma mai-le yi-jian Akiu feng **de** e$_k$.   (topicalization)
        skirt   Zhaoma buy-Prf one-Cl Akiu sew DE
        '(As for) skirts, Zhaoma bought one which Akiu sewed.'

    b. Zhaoma mai-le yi-jian Akiu feng **de qunzi**,   (ellipsis)
        Zhaoma buy-Prf one-Cl Akiu sew DE skirt
        ye mai-le yi-jian Xiaodi feng **de** ~~qunzi~~.
        also buy-Prf one-Cl Xiaodi sew DE skirt
        'Zhaoma bought a skirt which Akiu sewed, and also bought one which Xiaodi
        sewed.'

On the other hand, relative *de* of RC$_1$ licenses neither topicalization nor ellipsis, as shown by the ungrammaticality of (47a, b):

(47) a. *[**nei-jian qunzi**]$_k$, Zhaoma mai-le Akiu feng **de** e$_k$.   (topicalization)
        that-Cl skirt   Zhaoma buy-Prf Akiu sew DE
        '(As for) that skirt, Zhaoma bought it, which Akiu sewed.'

    b. *Zhaoma mai-le Akiu feng **de nei-jian qunzi**,   (ellipsis)
        Zhaoma buy-Prf Akiu sew DE that-Cl skirt
        ye   mai-le Xiaodi feng **de** ~~nei-jian qunzi~~.
        also buy-Prf Xiaodi sew DE that-Cl skirt
        'Zhaoma bought a skirt which Akiu sewed, and also bought one which Xiaodi sewed.'

We therefore propose instead that RC$_2$ are situated in the SPEC of ModP headed by *de*. Here *de* serves as a formal licenser (or a head-governor in GB-theoretical terms),[3] while triggering the matching type of relativization (cf. Aoun and Li 2003). The idea is sketched in the following diagram:

(48)

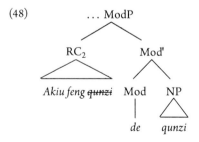

---

[3] For a minimalist account of the head-government effects displayed by modifier *de*, see Tsai (2011), where formal licensing in Rizzi's (1990) sense is reinvented as an "insurance" bought by Merge so that the No Tampering Condition (NTC) is strictly observed by subsequent operations such as deletion under identity at PF. As formulated in Chomsky (2007, 2008), NTC requires that Merge of X and Y leaves the two syntactic objects unchanged.

Relative *de* of RC$_1$, on the other hand, may well function as a particle cliticized to the relative clause in question, and trigger the raising type of relativization, as illustrated below:

(49)

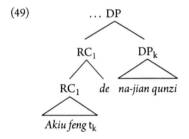

5.2. WHERE HAVE ALL THE NON-RESTRICTIVES GONE?

One of the important observations made in Huang (1987) concerns the parallelism between the pair of sentences in (50a, b) and those in (51a, b):

(50) a. There is a flying plane.   (restrictive)

     b. There is a plane flying.   (descriptive)

(51) a. tian-shang you yi-jia [ziyou aoxiang de] feiji.   (restrictive)
         sky-top   have one-Cl free   fly   DE plane
         'In the sky there is a plane which is flying freely.'

     b. tian-shang you yi-jia feiji [ziyou aoxiang]   (descriptive)
         sky-top   have one-Cl plane free   fly
         'In the sky there is a plane (and it's) flying freely.'
         'In the sky there is a plane, which is flying freely.'

Huang points out that the adjectival of (50a) patterns with the RC$_2$ of (51a) in terms of their restrictive function, whereas the secondary predicates of (50b) and (51b) are both descriptive in nature. This gives us necessary leverage to study the predicative properties of RC$_1$.

First, it has been established by Huang (1987) that Chinese secondary predication observes some form of (in)definiteness restriction, as illustrated by the pair of sentences below:

(52) a. wo jiao-guo   san-ge   xuesheng [conglai bu xizao].
         I   teach-Exp three-Cl student   ever   not bathe
         'I taught three students, who never bathed.'

     b. *wo zai zhao san-ge   xuesheng [conglai bu xizao].
         I   Prg find three-Cl student   ever   not bathe
         'I am looking for three students, who never bathed.'

For the construal of (52a) to be valid, the subject of secondary predication (i.e., the object *san-ge xuesheng* 'three students') must acquire specificity through aspectual licensing from the main predicate. Otherwise, the predication would fail, as is the case with (52b), where the progressive aspect on the *create*-type verb simply lacks the capacity of making the object specific. Curiously enough, the same effect shows up for either a proper name or a definite expression as the subject of secondary predication, as evidenced by (53a, b):

(53) a. *wo jiao-guo Akiu [conglai bu xizao].
          I   teach-Exp Akiu ever   not bathe
          'I taught Akiu, who never bathed.'

      b. *wo jiao-guo na-san-ge   xuesheng [conglai bu xizao].
          I   teach-Exp that-three-Cl student   ever   not bathe
          'I taught those three students, who never bathed.'

Huang attributes the kind of effects to a conflict between the existential force carried by the experiential aspect *-guo* and the definiteness of the object (cf. Barwise and Cooper 1981).

Along this line of inquiry, Tsai (1994) points out another curiosity: RC_1 behaves very much like Chinese secondary predicates in regard to the (in)definiteness restriction, notably in unaccusative constructions such as (54a, b):

(54) a. *zuotian   si-le   [[conglai bu xizao de] Akiu].
          yesterday die-Prf ever   not bathe DE Akiu
          'Yesterday three people who never bathed died.'

      b. *zuotian   si-le   [[conglai bu xizao de] na-san-ge   ren].
          yesterday die-Prf ever   not bathe DE that-three-Cl person
          'Yesterday those three people who never bathed died.'

Here the existential force comes from the unaccusative predicate *si-le* 'die-Prf' instead, but the effect remains the same nonetheless. By contrast, RC_2 never causes any trouble in this respect, and seems totally immune to the restriction, as evidenced by the following example:

(55) zuotian   si-le   [san-ge [conglai bu xizao de] ren].
      yesterday die-Prf three-Cl ever   not bathe DE person
      'Yesterday three people who never bathed died.'

This parallelism strongly suggests that RC_1 and secondary predicates may indeed belong to the same class of descriptive expressions in Chinese, namely, integrated non-restrictives of some sort.

6. Semantic Composition of Integrated Non-Restrictive Modification

6.1. A DIFFICULTY

Having argued that RMPs can be non-restrictive and having proposed a syntax for non-restrictive modification, we now turn to semantic composition of such constructions. Before engaging in it, let us make a brief digression about semantic composition of restrictive modification. A well-accepted assumption about restrictive relatives (RR) is that they denote properties of individuals, just as adjectival modifiers, and the semantics of an 'RR + Noun' construction is obtained via Heim and Kratzer's (1998) rule of Predicate Modification, where the denotation of the restrictive relative intersects with that of the common noun it modifies.[4] For example, the meaning of *renzhen dushu de xuesheng* 'students who study hard' is compositionally derived as follows, where $[\![a]\!]$ means the denotation of a:

(56)   renzhen dushu de xuesheng
    a. $[\![[_{CP}$ renzhen du shu de$]]\!] = \lambda x.x$ studies hard

    b. $[\![[_{NP}$ xuesheng$]]\!] = \lambda x.x$ is a student

    c. $[\![$renzhen dushu de xuesheng$]\!]$ (by Heim and Kratzer's Predicate Modification)
      $= \lambda x.[\![[CP]]\!]$ (x) = 1 and $[\![[NP]]\!]$ (x) =1
      $= \lambda x.x$ studies hard and x is a student

There are several possibilities concerning how a relative clause is turned into a property. It might be that the functional word *de* serves as a lambda abstractor binding the gap inside the relative clause, or it might be that *de* is semantically vacuous but the relative clause involves a null *wh*-operator interpreted as a lambda binder. In this chapter, we will not try to decide how the meaning of a relative clause is derived. For the purpose of this chapter, it suffices to assume that a Chinese relative clause denotes a property of individuals just like English relative clauses.

Returning to RMPs, we propose that they are adjoined to the proper names they modify as illustrated in (57):

(57)

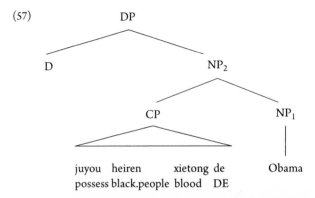

---

[4] Note that relative clauses are of type <e,t> and common nouns are also of type <e,t>. Two type <e,t> expressions cannot combine via functional application. Therefore, the rule of Predicate Modification, given in (i) below, is designed to deal with this type of mismatch.

The usual assumption for the meaning of proper names is that they denote the unique referent named by the proper name. For example, *John* means the individual named 'John.' If this direct reference theory such as Kripke (1980) is adopted, this means that the meaning of the DP node (and NP_2 as well) in (57) is a truth value, because the relative clause is a property of type <*e,t*> and the proper name is an individual of type *e*. This is an undesirable result, as this implies that no further semantic computation is possible beyond the DP. For example, if the DP in (57) is the subject of *dangxuan meiguo di sishisiren zongtong* 'was elected the forty-fourth president of America,' the two constituents can't combine because the subject is a truth value of type *t* but the VP is a property of type <*e,t*>, which requires an individual as its argument. Confronting such an obstacle, we have two choices: either we give up the denotation of proper names as an individual or we give up the denotation of a non-restrictive relative clause as a property of type <*e,t*>. In what follows, we would like to explore the first strategy, based on Matushansky's (2006) cross-linguistic study of proper names.

6.2 MATUSHANSKY'S (2006) TREATMENT OF PROPER NAMES AS TYPE <E,T> EXPRESSIONS

According to Matushansky's (2006) study, in some languages such as European Portuguese, Pima, some Italian, Spanish, Scandinavian and German dialects, Catalan, and so on, proper names in argument positions obligatorily come with a definite article as in (58), a Portuguese sentence:

(58) o   president nomeou   a   Maria ministra.
      the-M.SG   president named-3SG   the-F.SG Maria minister
      'The president named Mary the minister.'   (Matushansky 2006: 285)

The standard approach to this fact is to assume that the definite article is semantically vacuous, as in Longobardi (1994).

However, based on naming constructions across languages, Matushansky (2006) provides evidence showing that proper names are no different from common nouns in that both are underlyingly predicates of type <e,t>. One piece of evidence comes from Modern Greek, where proper names are subject to case-agreement. In Modern Greek (and Latin, Icelandic, and Albanian as well), the definite article is obligatorily with proper names in argument positions as in the object in (59a) and the subject in (59b). But in naming constructions unmodified proper names appear without an article, such as *Petro* in (59a, b):

(59)   Naming constructions
        a. vaftisa   to   Yani   Petro.
            baptized-1sg the-Acc Yani-Acc Petro-Acc
            'I baptized Yani Petro.'

(i)   Predicate Modification (PM)
        If α is a branching node, {β,γ}is the set of α's daughters and $[\![β]\!]$ and $[\![γ]\!]$ are both in D_{et}, then $[\![α]\!] = λx∈ De: [[\![β]\!](x) = [\![γ]\!](x) = 1]$

    b.   O   Yanis   vaftistike   Petros.
        The-Nom Yanis-Nom baptize-Pass.3sg Petros-Nom
        'Yanis was baptized Petro.'   (Matushansky 2006: 286)

Note that in Modern Greek, the case of a nominal predicate in a small clause must be the same as that of the small clause subject. Thus, in (60a), the nominal predicate of the small clause complement of the ECM verb *consider* case-agrees with the ACC feature of the small clause subject. When passivization renders the small clause subject nominative, the small clause predicate becomes nominative, too.

(60) a.   theoro   to   Yani   ilithio.
            consider-1sg the-Acc Yani-Acc idiot-Masc-Acc
            'I consider Yani an idiot.'

       b.   o   Yanis   theorite   ilithios.
            The-Nom Yanis-Nom consider-Pass.3sg idiot-Nom
            'Yanis is considered an idiot.'   (Matushansky 2006: 287)

The parallel between (59a, b) and (60a, b) shows that the proper name in a naming construction behaves exactly like a small clause predicate.

    In addition to Case-agreement languages, Matushansky also points out that in Case-marking languages without Case-agreement, the case on the proper name is the general predicative case, as is shown by languages as diverse as Hungarian, Syrian Arabic, and Russian:

(61) a   la'ny-om,-at   Mari-nak nevezt-em el.
       the daughter-1sg-Acc Mary-Dat named-1sg PREVERB
       'I named my daughter Mary'   (Matushansky 2005)

    Naming constructions in Korean (and Welsh as well) also give support for the predicative function of proper names in that they appear with the copular particle, as shown in (62):

(62) ku-nun caki-uy ttal-lul   Miran-i-la-ko   pwull-ess-ta.
       he-Top self-Gen daughter-Acc Miran-be-Assertive-Quot call-Past-Decl
       'He called his daughter Miran.'   (Matushansky 2005)

    In view of the above evidence, Matushansky (2006) concludes that proper names should be analyzed as bare nouns, that is, predicates, just as common nouns are. Therefore, languages where a definite article appears with proper names are the normal situation, and it is the absence of the definite article in most European languages such as English that must be explained. According to this view, the definite article that occurs with proper names has the standard semantics rather than being semantically vacuous. He also proposes an interesting explanation of the absence of the definite article in languages such as English in terms of m-merger. To discuss the details of his analysis is beyond the scope of this chapter. It suffices for us to assume that proper names are predicates underlyingly, at least in some languages.

6.3. SEMANTIC COMPOSITION OF NON-RESTRICTIVE RMPs

Given Matushansky's analysis of proper names, we assume that proper names are predicates of type *<e,t>* just like bare nouns, as given in (63):

(63)   a. $[\![\text{Zhangsan}_i]\!] = \lambda x. x = \text{Zhangsan}$
       b. $[\![\text{xuesheng}]\!] = \lambda x. x \text{ is a student}$

One difference between bare nouns and proper names is that the latter denote a single-ton set, that is, a set consisting of only the referent named by the proper name, whereas the former normally have more than one member in their denotation. Recall that ear-lier we said that an individual consists of temporal-spatial slices, which are stages real-izing the individual. In (63a), the subscript '*i*' is used to indicate the individual as a whole rather than the stages realizing that individual. In the latter case, a proper name has a common noun denotation as given in (64), where the subscript *s* indicates stages:

(64) $[\![\text{Zhangsan}_s]\!] = \lambda x. R(x, \text{Zhangsan}_i)$

Here the symbol 'R' in 'R(x, Zhangsan$_i$)' is Carlson's (1977) realization relation. 'R(x, Zhangsan$_i$)' means that x is a realization, that is, stage, of the individual Zhangsan$_i$. So under our approach, proper names are always predicates of type <e,t>.

But if individual-denoting proper names are predicates of type <e,t>, how do they end up denoting an individual? Here we will follow Matushansky (2006) in assuming that they are closed by a definite article with a standard semantics. More precisely, we assume that there is a null iota operator under the head D, in spite of the fact that there is no overt article at all in Mandarin Chinese. An illustration of the meaning of a DP containing a proper name is given in (65):

(65)   a.

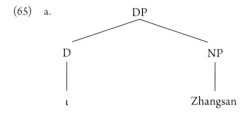

       b. $[\![\text{Zhangsan}_i]\!] = \lambda x. x = \text{Zhangsan}$
       c. $[\![[_D \iota]]\!] = \lambda P_{<e,t>}. \text{ the x such that } P(x)$
       d. $[\![[DP]]\!] = [\lambda P_{<e,t>}. \text{the x such that } P(x)](\lambda x. x = \text{Zhangsan})$
              $= \text{ the x such that x = Zhangsan}$

Note that the iota operator is not only available for proper names but also for common nouns. It is a well-known fact that bare nouns in Chinese may refer to definite enti-ties. For example, the subject *ji* 'chicken' in (66a) and the object *shu* 'book' can be construed as definite noun phrases:

(66)   a.   ji   chi-le.
              chicken   eat-Asp
              'The chicken already ate.'

b.   wo zhaodao shu   le.
     I   find   book Asp
     'I found the book.'

Therefore, the iota operation is an independently needed mechanism to obtain the definite interpretation for bare nouns.

With the preceding as background, we now discuss the semantic composition of non-restrictive relatives. We propose that non-restrictive modification involving RMPs has a syntactic representation like (67a) and is semantically computed as in (67b–d):

(67) a.

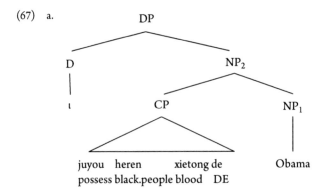

b. $[\![Obama]\!] = \lambda x. x = Obama$
c. $[\![_{CP} juyou heren xietong de]\!] = \lambda x.x$ has the blood of black people
d. $[\![NP_2]\!] = \lambda x. [\![CP]\!](x) = 1$ and $[\![NP_1]\!](x) = 1]$ (Predicate Modification)
          $= \lambda x. x$ has the blood of black people and $x = Obama$
e. $[\![DP]\!] = $ The x such that x has the blood of black people and $x = Obama$

In the above computation, it is worth special noting about the combination of the relative clause with the proper name. The non-restrictive relative is a predicate of type <e,t> and the proper name is also a predicate of type <e,t>. Therefore, they cannot combine directly. But the configuration matches Heim and Kratzer's rule of Predicate Modification, which was originally designed for restrictive modification. So the two type <e,t> expressions can combine, yielding an output that is again a type <e,t> predicate, which is closed by the iota operator. Therefore, the final denotation of the DP in (67a) is an individual with the property denoted by the relative clause. This makes further semantic computation possible, as desired.

It is worth emphasizing that non-restrictive modification, as proposed in (67), involves exactly the same rule of Predicate Modification as restrictive modification. The only difference is that non-restrictive relatives modify a noun denoting a singleton set, whereas restrictive relatives modify a noun denoting a non-singleton set. We believe that this result is a welcome one. In Mandarin Chinese, prenominal non-restrictive modification doesn't seem to be syntactically distinct from prenominal restrictive modification. If the syntax is the same for both restrictive and non-restrictive modification, there is no reason to expect a different syntax-semantics mapping rule. On the other hand, the difference between restrictive modification and non-restrictive modification can be ascribed to a minimal meaning difference between the nouns modified. When the noun modified by the relative denotes a (contextually restricted) singleton set, the meaning is non-restrictive. When the noun modified by the relative denotes a non-singleton set, the meaning is restrictive.

The proposed analysis of non-restrictive modification actually has cross-linguistic support. In English, in addition to post-nominal non-restrictive relatives, we also find non-restrictive adjectives in a prenominal position. Here are some examples:

(68)   a.   The Texan president returned to Houston.   (Leffel 2011: 1)

       b.   The industrious Greeks built beautiful monuments.   (Solt 2011)

The adjective *Texan* in (68a) must be non-restrictive in that there was only one president. (68b) is ambiguous in that it can be understood either as some industrious Greeks, as opposed to the lazy ones, who built the monuments or as Greeks as a whole. The Chinese RMPs can be said to be parallel to the above examples. In particular, it should be noted that the position of a non-restrictive adjective is also a position for restrictive adjective, as the ambiguity of (68b) shows. This indicates that our proposed analysis of Chinese RMPs is not without grounds in terms of both the syntax and the semantics.

The proposed semantics of RMPs has an important implication on the debate that we mentioned at the outset with respect to the interpretation of RC_1 and RC_2, especially RC_2. Recall that Chao (1968) claimed that RC_2 has a descriptive interpretation when not stressed. Given our analysis of non-restrictive modification, his claim seems to be correct, because RMPs as discussed in this chapter occupy exactly the RC_2 position following a null iota operator. RC_2 gets a descriptive interpretation when the common noun is confined to denote a single individual by the context of utterance.

7. Cross-Linguistic Variations

It has been occasionally reported that prenominal relatives cannot be non-restrictive, and attempts have been made to explain this claim (Del Gobbo 2005; Potts 2005; De Vries 2006). In particular, these studies suggest that linear ordering of non-restrictive modifiers can only be fixed as rightward of the anchor. Del Gobbo (2005) further suggests that non-restrictive relatives are instances of E-type anaphora and a non-restrictive E-type relative pronoun must temporally follow the head it modifies. Since Chinese relatives are prenominal, the relative always precedes the head, thus disallowing the possibility of non-restrictive relatives.

Despite the above studies, prenominal relatives in some languages have been reported to be either restrictive or non-restrictive, for example, Malayalam (Asher and Kumari 1997: 55), Marathi (Pandharipande 1997: 80–84), Kannada (Sridhar 1990: 51–52), and Turkish (Kornfilt 1997: 1.1.2.3.2; Göksel and Kerslake 1998: §25.2). For example, in the absence of any determiner, the following Amharic sentence is ambiguous between the restrictive and non-restrictive reading, according to Prenominal Relative Clauses (2010: example (239)):

(69)   *yä-näggäraññ*   *Desta*
        COMP-tell.PERF.S3SG.O1SG   Desta
        'Desta, who told it to me' or 'the Desta who told it to me'

If these authors are correct, the (im)possibility of a non-restrictive relative is not a simple matter of the linear ordering of the relative clause in relation to the head it modifies. This in turn implies that Del Gobbo's E-type strategy to account for the cross-linguistic variation of non-restrictive modification might not be on the right track (also see Constant 2011a for an empirical argument against this approach). In light of this, we would like to make an alternative parameter to account for cross-linguistic variation on non-restrictive relatives based on the semantics of proper names.

Longobardi (1999) argues that object and kind reference to nominal structures is cross-linguistically parametrized. In English, referential status of a proper name may occur with no overtly realized D, whereas in Romance it necessarily depends on a D position overtly occupied either by the noun itself or by an expletive article. This analysis suggests that a proper name in a given language can be assigned referential status with no overtly realized D or is dependent upon D to obtain referential status. In other words, the denotation of a proper name can be of type e, type $<e,t>$, or ambiguous. Restrictive or non-restrictive interpretation of a relative can be taken as consequences of the denotation of the proper name in a given language. If a proper name is of type e inherently, as Longobardi (1999) suggests for English, then the relative must be non-restrictive. In contrast, if a proper name is inherently of type $<e,t>$ and has no N-to-D movement, as we propose for Mandarin Chinese, then the relative must be restrictive. In such languages, superficial non-restrictive modification is derived from the fact that proper names denote singleton sets. Finally, if a proper name is ambiguous between type e and $<e,t>$, as is possibly the case for Amharic, then either restrictive or non-restrictive interpretation is possible depending upon which semantic type of the proper name is involved.[5]

8. Conclusion

In this chapter, we reviewed the debate over the restrictive versus non-restrictive distinction of Chinese prenominal relatives with a special focus on name-modifying relatives. Evidence shows that relatives modifying a proper name possess more properties of restrictive relatives than those of non-restrictive relatives. Semantically, however, there are clear cases where a name-modifying relative is not used to restrict the reference of the proper name. We thus agree with Del Gobbo (2010) that name-modifying relatives are a type of "integrated non-restrictives." The restrictive versus non-restrictive dilemma receives a plausible account under the treatment of proper names as predicates of type $<e,t>$. On the assumption that proper names are type $<e,t>$ expressions, name-modifying relatives can be semantically computed

---

[5] English proper names might be ambiguous between type e and $<e,t>$, too, because of examples such as *the John that I met yesterday*.

via exactly the same rule of restrictive predicate modification proposed by Heim and Kratzer (1998). The restrictive versus non-restrictive distinction is ascribed to the fact that proper names may denote singleton sets in addition to a non-singleton set (when understood as stages of individuals), whereas common nouns normally denote non-singleton sets. When the predicate modified by a relative denotes a singleton set, the non-restrictive interpretation is derived; when the predicate modified by a relative denotes a non-singleton set, a restrictive interpretation is derived. In this sense, the non-restrictive interpretation is still a restrictive modifier. Perhaps this analysis may explain why people's intuitions about the distinction between RC_1 and RC_2 vary so much from speaker to speaker. Along the above line of thought, we also propose that cross-linguistic variations in the (im)possibility of non-restrictive relatives can be ascribed to the inherent semantic type of proper names, which can be either type e, type $<e,t>$, or ambiguous. Finally, we present a syntactic distinction between RC_1 and RC_2 with respect to their capacity of formal licensing. That is, while RC_2 allows topicalization/ellipsis of its head noun, RC_1 does not carry the same clout. Furthermore, we point out that RC_1 and secondary predicates share the same trait in Chinese, that is, the (in)definiteness restriction in Huang's (1987) sense. All these point to the conclusion that RMPs may indeed belong to a special type of descriptive expressions, namely, integrated non-restrictives with properties of restrictive relatives.

References

Aoun, Joseph, and Yen-hui Audrey Li. 2003. *Essays on the Representation and Derivational Nature of Grammar: The Diversity of Wh-Constructions.* Cambridge, MA: MIT Press.

Asher, R. E., and T. C. Kumari. 1997. *Malayalam.* London and New York: Routledge.

Barwise, Jon, and Robin Cooper. 1981. Generalized quantifiers and natural language. *Linguistics and Philosophy* 4, 159–219.

Carlson, Gregory. 1977. *Reference to Kinds in English.* Doctoral dissertation. University of Massachusetts, Amherst.

Chao, Yuan Ren. 1968. *A Grammar of Spoken Chinese.* Berkeley: University of California Press.

Cheng, Lisa. Lai-Shen. 1991. *On the Typology of Wh-Questions.* Doctoral dissertation. MIT (published by Garland, New York, 1997).

Chomsky, Noam. 2007. Approaching UG from below. In *Interfaces + recursion = language?,* ed. Uli Sauerland and Hans Martin Gärtner, 1–29. New York: Mouton de Gruyter.

Chomsky, Noam. 2008. On phases. In *Foundational issues in linguistic theory. Essays in honor of Jean-Roger Vergnaud,* ed. Robert Freidin, Carlos P. Otero, and Maria Luisa Zubizarreta, 133–166. Cambridge, MA: MIT Press.

Cinque, Guglielmo. 2005. Deriving Greenberg's universal 20 and its exceptions. *Linguistic Inquiry* 36, 315–332.

Cinque, Gugliemo. 2006. Two types of appositives. *University of Venice Working Papers in Linguistics* 16, 7–56.

Cinque, Guglielmo. 2008. Two types of nonrestrictive relatives. In *Empirical Issues in Syntax and Semantics* 7, ed. Olivier Bonami and Patricia Cabredo Hofherr, 99–137. Accessed January 14, 2009. http://www.cssp.cnrs.fr/eiss7.

Constant, Noah. 2011a. *Appositives after All.* Ms., University of Massachusetts, Amherst.

Constant, Noah. 2011b. Re-diagnosing appositivity: Evidence for prenominal appositives from Mandarin. *Papers from the 47th Regional Meeting of the Chicago Linguistic Society.*

De Vries, Mark. 2006. The syntax of appositive relativization: On specifying coordination, false free relatives, and promotion. *Linguistic Inquiry* 37, 229–270.

Del Gobbo, Francesca. 2003. *Appositives at the Interface*. Doctoral dissertation, University of California, Irvine.

Del Gobbo, Francesca. 2004. On prenominal relative clauses and appositive adjectives. In *WCCFL 23 Proceedings*, ed. B. Schmeiser, Vineeta Chand, Ann Kelleher, and Angelo Rodriguez, 182–194. Somerville, MA: Cascadilla Press.

Del Gobbo, Francesca. 2005. Chinese relative clauses: Restrictive, descriptive or appositive. In *Contributions to the XXX Incontro di Grammatica Generativa*, ed. L. Brugè, G. Giusti, N. Munaro, W. Schweikert, and G. Turano, 287–305. Venezia: Cafoscarina.

Del Gobbo, Francesca. 2010. On Chinese appositive relative clauses. *Journal of East Asian Linguistics* 19, 385–417.

Emonds, Joseph. 1979. Appositive relatives have no properties. *Linguistic Inquiry* 10, 211–243.

Fang, Mei. 2008. Two emerging grammatical structures motivated by background information packaging: A case study on the cataphoric zero subject clause and the descriptive clause. *Zhongguo Yuwen* 325, 291–303.

Fox, Danny. 2000. *Economy and Semantic Interpretation*. Cambridge, MA: MIT Press.

Giorgi, Alessandra. 1984. Towards a theory of long-distance anaphors: A GB approach. *The Linguistic Review* 3, 307–362.

Göksel, A., and C. Kerslake. 2005. *Turkish: A Comprehensive Grammar*. London and New York: Routledge.

Greenberg, Joseph H. 1963. Some universals of grammar with particular reference to the order of meaningful elements. In *Universals of Language*, ed. Joseph H. Greenberg, 73–133. Cambridge, MA: MIT Press.

Heim, Irene, and Angelika Kratzer. 1998. *Semantics in Generative Grammar*. Malden, MA: Blackwell.

Hu, Xiaoliang. 2008. *A Contrastive Study of English and Chinese Relative Clauses*. Master's thesis, Hunan Normal University, Hunan, China.

Huang, C.-T. James . 1982. *Logical Relations in Chinese and the Theory of Grammar*. Doctoral dissertation, MIT.

Huang, C.-T. James. 1987. Existential sentences in Chinese and (in)definiteness. In *The Representation of (In)Definiteness*, ed. Eric Reuland and Alice ter Meulen, 226–253. Cambridge, MA: MIT Press.

Huang, C.-T. James, Audrey Li, and Yafei Li. 2009. *The Syntax of Chinese*. Cambridge: Cambridge University Press.

Huang, C.-T. James, and C.-S. Luther Liu. 2001. Logophoricity, attitudes and *ziji* at the interface. In *Long-distance reflexives*, Syntax and Semantics, vol. 33, ed. P. Cole, G. Hermon, and C.-T. J. Huang, 141–195. New York: Academic Press.

Kornfilt, J. 1997. *Turkish*. London and New York: Routledge.

Kripke, Saul. 1980. *Naming and Necessity*. Oxford: Blackwell.

Leffel, Tomothy. 2011. *Nonrestrictive Adjectives and the Theory of Scalar Implicature*. Unpublished manuscript, New York University.

Li, Yen-hui Audrey. 1992. Indefinite wh in Mandarin Chinese. *Journal of East Asian Linguistics* 1, 125–155.

Lin, Jo-wang.1996. *Polarity Licensing and Wh-Phrase Quantification in Chinese*. Doctoral dissertation, University of Massachusetts at Amherst.

Lin, Jo-wang. 2003. On restrictive and non-restrictive relative clauses in Mandarin Chinese. *Tsinghua Journal of Chinese Studies*, New Series, 33, 199–240.

Longobardi, Giuseppe. 1994. Reference and proper names. *Linguistic Inquiry* 25(4), 609–665.

Longobardi, Giuseppe. 1999. Bare nouns, proper names, and the syntax-semantics mapping: Toward a unified parametric approach. *Rivista di Grammatica Generativa* 24, 45–76.

Lü, Shuxiang. 1999. Xiushiyu [Modifiers]. In *Xiandaihanyu yufajianghua* [Lectures on Modern Chinese Grammar], ed. Ding Shengshu et al., 42–55. Beijing: The Commercial Press.

Matushansky, Ora. 2005. *Why Rose Is the Rose*. Abstract. Retrieved from http://www.cssp.cnrs. fr/cssp2005/abstracts/Matushansky.pdf.

Matushansky, Ora. 2006. Why Rose is the rose: On the use of definite articles in proper names. In *Empirical Issues in Syntax and Semantics* 6, ed. O. Bonami and P. Cabredo Hofherr, 285–307. Retrieved from http://www.cssp.cnrs.fr/eiss6/index_en.html.

McCawley, James D. 1981. The syntax and semantics of English relative clauses. *Lingua* 53, 99–149.

Ning, Chunyan. 1993. *The Overt Syntax of Topicalization and Relativization in Chinese*. Doctoral dissertation, University of California, Irvine.

Pandharipande, R. 1997. *Marathi*. London and New York: Routledge.

Potts, Christpher. 2003. *The Logic of Conventional Implicatures*. Doctoral dissertation, University of California, Santa Cruz.

Potts, Christopher. 2005. *The Logic of Conventional Implicatures*. Oxford: Oxford University Press.

Prenominal relative clauses: a typology study. [Anonymous 2009]. Retrieved from http://www. ddl.ish-lyon.cnrs.fr/fulltext/.../Prenominal_relative_clauses.doc.

Rizzi, Luigi. 1990. *Relativized Minimality*. Cambridge, MA: MIT Press.

Safir, Ken. 1986. Relative clauses in a theory of binding and levels. *Linguistic Inquiry* 17, 663–689.

Sells, Peter. 1987. Aspects of logophoricity. *Linguistic Inquiry* 18, 445–479.

Shi, Dingxu. 2010. Xianzhixing dingyu han miaoxiexing dingyu [Restrictive and descriptive modifiers], *Foreign Language Teaching and Research* 42(5), 323–328.

Solt, Stephanie. 2011. Attributive quantity words as nonrestrictive modifiers. To appear in *Proceedings of the 39th Meeting of the North East Linguistic Society (NELS39)*.

Sridhar, S. N. 1990. *Kannada*. London and New York: Routledge.

Thorne, James Peter. 1972. Nonrestrictive relative clauses. *Linguistic Inquiry* 3, 552–556.

Tsai, Wei-Tien Dylan. 1994. *On Economizing the Theory of A-Bar Dependencies*. Doctoral dissertation, MIT.

Tsai, Wei-Tien Dylan. 2011. *Rethinking Formal Licensing*. Paper presented at the 5th International Conference on Formal Linguistics, Guangdong University of Foreign Studies, Guangzhou, December 2011.

Zhang, Niina. 2001. *On the Absence of Nonrestrictive Relatives in Chinese*. Ms., ZAS, Berlin.

5

The *same* Difference: Comparative Syntax-Semantics of English *same* and Chinese *tong/xiang-tong*

WEI-WEN ROGER LIAO AND YUYUN IRIS WANG

1. Introduction

Three decades ago, the seminal work of Huang (1982) opened a new window into the study of comparative syntax. Huang (1982) convincingly argues that *wh*-movement, which is not observed in the surface patterns of Chinese *wh*-questions, takes place "covertly" at an inaudible syntactic level (i.e., the LF interface). Huang's theory of LF brings us to a core assumption of Universal Grammar: that the underlying syntax in human languages is actually uniform, despite surface discrepancies. More specifi-cally, Huang's theory shows that "LF-PF mismatches" do exist in natural languages—that is, a syntactic operation that displays an obvious LF effect does not always have an observable PF counterpart—and we may assume that "silent" elements and opera-tions are prevalent in natural languages. In particular, Huang's (1982) study argues convincingly that *wh*-movements are overt in English, but are silent in Chinese. An-other significant study made some years later, Pollock (1989), proposed that finite verbs move to Tense "audibly" in French, but "silently" in English, and more recently works by Kayne (2005, 2007, 2008), Riemsdijk (2002, 2005), and Sigurðsson (2004) and others have argued that there are many more silent elements than previously thought (and yet to be discovered) in syntax, and such silent elements are key to un-derstanding linguistic variation.

In this chapter, we follow these "silent" steps, and present a comparative syntax-semantic study of the adjective *same* in English and its equivalent, *tong/xiang-tong*, in (Mandarin) Chinese.[1] We argue that *same* is not always an NP-level adjective in English, nor is it one in Chinese, and that *same* can modify different functional cat-egories in the nominal syntax, both classifiers (CL) and determiners (D). Our central claim will be evidenced by the behaviors of *same* in Chinese, which has two different lexical realizations, *tong* and *xiang-tong*. The fact that each of these elements modifies

---

[1] 'Chinese' is used in this chapter simply to refer to Mandarin Chinese.

different syntactic structures offers a useful clue for detecting silent functional projections in English and Chinese. Given the syntax-semantics mapping between the syntactic NP-DP hierarchy and the semantic type-token distinction (Carlson 2003; Higginbotham 1985; Longobardi 1994; Vergnaud and Zubizarreta 1992; Zamparelli 2000; among others), we conclude that *tong* modifies a silent determiner in Chinese, while *xiang-tong* may freely modify other syntactic structures. In English, *same* may also modify a silent classifier projection, in addition to being the modifier of an overt determiner. Our theory thus ultimately provides strong empirical evidence for the claim that Chinese and English share the same functional inventories in their nominal syntax (Borer 2005; Li 1999; Simpson 2005; Tang 1990; Watanabe 2006; among others), and cross-linguistic variation is reduced to surface realization forms.[2]

The chapter is organized as follows. We introduce the syntactic and semantic properties of Chinese *same* (*tong* and *xiang-tong*), and provide a comparison with English *same* in section 2. In section 3, adopting the theory of silent projections (Kayne 2005; Leu 2008), we pursue a uniform syntactic analysis of Chinese and English *same*, and show that our syntactic analysis is fully supported by a mapping theory between the syntactic NP-DP hierarchy and the semantic type-token distinction (Vergnaud and Zubizarreta 1992). Section 4 concludes our analysis.

2. *Same* in English and in Chinese

2.1. *SAME* IN ENGLISH

Same in English appears to be an adjective, as it can be modified by *very*:

(1) John dated the *very same* girl as Tom did.

However, *same* also behaves very differently from typical adjectives in many respects. *Same* appears in a higher structural position than typical adjectives do, for instance, and while typical adjectives are adjacent to NP, *same* appears further away. The contrast is clear when a numeral appears, as shown in the following examples:

(2) a. John bought the *(*blue) three blue* shirts.

  b. John bought the *same three (*same)* shirts.

Additionally, *same* imposes a selectional restriction on its preceding determiners/quantifiers, and it only co-occurs with the definite article *the*, while such a selection is not observed in typical adjectives. Consider the following minimal pairs:

(3) a. John wore the/*a/*every/*some/*all same blue shirt(s).

  b. John wore the/a/every/some/all blue shirt(s).

---

[2] In Jean-Roger Vergnaud's theory of structural Case, reprinted in Vergnaud (2008), a universal principle of abstract structural Case is postulated, even in languages without overtly realized Case morphology. Such a view of linguistic variation in surface realization forms is revived in the Strong Minimalist Thesis under the name of the Uniformity Principle (see Chomsky 2001).

The co-occurrence of *same* with the definite article is also observed when *same* functions as a predicate. This, again, contrasts with typical adjectives:

(4) a. The shirts that John and Bill wore are *(the) same.

   b. The shirts that John and Bill wore are (*the) blue.

The strong selection between *same* and *the* therefore suggests that *same* and the determiner *the* form a syntactic complex, unlike other adjectives. We shall return to the specific structures in more detail below, but the contrasts can be roughly illustrated as follows:

(5) a. typical adjectives
       $[_{DP}$ the $[_{NP}$ red car$]]$

   b. *the same* complex
       $[_{DP}$ [the same] $[_{NP}$ car$]]$

2.2. ON TYPES AND TOKENS

Semantically, *same* also involves an interesting ambiguity that sets it apart from typical adjectives: it is ambiguous between sameness in "token" and sameness in "type." Here, we shall refer to types and tokens in their linguistic/grammatical senses, which are made precise in generative linguistics in Vergnaud and Zubizarreta (1992).[3] Adopting Vergnaud and Zubizarreta (1992), types are conceptual entities that refer to properties or concepts expressed by nominal expressions, and tokens refer to entities that are instantiations of types. The meaning of *same* may refer to either class— that is, objects of the "same type" are a set of entities that share some property or concept and are expressed by a nominal expression, while objects of the "same token" denote entities that share the same instantiation of some type. It is useful to visualize the type-token distinction as in the following sentences:

(6) a. We like the same (type of) music.   [same type]

   b. We live in the same house.   [same token]

In (6a), where the same type of music is intended, we may think of a set of mental/grammatical entities (nominal expressions) that share the property of being music:

(7) a. {[rock], [hip-hop], [classical music], [jazz] ...}

   b. {[rock], [hip-hop], **[classical music]**, [jazz] ...}

Sameness in type then means that a certain nominal expression that is a type of music is picked up. For example, if we both like classical music, then the nominal expression [classical music] is picked up. As we know, classical music may have many

---

[3] That is to say, we shall depart from the object-oriented view on types and tokens that is generally adopted in the Fregean traditions. See Vergnaud and Zubizarreta (1992) and Wetzel (2009) for further discussion.

different instantiations, or tokens (e.g., Mozart's *The Magic Flute*, Beethoven's *Symphony No. 5*, Schubert's *The Trout Quintet*, and so on); but these are of no concern here, since it is the type information that is salient in the core meaning of (6a).[4] On the other hand, in (6b), where the token information is intended, it is a specific instantiation of the type "house" that matters. The instantiation is indicated through numeral indexing, as in (8):

(8)

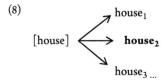

Therefore, *the same house* in (6b) not only denotes the same type of thing called *house*, but also makes reference to the same instantiation, a particular house (say, $house_2$ in (8)).

In English, the expression "*the same* NP" is ambiguous with respect to the type-token distinction, and the ambiguity may appear to be a lexical one. However, we shall argue that the type-token distinction of *(the) same* is not trivial in syntax. As we will see in the next section, 'same' in Chinese allows us to observe the type-token distinction transparently in syntax.

2.3. 'SAME' IN CHINESE: *TONG* VS. *XIANG-TONG*

In this section, the morphosyntactic and semantic properties of Chinese *same* will be examined. Chinese has two words for 'same,' *tong* and *xiang-tong*. We shall see that the former behaves as a determiner-like element (D-elements, including demonstratives and quantifiers), and the latter behaves like an adjective. Semantically, the former (*tong*) always refers to sameness in token, while the latter (*xiang-tong*) refers to sameness in type.

2.3.1. On the Morphosyntax of 'Same' in Chinese
Before we look into the semantic type-token distinction in Chinese 'same,' let us first examine its syntactic and morphological properties. The two morphological variants, *tong* and *xiang-tong*, share the same root, √tong 'same,' a morphologically bound form. In Chinese, bound forms typically operate as functional items and compounds. On the other hand, *xiang-tong* is a free morpheme (a compound form of *xiang* and

---

[4] Note that the definition of the type-token distinction, as defined by Vergnaud and Zubizarreta (1992), allows a certain level of recursion. For example, the musical compositions can also be viewed as types per se, instantiated by different (event) tokens (such as the *Symphony No. 5* performance I listened to at a concert, and a different one I heard last night on the radio). Likewise, natural kinds can be viewed either as tokens or as types. In English, for example, one can refer to natural kinds through definite singular nouns (*The dodo is extinct*), corresponding to "proto-typical tokens," or through bare plural nouns (*Dodos are extinct*), corresponding to types (Vergnaud and Zubizarreta 1992; Zamparelli 1998; among others). We thank Henry Y- L. Chang for pointing out this issue to us.

tong) that functions as a substantive adjective. In its origin, *xiang* has a literal meaning of 'each other,' but this meaning has been lost in modern Mandarin Chinese, and therefore, both *xiang-tong* and *tong* have the meaning of 'same.'[5,6] Their morphosyntactic differences can be observed in two ways. First, the free form *xiang-tong* can function as an adjectival predicate, but the bound form *tong* cannot. This contrast is shown in (9):

(9) Wo gen ni   xihuan de canting   shi xiang-tong/*tong de.
     I   and you like   DE restaurant be same/same   DE
     'The restaurant that you and I like is the same.'

Furthermore, as (10a) below shows, only the free adjective *xiang-tong* can modify the noun, and only *xiang-tong* can appear in positions that allow adjectives, which are indicated by the positions *I, II,* and *III* in (10b). In each of these positions, the modificational *de* marker is obligatory, as it is for other Chinese adjectives (for discussions of adjectives in Chinese, see Aoun and Li 2003; Huang, Li, and Li 2009).

(10)   Possible positions for adjectives: *I* + Dem + *II* + Num + CL + *III* + N[7]

    a. Zhangsan mai-le   **(xiang-tongde)** na %**(xiang-tong de)** yi   zhi
        Zhangsan buy-Asp same   DE that same   DE one CL
        (xiang-tong de)   gou.
        same   DE   dog.
        'Zhangsan bought the same dog.'

    b. Zhangsan mai-le   **(keai de)** na %**(keai de)** yi   zhi **(keai de)** gou.
        Zhangsan buy-Asp cute DE that   cute DE one CL cute DE do
        'Zhangsan hugged a cute dog.'

In contrast, (11) shows that the bound form *tong* appears in a fixed position before the numeral-classifier, and the *de* marker does not appear:

(11)   Zhangsan bao-le   **tong** (*de) yi   zhi (*tong) gou.
       Zhangsan hug-Asp same DE   one CL same   dog
       'Zhangsan hugged the same dog.'

---

[5] This kind of morphological variation is prevalent in Chinese morphosyntax (see Zhang 2007). One of the classic examples illustrating the close relationships between bound and free forms is the classifier in Chinese. Bound classifiers (a functional item) and free nouns (a substantive item) share the same nominal roots. For example, the nominal root √*ge*, which has a lexical meaning of 'single/individual,' can be used in compounds to form nouns like *ge-ti* 'individual-body, individual(s)' and *ge-bie* 'individual-separate, separate(ly).' At the same time, it can also occur in the simple form, where it functions as a bound classifier.

[6] Other lexical items in Chinese that have the meaning of 'same' include *tong-yang* 'same (lit. same-type)' and *yi-yang* 'same (lit. one-type),' which can be considered a reduced relative clause or a lexicalized form of the phrase [*tong yi yang*] 'same one type$_{CL}$' (James Huang, p.c.). Notably, both of them are free adjectivals that behave on a par with *xiang-tong*.

[7] Not all speakers identify as grammatical those sentences containing a demonstrative with an adjective in position II.

In addition to their differing syntactic distributions, *tong* and *xiang-tong* also display different co-occurrence restrictions. *Tong* cannot co-occur with any D-elements (including demonstratives and quantifiers) in Chinese, as shown in (12a), while *xiang-tong* has no such restrictions, as in (12b):

(12) a. Zhangsan mai-le   tong (*zhe/*na/*mei/*mou) yi   zhi gou.
          Zhangsan buy-Asp same this/that/every/some   one CL dog
          'Zhangsan bought the (*this/*that/*every/*a certain) same dog.'

      b. Zhangsan mai-le   xiang-tong de zhe/na/mei/mou   yi zhi gou.
          Zhangsan buy-Asp same   DE this/that/every/some one CL dog
          'Zhangsan bought this/that/every/a certain dog (of the same token or type).'

With respect to the definiteness, although *tong* is not compatible with D-elements, nominal phrases containing *tong* are always definite. The definiteness is brought about by *tong*, since without it, bare numeral-classifier NPs (with numerals other than *yi* 'one'; see our footnote 8) in Chinese are always interpreted as indefinite expressions (Li 1998; Tsai 2001). This contrast can be clearly illustrated in environments with definiteness effects (DE), discussed at length in Huang (1987). Of the examples from Huang's (1987) study, three DE-environments that do not allow definite expressions are listed in (13): subjects of existential *you*-sentences, as in (13a); internal arguments of unaccusative appearance/disappearance verbs (e.g., *come* and *die*), as in (13b); and subjects of secondary predicates, as in (13c). Notably, these environments allow neither *tong* nor a demonstrative:

(13) a. You (*na/*tong) yi ge xuesheng lai-guo.
          have that/same one CL student come-Asp
          'There has come a student.'

      b. Lai-le   (*na/*tong) yi ge xuesheng.
          come-Asp that/same   one CL student
          'A student came.'

      c. Wo jiao-guo (*na/*tong) yi ge xuesheng hen congming.
          I teach-Asp that/same   one CL student very clever
          'I have taught a student who is very clever.'

On the other hand, *xiang-tong* does not affect the definiteness of its modified phrases, and modified phrases simply retain their definiteness. Therefore, even with modification of *xiang-tong*, indefinite nominal phrases can still appear in DE environments, as shown in (14):

(14) a. You (xiang-tong de) yi ge (xiang-tong de) xuesheng lai-guo.
          have same   DE one CL same   DE student come-Asp
          'There has come a student of the same type.'

      b. Lai-le   (xiang-tong de) yi ge (xiang-tong de) xuesheng.
          come-Asp same   DE one CL same   DE student
          'A student (of the same type) came.'

    c. Wo jiao-guo (xiang-tong de) yi ge (xiang-tong de)
       I   teach-Asp same   DE one CL same   DE
      xuesheng hen congming.
      student   very clever
      'I have taught a student of the same type who is very clever.'

The last syntactic difference between *tong* and *xiang-tong* lies in their respective abilities to license *one*-omission. *Tong*, on a par with D-elements, allows *one*-omission, while *xiang-tong* does not allow *one*-omission by itself. The contrast is illustrated in (15):

(15)   a.   Zhangsan jian-guo   tong/na/mei/mou   (yi) ge laoshi.
             Zhangsan meet-Asp same/that/every/certain one CL teacher
             'Zhangsan met with the same/that/every/some teacher before.'

        b.   Zhangsan jian-guo xiang-tong de *(yi) ge laoshi.
             Zhangsan meet-Asp same   DE one CL teacher
             'Zhangsan met with the same teacher before.'

The following chart summarizes the morphosyntactic contrasts between *tong* and *xiang-tong*. The contrasts uniformly point to the conclusion that *tong* should be analyzed as a D-element, especially on a par with demonstratives. *Tong* and demonstratives are alike in their morphological status, share the same syntactic distributions, result in definite expressions, are in complementary distribution, and can license *one*-omission. On the other hand, characteristics of *xiang-tong* indicate that it should be analyzed as an adjective:

(16)   *tong* vs. *xiang-tong*

tong	*xiang-tong*
Bound form	Free morpheme
Does not occur with *de*	Must occur with *de*
Occurs before Num-CL	Occurs in adjective positions
Incompatible with D-elements	Compatible with D-elements
Licenses *one*-omission	Does not license *one*-omission

2.3.2. On Type-Token Distinction and 'Same' in Chinese

With respect to the semantic type-token distinction, *tong* and *xiang-tong* also display very different behaviors. *Tong* phrases always denote the same token, as shown in (17), and *xiang-tong* phrases may denote the same type or the same token, depending on their syntactic hierarchy, as shown in (18):

(17)   Mei ge ren   dou zhu zai tong yi jian fangzi.
       every CL person all   live in same one CL house
       a. 'Everyone lives in the same house.'   [same token]

       b. #'Everyone lives in the same type of house.'   [same type]

(18) a. Mei   ge   ren   dou zhu zai xiang-tong de na yi   jian fangzi
          every CL person all live in same   DE that one CL house
          i. 'Everyone lives in the same house.'   [same token]
          ii. #'Everyone lives in the same type of house.'   [same type]

      b. Mei   ge   ren   dou zhu zai xiang-tong de yi jian fangzi.
          every CL person all live in same   DE one CL house
          i. *'Everyone lives in the same house.'   [same token]⁸
          ii. 'Everyone lives in the same type of house.'   [same type]

      c. Mei   ge   ren   dou zhu zai yi jian xiang-tong de fangzi.
          every CL person all live in one CL same   DE house
          i. #'Everyone lives in the same house.'   [same token]
          ii. 'Everyone live in the same type of house.'   [same type]

We can therefore make the following generalizations about the relationship between Chinese 'same' and the type-token distinction:

(19) a. *Tong* always gives rise to a token-related interpretation (i.e., the sameness of token).
      b. *Xiang-tong* gives rise to a type-related interpretation by default (it may give rise to a token-related interpretation only indirectly, through a token-denoting D-element that is already in the structure).

More tests are given in the following examples to confirm these generalizations. The first test adopts a multiple-character scenario involving a person (i.e., an identical token) who embodies two characters of different types. Representative examples are Superman and Clark Kent, or Dr. Jekyll and Mr. Hyde. We predict that in Chinese, only *tong* can be used in such a scenario, and the prediction is borne out in (20):

(20) a. Chaoren   gen Kelake shi tong yi   ge ren.
          Superman and Clark be same one CL person
          'Superman and Clark are the same person.'

      b. #Chaoren   gen Kelake shi (yi ge) xiang-tong de ren.
          Superman and Clark be one CL same   DE person
          'Superman and Clark are the same type of person.'

---

⁸ Some speakers allow the sentence to have a token-related reading when they interpret 'a house' as a specific expression. In Chinese, some speakers allow bare [*yi*-CL NP] to have a specific interpretation (Tsai 2002). We shall assume that in this case, the numeral 'one' has moved to the D position (Borer 2005). Note that this specificity effect is weakened when the numeral is not 'one':

(i) Mei Ge ren   dou zhu zai xiang-tong de san   jian fangzi.
     every CL person all live in same   DE three CL house
     'Everyone lives in the three houses of the same type.' [sameness in type]

Sentence (i) may only have the type-related reading, but not the token-related reading. Due to this intervention by 'one,' we shall avoid using examples with xiang-tong modifying bare 'one'-CL NPs in the following.

An opposite scenario involves different tokens of the same type. For example, both Superman and Batman are superheroes (a type notion); and as we would predict, only *xiang-tong* can be used in this kind of scenario:[9]

(21) a. Chaoren   gen Bianfuxia shi (ge-xing)   xiang-tong de ren.
          Superman and Batman   be personality same   DE person
          'Superman and Batman are people with the same personality'

      b. #Chaoren gen Bianfuxia shi tong yi ge ren.
          Chaoren and Batman   be same one CL person
          'Superman and Batman are the same person.'

In addition, with a first-person speaker and a second-person hearer, it is not possible that *you* and *I* denote the same token, but it is possible that *you* and *I* belong to the same type (e.g., we are both linguists). As expected, only *xiang-tong* can be used in this scenario:

(22) a. #Wo gen ni shi tong yi ge ren.
          I   and you be same one CL person
          'You and I are the same (identical) person.'

      b. Wo gen ni   shi (gexing)   xiang-tong de ren.
          I   and you be personality same   DE person
          'You and I are the same (type of) person.'

The second test, pointed out to us by Maria Luisa Zubizarreta (p.c.), involves "inalienable possession" terms. Body parts like *hearts* and *eyes* cannot be objects shared by different individuals, and if one wishes to describe the similarity (or sameness) of body parts, we expect that only type-referring *xiang-tong* can be used, but not token-referring *tong*. Again, the prediction is borne out, as in (23):

(23) a. Archie gen mama you yi shuang xiang-tong de yanjing.
          Archie and mother have one pair$_{CL}$ same   DE eyes
          'Archie and his mother have the same (type of) eyes.'

      b. #Archie gen mama you tong yi shuang yanjing.
          Archie and mother have same one pair$_{CL}$ eyes
          '#Archie and his mother use the same eyes.'

The third test involves type-referring and token-referring *wh*-questions, suggested in Bromberger (1992). *Wh*-questions like 'who' (*shei* in Chinese) and 'what' (*shenme* in Chinese) generally require an answer that makes reference to token information; and *wh*-questions like 'what type' and 'how' (*zenmeyang* or *zenyang* in Chinese)

[9] Dylan Tsai (p.c.) points out that some speakers prefer to have overt specifications of type information in the same-type readings of *xiang-tong*, such as adding *gexing* 'personality' before *xiang-tong* 'same' in (21a), where *gexing* can be analyzed as a specifier of the adjective *xiang-tong*. Another strategy to specify the type information is to resort to the 'external' reading of *same*, as in (i):

(i) Chaoren shi yi ge yonggan de ren.
     Superman be one CL brave   DE person
     Bianfuxia shi yi ge xiang-tong de ren
     Batman   be one CL same   DE person
     'Superman is a brave person. Batman is the same.'

generally expect an answer that makes reference to type information. Again, evidence shows that *tong* and *xiang-tong* behave as expected:

(24)   token-referring question: *tong*
    A.   Chaoren   shi shei?
        Superman   be   who
        'Who is Superman?'

    B.   Chaoren   gen Kelake shi **tong** yi   ge   ren.
        Superman and Clark   be   same one CL   person
        'Superman and Clark are the same person.'

(25)   type-referring question: *xiang-tong*
    A.   Chaoren   shi zenyang   de   ren?
        Superman   be   how.type DE   person
        'What type of person is Superman?'

    B.   Chaoren   gen Bianfuxia shi **xiang-tong** de   ren
        Superman and Batman   be   same   DE   person
        'Superman and Batman are the same type of person.'

All of the above tests confirm our generalizations in (19): *tong* and *xiang-tong* by default give rise to token and type interpretations, respectively.

3. Toward a Syntax-Semantic Analysis

In this section, we aim to provide a unified syntactic analysis of *(the) same* in English and Chinese. Our analysis draws on the theory of a uniform mapping of syntax and semantics to provide a cross-linguistic perspective on "same"-ness.

3.1. FROM DEMONSTRATIVES TO A SILENT ARTICLE IN CHINESE

It is rather uncontroversial that *xiang-tong* can be analyzed as an adjective. This section therefore focuses on the analysis of *tong*. We have argued that *tong* and demonstratives behave on a par, both in their morphosyntactic distributions and their definiteness restrictions. Although a demonstrative and a modifier like *same* may seem to be quite different syntactic objects, we argue that a recent proposal by Leu (2008) may provide a clue (or glue) that unifies the two types of objects with respect to their internal syntactic makeup.

Extending the proposal of silent PLACE in Kayne (2005), Leu (2008) argues that a demonstrative should not be treated as a lexical primitive, but should rather be analyzed as a phrasal complex consisting of an agreement marker on the definite article and a silent PLACE argument, as represented in (26):[10]

---

[10] We present a simplified version of Leu's analysis here in order to accommodate our DM analysis. Leu's original analysis is that the *th-* parts of demonstratives are agreement markers within the structure [$_{DP}$[th-AGR$_A$ HERE/THERE] D NP], where the phrasal demonstrative complex is located in Spec, DP, and it may license an (un)pronounced D in language-specific ways. For example, in Greek, it is possible to say *afto to vivlio* 'this the book,' where the demonstrative licenses a

(26)   [$_{DP}$ [*the*-AGR HERE/THERE] NP]

The idea is that the demonstratives *this* and *that* are the surface forms of the under-lying syntactic complex [*the* HERE] and [*the* THERE], respectively. The idea can be transferred to Chinese, since demonstratives and locative nouns in Chinese also share the same morphological roots. We shall reinterpret Leu's theory under a ver-sion of the Distributed Morphology (DM) (Borer 2003; Halle and Marantz 1993; Pesetsky 1995), where roots are not specified with respect to syntactic categories and morphological realizations. Instead, the syntactic categories or functional roles of the morphological roots are determined by the functional environments they are inserted in, after which morphological rules are applied. Consider the following paradigms:

(27)   √*zhe/na* 'this or here' / 'that or there'
   a.   √*zhe/na* + locative suffixes → a locative noun: *zhe/na-er, zhe/na-li* 'here/there'
   b.   [$_{DP}$ [D + √*zhe/na*] NP] → a demonstrative: *zhe/na* 'this/that'

In this sense, the root √*zhe/na* is understood as a type of demonstrative because it appears in the functional environment of D (through head adjunction with D). Nota-bly, such an analysis entails that D in Chinese has no overt morphological form. Let us call it a silent THE (in capital letters), which is an unpronounced counterpart to *the* (or *th-*) in English. The contrasts between demonstratives in Chinese and in English are therefore reduced to opposite pronunciation patterns of their internal members. Where English employs a silent PLACE and a pronounced *the* (or *th-*), Chinese has a pronounced place morpheme, and a silent THE.

As Leu (2008) notes, the analysis can be extended to other D-elements with different semantic contents (other than PLACE arguments). His analysis thus provides a plausible way to analyze *tong* in Chinese. Leu (2008) does not dis-cuss *the same* in English, but he does touch upon the issue in other Germanic languages. Specifically, in Swiss German, *də-säb* 'the.MAS-self' and *di-säb* 'the.FEM-self' (with the meaning of *the same*) also behave on a par with other D-elements, and interestingly, Leu notes that the definite marker can be dropped in Swiss German without a noticeable effect on meaning. We may therefore en-visage a unified analysis of *də/di-säb* in Swiss German, *the same* (token-denoting) in English, and *tong* in Chinese. Like the contrast between English and Chinese demonstratives, the variations lie in surface pronunciation patterns of definite articles:[11]

pronounced 'the.' Tommi Leung points out to me that the same distribution is also found in Arabic (e.g., *hadha al-kitab* 'this.masc det-book.masc' vs. **hadha kitab*). The same expression, however, is not possible in English, where Leu assumes that *this* licenses an unpronounced *the*. We think that it is also plausible to assume that in languages that do not allow multiple definite markers (e.g., Eng-lish), the (silent) place head actually forms a syntactic complex directly with the D head (possibly through head adjunction). Note that the head-adjunction analysis does not clash with Leu's origi-nal proposal in any major way, and we shall assume the head-adjunction analysis throughout this chapter.

   [11] We return to the type-denoting *the same* in English later in our discussion.

(28) a. English: [[*the same*]NP]   ('the' is pronounced)

   b. Swiss German: [[(*də-*)*säb*] NP]   ('the' is optionally pronounced)

   c. Chinese: [[THE-*tong*] NP]   ('the' is not pronounced)

Again, assuming DM, the morphological distinctions between *tong* and *xiang-tong* in Chinese are only apparent, in the sense that they share the same root √*tong*, and their syntactic categories are determined by their functional environments in the morphosyntax. Thus, *tong*, occurring in a functional environment of D, becomes a D-element and has a morphological bound form; while *xiang-tong* in the environment of an adjective modifier (arguably due to the modifier marker *de*), requires a root/prefix *xiang-* in order to support its morphological requirements. Returning to the syntax of *tong* and *xiang-tong* in Chinese, then, we propose the following structures:[12]

(29) a. *tong*

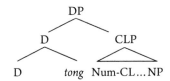

   b. *xiang-tong*

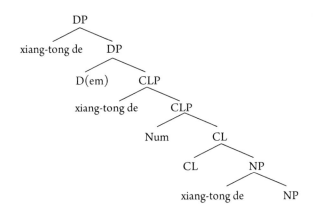

All of the morphosyntactic properties of *tong* (and *xiang-tong*) follow naturally from such an analysis. Specifically, *tong* and D-elements are in complementary distributions because the modifiers of D compete for the same syntactic

---

[12] We assume, according to standard theory, that modifiers create syntactic adjunctions. We also assume that a numeral is located in Spec, CLP (Liao and Wang 2011; Watanabe 2006), given that no adjunction is possible between Num and CL, and that they are not separable by any syntactic operations. However, note that no significant difference would occur should we assume that a numeral can project its own NumP phrase.

position (assuming that a head may allow only one modifier, as in Cinque 1999). The obligatory definiteness of *tong* is also accounted for: definiteness does not come from the root √*tong*, because *xiang-tong* does not necessarily result in a definite expression; rather, the definiteness comes from the unpronounced THE in Chinese.

3.2. FROM TYPE-TOKEN DISTINCTION TO NP-DP HIERARCHY

The semantic type-token distinction and its syntactic implications also lend strong support to our syntactic proposals for *tong* and *xiang-tong*. It has been suggested by a number of linguists that the semantic notions of type and token correspond to the syntactic projections of N(P) and D(P), respectively (see Carlson 2003; Higginbotham 1985; Longobardi 1994; Vergnaud and Zubizarreta 1992; Zamparelli 2000; among others).

Vergnaud and Zubizarreta (1992) construct a logical-conceptual denotata theory to describe the mappings between the semantic type-token distinction and the syntactic NP-DP hierarchies. The systematic mapping rule in (30) is dubbed the Correspondence Law (Vergnaud and Zubizarreta 1992: 612), which can be formalized as the denotation cycle in (31). Following Vergnaud and Zubizarreta (1992), we shall use numbers (1, 2, 3, . . .) to represent token-indices, and lowercase letters ($i, j, k, . . .$) to represent type-indices:[13]

(30) *Correspondence Law*
When a DP or an NP denotes, the DP denotes a token and the NP denotes a type.

(31)

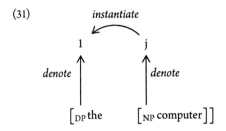

Therefore, the hierarchies of DP and NP are directly associated with token and type readings in semantics, respectively. Thus (31) can be simplified as in the structure in (32), where the DP denotes a token *1*, instantiated as a type *j*:

(32)

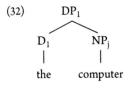

---

[13] See Vergnaud and Zubizarreta (1992) for the discussion of the kind-reading of [*the* NP] in English.

In Chinese, one more complication needs to be considered, namely, the classifiers projection. Following Li (1998) and Liao and Wang (2011), we assume that numeral-classifiers are not token-denoting, but type-denoting, and the numeral-classifiers only provide additional information (regarding counting levels and numbers) of types. The type-denoting (but not token-denoting) properties of numeral-classifier phrases are further evident in Li's (1998) study of quantity-denoting arguments:

(33) [San ge ren] chi-de-wan [yi wan fan].
      three CL person eat-can-finish one CL$_{bowl}$ rice
      '(Any) three people are generally able to finish (any) one bowl of rice.'

Li (1998) argues that these phrases do not project D in their syntactic structures, so these quantity-denoting phrases fit very naturally with our analysis. Unquestionably, these bare numeral-classifier phrases denote type-information. The sentence in (33) does not refer to certain tokens of three people or a certain bowl of rice, but rather types that are compatible with the expressions of [three people] and [one bowl of rice]. We therefore make the following amendment to the Correspondence Law:

(34) *Correspondence Law (amended)*
      When a nominal element (DP, NP, CLP) denotes, only DP can denote a token, and the other categories denote types.

Returning to the modifier *same*, the functions of *same* in English or *tong/xiang-tong* in Chinese are to map a set of types or tokens to an identical type or token, respectively, by operating on different kinds of indices. We therefore formulate the equivalence function as in (35):[14]

(35) The modifier *same* is an equivalent function that applies to type- or token-indices.
      [same](x)(y)... → x=y... (where x and y are type- or token-indices)

Now the syntax-semantic mappings between *tong/xiang-tong* and DP/NP(CLP) become transparent. In the case of *tong*, where a token-denoting D is modified, *tong* takes two or more token indices and equates the instantiations. Let us use (36) to illustrate the syntax-LF operation:

(36) a. Mei-ge   ren   dou xihuan tong yi ge nuhai
          every-CL person all like   same one CL girl
          'Everyone likes the same girl.'

      b. [Mei-ge ren]$_{1,2,3...}$ xihuan   [$_{DP}$ D$_{(n')}$-tong $_{(1'=2'=3'...)}$ [$_{CLP}$ yi ge nuhai]$_g$].

In (36), the singular object [*tong yi ge nuhai*] 'same girl' is bound by 'everyone' through predication (Williams 1981, 1994), yielding a plural set of objects carrying

---

[14] See Brasoveanu (2008) for a similar analysis for sentence-internal readings of *same/different* in English.

token-indices. Let us use (n') to represent the token-indices being bound by the universal quantifier, so that each person $(1, 2, 3, \ldots)$ likes a girl $(1', 2', 3', \ldots)$, each of which is an instantiation of the girl-type g, given by the following CLP. The equivalent function [**same**] $(1')(2')(3') \ldots$ returns $(1'=2'=3' \ldots)$, and as a result, every token-index is instantiated by a unique girl. The conceptual form of (36) can be represented as in (37):[15]

(37)   (1 likes 1') & (2 likes 2') & (3 likes 3') & ... $(1'=2'=3' \ldots)$

On the other hand, in cases where *xiang-tong* is used and either NP or CLP is modified, it is the type-information that is accessible. Again, adopting the logical-conceptual denotata theory, the type-related readings are illustrated as in (38) (for ease of exposition, we disregard the numeral-classifier phrase here):

(38) a.   Mei-ge   ren   dou xihuan xiang-tong de nuhai
             every-CL person   all like   same   DE girl
             'Everyone likes the same (type of) girl.'

      b. [Mei-ge ren]$_{1,2,3...}$ xihuan   [$_{NP}$ **xiang-tong**$_{(g'=g''=g'''...)}$ de [$_{NP}$ nuhai]$_{(g',g'',g''')}$].

The object bound by 'everyone' does not carry token information (since it does not have a token-denoting D-element).[16] On the other hand, being predicatively bound by the subject 'everyone,' the object *nuhai* 'girl' denotes an implied plural set of types that involves different types of girls (e.g., long-haired girls, short-haired girls, curly-haired girls, etc.). We shall use (x') to designate different type-indices. Therefore, (38) means that each person likes a type of girl, and all of the types are identical (due to the equivalent function of 'same'):

(39)   (1 likes g') & (2 likes g'') & (3 likes g''') ... & (g'=g''=g''')

However, in the special case where *xiang-tong* modifies a demonstrative, as in (18a), the demonstrative (a D-element) already gives rise to a specific token of 'house,' so naturally, [*xiang-tong de na yi dong fangzi*] '(lit.) that same house' can only refer to the same token.

We see that the Correspondence Law allows us to establish a seamless link between the syntax and semantics of *tong* and *xiang-tong*. The following structures summarize this section:

---

[15] In some cases, the token-index that serves as antecedent of the function of *tong* 'same' may come from cross-sentential domain. Consider the following example, where the antecedent token-index (1') is present in the preceding sentence (we are indebted to Hajime Hoji for this point):

(i)   Zhangsan$_1$ xihuan [na ge nuhai]$_{1'}$; Lisi$_2$ xihuan [D$_2$-tong$_{(1'=2')}$ [yi ge nuhai]].
        Zhangsan like   that CL girl   Lisi   like   same   one CL girl
        'Zhangsan likes that girl; Lisi likes the same girl.'

[16] We assume that bare NP arguments are DPs with null D heads that cannot denote tokens (Li 1999; Longobardi 1994). However, the issue of whether or not bare nouns project to DP has no bearing on our analysis here.

(40)   a. *tong*

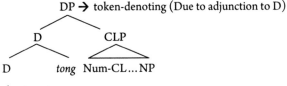

b. *xiang-tong*

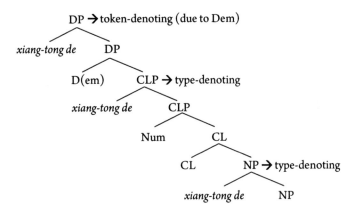

3.3. TYPE-RELATED 'SAME' IN ENGLISH

Let us now return to *the same* in English. A plausible assumption is that the token-related reading of *the same* results from a structure identical to that for *tong* phrases in Chinese, illustrated in (40a); yet, in English, both *the* and *same* are pronounced. The question is whether English also has a type-related 'same' that is lower in the structure, that is, as a modifier of NP or CLP.

Such a possibility (*same* as NP-modifier) can be ruled out because a numeral cannot appear between *the* and *same*:[17]

(41)   a.   The police officers arrested [**the same** [**three** thieves]].

b.   *The police officers arrested [**the** [**three** [**same** thieves]]].

On the other hand, we argue that *same* (under type-related readings) may adjoin to a silent CLP in English. The assumption is backed up by the following observations. First, in English, demonstratives and the type-denoting *same* may co-occur (e.g., *this same book* and *that same dress*), indicating that *same* and the silent modifier HERE/THERE of D do not compete for the same position. Like the CLP-modifying *xiang-tong* in Chinese, only type-related readings are allowed in these expressions. In strict token-related readings, the combinations of demonstratives and *same* sound odd:[18]

---

[17] An a priori reason to rule out DP-adjunction of *same* in English (Position I in Chinese) is that adjectives in English simply do not occur in that position: *beautiful the house, *red that flower, and *fast a car, etc.

[18] We would like to thank Andrew Simpson and Roumyana Pancheva (p.c.) for pointing this out to us.

(42) a. ??/*John bumps into this same person every day.

      b. ??/*We all live on *this same* planet.

A similar contrast is observed in Dutch, another Germanic language. In (43), the sentences may only refer to a particular type of car and a particular type of book, but not to a specific car or book (Broekhuis and Keizer 2012: 382):

(43) a. **Deze (zelfde) auto** met airconditioning is haast niet te verkrijgen.
          this same   car   with air.conditioning is almost not to obtain
          'This (same) car with air conditioning is hardly available.'

      b. **Dit(zelfde) boek** met een harde kaft is veel duurder.
          this.same   book with a   hard cover is much more.expensive
          'This (same) book in hardcover is much more expensive.'

These contrasts are accounted for if we assume that the type-related *same* in English (and *zelfde* in Dutch) actually modifies a (silent) classifier phrase, on a par with the CLP-modifying *xiang-tong* in Chinese.

4. Conclusion

Our discussion has compared the adjective 'same' in English and Chinese, and we have shown that the two varieties of 'same' in Chinese, *tong* and *xiang-tong*, display entirely different morphosyntactic and semantic properties. Based on these properties, we argue that *tong* should be analyzed as a D-element and *xiang-tong* as an adjective. By adopting a DM analysis, we propose that *tong* and *xiang-tong* are different realizations of the same morphological root, and the surface morphological form of the root varies in its place of insertion in syntax. Furthermore, establishing a syntax-semantic mapping theory under the Correspondence Law proposed in Vergnaud and Zubizarreta (1992), we argue that *tong* in Chinese and the token-related *same* in English share a unified syntax. Both are modifiers of D, in a way that is similar to the analyses of determiners in Kayne (2005) and Leu (2008). On the other hand, *xiang-tong* in Chinese is a modifier of different nominal projections (NP, CLP, and DP), and its readings with respect to type-token distinctions directly reflect its syntactic positions. We also show that the type-related *same* in English should be analyzed on a par with the Chinese *xiang-tong*, modifying a classifier phrase. Our analysis therefore leads to the conclusion that Chinese has a silent determiner, and English has a silent classifier. Our exploration of their "same" qualities (and their differences) offers further potential evidence in support of the universalist view that languages share the same functional inventories.

Acknowledgments

We have benefited greatly from discussions with Michael Barrie, Henry Chang, Lisa Cheng, Hajime Hoji, James Huang, Hilda Koopman, Tommi Leung, Audrey Li, Chen-Sheng Liu, Roumi Pancheva, Mamoru Saito, Dingxu Shi, Chih-hsiang Shu,

Andrew Simpson, Wei-tien Tsai, Maria Luisa Zubizarreta, and Niina Zhang. Earlier versions of this chapter were presented in WCCFL-31, FOSS-9, and TEAL-8, and as guest lectures at National Tsing Hua University and at USC. We would like to thank the audience there for many constructive comments. All errors, however, remain ours alone.

References

Aoun, Joseph, and Yen-hui Audrey Li. 2003. *Essays on the Representational and Derivational Nature of Grammar: The Diversity of Wh-Constructions*. Cambridge, MA: MIT Press.

Borer, Hagit. 2003. Exo-skeletal vs. endo-skeletal explanations: Syntactic projections and the lexicon. In *The Nature of Explanation in Linguistic Theory*, ed. John Moore and Maria Polinsky, 31–67. Stanford, CA: CSLI Publications.

Borer, Hagit. 2005. *In Name Only: Structuring Sense*. Vol. 1. Oxford: Oxford University Press.

Brasoveanu, Adrian. 2008. Sentence-internal readings of same/different as quantifier-internal anaphora. *WCCFL* 27, 72–80.

Broekhuis, Hans, and Evelien Keizer. 2012. *Syntax of Dutch: Nouns and Noun Phrases*. Vol. 1. Amsterdam: Amsterdam University Press.

Bromberger, Sylvain. 1992. *On What We Know We Don't Know: Explanation, Theory, Linguistics, and How Questions Shape Them*. Chicago: University of Chicago Press.

Carlson, Gregory. 2003. Interpretive asymmetries in major phrases. In *Asymmetry in Linguistic Theory*, ed. Anna-Maria Di Sciullo. Amsterdam: John Benjamins.

Chomsky, Noam. 2001. Derivation by phase. In *Ken Hale: A Life in Language*, ed. Michael Kenstowicz, 1–52. Cambridge, MA: MIT Press.

Cinque, Guglielmo. 1999. *Adverbs and Functional Heads*. Oxford: Oxford University Press.

Halle, Morris, and Alec Marantz. 1993. Distributed morphology and the pieces of inflection. In *The View from Building 20*, ed. Kenneth Hale and S. Jay Keyser, 111–176. Cambridge, MA: MIT Press.

Higginbotham, James. 1985. On semantics. *Linguistic Inquiry* 16, 547–594.

Huang, C.-T James. 1987. Existential sentences in Chinese and (in)definiteness. In *The Representation of (In)Definiteness*, ed. Eric Reuland and Alice Ter Meulen, 226–253. Cambridge, MA: MIT Press.

Huang, C.-T. James. 1982. *Logical Relations in Chinese and the Theory of Grammar*. Doctoral Dissertation, MIT.

Huang, C.-T. James, Yen-hui Audrey Li, and Yafei Li. 2009. *The Syntax of Chinese*. Cambridge, UK; New York: Cambridge University Press.

Kayne, Richard. 2005. *Movement and Silence*. Oxford: Oxford University Press.

Kayne, Richard. 2007. Several, *few* and *many*. *Lingua* 117, 832–858.

Kayne, Richard. 2008. Some preliminary comparative remarks on French and Italian definite articles. In *Foundational Issues in Linguistic Theory*, ed. Robert Freidin et al., 291–321. Cambridge, MA: MIT Press.

Leu, Thomas. 2008. *The Internal Syntax of Determiners*. Doctoral Dissertation, New York University.

Li, Yen-hui Audrey. 1998. Argument determiner phrases and number phrases. *Linguistic Inquiry* 29, 693–702.

Li, Yen-hui Audrey. 1999. Plurality in a classifier language. *Journal of East Asian Linguistics* 8, 75–99.

Liao, Wei-wen Roger, and Yuyun Iris Wang. 2011. Multiple-classifier constructions and nominal expressions in Chinese. *Journal of East Asian Linguistics* 20, 145–168.

Longobardi, Giuseppe. 1994. Reference and proper names: A theory of n-movement in syntax and logical form. *Linguistic Inquiry* 25, 609–665.

Pesetsky, David. 1995. *Zero Syntax: Experiencers and Cascades*. Cambridge, MA: MIT Press.

Pollock, Jean-Yves. 1989. Verb movement, universal grammar, and the structure of IP. *Linguistic Inquiry* 20, 365–424.

Riemsdijk, Henk C. van. 2002. The unbearable lightness of GOing. *Journal of Comparative Germanic Linguistics* 5, 143–196.

Riemsdijk, Henk C. van. 2005. Silent nouns and the spurious indefinite article in Dutch. In *Grammar and Beyond: Essays in Honour of Lars Hellan*, ed. Mila Vulchanova and Tor A. Afarli, 163–178. Oslo: Novus Press.

Sigurðsson, Halldor Armann. 2004. Meaningful silence, meaningless sounds. *Linguistic Variation Yearbook* 4, 235–259.

Simpson, Andrew. 2005. Classifiers and DP structure in Southeast Asian languages. In *The Oxford Handbook of Comparative Syntax*, ed. Guglielmo Cinque and Richard Kayne, 806–838. Oxford: Oxford University Press.

Tang, C.-C. Jane. 1990. A note on the DP analysis of the Chinese noun phrase. *Linguistics* 28, 337–354.

Tsai, Wei-tien Dylan. 2001. On subject specificity and theory of syntax-semantics interface. *Journal of East Asian Linguistics* 10, 129–168.

Tsai, Wei-Tien Dylan. 2002. Yi, er, san [one, two, three]. *Yuyanxue Luncong [Journal of Linguistics]* 26, 301–312.

Vergnaud, Jean-Roger, and Maria Luisa Zubizarreta. 1992. The definite determiner and the inalienable constructions in French and English. *Linguistic Inquiry* 23, 595–652.

Vergnaud, Jean-Roger. 2008. Letter to Noam Chomsky and Howard Lasnik on "filters and control," April 17, 1977. In *Foundational Issues in Linguistic Theory*, ed. Robert Freidin et al., 3–16. Cambridge, MA: MIT Press.

Watanabe, Akira. 2006. Functional projections of nominals in Japanese: Syntax of classifiers. *Natural Languages and Linguistic Theory* 24, 241–306.

Wetzel, Linda. 2009. *Types and Tokens: On Abstract Objects.* Cambridge, MA: MIT Press.

Zamparelli, Roberto. 1998. A theory of kinds, partitives and of/z possessives. In *Possessors, Predicates and Movement in the Determiner Phrase*, Vol. 22 of *Linguistics Today*, ed. Artemis Alexiadou and Chris Wilder, 259–301. Amsterdam: John Benjamins.

Zamparelli, Roberto. 2000. *Layers in the determiner phrase.* New York: Garland.

Zhang, Niina. 2007. Root merger in Chinese compounds. *Studia Linguistica* 61, 170–184.

6

How Universal is the Mass/Count Distinction? Three Grammars of Counting

GENNARO CHIERCHIA

1. On the (Non)Universality of How We Count

The mass/count distinction manifests itself in very different ways across different languages, to the point that doubts have repeatedly been raised as to whether such a distinction is universal.[1] This is what this chapter investigates: Is there a universal mass/count distinction, in spite of a prima facie huge diversity in the grammars of counting? If so, what is its basis?

The heart of the mass/count distinction is how we count. Things in the world arguably fall into natural kinds, classes, or sorts: sets whose members are identified by common qualitative traits. Cats, chairs, sailors, Italians, and so forth, are kinds of things. Gold, sand, blood, and so on, are kinds of substances or 'stuff.' Cats and the like come organized into units that can be counted. Gold and the like do not. Gold can, of course, be measured along several dimensions: its mass can be measured in, for example, kilos; its purity can be measured in carats. 'Measures' or 'ways of measuring' can be thought of as functions from entities into numbers; for example $\mu_{KG}(x) = n$ tells us that the mass (or weight) of x in kilos is n. Another important example of a measure function is 'cardinality,' which applies to sets or classes; if x is a set, its cardinality $\mu_{CARD}(x)$ (often notated in set theory as $|x|$) is the number of its members. The universe of measures is as diverse as the universe itself.

The view just sketched presupposes two macro categories, loosely denoted as 'things' (or 'objects') versus 'substances' (or 'stuff'), where objects come in natural units and substances do not. In particular, cats are pluralities of individual cats, which have a natural cardinality-based measure: the number of cats in a particular plurality. This macro-distinction between objects and substances can be made in slightly different but ultimately equivalent terms as follows. There are natural ways of measuring things along some of their most salient dimensions. Cats can, in principle, be

[1] For recent stands on this, see Wiltschko (2010), Lima (2010), and Darlymple and Morfu (2012). For an early discussion of the relevant issues, see the essays in Pelletier (1979), and Pelletier and Schubert (1989).

measured in terms of their mass (kilos, or the like); but they are most typically measured in terms of their natural units; if x is a plurality of cats, we tend to 'measure' it in terms of a function like $\mu_{NU}(x)$, which gives us the number of cats in x (a cardinality based measure); gold, on the other hand, is measured most naturally through a mass-based measure (like grams or the like); if x is gold, it is hard to imagine what $\mu_{NU}(x)$ would yield, for there are many ways in which gold comes in nature or conventionally packaged.

An important point that I think has emerged from much research over the past 30 years or so is that the distinction between objects and substances, as outlined in the preceding text, is not about a 'way of speaking.' It is not, that is, a distinction based in language/grammar. This is so because human infants seem to make it at a few months of age, *before* developing language. And so do other non-human species, which cannot be said to have language in the same sense in which humans do. Research by cognitive psychologists like S. Carey and E. Spelke provides rich evidence that preverbal infants make a distinction between objects and substances very close to the one we are after.[2] Objects are expected to be 'bounded' (i.e., endowed with natural boundaries), cohesive (i.e., with parts that 'stick together'), to move across space along continuous paths, and to retain their identity upon aggregating (or colliding) with other objects, while substances have none of the above properties. The evidence that shows that preverbal children make this distinction is varied and carefully controlled. A typical experimental paradigm used in this connection is the following. An object (say a teddy bear or a toy car) is displayed in front of an infant. Then a screen goes up and the child sees a second object of the same type being placed behind it. At this point, the screen goes down and one of two things happens, depending on the experimental condition. In the 'expected' condition, the child sees *two* objects and she shows no sign of surprise. In the unexpected condition, thanks to an experimental manipulation, the child finds only *one* object; and she reacts with great surprise. No similar reaction is found in control conditions with substances like sand or clay. The conclusion is that the preverbal child, as it were, expects or 'knows' that if you add a toy car to a toy car you should get *two* toy cars; and if you add one car to two cars you should find *three* cars. But if you add sand to sand, you do not get two sands. Similar experiments have been replicated with rhesus monkeys and even with mammals lower down on the evolutionary scale.[3] This capacity is linked to the existence of two different modes of counting/measuring that humans share with non-human mammals (two counting/measuring functions, if you wish). One is precise and applies to discrete objects, and only works for up to three objects (e.g., the rat knows that one cheese ball plus one cheese ball is two cheese balls, and if you add one more you get three; after three its tracking system crashes); the other measure function is continuous and approximate and applies to any amount of objects or stuff (if two piles of food are sufficiently

---

[2] The bibliography on this is abundant. See, for example, Carey (1985), Carey and Spelke (1996), Soja, Carey, and Spelke (1991).

[3] See, e.g., Hauser and Carey (2003), Hauser and Spaulding (2006).

different, the mouse rapidly learns to hone onto the larger one). These two ways of measuring enable preverbal children and non-human primates to track objects and substances differently.[4]

So there are two categories, linked to two modes of measuring/counting, present across a variety of human and non-human species, and this brings up considerations directly relevant to our inquiry. The first is that the distinction between objects and substances, as outlined, is not in any sense 'conventional' or 'formal' or 'arbitrary.' A car is an object, some sand or some clay is not. The human infant or the rhesus monkey has no choice on whether to categorize something as an object versus a substance. The second consideration is that we are clearly dealing with a pre- or extra-linguistic distinction. This is not the place to speculate on whether the object/substance distinction is rooted in some extra-mental aspect of reality or in some very general categorization schema shared across species and widely used to conceptualize reality. What matters in the present context is that there is no other reasonable conclusion but the independence of the categories of substance versus object from linguistic categories in the narrow sense, if this line of research is on the right track.

Usually, by mass/count distinction one refers to linguistic phenomena that somehow track the substance/object distinction. And now perhaps the question of whether such a distinction manifests itself across all languages acquires a more determinate sense. Generally speaking, we may wonder how systematically the contrast between substances and objects is reflected in grammar, particularly in those aspects of language having to do with counting, quantifying, and measuring. Let us refer to all of those jointly as the 'grammar of counting.' It is evident that the English grammar of counting seems to be pervasively affected by the contrast (and we shall review how shortly). Put in other terms, English has a robust grammar of mass versus count. So do all other Indo-European languages. The next question is: Is every language similarly affected? What are the ways in which a language may code the distinction between substances and objects? Are there languages in which *no* systematic reflection of the distinction is found? The hope is that by asking questions such as these we may find a particularly perspicuous way of understanding the relationship between grammatical categories in the narrow sense and extragrammatical ones.

In what follows, I will first discuss the mass/count distinction in English and sketch an epistemic approach to it (where it is not 'atomicity' per se that matters but 'epistemically ascertained' atomicity/lack thereof). Then I will compare the English grammar of mass/count with that of rich classifier languages, such as Mandarin, on the one hand, and with languages with a 'sparse' classifier system, such as Yudja, on the other.[5] Both such languages have been claimed to lack the mass/count distinction. The epistemic take to be presented below lends itself to accounting for these three extremely diverse language systems in terms of elementary parametric switches. This will facilitate an assessment of the (non)universality of the mass/count distinction.[6]

---

[4] Cf. Spelke and Dehaene (1999), Feigeson, Carey, and Spelke (2002).

[5] For Yudja, I will heavily rely on Suzi Lima's work, as it appears through, e.g., Lima (2010) and through our conversations on this matter.

[6] The approach I will be presenting is based on Chierchia (2010).

2. Mass Versus Count in English

The mass/count distinction in English is extremely rich and fairly well chartered, so much so that we won't be able to do full justice to it within the limits of the present chapter. I will presently review five aspects of the mass/count distinction that jointly serve well the purpose of illustrating its most problematic aspects. The five properties I will discuss involve (a) pluralization and counting, (b) measure phrases, (c) so-called psuedopartitive constructions with phrases like *quantity of, amount of,* and so on, (d) so-called fake mass nouns (like *furniture, footwear,* etc.), and (d) ambiguous nouns (like *beer, rope,* or *chicken*) and coercion (like *there is apple in the salad*). In presenting this phenomenology, I will have to oversimplify things greatly but, I hope, without being too misleading.

2.1. SOME DIFFICULT TEST CASES FOR THE MASS/COUNT DISTINCTION

Pluralization and counting are a primary way of teasing apart count nouns from mass ones, at least in languages that obligatorily mark number on nouns. Lexical count nouns naturally pluralize and directly combine with numerals; lexical mass nouns do not. The former typically denote objects, the latter substances:

(1) Pluralization and counting.
    a. i. table/tables; cat/cats, etc.
       ii. blood/*bloods; salt/*salts, etc.

    b. i. Those tables are three.   ii. I bought three tables.

    c. i. *That blood is three.   ii. *I donated three bloods.

    d. i. That blood is three ounces/drops. ii. I donated three ounces of blood.

I refer to numeral-noun constructions like *three cats* as NumPs ('Number Phrases'). Measure Phrases like *three kilos of* typically form so-called pseudopartitive constructions;[7] they combine with both lexically count nouns, which have to appear in the plural, like *apples* (2a), and with mass nouns (2b). In the case of mass nouns, the insertion of a measure phrase is obligatory if one is to use a number:

(2) Measure phrases in psuedopartitive constructions
    a. three (kilos of) apples   b. three *(kilos of) salt

---

[7] A precise characterization of partitive vs. pseudopartitive is a complex matter. At a descriptive level, partitive constructions are those in (a), with a definite inner noun; pseudopartitives (cf. b.i–ii) differ from the former in that the inner noun is determinerless (and hence indefinite).

(a) i. three kilos of that flour
    ii. two quantities of the pizza

(b) i. three kilos of flour
    ii. two quantities of pizza

An early and still very useful characterization of the constructions in (a) and (b) can be found in Selkirk (1977); for a more recent discussion, see, for example, Stickney (2009).

A special class of pseudopartitives involves words like *quantity* or *amount*. Like genuine measure phrases, they can combine with both mass and count nouns.

(3)   Quantities and amounts
    a.   i.   that quantity of apples   ii.   those apples
    b.   i.   that quantity of water   ii.   that water

The characteristic of these constructions is that they are typically used to refer to the very same things as the corresponding noun they are in construction with; the word *quantity* doesn't seem to add much to the noun it modifies.[8] For example, the noun phrases in (3a.i) and (3a.ii) will denote the same plurality of apples; yet (3a.i) is grammatically singular, while (3a.ii) is grammatically plural. Accounting for this observation is not trivial, as it turns out.[9] By the same token, (3b.i) and (3b.ii) refer to the same stuff; but (3b.i) is grammatically a count construction (it pluralizes, etc.), while (3b.ii) is grammatically mass (it doesn't pluralize, etc.). At one level, one may want to think of *quantity of* and the like as measure phrases; but they also have something in common with words like *group of, aggregate of*, and so on. The reason to bring them up is that they seem to raise special problems, in that it appears that the plural/singular and object/substance contrasts become void of semantic content when such words are involved. Understanding *quantity of*-phrases is important also from a cross-linguistic point of view as they may be playing a key role in the grammar of languages with a 'sparse' mass/count phenomenology like Yudja, to be reviewed later in this chapter.

The fourth phenomenon mentioned in the preceding list involves nouns that are associated with kinds of objects but that appear to act as grammatically mass. They typically involve superordinate nouns like *furniture, jewelry, footwear*, and so on.

(4)   Fake mass nouns
    a.   *I bought three furniture yesterday.
    b.   This table is good furniture.
    c.   *This piece of my desk is good furniture.

Examples like (4b) are meant to show that nouns like *furniture*, though 'superordinates,' are not collective: a single table or chair is furniture; examples like (4c) show that *furniture* does come in natural units much like count nouns do: a part of a table is not furniture, just like it is not a table.[10] These nouns are interesting because they clearly show that grammar introduces a degree of freedom of categorization with

---

[8] As Greg Scontras pointed out to me, the noun phrases in (3a.i) and (3b.i) also have a very different reading that can be made salient in contexts of the following sort:

(a) Tomorrow, I would like you to bring me that quantity of apples again

This 'amount' reading requires a different analysis, which we cannot get into here.

[9] For example, on Sauerland's (2003) interesting approach, the semantic contribution of singular and plural takes place at the level of the maximal Determiner Phrase, via functions of type $<e,e>$ that check whether the DP denotes an atom or not. Clearly, at that level the denotation of (3a.i) would not be distinguishable from that of (3a.ii) and the two nouns would have to come out either both singular, or both plural. Sauerland is aware of this issue. While otherwise following the general take of Sauerland's on singular/plural checking, we will modify this aspect of his proposal.

[10] See on this Barner and Snedeker (2005).

respect to the distinction between individuals versus substances. While the preverbal child has no choice as to how to conceptualize a table (it has to be an object, not a substance), an English speaker does have a choice here: tables can be conceptualized as pieces of furniture or as furniture.

Finally, some nouns appear to be just about equally felicitous in mass or count frames. Moreover, mass nouns can be coerced into count ones and count nouns into mass ones, with greater or lesser degrees of felicity, depending on the context.

(5)   Noun ambiguity and coercion
    a.   Ambiguous nouns: rope, rock, beer, chicken, . . .
        i. I got three ropes/a lot of rope at the convenience store.
        ii. This is good rope/these are good ropes. I wish we had more of it/them.

    b.   Coercion: mass-to-count
        i. At a vampire bar: They ordered three bloods on the rocks.
        ii. In a lab: We store three bloods here.

    c.   Coercion: count-to-mass
        i. There is apple in the salad.
        ii. There was cat all over the floor.

Ambiguous nouns such as those in (5a) appear to have distinct meanings. Imagine a long rope wrapped in a coil at the convenience store. A part of it is not *a* rope, though it is rope. If you cut a piece from the rope coil, you bring about a change in the world, and what was merely rope now becomes *a* rope in its own right (at least, if it is long enough to tie something with). But this involves a real change of state. The mass uses and the count uses of *rope* may involve the same spatiotemporal entity, but they focus on different aspects or dimensions of it. A rope has naturally set boundaries; rope is material from which we can potentially extract many different ropes (by cutting it into pieces). Also the count sense and the mass sense of chicken are quite different. One is a biological species, the other is food material. Coercions happen by analogy with these ambiguities. Count-to-mass coercion involves shifting from individuated objects that form natural units to materials, typically foodlike. D. Lewis coined the name 'grinding' for this type of shift.[11] Mass-to-count involves going from a substance to types thereof (as in (5b.ii)) or to standardized servings thereof (as in (5b.i), where the intended analogy is with *whisky*). Pelletier uses the term 'packaging' for this kind of shift. In the case of packaging, standardization appears to be crucial, as witnessed by contrasts of the following sort:

(6)   a.   Three quantities of blood were found on OJ's sock.

    b.   * Three bloods were found on OJ's sock.

Sentence (6a) is natural. Sentence (6b) is ungrammatical, presumably because no plausible 'standardization' is available. The fact that there are three continuous stains of blood is not enough for us to speak of *three bloods*. [A heads-up: the

---

[11] See the essays in Pelletier (1979); for a comprehensive overview, see Pelletier and Schubert (1989).

word-by-word translation of (6b) in languages like Yudja is grammatical.] It is worth emphasizing in this connection that fake mass nouns do not involve 'ambiguity' or coercion. The difference between, say, shoes versus footwear appears to be solely a difference of form; no grinding or packaging is going on. Similarly, nothing changes in the world if you regard something as a piece of furniture or as furniture.

These cursory remarks suffice to show the great complexity of the problem. The main question that arises from a linguistic point of view is whether there is a way of regarding the contribution of pluralization, numerals, and so on, in a consistent and uniform way across this range of phenomena.

2.2. BACKGROUND

Let us start by reviewing some assumptions that we need to get started. Everything I will present is an object of controversy. But this background part is meant to be relatively less controversial, or, to put it differently, whatever controversy there might be is orthogonal to the mass/count issue. Any modern account of the plural-singular distinction, since at least Link (1983), adopts models that are isomorphic to the following:

(7)   Plural-singular structures.
   a. $a \cup b \cup c, a \cup b \cup d, \ldots$ SUMS
        $a \cup b, b \cup c, a \cup c, a \cup d, \ldots$
        a,   b,   c,   d, ...   ATOMS
   b.   Relevant features of singular/plural structures.
        i.   a binary join operation : $a \cup b$ (commutative, associative, idempotent)
        ii.   atomic: there are elements that aren't sums
        iii. generated: every sum is generated out of AT (via iterated applications of $\cup$),
        iv.   partially ordered: $a \leq a \cup b$

The universe is classified as constituted by a set of 'atoms' (= singularities) and all of their joins (groups thereof, the pluralities). Formally, an 'absolute' atom is anything that has only itself as a part in the above structure. It should be noted that these structures are not mereologies: the 'part of' relation is not to be identified with 'material part of.' Among the atoms there are things that are mereological parts of each other (e.g., me and my right arm could both be atoms, in spite of the fact that the latter is spatiotemporally included in the former). These structures are used to individuate the semantic contribution of pluralization along the following lines. A singular count noun is taken to denote a set of qualitatively uniform atoms (in each world/situation). For example, the singular noun *cat* will be true only of (absolute) atoms.[12]

---

[12] My insistence on the term 'absolute' will become clearer shortly. But roughly speaking, 'absolute' atoms are the atoms in the whole structure. 'Relative' atoms are the smallest members of a property denotation. Imagine a property true of pluralities/groups with the following denotation:

$$a \cup b \cup c$$

$P =$

$$a \cup b, b \cup c$$

The individuals $a \cup b, b \cup c$ are not absolute atoms (i.e., atoms relative to the whole structure). They are, however, relative P-atoms, that is, the smallest things of which P is true.

Its pluralization denotes the closure of that set under join. In other words, a plural noun is true in an undifferentiated manner of both atoms and all the pluralities thereof.[13]

(8)   A standard take on singular versus plural nouns.
      In a world w with three cats:
      i.   cat = {a, b, c}   ii.   cats = { a, b, c, a∪b, b∪c, a∪c, a∪b∪c }

We should find a place in the structures in (7) also for kinds. Kinds are involved in understanding what sentences like those in (9), and related examples, mean:

(9)   a.   i.   Dogs evolved from wolves   (from Carlson 1977)
            vs.:
            ii. Those are nice dogs.
            iii. The dogs you see
      b.   Dinosaurs are extinct.
      c.   Green bottles come in three sizes.

Sentences such as those in (9a.i)–(9c) appear to be saying something of the kind as a whole. Only a whole kind can evolve from wolves, become extinct, or come in three sizes. As the examples in (9a) illustrate, sometimes (plural) nouns are kind denoting (in (9a.i), (9b) and (9c)), in other contexts (e.g., in postcopular position (9a.ii) or after a determiner (9a.iii)) they denote predicates (or properties). Kinds and properties are different types of semantic creatures. For our purposes, we can think of kinds (in a world w) as the maximal plural individual that comprises all of the manifestations of the kind (in w). Predicates (i.e., the extension of a property in a given world/situation) can be modeled as sets (or characteristic functions thereof). Thus, we wind up with a 'semantic triad,' which can be represented as follows:

(10) The semantic triad (from Chierchia 2010).
      a.   In any context/situation/world w_0,

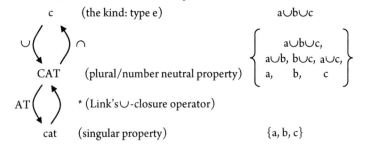

---

[13] The inclusion of atoms in the denotation of plurals is to get contrasts like (a)–(b) right:

(a)   There were no cats on the mat.
(b)   There was no group of cats on the mat.

Sentence (a) would be false if there is a single cat on the mat; sentence (b) would be true in such a case.

b. Definitions of the morphisms in (a):

$\cap$: i. Type = $<<s,<e,t>>, e_k>$
    ii. $\cap P = \lambda w.\, \iota P_w$

$\cup$: i. Type = $<e_k, <s,<e,t>>>$

    ii. $\cup k = \lambda w.\begin{cases} \lambda x.\, x \leq k_w \text{ , if } k_w \text{ is defined} \\ \\ \varnothing \text{ , otherwise} \end{cases}$

AT: i. Type = $<<s,<e,t>>, <s,<e,t>>>$

    ii. $AT(P) = \lambda w \lambda x[\, P_w(x) \wedge \forall z[P_w(z) \wedge z \leq x \to z = x]]$[14]

$*$: i. Type : $<<s,<e,t>>, <s,<e,t>>>$

    ii. $\lambda w \lambda x \exists Y[\, Y \subseteq AT(P)_w \wedge x = \cup Y]$

    [Link's (1983) puralization operator]

The members of a semantic triad are intensional structures: functions from worlds/ situations into extensions of the appropriate type. A simple, singular property cat_w denotes in any world w a (possibly empty) set of atoms. A plural property CAT_w denotes the closure under $\cup$ of a set of atoms. A kind c_w denotes a (maximal) plural individual. (I will sometimes omit reference to the world/situation, dropping the w-subscript). The entities in the semantic triad ultimately code the same worldly information, in the sense that they are linked via natural morphisms, as indicated in (10b). '$\cap$' maps a (plural) property into the corresponding kind; '$\cup$' a kind into the corresponding (plural) property; 'AT' extracts the smallest members out of a property denotation; '*' closes a property denotation under join. The semantic triad constitutes the logical space in which noun denotations live.

Let us turn now to the interpretation of numbers. Several options are open and viable. For our purposes, we shall regard them as adjectival, property-modifiers (ultimately based on cardinality predicates). For any property P, 3(P) is true of three membered pluralities of the smallest things to which P applies. For example, *three cats* = 3(CAT) will be true of all pluralities in CAT constituted by exactly three CAT-atoms. Here is an example, in a situation with only three cats a, b, and c.

(11) a. Example of how *n cats* work (in a world with three cats)

    $a \cup b \cup c$ $3(CAT) = \{\, a \cup b \cup c\}$
    $CAT = a \cup b, b \cup c, a \cup c$ $2(CAT) = \{\, a \cup b, b \cup c, a \cup c\,\}$
        $a, \quad b, \quad c$

    b. General definition of *three* as predicate modifier

    $3_{<<s,<e,t>>,<s,<e,t>>>} = \lambda P \lambda w \lambda x \exists Y[x = \cup Y \wedge Y \subseteq AT(P)_w \wedge \mu_{CARD}(Y) = 3\,]$[15]

[14] The notion of absolute atom, as used in (7) becomes then:

(a) $AT(\lambda w. D_w)$

were $\lambda w. D_w$ is a function from worlds/situations in the total domain D_w of individuals in w.

[15] I follow on numbers the basic line of Ionin and Matushansky (2006). Treating numbers as predicate modifiers paves the way for a compositional analysis of complex numerals (like *two hundred and thirty three*), which we cannot pursue here.

It should be noted that 3 in (11b) is used differently in the right (the *definiens*) and in the left (the *definiendum*) of the identity sign. The occurrence to the left is of the type of predicate modifiers, the one to the right is of type e (an ordinal).

    c.   Three uses of NumPs in simple clauses

        i.   Those are three cats.   Predicative

        ii. $3(CAT)(those)$

        iii. The three cats are ugly.   Argumental, definite

        iv. $ugly(\iota 3(CAT))$

        v.   Two cats stole the sausage.   Argumental, indefinite

        vi. $\exists x[\ 2(CAT)(x) \wedge \text{stole the sausage}(x)]$

Number Phrases like *two cats* or *three cats* denote a 'quantized' property (cf. (11c.i–ii)). In the example in (11a) there is only one group of three cats. Hence, *three cats* is a singleton property and it would be appropriate to use it in a definite description like *the three cats* (cf. (11c.iii–iv)). In contrast, *two cats* has three pluralities in its extension in the above situation. Accordingly, it would be infelicitous to use the noun phrase *the two cats*, though we could say things like *two cats stole the sausage*. In absence of a determiner, *two cats* in argument position undergoes $\exists$–closure, winding up with the truth conditions in (11c.vi).

As mentioned above, this general story can be varied upon in a number of ways, but it is not hugely controversial. One would like to maintain something like it as much as possible in the presence of more complex cases. Consider in this light the word *quantity* in constructions like *two quantities of apples*. Imagine a situation in which there are four apples on the table: two (say, a and b) are in a bowl, two (c and d) in a packaged carton. In such a situation we might equally felicitously utter (12a) or (12b).

(12) a.   There are two quantities of apples on the table. You guys take that one, we the other.

      b.   You guys take those apples, we take those others.

      c.   Denotation of *quantity/ies of apples* in context:

         i.   quantity of apples $= f_n(APPLE) = \{\ a\cup b,\ c\cup d\}$

         ii.   quantities of apples $= {}^*f_n(APPLE) = \{\ a\cup b,\ c\cup d,\ a\cup b\cup c\cup d\}$

      d.   i.   those apples $= those_j(APPLE) = a\cup b$

         ii.   that quantity of apples $= that_i(f_n(APPLE))) = a\cup b$[16]

How can we maintain the above theory of plurality in such a way that the sentences in (12a) and (12b) come out as truth-conditionally equivalent? How can it be that *that quantity of apples* and *those apples* can denote the same thing, but one is a singular Determiner Phrase (DP) and the other a plural one? A reasonable idea is that plurality versus singularity is factored in *before* the contribution of the determiner, at the level of the

---

[16] Here is a general definition of *quantity* (of type $<<s,<e,t>>, <s,<e,t>>>$):

(a)   General definition of *quantity*:

        $quantity_n = \lambda P\lambda w[f_n(P_{w@})]$

        where f is a variable of type $<<e,t>,<e,t>>$ such that for any $X_{<e,t>}$, and any y and z in $f_n(X)$, $x\cap y = \bot$; $w_@$ is the world of the context.

This definition guarantees that *quantity of water* is a constant property with an (indexically fixed) extension.

property. Here is the story in informal terms. Imagine that *quantity* applies to a plural count noun and partitions its denotation in contextually salient ways (with the preposition *of* just a semantically vacuous case marker). Think of the word *quantity*, if you like, as ranging over variables on partition functions. There are many ways of partitioning a property, whence the n-subscript *quantity*$_n$; only some of them will be salient in any given context. In the case at hand, with our four apples, the denotation of the noun is partitioned between the apples in the bowl (a$\cup$b) and those in the carton (c$\cup$d), as indicated in (12c.i). While the (context-dependent) property *quantity of apples* is true of plural individuals, it still may qualify as a *singular* property because it is not closed under join. In other words, it is not an individual entity that is to be regarded as plural or singular, but a property. A property is singular whenever it is not closed under join, plural when it is.[17] The denotation of a morphologically singular count noun like *cat* remains singular under this revised definition of singularity (and, of course, *cats* remains plural). Pluralization, then, follows its usual course and closes *quantity of apples* under join as in (12c.ii). On top of it all, determiners do their usual thing. In particular, demonstratives extract from a property extension the individual that is being pointed at, and one may wind up with situations like the one exemplified in (12d), with a plural and a singular DP denoting the same entity. We can thus retain a uniform theory of pluralization, where the contribution of the plural and singular morpheme is always the same under a fairly natural analysis of the *quantity of* construction. But we need to assume that properties are plural or singular (and individuals may be only in a derivative sense).

2.3. AN EPISTEMIC TAKE ON MASS NOUNS

It's time to address the mass/count contrast in English. This part of the proposal is going to be way more controversial than the background reviewed in the preceding section. Ideally, in developing an analysis of mass versus count, we would like to retain as much of our background as possible. In particular, we would like to maintain insofar as possible the analysis we have sketched of kinds, pluralization, and *quantity of* constructions. Note in this connection that mass nouns appear to be either property or kind denoting in ways that are fully parallel to those of count nouns:

(13) a.   gold is scarce/comes in different alloys   Kind

  b.   i.   This is pure gold.   Property
      ii. The gold in this ring comes from South Africa.

So, we should think in terms of mass properties and mass kinds. The big question is, what is it that makes a mass property uncountable? There are, of course, many ways to go and many proposals out there from which to draw. Let me mention two prima facie tempting strategies. One is to assume that mass properties (and, eventually,

---

[17] The proper definition should more be like:

(a)   P is singular iff it is not closed under join or trivially so.

The part after the disjunction is to allow empty or singleton properties to count as singular (in spite of being technically $\cup$-closed), as singular properties can, of course, turn out to have singleton or empty denotations.

mass kinds) are constructed from a different, somehow non-atomic domain of entities.[18] The question that arises in this connection is, what would make such a domain
'non-atomic'? A domain D with an ordering relation ≤ is non-atomic iff no member
of it is minimal with respect to ≤. If we take this literally, it would entail that any
member of x of D would have to have an infinite number of smaller and smaller
parts. Such domains can be constructed.[19] But how plausible is such a move? Any
physical entity does have minimal parts. The above model would force us to think
of material substances like gold or water as being composed of never ending smaller
and smaller gold/water particles. A second strategy is to simply 'paint' mass properties of a different color from the count ones in some formal way. We could easily
bend the 'separate domain' approach to this purpose. We say that count nouns get
their denotation from a domain C with the structure above and mass nouns from
a separate domain M (with a structure to be negotiated). Taking your denotation
from M makes you uncountable.[20] But this looks arbitrary. In particular, nothing
would prevent, it would seem, a language from interpreting all the nouns for objects
in the mass domain M (making them all mass) and all the nouns for substances in
the count domain C (making them count). We surely do not want our theory to give
us such interpretive freedom. Yes, English does allow nouns of objects like *furniture*
to act like mass nouns (and we need to understand how and why)—but on a limited
scale. Most basic mass nouns in English are nouns of substances. And no known language that has some grammatical manifestation of the distinction mixes things up
by letting its grammatically count nouns denote substances and vice versa. For that
matter, no known language that has some manifestation of the contrast is indiffer-
ent to the object/substance dichotomy, in the sense that it doesn't care how its basic
nouns are lexicalized.[21]

Given these non-trivial constraints, a move that strikes me as particularly plausible is to set the mass/count contrast on an epistemic grounding. If we know that
x is a cat, we know that in no world/situation can that very same object be two or
more cats. This is even true of earthworms. No individual earthworm is a plurality of
earthworms, even if it so happens that I can take an earthworm, cut it in half, and get
two earthworms (unlike what happens with cats). An important note: we may well be
uncertain as to whether a particular object is a cat or not (think of dead cats, cat em-
bryos, or what have you). The point is that it is part of how we use words like *cat* that
if we decide/determine x to be a cat, then we can no longer regard it as a plurality of
cats. For mass nouns, things work out differently. If x is water, we must countenance
that for all we know it might be an aggregate (i.e., a plurality of smaller water quantities). Again, this is a characteristic of how we use the noun *water*, not a claim about

---

[18] Link (1983) has inspired many theories of this sort. See also Landman (1991) for important
modifications of Link's original proposals.

[19] Bunt (1979) explicitly models mass nouns in this way, using his concept of ensemble (a set
with infinitely descending ∈ -chains).

[20] Landman's (1991) can be interpreted in this way. Cf. also the approach developed in Higginbotham (1994).

[21] Even though technically not a 'double domain' theory, the proposal developed in Chierchia
(1998a) does allow this type of interpretive freedom. So do the approaches developed in Rothstein
(2010) and Landman (2011), insofar as I can see.

the chemical makeup of water. The intuition is simple, and its formal rendering is also fairly simple. Here is our proposed definition of what it is to be count versus mass:

(15)　a.　COUNT(P) = $\forall w \forall x[P_w(x) \wedge \forall z[P_w(z) \wedge z \leq x \to z = x] \to \Box \, \forall y[P(y) \wedge y \leq x \to y = x]]$[22]

　　　　If x is a P-atom in any world w it must be a P-atom in every world compatible with what is known in w.

　　b.　MASS.(P) = $\forall w \forall x [P_w(x) \wedge \forall z[P_w(z) \wedge z \leq x \to z = x] \to \neg \Box \, \forall y[P(y) \wedge y \leq x \to y = x]]$

　　　　= $\forall w \forall x [P_w(x) \wedge \forall z[P_w(z) \wedge z \leq x \to z = x] \to \Diamond \exists y [P(y) \wedge y < x]]$

　　　　If x is a P-atom in w it is consistent with what is known in w that x may be a plurality of smaller Ps.

Everything stays the same in our semantics. We work with a totally canonical atomic domain D of the kind described earlier. What do the constraints in (15) concretely demand of noun denotations? Take a prototypical count noun, say *cat*. What (15a) requires is that if something is a cat-atom (i.e., a single cat) in no epistemically accessible world that cat-entity turns out to be more than one cat. On the other hand, if something is a minimal quantity of water, say a drop of water, you have to be able to view it as a plurality of smaller quantities thereof.

An immediate question that arises in this connection is, what about water molecules? Isn't a single H_2O molecule water in any w? And won't it be required by (15b) to be constituted of submolecular water particles, which is, we are told, a chemical impossibility? My line of reply to this is that I do not know the answer to these questions. I do not know whether a single water molecule (that in my very poor understanding is something like a probability distribution in space of the position and momentum of subatomic particles) counts as water or not given the way normally competent speakers use this term. What I know is that we do not have to settle this matter to competently use the noun *water*. The constraint in (15) is to be understood as relativized to 'natural contexts', that is, common grounds (/set of worlds) that are shared by competent (but typically scientifically naïve) speakers.[23] In such contexts, a smallest water quantity will have to be large enough (however the vagueness of 'large enough' is resolved) to be perceived without the aid of complex experimental machinery. So (15b) winds up requiring that any smallest *perceivable* water quantity can be conceived of

---

[22] A note on notation: Formula (15a) in the text (and similar formulas I use throughout) should be written as follows:

(a)　$\forall w \forall x[P_w(x) \wedge \forall z[P_w(z) \wedge z \leq x \to z = x] \to \forall w' \in K_w \forall y[P_{w'}(y) \to \wedge y \leq x \to y = x]$

where K is the relevant accessibility relation (of type <w, <w,t>>, w the type of words/situations).

In the abbreviation in (15a) I omit the w-subscript after '$\Box$,' because that is what the latter operator binds (and hence notating w on P as a free variable would be misleading). If the convention adopted in the text confuses you, just replace it with (a) throughout.

[23] By 'relativized to natural context' I mean that the initial quantifier over worlds in (15a–b) ought to range over worlds of the common ground:

(a)　$\forall w \in CGR_{w@} \ldots$

Where $CGR_{w@}$ is the set of worlds that constitutes mutually shared knowledge across speakers in the actual world w@.

as being composed of smaller unperceivable ones. This is how (15b) goes, insofar as 'concrete' mass properties are concerned. For abstract ones (like, say, *honesty*, or, perhaps, *space*), nothing prevents us from thinking of them as being made up of an infinite set of smaller and smaller abstract units. Thus, insofar as I can see, modalizing our understanding of what is it to be mass versus count affords us a reasonable take on the distinction that works for both concrete and abstract nouns. The constraints in (15) are meant to reflect how nouns are used; as such, they should to be consistent with laws of nature without unduly restricting how such laws may turn out to be.[24]

Let us construct an example. Suppose we are in a context with just three grains of rice: a, b, and c. In such a context, there will be *many* grain-sized quantities of rice. There will be the three grains, of course. But one-half of grain a and one-half of grain b (i.e., ($\frac{1}{2}$ a + $\frac{1}{2}$ b)) is also a grain-sized quantity of rice. And so is one-third of grain a and two-thirds of grain b; and so on. All of these many grain-sized quantities of rice can constitute our minimal rice quantities (and we could go smaller, of course). The point is that each minimal quantity of rice can be viewed as an aggregate of smaller amounts of rice in an endless number of ways.

(16)   A mass triad.
        Rice in a world w_0 with 3 grains of rice

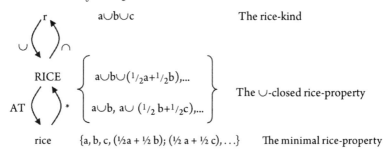

The total sum that constitutes all of the rice in this world w spatiotemporally coincides with the sum of the three grains $a \cup b \cup c$ (and that is why I am representing it that way in (16)); but rice has many more parts than a, b, and c (including spatially discontinuous ones, likes one-half of grain a and one-half of grain b). And all such parts, for all we know, may turn out to be aggregates of smaller rice parts. So, on this view, there are two sorts of P-atoms in correspondence with two sorts of natural properties: the P-atoms that are epistemically stable and those that are not. Cat-atoms are stable; rice-atoms are not. Conversely, if a property has stable relative atoms, it is count. If all of its minimal instances are epistemically unstable, it is mass. We have now reconstructed the mass/count distinction as a formal-grammatical one.

This view has several interesting consequences. Let me discuss four of them.

---

[24] I think the proper way of developing the present approach is as a contraint on how vagueness is to be resolved for mass nouns vs. count nouns. For mass nouns, all minimal instances fall within the vagueness band. The axioms in (15) are axioms on 'ground worlds/contexts' and the modal in them ranges over 'precisifications' of the latter, in the spirit of supervaluation semantics. See Chierchia (2010) for a development of this line of argumentation.

First, we can now think of mass-kinds/properties in a way fully parallel to their count counterparts (thereby providing a basis for a uniform account of bare plurals and bare mass nouns in English, and across languages that have the singular/plural distinction and allow for bare arguments). Mass kinds are qualitatively homogenous, maximal plural individuals with unstable minimal instances/parts.

Second, the present approach strongly constrains the mapping between mass/ count qua language internal categories (as defined in (15)) and substances/objects. If something is a substance, we won't know what its minimal parts look like (scientists may; but that is irrelevant). Hence we have no choice but to categorize them as mass. For objects, it will certainly be natural to categorize them as count; but we might be able to categorize them as mass, if the language gives us a way of doing so, as English does (and we still have to see how that is possible).

Third, counting the members of P means counting P-atoms (cf. the definition of numbers in (11) above).[25] But if P-atoms are structurally undetermined (i.e., epistemically unstable), we cannot do it. We can only count the minimal instances of a property that is known to have them; we cannot count the minimal instances of a property that is not known to have any. Differently put, counting goes via AT. If *blood* is mass in the sense of (15b), it follows from logic alone that AT(blood) is necessarily empty. Hence n(AT(blood)) is a logically contradictory property. This constitutes an arguably elegant explanation for why things like *three bloods* are weird.

Fourth, suppose that *quantity* works on mass nouns just as it does on count ones: it partitions its denotation along contextually determined lines. Then it will follow that the result of this partition will have stable minimal atoms. Being contextually set, such a property has to have stable minimal parts. So while AT(blood) is necessarily empty, $AT(quantity_n(blood))$ will not be; and counting with it will produce interpretable results.[26]

All of these are quite direct consequences of our epistemic take. What about pluralization? Here we have some leeway. We have seen that a substance must be categorized as mass. But as a mass what? Sticking to properties, there are two choices. A mass property like *rice* in (16) is true of just the (unstable) minimal rice quantities. If we choose *rice* as denotation for the corresponding noun, nothing would prevent it from pluralizing (i.e., getting closed under '$\cup$' via the *-operator). Perhaps, some languages take this route; it is a fact that several languages do allow their mass nouns to pluralize, without allowing direct combinations with numbers (cf. Tsoulas 2006 on modern Greek; Gillon 2010 on Innu Aimun, an Algonquian language).[27] Or maybe a language may choose to lexicalize its mass nouns as $\cup$–closed mass properties, such as RICE in (16). In such a case, pluralization would perhaps become impossible because mass nouns

---

[25] In the new modal setting the definition of the AT function becomes (a) (or, in primitive notation (b)):

(a) $AT(P) = (a) \lambda w \lambda x[\ P_w(x) \wedge \square \ \forall z[P(z) \wedge z \leq x \rightarrow z = x]]$

(b) $AT(P) = (b) \lambda w \lambda x[\ P_w(x) \wedge \forall w' \in K_w \forall z[P_{w'}(z) \wedge z \leq x \rightarrow z = x]]$

[26] Cf. fn 16 for a formal definition of 'quantity of X,' which has this consequence.

[27] Also Ojibwe has a singular/plural contrast on mass nouns, but with a different semantics than the one found in Greek and Innu Aimun; on this, see Mathieu (2012).

would already be plural, as it were. One would have to work out an economy condition that prevents pluralizing something that is lexically ∪-closed, a not implausible move.

I see one drawback to the proposal that mass nouns in English (or Italian, etc.) are lexicalized as being ∪-closed. The drawback is that singular morphology has been defined above as semantically requiring that a property be *not* ∪-closed. In languages like English (unlike modern Greek), mass nouns carry invariably singular morphology. So we would be forced to say that singular morphology on mass nouns does not have its usual semantic import. While this is perhaps acceptable, one might want to explore an alternative that does not have such a consequence. G. Magri (p.c.) has proposed an interesting take on this issue. A singular property is, according to our definition, a property that is not ∪-closed or it is trivially ∪-closed. The disjunction is necessary to let empty sets and singletons count as singular (a singular noun may turn out to have an empty or a singleton denotation). Now we might stipulate that all mass nouns are coded in English as singleton properties, thereby making them semantically singular: they are true just of the *totality* of the instances of the properties.[28] For example, *water* would be true of the totality of water, *blood* of the totality of blood, and so on. This would require some fiddling with the definition of some quantifiers, but nothing really major. It would make mass properties 'proper name'–like.[29] It would also give us an additional reason why numerals cannot combine with mass properties: mass properties, when non-empty, would have a logically fixed cardinality, and combining such properties with numerals seems pointless (a functional observation that can be readily turned into a formal one). This approach would enable us to maintain a uniform, exceptionless meaning for singular morphology. As may be evident from my way of presenting it, I am unable hide my sympathy for this proposal.

Magri's suggestion has a further advantage. It would allow us to make sense of the phenomenon of fake mass nouns. If mass nouns are singleton properties, some nouns associated with objects (like *furniture, footwear*, etc.) might take on the same shape as mass nouns and be coded as singleton properties. That way they would be forced to behave just like mass nouns: they would fail to pluralize, they would not be able to combine with numerals, and so on.[30] The prediction of this approach is

---

[28] Recall that properties and kinds are of different semantic types: <s, et> vs. <s,e>. We are assuming that mass nouns in English start out their semantic life as properties, though they wind up denoting kinds in specific contexts.

For a suggestion similar to Magri's, see Zamparelli (2008).

[29] In many languages (northern Italian, Portuguese, modern Greek) proper names require the definite article. It is natural to analyze proper names in these languages as singleton properties. Cf. on this, e.g., Chierchia (1998b). For a different take, cf., e.g., Longobardi (1994).

[30] Notice that on the present approach, 3(FURNITURE), where FURNITURE is the ∪-closed property true of all pieces of furniture, would come out as well defined, because FURNITURE has stable atoms. This is fully consistent with the fact, amply documented in Barner and Snedeker (2005), that the units of furniture are accessible to counting and provides a further argument against modeling fake mass nouns as ∪-closed properties, as proposed by Chierchia (1998a). On the singleton property approach, furniture would denote:

(a) $\lambda w \lambda x[\, x = \cup FURNITURE_w]$

As argued in the text, we can readily build into the definition of number the idea that they are infelicitous with properties with a logically fixed cardinality.

that the phenomenon of fake mass nouns could arise only in those number-marking languages that disallow pluralization of mass nouns, for only in such languages would mass nouns have to be coded as singleton properties. To the extent that I know, this prediction is borne out. In particular, modern Greek just does not have fake mass nouns (Tsoulas, p.c.). If on the right track, this would constitute strong support in favor of Magri's conjecture.

Be that as it may, I think that any theory will want to differentiate fake mass nouns from standard ones. When it comes to standard mass nouns, languages appear to have little choice. If a language has the mass/count distinction at all, substances must be lexicalized as mass. When it comes instead to coding kinds of objects as mass, there is huge variation, even across closely related languages, and in many languages fake mass nouns appear to be unattested. This suggests that the difference should be captured in type theoretic terms, without loosening too much the mapping from linguistico-semantic categories into extra-linguistic ones.

Finally, the present approach can lift wholesale the traditional view of grinding and packaging. Standardized grinding is a highly partial and context-dependent type-shifting function gr such that for any count property P_{COUNT}, $gr(P_{COUNT})$, if defined, is a mass property (rooted in unstable atoms). For example, we might assume that *chicken* refers primarily to the biological species, and gr(CHICKEN) maps the biological species into chicken meat. Gr is not shape or function preserving; though it is typically 'matter' preserving, in the sense that anything which is gr(CHICKEN) must be a spatiotemporal part of a chicken (albeit, a dead one). Similar considerations apply to packaging. For any mass property P_{MASS}, $pk(P_{MASS})$, if defined, is a count one, with stable atoms. For example, one might argue that count versus mass senses of *beer* are modulated via pk. BEER is a kind of alcoholic substance and pk(BEER) is the property of being a (contextually salient) standard serving of beer; ROPE and pk(ROPE) can be viewed along similar lines, with the latter as the property of being a physically bounded and connected piece of rope, and so on. For 'ambiguous' nouns P_{COUNT} / $gr(P_{COUNT})$ or P_{MASS} / $pk(P_{MASS})$ are equally salient, natural, frequent, and so on. For most properties, a special context is required for felicitous shifting, as some properties are more resilient to it than others. Pk doesn't apply easily to snow, blood, or honesty.[31] Gr does not apply in a natural way to triangles, kilos, or computer programs, for example.

---

[31] As mentioned in the text, there is a further type-shift *kd* that maps sortal properties into kind-level ones. Such a type shift probably applies to both count and mass properties. If WHALE is true of whales, kd(WHALE) will apply to subkinds thereof (sperm whales, hump backs, etc.). And if BLOOD is true of quantities of blood, kd(BLOOD) is true of types or sub-kinds of blood. Kd is involved in the interpretation of sentences like (a). According to Dayal (2004), it is also involved in the interpretation of (b), and in the interpretation of definite singular generic uses of the definite article (c).

(a) We keep three bloods in this lab.

(b) Most whales are extinct.

(c) The dodo is extinct.

Summarizing, the English system might look roughly as follows.

(17)   three cats

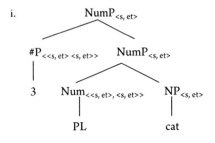

i.

ii.   PL(P) = P if *AT(P) = P
iii.   SG(P) = P if AT(P) = P

Following tradition, nouns in English are (or enter the semantic computation as) property denoting. In order to be turned into an argument, an NP will eventually need a determiner (or covert type shifting along the lines of Chierchia 1998b; Dayal 2004). Number marking encodes a function from properties into properties that checks whether a property has the right semantic structure. A singular property must be non $\cup$-closed (or trivially so), as per (17.iii); a plural property must be $\cup$-closed (as per (17.ii)). Mass nouns fail to combine with numerals, because numerals have built into their semantics the AT function, which requires stable P-atoms. Concerning PL and SG morphology, at least a couple of options may be available, only one of which is implemented in (17). In (17), both SG and PL require that the property be stably atomic (as they are based on AT). Mass nouns fail this test, because they are not stably atomic. To use mass nouns in such languages, they must be made uniformly stably atomic, but without changing their basic meaning. The repair strategy is to code mass nouns as singleton properties true of maximal plural individuals, which can be regarded as stably atomic. So if a language makes the choice in (17) concerning its singular-plural morphology, three consequences follow: (a) its mass nouns must be coded as singleton properties, (b) mass nouns cannot pluralize (because pluralization cannot change the basic meaning—the $\cup$-closure of a singleton is a singleton), and (c) fake mass nouns will come about. A second strategy is to weaken the meaning of PL versus SG so that it still requires $\cup$-closure versus lack thereof, but without going through AT, that is, without requiring of properties to be stably atomic.[32] In such a case, mass nouns will be expected to pluralize (and no fake mass nouns are expected to be attested), but they will still be unable to combine with numerals (which universally go through AT). Finally, on top of this, meaning-changing lexical shifts from mass to count and vice versa are possible on a context-dependent basis; and *quantity of* (and other similar constructions like *amount of, part of*) can turn a mass

---

[32] The weakening in question can, for example, be along the following lines:

i.   PL(P) = P if *P = P
ii.   SG(P) = P if $\forall w \forall x [P_w(x) \rightarrow \forall z[P_{w'}(z) \wedge z \leq x \rightarrow z = x]]$

(ii) corresponds to the non modal characterization of (relative) atomicity AT in (10c).

noun into a count one, by anchoring its denotation to a contextually salient partition of the property (which by construction will have stable atoms).

3. Two More Nominal Systems

In the present section I will review in an even more cursory way than what I did for English two very different nominal systems, and show how the mass/count distinction may come through. This will also provide us an interesting way of testing the theory of mass nouns sketched in section 2.

3.1. CLASSIFIER LANGUAGES

Classifier languages (ClLs) are those in which no noun can directly combine with a numeral. The word-by-word translation of *three cats* is ungrammatical in a ClL; one must always use a classifier in such combinations, yielding something that in English would look like 3 *units of cat*. Mandarin, Japanese, Korean, and Bangla are examples of ClLs. In light of this restriction, the macrogrammar of counting in ClLs resembles that of mass nouns in English, and this has prompted the speculation that these languages lack the mass/count distinction, in that all nouns are coded as mass. While it may be descriptively accurate to maintain that in ClLs all nouns are mass-*like* from an Anglocentric point of view, it turns out to be wrong to claim that all nouns are literally mass, and thus that ClLs do not have a grammatical manifestation of the mass/count distinction. The distinction in question manifests itself mostly through the classifier system. This point has been repeatedly shown in the literature, starting with Cheng and Sybesma (1998, 1999), and here is a summary of their main line of argumentation. ClLs turn out to have many families of classifiers, two of which are relevant to our discussion. Taking Mandarin for illustration, the first class involves classifiers like the generic one *ge* and more specific ones like *zhi* (that goes with words like *bi* 'pen') or *ben* (that goes with words like *shu* 'book'). These are sometimes referred to as 'individual' classifiers. The second class involves measure functions like *bang* 'pound' or *mi* 'meter.' Just like in English, classifiers of this second type go with either substances (like *meat* in (18a)) or objects (like *cherries* in (18b)).

(18) a. san bang rou
          three pound meat   'three pounds of meat'

      b. san bang yintao
          three pound cherry   'three pounds of cherries'

Individual classifiers, on the other hand, only go with kinds of objects. When combined with a substance noun, reinterpretation of the noun (i.e., shifting) is required. If standardized packaging is not available, use of a mass noun with a count quantifier is deviant (cf. (19b)).

(19) a. Successful standardized packaging
          (In a hospital):
          gei won na   san ge xie
          to me bring three Cl blood   'bring me three bags of blood'

   b. Unsuccessful packaging:
     (After getting cut):
     *wo diu le   san ge xie
     I   loose Asp three Cl blood

   c. 'Ambiguous' nouns
     i. wo mai le   san   bang xia
         I   buy Asp three pound shrimp 'I bought three pounds of shrimp.'
     ii. wo you san zhi/?ge xia
         I   have three Cl   shrimp   'I have three shrimps.'

On top of this main contrast, the syntax and semantics of individual classifiers versus measure-classifiers differ in a number of other ways, which we won't review here.[33] What matters to us is that the natural way to tease apart individual classifiers from measure-based ones relies on the semantic properties of the nouns they combine with; individual classifiers only go with nouns associated with kinds that come in natural units. As individual classifiers have a different syntactic distribution from measure-based ones, this constitutes clear evidence of a grammaticized manifestation of the mass/count distinction in ClLs.

From the present point of view, a natural way to conceptualize ClLs is by marrying the theory of mass/count sketched in section 2 with the Nominal Mapping Parameter, developed in Chierchia (1998b). The core idea of the latter proposal is that languages may vary in the way their nouns choose their lexical denotation from semantic triads. English, as we saw, requires its nouns to be property denoting, and number morphology is a function that checks whether such properties are singular or plural. ClLs require their nouns to be kind denoting. This hypothesis provides a natural account for the obligatory existence of classifiers, along the following lines. Numerals, we have hypothesized, are functions from properties into quantized properties. If this is universal (as one might want the semantics of numbers to be) and some languages insist on their nouns being kind denoting, a mismatch will arise preventing numbers from directly combining with nouns. It is natural to conjecture that classifiers become necessary in such languages to obviate this type mismatch. While there are several ways in which classifiers might be viewed as fulfilling such a requirement, one that strikes me as particularly effective has been developed in Jiang (2012), who in turn builds

---

[33] An important syntactic difference between individual and measure classifiers is that the latter but not the former can combine with the noun modifier *de*:

(a) *san ge de ren
     three cl DE person
(b) san bang de yintao
     three pound DE cherry 'three pounds of cherries'

For relevant discussion, see Cheng and Sybesma (1998, 1999), Jiang (2010). A number of authors have provided counterexamples to this generalization; cf., e.g., X. Li (2011):

(c) ta yilian   xie le liang-bai   duo feng de xin
     she continuously write Perf two-hundred more Cl DE letter.
     'She continuously wrote more than 200 letters.'

These counterexamples are limited, however, just to 'high' numbers.

on Krifka's (1995) classic proposal. Jiang argues that all classifiers can be viewed as binary functions that take a kind and a number to yield a (quantized) property. Here is an illustration with both individual and measure classifiers (cf. also X. Li 2011).

(20) a. Structure of ClPs

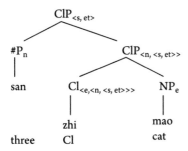

(Tang 1990, Cheng and Sybesma 1999, Jiang 2012, among many others)

b. Individual Classifiers (Jiang 2012)

   i. san zhi mao → $\lambda w \lambda x [\text{three}(\text{AT}(^\cup c))_w(x)]$
   ii. zhi mao → $\lambda n \lambda w \lambda x [n(\text{AT}(^\cup c))_w(x)]$
   iii. zhi → $\lambda k \lambda n \lambda x [n(\text{AT}(^\cup k))_w(x)]$

c. Measure Classifiers

   i. san bang rou → $\lambda w \lambda x [^\cup \text{meat}_w(x) \wedge \mu_{pound}(x) = 3]$
       three pound meat
   ii. bang rou → $\lambda n \lambda w \lambda x [^\cup \text{meat}_w(x) \wedge \mu_{pound}(x) = n]$
   iii. bang → $\lambda k \lambda n \lambda w \lambda x [^\cup k_w(x) \wedge \mu_{pound}(x) = n]$

Classifier phrases have a structure that is fully parallel to that of NumPs in English. In particular, ClPs built out of individual classifiers are analyzed as quantized properties that can be used in the typical ways of NumPs in English: predicatively, or in generic sentences, or as restrictors of quantifiers, or undergoing ∃-closure in argument position. In (20a.ii–iii) we track the compositional makeup of classifier phrases, following the hypothesized structure in (20a). The lexical classifier *ge* applies to kinds, and turns them into number-seeking properties using '$^\cup$' and the AT-function. The *zhi mao* subconstituent looks for a number; by applying it to *san* 'three,' we obtain a quantized property. It follows from the use of AT in definition (20b) that individual classifiers like *zhi* (or *ge*) will be defined only for count-kinds, endowed with stable minimal parts. Uses with mass-kinds will be possible only through the canonical mass-to-count shifts. Measure classifiers have the same logical type as individual ones and are analyzed by analogy with measure phrases in English. They combine with a kind first, then with a numeral and yield a quantized property that uses a non-atom-based measuring function (in the case at hand, something like *kilo* or *pound*).[34]

---

[34] The main argument in favor of adopting the one in (20) as the basic type of classifiers is that structures parallel to (20), with possible word order variations, are attested in every ClL. On the other hand, only some ClLs allow also bare (i.e., numberless) classifier noun sequences. For example:

(a) zek gau zungji sek juk (Cantonese)   Cheng and Sybesma (1998)
     CL dog like   eat meat 'The dog likes to eat meat.'

On the present take, the existence of a generalized classifier system is triggered by a type mismatch: ClLs have kind-denoting nouns. Numbers combine with properties, and hence in ClLs they cannot directly combine with nouns. The classifier is required to lift noun denotations to the right type for combining with numbers (creating, moreover, number-taking functions); if they do so via AT, they will only combine with kind-denoting nouns that have stable atoms (count kinds); if they do so via some other, non-cardinality based measure function, they will be able to combine with nouns of any type (mass or count), to the extent that such nouns have the relevant dimension (weight, length, or what have you). Now, there clearly are many conceivable alternatives or variants to this general approach. However, the present one has a consequence that other proposals I am familiar with fail to have.[35] It derives in an arguably principled manner the observation that every ClL allows bare arguments.

(21) a. Every ClL allows verbs to merge with bare nouns.
      b. i.   xiong jue-zhong   le   Krifka (1995)
               bear vanish-kind ASP   'bears are extinct'
          ii. waiman gou zai   jiao
               outside dog PROG bark   'dogs/the dog are/is barking outside'

The converse of (21a) does not hold: there are plenty of languages that allow bare arguments, and are not ClLs. A prime example is that of languages like Russian or Hindi that have no overt determiners and freely allow numbers to directly combine with their count nouns. To see the empirical robustness of the generalization in (21a), notice that there is no a priori reason why there couldn't be a ClL, which disallows bare arguments and requires some overt structure (a determiner or a classifier) of all its nominals in argument position (the way in which, say, French always requires an overt determiner). The generalization in (21a) follows from the present approach in a straightforward manner. Nouns in ClLs are kind denoting, and kinds are of an argumental type. Under the hypothesis that categories can be freely syntactically merged with each other, modulo type consistency, we come to expect structures such as those in (21b) to be well formed in every ClL. Our parametric setting on noun denotations catches two birds with one stone: the obligatory presence of a classifier in the grammar of counting has to come with the availability of bare arguments.

(b) *jia gau be   lim   zhui   (Mandarin)
     CL dog want drink water   Intended: 'The dog wants to drink water.'
The interpretation and distribution of bare classifier-noun sequences vary significantly across classifier languages. Jiang (2012) proposes that this asymmetry between numeral-classifier-noun structures (always attested with a uniform interpretation) and bare classifier-noun ones (attested on a language particular basis and with varying interpretations) is due to the fact that the latter is derived from the former through a process of 'detransitivization' of classifiers (that amounts to plugging into a classifier the numeral *one*), and is available on a parametric basis.
    Also relevant to the present discussion is the distribution and interpretation of 'plural' noun phrases in ClLs. Cf. Li (1999) for an influential proposal. See Jiang (2012) for a reanalysis of Li's generalizations along lines consistent with the present approach.
    [35] Cf., e.g., Longobardi (1994), Borer (2005).

In Chierchia (1998b) I speculate that since ClLs do not need determiners to turn their nouns into arguments, they will never develop lexical determiners on economy grounds. This speculation turns out to be wrong. Jiang and Hu (2010) and Jiang (2012) show that Yi, a ClL historically related to Mandarin, does have a lexical definite determiner, namely *su* 'the.' Jiang (2012) argues that this is in fact to be expected, contra Chierchia (1998b)'s speculation: if ClPs are of a predicative type, determiners may well develop to turn them into arguments. She makes the further interesting prediction that if a ClL develops a determiner, it will be able to apply only at the level of ClPs, which is property-denoting, and not at the level of the bare noun, which is kind-denoting, under the plausible assumption that determiners are universally property-seeking functions.

The present sketchy remarks should suffice to illustrate how the mass/count distinction turns out to be grammatically encoded in ClLs in ways that are very different from the English one. Such a distinction is encoded in the classifier system: individual and measure classifiers, while partaking in structures like (20), have otherwise widely diverging syntactic and semantic properties, all traceable back to the presence of the atomizing function in individual classifiers but not in the measure ones. The present approach to mass/count that relies on a basic, universal distinction between properties/kinds with epistemically stable minimal instances and properties/kinds with epistemically unstable ones, appears well designed to capture such variation through a conceptually minimal shift in the denotation of nouns.

3.2. A PLUNGE IN A 'LESS FAMILIAR' LANGUAGE

In the following brief paragraphs I am going to report on Suzi Lima's research on Yudja, a language of the Juruna family, Tupi stock, spoken by 294 people in the Xingu Indigenous Park in Brazil. My goal is to explore, in a very preliminary way, the consequences of Lima's findings for the present approach to mass and count. All the examples below are from her fieldwork. Yudja is a determinerless language whose nouns are number neutral.[36] Bare arguments are freely allowed.

(22)   ali   ba'   ï   ixu
       child paca to eat   'The/a/child(ren) eat(s)/ate the/a paca(s).'

The language has a few classifiers, but they are typically not obligatory. A most striking characteristic of this language is that numerals can freely combine with nouns of any type. With notionally count nouns, numerals have their usual meaning. With mass nouns, the readings one systematically gets are two: one is the 'standardized packaging' reading. The other, however, involves 'unconventional contexts,' as Lima puts it:

(23)   a.   Conventional container reading.
            Txabïu ali   eta   awawa
            three child sand to get   'Children got three sand(s) in the beach.'[37]
            (The) children got three containers with sand from the beach.

---

[36] There is a morpheme -i- associated with plurality, but it is always optional and restricted to human nouns.

[37] As is evident from these examples, numerals in Yudja preferentially float at the beginning of the clause.

b.   Context: the children dropped a little bit of sand near the school and a little bit
     near the hospital (the drops have different sizes and shapes):
     Yauda ali   eta apapa
     two   child sand drop.redupl   'Children drop two sand(s).'
     The children dropped two quantities of sand.

The behavior in (23a) is sort of expected. The mass noun *sand* can in principle be
mapped onto the meaning 'standardized container of sand' by the packaging function. Packaging into standardized containers/units may happen more easily in
Yudja than in, say, English, but the general phenomenon appears to be the familiar
one. The case of unconventional contexts is, however, clearly different from what
happens in Indo-European and in ClLs, where construals such as those in (23b)
are disallowed. Lima has tested it carefully with a wide variety of unconventional
contexts and mass nouns, including *water, flour, blood*. Here is an example with
blood:

(24)   Context: someone cut his finger and dropped a little bit of blood near the school, and
       also dropped blood near the hospital and near the river (the blood drops have
       different sizes and shapes):
       Txabïu apeta ipide   pepepe
       three   blood on the floor to drip.redupl (three events)
       'Three bloods dripped on the floor.'

Should we conclude that Yudja lacks the mass/count distinction altogether? Have
we finally found a language that doesn't care how its nouns are lexicalized? Even
though the evidence is somewhat sparse, upon closer inspection it looks like the
answer should be 'no.' There are at least two pieces of evidence that point in this
direction. The first is the behavior of numerals in combination with count nouns;
such combinations do have the canonical interpretation, even when the context
might make a non-standard interpretation salient. One cannot take a table, cut it in
three parts, and then say something like "now we have got three tables," meaning
'now we have got three quantities/parts of table.' By the same token, one cannot
assign three places on a canoe to three boys and say "the boys are occupying three
canoes," meaning 'the boys are occupying three parts of a canoe.' Nor can one
divide a whole lot of canoes into three sets, assign each set to a team, and say "each
team got one canoe," meaning 'each team got one quantity of canoes.' If the language really didn't care about mass versus count, these things ought to be possible
(particularly given the flexibility we observe with mass nouns). Or to put it differently, the construction *three N* means 'three quantities of N,' if N is mass; but it
does not (and cannot) mean 'three quantities of N,' if N is count. This is evidence
that the mass/count distinction is lexicalized in the language. The second piece of
evidence involves the pair of quantifiers *urahu* 'a lot' and *xinahu* 'little/few.' These
quantifiers can freely combine with either mass or count nouns, but with different meanings. In combination with mass nouns the quantifier pair means 'a lot/a
little'; with count nouns, however, they can only get an adjectival reading ('big/
small'):

(25)   a.   Urahu ahuanama txa
            A lot milk   'A lot of milk in a single place'

       b.   Xinaku ahuanama txa
            Little   milk   'Little milk in a single place'

       c.   Urahu ali
            big   child   'The child is big.'

       d.   xinaku ali
            small   child   'The child is small.'

Even though the nouns of the language are number neutral, something like (25c) cannot be interpreted as 'a lot of children.' This generalization about quantification with *urahu/xinaku* could not be stated without the substance/object contrast and constitutes a way of coding it into grammatical morphemes.[38]

Considerations of this sort suggest that even in Yudja grammatical manifestations of the mass/count distinction are attested. What Lima is exploring in this connection is an analysis in terms of a very general classifier that modulates counting in Yudja. Within the present set of assumptions, Lima's insight could be couched along the following lines. Nouns in Yudja are kind denoting, like in Mandarin. This enables them to occur as bare arguments and requires classifiers for counting. But Yudja, unlike Mandarin, has a poor classifier system, because it relies on an unrestricted 'logical' one that typically can be dropped. The structure of Yudja's ClPs might be something like:

(26)   Cl-drop languages[39]

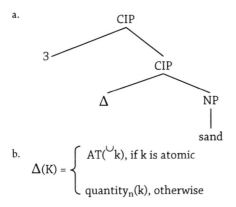

a.

b. $\Delta(K) = \begin{cases} AT(\breve{\ }k), \text{ if k is atomic} \\ \\ \text{quantity}_n(k), \text{ otherwise} \end{cases}$

---

[38] There is a third relevant data set, involving the rest of the quantifier system, for example the quantifiers *itxïbï* 'many' and *kïnana* 'few.' Such quantifiers in combinations with mass nouns of the form *itxïbï ahuanama txa* 'many milk' are glossed as 'many containers of milk.' It would seem from these glosses that such quantifiers force mass-to-count shifts of the canonical kind and would be deviant in unconventional contexts. If this turns out to be so, it would constitute a further piece of evidence for a grammatical manifestation of the mass/count distinction.

[39] I am assuming that the surface word order is obtained by floating the numeral to a clause initial position.

The term 'classifier drop' is by analogy with 'pro drop.' The idea is that Yudja's main classifier has a logically set meaning and, in view of its great generality, it goes unpronounced (it is 'retrievable'). With count nouns, such a classifier simply extracts the natural units/atoms; with mass nouns it has the same semantics as 'quantity of,' which makes the noun count by linking it to a contextually salient partition of the noun-denotation. Crucially, 'quantity of' includes but is not limited to standardized servings/containers and the like. The latter is the main difference between 'Δ' and *ge*: *ge* goes with count nouns or forces reinterpretation of mass nouns in terms of standardized units/containers); 'Δ' means *atom of* with count nouns and *quantity of* with mass nouns, without being restricted to standardized servings/containers. The structure in (26) would explain the flexibility of Yudja's grammar of counting, while at the same time accounting for the constraints discussed earlier that seem to characterize the behavior of count nouns and of quantifiers. It also enables us to retain the same semantics for numerals as for English and Mandarin. It is clear that this is not the only possible analysis of Yudja. At the same time, it is a fairly simple one that fits nicely in an arguably general, semantically driven typology.

4. Concluding Remarks

We have explored in a cursory way three very different grammars of counting insofar as they concerns the mass/count distinction. Our tentative conclusion on this limited basis is that such a distinction is attested, in parameterized form across these three types of languages, contrary to what it may prima facie appear.

Our starting point is the observation is that there exists a pre-linguistic categorial distinction between 'objects,' structured in qualitatively uniform natural classes with cognitively salient minimal parts, and 'substances' that are not so structured. This pre-grammatical distinction turns through grammar into a formal, epistemically grounded one. Count nouns have to map onto properties or kinds with minimal instances that are known to be such across contexts. Mass nouns have to map onto properties/kinds whose minimal instances are epistemically unstable. A minimal instance of a mass property has to be set to something that may turn out to be constituted by smaller units. The reason that counting with mass nouns tends to be disallowed by grammar is that we cannot count minimal instances of properties, if such instances are epistemically undetermined.

This proposal is similar to traditional approaches in that it differentiates among count (i.e., atomic) and mass (i.e., non-atomic) properties/kinds in terms of the things they apply to. It differs from them in that it has a built-in mapping onto the extra-linguistic distinction between objects and substances, provided by its modal, epistemic standpoint: a property/kind whose minimal instances are inaccessible to our cognitive system must be construed as mass in the formal sense.

At the same time, we have explored a number of possible parameters that can condition aspects of this mapping and thereby the grammar of counting. A primary divide is between property-oriented and kind-oriented languages. In property-oriented languages, numbers will be able to combine directly with count nouns on type theoretic grounds. In kind-oriented ones, they will not be able to, and classifiers (overt or null) will be needed. Kind-oriented languages are expected to freely allow bare arguments, and the mass/count distinction is expected to manifest itself in the grammar of the classifier system and of quantifiers.

In the two kind-oriented languages we have looked at, this takes place in different ways. If the language has a rich classifier system, there will emerge (at least) two classes of classifiers: one, atom based, will combine with count kinds; the other, measure and container based, will be able to combine with a broader set of nouns; such classes will have a partially overlapping, but diverse distribution. At the opposite end, we found a language that uses a very general way of extending countability to the mass portion of its lexicon (through the interpolation of something like the context dependent 'countifying' function *quantity of*). In such a language, we still detect the mass/count distinction through the different interpretation of numbers with count versus mass nouns (and through the quantifier system).

Finally, it is worth recalling a parametric difference internal to property-oriented languages. Some such languages (like modern Greek) apply number marking uniformly across mass and count nouns, allowing their mass noun to pluralize. Most languages with the singular/plural distinction, however, use it to enforce some kind of obligatory singularity on mass nouns. Following Magri, we have conjectured that mass nouns in languages of this second type are coded as singleton properties in order to meet the singularity requirement. It is in languages of this second type that the phenomenon of fake mass nouns may arise, as a sort of 'copy-cat' effect.

The study of further nominal systems may well lead to a radical reorganization of this picture. For the time being, however, it seems to me that the mass/count distinction holds up across quite a diverse range of nominal system, and that an epistemic take to it might be useful in understanding what is going on.

Acknowledgments

Thanks to Amy Rose Deal, Julie Li Jiang, Suzi Lima, Roberta Pires, Greg Scontras, Jesse Snedeker, and George Tsoulas for very helpful discussions on this topic.

Jim Huang and I met 30 years ago and we have been close colleagues and friends throughout. I owe him a lot for his insight, his teaching, and his friendship.

References

Barner, D., and J. Snedeker. 2005. Quantity judgments and individuation: Evidence that mass nouns count. *Cognition* 97, 41–66.

Borer, H. 2005. *Structuring Sense*. Oxford: Oxford University Press.

Bunt, H. 1979. *Ensembles* and the formal semantic properties of mass terms. In *Mass Terms: Some Philosophical Problems*, ed. F. J. Pelletier. Dordrecht: Kluwer, 249–277.

Carlson, G. 1977. *Reference to Kinds in English*. Doctoral dissertation, University of Massachusetts at Amherst. (Published in 1980 by Garland, New York).

Carey, S. 1985. *Conceptual Change in Childhood*. Cambridge, MA: Bradford Books, MIT Press.

Carey, S., and E. Spelke. 1996. Science and core knowledge. *Philosophy of Science* 63(4), 515–533.

Cheng, L., and R. Sybesma. 1998. Yi-wang Tang, yi-ge Tang: Classifiers and massifiers. *Tsing Hua Journal of Chinese Studies* XXVIII(3), 385–412.

Cheng, L.-S., and R. Sybesma. 1999. Bare and not-so-bare nouns and the structure of NP. *Linguistic Inquiry* 30(4), 509–542.

Chierchia, G. 1998a. Plurality of mass nouns and the notion of 'semantic parameter.' In *Events and Grammar*, ed. S. Rothstein. Dordrecht: Kluwer.

Chierchia, G. 1998b. Reference to kinds across languages. *Natural Language Semantics* 6, 339–405.

Chierchia, G. 2010. Mass nouns, vagueness, and semantic variation. *Synthese* 174, 99–149.

Darlymple, M., and S. Morfu. 2012. Plural semantics,reduplication, and numeral modification in Indonesian. *Journal of Semantics* 29(2): 229–260.

Dayal, V. 2004. Number marking and (in)definiteness in kind terms. *Linguistics and Philosophy* 27(4), 393–450.

Feigeson, L., S. Carey, and E. Spelke. 2002. Infants' discrimination of number vs. continuous extent. *Cognitive Psychology* 44, 33–66.

Gillon, C. 2010. The mass/count distinction in Innu-aimun: Implications for the meaning of plurality. In *Proceedings of WSCLA 15*, ed. B. Rogers and A. Szakay. University of British Columbia, 12–29.

Hauser, M., and S. Carey. 2003. Spontaneous representations of small numbers of objects by rhesus macaques: Examinations of content and format. *Cognitive Psychology* 47, 367–401.

Hauser, M., and B. Spaulding. 2006. Wild rhesus monkeys generate causal inferences about possible and impossible physical transformations in the absence of experience. *Proceedings of the National Academy of Science* 103, 18, 7181–7185.

Higginbotham, J. 1994. Mass and count quantifiers. *Linguistics and Philosophy* 17, 447–480.

Jiang, L. J. 2010. Monotonicity and measure phrases in Chinese. *Proceedings of the Chicago Linguistics Society* 45, 303–317.

Jiang, L. J. 2012. *Nominal phrases and language variation*. Doctoral dissertation, Harvard University.

Jiang, L. J., and S. Hu. 2011. *An Overt Determiner in a Classifier Language*. In *Proceedings of Glow VII in Asia 2010*, ed. M.- G. Gao, Beijing: Beijing Languages and Cultures University Press.

Krifka, M. 1995. Common nouns: A contrastive analysis of Chinese and English. In *The Generic Book*, ed. G. Carlson and F. J. Pelletier. Chicago: University of Chicago, 398–411.

Landman, F. 1991. *Structures for Semantics*. Dordrecht: Kluwer.

Landman, F. 2011. Count nouns – mass nouns – neat nouns – mess nouns. In *Formal Semantics and Pragmatics: Discourse, Context and Models, The Baltic International Yearbook of Cognition, Logic and Communication*, ed. M. Glanzberg, B. H. Partee, and J. Šķilters, Vol. 6, 1–67.

Li, Yen-Hui Audrey. 1999. Plurality in a classifier language. *Journal of East Asian Language* 8, 75–99.

Li, Xu-Ping. 2011. *On the Semantics of Classifiers in Chinese*. Doctoral dissertation, Bar Ilan University, Israel.

Lima, S. 2010. About the mass-count distinction in Yudja: A description. In *Proceedings of WSCLA 15*, ed. B. Rogers and A. Szakay, University of British Columbia, 157–176.

Link, G. 1983. The logical analysis of plural and mass terms: A lattice theoretic approach. In *Meaning, Use and Interpretation of Language*, ed. R. Bäuerle, C. Schwarze, and A. von Stechow, 302–323. Berlin: de Gruyter.

Longobardi, G. 1994. Reference and proper names: A theory of N-movement in syntax and logical form. *Linguistic Inquiry* 25, 609–665.

Ionin, T., and O. Matushansky. 2006. The composition of complex cardinals. *Journal of Semantics* 23, 315–360.

Mathieu, E. 2012. Flavors of division. *Linguistic Inquiry* 43, 650–679.

Pelletier, J., ed.1979. *Mass Terms: Some Philosophical Problems*. Dordrecht: Reidel.

Pelletier, J., and L. Schubert. 1989. Mass expressions. In *Handbook of Philsophical Logic*, ed. D. Gabbay and F. Guenthner, Vol. IV. Dordrecht: Kluwer.

Rothstein, S. 2010. Counting and the mass count distinction. *Journal of Semantics* 27(3), 343–397.

Sauerland, U. 2003. A new semantics for number. In *Proceedings of SALT 13*, ed. R. Young and Y. Zhou. Ithaca, NY: CLC Publications, Cornell University.

Selkirk, E. 1977. Some remarks on noun phrase structure. In *Formal Syntax*, ed. A. Akmajan, P. Culicover and T. Wasow. New York: Academic Press.

Soja, N., S. Carey, and E. Spelke. 1991. Ontological categories guide young children's inductions of word meanings: Object terms and substance terms. *Cognition* 38, 179–211.

Spelke, E., and S. Dehaene. 1999. Biological foundations of numerical thinking. *Trends in Cognitive Sciences* 3, 365–366.

Stickney, H. 2009. *The Emergence of DP in the Partitive Structure*. Doctoral dissertation, University of Massachusetts at Amherst.

Tsoulas, G. 2006. *Plurality of Mass Nouns and the Grammar of Number*. Paper presented at the 29th Glow Meeting, Barcelona.

Wiltschko, M. 2010. How do languages classify their nouns? Cross-linguistic variation in the mass/count distinction. In *Proceedings of WSCLA 13 and 14*, ed. H. Bliss and R. Girard. University of British Columbia, 223–241.

Zamparelli, R. 2008. Bare predicate nominals in Romance languages. In *Essays on Nominal Determination*, ed. H. Müller and A. Klinge. Amsterdam: John Benjamins, 101–130.

Part Two

THE PREDICATE DOMAIN

7

Analysis versus Synthesis: Objects

MICHAEL BARRIE AND AUDREY LI

1. Introduction

Huang (2005, 2006, Chapter 1 in this volume) has proposed insightful and influential analyses of different types of constructions in different languages with the notions of micro-parameters and macro-parameters: some languages, like Chinese,[1] have more micro-parameters of analytic properties; others, like English, are more synthetic in the sense that they have more micro-parameters of synthetic properties. Analyticity generally has a more transparent matching of meaning-morpheme/word correspondence relation, whereas synthesis encodes more meanings into one morpheme/word. This contrast is manifested very well in the formation of accomplishment verbs in English and the use of bi-morphemic action + result expressions for the corresponding verbs in Chinese (Tai 1984):

(1) English Chinese
    learn   xue-hui 'study-capable'
    break   da-po   'hit-break'
    kill   sha-si   'kill-dead'

In light of this contrast, it is interesting to note that Chinese allows verbs to be immediately followed by noun phrases (NPs)[2] that are temporal, locative, or instrument expressions, which has sometimes been assumed to involve verbs combined with other light verbs (e.g., Lin 2001):

(2) a. ta xihuan zuo **baitian** -temporal
      he like   do daytime
      'He likes to work in the daytime.'

    b. ta xihuan chi **haohua canting.** -locative
      he like   eat fancy   restaurant
      'He likes to eat at fancy restaurants.'

---

[1] This work focuses on Mandarin Chinese.

[2] Because the distinction between DP and NP is not relevant in this work, we use the label NP throughout the work as an abbreviation for argumental nominal expressions.

    c. ta xihuan xie   **zhe-zhi maobi.**   -instrument
        he like   write this-CL brush.pen
        'He likes to write with this brush pen.'

Such postverbal NPs roughly correspond to adjunct PPs, which generally occur pre-verbally in Chinese:

(3) a. ta xihuan **zai baitian** zuo (shi)
        he like   at daytime do work
        'He likes to work in the daytime.'

    b. ta xihuan **zai haohua canting**   chi fan.
        he like   at fancy   restaurant eat meal
        'He likes to eat at fancy restaurants.'

    c. ta xihuan **yong zhe-zhi maobi**   xie (zi)
        he like   use   this-CL brush.pen write word
        'He likes to write with this brush pen.'

To accommodate such facts, Lin (2001) proposes that verbs in Chinese in the following structure can be incorporated with the light verb that licenses the relevant adjunct expression:

(4)

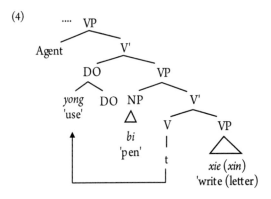

The postverbal NPs in (2a–c) generally correspond to PPs in English, as indicated by the translation for the sentences. This categorical difference between Chinese and English and the derivation captured in (4) are not expected if we consider the morphological analyticity just mentioned. However, Lin (2001) and Huang (2005, 2006) note that the possibility of (2a–c) is in fact an illustration of another analytic property: Chinese verbs are more bare and do not contain thematic features. Therefore, typical objects (objects subcategorized for by verbs) are not needed (see also Williams, Chapter 11 of this volume). The postverbal adjunct NP takes the place of the normally subcategorized object. Let us refer to the subcategorized objects as canonical objects and the adjunct NPs taking the place of canonical objects as non-canonical objects. As a comparison, English generally does not license non-canonical objects because this language is more synthetic in the sense that its verbs do contain thematic features.

If non-canonical objects are possible because no thematic features are specified as lexical properties of verbs one might wonder why the relevant light verbs are needed at all. Why do non-canonical objects need light verbs to license them thematically? Moreover, there are interesting constraints on what can be a non-canonical object; that is, not all preverbal adjunct PPs can have a non-canonical object counterpart:[3]

Comitatives

(5) a. wo **gen** hao wuban   tiao wu.
          I   with good dance.partner dance dance
          'I dance with good dancing partners.'

     b. *wo tiao   hao wuban.
          I   dance good dance.partner
          intended to mean 'I dance with good dancing partners.'

Benefactives

(6) a. wo **wei** luke   kan   xingli
          I   for travelers watch luggage
          I watch luggage for travelers.'

     b. *wo kan   luke.
          I   watch traveler
          intended to mean 'I watch (luggage) for travelers.'

What is even more interesting and striking is that a similar contrast in the availability of a non-canonical object roughly corresponding to an adjunct PP is found in noun incorporation (NI) languages, such as Northern Iroquoian languages.

This work argues that non-canonical objects do not behave like adjunct PPs. Instead, they are more like canonical objects syntactically, although the two are not identical in every aspect. The (un)availability of non-canonical objects depends on the role of Ps, applicatives, or case markings. We will refer to these functional categories such as Ps, applicatives, case, and agreement markings as functors. An argument not licensed by a functor can be the syntactic object of a verb, interpreted according to institutionalized conventions (grammaticalized world knowledge).

---

[3] The judgment with sources is not as clear. For instance, the following sentence is generally not acceptable to the consultant that we worked with:
Source

(i) a   wo **xiang tushuguan** jie   shu.
          I   from library   borrow book
          'I borrow books from libraries.'

     b. *wo jie   tushuguan.
          I   borrow library
          intended to mean 'I borrow (books) from libraries.'

However, if the object is a specific bank name, the acceptability improves for some speakers:

(ii) wo jie   Meiguo Yinhang.
          I   borrow America bank
          'I borrowed from Bank of America.'

The presence/absence of case morphology will be a focus of our discussion, and will be shown to be a property of particular constructions, rather than specific languages. Therefore, we will find the counterpart of Chinese non-canonical objects in English compounding (N-V-*er/ing*) and noun incorporation structures in Northern Iroquoian languages. This will lead us to conclude that "analysis versus synthesis" should consider specific constructions, rather than types of languages. It would be important to examine micro-variations (micro-parameters) and take "macro-parameter" as an aggregation of correlating variations (see Huang, Chapter 1 of this volume).

2. Non-Canonical Objects in Chinese

The notion of objects of verbs seems to be intuitively clear. Native speakers seem to know when and where there is an object. When one hears sentences such as those in (7a, b), the understanding is that probably something is missing. The interpretation should include something about what was done by him or liked by him—objects of verbs. In contrast, the sentences in (8a, b) do not seem to be missing an object.

(7) a. ta zuo le.
         he do   LE⁴
         'He did (something).'

     b. ta xihuan.
         he like
         'He likes (something).'

   vs.

(8) a. ta shui le.
         he sleep LE
         'He slept.'

     b. ta xiangdang yingjun.
         he quite   handsome
         'He is quite handsome.'

What is interesting in Chinese, as noted in many linguistics works, is that the division in Chinese between transitive and intransitive verbs is not very clear, and argument structure in Chinese is not easy to define (see Chen 2004; Cheng 2009; Guo 1999; Hu 2007, 2008, 2010; Lin 2001; Shen 2006; Teng 1975; Xiong 2009; Xu and Shen 1998; Yang 2007a, 2007b; Yuan 1998, 2003, 2004; Zhan 1999, 2004; Zhou 1997; among many others). For instance, even though *shui* 'sleep' in (8a) is generally considered intransitive, it allows a noun phrase immediately following it:

(9) a. ta shui da chuang.
         he sleep big bed
         'He sleeps on the big bed.'

---

⁴ *Le* in Chinese can occur either as a sentence-final particle indicating change of state or can be suffixed to a verb as a perfective aspect marker. When *le* follows a non-stative verb at the end of a sentence, its function is less clear. It could be the combination of both *le*'s or one of them. We leave the distinctions aside and simply gloss all the occurrences of *le* as LE.

b. ta zhi shui baitian.
    he only sleep day.time
    'He only sleeps in the daytime.'

Moreover, as noted in the works cited earlier and others, the types of nominal phrases (NPs) in the object position in Chinese raise interesting questions, as the position seems to allow a variety of NPs in place of canonical objects, in contrast to the relative rigidity of complement selection in English.[5] The examples in (2a–c) illustrate the possibility of a temporal, locative, and instrument NP in place of canonical objects, and these NPs roughly correspond to preverbal PPs modifying the verb phrase (preverbal adjunct PPs), as in (3a–c). The question is what the postverbal nominal phrases in (2a–c) are. Are they objects or not? In what sense are they or are they not objects?[6]

---

[5] English allows a certain degree of flexibility with certain verbs, such as the following examples: *He likes to fly a Boeing. He works evenings and weekends.* However, they are much more restricted than in Chinese.

[6] Lin (2001) claims that a non-canonical object can also be a reason expression, expressed by the light verb FOR. Examples are like (i–ii):

(i)   ta shi chi haowan de.
      he be eat fun   DE
      'He was eating for fun.'

(ii) tamen ku   guo-po-jia-wang
      they cry country-break-home-perish
      'They cried for the disintegration of country and the perish of home.'

According to Lin, (i–ii) correspond to (iii–iv) with a preverbal *wei* 'for'-phrase:

(iii) ta wei haowan chi.
       he for fun   eat
       'He was eating for fun.'

(iv)   tamen wei guo-po-jia-wang   ku
       they for country-break-home-perish cry
       'They cried for the disintegration of country and the perish of home.'

However, (i) and (ii) are not quite the same. The former generally has a predicate following the verb (*haowan* 'good to play') and occurs in the (*shi*) ... *de* 'copula ... sentence-final-particle' construction. The latter has the typical V-Object form and does not have to occur in the (*shi*)... *de* pattern:

(v) a. tamen zai ku shenme?   cf. b. ta chi shenme?
         they at cry what   he eat what
         'What are they crying at?'   'What does he eat?' (no reason reading)

We will take (v.a) (and therefore (ii)) as a regular transitive verb construction, like (vi.a) in English:

(vi) a. He mourned the loss.
cf.   b. He cried   at the loss.

Similarly *xiao* 'laugh' can be the equivalent of the English *laugh at/ridicule,* as in *ta xiao wo* 'he ridiculed me.' That is, *ku/xiao*, etc., in such constructions can simply be transitive verbs. The objects following such verbs are typical objects.

The construction in (i) can be analyzed as a structure containing a stative predicate (the predicate following the verb), which accommodates the fact that it occurs in the (*shi*) ... *de* pattern.

3. Non-Canonical Objects

Syntactically, a postverbal non-canonical object NP behaves very much like a canonical object,[7] because it has the same properties as a canonical object such as the ones in the following examples (see Li 2011):

(10)   a.   Non-canonical objects, like canonical objects, can be any type of nominal expression, definite, indefinite, or quantificational.

   b.   A non-canonical object is an NP. It is not an Adv or PP (the P of the corresponding preverbal adjunct PP does not appear postverbally).

   c.   It is in complementary distribution with a canonical object.

   d.   It can occur with a postverbal duration/frequency phrase, taking the same position as a canonical object relative to these other postverbal phrases. V-reduplication is possible in these cases, just like canonical objects. This is also true when the V is directly followed by a *de* phrase of description or result.

   e.   It can have narrow scope with respect to the duration/frequency phrase, like a canonical object.

   f.   It allows object deletion, just like canonical objects.[8]

   g.   Like a canonical object, a non-canonical object can also combine with V to take an affected outer object.

Note that for some speakers (especially northern Chinese), the verb preceding the stative predicate needs to be followed by the durative aspect marker *zhe*,

(vii)   ta shi chi-zhe haowan de.
    he be eat-ing fun   DE
    'He was eating for fun.'

This is not a V-Object construction and will not be included in the constructions illustrating non-canonical objects.

   [7] Zhang (2005) observes that a non-canonical object differs from the corresponding adjunct semantically in that a verb generally should have an effect on a non-canonical object. Unfortunately, it is not easy to define what it means for a verb to have an effect on a non-canonical object, making this intuition difficult to state clearly. For instance, it is not clear what this would mean for a sentence like *wo xihuan shui baitian* 'I like to sleep (in the) daytime.'

   [8] However, not all non-canonical objects can be deleted equally. The more established, institutionalized, or commonly used the form [V + non-canonical object] is, the easier it is to have the object missing. It could be that object deletion is more closely related to lexical subcategorization (Li 2005). This qualification applies to (h) as well.

Moreover, the use of the experiential aspect marker *guo* tends to make the deletion of non-canonical objects better. For instance, (ii) is not as good as (i); but (iii) is quite acceptable:

(i)   ta kan   na-bu dianying, wo ye   kan.
    he watch that-CL movie   I   also watch
    'He watched that movie; I also watched (that movie).'

(ii)   ??ta kan   zaoshang, wo ye   kan.
    he watch morning   I   also watch
    'He watched (something) in mornings; I also watched.'

(iii)   ta kan-guo zaoshang, wo ye   kan-guo.
    he watch-ASP morning   I   also watch-ASP
    'He has watched (something) in mornings; I have also watched.'

h. Like a canonical object, a non-canonical object can occur in the construction [. . . de Ø], (a structure distinguishing arguments and adjuncts (see, among many others, Zhu 1961). That is, if an argument undergoes relativization, the relativized argument can be deleted. In contrast, a relativized adjunct cannot be deleted (see Aoun and Li 2003, chapter 5, for detailed discussion on this argument/adjunct asymmetry).

i. As with arguments (objects), long-distance topicalization or relativization of such a non-canonical object is possible.

Property (10a) is illustrated with the following examples:

(11) a. yao hua ji-zhang   zhi ne?   -quantificational
     need draw how.many-CL paper Q
     'How many pieces of paper to draw on?'

    b. buyao hua na-mian qiang.   -definite
     don't draw that-CL wall
     'Don't draw on that wall.'

    c. jiao bang-tiao. hong shengzi.   -indefinite
     foot tie-CL   red   string
     'The foot was tied with a red string.'

The impossibility of an adverb or the P of the corresponding preverbal PP in (10b) is demonstrated in the following examples:

(12) a. ta changchang chi mian   ---Adv-V
     he often   eat noodle
     'He eats noodle often.'

    b. *ta chi changchang   --- *V-Adv
     he eat often

(13) a. ta cong qi dian dao jiu dian chi zaofan.   ---PP-V
     he from 7 o' clock to 9 o' clock eat breakfast
     'He eats breakfast from 7 to 9 o'clock.'

    b. ta chi (*cong) qi dian dao jiu dian   ---*V-PP
     he eat from 7 o' clock to 9 o' clock

A non-canonical object and a canonical object are in complementary distribution—property (10c):

(14) *wo chi wancan fandian/fandian   wancan   —*complementary distribution*
     I   eat dinner restaurant/restaurant dinner

Just as a canonical object is able to occur with a frequency/duration phrase, so can a non-canonical object (a definite one tends to precede the duration/frequency phrase and a bare nominal object follows the duration/frequency), as stated in (10d):

(15) a. wo shang xingqi chi-le san-ci/tian   mian/fandian.   *- fre/dur + bare object*
     I   last   week eat-LE three-times/day noodle/restaurant
     'I ate noodles/at restaurants three times/days last week.'

    b. wo shang xingqi chi-le na-zhong mian/na-jia   fandian
     I   last   week eat-LE that-CL   noodle/that-CL restaurant
     san-ci/tian.   *– def obj + fre/dur*
     three-times/day
     'I ate that noodle/at that restaurant three times/days last week.'

V-reduplication is possible with non-canonical objects and other postverbal phrases such as duration/frequency and *de* expressions, just like the cases involving canonical objects:

(16)   wo **chi** mian/haohua fandian   **chi**-le henduo ci/tian   —*V-reduplication with fre/dur*
      I   eat noodle/fancy restaurant eat-LE many   time/day
      'I ate noodle/at fancy restaurants many times/days.'

(17)   wo **chi** mian/haohua fandian   **chi**-de hen
      I   eat noodle/fancy restaurant eat-DE very
      gaoxing/lei   —*V-reduplication with de-phrases*[9]
      happy/tired
      'I am happy/tired from eating noodle/at fancy restaurants.'

In the same way that a canonical object can have narrow scope with respect to a duration/frequency phrase, a non-canonical object can also take narrow scope, as noted in (10e):

(18)   a.   ta chi-guo liangci niurou huo/he zhurou   —*canonical object narrow scope*
         he eat-ASP twice beef   or/and pork
         'He ate twice beef or/and pork.'

      b.   ta chi-guo liangci zhong   canting   huo/he
         he eatASP twice   Chinese restaurant or/and
         xi canting.   - *non-canonical obj. narrow scope*
         western   restaurant
         'He ate twice in Chinese or/and Western restaurants.'

Some non-canonical objects can also undergo object deletion, like canonical objects (10f) (see note 8):

(19)   ta chang chi mian/haohua canting; wo bu chang chi ___. —*object deletion*
      he often eat noodle/fancy restaurant I   not often eat
      'He often eats noodle/at fancy restaurants; I don't often eat (noodle/at fancy restaurants)'

In addition, as noted in (10g), a non-canonical object can behave like a canonical object and combine with a verb to take an "affected" object (inner and outer object; cf. among many others, Thompson 1973; Lu 2002; Zhan 1999; Huang 2007). For instance, the canonical inner object in (20a, b) can be replaced with a non-canonical object (the examples in (20) are adapted from Lu 2002):

(20)   a.   wo chi-le ta   san-ge   pingguo.
         I   eat-LE him three-CL apple
         'I ate him three apples = he was affected by my eating (his) three apples.'

      b.   wo jian-le ta   shi-gongchi bu.
         I   cut-LE him ten-meter   cloth
         'I cut ten meters of cloth from him.'

(21)   a.   wo (cai) chi-le ta   san-tian Fanguan (ta jiu yijing shou-bu-liao le)
         I   only eat-LE him three-day restaurant he then already put-not-up LE
         'I (only) ate at restaurants for three days on him (and he already could not take it).'

---

[9] In Chinese, what occurs postverbally is limited. In addition to objects, a verb can be followed by the grammatical marker *de* and an adjectival phrase or clause expressing the manner, extent, or result of an action/event.

b. wo (cai) jian-le ta   san-ba   jiandao (ta jiu yijing bu gaoxing le)
    I   only cut-LE him three-CL scissors he then already not happy   LE
    'I (only) cut with three pairs of scissors on him (and he already was not happy).'

The following are some more examples illustrating the ability of a non-canonical object combining with a V to license an affected object:[10]

(22) a. wo xie-le   ta   yigong   san-zhi maobi
          I   write-LE him altogther three-CL brush.pen
          'I wrote with three brush pens (of his) altogether.'

      b. wo jiu   qie-le ta   san-ba   daozi
          I   only cut-CL him three-CL knife
          'I only cut with three knives (of his).'

      c. wo xie-le   ta   san   da-zhang zhi.
          I   write-LE him three big-CL   paper
          'I wrote on three big pieces of paper on him.'

The examples above show that canonical objects syntactically behave like non-canonical objects.

Regarding (10h), there is a substantial number of cases showing that non-canonical objects are like arguments, according to the test using the relativization construction without an overt noun phrase following *de*. Briefly, if an argument undergoes relativization to appear in the position following *de* [[$_{rel. cl.}$ ... t$_i$...] *de* [NP$_i$]], the relativized NP can be deleted. However, relativization of an adjunct does not allow the noun phrase following *de* to be empty (see Aoun and Li 2003, chapters 5–6 for details).[11]

(23) a. [ta chi de] dou shi hao   dongxi. --- *argument relativization*
          he eat DE all   be good thing
          'All he eats are good things.'

      b. *[ta chi fan   de] (dou) shi hao   liyou. --- *adjunct relativization*
          he eat meal DE all   be good reason
          intended to mean 'The reasons why he eats meals are good reasons.'

A non-canonical object can undergo relativization and be deleted, just like an argument:

(24) a. ta chi de (canting)   dou shi haohua canting.
          he eat DE (restaurant) all   be fancy   restaurant
          '(The restaurants where) he ate were fancy restaurants.'

      b. zhe-shuang kuaizi   jiu   shi ta chi de (kuaizi).
          this-CL   chopsticks exactly be he eat DE chopsticks
          'This pair of chopsticks was (the chopsticks) he ate with.'

---

[10] It is difficult to find examples with time expressions as non-canonical objects in such constructions because generally the inner and outer object bear some relation, such as a possession or affectedness relation (see Huang 2007 for examples not bearing a possession relation, even though an "affected" relation still holds).

[11] The *de* in this construction is a modification marker within a noun phrase, different from the *de* mentioned in note (8).

   c. zhe-ba dao jiu   shi ta qie de (dao).
       this-CL knife exactly be he cut de knife
       'This knife was exactly (the knife) he cut with.'

   d. ta xie   de (zhi) jiu   shi zhe-zhong zhi.
       he write DE paper exactly be this-kind paper
       '(The paper) he wrote on was exactly this kind of paper.'

   e. ta kan de (shijian) shi wanshang, bu shi zaoshang.
       he see DE time   be evening   not be morning
       '(The time when) he saw (something) was in the evening, not in the morning.'

Finally, long-distance relativization or topicalization of a non-canonical object is illustrated in the following:

Long-distance topicalization of a non-canonical object:

(25) a. zhe-zhi bi, wo zhidao dou hai meiyou ren   xie-guo.
       this-CL pen I   know all yet not.have person write-ASP
       'This pen, I know that nobody has ever written (with) ＿＿＿ yet.'

   b. na-jia   gongsi, wo zhidao ta zuo-guo.
       that-CL company I   know he work-ASP
       'That company, I know that he has worked (at) ＿＿＿ .'

   c. qi-dian   dao jiu-dian, wo zhidao meiyou ren   yuanyi zuo.
       7-o'clock to   9-o'clock I   know not.have peson willing do
       '7 to 9 o'clock, I know that nobody would be willing to work (at) ＿＿＿ .'

Long-distance relativization of a non-canonical object:

(26) a. wo zhidao dou hai meiyou ren   xie-guo de zhe-zhi bi
       I   know all yet not.have person write-ASP DE this-CL pen
       'the pen that I know that nobody has ever written (with) ＿＿＿ yet'

   b. wo zhidao ta zuo-guo de na-jia   gongsi
       I   know he work-ASP DE that-CL company
       'the company that I know that he has ever worked (at) ＿＿＿ '

   c. wo zhidao meiyou ren   yuanyi zuo de na-duan   shijian
       I   know not.have peson willing do DE that-period time
       'the period of time when I know that nobody would be willing to work (at) ＿＿＿ .'

In short, the examples in (12)–(26), illustrating the points in (10a–i), identify the similarities between non-canonical objects and canonical objects.[12] Their identical behavior and their complementary distribution suggest that the two types of objects should occupy the same syntactic position.

4. PPs Without Corresponding Non-Canonical Objects

The examples above show that the "adjunct-like" temporal, locative, and instrument phrases can occupy the postverbal object position. They roughly correspond to

---

[12] Due to limited space, not every point is illustrated with examples comparing the behavior of canonical with non-canonical objects.

preverbal PPs. However, not all types of preverbal PPs behave alike. Some do not have the possibility of a corresponding postverbal non-canonical NP, such as benefactives, comitatives, goals(recipients) in non-subcategorized cases. The cases with benefactives and comitatives are illustrated in (5)–(6).[13] Goals are more complicated. They can occur in the bare NP form postverbally with a few verbs that are subcategorized for double objects, such as *song* 'give' (see, for instance, Tang 1978 for the different types of double object constructions in Chinese).

(27) a. wo song zhe-ben shu   gei shu-shang.
     I   give this-CL book to book-merchant
     'I gave this book to book merchants.'

   b. wo song (gei) shu-shang   zhe-ben shu.
     I   give to   book-merchant this-CL book
     'I gave book merchants this book.'

   c. zhe-ben shu   song (gei) shu-shang.
     this-CL book give to   book-merchant
     'This book was given to book merchants.'

Verbs that can be directional in interpretation, such as *qu* 'go', *fei* 'fly', *diao* 'drop,' can also be followed by a locative noun phrase and can be interpreted as the destination of the event:[14]

(28) a. ta qu shudian.
     he go book.store
     'He goes to the bookstore.'

   b. ta fei Shanghai.[15]
     he fly Shanghai
     'He flies to Shanghai.'

   c. shu   diao di-shang   le.
     book drop ground-top LE
     'The book fell on the ground.'

---

[13] Even when the canonical object is present, made possible by an additional copy of the verb, a benefactive still cannot occur as a non-canonical object (cf. Pylkkänen 2008 on the need of an object to license a low applicative):

(i) *zhu jiaren zhu fan   or   *zhu fan zhu jiaren
    cook family cook meal   cook meal cook family

[14] Chia-fen Wu (personal communication) raised the question of whether the postverbal locative phrases in these cases were non-canonical objects. It is possible to take these as non-canonical objects because the relevant verbs 'go/fly/fall' can occur without any complements, just like their counterparts in English, which requires prepositions to occur with the locative noun phrases. Nonetheless, distinguishing between canonical objects and non-canonical objects might not be significant grammatically—both are the noun phrases that can take the object position.

[15] *Fei* 'fly' need not be directional, illustrated by the following sentence:

(i) taikongsuo   fei wai   taikong
    space.shuttle fly outer space
    'Space shuttles fly in the outer space.'

For the verbs not subcategorized for double objects, such as *ji* 'mail,' *da* as in *da-dianhua* 'make-phone call,' the goal marker *gei* 'give, to' is required and [V-goal NP] is not possible:

(29) a. wo ji   zhe-ben shu *(gei) shu-shang.
         I   mail this-CL book to   book-merchant
         'I mailed this book to book merchants.'

      b. wo/zhe-ben shu ji *(gei) shu-shang.
         I/this-CL   book to book-merchant
         'I mailed (something) to book merchants/This book was mailed to book merchants.'

(30) a. wo da   dianhua *(gei) kehu.
         I   make call   to   client
         'I made phone calls to clients.'

      b. zhe-ge dianhua da   *(gei) kehu.
         this-CL call   make to client
         'This call was made to clients.'

In addition, it seems that recipient-goals and destination-goals should be distinguished. Compare (27)–(29) with (31):

(31) a. wo ji   zhe-ben shu dao Luoshanji.
         I   mail this-CL book to LosAngeles
         'I am mailing this book to Los Angeles.'

      b. zhe-ben shu ji   Luoshanji.
         this-CL book mail LosAngeles
         'This is to mail to Los Angeles.'

The examples in this section show that, in contrast to those in the previous section, some PPs do not have corresponding non-canonical objects.

5. "Institutionalized" Non-Canonical Objects

The interpretation of a non-canonical object, that is, its relation with the related verb, is generally "conventionalized" or "institutionalized." This is not different from how canonical objects are interpreted. After all, the relation between a verb and its subcategorized object probably is the most established and conventionalized. In contrast, the PPs corresponding to non-canonical objects are interpreted according to the Ps. The relation with the related verb is not subject to the notion of "conventionalized/institutionalized." The difference in interpreting non-canonical objects and adjunct PPs can be illustrated by the contrast in the pairs of examples below.

(32) a. wo (cong) qi dian dao jiu dian kan haizi.   -the time of the event
         I   from   7 o' clock to   9 o' clock care children
         'I care(d) for children from 7 to 9 o'clock.'

      b. wo kan qi   dian dao jiu dian. -the 7-9 shift/work
         I   care 7 o' clock to   9 o' clock
         'I care(d) from 7 to 9 o'clock.'

The sentence in (33a) below with a non-canonical object denotes a guard's duties. In contrast, (33b) with a preverbal adjunct simply describes the time/location of the activities.

(33) a ta zhan zaoshang/waimian.
            he stand morning/outside
            'He stands (guard) in the mornings/outside.'

      b. ta zai zaoshang/waimian zhan (gang).
            he at morning/outside stand (guard)
            'He is standing (guard) in the morning/outside.'

The non-canonical object (34a) below denotes restaurant food (which can be take-outs and eaten at places other than restaurants), in contrast to the adjunct PP expressing the place of eating.

(34) a. ta chi canting
            he eat restaurant -meals are restaurant food (see Zhang 2005)

      b. ta zai canting chi
            he at restaurant eat -the place of eating is at restaurants
            'He ate at restaurants.'

Sun and Li (2010, 22) note that the non-canonical object construction generally expresses types, categories (*leibie*). The type reading is also clear in (35a), which expresses the type of flights, 'evening flights,' in contrast to morning flights, for instance.[16] The adjunct PP in (35b) simply expresses the time of flying.

(35) a. wo fei wanshang.
            I fly evening
            'I fly evenings = fly evening flights.'

      b. wo zai wanshang fei.
            I at evening fly
            'I fly/am flying in the evening.'

In addition, if the relation between the verb and a potential non-canonical object is not conventionalized or institutionalized, then the use of such a non-canonical object is much less acceptable (see Lin 2001 on conventionalized meanings). For instance, (36b) is much less acceptable than (36a) because eating with chopsticks is much more established than eating with a fork in the Chinese culture.

---

[16] The translation should not suggest that the non-canonical object is the XP in a noun phrase [XP *de* YP], with XP modifying the noun phrase YP and [*de* YP] being deleted:

(i) wo zuo [wanshang ~~de gongzuo~~]
    I do evening DE work
    I do evening work.'

Were (i) a possible derivation, it would not be expected why such a temporal phrase cannot occur in other positions and be interpreted as [XP *de* YP] with [*de*YP] deleted.

(ii) wo ba [wanshang ~~de gongzuo~~] zuo le.
     I BA evening DE work do LE
     'I did evening work.'

(36) a. ni   jiu   chi zhe-shuang kuaizi   ba!
          you then eat this-pair   chopsticks Particle
          'You eat with this pair of chopsticks!'

      b. ni   jiu   chi zhe-ba chazi ba!
          you then eat this-CL fork Particle
          'You eat with this fork!'

The discussions so far demonstrate that some adjunct-looking expressions (temporal, locative, and instrument) can take the object position, with requirements on their meanings being conventionalized or institutionalized. However, there are some others that systematically lack the possibility of being a non-canonical object—benefactives, comitatives, recipient-goals.

6. Noun-Incorporation

Very interestingly and even strikingly, a similar contrast in the availability of a non-canonical NP roughly corresponding to an adjunct PP discussed in the previous sections is found in noun incorporation (NI) languages, and NI exhibits a very similar range of (im)possibilities as non-canonical objects.

NI is attested in numerous languages around the world (Mithun 1984; Massam 2009; Gerdts 1998). In many languages with NI, the incorporated variant exists alongside an analytic variant.[17] The nominal root *nakt* ('bed') has been incorporated into the verbal complex in (37b).

(37) a. Wa'-k-hnínu-'   ne ka-nákt-a'.   [Mohawk, Iroquoian]
          FACT-1.SG-buy-PUNC NE 3.SG.NT.AG-bed-NFS
          'I bought a/the bed.'

      b. Wa'-ke-**nakt**-a-hnínu-'.
          FACT-1.SG-bed-JOIN-buy-PUNC
          'I bought a/the bed.'   (Baker 1996: 279)

NI has been shown to exhibit several properties cross-linguistically. First, NI constructions typically have non-compositional, idiomatic, or institutionalized meanings (Mithun 1984, Dayal 2011). Note the idiosyncratic and institutionalized readings in the following Onondaga examples (Woodbury 2003).

(38) a. wa' gǫya' dahdǫ' da'
          wa'- kǫ- ya't- ahtǫ-   't-   a'
          FACT- I:you- body- disappear- CAUS- PUNC
          'I lost you (e.g., in a crowd).'

---

[17] Glosses from Iroquoian examples have been altered to be uniform with the rest of the text here. Glosses from examples from other languages are retained in their original forms. The following non-obvious abbreviations are used. AG = agent (S in Baker); CIS = cislocative; FACT = factual; JOIN = joiner vowel (an epenthetic vowel in NI constructions in Iroquoian languages); LV = light verb; NE = ne' (a nominal particle); NFS = noun forming suffix; NT = neuter (N in Baker); PAT = patient (O in Baker); PUNC = punctual.

b. hathwisdanųhna⁷
ha-   at-   hwist- a-   nųhn -a⁷
3.SG.M.AG- SRFL- money- JOIN- guard -STAT
'He is a treasurer.'

Second, NI constructions are typically found to be not fully productive (cf. *at school* or *at church* but not **at airport*; see Stvan 2009. See Mithun 1984 for a discussion on the range of productivity of NI in Northern Iroquoian and other languages). A further significant property, relating to the occurrence of NI with elements other than themes, is discussed less frequently. However, it is pervasively noted in the literature. NI in many languages is typically illustrated with a canonical direct object— a theme—as the incorporated noun (IN), but NI is not restricted to direct objects. Instruments, paths, and locatives also often productively incorporate (Mithun 1984, 2004; Spencer 1995; Muro 2009). We illustrate this with Onondaga (Woodbury 2003: 282, 928, respectively), (39); Chukchi (Spencer, ex (58a)), (40); and Southern Nahuatl (Merlan 1976), (41).[18]

(39) a. honathahidákhe⁷
          hon-   at-   hah- itakhe -⁷
          3.PL.M.NOM-SREFL-path-run   -PUNC
          'They are walking on a path.'

      b. wa⁷hage⁷nhyayę́ hda⁷
          wa⁷-   hak-   ⁷nhy- a-   yęt-ha⁷
          FACT-3.SG.M.AG:1.SG.PAT-stick- JOIN-hit   -PUNC
          'He hit me with a stick.'

(40) gətg=əlqət-g?e walwəŋən
      lake=go-3.SG. sraven.ABS.SG
      'Raven went to the lake.'

(41) ya? kikočillotete?ki panci
      3.SG 3.SG-it-knife-cut bread
      'He cut the bread with the knife.'

Note, however, that comitatives, benefactives, and recipient-goals cannot undergo NI in virtually any language. We illustrate this with Mohawk (Baker 1996: 207), (42), which is ungrammatical on the intended reading, but possible with the nonsensical reading in square brackets. Observe also the data from Onondaga (Gloria Williams, Nora Carrier, speakers), and Cayuga (Barb Garlow, speaker).

(42) *t-   a'-   ke- wir- u-   '   ne athvno
      CIS- FACT- 1sS- baby- give- PUNC NE ball
      ('I gave the ball to the baby.') [ok as, 'I gave the baby to the ball.']

(43) a. ękhewíhsa:tha:s   ne⁷Meri
          ę-khe-wíhsa:th-aR-s-Ø   ne⁷ Mary
          FUT-1SG:3FEM.INDEF-butter-apply-BEN-PUNC ne Mary
          'I will butter it for Mary.'

---

[18] We have found very few examples of the incorporation of true temporals in Northern Iroquoian. We attribute this gap to the fact that many of the nouns relating to time in Northern Iroquoian are not of the right shape morphologically to be incorporated.

b. wa²hetcihsag²hgwa²
   wa²-   he-   atci-   hsR-   a-   k²hkw -a²
   FACT- 1SG:3M.SG- friend- NZRL- JOIN- hit-   -PUNC
   'I hit my friend.'

c. *ękhetcihsa:sne²owíhsa²
   ę-khe-atci-hsR-aR-s-Ø   ne² o-wihs-a²
   FUT-1SG:3FEM.INDEF-friend-NZLR-apply-BEN-PUNC NE butter
   'I will butter it for my friend.'

d. *ękhetcihsa:kne²owíhsa²
   ę-khe-atci-hsR-aR-k   ne² o-wihs-a²
   FUT-1SG:3FEM.INDEF-friend-NZLR-apply-PUNC NE butter
   'I will butter it for my friend.'

(44) a. John tóhháhe: ²Ganáthae:²
        John toh   he-a²-ha-e:²   Ganáthae:²
        John there   TRANSLOC-FACT-3.SG.M.AG-go-PUNC Brantford
        'John went to Brantford.'

     b. John ne² hni² honatsih Ganáthae: ²tóhha² hęne²
        John ne² hni² honatsih Ganáthae:² toh   he-a²-hęne²
        John NE and his.friend Brantford   there TRANSLOC-FACT-3.PL.M.AG-go-punc
        'John went to Brantford with his friend.'

     c. *John tóh   hatsihę: ²Ganáthae:²
        John toh   ha-tsi-hę:²   Ganáthae:²
        John there 3.SG.M.AG-friend-go-PUNC Brantford
        ('John went to Brantford with a friend.')

Combining the observations regarding the NI and non-canonical object constructions, we can reach the following generalization:

(45)   *Object Usurper Generalization*

   Locatives (including paths, destinations), instruments, and temporals can behave as direct objects syntactically. Benefactives, recipients, and comitatives cannot.

How can such a generalization be understood and accounted for? We approach this issue in section 7.

7. Toward an Account

We begin this discussion with the following questions.

(46) a. Why is it that some adjuncts seem to be able to take the object position (function as object usurpers) but others cannot?

     b. What is common to NI in Northern Iroquoian languages and non-canonical objects in Chinese such that they show the same behavior with respect to (a)?

We propose that what is common to these constructions is the availability of an argument position not occupied by canonical objects and the object usurper's ability to take advantage of this opportunity because they do not have to be licensed by Ps (or other functors such as applicatives) thematically.

7.1. AVAILABLE ARGUMENT POSITION

In Northern Iroquoian it is generally possible to incorporate a noun to a verb. The verb can be intransitive and therefore does not have a canonical object. The verb can also be transitive and the canonical object occurs in a non-incorporated, verb-external object position. In either of these two cases, there is no object incorporated to the verb and another noun can take advantage of the vacancy and be incorporated. Consider the following examples.

(47) a. honathahidákhe⁷
  hon-   at- hah- itakhe- ⁷
  3.PL.M.NOM-SREFL-path-run -PUNC
  'They are walking on a path.'

 b. wa⁷hage⁷nhyayę́hda⁷
  wa⁷- hak-   ⁷nhy- a- yęt -ha⁷
  FACT-3.SG.M.AG:1.SG.PAT- stick-JOIN- hit -PUNC
  'He hit me with a stick.'

In Mandarin Chinese, the postverbal object position does not have to be occupied by a canonical object. When there are two phrases in the postverbal position that need to be adjacent to the verb, there can be two copies of the verb to license each of the two phrases:

(48) a. ta meitian **kan** shu **kan** san-ge xiaoshi.
  he everyday read book read three-CL hour
  'He reads books for three hours every day.'

 b. ta laoshi **chi** rou **chi** da-kuai, **he** tang **he** xiao-wan
  he always eat meat eat big-piece drink soup drink small-bowl
  'He always eats big pieces when eating meat, drinks small bowls when drinking soup.'

The canonical object can also be a topic (with or without the verb accompanying the topicalized object).

(49) a. (kan) dianshi ta zhi kan banye.
  watch TV he only watch mid-night
  '(Watching) TV, he only watches (TV at) midnight.'

 b. (kan) yuan-de dongxi ta laoshi kan zuo yan.
  watch far-DE thing he always watch left eye
  '(Watching) things at a distance, he always watches (with) the left eye.'

 c. (he) cha, zaoshang he da bei, wanshang he xiao bei.
  drink tea morning drink big cup evening drink small cup
  '(For drinking) tea, drink big cups in the morning, drink small cups in the evening.'

In addition, the object of certain verbs can sometimes be the subject of the sentence and a non-canonical object appears postverbally:

(50) yuan-de dongxi kan zuo yan; jin-de   dongxi kan you   yan.
      far-DE   thing   see left eye   near-DE thing   see right eye
      'Things at a distance are seen with the left eye; things near are seen
      with the right eye.'

Alternatively, one may simply say that objects do not have to be realized in Chinese, because verbs in Chinese, an analytic language in the sense that verbs are quite bare in feature specifications, are not specified with thematic features (Lin 2001; Huang 2005, 2006, Chapter 1 of this volume; also Williams, Chapter 11 of this volume).

In short, the postverbal object position in Chinese and the incorporated nominal position in NI languages are possible positions for nouns or noun phrases that are not canonical objects because the latter can be realized elsewhere or need not occur.

7.2. OBJECT USURPERS VERSUS OBJECT NON-USURPERS

We propose that there are certain prepositions that carry only a case-assigning function and do not assign thematic roles to their objects. These include temporals and locatives in the following examples.

(51) a. zai zhuo-shang zai xuexiao-waimian
          at table-top   at school-outside
          'on the table'   'outside the school'

      b. zai zhuo-xia   zai xuexiao-limian
          at table-under at school-inside
          'under the table' 'inside the school'

A localizer combines with a (common) noun to become a locative noun. Together they can be the object of *zai* '(be) at.' The need for the preposition *zai* depends on where the locative noun phrase appears. It is needed when the expression is a preverbal adjunct. If it occurs in the subject or object position, the preposition *zai* does not occur. Thus, the preposition *zai* is responsible only for Case assignment (Li 1985, 1990).

(52) a. women yixiang *(zai) xuexiao-waimian chi fan.
          we   always   at   school-outside   eat meal
          'We always eat outside the school.'

      b. women yixiang chi (*zai) xuexiao-waimian.
          we   always   eat at   school-outside.
          'We always eat outside the school.'

(53) a. women zhi   *(zai) wanshang zuo shi.
          we   only   at   evening   do work
          'We only work at evenings.'

      b. women yixiang zuo (*zai) wanshang.
          we   always   do   at   evening
          'We always work at evenings.'

This is reminiscent of bare NP adverbs in Larson (1985), which are noun phrases with a feature that allows them not to require prepositions for Case assignment. What we have here is an adverb-like noun phrase that does not need a P for thematic assignment. Observe also that an instrument P is not always needed to express the instrument interpretation in English.

(54) a. This pen generally writes smoothly.

  b. That knife cuts beautifully.

  c. A sharp knife cuts better than a dull knife.

Our examples have demonstrated that temporals, locatives, and instruments can be object usurpers. In contrast, it seems difficult to find any instances using a noun phrase as a comitative without any comitative marking (marking by a distinct comitative Case or P, or an applicative). We refer to this type as "object non-usurper" based on the observations in the previous section. These elements require some marking to make a noun phrase obtain the intended adjunct interpretation. Another example is that of benefactives. Unless there is an applicative construction or a benefactive marked by Case or P, it seems impossible to find an instance of a non-marked nominal interpreted as a benefactive. Recipients seem to generally require some marking as well—applicative, (inherent) Case or a special preposition.

For convenience, we refer to the special markings such as applicatives, adpositions, and case markers that mark the grammatical functions of arguments as functors. Arguments with functors are interpreted according to their co-occurring functors. In contrast, those without functors are not accompanied with grammatical indications of the thematic roles they play. They are interpreted according to an institutionalized or conventionalized relation with the related verb (or the event), that is, our institutionalized world knowledge of how participants are related to activities or events. For instance, an activity of writing, cutting, and so on, conventionally takes place with an instrument, and a particular instrument is conventionally associated with such an activity. An activity can also be conventionally situated in a time or place. Accordingly, instrument, temporal, and locative phrases are typically associated with activity verbs. Types of activities may also be associated with different locative expressions. For instance, with a directional movement verb, the locative nominal related to it without a functor is interpreted as the destination of the movement, as illustrated by the Chinese directional verb like *qu* 'go' or *lai* 'come.'

(55) qu/lai   xuexiao/jiaotang/yiyuan
go/come   school/church/hospital
'go/come to school/church/hospital'

(56) a. qu ta   nali
go him there
'go to him'

  b. lai   wo zher
come me here
'come to me'

The locative noun phrases in these cases must be interpreted as destination points. In contrast, the locative noun phrase in the object position of a non-directional activity verb can only denote the location where the activity takes place, as in (57), because the activity of running is non-directional.

(57) ta xihuan pao gongyuan.[19]
    he like   run park
    'He likes to run in the park.'

The way to interpret non-canonical objects may be naturally extended to interpreting other arguments without functors, such as canonical objects. That is, there should be no significant differences in the mechanisms for interpreting canonical and non-canonical objects in Chinese, as noted in passing in note (14) and the beginning of section 5. Both sets do not have co-occurring functors specifying interpretations (applicatives, specific case markers, Ps). They both denote the participants whose relations with the activities expressed by the related verbs are conventionally established. This may also give us an answer as to why Chinese prominently allows non-canonical objects when many other languages do not, which is elaborated below.

Let us compare English and Chinese. English has verbs that optionally take objects. The question is why the non-occurrence of an object in such cases does not productively allow a non-canonical object to occur. For instance, the verb *eat* in English is not required to take an object; but a non-canonical object in its object position is still difficult. A preposition generally cannot be deleted. The sentence in (58b) is acceptable without *at* only if *fancy restaurants* is interpreted as the object that is eaten.

(58) a. John likes to eat.

    b. John likes to eat *(at) fancy restaurants.

Why is it that the noun phrase following the verb in the English sentence in (58b) has to be interpreted as the canonical object of the verb, but the corresponding Chinese one need not be? We propose that this is due to the absence of case morphology in Chinese.

7.3. CASE MORPHOLOGY

A prominent common property shared by non-canonical objects in Chinese and the incorporated noun in NI languages is the absence of case morphology. As is well known, Chinese does not have any overt case markings.[20] Incorporated nouns in NI constructions do not have any case markings, either.[21] We show next that the absence

---

[19] When more than one conventional relation is institionalized between an activity and a participant, ambiguity arises. For instance, the following sentence is three-way ambiguous.

(i) qing ni xie   zhe-zhi maobi.
    please you write this-CL brush.pen
    'Please write with this brush pen.'

'This brush pen' in this example can indicate a locative, an instrument, or a theme: write on this brush pen, write with this brush pen, write the words 'this brush pen.'

[20] In fact, it has been suggested that the notion of abstract Case is not relevant in Chinese (Hu 2007; Markman 2009). We will return to this issue in section 8.

[21] The full NP in the canonical object position is not overtly case-marked, either. However, it triggers agreement (Northern Iroquoian has both subject and object agreement); whereas incorporated nouns consistently fail to trigger agreement.

of case morphology allows a noun phrase without a functor to occur in the object position.

Recall that if functors exist, the interpretation of the related arguments would be restricted by such functors. Ps, overt case morphology and applicatives are functors (or at least are indicative of the existence of a functor). In noun incorporation patterns, the noun is not case marked. The observed non-canonical objects occur in Chinese, which is a language that does not have any overt case markings. In other words, in both noun incorporation and non-canonical object constructions, case morphology does not exist. A locative/temporal/ instrument noun (phrase) occurs in a position for a noun (phrase) without functors—incorporated position or object position. Therefore the interpretation is not limited by functors. As long as there is a conventional or institutionalized relation with the related verb, the noun (phrase) can be interpreted.

This predicts that even English, a language that has case morphology, should also allow object usurpers in constructions without case markings.[22] This turns out to be true. English N-V-*er/ing* compounding patterns not only allow thematic objects to occur in the N position, but also temporal, locative, and instrumental expressions. Notably, only object usurpers are possible in such a pattern.

(59) a. truck-driver/driving, apple-picker/picking, stamp-collector/collecting, dishwasher/washing, lawn mower/mowing, ice-breaker/breaking, etc.

   b. axe-murderer/murdering, street-walker/walking, Sunday driver/driving, bed-hopper/hopping, church-goer/going, etc.

   c. *child-giver/giving; *friend-goer/going (someone who goes places with friends); *elderly-worker/working (someone who does work for the elderly), etc.

In addition, like NI and non-canonical objects, these forms exhibit some degree of productivity and typically have an institutionalized meaning.

(60) a. Is that the kind of mother you want? Some boring, old, normal, old toilet-goer? [heard on a British sitcom]

   b. The gear necessary for night hunting is often cumbersome and it is sometimes awkward to carry afield. [from a website for a hunting club in the US]

Moreover, we should predict that in a language with case morphology consistently, a non-canonical object is not possible, even when there is an additional accusative position. This is borne out in a language like Korean. Korean is very much like Chinese in many ways (such as bare nouns having definite and indefinite interpretations, use of classifiers, *wh*-phrases used as non-interrogative universal or existential expressions, use of sentence-final particles, among many other shared characteristics).

---

[22] What matters is the position that shows case markings, not that every item in that position needs to carry case morphology. Thus, even though only pronouns in English show overt case markings, it is assumed that all NPs carry accusative case marking when they occur in object positions. Objects in English therefore are positions with case markings. This contrasts with the compounding pattern, which does not case-mark the compounded noun and is insensitive to case morphology.

However, it differs from Chinese in the prominent use of morphological cases. It also allows two nominal phrases with accusative case marking in a verb phrase. The two accusative case-marked NPs can occur in either ordering, as in (61a, b).

(61) a. John-i   chayk-ul sey sikan-ul   ilk-ess-ta
          John-NOM book-ACC three hours-ACC read-PST-DECL

      b. John-i   sey sikan-ul   chayk-ul ilk-ess-ta
          John-NOM three hours-ACC book-ACC read-PST-DECL
          'John read the book for three hours.'

Given the availability of two instances of accusative marking within one VP, one might wonder whether a non-canonical object is possible because an additional accusative case position is available other than the one for the canonical object. Very interestingly, Korean does not allow the type of non-canonical objects we saw in Chinese.

(62) John-un nac-ey/*ul   ca-ko   siphe-ha-n-ta.
      John-TOP daytime-at/*ACC sleep-COMP want-LV-PRS-DECL
      'John wants to sleep in the daytime.'

In short, we have seen that NI constructions, non-canonical objects in Chinese, and compounds in English all allow the same range of elements—object usurpers. What is shared by these constructions is the absence of case morphology. In contrast, a language with case morphology like Korean does not have object usurpers, even though such a language may have two accusative case-marked positions.[23] This shows that the availability of a non-canonical object is related to the lack of case morphology (functors). The NP position licensed by verbs can be occupied by a non-canonical object as well as a canonical object.

This question should be asked: Is an object position in Chinese like an incorporated noun or compounded noun, which is not even assigned abstract Case? That is, should we conclude that the notion of abstract Case is irrelevant in Chinese?

8. Abstract Case in Chinese

We argue that the absence of case morphology in Chinese does not mean that the notion of abstract Case is irrelevant to this language (see Hu 2007; Markman 2005, 2009).[24]

As Li (1985, 1990) demonstrates, the notion of abstract Case is crucial in Chinese for capturing word order facts regarding arguments. Briefly, if we take the theory of abstract Case to govern the distribution of noun phrases, applying the notion of

---

[23] We were not able to clearly define the behavior of compounds in Korean, corresponding to that in English, due to the absence of clear empirical generalization.

[24] Legate (2008) argues that morphological case and abstract Case are not identical, but both are needed by NPs, resulting in mismatches of abstract Case and morphological cases in some instances. The need for both forms of Case accounts for numerous puzzling facts regarding agreement and case realizations in many different types of languages.

abstract Case to Chinese allows us to capture the use or non-use of Ps in different syntactic positions in this language. It also allows a non-canonical object to occur in the postverbal position where a canonical object occurs because the Case requirement on noun phrases is satisfied. A canonical and a non-canonical object do not co-occur after the same verb because there is generally only one Case available from the verb to one noun phrase.[25] The Case-marker P does not occur with a non-canonical object, as the verb has already provided the needed Case.

Moreover, the arguments against the existence of abstract Case in Chinese found in the literature actually do not hold up well. Markman (2009) links abstract Case with case morphology. She proposes that the absence of case morphology implies the absence of abstract Case, and suggests that Case and agreement features are not universal. She groups languages into the following types according to their Case and agreement properties.

(63)   Type A: Northern Iroquoian, Agreement marking, no Case; NP dislocation obligatory

   Type B: Indo-European, both Agreement and Case; NP dislocation available

   Type C: Japanese, Case, no Agreement; NP dislocation available

   Type D: Chinese, no Agreement or Case; NP-dislocation highly restricted

Chinese (Type D) is a language without agreement or Case, the latter due to the lack of case morphology, according to Markman. The proposal is claimed to be supported by the rigidity of word order in this language: ". . . word order is a way to preserve thematic relations at PF in the absence of case and/or agreement marking. . . . Case and agreement morphemes can be viewed as the PF reflexes of thematic relations that hold within the vP between the verb and at least one of its arguments. However, in the absence of Case and agreement features, thematic relations at PF can be preserved via a rigid relative word order of constituents within the vP" (p. 417).

Unfortunately, contrary to the claim by Markman, English (Markman's type B language) is actually more rigid in word order than Chinese. English essentially has rigid SVO word order, whereas Chinese has the following frequently-occurring word orders, in addition to SVO.

(64)   a.   niurou, ta bu chi. ---OSV
         beef   he not eat
         'Beef, he does not eat.'

     b.   ta niurou bu chi. ---SOV
         he beef   not eat
         'He does not eat beef.'

Chinese also has pairs of reversible word orders not found in English (examples from Huang, Li, and Li 2009, chapter 2, (58)–(60)).

(65)   a.   xiao bei he   lücha.
         small cup drink green.tea
         'Use the small cup to drink the green tea.'

---

[25] Double object verbs of the form [V + Indirect Object + Direct Object] are lexically specified as such.

b. lücha   he   xiaobei.
green.tea drink small cup

(66) a. ni-de keren shui na-zhang chuang ba.
your guest sleep that-CL bed   SFP
'Let your guest sleep on that bed.'

b. na-zhang chuang shui ni-de keren ba.
that-CL   bed   sleep your guest SFP

(67) a. jieri   liwu dou gei-le pengyou-men le.
holiday gift all give-LE friend-pl   SFP
'Holiday gifts were all given to the friends.'

b. pengyou-men dou gei-le   jieri   liwu le.
friend-PL   all give- LE holiday gift SFP
'Friends were all given gifts.'

Markman's reasoning based on rigidity of word order should actually lead to the claim that Chinese must have Case.

Briefly summing up, the theory of abstract Case can accommodate the distribution of noun phrases and the presence/absence of Ps in Chinese. In addition, the kinds of arguments for the lack of abstract Case in Markman's works would actually lead one to expect that the notion of abstract Case should be relevant in Chinese. In short, we maintain the claim that the notion of abstract Case is relevant in Chinese. It is just that it does not manifest itself with any overt case markings. Then, in terms of "functors" assumed in this work, how do we distinguish the patterns with case morphology (English/Korean patterns distinguishing nominative and accusative cases) and those without (English compounding, NI in Northern Iroquoian and Chinese) such that only the latter allow object usurpers? We suggest the following structural distinction between abstract Case and morphological case: only the constructions with case morphology project agreement projections that can be realized as nominative or accusative case markings. The patterns that do not have case morphology at all do not project such agreement projections. The notion of abstract Case is expressed in terms of relation with a certain head (v or Tense)—arguments in the Specifier position of these heads satisfy the requirement of having an abstract Case. In the patterns with case morphology, arguments need to move to the relevant agreement projections in order to obtain the proper case morphology. In other words, it is the presence versus absence of agreement projections in the relevant constructions that gives rise to the realization of case morphology.[26] Agreement is a functor assumed in this work but not the structural relation between an argument with respect to a verb or Tense (notion of abstract Case).

---

[26] Alternatively, the agreement projection may give rise to agreement morphology. In other words, if a construction has either case or agreement morphology, agreement projections exist and object usurpers are not possible. Furthermore, the presence of an agreement projection does not necessarily mean that there must always be overt case or agreement morphology. For instance, non-pronominal NPs in object positions in English do not have any morphological markings. The clue to the existence of an agreement projection is the case morphology required for pronouns in the relevant positions.

9. Conclusions

Chinese has similar possibilities and constraints in licensing non-canonical objects as in NI in Northern Iroquoian languages. NI and non-canonical objects allow themes, locatives, temporals, and instruments, but not benefactives, recipients, or comitatives. English compounds were also shown to exhibit the same range of restrictions—object usurpers versus object non-usurpers. We propose that these striking similarities can be traced to the possibility of object usurpers occurring without functors and the absence of case morphology—further confirmed by the impossibility of non-canonical objects in Korean, despite the fact that it allows two accusative marked noun phrases within a verb phrase. In regard to the interpretation of object usurpers, functors indicating the specific functions of the object-usurpers are missing. Following Borer (2005), for instance, we assume that the interpretative possibilities are supplied by world knowledge/pragmatics. Non-canonical objects, NI, and compounds are subject to cultural and institutionalized norms within their languages. Directly relating a verb and an NP without a functor means that the interpretation is generally conventionalized or institutionalized.[27]

The fact that Chinese and Northern Iroquoian languages have similar object usurpers, as well as English compounding, has interesting implications for the notion of analysis and synthesis in describing types of languages. Chinese is a language that tends to be an example of an isolating or analytic language, whereas Northern Iroquoian languages have many inflections attached to verbs, and nouns are often incorporated to verbs—highly synthetic languages. English is not as synthetic as Northern Iroquoian languages but not as analytic as Chinese, according to morphological complexities. Yet, all these languages have the same possibilities and constraints in some constructions: verb-object constructions in Chinese, noun incorporation in Northern Iroquoian languages, and compounding in English. Recall that the possibility of non-canonical objects in Chinese has been attributed to the analytic nature of Chinese, in contrast to the synthetic nature of English, which has been claimed to disallow non-canonical objects; that is, whether lexical verbs are specified with thematic features (e.g., Lin 2001). This chapter shows that if such an analysis versus synthesis distinction (analysis-synthesis parameter) is adopted, it should not apply to languages as a whole (macro-parameter to distinguish types of languages). Rather, it is the individual constructions that need to be considered. We propose that the relevant constructions in Chinese, Northern Iroquoian, and English are unified by the lack of case morphology. They contrast with the constructions with case morphology, such as verb-object constructions in English and Korean. Because individual constructions should be considered, micro-parameters are relevant. Macro-parameters would be aggregation of correlated differences, as discussed in length in Huang (Chapter 1 of this volume).

---

[27] As Chinese does not have case morphology at all, we should also expect to see non-canonical subjects. This is true (Lin 2001). We will extend our account to non-canonical subjects in a separate work.

Acknowledgment

We would like to thank Lisa Cheng, James Huang, Bingfu Lu, Jane Tang, Tingchi Wei, Chiafen Wu, and the audience at TEAL 8 in Tsing-Hua University, 2012 International Conference on Bilingualism and Comparative Linguistics at the Chinese University of Hong Kong, the 2011 West Coast Conference on Formal Linguistics at Santa Cruz, and the Institute of Linguistics at Academia Sinica for their comments and suggestions. The first author wishes to acknowledge the generous financial support of SSHRC (#410-2011-2417). The second author would like to especially thank James Huang for his mentorship, friendship, support, and inspiration through the decades.

References

Aoun, Joseph, and Yen-Hui Audrey Li. 2003. *Essays on the Representational and Derivational Nature of Grammar: The Diversity of Wh-Constructions.* Cambridge, MA: MIT Press.

Baker, Mark C. 1996. *The Polysynthesis Parameter.* Oxford: Oxford University Press.

Barrie, Michael. 2012. Noun incorporation and the lexicalist hypothesis. *Studies in Generative Grammar* 22(2), 235–261.

Borer, Hagit. 2005. *Structuring Sense, Volume 1: In Name Only.* Oxford: Oxford University Press.

Chen, Ping. 2004. Hanyu shangxiang mingciju yu huati - chenshu jiegou [Double NP constructions and topic-comment articulation in Chinese] *Zhongguo Yuwen [Studies of the Chinese Language]* 6, 493–507.

Cheng, Jie. 2009. Xu jieci jiashe yu zengyuan jiegou - lun bu jiwu dongci hou fei hexin lunyuan de jufa shuxing [The null preposition hypothesis and the applicative consruction: a syntactic study of the post-intransitive-verb non-core arguments]. *Modern Foreign Languages* 32(1), 23–32.

Dayal, Veneeta. 2011. Hindi pseudo-incorporation. *Natural Language & Linguistic Theory* 29(1), 123–167.

Gerdts, Donna B. 1998. Incorporation. *The Handbook of Morphology*, ed. Andrew Spencer and Arnold M. Zwicky, 84–100. Malden, MA: Blackwell.

Guo, Jimao. 1999. Shi Tan "Fei Shanghai" Deng Bu-Jiwu Dongci Dai Binyu Xianxiang [On the Phenomena of Intransitive Verbs Taking Objects as i "Flying Shanghai"]. *Zhongguo Yuwen [Studies of the Chinese Language]* 5, 337–346.

Hu, Jianhua. 2007. Tiyuan lunyuan he yufa gongneng xiang - gebiao xiangying yu yuyan chayi [Thematic roles, arguments, and GF - Case-marking effect and language variation] *Foreign Language Teaching and Research* 3, 163–168.

Hu, Jianhua. 2008. Xiandai hanyu bu jiwu dongci de lunyuan he binyu - cong chouxiang douci 'you' dao jufa-xinxi jiegou jiegou [Mandarin object-taking intransitivee constructions at the syntax-information structure interface]. *Zhongguo Yuwen [Studies of the Chinese Language]*. 5, 396–409.

Hu, Jianhua. 2010. Lunyun de fenbu yu xuanze [The distribution and selection of arguments]. *Zhongguo Yuwen [Studies of the Chinese Language]* 1, 3–20.

Huang, C.-T. James. 2005. *Syntactic Analyticity and the Other End of the Parameter.* Lecture handouts distributed at 2005 LSA Linguistic Institute for course by the same title, MIT and Harvard University.

Huang, C.-T. James. 2006. Resultatives and unaccusatives: A parametric view. *Bulletin of the Chinese Linguistic Society of Japan* 253, 1–43.

Huang, C.-T. James. 2007. Hanyu dongci de tiyuan jiegou yu qi jufa biaoxian [The thematic structures of verbs in Chinese and their syntactic projection]. *Linguistic Sciences* 6(4), 3–21.

Kiparsky, Paul. 1998. Partitive case and aspect. In *The Projection of Arguments: Lexical and Compositional Factors*, ed. Miriam Butt and Wilhelm Geuder, 265–307. Stanford, CA: Center for the Study of Language and Information.

Kratzer, Angelika. 2004. Telicity and the meaning of objective case. *The Syntax of Time*, eds. Jacqueline Guéron and Jacqueline Lecarme., 389–424. Cambridge, MA: MIT Press.

Larson, Richard. 1985. Bare-NP adverbs. *Linguistic Inquiry* 14, 595–621.

Legate, Julie Anne. 2008. Morphological and abstract case. *Linguistic Inquiry* 39, 55–101.

Li, Yen-Hui Audrey. 1985. *Abstract Case in Chinese*. Doctoral dissertation, University of Southern California.

Li, Yen-Hui Audrey. 1990. *Order and Constituency in Mandarin Chinese*. Dordrecht: Kluwer.

Li, Yen-Hui Audrey. 2005. VP-deletion and null objects. *Linguistic Sciences* 15, 3–19.

Li, Yen-Hui Audrey. 2010. Case and objects. *GLOW in Asia VIII*. CD 8.

Li, Yen-Hui Audrey. 2011. Non-canonical objects and case. *Korea Journal of Chinese Language and Literature* 1, 21–51.

Lin, Tzong-Hong. 2001. *Light Verb Syntax and the Theory of Phrase Structure*. Doctoral Dissertation. University of California, Irvine.

Lu, Jianming. 2002. Zai tan "chi-le ta san-ge pingguo" yilei jigeou de xingzhi [On *chi-le ta san-ge pingguo* type of constructions] *Zhongguo Yuwen* [*Studies of the Chinese Language*] 4, 317–325.

Markman, Vita. 2005. *The Syntax of Case and Agreement: Its Relationship to Morphology and Argument Structure*. Doctoral dissertation, Rutgers.

Markman, Vita. 2009. On the parametric variation of case and agreement. *Natural Language & Linguistic Theory* 27(2), 379–429.

Massam, Diane. 2009. Noun incorporation: Essentials and extensions. *Language and Linguistics Compass* 3(4), 1076–1096.

Merlan, Francesca. 1976. Noun incorporation and discourse reference in modern Nahuatl. *International Journal of American Linguistics* 42(3), 177–191.

Mithun, Marianne. 1984. The evolution of noun incorporation. *Language* 60(4), 847–894.

Mithun, Marianne. 1991. Active/agentive case marking and its motivations. *Language* 67(3), 510–546.

Mithun, Marianne. 2004. The non-universality of obliques. *Syntax of the World's Languages*. CD 10.

Muro, Allesio. 2009. Noun incorporation: A new theoretical perspective. Doctoral dissertation. Universitá degli Studi di Padova.

Pylkkänen, Liina. 2008. Introducing arguments. Cambridge, MA: MIT Press.

Shen, Jiaxuan. 2006. *WangMian* si le fuqin de shengcheng fanshi [The generation of *WangMian died father*]. *Zhongguo Yuwen* [*Studies of the Chinese Language*] 4, 291–300.

Spencer, Andrew. 1995. Incorporation in Chukchi. *Language: Journal of the Linguistic Society of America* 71(3), 439–489.

Stvan, Laurel Smith. 2009. Semantic incorporation as an account for some bare singular count noun uses in English. *Lingua* 119(2), 314–333.

Sun, Tianqi, and Yafei Li. 2010. Hanyu fei hexin lunyuan yunzhunjiegou chutan [Licensing noncore arguments in Chinese]. *Zhongguo Yuwen* [Studies of the Chinese Language]. 2010(1), 21–33.

Tai, James. 1984. Verbs and time in Chinese: Vendler's four categories. CLS 20: *Parasession on lexical semantics*, 289–296. ed. D. Testen, V. Mishra, and J. Drogo, Chicago Linguistic Society.

Tang, Ting-Chi. 1978. Double object constructions in Chinese. In *Proceedings of Symposium of Chinese Linguistics*, ed. R. C. Cheng, Y. C. Li, and T. C. Tang, 67–96. Taipei: Student Books.

Teng, Shouhsin. 1975. *A Semantic Study of Transitivity Relations in Chinese*. Berkeley: University of California Press.

Thompson, Sandra A. 1973. Transitivity and some problems with the *ba* construction in Mandarin Chinese. *Journal of Chinese Linguistics* 1, 208–221.

Woodbury, Hanni. 2003. *Onondaga-English/English-Onondaga Dictionary*. Toronto, ON: University of Toronto Press.

Xiong, Zhongru. 2009. Waieige de lunyuan diwei [The peripheral cases as non-core arguments]. *Journal of Anhui Normal University (Humanties and Social Sciences).* 37(5), 560–566.

Xu, Lijiong, and Yang Shen. 1998. Tiyuan lilun yu hanyu peijia wenti [Thematic theory and argument structure in Mandarin Chinese]. *Contemporary Linguistics* 3, 1–21.

Yuan, Yulin. 1998. Hanyu dongci de peijian yanjiu [The study on the argument structure of verbs in Mandarin Chinese]. Jiangxi: Jiangxi Educational Publishers.

Yuan, Yulin. 2003. Yitao hanyu dongci lunyuan jiaose de yafa zhibiao [A set of grammatical guidelines to the thematic roles in Chinese]. *Shijie Hanyu Jiaoxue* [World Chinese Language Teaching] 3, 24–36.

Zhan, Weidong. 1999. Yige hanyu yuyi zhishi biaoda kuanjia: guangyi peijia moshi [A framework of Chinese semantic representation: Generalized valence mode]. *Jisuanji yuanyanxue wenji* [*Selections on Computational Linguistics*] Beijing: TsingHua University Publisher.

Zhan, Weidong. 2004. Lunyuan jie yu jushi bianhuan [Argument structure and constructional transformation]. *Zhongguo Yuwen* [*Studies of the Chinese Language*] 3, 209–221.

Zhang, Ren. 2005. *Enriched Composition and Inference in the Argument Structure of Chinese.* New York: Routledge.

Zhou, Guoguang. 1997. Gongjuge zai hanyu jufa jiegou zhong de diwei [The grammatical status of the instrumental case in Mandarin] *Zhongguo Yuwen* [*Studies of the Chinese Language*] 3, 215–218.

Zhu, Dexi. [朱德熙] 1961. Shuo *de* [On Chinese *de*]. *Zhongguo Yuwen* [*Studies of the Chinese Language*] 110, 1–15.

8

Transitive Psych-Predicates

LISA LAI-SHEN CHENG AND RINT SYBESMA

1. Introduction: Chinese Objects

In Chinese languages we find a number of interesting phenomena when we look at objects. First of all, verbs in Mandarin (as well as in other Chinese languages) seem to have a lot of freedom in taking non-thematic objects, that is, locative, temporal, instrumental and reason objects, as shown in (1). Huang (2006) attributes this freedom to the high degree of analyticity that Chinese is supposed to have: lexical verbs in Chinese are not conflated in the lexical structure, and this allows them to have more freedom in the type of objects they take. Barrie and Li (Chapter 7 of this volume) link this property to the lack of Case morphology in Chinese.

(1) a. tā kāi-le   yī-liàng tǎnkèchē.   (data from Huang 2006; tones added)
        he drive-PERF one-CL tank
        'He drove a tank.'

     b. tā kāi   zuǒbiān, wǒ kāi   yòubiān.
        he drive left-side, I   drive right-side
        'He drives [on] the left side, I drive [on] the right side.'

     c. tā kāi   báitiān, wǒ kāi   wǎnshang.
        he drive day,   I   drive night
        'He drives [in] daylight, I drive [at] night.'

     d. tā kāi   jiàzhào, wǒ kāi   shēnfènzhèng.
        he drive license, I   drive ID-card
        'He drives [with] a driver's license, I drive [with] an ID card.'

     e. wǒ kāi   hǎo-wán.
        I   drive good-play
        'I drive [for] fun.'

Second, there are verbs (generally counterparts of unergative verbs in English) that have a "dummy" object, that is, an object that does not seem to contribute much meaning (Cheng and Sybesma 1998). Here are some examples:

(2) chī-fàn 'eat-rice = eat'
     kāi-chē 'drive-car = drive'
     bān-jiā 'move-house = move'
     pǎo-bù 'run-step = run'
     zǒu-lù 'walk-road = walk'

For a more complete discussion of these VO-combinations, we refer to Cheng and Sybesma (1998), but here we want to stress, first, that the dummy objects are syntactically active objects (they are, for instance, in complementary distribution with other, more referential or more contentful objects, as illustrated in (3), order irrelevant) and, second, that in the relevant meaning these verbs require an object. In relation to the latter point, it must be noted that this class of dummy objects falls into two categories: for some, deletion of the object leads to a change in meaning. For instance, whereas *pǎo-bù* means 'run, jog,' *pǎo* by itself means 'run away, escape.' The other class keeps its original meaning when there is no overt object but, significantly, it is interpreted as if there is an empty object, which, in Chinese, is automatically referential (Huang 1982). Thus, while *chī-fàn* means 'eat,' *chī* by itself is interpreted as *chī ø* 'eat it.' We return to this point below.

(3) a. pǎo (*bù) shāngdiàn
         run step shop
         'run from shop to shop'

     b. zǒu (*lù) hòu-mén
         walk road back-door
         'go through the (unofficial) backdoor'

     c. chī (*fàn)/yī-wǎn chǎo-miàn
         eat rice/one-bowl fried-noodles
         'eat a bowl of fried noodles'

The third interesting phenomenon involving objects, and the topic of this chapter, is illustrated by the following examples (for *hěn* glossed as 'very,' see the following examples):

(4) a. tā hěn dānxīn
         he very worried[1]
         'He is (very) worried.'

     b. tā hěn dānxīn xiǎoháir
         he very worried child
         'He is (very) worried about his child.'

(5) a. tā hěn gāoxìng
         he very happy
         'He is (very) happy.'

---

[1] *Dānxīn* will be glossed as 'worried' or as 'worry.' This is to acknowledge that in some uses, it has a more "verby" activity sense than in other contexts, when it is more stative, in correlation with the fact that English has two lexical items for these. Nothing hinges on the gloss, but we come back to it, briefly, in the final section.

b. tā hěn gāoxìng zhè-jiàn shì
   he very happy   this-CL affair
   'He is (very) happy about this.'

What these examples show is that there are stative predicates, which can appear, in the same meaning, as intransitive as well as transitive. What we will discuss in this chapter is how the objects are licensed, both formally and qua content. We argue that the phenomenon is limited to psych-predicates and that they can take an object complement because of the presence of an applicative projection in the structure.

In the following discussion, we first discuss a number of properties associated with the Mandarin psych-predicates, the objecthood of the objects following the psych-predicates, as well as the different types of psych-predicates. In section 3, we take some preliminary steps toward an analysis by examining structures with experiencers. We take into account comparable data in Bantu languages and explore an analysis of adding an applicative layer in Mandarin to accommodate the "extra" object with psych-predicates in section 4, and we discuss the implications of this analysis with respect to analyticity as well as the differences between Cantonese and Mandarin in section 5.

2. Properties

2.1. PRELIMINARIES

In this section we present and discuss a number of properties associated with the psych-predicates in (4) and (5). A recurrent theme in this section will be that the predicates we may lump together under the label "psych-predicates" for semantic reasons (they describe a mental state[2]) actually constitute a mixed bag if we look at the properties they have. In addition to *dānxīn* 'worried' and *gāoxìng* 'happy,' elements we will be taking into consideration in this chapter include *fán* 'annoyed,' *hàipà/pà* 'afraid,' *hàoqí* 'curious,' *mǎnyì* 'satisfied,' *shēngqì/qì* 'angry,' *xiǎoxīn* 'careful,' and *xǐhuān* 'like.'

The bi-syllabic elements among them are also bi-morphemic, but the internal structure is not the same. While some are VO compounds, for example, *dānxīn* 'worried' ('carry' + 'heart') and *hàoqí* 'curious' ('like' + 'strange'), others are AN compounds, such as *gāoxìng* 'happy' ('high' + 'mood') and *mǎnyì* 'satisfied' ('full' + 'desire'). *Xǐhuān* 'like' consists of two A's: 'happy' + 'merry'. However, as we will see, the differences in internal structure do not correlate systematically with any of the other differences we will discuss.[3]

We will not go into a discussion regarding the categorial status of these elements, whether they are verbs or adjectives. In the literature, there is discussion on the

---

[2] Or, in the words of Landau (2010, 137): "A psych verb is any verb that carries psychological entailments with respect to one of its arguments (the experiencer). A psychological entailment involves an individual being in a certain mental state."

[3] Later in the chapter, we also discuss cases such as *gǎn-dòng* 'feel-move: touch,' which have a verb-result makeup.

question of whether Chinese has a separate category comparable to adjective at all; see Chao (1968) and McCawley (1992), who say there is not; and S. Huang (2006) and Paul (2005, 2010), for the opposite view. One argument for treating stative predicates as verbs is that in their predicative use, they do not need a copula. On the other hand, most stative predicates when used as a predicate in a non-comparative environment require the presence of the element *hěn* 'very' (which is generally unstressed, in which case it does not mean *very*).

(6)   a.   Zhāngsān hěn gāo
           Zhangsan very tall
           'Zhangsan is tall.'
           NOT: 'Zhangsan is *very* tall' unless *hěn* is stressed.

      b.   Zhāngsān gāo
           Zhangsan tall
           'Zhangsan is taller (than someone known from context).'
           NOT: 'Zhangsan is tall.'

S. Huang (2006) treats *hěn* as a type-raiser: it raises in principle non-predicative elements to the status of predicate. Grano (2012) proposes that *hěn* has both a semantic and a syntactic role. On the one hand, *hěn* approximates positive semantics (see also Sybesma 1999).[4] On the other, syntactically, *hěn* allows an adjective to be a complement of T^0 (which comes close to what S. Huang says). Grano (2012) claims that T^0 in Mandarin only selects for a verbal element, and *hěn* is a functional morpheme that allows an adjective to combine with T^0.[5] In other words, for S. Huang and Grano, there is a class of elements we may call adjectives, separate from verbs. As mentioned earlier, we will not get involved in this discussion here. We do, however, want to point out that *hěn* can be seen as an element that is only compatible with predicative elements that are gradable and have an open range, and it closes that range. We see that it is no longer acceptable with words whose open range has been closed in another way. Consider the following examples. In sentences such as (7a, b) the presence of *hěn* is strongly preferred.

(7)   a.   tā hěn dānxīn (wǒ)
           he very worried me
           'He is very worried (about me).'

      b.   tā hěn hàoqí   (zhè-jiàn shì)
           he very curious this-CL matter
           'He is very curious (about this matter).'

---

[4] Kennedy and McNally (2005) and Kennedy (2007) propose that degree adjectives used in non-comparative environments have "positive predication": what is predicated of stands out along the dimension with respect to a contextually determined comparison class.

[5] Grano (2012) proposes the "T [+V] constraint": "In Mandarin, the direct complement to T(ense) (or something like Tense) must either be (an extended projection of) a verb or a functional morpheme that can in principle combine with (an extended projection of) a verb." (p. 518) In the case of comparatives, a null morpheme does this job.

However, when we close the open range using a structure that is generally used for resultatives (which have the same function: providing an end to an open-ended predicate), *hěn* cannot be present:

(8) a. zhè-jiàn shì   (*hěn) dānxīn-sǐ   wǒ le
       this-CL matter very   worry-dead I LE
       'This matter makes me worried to death.'

  b. tā (*hěn) qì-huài   wǒ le
     he very   angry-broken I LE
     'He makes me angry to the extent that I'm broken.'

On the other hand, we note that it is not the case that all predicates that combine with *hěn* would fall in the category of adjective if there were such a category. Certain modal verbs are also compatible with *hěn*, including *yuànyì* 'want' and *xiǎng* 'would like.'

In any case, we treat the psych-predicates we will be discussing in this chapter as predicative elements, without worrying about their categorial status.

2.2. TRUE OBJECTS

The examples presented so far illustrate transitive use of *dānxīn* 'worried,' *gāoxìng* 'happy,' *qì* 'angry,' and *hàoqí* 'curious.' Here are some more examples, with different predicates.

(9) a. tā hěn fán   zhè-jiàn shì
       he very annoyed this-CL matter
       'He is (very) annoyed by this matter.'

  b. tā hěn *mǎnyì*   tā de chéngjī
     he very satisfied he DE result
     'He is (very) satisfied about his result.'

  c. nǐ yào xiǎoxīn zhè-ge rén
     you need careful this-CL person
     'You should be careful about this person.'

The first thing to note about these objects is that the thematic role they have is that of what we will call, following Pesetsky (1995), "the subject matter": it is what we are happy, worried, careful, or curious about. This is true for all psych-predicates discussed in this chapter. Although it is clear from the examples, we do want to point out that these predicates are not causative like transitive de-adjectival verbs in English, such as *clear* in *they cleared the screen* (more on this later).

Second, we need to establish the syntactic status of these objects. Just like Cheng and Sybesma (1998) show that dummy objects are real objects, Barrie and Li (Chapter 7 of this volume) provide a list of properties of canonical, thematic objects, and show that non-thematic objects such as the ones in (1) also have these properties. We briefly discuss a number of the properties they mention here and apply them to our objects.[6]

First, the object noun phrase can be any type of nominal expression. This is illustrated in (10).

(10) a. tā hěn qì   suǒyǒude xuéshēng   –quantificational
          he very angry all   student
          'He is angry at all the students.'

      b. tā hěn pà   nèi-ge rén   –definite
          he very afraid that-CL person
          'He is afraid of that person.'

      c. tā bù   dānxīn rènhé shì   –indefinite
          he NEG worried any   matter
          'He doesn't worry about anything.'

Second, we observe that their distribution differs from adverbials. This is shown in (11).

(11) *tā hěn qì   chángcháng
       he very angry often

Furthermore, reduplication of the predicate is possible with the addition of a *de*-expression to the second copy, just like predicates with canonical objects:

(12) a. tā   dānxīn nèi-jiàn shì   dānxīn de chī bu xià   fàn
          s/he worry   that-CL matter worry DE eat not down rice
          'S/he worries about that matter to the extent that s/he can't eat.'

      b. tā qì   nèi-ge rén   qì   de jiǎng bu chū huà lái
          he angry that-CL person angry DE speak not out word come
          'S/he is so angry at that person that s/he can't say a word.'

The object complement of psych-predicates can also appear in elided contexts:

(13) tā chángcháng dānxīn tā de jiànkāng, wǒ bìng bù   nème dānxīn
      he often   worry   he DE health   I rather NEG so   worry
      'He often worries about his health, but I don't worry much (about that).'

Finally, just like canonical objects, the object of psych-predicates can also be relativized:

(14) tā zuì pà   de lǎoshī shi Huáng lǎoshī
      he most afraid DE teacher COP Huang teacher
      'The teacher that he is most afraid of is Teacher Huang.'

This overview shows that the post-adjectival object is on a par with a canonical object of a transitive verb. This applies to all objects of all predicates under discussion here.

---

[6] Some of the properties do not apply to the case of the stative predicates discussed here, for instance, the property of being in complementary distribution with a canonical object. We only take those that apply to our cases straightforwardly.

2.3. OBLIGATORY TRANSITIVITY

After having presented some properties that all predicates have in common, we will now look at two properties that divide the psych-elements in different groups. The first has to do with the transitivity of these elements, the second, in the next section, with *duì* 'towards.'

In (4) and (5) we illustrate the intransitive and transitive use of *dānxīn* 'worried' and *gāoxìng* 'happy.' What we mean with intransitive use is the use with no object at all, also no covert, phonologically empty "understood" object. When we discussed the verbs with dummy objects, we noticed that a verb like *chī* 'eat' is obligatorily transitive in the sense that when no overt object is present, the utterance is understood as if there is a (referential) empty object present. As a result, such utterances are only understandable in context. If someone bursts into a room and cries *wǒ chī le!*, this sentence is uninterpretable unless the hearers know what he was supposed to be eating, as it means 'I ate it!' The sentences in (4a) and (5a) with intransitive *dānxīn* 'worried' and *gāoxìng* 'happy' are perfect even without a context providing a referent for an empty object. One may wonder why someone is worried or happy, but the sentences are interpretable. In other words, *dānxīn* 'worried' and *gāoxìng* 'happy' are not obligatorily transitive. Other such elements are *fán* 'annoyed,' *hàoqí* 'curious,' *mǎnyì* 'satisfied,' *shēngqì* 'angry,' and *xiǎoxīn* 'careful.' (Note that they can have empty objects as well: this was illustrated in (13).) On the other hand, other psych-predicates are just like most other predicates in Chinese, obligatorily transitive. Thus, one cannot burst into a room saying *tā xǐhuān* 'he likes' if there is no previously established referent for the empty object of *xǐhuān*. *Pà* 'fear, afraid' is also like this.

2.4. *DUÌ* 'TOWARD'

The second property that divides the psych-predicates into different groups is the co-occurrence with the preposition/coverb *duì* 'toward.'[7] Most of the elements listed above allow the "object" to appear preverbally preceded by *duì* 'toward.' Here are some examples:

(15)   a. tā duì xiǎoháir hěn dānxīn
            he to   child   very worried
            'He is (very) worried about his child.'

       b. tā duì zhè-jiàn shì   hěn gāoxìng
            he to   this-CL matter very happy
            'He is (very) happy about this matter.'

       c. wǒ duì zhè-jiàn shì   hěn fán
            I   to   this-CL matter very annoyed
            'I am (very) annoyed about this matter.'

       d. tā duì nǐ hěn mǎnyì
            he to   you very satisfied
            'He is (very) satisfied about you.'

---

[7] There may be three groups: no *duì* (that is, they only allow for VO), optional *duì*, and obligatory *duì* (there is no VO variant). We leave this uninvestigated.

Not all elements allow for this alternation. As far as we have been able to establish (but more empirical investigation is necessary), the predicates that are obligatorily transitive resist co-occurrence with *duì*. In our analysis we will capitalize on the alternation and try to explain why not all types of predicates allow for it.

3. Toward an Analysis: Preliminaries

3.1. DE-ADJECTIVAL VERBS?

The central question we would like to answer is how the objects of psych verbs (especially the optionally transitive ones) are licensed, both formally and qua content (Rizzi 1986).

Since the psych-elements under consideration here are stative predicates, it seems reasonable to explore the option of treating them as transitive adjectives, that is, like de-adjectival verbs such as *clear* and *tighten* in English. Hale and Keyser (1993) argue that intransitive de-adjectival verbs such as (16a) result from a conflation process as shown in (17).

(16)   a.   The screen cleared.

        b.   I cleared the screen.

(17)

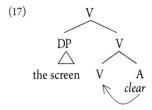

The transitive version (16b) involves a higher level of verb (causative or little *v*), in which the de-adjectival verb is incorporated, as follows:

(18)

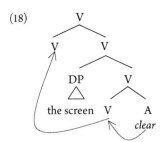

Importantly, the object in (16b) is the original single argument in (16a); the argument that is added through the process of adding the *v*P-layer is the external argument.

As we noted above, the cases at hand, like *dānxīn* 'worried,' are different in their semantics: they are not causative. Importantly, another, no doubt related, difference is that when we compare the transitive-intransitive pairs in (4) and (5), it is the object that is added, not the subject. In short, the cases at hand cannot be analyzed in a fashion parallel to *clear* (others may be, see later discussion).

3.2. EXPERIENCERS

Since we are dealing with psych-predicates, it is reasonable to look at Belletti and Rizzi's (1988) influential analysis of psych-verbs in Italian. Belletti and Rizzi show that there are two types of psych predicates: for some the subject is the experiencer; for others the object is. The former is exemplified by (19a), the latter by (19b).

(19) a. Gianni teme questo   (Experiencer subject)
          Gianni fears this

      b. questo preoccupa Gianni   (Experiencer object)
          this   worries   Gianni

      c. questo piace   a Gianni
          this   pleases to Gianni

In fact, there is a third type, exemplified in (19c), with the experiencer introduced by the preposition *a* 'to' (and with an alternative order: *A Gianni piace questo*). Belletti and Rizzi argue, however, that both (19b) and (19c) have the same underlying structure (though we ignore (19c) in our subsequent discussion).

Under their analysis, experiencer object sentences have the base structure given in (20a). Thus, (19b) has the base structure in (20b). In other words, in their view, an element such as *preoccupare* 'worry' has two internal arguments, though one is an argument of the V, while the other is an argument of V-bar.

(20) a. [$_{VP}$ [verb theme] experiencer] (2 argument-unaccusatives)

      b. [$_{VP}$ [worry this] Gianni]

In the subsequent derivation, the theme object (*this* in the case of (20b)) moves to the subject position for Case assignment, just like *the door* in (21) is supposed to have moved from the underlying complement position (since the verbs *open* and *preoccupare* are both unaccusative, they do not assign Case to the object). Crucially, in their analysis, it is not possible for the experiencer to raise to the subject position as it has inherent Case, predicting that **Gianni preoccupa questo* (intended to mean: 'Gianni worries about this') is ungrammatical.

(21) the door opened

As for experiencer subject sentences as in (19a), under Belletti and Rizzi's analysis, the subject is base-generated. In other words, there are transitive psych-verbs and unaccusative psych-verbs.

Coming back to Mandarin psych-predicates, especially in comparison with Italian and English, what we would like to point out is that (i) the Mandarin counterpart of (19b) is ungrammatical—thus an experiencer-object sentence like (19b) is not possible, as shown in (22a, b); and (ii) that in all Chinese cases, as illustrated in (4) and (5), the experiencer is generated in subject position, just like (19a).

(22) a. *zhè-jiàn shì   dānxīn-le   wǒ
          this-CL matter worry-PERF   I
          Intended: 'This matter worries me.'

      b. *tā gāoxìng-le   wǒ
          he happy-PERF   I
          Intended: 'He made me happy.'

Note that the intended meaning of (22a) can only be expressed using a periphrastic causative, as in (23).

(23) zhè-jiàn shì   ràng wǒ dānxīn
      this-CL matter let   I   worry
      'This matter makes me worry.'

This brings us to Pesetsky's (1995) analysis of psych-verbs. He argues that experiencer-object sentences such as (19b) are not derived from the structure in (20b), as suggested by Belletti and Rizzi; instead, experiencer-object sentences are causatives. That is, these sentences are basically transitives, that is, experiencer-objects are objects. Thus, for an experiencer-object sentence such as (24a), we can have a passive counterpart, as in (24b).

(24) a. Your remark frightened John.

      b. John was frightened by your remark.

Under Pesetsky's analysis that experiencer-object sentences are causatives, we expect Mandarin to have experiencer-objects since aside from periphrastic causatives such as (23), Mandarin allows causatives such as (25a, b), and, as we will see below, the only type of "experiencer-objects" we find in Mandarin are in causative-resultative sentences. In Chinese, a straightforward object is never an experiencer.

(25) a. zhè-píng jiǔ   hē-zuì-le   Zhāngsān
          this-bottle wine drink-drunk-PERF Zhangsan
          'This bottle of wine made Zhangsan drunk.'

      b. zhè-běn shū kàn-lèi-le   wǒ-de yǎnjīng
          this-CL book read-tired-PERF   I-DE   eye
          'This book makes my eyes tired (by my reading it).'

In contrast to what we have indicated above in (22), Cheung and Larson (2006) claim that Chinese does have experiencer-objects, illustrating this claim with the following examples (from Chen 1995, ex. (8b)):

(26) a. Zhāngsān gǎn-dòng-le Lǐsì.
          Zhangsan touch-PERF   Lǐsì
          'Zhangsan touched Lisi.'

b. Zìjǐ₁de chénggōng zhènfèn-le   Fāngfāng₁.
    self's   success   excite-PERF Fangfang
    'Her₁ (own) success excited Fangfang₁.'

Note that both examples involve resultative compound verbs. Both verbs consist of a V-R combination, V denoting an activity of some sort, R the result (e.g., for (26a): *gǎn* 'feel' with *dòng* 'moved'). They are in this respect the same as the sentences we presented in (8), repeated here:

(27) a. zhè-jiàn shì   dānxīn-sǐ   wǒ le
          this-CL matter worry-dead I   PERF
          'This matter worried me to death.'

      b. tā qì-huài   wǒ le
          he angry-broken I   SFP
          'He makes me angry to the extent that I'm broken.'

The questions we need to address are: Why is there a contrast in (28)? Why does the addition of a resultative verb make the experiencer-object sentence licit?

(28) a. *zhè-jiàn shì   dānxīn-le   wǒ (=(22a))
           this-CL matter worry-PERF   I
           'This matter worries me.'

      b. zhè-jiàn shì   dānxīn-sǐ   wǒ le   (=(27a))
          this-CL matter worry-dead I   PERF
          'This matter worried me to death.'

To answer these questions, we need to have a look at resultative structures. We adopt the analysis for such structures that was developed in Sybesma (1992, 1999; for the full account, the reader is referred to these works; see also Shen and Sybesma 2006). In this analysis, intransitive resultative structures such as the ones in (29) have the underlying structure in (30): a V with as its complement a small clause consisting of a subject and a predicate; the sole argument of the sentence is the subject of the small clause.

(29) a. Zhāngsān hē-zuì-le
          Zhāngsān drink-drunk-PERF
          'Zhang San drank himself drunk/is drunk from drinking.'

      b. wǒ-de yǎnjīng kàn-lèi-le
          I-DE eye   read-tired-PERF
          'my eyes tired from reading'

      c. Lìsì gǎn-dòng-le
          Lìsì feel-move-PERF
          'Zhangsan touched Lisi.'

      d. wǒ dānxīn-sǐ-le
          I worried-die-PERF
          'I'm worried to death.'

(30) a. [hē   [sc Zhāngsān zuì]]
         drink   Zhāngsān drunk

   b. [kàn [sc wǒ-de yǎnjīng lèi]]
      read   I-DE eye   tired

   c. [gǎn [sc Lǐsì dòng]]
      feel   Lǐsì move

   d. [dānxīn [sc wǒ sǐ]]
      [worried   1s die

One of the things that happen subsequently so as to derive the surface order is that the subject of the small clause moves out of the small clause to the matrix subject position for licensing reasons. Transitive resultatives in this analysis are formed by incorporating the structures in (30) under a *v*P, which provides the external agentive-causative argument. The base structure is given in (31), with the lexical elements of (32d) (which is the same as (28b)).

(31)

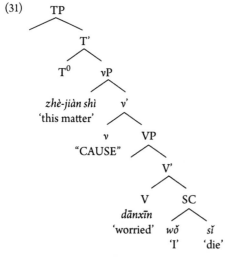

To derive (32d), *zhè-jiàn shì* 'this matter' moves to the matrix subject position for Case (SpecTP); *wǒ* 'I' moves to SpecVP for the same reason, and the V-R cluster *dānxīn-sǐ* 'worried to death' forms a complex head and subsequently moves to the head of *v*P (for discussion, see Sybesma 1992). The transitive counterparts of the sentences in (29) are:

(32) a. zhè-píng jiǔ   hē-zuì-le   Zhāngsān
        this-CL   wine drink-drunk-PERF Zhangsan
        'This bottle of wine made Zhangsan drunk.'

   b. zhè-běn shū   kàn-lèi-le   wǒ-de yǎnjīng
      this-CL book read-tired-PERF I-DE eye
      'This book makes my eyes tired (by my reading it).'

c. Zhāngsān gǎn-dòng-le   Lǐsì. (= (26a))
   Zhangsan feel-move-PERF Lǐsì
   'Zhangsan touched Lisi.'

d. zhè-jiàn shì   dānxīn-sǐ   wǒ le (= (27a))
   this-CL matter worry-dead I   LE
   'This matter worried me to death.'

In this analysis, transitive resultatives have a variant with *bǎ*. The derivational difference with the sentences in (32) is that *bǎ* is inserted in v^0 as a kind of dummy
instead of the V-R cluster moving into it. Here are the *bǎ*-variants of the sentences
given in (32):

(33) a. zhè-píng jiǔ   bǎ Zhāngsān hē-zuì-le
        this-CL   wine ba Zhangsan drink-drunk-PERF
        'This bottle of wine made Zhangsan drunk.'

    b. zhè-běn shū   bǎ wǒ-de yǎnjīng kàn-lèi-le
       this-CL book ba I-DE   eye   read-tired-PERF
       'This book makes my eyes tired (by my reading it).'

    c. Zhāngsān bǎ Lǐsì gǎn-dòng-le.
       Zhangsan ba Lǐsì feel-move-PERF
       'Zhangsan touched Lisi.'

    d. zhè-jiàn shì   bǎ wǒ dānxīn-sǐ   le
       this-CL matter ba I   worry-dead PERF
       'This matter worried me to death.'

These sentences show that the experiencer in (32c, d) and (33c, d) behave in exactly
the same way as the "objects" (underlyingly the subject of the resultative small clause)
in other resultative sentences. In other words, Mandarin does have experiencer objects, but only with resultatives.

Turning now to the question of why there is a difference between the sentences
in (28), the answer is that only unaccusative predicates can be subsumed under *v*P,
and V-R compounds are unaccusative, as they have no external argument. The V-R
compound in (28b), *dānxīn-sǐ* 'worry to death,' is thus compatible with a causative
structure, while *dānxīn* 'worry' alone, as an unergative, with its own external argument, is not. We return to this question later, after we have discussed in more detail
the structure we have in mind for Chinese transitive psych-predicates in the next
section.

In any case, what we have established in this section is that the experiencer subject
of psych-predicates like *dānxīn* 'worry' are base-generated subjects.

4. The Proposal: An Applicative Layer

One well-known way of adding an argument to a verbal argument structure is the
use of applicatives. Pylkkänen (2008) distinguishes two types of applicative heads.

The low applicative head is situated within the VP, and denotes a relation between two individuals (with a transfer-of-possession relation). The high applicative head, on the other hand, is positioned above the VP, adds another participant to the event described by the verb, and denotes a relation between an event and an individual. Given this distinction, applicatives added to a verb that does not already have an argument must be high applicatives. Indeed, Pylkkänen (2008) shows that unergatives and statives combine with high applicatives, not low applicatives. Example (34) illustrates an example of a high applicative in Luganda with an unergative verb (data from Pylkkänen 2008).

(34)   High applicative (Luganda)
       Mukasa ya-tambu-le-dde   Katonga
       Mukasa 3SG.PAST-walk-APPL-PAST   Katonga
       'Mukasa walked for Katonga.'

The typical participant discussed in the literature for high applicatives is a benefactive, as in (34), though locatives and instrumentals are also mentioned. However, in the literature on Bantu languages, other types of participants can be easily found. For instance, aside from locations and instruments, such participants can be goals, purposes, and reasons (see Du Plessis and Visser 1992). In fact, the addition of a subject matter or theme can also easily be found with psych-adjectives/verbs. Consider the following examples from Xhosa; the applicative affis -*el* precedes the final vowel *a*:

(35)   Xhosa (data from Du Plessis and Visser 1992)
       a.   úmqhúbì úkhàlázèlà   úmqéshì
            1.driver 1.complain.APPL   1.employer
            'The driver complains about the employer.'

       b.   ísíbóndà   síkròkrélà   émzìnì
            7.headman 7.suspicious.APPL village.LOC
            'The headman is suspicious of the village.'

Pylkkänen proposes that the high applicative projection is projected above the lexical VP (and below VoiceP (i.e., vP)), thus it is projected between the vP and the VP.

Recall that psych-predicates in Mandarin like *dānxīn* 'worried' are in principle intransitive, and that an object can be added. This is comparable to the Xhosa data in (35).

We thus propose that the addition of the object in these cases is also through the addition of a high applicative layer.[8] Consider first the structure of an intransitive adjective in (36).

---

[8] See Paul and Whitman (2010) for an analysis of Mandarin double object sentences as having an applicative structure, though they argue for making no distinction between a high and a low applicative.

(36) 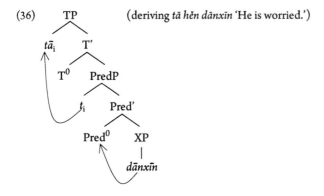 (deriving *tā hěn dānxīn* 'He is worried.')

In this structure, we assume along the lines of Bowers (1993) that predicates have a functional layer.[9] Assuming that a high applicative head is merged above the VP, introducing an extra argument (e.g., the subject matter), a subject-experiencer sentence with an object complement can have the structure in (37).

(37) 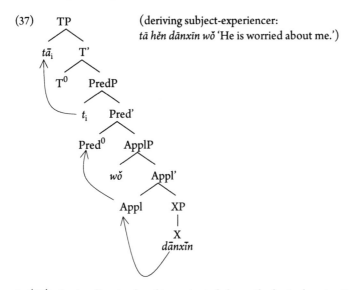 (deriving subject-experiencer: *tā hěn dānxīn wǒ* 'He is worried about me.')

In (37), the Applicative head is projected above the lexical projection[10] and below the PredP, which hosts the subject of the predicate. The structure is thus quite similar to a high applicative structure in other languages with high applicatives.[11]

Given a structure such as (37), the fact that a psych-predicate can take an object complement seems to be straightforward. We propose to connect this to the fact

---

[9] As indicated above, Grano (2012) considers *hěn* to be an Adjective-to-Verb shifter. His structure for the same sentence will only be different in that PredP will be a VP.

[10] We have not provided a category label for the psych-predicates, leaving the question of whether they are adjectives or verbs outside the discussion.

[11] We haven't indicated where *hěn* is inserted in this structure. We consider this to be a point that, though very interesting, is not directly relevant to the transitivity issue at hand.

mentioned earlier, that the non-obligatorily transitive psych-predicates (and only those!) can also add the subject matter argument in preverbal position preceded by *duì* 'toward.' More specifically, we propose that the sentences in (38) have the same underlying structure. The derivation of (38b) was given in (37), and that of (38a) is given in (39), which is the same as (37) except that the lexical head does not raise to Appl^0 and that, instead, *duì* 'toward' is inserted (just like *bǎ* was inserted in v^0 in (33)) into this position, after which it moves to Pred^0.

(38) a. tā duì xiǎoháir hěn dānxīn
          he   to   child   very worried
          'He is (very) worried about his child.'

    b. tā hěn dānxīn xiǎoháir
          he   very worried child
          'He is (very) worried about his child.'

(39)

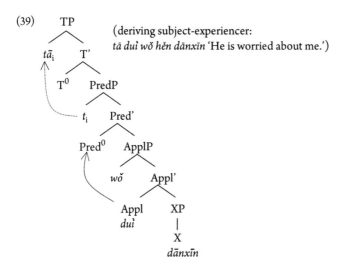

This is almost identical to the analysis proposed for *yǐ* in pre-modern Chinese in Aldridge (2012): she proposes to put *yǐ* in the head of ApplP.

The fact that only the non-obligatorily transitive psych-predicates display this alternation between [*duì* O X] and [X O] suggests that the addition of the object is indeed due to the addition of an extra layer. Intrinsically, and consequently obligatorily, transitive predicates do not derive their transitivity from an extra layer.

Given the above analysis, the question arises of when a high applicative projection is available. Can it be added to all stative predicates? The answer is no. It cannot, for instance, be added to non-psych-predicates like *zhòng* 'heavy':

(40) zhè-běn shū hěn zhòng (*Zhāngsān)
      this-CL book very heavy   Zhangsan
      'This book is (very) heavy (for Zhangsan).'

Note that the addition of a *duì* phrase is possible with non-psych predicates:

(41) zhè-běn shū   duì Zhāngsān hěn zhòng
      this-CL book to   Zhangsan very heavy
      'This book is (very) heavy for Zhangsan.'

However, in cases like this, the complement of *duì* is not the subject matter. In other words, *duì* in these cases is not the head of an ApplP. It should be noted that (41) can be paraphrased with (42).

(42) zhè-běn shū   duì Zhāngsān lái   shuō hěn zhòng
      this-CL book to   Zhangsan come say   very heavy
      'This book is (very) heavy for Zhangsan/in the perspective of Zhangsan.'

This means that the applicative layer can only be added to predicates that allow for a "subject matter" interpretation of the extra argument, which limits it to psych-predicates. Note that Landau (1999) makes a distinction between psych-adjectives and non-psych-adjectives: psych-adjectives are relational and minimally dyadic, while non-psych-adjectives are monadic.

In contrast to high applicatives, according to Pylkkänen, in our case, the applicative layer cannot be added to just any predicate; instead it is limited to predicates that, thematically speaking, have room for an internal argument.

As far as the formal licensing is concerned, it is either the case that the extra layer, just like *v*P, not only provides an extra argument but also an extra Case, or the psych-predicates, being unergatives, can license these objects by themselves.

5. Conclusions and Discussion

In this chapter we have put forth a proposal to account for the occurrence of an object with unergative, stative, and in principle intransitive psych-predicates in Mandarin. The proposal involves the postulation of an applicative-like layer between XP (a lexical projection) and *v*P, the head of which is filled either by the verb (via movement) or the element *duì*. In this section we discuss a number of consequences of the different aspects of the proposal, which can be used, among other things, to evaluate it.

One of the assumptions that underlie the proposal is that transitivity can be derived in different ways, leading to different structures. In this chapter we have discussed transitive/causative resultatives, the object in which is underlyingly the subject of the resultative small clause. Second, we have also assumed the existence of "obligatorily transitive" predicates, which have an object even if there is no resultative phrase: they may be subcategorized for one. And finally, we have the psych-predicates whose object is added through the addition of an applicative type of projection. (And these three situations do not even include the "non-thematic" objects in (1), discussed in more detail in Barrie and Li (Chapter 7 of this volume).) The question here is whether these differences are related to the nature of the lexical elements involved or to the nature of the structures they are inserted into (e.g., (31) or (37)). With Marantz (2013), we think the latter is the case (see Sybesma 1992,

1999 for discussion of similar ideas), if only because we see that certain elements can appear in different structural environments. Insertion in different slots in different structures possibly leads to different additional semantics (e.g., more active or more stative). This may explain what we mentioned in footnote 1: that sometimes *dānxīn* seems more like an activity verb, while at other times it is more like a stative; it is simply in a different structure in each case.

Another consequence of our proposal, mentioned earlier, is that there are two different *duì*'s, or, phrased differently, that, as a consequence of being inserted into different positions, *duì* has a different relationship with the nominal element following it. Sometimes (as in (41)) it is like a preposition and forms a constituent with the noun it precedes, while in our applicative cases, it does not.

Another consequence we also already mentioned is that our applicative is not entirely the same as Pylkkänen's in the sense that, in our case, whether an applicative can be added or not is determined by the thematic nature of the lexical element. This may, however, also be the case in (some) Bantu languages. In Zulu (which, like Luganda and Xhosa, also uses the applicative morpheme *-el* for the addition of an argument),[12] the applicative morpheme *-el* can be added to psych-predicates such as *dabuka* 'sad' and *thukuthela* 'angry,' as shown in (43) and (44).

(43) a. u-dabuk-ile
          1SM-break-DISJ.PAST
          'He was sad.'

      b. u-dabuk-el-a   iz-ingane
          1SM-break-APPL-FV   10-child
          'He's sad about the children.'

(44) a. ngi-thukuthel-e
          1SG-be.angry-FV
          'I am angry.'

      b. ngi-thukuthel-el-e   uSipho
          1SG-be.angry-APPL-FV   1.Sipho
          'I am angry with Sipho.'

However, preliminary results (based on Cheng's own field notes) show that the use of applicatives with psych-predicates is not without restrictions. Some psych-predicates allow an object to be added directly (e.g., *afraid*), while others (e.g., *anxious, worried, happy*) require a preposition kind of element. More research is needed to determine the nature of the difference.

Next, Huang (2012) argues that there are macro-parametric properties of modern Chinese that are linked to a high degree of analyticity. The properties range from having light verb constructions (e.g., *dǎ yú* 'do/hit fish: to fish'), generalized classifiers for count nouns, to *wh*-in-situ. Holmberg and Roberts (2010) and Huang (2012) suggest that the cluster of properties can all be connected to the lack of head movement. This can be in the lexical structure, leading to the lack of denominal verbs

---

[12] We would like to thank Meritta Xaba for her patience and wisdom in discussing the Zulu data.

(and having "light" verbs instead, as in *dǎ yú* 'do/hit-fish: to fish'). In the inflectional functional domain, head movement is also missing, yielding the lack of V to T to C movement.

However, the above analyses of transitive resultatives and transitive psych-predicates involve V/Adj to *v*/Pred/Appl movement. In other words, though there is no V/*v* to T movement, there is movement within the projection below TP. Note that we think that Huang (2012) is right in saying that there is no conflation type of process in lexical syntax in Chinese, yielding the lack of denominal verbs. This means that in Chinese, head-movement is limited to the lower (i.e., more lexical) end of the extended projection in the sense of Grimshaw (1991/2005), including V-to-*v* and A/V-to-Pred, but excluding (a) N-to-V, N being the thematic complement of V, because VP is not part of the extended projection of N, and (b) *v*/V to T, as this involves movement to the higher, functional end of the extended projection of V.

Talking about parametric and cross-linguistic considerations in relation to the proposals presented in this chapter, we would like to point out the following. First, positing a high applicative projection raises the question of whether such a projection is available cross-linguistically. We have seen from Pylkkänen (2008) that Bantu languages, for example, have high applicatives, but languages such as English do not. It is, however, unclear why such projections are not available in some languages. In Barrie and Li (Chapter 7 of this volume), a similar question is asked: Why are non-canonical objects so easily available in Chinese? Their answer is that Chinese has no Case morphology, though they state this in connection to objects without functors (i.e., licensers such as applicatives). We think that the availability of Case and the presence of functors should in principle be treated separately: arguments must be formally licensed as well as content-licensed. That is, the presence of a high applicative head allows the introduction of an extra argument (e.g., a subject matter argument). However, the applicative head itself is not necessarily a Case-marker. Thus, it may be the case that the lack of Case morphology allows languages like Chinese and Bantu to accommodate extra arguments with applicatives, and it is not possible for English and other Case languages to do that, unless extra Case markers are available.[13]

When we compare Cantonese and Mandarin in the light of our analysis of transitive psych-predicates, we note that Cantonese differs in an interesting way from Mandarin. Like Mandarin, it has transitive psych-predicates, with the object denoting the subject matter (as in (45)), but unlike Mandarin, it does not have a variant with *duì* (as illustrated in (46)).

(45) a. keoi⁵ hou² daam¹sam¹ keoi⁵ go³ zai²
        he   very worry   he   CL son
        'He's worried about his son.'

     b. keoi⁵ hou² lau¹ li¹-gin⁶ si⁶
        he   very angry this-CL matter
        'He's angry about this.'

---

[13] See Diercks (2012), who argues that Bantu languages lack abstract Case.

    c.   lei⁵ jiu³ siu²sam¹ go²-go³ jan⁴
       you need careful   that-CL person
       'You need to be careful about that person.'

(46) a. *keoi⁵ deoi³ keoi⁵ go³ zai² hou² daam¹sam¹
        he   to   he   CL son very   worry
        Intended: 'He's worried about his son.'

    b. *keoi⁵ deoi³ li¹-gin⁶ si⁶   hou² lau¹
        he   to   this-CL matter very angry
        Intended: 'He's angry about this.'

    c. *lei⁵ deoi³ go²-go³ jan⁴   jiu³ siu²sam¹
        you to   that-CL person need careful
        Intended: 'You need to be careful about that person.'

Under our analysis, this means that in Cantonese the verb invariably moves into the Pred⁰-position. Note, however, that Cantonese does have prepositional *deoi⁶* in other contexts, comparable to *dui* illustrated in (41).

(47) a. keoi⁵ deoi³ ngo⁵ hou² hou²
        he   to   me   very good
        'He is very good to me.'

    b. hoeng¹gong²-jan⁴ deoi³ bat³gwaa³ san¹man² hou² jau⁵ hing³ceoi³
        Hongkong-people to   gossip   news   very have interest
        'Hong Kong People are very interested in gossip.'

                     (adapted from Matthews & Yip 1994)

Thus, as was pointed out by a reviewer, both Cantonese and Mandarin have the true preposition *dui/deoi⁶*, but only Mandarin has the Applicative *dui*, which can be seen as support for the claim that there are two different (positions for) *dui*'s.

What may be significant as well in this context is that colloquial Cantonese also lacks a counterpart of the *bǎ* construction (we say "colloquial Cantonese" because there *is* a counterpart in the Mandarin/Mandarinized more formal/written registers). This means that in all such cases, Cantonese opts for head-moving V, instead of inserting a dummy in some target position.[14]

Incidentally, underscoring the differences between the nominal and verbal domain, we see the opposite in the nominal domain. At least, according to Cheng and Sybesma (1999, 2005, and 2012) Mandarin bare nouns (N⁰) undergo movement to the classifier head (Cl⁰) to generate a definite bare noun, while in Cantonese, the classifier head has to be filled and a classifier is inserted.

---

[14] See Tang (2006), who argues that in Cantonese, the verb moves higher than the verb in Mandarin (and other Chinese languages). Note that under our analysis, Mandarin verbs can move but don't have to.

Acknowledgement

We would like to thank Norbert Corver, Roberta D'Alessandro, Audrey Li, Jane Tang, and Dylan Tsai, as well as the audience in the Institute of Linguistics at Academia Sinica, TEAL 8 in Tsing-Hua University and Utrecht University for their comments and suggestions.

References

Aldridge, Edith. 2012. PPs and applicatives in Late Archaic Chinese. *Studies in Chinese Linguistics* 33(3), 139–164.

Belletti, Adriana, and Luigi Rizzi. 1988. Psych verbs and theta-theory. *Natural Language and Linguistic Theory* 6, 291–352.

Bowers, John. 1993. The syntax of predication. *Linguistic Inquiry* 24, 591–656.

Chen, Dong-dong. 1995. UTAH: Chinese psych verbs and beyond. In *Proceedings of the North American Conference on Chinese linguistics*, ed. J. Camacho and L. Choueini, 15–29.

Cheng, Lisa Lai-Shen. 2007. Verb copying in Mandarin Chinese. In *The Copy Theory of Movement*, ed. Norbert Cover and Jairo Nunes, 151–174. Amsterdam: John Benjamins.

Cheng, Lisa Lai-Shen, and Rint Sybesma. 1998. On dummy objects and the transitivity of *run*. *Linguistics in the Netherlands 1998*, ed. R. van Bezooijen and R. Kager, 81–93. Amsterdam: AVT/John Benjamins.

Cheng, Lisa L.-S., and Rint Sybesma. 1999. Bare and notso-bare nouns and the structure of NP. *Linguistic Inquiry* 30, 509–542.

Cheng, Lisa L.-S., and Rint Sybesma. 2005. Classifiers in four varietes of Chinese. In *Handbook of Comparative Syntax*, ed. G. Cinque and R. S. Kayne, 259–292. Oxford: Oxford University Press.

Cheng, Lisa Lai-Shen, and Rint Sybesma. 2012. Classifier and DP. *Linguistic Inquiry* 43(4), 634–650.

Cheung, Candice, and Richard Larson. 2006. *Chinese Psych Verbs and Covert Clausal Complementation*. Paper presented at the Chicago workshop on Chinese Linguistics.

Grimshaw, Jane. 1991/2005. Extended projection. In *Words and Structure*, ed. J. Grimshaw, 1–73. Stanford, CA: CSLI.

Grano, Thomas. 2012. Mandarin *hen* and universal markedness in gradable adjectives. *Natural Language & Linguistic Theory* 30(2), 513–565.

Hale, Kenneth, and Samuel Jay Keyser. 1993. On argument structure and the lexical expression of syntactic relations. In *The View from Building 20*, ed. K. Hale and S. J. Keyser. 53–110. Cambridge, MA: MIT Press.

Hoekstra, Teun, and René Mulder. 1990. Unergatives as copular verbs: Location and existential predication. *The Linguistic Review* 7, 1–79.

Holmberg, Anders, and Ian Roberts. 2010. Introduction: Parameters in minimalist theory. In *Parametric Variation: Null Subjects in Minimalist Theory*, ed T. Biberauer, A. Holmberg, I. Roberts, and M. Sheehan, 1–57. Cambridge: Cambridge University Press.

Huang, C. T. James. 1982. *Logical Relations in Chinese and the Theory of Grammar*. Doctoral dissertation, Massachusetts Institute of Technology.

Huang, C. T. James. 2006. Resultatives and unaccusatives: A parametric view. *Bulletin of the Chinese Linguistic Society of Japan* 253, 1–43.

Huang, C. T. James. 2012. On macrovariations and microvariations in parametric theory. In *Proceedings of the 13th International Symposium on Chinese Language and Linguistics*, ed. Yung-O Biq and Lindsey Chen, 1–18.

Huang, Shi-Zhe. 2006. Property theory, adjectives, and modification in Chinese. *Journal of East Asian Linguistics* 15, 343–369.

Kennedy, Christopher. 2007. Vagueness and grammar: The semantics of relative and absolute gradable adjectives. *Linguistics and Philosophy* 30, 1–45.

Kennedy, Christopher, and Louise McNally. 2005. Scale structure, degree modification, and the semantics of gradable predicates. *Language* 81, 345–381.

Landau, Idan. 1999. Psych-adjectives and semantic selection. *The Linguistic Review* 16(4), 333–358.

Landau, Idan. 2010. *The Locative Syntax of Experiencers*. Cambridge, MA: MIT Press.

Matthews, Stephen, and Virgina Yip. 1994. *Cantonese: A Comprehensive Grammar*. London: Routledge.

McCawley, James. 1992. Justifying part-of-speech assignments in Mandarin Chinese. *Journal of Chinese Linguistics* 20(2), 211–246.

Marantz, Alec. 2013. Verbal argument structure: Events and participants. *Lingua* 130, 152–168.

Paul, Waltraud. 2005. Adjective modification in Mandarin Chinese and related issues. *Linguistics* 43, 757–793.

Paul, Waltraud. 2010. Adjectives in Mandarin Chinese: The rehabilitation of a much ostracized category. In *Adjectives: Formal Analyses in Syntax and Semantics*, ed. Patricia Cabredo-Hofherr and Ora Matushansky, 115–152. Amsterdam: John Benjamins.

Paul, Waltraud, and John Whitman. 2010. Applicative structure and Mandarin ditransitives. In *Argument Structure and Syntactic Relations*, ed. M. Duguine, S. Huidobro, and N. Madariaga, 261–282. Amsterdam; Philadelphia: John Benjamins.

Pesetsky, David. 1995. *Zero Syntax: Experiencers and Cascades*. Cambridge, MA: MIT Press.

Pylkkänen, Liina. 2008. *Introducing Arguments*. Cambridge, MA: MIT Press.

Rizzi, Luigi. 1986. Null objects in Italian and the theory of *pro*. *Linguistic Inquiry* 17: 501–557.

Shen, Yang, and Rint Sybesma. 2006. 结果补语小句分析和小句的内部结构 Jiéguǒ pǔyǔ xiǎojù fēnxī hé xiǎojù de nèibù jiégòu. [Small clause results and the internal structure of the Chinese resultative small clause]. 华中科技大学学报 (社会科学版) *Huázhōng kējì dàxué xuébào (shèhuikēxué bǎn)* [*Journal of the Huazhong University of Science and Technology (Social Sciences volume)*] 20(4), 40–46.

Sybesma, Rint. 1992. *Causatives and Accomplishments: The Case of Chinese* ba. Doctoral dissertation, Leiden University.

Sybesma, Rint. 1999. *The Mandarin VP*. Dordrecht: Kluwer.

Tang, Sze-Wing. 2006. "汉语方言受事话题句类型的参数分析 Hanyu fangyan shoushi huatiju leixing de canshu fenxi [A parametric approach to the typology of subtopics in Chinese dialects]. *Yuyan Kexue* 5–6, 3–11.

9

Light-Verb Syntax Between English and Classical Chinese

SHENGLI FENG

1. Different Types of Light Verbs in English

In English, there are different types of predicates that can be analyzed in terms of the empty verbal head of Larson's (1988) (and subsequently Hale and Kayser 1993; Huang 1997; and many others), which empty verb structures involve, for example, ditransitive verbs (1a), resultative verbs (1b), object control verbs (1d), monotransitive verbs (1e), ergative verbs (1f), unergative verbs (1g), and unaccusative verbs (1h), and so on, as seen in (1):

(1)   a.   Ditransitive verbs
        I will get you a present.
        I will show you a picture.

      b.   Resultative verb
        He painted the house green.
        The ink turned the paper black.

      c.   V + PP(DP) + CP
        He agrees with me that the paper will turn bad.
        He learned from his brother that study has no fine.
        He suggested to him that they should try safe argument.

      d.   Object Control
        What decide you to take linguistics?
        She persuaded me to try phonology-free syntax.

      e.   Monotransitive → Ditransitive
        He read me the letter.
        He ordered me a taxi.
        He sent me a card.

      f.   Ergative Verbs
        The window breaks.
        He broke the window.

g. Unergative Verbs
Let's party!   Let's have a party
I am fishing.   I am catching fish.
They are lunching.   They are having lunch.
He may protest.   He may make a protest.
He was lying.   He was telling lies.
Why not guess?   Why not make a guess?

h. Unaccusative Verbs
There stands a man.
There comes a stranger from outside.
There appeared a ghostly face at the window.
There have arisen several problems.

According to Huang (2009), the syntactic function of light verbs is on a par with light nouns (classifiers). While the light nouns help to classify nouns and function to atomicize or individuate an otherwise homogenous entity for the purpose of counting, light verbs, on the other hand, select verb roots, in the sense that DO selects activities, CAUSE selects accomplishments, and so on, and also help select verb roots by adding the required semantic components, as shown in (2).

(2) Light noun: ... $[_{clP}$ cl $[_{NP}$ [N]]]
     Light verb: ... $[_{vP}$ v $[_{VP}$ [V]]]

Based on this analysis, we see that there are different types of light verbs that are utilized for selecting different verb roots. For example:

(3) a. Causative light verbs
         To CAUSE the gravy ~~to~~ thin ➔ To thin the gravy

     b. The Performative light verbs
         To PERFORM an act [of hitting him] ➔ She hit him.
         To PERFORM(-ize) an act [of apology] ➔ She will apologize.

     c. Eventive Lightverbs
         There happens an event [that a man comes] ➔ A man comes.

     d. Experiential Lightverbs
         You surprised me.
         It horrifies people.

     e. Inchoative Light Verbs
         I can blind him.
         The sky will clear.

The event-aspectual property of light verbs characterized by Lin (2001) can also be understood in terms of the action-classifier style of Huang's system. Under these theoretical explorations, however, one may wonder what would be the action-classifier syntax in Classical Chinese, given the observation that Classical Chinese is more like English (i.e., a synthetic language, as compared with medieval and Modern Chinese, which have become more and more analytical).

In what follows, I will provide, based on Feng (2000, 2005), various examples from Archaic Chinese to show that light-verb syntax with an abstract "generic light verb" (on par with the generic light noun like *ge* in Modern Chinese) was freely operative in pre-Buddhism Chinese (i.e., before the first century A.D.), and is different from medieval and Modern Chinese.

2. Light Verbs in Classical Chinese: Traditional Observations

There has been some confusion regarding the grammar of Chinese, which is conceived as "practically the same not only among the dialects but even between modern speech and the classical language" (Chao 1976: 99). In fact, there is at least a crucial difference between modern speech and the classical language that has well been recognized by traditional linguistics, namely, the causative, putative, purposive, and denominative structures, as seen in (4).

(4) a. Causative   斫而小之
                     Zhuó ér   xiǎo zhī.
                     Cut   and small it
                     'cut it and make it smaller'

     b. Putative   登泰山而小天下
                     Dēng   Tài shān   ér   xiǎo tiānxià
                     Climbing Tai Mountain and small world
                     'On top of the Tai Mountain you will feel the world is so small.'

     c. Purposive   死國可乎?
                     Sǐ   guó   kě   hu
                     Die country can Q
                     'Can I die for the country?'

     d. Denominative 君子不器
                     Jūnzǐ   bú qì
                     Learned-men not utensil.
                     'An honorable man is not an utensil.'

The syntactic operation of the above sentences had vanished after the Han Dynasty (206 B.C.–220 A.D.), even if there are sporadic examples of light-verb structures observed in Modern Chinese, for example:

(5) Causative   Lǜ-huà   xiàoyuán
                   Green-ize campus
                   'to make campus green'
     Putative   Zhòng lǐ   qīng wén
                   Heavy science light humanity
                   'to consider science more important than humanities'
     Benefactive   Fúwù   zǔguó
                   Service country
                   'to do service for one's country'

Nominative Dōu dàrén le,   zénme hái   niào chuáng ne ?
Even adult Asp. Why   still pee bed   Q
'S/h e is an adult already, how come s/he still wets the bed?'

Note that the examples given in (5) are not freely (or systematically) formed in Modern Chinese, even if some linguists considered examples in (5) and particularly in (6) to be derived by light-verb movement (Feng 2000; Lin 2001), as shown in the tree structure of (6a):

(6)

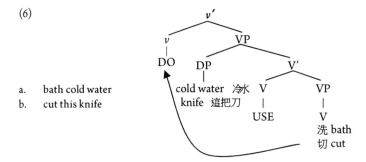

a.   bath cold water
b.   cut this knife

c.   Pái   tóugè
      Line first
      'To line up as the first one.'

d.   Kāi   yè   bān
      Drive night work
      'To drive for one's duty of the night assignment.'

e.   Chī shítáng
      Eat cafeteria
      'To eat at a cafeteria.'

All these examples may give analysts an impression that the same syntactic operation observed in Archaic Chinese is still operative in modern times. However, it is important to note that the grammar of light verbs (or the "non-canonical objects") is not freely operable in Modern Chinese without an idiomatic or conventionalized context. For example:

(7) a. *Tā jīngcháng chī Dìdū Fàndiàn
         He oftern   Eat Royal Restaurant.
         'He often eats at Royal Restaurant.'

     b. *Zhège sījī   yìzhí kāi   1:30.
         This   driver always drive 1:30
         'This driver always drives for the 1:30 Duty.'

     c. Nǐ   qiē zhèbǎ dāo / *chāzi.
         You cut this   knife/ *fork
         'You cut with this knife /*fork.'

    d. Chī dà wǎn /*pánzi
        Eat big bowl / plate
        'To eat with a big bowl / *plate.'

Feng (2000) characterizes the type of phenomena given (7) in terms of "idiosyncratic or idiomatic usages" (成語化), while "conventionalized meaning" (Lin 2001) and "institutionalized meanings" (A. Li 2012) are also used to generalize the properties of the light-verb syntax in Modern Chinese. The question is this: Is Archaic Chinese more like Modern Chinese in the sense that the light-verb syntax is idiomatized or conventionalized, or is it more like English in that light-verb structures are relatively free productions of the syntax? Before we answer these questions, let us look at the data from Archaic Chinese in the following section.

3. Light Verbs in Classical Chinese: New Observations

In Feng (2005), I proposed that the light-verb syntax in Classical Chinese is freely operative, substantially similar to English. In fact, there have been tremendous works done on the subject of light-verb syntax, not only synchronically and diachronically, but also empirically (Shi 2007) and theoretically (Tsai 2007, 2009, 2012; A. Li 2012; and references cited therein). As we will see below, an increasing number of light-verb structures in Classical Chinese have been uncovered, and the following examples represent most of the cases that have been observed in the literature on light-verb expressions in Archaic Chinese (among others, see Chen 1999; Feng 2003/2005; Shi 2007; and references cited therein). For example:

(8) a. **Place:[at在 N V]**
      旦刷幽燕，晝秣荊越。(顏延年《赭白馬賦》)
      Dàn shuā yōu yān, zhòu mò   jīngyuè (*Yán Yán nián, Zhě bái mǎ fù*)
      Dawn scrub You yan, day   Fodder Jingyue
      'At dawn (I) scrub (the horses) in Youyan and by noon (I) fodder them in Jingyue.'

      (費遂)乃與公謀逐華貙，將使田孟諸而遣之。 《左傳·昭公21》
      (Fèi Suì) nǎi yǔ   gōng móu zhú Huāchū, Jiāng shǐ   tián Mèngzhū ér
      (Fèi Suì) then with duke plan expel Huachu, will   Send hunt Mengzhu and
      qiǎn   zhī.
      dismiss him.
      '(Huā Fèi Suì) then planned with the duke to expel Huachu (from the state), and was about to send him to hunt at Mengzhu area and thence banish him.'
      Zuǒzhuàn-zhāogōng 21nián.

      死長安即葬長安，何必來葬為？《史記·吳王濞列傳》
      Sǐ Cháng'ān jí   zàng Cháng'ān, hé   bì   lái   zàng wéi?
      Die Chang'an city then bury Chang'an city, what must come bury for
      'If I die in Chang'an then I will be buried in Chang'an, why must I come back to be buried here?' *Shǐjì·wú wáng bì liè zhuàn.*

b. **Source: [from從 N V]**

日出東方。《莊子·田子方》

Rì   chū dōng fāng

Sun rise east   direction

'The sun rises from the east.' *Zhuāngzǐ·tián zǐ fang.*

朝發白帝，暮到江陵。《水經注·江水》

Zhāo   fā   Báidì, mù   dào   jiānglíng   (*Shuǐ jīng zhù··jiāng shuǐ*)

Morning depart Baidi, evening arrive Jiangling

'(One) departs from Baidi in the morning and arrives at Jiangling in the evening.'

予取予求，不女疵瑕，《左傳·僖公7》

Yú qǔ   yú qiú   bù nǚ(rù) cīxiá   (*Zuǒzhuàn·xī gōng 7 nián*)

Me take me seek not you   fault

'(You) took from me and pleaded to me, (but I) didn't find fault with you.'

c. **Target[face /toward向/朝 N V]**

使人召犀首，已逃諸侯矣。《韓非子·外儲說右上》

Shǐ rén   zhào   Xīshǒu,   yǐ   táo   Zhūhóu   yǐ

Send someone summon Xishou,   already escape feudal lord Prt.

'(He) sent someone to summon Xishou, but (Xishou) had already fled to the feudal lord' *Hánfēizǐ·wài chǔ shuō yòu shang.*

沛公至咸陽，諸將皆爭走金帛財物之府分之。《漢書·蕭何傳》

Pèi gōng zhì   Xiányáng, zhū jiāng   jiē   zhēng   zǒu jīn   bó   cáiwù zhī

Pei duke arrive Xian'yang, all general each compete run gold silk wealth 's

fǔ   fēn   zhī

storehouse share them.

'When Duke Pei arrived at Xian'yang, all the generals rushed at the (royal) storehouse of gold, silk and valuables to share them.' *Hànshu Xiāohe Zhuàn*

趙簡子令諸侯之大夫輸王粟。《左傳·昭公25 年》

Zhào Jiànzǐ lìng zhūhóu zhī   dàfū   shū   wáng sù   (*Zuǒzhuàn·zhāo gōng 25 nián*)

Zhao Jianzi order feuldal-Lord 's   officer contribute king grain

'Zhao Jianzi gave orders to the officers of feudal lord to contribute grain to the king.'

欲其入而閉之門。《孟子·萬章下》

Yù   qí rù   er   bì   zhī mén   (*Mèngzǐ· wàn zhāng xià*)

Desire his enter but close him gate

'To want him to enter but close the door on him.'

秦饑，晉閉之糴。《左傳·僖公15》

Qín jī,   Jìn bì   zhī dí   (*Zuǒzhuàn· xī gōng 15 nián*)

Qin no harvest, Jin block it grain-sale

'When Qin suffered from a bad harvest, the Jin state blocked its grain sale to Qin.'

d. **Effectee of action[to 對 N V]**

誓之曰："不及黃泉無相見也。" 《左傳·隱西元年》

Shì   zhī yuē bù jí   huáng quán wú xiāng jiàn yě   (*Zuǒzhuàn·yǐn gōng yuán nián*)

Oath her say not reach yellow spring no each   meet Prt.

'(He) swore an oath to her and said: "until we reach the underworld, we shall never see each other."'

厲公 怒紏曰 "謀及婦人, 死固宜哉".《史記·鄭世家》

Lì gōng nù   Jiū yuē: móu jí   fùrén   sǐ   gù   yí   zāi

(*Shǐjì·zhèng shì jiā*)

Li duke angry Jiu say: plan with women death certainly should Prt.

'Duke Li was angry at Jiu and said, "He made plan with his wife, so he deserves to die!"'

夫義人者, 固慶其喜而吊其憂.《國語·魯語下》

Fú yì   rén   zhě, gù   qìng   qí   xǐ ér diào   qí

such righteousness people Prt. indeed celebrate their joy and mourn their

yōu   (*Guóyǔ·lǔyǔ xià*)

sorrow

'A person who is trustworthy to others will surely rejoice at their joy and mourn for their sorrow.'

我幾禍子, 子將為子不利.《左傳··昭公27年》

Wǒ jī   huò   zǐ, zǐ jiāng wéi zǐ   bù lì (*Zuǒzhuàn·zhāo gong 27 nián*)

I   nearly misfortune you, you will do you not profitable

'I have almost brought misfortune on you. You will do something unfavorable to yourself.'

驕其妻妾《孟子·離婁下》

Jiāo   qí qī   qiè

Arrogant his wife concubine

'(He) behaved arrogantly towards his wife and concubine.' *Mèngzǐ·lí lóu xià.*

且君而逃臣, 若社稷何?《左傳·宣公12年》

Qiě   jūn ér táo chén,   ruò shèjì   hé

Moreover ruler and flee subject, how state (gods of soil and grain) what

'Moreover, if a ruler flees in facing a subject (or, run away on the subject), what do you say to the gods of the land and grain?' *Zuǒzhuàn·xuān gong 12 nián.*

e. **Comitative [with 與N V]**

君討臣, 誰敢仇之?《左傳·定公4年》

Jūn   tǎo   chén,   shuí gǎn chóu   zhī   (*Zuǒzhuàn·dìng gōng 4 nián*)

Ruler attack Subject, who dare enemy him

'A ruler punishes his subject, there is no one who dares to be his enemy.'

君子成人之美, 小人反是.《論語·顏淵》

Jūnzǐ   chéng rén zhī   měi,   xiào rén fǎn   shì. (*Lún yǔ·Yányuān*)

Honored men complete people's success, small men opposite it.

'Honorable men fulfill people's success, and small men are opposing to it.'

f. **Reason:[for (因)為N V]**

歸而飲至.《左傳·隱公5年》

Guī   ér   yǐn   zhì   (*Zuǒzhuàn·yǐn gōng 5 nián*)

Return and drink (over) arrival (cf. On your victory we have a drink)

'(The troops) returned and a sacrificial drinking was held because of their arrival.'

討其二于楚也.《左傳·成公9年》

Tǎo   qí   èr   yú Chǔ yě (*Zuǒzhuàn·chéng gong 9 nián*)

Attack their two at Chu Prt.

'(Chu State) attacked them for their betrayal of the Chu.'

冬暖而兒號寒，年豐而妻啼饑。（韓愈《進學解》）

Dōng nuǎn ér ér háo hán, nián fēng ér qī tí jī (Hán yù,

Jìn xué jiě)

Winter warm but child howl cold, year abundant but wife weep hungry

'Although the winter is warm, your children howl because of coldness; although the year brings a bumper harvest, your wife weeps because of hunger.'

王怒曰：“大辱國，詰朝爾射，死藝。”《左傳·成公10年》

Wáng nù yuē: dà rǔ guó, jié cháo ěr shè sǐ yì

King angry say: great disgrace state, next morning you discharge die art

'The king got angry and said, "(you are) a great disgrace to the state. Tomorrow morning you will shoot and die of the art (of archery) (cf. Go to play, okay, but you will die for the play)."' *Zuǒzhuàn·chéng gōng 10 nián.*

逍遙乎寢臥其下，不夭金斧......安所困苦哉？《莊子·逍遙遊》

Xiāoyáo hū qìn wò qí xià, bù yāo jīn fǔ... ān suǒ

Roam around sleep lie-down its under, not die young metal axe... where Prt.

kùn kǔ zāi

difficult bitter prt.

'Roam around and fall asleep under it. It survived from early death by the axe. Where is the reason to be endangered and suffer?' *Zhuāngzǐ·xiāo yáo yóu.*

g. **Recipient:**[give與A以B]

宋百牢我 《左傳·哀公7》 (cf. Hamburger me!)

Sòng bǎi láo wǒ

Song (state) hundred (set of) sacrificial animals us

'Song (state) gave us a hundred sets of animals.' *Zuǒ zhuàn·āi gōng 7 nián.*

牛羊父母、倉廩父母…。 《孟子·萬章上》

Niú yáng fù mǔ cāng lǐn fù mǔ (Mèngzǐ· wàn zhāng shang)

Ox sheep father mother barn storehouse father mother

'Give the oxen and sheep to my parents, and the storehouses also to my parents.'

胙之土 而命之氏。《左傳·隱公8年》

Zuò zhī tǔ ér mìng zhī shì (Zuǒ zhuàn·yǐn gōng 8 nián)

Grant them land and designate them clan name

'(He) grants them territory and designates them clan name.'

h. **Purposive:** [為(for) N V]

召忽死之，管仲不死。《論語·憲問》

Shào hū sǐ zhī Guǎn zhòng bù sǐ

Shao Hu die him Guan Zhong not die

'Shao Hu died for him, but Guan Zhong did not.' *Lún yǔ·xiàn wèn.*

文嬴請三帥。《左傳·僖公33年》

Wén yíng qǐng sān shuài (zuǒ zhuàn·626 B.C.)

Wen Ying petition three commander

'Wen Ying petitioned for the three commanders.' *Zuǒ zhuàn·xī gōng 33 nián.*

丈夫死國，婦人死夫，義也。《元史·忠義》

Zhàngfū sǐ guó, fùrén sǐ fū, yì yě (Yuán shǐ·zhōng yì)

Men die state, women die husband, righteous Prt.

'It is righteousness that men die for their state and women for their husbands.'

i. **Resemble: [N（不）如/像N]perform/resemble**
   (i). A resembles B

君君臣臣父父子子《論語・顏淵》

Jūn jūn chén chén fù fù zǐ zǐ

Lord lord, subject subject, father father, son son

'Lords behave like lords, subjects behave like subjects, fathers behave like fathers, sons behave like sons.' *Lún yǔ·yányuān.*

觚不觚，觚哉觚哉《論語・雍也》

(Cornered) gū bù gū, gū zāi gū zāi (*Lún yǔ·yōng yě*)

(Cornered) beaker not beaker, beaker Prt beaker Prt.

'The cornered beaker does not look like a beaker. What a beaker! What a beaker!'

君子不器《論語・為政》

Jūnzǐ bù qì

Honorable men not utensil

'Gentlemen (learned men) do not behave like instruments.' *Lún yǔ·wéi zhèng.*

晉靈公不君《左傳・宣公二年》

Jìn líng bù gōng jūn

Jin Ling duke not lord

'Duke Ling of Jin state does not behave like a lord.' *Zuǒ zhuàn·xuān gong 2 nián.*

(ii). A resembles B Adjective[如N有N]

山中人兮芳杜若《楚辭・九歌・山鬼》

Shān zhōng rén xī fāng Dùruò (*Chǔ cí·jiǔ gē·shān guǐ*)

Mountain inside person Prt. fragrant flower (Duruo)

'The mountains lady is fragrant like the Duruo flower.'

諸君徒能得走獸耳，功狗也。《史記・蕭相國世家》

Zhū jūn tú néng dé zǒu shòu ěr, gōng gǒu yě

(*Shǐ jì·xiāo xiāng guó shì jiā*)

All you merely can get run beast only, achievement dog Prt.

'All of you could only capture the scampering beast, and so your achievement is that of (hunting) dogs'

j. **Causative: [make使NV]**
   (i). A causes B to be(come) C

匠人斫而小之。《孟子・梁惠王下》

Jiàng rén zhuó ér xiǎo zhī (*Mèngzǐ·liáng huì wáng xià*)

Carpenter man strike and small it

'The carpenters cut and made it small.'

因其所大而大之，因其所小而小之。《莊子・秋水》

Yīn qí Suǒ dà ér dà zhī, yīn qí suǒ xiǎo ér xiǎo zhī (*Zhuāngzǐ·qiū shuǐ*)

Based its prt. big and big it, by its Prt. small and small it

'To make it bigger based on where the size is big and make it smaller based on where the size is smaller.'

勞師以襲遠。《左傳・僖公32》

Láo shī yǐ xí yuǎn (*Zuǒzhuàn·xī gōng 32 nián*)

Fatigue army thereby raid distant

'To toil an army (with a long march), and raid a distant place with it.'

齊襄公與魯君飲，醉之。《史記·齊太公世家》

Qì Xiāng Gōng yǔ lǔ jūn yǐn, zuì zhī   (Shǐjì·jì tài gōng shì jiā)
Qi Xiang Duke with Lu ruler drink, drunk him
'Duke Xiang of Qi state drank with the ruler of Lu state and made him drunk.'

(ii). A causes B to be (come/with) C

公戟其手曰："必斷而足！"《左傳·哀公25年》

Gōng jǐ   qí shǒu yuē bì   duàn ér zú   (Zuǒ zhuàn·āi gong 25 nián)
Duke halberd his hand say must cut you foot
'The duke bends his fingers like a halberd and said: "I will certainly cut your feet!"'

解衣衣我，推食食我。《史記·淮陰侯列傳》

Jiě   yī   yì   wǒ tuī shí sì   wǒ   (Shǐ jì·huái yīn hóu liè zhuàn)
Remove clothes clothe me push food feed me
'(He) took off his garments to clothe me, and gave up his food to feed me.'

生死而肉骨也。《左傳·襄公22》

Shēng sǐ   ér ròu gǔ yě   (Zuǒzhuàn·xiāng gong 22 nián)
Life death and meat bone Prt.
'(He) let the dead have life, and the bare bones have flesh.'

夫人之，我可不夫人之乎？ 《谷梁傳·僖公8年》

Fūren zhī, wǒ kě bù fūren zhī hū   (Gǔ liáng zhuàn·xī gong 8 nián)
Wife her, I can not wife her Prt.
'(When the text) calls her 'the wife,' can I avoid calling her 'the wife'?'

k. **Treatment: [take以Ato be為B]**
時充國年七十餘，上老之。《漢書·趙充國傳》

Shí   Chōngguó nián qī-shí yú, shàng   lǎo zhī   (Hàn shū·zhào chōng guó
                                                      zhuàn)
Time Chongguo age   seventy over, emperor old him
'At that time, Chongguo was seventy odd years of age, and the emperor treated him
as an elderly.'

鼎鐺玉石，金塊珠礫。（杜牧《阿房宮賦》）

Dǐng   chēng   yù shí jīn kuài   zhū lì(Dù mù, Ēfáng gōng fù)
Cauldron shallow pan jade stone gold lump of earth pearl gravel
'(They) treat a cauldron as a pan, jade as stone, gold as a lump of earth, and pearl as
gravel.'

孟嘗君客我。《戰國策·齊策四》

Mèngcháng jūn kè   wǒ
Mengchang lord guest me
'Lord Mengchang treated me as a guest (respect me).' (Zhàn guó cè·jì cè 4)

甘其食，美其服，安其居，樂其俗。《老子·道德經》

Gān qí   shí měi qí   fú   ān   qí   jū   lè   qí
Sweet such food pretty such clothes comfortable such dwelling delightful such
sú
custom
'(They) consider such food delicious, such clothes beautiful, such dwelling
comfortable, and such custom delightful.' Lǎozi Dàodéjīng.

l. Being:[為 (be) A's 之 B]

故事半古之人，功必倍之。《孟子·公孫醜上》
Gù   shì bàn gǔ   zhī   rén, gōng   bì   bèi   zhī.
Therefore work half ancient 's   people achievement necessarily double it
'Therefore, his work is half the work of people of ancient times, but his achievement is
twice as much as that of people of ancient times.' *Mèngzǐ·gōng sūn chǒu shang.*

大夫倍上士，上士倍中士，中士倍下士。《孟子·萬章下》
Dàfū   bèi   shàng shì, shàng shì bèi   zhōng shì,   zhōng shì
Great-officer double high-officer, high officer double middle officer, middle officer
bèi   xià shì
double low officer
'Great officers' (income) is twice as much as high ranking officers', high rank officers'
(income) is twice as much as middle ranking officers', middle ranking officers'
(income) is twice as much as low ranking officers.' *Mèng zǐ·wàn zhāng xià*

武安由此滋驕，治宅甲諸第。《史記·魏其武安侯列傳》
Wǔ Ān yóu cǐ   zī   jiāo,   zhì   zhái   jiá zhū dì
Wu An from this more arrogant, govern residence first all   mansion.
'From then on (marquis) became even more arrogant, and built his residence to be
the best of all mansions.' *Shǐjì·wèi qí wǔ ān hóu liè zhuàn.*

布常冠軍。《漢書·黥布傳》
Bù cháng guān(guàn)   jūn
Bu often   hat (first place) army
'Bu often was a chief commander of army.' *Hàn shū·qíng bù zhuàn.*

惠子相梁，莊子往見之。《莊子·秋水》
Huìzǐ Xiāng   Liáng,   Zhuāngzǐ wǎng jiàn zhī (*Zhuāng zǐ·qiū shuǐ*)
Huizi minister Liang state Zhuangzi go   see him
'Master Hui became a minister of Liang state, so master Zhuang went there to see him.'

古之王者建國君民，教學為先。《禮記·學記》
Gǔ   zhī wáng zhě jiàn   guó jūn mín,   jiāo xué wéi   xiān
                                                          (*lǐ jì·xué jì*)
Ancient 's king Prt. establish state lord subjects, teach learn be   priority
'Those who were kings of the old times, in establishing a state and playing a ruler of
their subjects, made teaching and learning their priority.'

m. Instrument:[do A by B]

鴛鴦于飛，畢之羅之。《詩經·小雅·鴛鴦》）
Yuān yāng   yú fēi, bì zhī luó zhī   (*Shījīng· Xiǎoyǎ·Yuānyāng*)
Aix   galiericulata prt. fly, net it   and basket it.
'When the Aix galiericulata about to fly, (one may like) to net them and to basket
them.'

All the examples given above can be reformulated with following patterns:

(9) (a) Place: [at Place Vi/t]→ [Vi/t Place]
     (b) Source: [from Source V] → [V Source]
     (c) Target   [face/toward Direction V] → [to V Direction]
     (d) Comitative: [to be with someone V] → [to V someone]
     (e) Reason: [because N V] → [to V N]

(f) Recipient: [to give A to B] → [to B the A]
(g) Benefactive: [for (reason of) N V] → [to V the N]
(h) Resemble: i.   [to (not) act like A] → [(not) to A]
        ii.   [to resemble A being B] → [to B the A]
                     [to resemble A having B] → [to B the A]
(i) Causative: [to make N Adj.] → [to Adj. the N]
        i.   [to cause A to be (come) B] → [to B the A]
        ii.   .[to cause A to be with B] → [to B the A]
        iii.   [to cause A to like/have B] → [to B the A]
(j) Treatment: [to treat A using the way of treating B] → [to B the A]
(k) Being: [to be A's B] → [to B the A]
(l) Instrument: [to do A by B] → [to B A] (畢之羅之)

Needless to say, widespread light-verb phenomena existed in Archaic Chinese, which indicates that the light-verb structures were freely construed at that time (i.e., around 400 b.c.). Comparing Archaic Chinese with English, we see that there are many parallel light-verb expressions between the two languages as well. The following examples show the similarity of the two languages, and also a typological difference between Modern Chinese and Classical Chinese. For example:

(10)   **English**   **Archaic Chinese**   **Modern Chinese**
        a. Parents
        He fathered the Children   fù   wǒ 父我[1]   *baba wo 'father me'
                                    father me 'respect me'
        She mothers him.   mǔ   tiānxià 母天下[2]   *mama tamen 'mother them'
                                    mother world   'be world's mother'
        b. Animals
        Dog them/him   chú.gǒu   wànwù 芻狗萬物[3]   *gou laobaixing 'dog people'
                                    straw.dog world   'to treat the world like straw-dog'
        He fished yesterday.   shǐ   yú 始漁[3]   *qu yu 'go fish'
                                    start fish 'to start to fish'
        c. Body
        Don't eye me   mùˋ zhī 目之[4]   *yanjing ta 'eye him'
                                    eye her 'to eye her'
        Don't knee him   xī   xí 膝席[5]   *xigai chuang 'nee on the bed'
                                    knee rag 'knee on the rug'
        Don't elbow him   zhǒu zhī 肘之[6]   *gebo.zhou ta 'elbow him'
                                    elbow him 'to elbow him'
        Hand me the paper   shǒu jiàn 手劍[7]   *shou baojian 'hold the sword'
                                    hand sword 'to hold the sword.'

---

[1] 《汉书·萧望之传》: "侯年宁能父我耶！"
[2] 《汉书·刘辅传》 "欲以 (卑贱之女) 母天下。"
[3] 《礼记·月令》 "是月也, 命渔师始渔。"
[4] 《史记·卫康叔世家》 "瞷瞯数目之, 夫人觉之, 惧, 呼曰: 太子欲杀我！"
[5] 《史记·魏其武安侯列传》: "故人避席耳, 余半膝席。"
[6] 《左传·成公二年》 "从左右, 皆肘之。"

Shouldered a basket	Jiān	huò 肩貨[8]	*jian.bang dongxi 'to shoulder'
	shoulder goods 'to carry goods on the shoulder'		
Butt someone (頂)	Wú zhǒng Chú 吳踵楚[9]		*Riben jiaogen Meiguo 'Japan
	Wu heel Chu 'Wu follows Chu' follows America.'		
Horn in	bǐ tóng (ér) jiǎo 彼童		*jijiao ta 'to gore him'
	而角[10]		
	that enfant (and) horn		
	that (was a) boy and knotted his hair'		

d. Instruments

How dare you caned him!	zhàng zhī 杖之[11]		*gunzi ta 'cane him'
	cane him 'to beat him'		
Knife his chest	zì rèn 自刃[12]		*dao.ren ziji 'to suicide with
	self blade		blade (Knife)'
	'suicide with a knife'		

e. Cooking

He breads the children.	Fàn Xìn 飯信[13]		*mifan Zhangsan 'to feed Z'
	Food Xin 'to feed Mr. Xin'		
They are spooning.	shǎo jiāo jiāng勺椒漿[14]		*shaozi niunai 'to spoon milk'
	spoon spice milk		
	'to ladle out spice milk'		
She waters flowers.	huò zhī, shuǐ zhī 火之,		*shui ta 'to water it'
	水之[15]		
	fire it, water it		
	'to burn it (and) to water it'		

f. Clothing

I clothe myself	yī zhī Máng fú衣之		*yifu ta 'to cloth him'
	尨服[16]		
	clothe it Mang dress		
	'to dress him with Mang clothing'		
Mommy trousers me.	lǚ zhī 履之[17]		*xie ta 'to shoe him'
	shoe him 'to wear shoes for him'		

As seen above, there are identical structures between English and Chinese in terms of light-verb operations. On the other hand, the same (or similar) expressions are NOT allowed in Modern Chinese, indicating that the light-verb syntax must operate

---

[7] 《公羊傳·莊十三年》"曹子手劍而從之"。《司馬相如·上林賦》"手熊羆"。註: "言手擊之"。

[8] 《尚书·说命》"不肩好货"、"行, 肩而不并"。

[9] 《左传·昭公24年》"吴踵楚, 而疆场无备, 邑能无亡乎?"   《孟子·滕文公上》"自楚之藤, 踵门而告文公。"

[10] 《诗·大雅·荡》"彼童而角。"《左传·襄公14年》"譬如捕鹿, 晋人角之, 诸戎掎之。"

[11] 《子思子》"怒而杖之。"

[12] 《左传·襄公25年》"请自刃于庙, 勿许。"

[13] 《史记··淮阴侯列传》"有一母见信饥, 飯信."

[14] 《汉书·礼乐志》"勺椒浆."

[15] 《考工记》"刊阳木而火之, 剥阴木而水之。"《考工记》"水之以其平沈之均也。"《左传·昭公30年》"防山以水之。"

[16] 《左传·僖公·元年》"衣之尨服, 远其躬也。"《礼记·缁衣》"君子问人之寒, 则衣之"

[17] 《史记·留侯世家》"遂长跪履之"

differently between English and Archaic Chinese on the one hand, and Modern Chinese on the other hand.

Although Archaic Chinese and English exhibit similarities in light-verb syntax as seen above, the light-verb structures involving instruments, locatives (path, destination), and temporal in English, as indicated by A. Li (2012), are different from those involving benefactive, recipients, and comitatives because the former is acceptable, while the latter may cause ungrammatical results in compound formations. For example:

(11)   Instruments: Axe-murderer
        Temporals: Sunday driver/ring
        Locatives: sky-walker/ing
        Comitatives: *friend-goer/ing (someone who goes a place with friends)
        Benefactives: *Baby-worker/ing (someone who does work for the baby)

How can we account for the grammatical contrasts between English and Archaic Chinese? There have been proposals (A. Li 2012) explaining the differences in English and Modern Chinese. A. Li (2012) claims that in a synthetic language, the lexical items specify whether they are transitive (requiring a canonical object) or intransitive (not requiring a canonical object), or requiring lexical specification of the argument structures of verbs (verb vs. V-ing/er), while in analytic languages, on the other hand, the lexical items do NOT specify whether they are transitive (requiring a canonical object) or intransitive (not requiring a canonical object). Thus, there are different structures that are allowed by different languages (English is less analytic than Modern Chinese so the light-verb structures are more restricted than Modern Chinese).[18]

Although this hypothesis is insightful, we still face the question of whether Archaic Chinese is typologically more similar to English or Modern Chinese. Given that Archaic Chinese systematically permits light-verb operations, which is obviously different from the syntactic type of Modern Chinese but closer to the type of English, in the sense that more light-verb structures were permitted with richer morphological markers in that language (Classical Chinese had more affixes than medieval and Modern Chinese).[19] What is the difference between Classical Chinese and Modern Chinese, on the one hand, and Classical Chinese and English, on the other? The following section will deal with these questions.

---

[18] A. Li (2012) also observed that No-Case marking languages allow non-canonical objects, where Overt-Case-marking languages do not allow for such objects. Thus, case marking is another possible reason for non-canonical object (i.e., light verb) structures occurring in different languages. How to account for the difference between Classical Chinese (that permits free light-verb construction, i.e., all the non-canonical objects in Modern Chinese are indeed 'canonical' in Archaic Chinese) and Modern Chinese (that permits only non-canonical object construction through idiomatization or conventionalization) needs to be explored in future studies.

[19] For example, an *s-caustive prefix may exist in Archaic Chinese (see Yakhontov 1960; Mei 2012):

敗 OC *brads > MC bwai 'lose' / pwai 'defeat,' i.e., *s-brads > s-prads > prads > (MC) pwai
折 OC *djat > MC zjat 'broken' / tsjat 'to break,' i.e., *s-djat > s-tjat > tjat > (MC) tsjat
現 OC *gains > MC gien 'appear' / kien 'to see,' i.e., *s-giens > s-kiens > kiens > (MC) kien

4. A Tentative Explanation

Under a formal analysis (Feng 2005), examples of Classical Chinese seen in (8) and (9) are analyzed in terms of light-verb syntax. More specifically, the causative, putative, purposive, and denomination structures as seen in (4) are analyzed with the following tree diagrams.

(12) a.

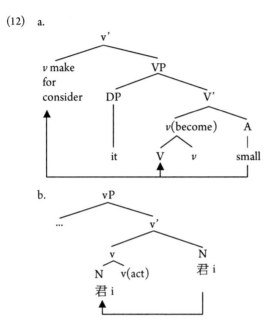

b.

These structures will generate what has traditionally been called CAUSATIVE (to make something physically into (be/become/be with) something else), PUTATIVE (to make something psychologically into (be/become/be with) something else), PURPOSIVE (to do something for someone/something), and DENOMINATIVE ('to perform an action as . . . ,' or 'to act as . . .') constructions in Classical Chinese. Examples given in (9) also show that more complex thematic relations may be involved in the V' events. That is, the extra-arguments selected by the light verbs have more complex theta-relations with the V' event. Let us first look at English:

(13) (a) Recipient NP: [. . . get [***the teacher***] [a present]]
      (b) Experiencer NP: [. . . persuade [***me***] [to take syntax]]
      (c) Participant NP: [. . . read [**me**][a book]], [. . .pass [**me**][salt]], [. . .buy [**me**][a book]]
      (d) Participant PP: [He agrees [**with me**] [that the paper turns red]]
                              [I learned [**from him**] [that study has no fine]]
                              [He suggested [**to him**] [that he does safe syntax]]
                              [He may lie [**to you**]]
                              [He protested [**to the prime minister**]]

The extra-arguments located under SPEC of VP have different thematic relations with their predicate V': it can be an experiencer, a recipient, or a participant, and sometimes called an outer object or 'non-canonical' object in Modern Chinese (Huang 2009; Li, 2012). When compared with the extra-arguments in Classical Chinese, we see that thematic relations between the NPs under SPEC are more complex than those in English, as seen in (9).

Comparing the thematic relations between elements under the SPEC of VP and the V' in both English and Classical Chinese, I would like to suggest that the structures in Classical Chinese may involve a more abstract light verb, say, INVOLVE or DO, that selects a DP/PP (as involver) and a VP (for the event that the involver is involved in),[20] that is:

(14)

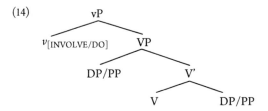

The tree diagram in (14) illustrates a thematic structure of the DP/PP in SPEC of VP with the event V'; and the whole thematic structure can be interpreted as follows: (there) INVOLVE (light-v) a participant (NP in Spec of VP) in an event/action (V-bar).

Evidence supporting this hypothesis comes from the fact that in Classical Chinese, the thematic relation of the NP in SPEC of VP may or may not be introduced by a phonetically realized light verb (or P, in traditional terms). In other words, there was no overt functor that assigned theta role to the NP in SPEC of VP in Archaic Chinese, and there was no corresponding P in later developments of the language to be used to specify the thematic relation between the participant NP and the V' action in medieval Chinese either. Let's look at the following examples first.

(15) a. 鄭公逃其師而歸。《左傳·僖公5年》
          Zhèng Gōng [táo qí shī]   ér guì   (*Zuǒzhuàn·xǐ gōng 5 niǎn*)
          Zheng Duke [run his army] and back.
          'Duke Zheng runs away from his army and went back to his home.'

      b. 使人召犀首，已逃諸侯矣。《韓非子·外儲說右上》
          Shǐ rén   zhào Xīshǒu, yǐ   [táo Zhūhóu]   yi.
          Send people call Xishou, already [run FeudalLords] prt.
          'When sending people to get Xishou, he has run to the Feudal Lord already.'
          Hánfēizǐ·wài chǔ shuō yòu shang.

---

[20] The abstract INVOLVE could simply be represented just by the DO. Thanks go to Jim Huang for this suggestion.

c. 且君而逃臣，若社稷何？《左傳·宣公12年》
qiě jūn ér [táo chén], ruò shèjì hé?
and lord but [run subject], to country what?
'Being a lord, if you run away (from our army) when there is a subject of the enemy, how can we report it to our ancestors?' *Zuǒzhuàn·xuān gōng 12 nián.*

The light verbs c-commanding the verb *táo* 'run away' can be specified with a thematic feature of 'from' in (15a) and 'to' in (15b). However, the thematic feature in (15c), that is, the thematic relation between the event *táo* 'run away' and the involver *chén* 臣 'subject,' cannot easily be specified by any existent (or later developed) prepositions as 'from,' 'to,' or even 'because.' Because the discourse sentence does not mean that the lord runs away because there is a subject. Instead, the sentence contrasts the lord with the subject, on the one hand, and on the other hand, it emphasizes the action 'run away' that took place just in front of the 'subject.' In other words, there is no one-to-one correspondence between a light-verb structure (in Archaic Chinese) and a PP-structure (in later development).[21] Without having a later developed (correspondent) preposition (from the covert light verb) as a theta-role assignment indicator, what would be the thematic relation between the action *táo* 逃 and the entity *chén* 臣 in (15c)? A more plausible answer, I would like to suggest, is to propose that an abstract relation INVOLVE is functioning here. That is, the subject *chén* is simultaneously involved in *táo* when the action took place. The specific relation between the involvee and the action is not what the structure is about.

Another support of this analysis comes from the fact that light-verb expressions like *miǎn wú sǐ* 免吾死 'relieve/cancel him death > free him from death penalty/cancel his death penalty' (16a) cannot be structured in Modern Chinese with a ditransitive verb structure (16c); instead, it can only be paraphrased with a pseudo-possessive form, as in (16b).

(16)　a.　賜我玉而免吾死也，敢不稽首以拜？《左·昭·十七年》
Cì wǒ yùér miǎn wú sǐ, gǎn bú jī-shǒu yí bài (*Zuǒzhuàn·zhāo gōng 17 nián*)
Give me jade and relieve me die, dare not head-down and make a courtesy call.
'(you have) given me the jade and freed me from death (or canceled my death penalty), how dare I do not down my head and make a courtesy call?'

　　　b.　免他的死
Miǎn tā de sǐ
Relieve he 's die
'To cancel his death penalty' or 'to free him from a death penalty'

　　　c.　*对他免死
*Duì tā miǎn sǐ
To him relieve death
'To free him from death penalty'

The example in (16a) shows that the historical transformation from a light-verb structure to a [PP+VO] structure, as seen in (8), did not take place on the verb *mian* 'to relieve/cancel,' indicating that not all of the semantic relations denoted by light-verb

---

[21] See Li A (2012) for a similar argument for Modern Chinese).

structures in Archaic Chinese are grammaticalized into [PP+VO] structures later on. It follows that although the thematic relation licensed by the abstract light verb INVOLVE were not grammaticalized totally during the typological change from syntheticity to analyticity, the new [PP+VO] structures during and after the Han Dynasty resulted from the grammaticalization of covert light verbs becoming overt ones (either a lexical verb, a functional light verb, or a co-verb).

Given the above analysis, expressions in Archaic Chinese such as *e sui*惡睢 'to evil Sui' will be analyzed as "performed an action of *zuo e*作惡 'make evil thing' where *sui*睢 is involved in that action." [22] What is the specific way that Sui is involved in that action? World knowledge will tell, for example, either as 'saying bad things to Mr. Sui' or as 'did bad things to Mr. Sui', and so on. It is not the responsibility of the light-verb syntax to give specifications as to how Mr. Sui is involved in the 'bad things'; rather, it is the world-knowledge that interprets the relations specifically in different situations (or contexts) where the action took place.

The INVOLVE can therefore be understood as a covert generic light verb, exactly on par with the generic light noun that functions to hold a syntactic position (for the light noun in Classical Chinese, see Huang 2009; Feng 2012). The generic light verb gives a broadest thematic relation to the NP under SPEC with the V' under the VP, and it acts just like the generic classifier *ge* that could replace different and specific classifiers in Modern Chinese. Thus, we have three types of parallelisms of light functors in the language: (1) light verb parallels light noun; (2) generic light nouns parallels generic light verb; (3) the grammaticalization of generic light nouns > specific light nouns parallels to that of generic light verbs > specific light verbs around the time of the Han Dynasty.

Given the above analysis, it becomes plausible that the abstract INVOLVE/DO is expected to have a counterpart when it became a phonologically realized one in medieval and Modern Chinese. In other words, if there is a phonetically covert generic light verb in Archaic Chinese, when the covert light verbs were grammaticalized into overt ones, there would also be a phonetically realized generic light verb later on, functioning as the counterpart of the covert one in Archaic Chinese. As seen in the following examples, this prediction is borne out.

The Modern Chinese light verb *gǎo* is an overt light verb, and it can be perfectly analyzed as an INVOLVE type light verb in Modern Chinese. Although *gǎo* is often translated as 'DO,' it has different connotations and interpretations when it occurs with different types of (non-canonical) objects in Modern Chinese, for example:

(17)   *gǎo*搞 = DO (cleaning/manufacture/work/activity搞衛生/生產/工作/活動, etc.)
    *gǎo*搞 = GET (water/material搞點水/材料, etc.)
    *gǎo*搞 = SET (firmly 搞定, etc.)
    *gǎo*搞 = PLAY (ghost/tricks 搞鬼, etc.)
    *gǎo*搞 = MAKE (joke/ 搞笑, etc.)
    *gǎo*搞 = CARRY OUT (business搞商業, etc.)

---

[22] 《史记・范睢列传》："公前以睢為有外心於齐而恶睢於魏齐，公之罪一也。"

gǎo搞 = FIND/DATE (lover/fiancee搞對象, etc.)
gǎo搞 = ESTABLISH (relationship搞關係, etc.)
gǎo搞 = PUNISH (people幾個人合起來搞他, etc.)

Regarding the different usages of *gǎo* in (17), one may say that there are nine (or more) different *gaos* in Modern Chinese. However, a simple and unified solution would be to consider *gǎo* as a generic light verb used for different thematic relations between the action and the entity involved in that action. Note that if light-verb typologies differ in terms of phonologically realized (overt) in Modern Chinese accord with its analytic properties, and phonetically unrealized (covert) in Archaic Chinese accord with its synthetic properties (Feng 2005, 2009; Huang 2009), then it is expected that there should be two types of generic light verbs given the hypothesis presented here, that is, one is overt (phonetically realized) in Modern Chinese and the other is covert (phonetically unrealized) in Archaic Chinese. Obviously, what is predicted by the theory is what we see in reality.

5. Theoretical Implications

The proposed generic light verb in this study has a number of theoretical implications. First, it is well known that there are ambiguous interpretations of a light-verb expression, for example:

(18) a. Qín mín 勤民 (*Zuo Zhuan*)
          Work people

          (i)   'To make people to work' ("秦違蹇叔，而已貪勤民"《左傳·僖33》)
          (ii) 'To work for people' ("令尹其不勤民，實自敗也"《左傳·僖28》)

      b. Wàng wǒ 王我
          King me
          (i)   'To consider me to be the king' ("縱江東父老憐而王我，何面目見之"《史記》)
          (ii) 'To make me to be the king' ("爾欲吳王我乎? "《左传》)
          (iii) 'To be a king of mine' (cf. 王天下)

      c. Qī zhī 妻之
          Wife her/him
          (i)   'To take her as a wife'
          (ii) 'To find a wife for him'

Theoretically, generic light verbs with an abstract content, regardless of whether it is phonetically realized or not, will inevitably be interpreted ambiguously as having different thematic relations between the entity and the action (under the V') in which the entity is involved, causing the light-verb construction to have different semantic effects. This is borne out by evidence from Archaic Chinese, as seen in (18).

The different semantic interpretations are also expected in contexts where the relations between the action (event) and the participant (involver) are established under different social-cultural conditions. In other words, the culture-dependent relation between the involver (the NP) and the event (V') can be established by world knowledge synchronically, diachronically, or even cross-linguistically. Thus:

(19) *fù zhī* 父之 'father him' in Classical Chinese : to respect him (like respecting a father)

     father him in English: to give birth to him [like what fathers do])

Of course, when one reads *lǎo wó lǎo* 老吾老 'to old my old > to respect my old man,' one cannot understand what it exactly means until one knows what the word 'old' means linguistically, culturally, as well as ethically in the society where the sentence is formed. Given the INVOLVE/DO light-verb hypothesis, this type of cultural-semantics is expected because the INVOLVE/DO light verbs are so generic and abstract that any form of possible relations between the event and the involver would be allowable by the generic light verb proposed here. In other words, syntax provides a structure, INVOVLE/DO (covert or overt) licenses possible thematic relations between an entity (the involver) and an action (denoted by the V'), and finally, it is the world-knowledge (about nature, society, culture, etc.) that interprets what a specific relation will be in the real world at that time and place. [23]

A further expectation under this analysis is that the semantic effects can be different between overt and covert light verbs. For example, 'to make the gravy thin' and 'to thin the gravy' could have two (even if slightly) different meanings: the former may be used to express a procedure (when teaching someone how to cook), while the latter can be used to express what one wants. [24] The different expressive effect can be seen again in the following examples:

(20) a. He taught me English.   = The process of teaching may be completed.

     b. He taught English to me. = It is in the process of teaching.

Given the light-verb syntax discussed in this chapter, the different semantic interpretations would be a natural consequence of a covert light-verb operation that triggers verb-movement and an overt light-verb operation in which no verb-movement is motivated. Thus, in Chinese, as Feng (2000) argued, *shuì xiǎo chuáng* 'sleep (on) a small bed' the light-verb construction is not equivalent to the counterpart of *zài xiǎochuáng shàng shuì* 'on a small bed sleep.' Different structures may motivate different interpretations semantically (see also A. Li 2012 for a similar argument).

Regarding the different semantic interpretations between overt and covert light-verb syntax discussed here, some of the questions raised by Culicover and Jackendoff (2005: 55) may be reconsidered under the current theory, for example: Which particular nouns can become verbs? Given a particular noun, which of many

---

[23] This is similar to the meaning difference between active and passive sentences that share the same underlying structure.

[24] We aware of the fact that the two sentences in (20) may not have two different interpretations for some native speakers. However, when speakers do interpret them differently, the two readings never crossed each other, indicating that the two structures are semantically distinct from each other.

possible derivations into a denominal verb is possible? And finally, given a particle structural realization of a denominal verb, how does the syntactic derivation encode all of the idiosyncratic information that can be expressed in a lexical entry, but that does not follow systematically from syntactic alternation? Obviously, these questions involve some important issues, as discussed in this chapter. As seen earlier, all nouns in Classical Chinese are syntactically permissible to become a verb (with speaker's motivation, of course),[25] and therefore there is no such question as to which noun can become a verb in Archaic Chinese. On the other hand, covert light-verb operations in Modern Chinese are created by idiomatization, which means that no noun is freely permissible to become a verb unless it is conventionalized (and idiomatized) in specific situations, a factor that activates the light-verb operation in L-syntax of Modern Chinese. As for English, it is possible that English is typologically neither so synthetic (as Archaic Chinese) nor so analytic (as Modern Chinese); as a result, the operation of covert light verb is neither so free (as it was in Archaic Chinese) nor so rigid (as it is in Modern Chinese), which may be on par with the different degrees of richness of INFL corresponding to different types of pro-drop effects among languages.

The current comparative study between classical and Modern Chinese, and between Chinese and English, however, shows how the analysis of light verb syntax in Classical Chinese can inform an understanding of syntactic phenomena in English and Modern Chinese, and how insights that are possibly gained in the study of classical languages can in turn shed interesting new light on patterns in modern languages like Mandarin Chinese and English. Although more research needs to be done in this area, the present study raises interesting and important questions for future studies, and the results of this research may provide some fresh perspectives not only on Chinese but also on other, genetically unrelated languages.

Acknowledgments

This chapter was presented at the TEAL-8 Conference and I would like to thank Jim Huang, Dylan Tsai, Niina Zhang, Li Shen. and Mamoru Saito for comments and suggestions that improved this work.

References

Bisang, Walter. 2008. Precategoriality and syntax-based parts of speech: The case of Late Archaic Chinese. *Studies in Language* 32(3), 568–589.

Chen, Puqing. 1999. *Wenyan Jinyi Xue*《文言今譯學》 [Study on Translation of Literary Chinese]. Yuelu Press.

Culicover, Peter, and Ray Jakendoff. 2005. *Simpler Syntax*. Oxford: Oxford University Press.

---

[25] For example, *huo* 'fire' were not used as a verb with a non-canonical object like a 'book' in Archaic Chinese (see [10d]); however, when the chance (or need) is there, it can be used as verb such as *huo qi shu* 火其書 'fire their book > to burn their books' written by Han Yu 韓愈 (768–824) of the Tang Dynasty.

Clark, Even V., and Herbert H. Clark. 1979. When nouns surface as verbs. *Language* 55, 767–811.

Chao, Yuen-Ren. 1976. Chinese national language movement. In *Aspects of Chinese Sociolinguistics*, ed. Y. R. Chao, 97–105. Stanford: Stanford University Press..

Feng, Shengli. 2000.寫毛筆" 與韻律促發的動詞併入 [*Xie maobi* and prosodically motivated verb-incorporation]. *Language Teaching and Linguistic Studies*《語言教學與研究》1, 25–31.

Feng, Shengli. 2003. *Light Verb Syntax in Classical Chinese*. Paper presented at the Conference on Research and Pedagogy in Classical Chinese and Chinese language History. March 28–30, 2003. Columbia University, New York.

Feng, Shengli. 2005. "輕動詞移位與古今漢語的動賓關係 [Light-verb movement in Modern and Classical Chinese]." *Linguistic Science*《語言科學》1, 3–16.

Feng, Shengli. 2012. The syntax and prosody of classifier in Classical Chinese . In *Plurality and Classifiers across Languages of China*, ed. Xu Dan, 67–99. Berlin: de Gruyter.

Hale, Ken, and Samuel Jay Keyser. 1993. On argument structure and the lexical expression of syntactic relations. In *The View from Building 20: Essays in Linguistics in Honor of Sylvain Bromberger*, ed. Kenneth Hele and Samuel Jay Keyser, 53–109. Cambridge, MA: MIT Press.

Hale, Ken, and Samuel Jay Keyser. 2002. *Prolegomenon to a Theory of Argument Structure*. Cambridge, MA: MIT Press.

Harley, H. 2003. Possession and the double object construction. In *Linguistic Variation Yearbook* 2, ed. P. Pica and J. Rooryck, 31–70. Amsterdam: John Benjamins.

Huang, C.-T. James. 1997. Lexical structure and syntactic projection. *Journal of Chinese Languages and Linguistics* 3, 45–89.

Huang, C.-T. James. 2009. Lexical decomposition, silent categories, and the localizer phrase. *Yuyanxu Luncong: Essays on Linguistics* 39, 86–122.

Larson, Richard. 1988. On the double object construction. *Linguistic Inquiry* 19, 335–391.

Li, Audrey 2012. *A Comparative Study of Argument Structure and Lexicon*. Talk at the Chinese University of Hong Kong. May 2012.

Lin, Tzong-Hong. 2001. *Light Verb Syntax and the Theory of Phrase Structure*. Doctoral dissertation, University of California, Irvine.

Mei, Kuang. 2003. Yingjie yi-ge kaozheng-xue he yuyan-xue jiehe de Hanyu yufa-shiyanjiu xin jumian [Anticipating a new horizon of the historical syntax of Chinese incorporating philology and linguistics]. In *Historical Development of Chinese Language*, ed. Dah-an Ho, 23–47. Papers from the Third International Conference on Sinology, Linguistics Section. Taipei: Institute of Linguistics, Academia Sinica.

Mei, Tsu-lin. 2012. The causative *-s and nominalizing *-s in Old Chinese and related matters in Proto-Sino-Tibetan. *Language and Linguistics* 13(1), 1–28.

Shi, Bing. 2007. 上古漢語雙 及物動詞結構研究 [Studies on the structure of ditranstive verbs in Archaic Chinese]. Hefei: Anhui Univeristy Press.

Tsai, W.-T. Dylan. 2007. *Four Types of Affective Constructions in Chinese*. FOSS-5, National Kaohsiung Normal University, Taiwan, April 2007.

Tsai, W.-T. Dylan. 2009. *High Applicatives Are Not High Applicatives: A Cartographic Solution*. FOSS-6. National Taiwan Normal University.

Tsai, W.-T. Dylan. 2012. *A Generative Approach to the Origin of Applicative Structure in Chinese*. Ms., National Chinghua University, Taiwan.

Wang, Siyuan. 1988. "古語文釋例 [Case Studies on Classical Literary Chinese.] Shanghai: Shanghai Classics Press.

Yakhontov, S. E. 1960. *Consonantal Combinations in Archaic Chinese*. Paper presented by the USSR Delegation at the 25th Congress of Orientalists, Moscow. *25th International Congress of Orientalists*, Vol. 5, 89–95. Moscow: Oriental Literature Publishing House.

10

Selection and Incorporation in Complex Predicate Formation

MAMORU SAITO

1. Introduction

The purpose of this chapter is to examine the roles of selection and incorporation in complex predicate formation.[1] I consider lexical complex predicates in Japanese, the resultative serial verb construction in Edo, and compound verbs in Chinese, exemplified in (1)–(3), respectively.

(1) Hanako-ga   Taroo-o   osi-taosi-ta
    Hanako-NOM Taroo-ACC push-make.fall-Past
    'Hanako pushed Taroo and made him fall.'

(2) Òzó suá Úyì dé
    Ozo push Uyi fall
    'Ozo pushed Uyi, which made him fall.'

(3) Ta he-zui   (jiu) le
    he drink-drunk wine Asp.
    'He drank (wine) and became drunk.'

(2) instantiates a serial verb construction with two independent verbs. But I assume, following the analysis proposed in Saito (2001), that the second verb covertly incorporates into the first and forms a complex predicate.

The three constructions are subject to different constraints. Thus, a Japanese lexical complex predicate cannot be formed with the two verbs in (2) or (3), as shown in (4).

[1] This is a revised version of part of the material presented in a colloquium at Harvard University in 2003 and in a syntax seminar at the University of Connecticut in 2005. I would like to thank Jim Huang, Jonathan Bobaljik, and Diane Lillo-Martin, among others, for helpful comments. I benefitted from discussions with many people at various occasions. Special thanks are due to Mark Baker and Jim Huang for their extensive help with the analysis as well as the data. Shengli Feng, Seng-hian Lau, and Dylan Tsai also kindly provided me with relevant data from Classical Chinese and Chinese dialects. I regret that I was unable to discuss them in this version of the paper.

(4) a. *Hanako-ga   Taroo-o   osi-taore-ta
         Hanako-NOM Taroo-ACC push-fall-Past
         'Hanako pushed Taroo, which made him fall.'

     b. *Hanako-ga   wain-o   nomi-yot-ta
         Hanako-NOM wine-ACC drink-get.drunk-Past
         'Hanako drank wine and got drunk.'

Although other factors may also be involved in these differences, I explore the hypothesis that they arise because of the ways in which derivations are constrained by selectional restrictions and the interpretive mechanism of chains formed by incorporation. Kageyama (1993) argues that Japanese lexical complex predicates are formed before they merge into larger syntactic structures, that is, in the lexicon in his terms. As mentioned above, the resultative serial verb construction in Edo arguably involves covert incorporation. And I explore the possibility, extending the ideas in Tang (1997) and Huang (2006), that Chinese compound verbs are derived by overt incorporation. The hypothesis pursued in this chapter is that selection and chain interpretation interact with these differences in derivation and yield the variations in the possible combinations of verbs.[2]

In the following section, I discuss the transitivity harmony principle, proposed by Kageyama (1993) as a generalization on Japanese lexical complex predicates, and argue that it follows from the selectional relation between v and V. Then, in section 3, I examine the consequences of this proposal for the Japanese light verb construction and the Edo resultative serial verb construction. The conclusion there is that selectional restrictions are constraints on the application of Merge, as opposed to the resulting phrase structure. In section 4, I turn to Chinese examples with compound verbs and illustrate their peculiarities in contrast with the phrasal resultative construction with two independent verbs in the language. Finally, I compare the Edo serial verbs with Chinese compound verbs in section 5 and suggest that their differences may be attributed to the covert versus overt distinction in complex predicate formation. Section 6 concludes the chapter.

2. Japanese Lexical Complex Predicates

In this section, I argue that the restrictions on Japanese lexical complex predicates follow, to a large extent, from the selectional requirements of v. I first briefly review Kageyama's (1993) analysis and then present the argument.

Japanese employs complex predicates extensively. Kageyama, first, divides them into two groups, lexical and syntactic. A syntactic complex predicate projects a

---

[2] Li (1993) presents the most detailed comparison of Japanese lexical complex predicates and Chinese compound verbs, to my knowledge. He assumes that both are formed in the lexicon with composite argument structures. His analysis for the differences between the two, roughly speaking, is based on the proposal that only the former is "doubly headed." Although the account to be proposed in this chapter is syntactic and is quite different from Li's, it does share some of his insights abstractly.

structure with clausal embedding, where each element of the complex predicate functions as an independent verb and projects a VP. Typical examples are shown in (5).

(5) a. Hanako-ga   Taroo-ni   wani-o   tabe-sase-ta
         Hanako-NOM Taroo-DAT alligator-ACC eat-make-Past
         'Hanako made Taroo eat alligator meat'

     b. Taroo-ga   wani-o   tabe-hazime-ta
         Taroo-NOM alligator-ACC eat-start-Past
         'Taroo started to eat alligator meat'

As Kageyama points out, the first verb projects an independent VP in these examples, and hence, a pro-VP (or V') form *soo su* 'do so' can substitute for the VP. This is
shown in (6).

(6) a. Hanako-ga   Taroo-ni   soo s-ase-ta
         Hanako-NOM Taroo-DAT so   do-make-Past
         'Hanako made Taroo do so.'

     b. Taroo-ga   soo si-hazime-ta
         Taroo-NOM so   do-start-Past
         'Taroo started to do so.'

A lexical complex predicate, on the other hand, projects a single VP. Examples are
provided in (7).

(7) a. Taroo-ga   ana-ni suberi-oti-ta
         Taroo-NOM hole-in slip-fall-Past
         'Taroo slipped and fell into a hole.'

     b. Hanako-ga   me-o   naki-harasi-ta
         Hanako-NOM eye-Acc cry-make.swollen-Past
         'Hanako cried and made her eyelids swollen.'

In this case, the pro-VP (V') form *soo su* cannot substitute for the first verb (and its
internal arguments) as in (6) because the first verb does not project a VP (V') by itself.
Thus, the examples in (8) are ungrammatical, as expected.

(8) a. *Taroo-ga   (ana-ni) soo si-oti-ta

     b. *Hanako-ga (me-o)   soo si-harasi-ta

Kageyama (1993), then, presents (9) as a generalization that applies to lexical
complex predicates.

(9) <u>Transitivity Harmony Principle</u>
     In a lexical complex predicate V_1+V_2, if one of the verbs takes an external argument, so does
     the other one.

This generalization is based on the observation that complex predicates that consist
of two unaccusative verbs and those that include two unergative/transitive verbs are

abundant, but we rarely find those that combine an unaccusative verb and an unergative/transitive verb. Relevant examples are listed in (10).

(10) a. transitive-transitive: *hiki-nuk* (pull-pull.out), *nigiri-tubus* (grasp-crash), *tataki-otos* (hit-make.drop), *kiri-tor* (cut-remove)

   b. unergative-unergative: *hasiri-yor* (run-go close), *tobi-ori* (jump-go down), *aruki-mawar* (walk-go.around), *mure-tob* (form.a.flock-fly)

   c. unaccusative-unaccusative: *suberi-oti* (slip-fall), *ukabi-agar* (float-rise), *umare-kawar* (be.born-change), *huri-sosog* (fall-flow)

   d. transitive-unergative: *moti-aruk* (carry-walk), *sagasi-mawar* (look.for-go.around), *mati-kamae* (wait.for-hold)

   e. unergative-transitive: *naki-haras* (cry-make swollen), *nori-kae* (ride.on-change), *nomi-tubus* (drink-waste)

Note that **osi-taore* 'push-fall' and **nomi-yow* 'drink-get.drunk' in (4) instantiate the transitive-unaccusative combination and are ill-formed. (11a–b), which contain complex predicates of unaccusative-transitive combination, are equally ungrammatical.

(11) a. **Kareha-ga   zimen-o   oti-kakusi-ta
       dead.leaf-NOM ground-ACC fall-hide-Past
       'Dead leaves fell and covered the ground.'

   b. **Taroo-ga   kuzira-o   ukabi-mi-ta
       Taroo-NOM whale-ACC float-see-Past
       'A whale came to the surface and Taroo saw it.'

Kageyama's generalization in (9) has been discussed extensively since it was proposed. Yumoto (1996) and Matsumoto (1998), for example, present detailed semantic analyses for lexical complex predicates, and point out some potential counterexamples to the generalization. However, as Kageyama (1999) notes, those examples, even if they are indeed problematic, are quite limited, and (9) clearly expresses a strong tendency that is observed uniquely with Japanese lexical complex predicates.[3] At the

---

[3] It seems to me that the most serious issue is the scope of the generalization rather than its accuracy. As far as I know, there are three kinds of potential counterexamples. The first includes cases where the same verb combines with an unergative verb as well as an unaccusative verb, as in *naki-sakeb* 'cry-scream' and *naki-kuzure* 'cry-collapse.' But *nak*, for example, can mean 'cry' or 'be in tears' and may be ambiguous between unergative and unaccusative. The second group consists of examples where the second verb is *aki* 'be bored with, be tired of', *tukare* 'be tired with' or the like, as in (i).

(i) Taroo-wa   gengogaku-no   hon-o   yomi-aki-ta
    Taroo-TOP linguistics-GEN book-ACC read-be.tired-Past
    'Taroo was tired of reading linguistics books.'

The *soo su* 'do so' test mentioned in the text would classify *yomi-aki* in (i) as a lexical complex predicate, but the possibility seems to remain that *aki* takes a full *v*P complement because the accusative on the object comes from the transitive *yom* rather than the unaccusative *aki*. That is, the failure of *soo su* substitution may be a necessary but not a sufficient condition for a complex predicate to be lexical. The last group consists of examples like *tobi-kom* 'jump-go.into,' where it is dubious that

same time, the generalization, if correct, calls for an explanation. Kageyama (1993) proposes (9) as a language-specific constraint on lexical complex verb formation. But this raises questions, as it is not clear why Japanese should have this constraint and how children acquire it, for example, based on positive evidence. Here, I propose that (9) is to be derived from selection.

It is widely assumed that both of the component verbs in a lexical complex predicate participate in θ-marking. Thus, in (1), repeated below as (12), *Hanako* is the subject and *Taroo* is the object of both *os* 'push' and *taos* 'make.fall.'

(12)   Hanako-ga   Taroo-o   osi-taosi-ta
       Hanako-NOM Taroo-ACC push-make.fall-Past
       'Hanako pushed Taroo and made him fall.'

The sentence cannot depict a situation in which Hanako pushed a chair and as a result made Taroo fall. This implies that each verb is visible in the interpretation of a larger structure. (13) illustrates how *os* and *taos* assign the theme role to *Taroo*.

(13) $[_{VP}$ Taroo $[_V [_V$ osi]-$[_V$ taos]]]

Further, Kageyama (1993) presents clear evidence that each verb in a lexical complex predicate participates in the selectional relations with the arguments. As Japanese morphology is head-final, it is not surprising that the second verb projects its argument structure in the syntax. But the following examples, adopted from Kageyama (1993) with slight changes, demonstrate that the arguments must satisfy the selectional requirements of the first verb as well:

(14)   a.   Tuta-ga   boo-ni maki-tui-ta
            ivy-NOM stick-to wind-attach-Past
            'An ivy twined around the stick.'

       b.   Abura-ga kabe-ni simi-tui-ta
            oil-NOM wall-to soak-attach-Past
            'The wall was stained with oil.'

(15)   a.   *Tuta-ga   boo-ni simi-tui-ta
            ivy-NOM stick-to soak-attach-Past
            'The stick was stained with an ivy.'

the second verb has an argument structure of its own. There is no independent verb *kom* with the appropriate meaning. If Kageyama's generalization has to do with the argument structures of the component verbs, it may not include these examples in its scope to begin with. Kageyama (1993) in fact proposes to analyze *kom* as a verbal suffix that adds information to the lexical-conceptual structure. Finally, as compounds are at issue, it is not surprising if there are cases where they are lexicalized and registered in the lexicon independently of the parts they seem to be composed of. Once this possibility is granted, the generalization loses its strict falsifiability. But it is difficult to avoid the situation with the investigation of compounds, and as stated in the text, the generalization holds over a large domain with at most limited potential counterexamples. See the references cited for more detailed discussion on this issue.

    b. *Abura-ga kabe-ni maki-tui-ta
        oil-NOM wall-to wind-attach-Past
        'The oil twined around the wall.'

(15a) is ungrammatical because an ivy cannot soak into a stick, and (15b) because oil cannot twine around a wall.

    But if both verbs in a lexical complex predicate have selectional relation with the object, they must also participate in the selectional relation with v when v and VP are merged. (16) illustrates this with *osi-taos* 'push-make.fall' in (12).

(16) $[_{v'} [_{VP} \text{Taroo} [_V [_v \text{osi}]\text{-}[_V \text{taos}]]] v]$

Here, v comes in two varieties, v^* and v, as proposed in Chomsky (1995). v^* selects for a transitive/unergative V and hosts an external argument, while v selects for an unaccusative V. Then, the v in (16) must be v^* and the structure is well formed as it enters into proper selectional relation with two transitive verbs. When the complex predicate consists of two unaccusative verbs, the structure should also be legitimate with v selecting for unaccusatives. But when the complex predicate consists of an unaccusative verb and a transitive/unergave verb, a conflict in the selectional relation with v arises. If the VP merges with v^*, then the v^* does not select for the unaccusative verb. On the other hand, if v is employed, its selectional requirement fails with the transitive/unergative verb. Thus, Kageyama's transitivity harmony principle is derived.

3. Complex Predicate Formation with Covert Incorporation

In this section, I assume the account for the restriction on the Japanese lexical complex predicates just presented, and explore its consequences for the analysis of the Japanese light verb construction and the Edo resultative serial verb construction. I argued in Saito (2001) that these constructions involve formation of complex predicates by covert incorporation.[4] I first show that the Japanese light verb construction exhibits a restriction similar to "transitivity harmony," and argue that the account proposed in the preceding section extends to this case. Then, I discuss the Edo resultative serial verb construction, and draw the conclusion that selection is a derivational constraint that applies to the application of Merge.

---

[4] I do not repeat the arguments here and refer the reader to Saito (2001). See also Grimshaw and Mester (1988), Hoshi (1995), and Saito and Hoshi (2000) for detailed discussion on the Japanese light verb construction, and Stewart (1998), and Baker and Stewart (1999) for comprehensive examination of the Edo serial verb constructions.

Let us start with the Japanese light verb construction. Typical examples are shown in (17).

(17)   a.   Hanako-ga   Taroo-ni   [_{NP} toti-no   zyooto]-o   si-ta
           Hanako-NOM Taroo-DAT   land-GEN giving-ACC do-Past
           'Hanako gave a piece of land to Taroo.'

       b.   Hanako-ga   Taroo-kara [_{NP} hooseki-no   ryakudatu]-o si-ta
           Hanako-NOM Taroo-from   jewelry-GEN robbery-ACC do-Past
           'Hanako robbed Taroo of jewelries.'

The peculiarity of this construction, as discussed in detail in Grimshaw and Mester (1988), is that the goal argument in (17a) and the source argument in (17b), *Taroo*, are θ-marked by the head noun of the direct object, *zyooto* in (17a) and *ryakudatu* in (17b), respectively. Given this, it is proposed in Saito and Hoshi (2000) that the head noun of the direct object covertly incorporates into the light verb *su* 'do' and θ-marks *Taroo*.

(18) shows the structure of *v*P in (17a).[5]

(18)

[_{vP} Hanako-ga [_{v'} [_{VP} Taroo-ni [_{V'} [_{NP}toti-no [_N zyooto]]-o [_V [_N zyooto] [_V su]]]] v]]

The head noun *zyooto* 'giving' assigns the theme role to *toti* 'land' in the initial position, and then, covertly incorporates into the verb *su* 'do' and assigns the goal role to *Taroo* from the landing site. If the initial merger of an argument into a structure is confined to its θ-position, as proposed in Chomsky (1995), then the covert incorporation must take place cyclically, that is, as soon as the verb *su* merges with the complement accusative NP. This is so because the position of *Taroo* becomes a θ-position only after the incorporation of *zyooto* into *su*. The cyclic application of covert movement is indeed possible, given the single-cycle model of Bobaljik (1995), where the only distinction between overt and covert movements is whether the phonetic features are realized at the landing site or the initial site.

Grimshaw and Mester (1988) point out a number of interesting constraints on the light verb construction. Among them is that the head noun of the accusative NP cannot be unaccusative. This is illustrated in (19).

(19)   a.   *Mizu-ga   (sara-kara) zyoohatu-o   si-ta
           water-NOM dish-from evaporation-ACC do-Past
           'The water evaporated from the dish.'

       b.   *Antena-ga   (yane-kara) rakka-o   si-ta
           antenna-NOM roof-from falling-ACC do-Past
           'The antenna fell from the roof.'

---

[5] Saito and Hoshi (2000) assume the classical VP-internal subject hypothesis, and hence, place the subject within VP. I assume here that it is merged at *v*P Spec.

These examples receive a straightforward account along the lines proposed in Miya-gawa (1989) and Tsujimura (1990). The v in these sentences must be a v^* as an accusa-tive NP is present. Then, there must be an external argument, which is absent in both (19a) and (19b).

But interestingly, the light verb construction is incompatible with an unaccusative noun even in the presence of an external argument, as shown in (20).

(20) a. *Taroo-ga   sara-kara [$_{NP}$ mizu-no   zyoohatu]-o   si-ta
         Taroo-NOM dish-from   water-GEN evaporation-ACC do-Past
         'Taroo made the water evaporate from the dish.'

   b. *Hanako-ga   yane-kara [$_{NP}$ antena-no   rakka]-o   si-ta
         Hanako-NOM roof-from   antenna-GEN falling-ACC do-Past
         'Hanako made the antenna fall from the roof.'

In this case, there should not be any problem with θ-marking, as illustrated in (21) for (20a).

(21)

[$_{vP}$ Taroo-ga [$_{v'}$ [$_{VP}$ sara-kara [$_{V'}$ [$_{NP}$ mizu-no [$_{N}$ zyoohatu]]-o [$_{V}$ [$_{N}$ zyoohatu] [$_{V}$ su]]]] v]]

Zyoohatu 'evaporation' assigns the theme role to *mizu* 'water' in situ, and then assigns the source role to *sara* 'dish' after covertly incorporating into *su* 'do.' In addition, v hosts the required external argument, *Taroo*, in its Spec.

The analysis presented in the preceding section predicts the ungrammaticality of (20a, b) straightforwardly. Note that the covert incorporation of a noun into *su* cre-ates a complex predicate, and that the formed complex predicates in (20a, b) do not conform to Kageyama's (1993) transitivity harmony principle. In these examples, the complex predicate consists of an unaccusative noun and the verb *su*, which takes an external argument. Hence, the v, whether it is v^* or v, cannot have proper selectional relations with both. The grammatical (17a, b) do not face this problem because the incorporated noun is transitive in both cases.

It was shown that the account for Kageyama's transitivity harmony principle ex-tends to complex predicates formed by covert incorporation. In the remainder of this section, I argue that the Edo resultative serial verb construction, which seems prob-lematic on the surface, provides us with further insights into the role of selection in the derivation.

Representative examples of the Edo construction are shown in (22).

(22) a. Òzó suá Úyì dé
         Ozo push Uyi fall
         'Ozo pushed Uyi, which made him fall.'

   b. Òmó dé wú
         child fall die
         'The child fell and died.'

I proposed in Saito (2001) that this construction involves covert incorporation, just as in the case of the Japanese light verb construction. The derivation of (22a) is illustrated in (23).

(23) $[_{vP}$ Òzó $[_{v'} v \, [_{VP}$ Úyì $[_{V'} [_{V} [_{V}$ suá$]$ $[_{V}$ dé$]]$ $[_{VP} [_{V}$ dé$]]$ $]]]]$

(22a) exhibits the typical resultative paradox, that is, the object Úyì receives θ-roles from both *suá* 'push' and *dé* 'fall.' The paradox is resolved by covert incorporation in (23). The matrix verb *suá* takes the VP headed by *dé* as a complement and hosts Úyì in its Spec position. This configuration allows *suá* but not *dé* to θ-mark Úyì. But the incorporation of *dé* to *suá* creates the desired configuration that makes it possible for both *suá* and *dé* to θ-mark Úyì.[6]

This analysis appears to be in conflict with the proposal on "transitivity harmony" presented earlier because the complex predicate formed by covert incorporation consists of the transitive *suá* 'push' and the unaccusative *dé* 'fall.' But there is a crucial difference between this case and the Japanese light verb construction. In the latter, the covert incorporation was required for the merger of an internal argument in VP Spec. In (17a), repeated below as (24), the incorporation of *zyooto* 'giving' makes it possible for *Taroo* to merge into a θ-position.

(24) Hanako-ga   Taroo-ni $[_{NP}$ toti -no   zyooto]-o   si-ta
      Hanako-NOM Taroo-DAT   land-GEN giving-ACC do-Past
      'Hanako gave a piece of land to Taroo.'

Hence, the covert incorporation must apply cyclically prior to the merger of *Taroo*, and consequently before the merger of *v* into the structure. The situation in (23) is different. Since *suá* 'push' θ-marks Úyì, the incorporation of *dé* 'fall' is not required for the merger of Úyì into the structure. Then, the incorporation can apply after *v* is merged into the structure, as illustrated in (25).

(25)

a. $[_{v'} v \, [_{VP}$ Úyì $[_{V'} [_{V}$ suá$]$ $[_{VP} [_{V}$ dé$]]$ $]]$ $]$ (merger of *v* with VP headed by *suá*)

b. $[_{v'} [_{v} v \, [_{V}$ suá$]]$ $[_{VP}$ Úyì $[_{V'} [_{V}$ suá$]$ $[_{VP} [_{V}$ dé$]]$ $]]$ $]$ (overt incorporation of *suá* into *v*)

c. $[_{v'} [_{v} v \, [_{V}$ suá$]]$ $[_{VP}$ Úyì $[_{V'} [_{V} [_{V}$ suá$]$ $[_{V}$ dé$]]]$ $[_{VP} [_{V}$ dé$]]$ $]]$ $]$ (covert incorporation of *dé*)

---

[6] *Suá* raises overtly to *v*, yielding the surface word order.

This derivation allows v, or more precisely v^* in this case, to satisfy its selectional requirement at the point it is merged into the structure. Thus, there is a way for the Edo resultative construction to circumvent "transitivity harmony."

The account for the difference between Japanese and Edo proposed above has a few consequences. First, incorporation can apply as soon as the target is introduced into the structure, as in the case of the Japanese light verb construction, or wait until a later point, as in (25). Second, the analysis of Edo implies that selectional restrictions are constraints on the application of Merge, and not on the derived structure. This is so since v^* in (25) is in a proper selectional relation with the complement V at the point it is merged into the structure, as in (25a), but not after *dé* 'fall' incorporates into *suá* 'push,' as can be seen in (25c). This conclusion may seem surprising because selectional requirements are understood to be semantic in nature. However, it is in accord, for example, with the head movement of *be* to T as in (26).

(26)   Mary thinks [$_{CP}$ that [$_{TP}$ John is not the best candidate]]

The main verb *be* raises to T in the embedded clause of (26). Nevertheless, the embedded C is in selectional relation only with the embedded T and not with the raised verb. The conclusion indeed seems plausible.

4. Chinese Compound Verbs and the Object Restriction

Chinese compound verbs are not subject to transitivity harmony either. For example, the following examples cited from Huang (1992) contain compounds that consist of a transitive/unergative verb and an unaccusative verb:

(27)   a.   Ta chi-bao   (fan) le
               he eat-full   rice Asp.
               'He ate (rice) and became full.'

         b.   Ta he-zui   (jiu) le
               he drink-drunk   wine Asp.
               'He drank (wine) and became drunk.'

If these compounds are formed by overt incorporation, they can be accounted for in the same way as Edo. That is, the incorporation of the second verb into the first applies after v is merged into the structure. At the same time, Chinese resultatives with compound verbs exhibit an outstanding property that is not shared by the Edo resultatives: they are not subject to Simpson's (1983) object restriction. I discuss this property in this section and then compare Chinese and Edo in the next.

It is known that resultative constructions are, to a large extent, subject to the object restriction, as discussed in detail in Simpson (1983). The restriction states that the result predicate is predicated on the object. Thus, the contrast between (28) and (29) obtains.

(28) a. John painted the barn red

  b. The metal$_i$ was pounded t_i flat

  c. The liquid$_i$ froze t_i solid

(29) a. *John ran tired

  b. *Mary ate the rice full

The restriction applies to the Edo resultative serial verb construction as well, as pointed out in Baker and Stuart (1999).[7] The following examples illustrate this:

(30) a. *Òzó ré kp`Ol'O
     Ozo ate be.big
     'Ozo ate himself fat.'

  b. *Òzó dá (ày'On) mu`Emu'E
     Ozo drink palm wine be.sluggish
     'Ozo drank palmwine and became sluggish.'

On the other hand, Chinese compound verbs are not subject to this restriction, as discussed in detail in Li (1990; 1993) and Huang (1992). This is demonstrated by the examples in (27). The subject *ta* 'he' becomes full in (27a) and becomes drunk in (27b). In this section, I briefly go over the discussion in Huang (2006), which indicates that the object restriction is inapplicable to the Chinese examples in (27) because they employ compound verbs, unlike the English examples in (29) or the Edo examples in (30).

Huang (2006) examines the absence of the object restriction in Chinese in detail. He first notes that compound resultatives and non-compound, phrasal resultatives both apparently do not exhibit the object restriction. (31a) contains a compound *tiao-lei* 'dance-tired' whereas (31b) has two independent predicates *xiao* 'laugh' and *zhan-bu-qilai* 'cannot-stand-up' with the former followed by *de*.[8]

(31) a. Lisi tiao-lei le
     Lisi dance-tired Asp.
     'Lisi danced himself tired.'

  b. Zhangsan xiao-de zhan-bu-qilai
     Zhangsan laugh-till cannot-stand-up
     'Zhangsan laughed so much that he couldn't stand up.'

But the violation of the object restriction in phrasal resultatives, Huang argues, is only apparent.

The resultatives with compounds are not totally free of restrictions. For example, Huang (2006) notes that (27a) is acceptable in the presence of an object only when

---

[7] It is distinguished in this respect from the other serial verb constructions in the language, covert coordination and the consequential serial verb construction. See Baker and Stewart (1999) for detailed discussion.

[8] Huang's (2006) analysis crucially relies on the properties of *de*, which will be discussed later.

the object is a bare NP that is part of the expression *chi fan*, which simply means 'eat' or 'have a meal.' Thus, the following example is unacceptable:

(32) *Zhangsan chi-bao-le   na-wan   fan / liang-wan fan
      Zhangsan eat-full-Asp. that-bowl rice two-bowl rice
      'Zhangsan ate that bowl of rice / two bowls of rice and became full.'

However, he also notes that there are examples in which the result predicate can or even must be predicated of the subject, even when the object is referential. (33) is one of his examples.

(33) Zhangsan kan-lei-le   Lisi / na-ge ren
      Zhangsan chase-tired-Asp. Lisi that person
      'Zhangsan chased Lisi / that person and became tired.'

Given this, he concludes that the second verb in a resultative compound may sometimes be predicated of the subject even in the presence of an object.

The pattern that Chinese phrasal resultatives exhibit is quite different. Although the second verb can apparently be predicated of the subject, as in (31b), this is possible only when the first verb is unergative. When the first verb is transitive and an object appears, the object restriction is indeed observed. The following contrast between a compound resultative and a phrasal resultative illustrates this:[9]

(34) a. Lisi qi-lei-le   ma   le
          Lisi ride-tired-Asp. horse Asp.
          (i) 'Lisi rode a horse and got tired from it.'
          (ii) 'Lisi rode a horse and got the horse tired.'

      b. Lisi qi-de   ma   hen lei
          Lisi ride-till horse very tired
          'Lisi rode a horse and got the horse tired.'

In (34a) with the compound *qi-lei* 'ride-tired,' *lei* can be predicated of the subject, *Lisi*. But (34b) only has the reading in which *lei* is predicated of the object, *ma* 'horse.'

Having observed that subject predication is allowed in phrasal resultatives only when the first verb is unergative, Huang (2006) goes on to argue that the violation of the object restriction in this case is only apparent. He first notes that phrasal resultatives with unergative verbs exhibit inchoative-causative alternation, as shown in (35).

(35) a. Ta tiao-de   man-shen-da-han
          he dance-till whole-body-big-sweat
          'He danced [himself] all sweaty.'

      b. Yi-zhi   tangewu tiao-de   ta man-shen-da-han
          one-CL tango   dance-till he whole-body-big-sweat
          'A tango dance caused him to dance himself all sweaty.'

---

[9] Huang notes that there are limited potential counterexamples to this generalization and offers speculations on them.

Here, it is known that unaccusatives, but not unergatives, show alternation of this kind. (36b) is fine but (37b) is totally ungrammatical.

(36)   a.   The boat sank

       b.   The bomb sank the boat

(37)   a.   John laughed

       b.   *The joke laughed John

Then, the grammaticality of (35b) indicates that *tiao-de* in (35a) is unaccusative. At this point, Huang observes that *-de* evolved out of the verb *de* 'get,' which can be paraphrased as *bian-de* 'become' or *shi-de* 'cause,' just like its English translation *get*. He then proposes that *-de* with the unaccusative meaning 'become' heads *tiao-de* in (35a), and *tiao* modifies it indicating the manner in which the event happens.

   Huang's (2006) analysis of phrasal resultatives in Chinese implies that they are subject to the object restriction. Then, the violation of the restriction is a unique property of the compound resultatives. In the following section, I consider the difference between the Chinese compound resultatives and the Edo serial verb resultatives with respect to the object restriction. I entertain the possibility that the difference arises because incorporation is overt in the former while it is covert in the latter, and present an analysis in terms of chain interpretation.[10]

5. Comparison of Chinese Compound Resultatives with Edo Resultatives

As discussed in the preceding section, Edo resultative serial verb construction exhibits the object restriction, whereas the Chinese resultative construction with compounds does not. Relevant examples in (30) and (27) are repeated in (38) and (39).

(38)   a.   *Òzó ré kp'Ol'O
            Ozo ate be.big
            'Ozo ate himself fat.'

       b.   *Òzó dá   (ày'On)   mu'Emu'E
            Ozo drink palm wine be.sluggish
            'Ozo drank palmwine and became sluggish.'

(39)   a.   Ta chi-bao (fan) le
            he eat-full rice Asp.
            'He ate (rice) and became full.'

       b.   Ta he-zui   (jiu)   le
            he drink-drunk wine Asp.
            'He drank (wine) and became drunk.'

---

[10] The Edo construction is chosen as the target of comparison because I argued in Saito (2001) that it involves covert incorporation. It is argued there that English resultatives are not derived by covert incorporation but by NP movement. A discussion of the derivation of Chinese phrasal resultatives is beyond the scope of this chapter. I refer the reader to Huang (2006) for an analysis.

In this section, I investigate the source of this difference on the assumption that the compounds in (39) are formed by overt incorporation.

Let me first note that the incorporation analysis proposed in section 3, as it stands, allows both (38) and (39). A possible derivation for (38a) is shown in (40).

(40)

a. $[_{vP}$ Òzó $[_{v'}$ v $[_{VP}$ $[_V$ ré] $[_{VP}$ $[_V$ kp`Ol´O]]]]] (Merge to yield the base *v*P structure)

b. $[_{vP}$ Òzó $[_{v'}$ v $[_{VP}$ $[_V$ $[_V$ ré] $[_V$ kp`Ol´O]] $[_{VP}$ $[_V$ kp`Ol´O]]]]]

c. $[_{vP}$ Òzó $[_{v'}$ $[_v$ v $[_V$ $[_V$ ré] $[_V$ kp`Ol´O]]] $[_{VP}$ $[_V$ $[_V$ ré] $[_V$ kp`Ol´O]] $[_{VP}$ $[_V$ kp`Ol´O]]]]]

In (40b), *kp`Ol´O* 'be.full' covertly incorporates into *ré* 'ate.' Then, the complex V, *ré-kp`Ol´O* 'ate-be.full' overtly raises to *v* in (40c). The second verb *kp`Ol´O* should be able to θ-mark *Òzó* from this position, yielding the intended interpretation. The Chinese (39a) can be analyzed in exactly the same way. Its derivation is shown in (41).[11]

(41)

a. $[_{vP}$ Ta $[_{v'}$ v $[_{VP}$ fan $[_{V'}$ $[_V$ chi] $[_{VP}$ $[_V$ bao]]]]]] (Merge to yield the base *v*P structure)

b. $[_{vP}$ Ta $[_{v'}$ v $[_{VP}$ fan $[_{V'}$ $[_V$ $[_V$ chi] $[_V$ bao]] $[_{VP}$ $[_V$ bao]]]]]]

c. $[_{vP}$ Ta $[_{v'}$ $[_v$ v $[_V$ $[_V$ chi] $[_V$ bao]]] $[_{VP}$ fan $[_{V'}$ $[_V$ $[_V$ chi] $[_V$ bao]] $[_{VP}$ $[_V$ bao]]]]]]

In (41b), *bao* 'full' incorporates into *chi* 'eat' to form a compound. The compound, then, raises to *v* in (41c), and *bao* θ-marks *ta* 'he' from this position.

The fact that (39a) can be analyzed as in (41) suggests that this may indeed be a viable analysis for the example. The issue, then, is why (38a) cannot have the derivation in (40). Here, the obvious difference between Edo and Chinese is whether the incorporation in Step b is covert or overt. Let us then explore the possibility to attribute the contrast between (38) and (39) to this difference.

Throughout this chapter, I have been assuming Bobaljik's (1995) proposal that the only difference between overt movement and covert movement is whether the phonetic features are interpreted at the landing site or at the initial site. I express this as in (42), where α̶ is α with its phonetic features deleted.

(42)   a.   overt movement: α   ...   α̶

       b.   covert movement: α̶   ...   α

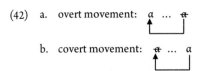

---

[11] I ignore the aspect *le* in (41), as it is irrelevant for the point made here.

Then, phonetic features are deleted at the initial site with overt movement, whereas they are deleted at the landing site with covert movement. Assuming that there is indeed deletion of phonetic features in this way, there are two possibilities with the timing of the deletion. First, the deletion of phonetic features can apply as soon as the movement takes place. Second, the deletion can apply at the phase level as part of the Transfer Operation in the sense of Chomsky (2005), which sends information to the C-I system and the S-M system. Let us consider these two possibilities for the derivations in (40) and (41) to see if they successfully distinguish these derivations.

The Chinese case in (41) is straightforward. The derivations in (40)–(41) can both be schematically expressed as in (43).

(43) $[\ ... \ v + [\underline{V_1 + V_2}] \ ... \ [\underline{V_1 + V_2}] \ ... \ V_2 \ ... \ ]$

For (41), if deletion takes place after each step of the derivation, then the phonetic features of V_2 are deleted at the initial site after the verb incorporates into V_1 as in (44a).

(44) a. $[\ ... \ [\underline{V_1 + V_2}] \ ... \ \cancel{V_2} \ ... \ ]$

  b. $[\ ... \ v + [\underline{V_1 + V_2}] \ ... \ [\underline{V_1 + V_2}] \ ... \ \cancel{V_2} \ ... \ ]$

  c. $[\ ... \ v + [\underline{V_1 + V_2}] \ ... \ [\cancel{\underline{V_1 + V_2}}] \ ... \ \cancel{V_2} \ ... \ ]$

Then, $V_1 + V_2$ incorporates into v as in (44b), and its phonetic features are deleted at the initial site as in (44c). Thus, the grammatical examples in (39) are successfully derived. But this does not provide evidence that deletion of phonetic features applies cyclically. This is because the same result obtains, even if deletion applies after the construction of the vP phase is completed. (43) contains two chains, (V_2, V_2) and $(V_1 + V_2, V_1 + V_2)$. The phonetic features of V_2 can be deleted at the initial site, and then, those of $V_1 + V_2$ can be deleted also at the initial site.

The situation with the Edo (40), however, is different. If deletion of phonetic features applies immediately after incorporation, then the incorporation of V_2 into V_1 yields (45a).

(45) a. $[\ ... \ [\underline{V_1 + \cancel{V_2}}] \ ... \ V_2 \ ... \ ]$

  b. $[\ ... \ v + [\underline{V_1 + \cancel{V_2}}] \ ... \ [\underline{V_1 + \cancel{V_2}}] \ ... \ V_2 \ ... \ ]$

  c. $[\ ... \ v + [\underline{V_1 + \cancel{V_2}}] \ ... \ [\cancel{\underline{V_1 + V_2}}] \ ... \ V_2 \ ... \ ]$

Then, $V_1 + \cancel{V_2}$ incorporates into v as in (45b), and its phonetic features are deleted at the initial site as in (45c). Hence, if this derivation is allowed, (40) should be grammatical.

On the other hand, a different result obtains if deletion of phonetic features applies after the completion of the vP phase. Consider the configuration in (43) again, repeated here as (46a).

(46) a. $[\ldots \ v + [\underline{V_1 + V_2}] \ldots [\underline{V_1 + V_2}] \ldots V_2 \ldots]$

    b. $[\ldots \ v + [\underline{V_1 + V_2}] \ldots [\underline{V_1 + \cancel{V_2}}] \ldots V_2 \ldots]$

    c. $[\ldots \ v + [\underline{V_1 + V_2}] \ldots [\underline{\cancel{V_1} + V_2}] \ldots V_2 \ldots]$

As the incorporation of V_2 is covert, its phonetic features must be deleted at the landing site. This yields (46b). But then, a problem arises with the chain $(V_1+V_2, V_1+\cancel{V_2})$. First, the two members of the chain are not identical with respect to phonetic features, and this by itself may cause a problem for the deletion operation. But even if the operation successfully applies, (46c) is derived with the phonetic features of V_2 remaining at the landing site. Note that the same problem arises even if deletion applies to the (V_1+V_2, V_1+V_2) chain first. In this case, the deletion directly yields (46c) from (46a). Since the leftmost V_2 in the v position and the rightmost V_2 at the initial site do not form a chain, there is no way to delete the former. Thus, the ungrammatical examples in (38) cannot be derived, a desirable result.[12]

It was shown above that the difference in (38) and (39) between Edo and Chinese can be successfully captured if deletion of phonetic features takes place upon the completion of phase. The contrast between (38) and (39), then, provides evidence that the deletion of phonetic features applies in this way. The mechanism is conceptually motivated as well, as long as the deletion of phonetic features is part of the Transfer Operation that sends information to the C-I and S-M interfaces.

Before I conclude this section, I would like to point out an implication for the analysis of V-T merger in Japanese. It is generally assumed that there are two distinct ways for V to merge with T, by incorporation of V to T, as in (47a), and by phonological merger (or affix hopping in the sense of Chomsky, 1957), as in (47b).

(47) a. John is quickly   solving the problem

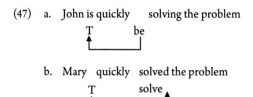

    b. Mary quickly solved the problem

Only auxiliary verbs and *be*-verbs take the first option in English, but as first observed by Emonds (1978), the option is widespread cross-linguistically. At the same time,

---

[12] A question arises as to why (46c) itself is not allowed with two copies of V_2 pronounced. I assume here that this is ruled out by an independent principle that restricts the realization of phonetic features at two positions.

it has not been clear which option Japanese employs because the language is strictly head-final, and adverbs, for example, cannot right-adjoin to any phrase. As nothing can intervene between V and T in Japanese, it is difficult to find evidence that distinguishes the two options.

But the discussion in this section implies that Japanese resorts to phonological merger. The account for the ungrammaticality of the Edo examples in (38), as illustrated in (46), implies that a covert incorporation cannot be followed by an overt incorporation in the way shown in (48).[13]

(48)   [... $\gamma + [\beta + \alpha]$ ... $[\beta + \alpha]$ ... α ...]

With this in mind, let us consider again the example of the light verb construction in (24), repeated here as (49).

(49)   Hanako-ga   Taroo-ni   [$_{NP}$ toti-no   zyooto]-o   si-ta
       Hanako-NOM Taroo-DAT   land-GEN giving-ACC do-Past
       'Hanako gave a piece of land to Taroo.'

According to the analysis presented in Section 3, *zyooto* 'giving' covertly incorporates into *su* 'do,' and makes the merger of the goal argument *Taroo* possible. If *su* is to eventually move to T, it must first overtly incorporate into *v* so that it is located at the phase edge of *v*P. But this is excluded because it creates the illegitimate configuration in (48). It follows then that phonological merger is the only option for the merger of *su* 'do' and *ta* 'Past' in this case.

6. Conclusion

In this chapter, I examined the roles of selectional restrictions and the interpretive mechanism of incorporation chains in the formation of complex predicates. Given the theory of Merge in Chomsky (2012), the operation applies freely in the construction of phrase structure. Then, much burden is placed on selection to distinguish legitimate and illegitimate derivations. I first argued in section 2 that Kageyama's (1993) transitivity harmony principle on Japanese lexical complex predicates can be derived from the selectional relation between *v* and V. This showed that the selectional

[13] The account implies more generally that covert movement cannot be followed by overt movement whether the movement is incorporation or not. Overt movement, by definition, retains the phonetic features at the landing site. Given this, if the second step of movement is overt, the first step must be as well because otherwise the phonetic features are realized at two positions, the final landing site and the initial site. It is probably of some interest that overt movement must precede covert movement even in a single-cycle model.

requirements of *v* constrain the possible forms of complex predicates. Then, I examined the Japanese light verb construction and the Edo serial verb construction in section 3, and concluded that selectional requirements constrain the application of Merge rather than the resulting phrase structure. In section 4, I briefly reviewed the discussion in Huang (2006) on Chinese resultatives. In particular, I introduced his argument that phrasal resultatives, as opposed to compound resultatives, are subject to the object restriction just like resultatives in Edo. Based on this, I concluded that the unique properties of compound resultatives in Chinese are due to the fact that they employ compounds. Finally, in section 5, I suggested an analysis for the difference between the Chinese compound resultatives and the Edo serial verb resultatives with respect to the object restriction. The analysis provided empirical support for the conceptually motivated assumption that the deletion of phonetic features, which distinguishes covert and overt movements, applies upon the completion of a phase as part of the Transfer Operation to the interfaces.

As noted at the outset of this chapter, Japanese lexical complex predicates, Edo resultative serial verbs, and Chinese compound verbs all exhibit different properties. I argued that no "language-specific principles" are necessary to account for those differences. The three types of complex predicates are formed differently. Japanese lexical complex predicates are formed before they are merged into a larger syntactic structure. Edo resultative serial verb construction involves covert incorporation. And I entertained the possibility that Chinese compound verbs are formed by overt incorporation. I argued that given this, the theories of selection and chain interpretation explain the different properties that these three constructions exhibit.

References

Baker, Mark, and Osamuyimen T. Stewart. 1999. *On Double-Headedness and the Anatomy of the Clause*. Ms., Rutgers University.

Bobaljik, Jonathan D. 1995. *Morphosyntax: The Syntax of Verbal Inflection*. Doctoral dissertation, MIT.

Chomsky, Noam. 1957. *Syntactic Structures*. The Hague: Mouton.

Chomsky, Noam. 1995. *The Minimalist Program*. Cambridge, MA: MIT Press.

Chomsky, Noam. 2012. *Problems of Projection*. Ms., MIT.

Emonds, Joseph. 1978. The verbal complex V'-V in French. *Linguistic Inquiry* 9, 151–175.

Grimshaw, Jane, and Armin Mester. 1988. Light verbs and θ-marking. *Linguistic Inquiry* 19, 205–232.

Huang, C.-T. James. 1992. Complex predicates in control. In *Control and Grammar*, ed. Richard K. Larson et al., 109–147. Dordrecht: Kluwer Academic Publishers.

Huang, C.-T. James. 2006. Resultatives and unaccusatives: A parametric view. *Bulletin of the Chinese Linguistic Society of Japan* 253, 1–43.

Kageyama, Taro. 1993. *Bunpoo to Gokeisei* [Grammar and Word Formation]. Tokyo: Hituzi Syobo.

Kageyama, Taro. 1999. *Keitairon to Imi* [Morphology and Meaning]. Tokyo: Kuroshio Shuppan.

Li, Yafei. 1990. On V-V compounds in Chinese. *Natural Language & Linguistic Theory* 8, 177–207.

Li, Yafei. 1993. Structural head and aspectuality. *Language* 69, 480–504.

Matsumoto, Yo. 1998. The combinatory possibilities in Japanese V-V lexical compounds (in Japanese). *Gengokenkyu* 114, 37–83.

Miyagawa, Shigeru. 1989. Light verbs and the ergative hypothesis. *Linguistic Inquiry* 20, 659–668.

Saito, Mamoru. 2001. Movement and θ-roles: A case study with resultatives. In *The Proceedings of the Second Tokyo Conference on Psycholinguistics*, ed. Yukio Otsu, 35–60. Tokyo: Hituzi Syobo.

Saito, Mamoru, and Hiroto Hoshi. 2000. The Japanese light verb construction and the minimalist program. In *Step by Step: Essays on Minimalist Syntax in Honor of Howard Lasnik*, ed. Roger Martin et al., 261–295. Cambridge, MA: MIT Press.

Simpson, Jane. 1983. Resultatives. In *Papers in Lexical-Functional Grammar*, ed. Lori Levin et al., 143–157. Bloomington: Indiana University Linguistics Club.

Stewart, Osamuyimen T. 1998. *The Serial Verb Construction Parameter*. Doctoral dissertation, Rutgers University.

Tang, Sze-Wing. 1997. The parametric approach to the resultative construction in Chinese and English. *UCI Working Papers in Linguistics* 3, 203–226.

Tsujimura, Natsuko. 1990. Ergativity of nouns and case assignment. *Linguistic Inquiry* 21, 277–287.

Yumoto, Yoko. 1997. Word formation and the lexical-conceptual structure (in Japanese). In *Gengo to Bunka no Shosoo* [Aspects of Language and Culture], ed. Publishing Committee, 105–118. Tokyo: Eihoosha.

11

Agents in Mandarin and Igbo Resultatives

ALEXANDER WILLIAMS

1. Introduction

Huang (1988) and (1992) are landmarks in the cross-linguistic analysis of complex predicates. The rigor and creativity of these studies made way for two fertile decades of further work in the area, on a wide array of languages. Together with their sequels, these papers have contributed inestimably to our understanding of verbs and the structure of predicates, drawing on the lessons of Chinese languages.

The topic of this chapter is clauses with resultative complex predicates in Mandarin, Igbo, and English. This chapter concerns only those with an agentive verb, such as English (1) and (2).

(1) Lee cut the bone open.

(2) Mo sang her throat hoarse.

I call *cut* and *sing* agentive both because cuttings and singings necessarily have agents, and because (3) and (4) are bad. These are transitive and unergative verbs.

(3) * The bone cut.
    'The bone got cut.'

(4) * The intro sang.
    'The intro got sung.'

In English, resultatives with such verbs have two features I want to discuss in a cross-linguistic context. First, when they inhabit a transitive clause, as in (1) and (2), the subject must name the agent of the verb's event.[1] (1) entails that Lee cut something and (2), that Mo sang. (5) and (6) are accordingly impossible. I explain the unusual glosses in section 2.

(5) * The bone cut his knives dull.
    'The bone made his knives dull from [their] cutting [it].'

---

[1] My use of "agent" is very broad (Baker 1997). It is not limited to volitional actors, and sometimes includes participants that might also be called instruments, in a different gloss on the same stretch of history.

(6)   * The intro sang her throat hoarse.
      'The intro made her throat hoarse from [her] cutting [it].'

In this respect the resultative clauses are just like those with the agentive verb on its own. In (7) and (8) as well, the subject must name the cutter or singer.

(7)   Lee cut the bone.

(8)   Mo sang (the intro).

Second, such resultatives cannot occur in unaccusative clauses, such as (9) or (10), without any dependent to name the agent implied by the verb. Again, this is like the verb on its own: (9) and (10) match (3) and (4), respectively.

(9)   * The bone cut open.
      'The bone got open from [someone] cutting [it].'

(10) * Mo's throat sang hoarse.
      'Mo's throat got hoarse from [someone] singing.'

These two features have had a decisive influence on theories of the resultative, and on general theories of argument structure, through works such as Dowty (1979), Levin and Rappaport Hovav (1995), and Kratzer (2005). In many theories, at least one of the two is grammatically or conceptually necessary. Yet this cannot be right, as they are not exhibited equally in every language. Neither feature is exhibited in Mandarin. First, the transitive clause in (11) does not entail that the bone did any cutting.[2]

(11) Na gen gutou qie dun -le   wode caidao.
      that CLS bone cut dull-PFV my   food knife
      'That bone made my knife dull from cutting.'

Second, the intransitive clause in (12) contains *tui* 'push,' which on its own occurs just in clauses with a subject naming the pusher.

(12) Na   liang che tui fan   -le.
      which CLS   car push reverse -PFV
      'Which car got upended from pushing [it]?'   (adapted from Tan 1991: 79)

---

[2] In glosses of Mandarin, PFV means 'perfective' and CLS means 'classifier.' For both Mandarin and Igbo, I use hyphens only with clitics and affixes. Glosses of Igbo use the following abbreviations. FACT means 'factative.' Roughly, a predicate in the factative has past time reference when eventive, and non-past time reference when stative. BVC means 'bound verb cognate' (Nwachukwu 1987; Emenanjọ 1987), a nominalization of the verb group. In all the data to be presented here, the BVC serves only to satisfy the requirement that a verb group in the factative not be clause-final (Nwachukwu 1987: 19–21). 3s(S) means 'third person singular (subject) pronoun,' and PREP means 'general preposition.' Igbo ([íbò]) is a Benue-Congo language spoken mainly in Nigeria. For my Igbo data, I thank Chidi Ukazim, Eric Nzeribe, Anthony Ihunnah, Chidi Nwaubani, Stella Eke-Okoro, Somto Akunyili, and Peter Ihiọnụ.

Igbo does share the first feature with English, so that (13) entails that Chidi dug out something, and (14) is accordingly impossible.

(13)   Chidi gwu   ji   -ri   ọgụ ya.
         C.   dig out snap -FACT hoe 3s
         'Chidi made his hoe snap from digging out [stuff with it].'

(14)   *Ji   ahụ gwu ji   -ri   ọgụ ya.
          yam that dig out snap -FACT hoe 3s
          'That yam made his hoe snap from digging out [with it].'

But like Mandarin, Igbo differs fromEnglish in allowing for sentences like (15), the unaccusative counterpart to (13), even though *gwu* 'dig out' alone is a transitive verb (Nwachukwu 1987; Ụwalaka 1988; Hale et al. 1995).

(15)   Ọgụ ya gwu   ji   -ri   egwuji.
         hoe 3s dig out snap -FACT BVC
         'His hoe snapped from digging out [stuff].'

The likeness on display in (12) and (15) is not, however, complete. In unaccusative clauses with resultative complex predicates, Igbo allows only a subset of the agentive verbs that are possible in Mandarin. For example, (16) replaces *gwu* 'dig out' in (15) with *zọ* 'tread on,' and the result is unacceptable (Hale et al. 1995). This contrasts with Mandarin (17).

(16)   *Ọgụ ya zọ   ji   -ri   egwuji.
           hoe 3s tread on snap -FACT BVC
          'His hoe snapped from treading on [it].'

(17)   Haojige pingguo cai   lan   -le.
         many   apples tread mushy -PFV
         'A good many apples got mushy from treading [on them].'

So along our dimensions of interest, we have minimal comparisons between these three languages. The contrast between Mandarin and Igbo is especially interesting, since their resultatives are otherwise quite similar (Lord 1975; Williams 2008).

    In this chapter I ask how to describe these facts theoretically, in light of the variation between languages. First, what is the grammar of Mandarin and Igbo such that (12), (15), and (17) are acceptable when Mandarin *tui* 'push' and *cai* 'tread on,' or Igbo *gwu* 'dig out,' are on their own transitive verbs, and when the same is not possible in English, or for Igbo *zọ* 'tread on' in (16)? Second, what requires the subject in Igbo (13) to name the agent of the digging, as in English (5), when this is not necessary in Mandarin (11)? Our answers should keep the grammar of each language simple. But they should also trace the variance among languages to plausible points of difference, keeping as much as possible constant. And this is not as easy as it looks, despite how banal the facts of English might appear. In my view, the basic case is laid bare for us by Mandarin. The patterns of English or Igbo are elaborations within the outlines that Mandarin makes plain, expressing additions either to the argument structure of verbs, or to the structure or meaning of the resultative. So the question is, which way of elaborating makes the most sense?

To focus, I will proceed in the context of a theory I have defended elsewhere (Williams 2008, 2009, 2014, accepted). In earlier expositions, I responded mainly to the interpretation of the underlying object in a resultative clause. I now attend to the underlying subject. The theory serves to illuminate the particular challenges of the data I have in my sights. But those challenges remain sharp even under accounts of the resultative other than my own, such as those in Li (1995), Levin and Rappaport (1995), Rappaport Hovav and Levin (2001), Rothstein (2004), Kratzer (2005), or Huang et al. (2009), though I will not pause to show this. My goal is not to prove my framework right, but at most to show how our data might be described in its terms. One part of this framework is the claim that verbs in Mandarin and Igbo characteristically do not have any arguments, while verbs in English do (Williams 2005, 2008). In this setting we have the question of whether facts like Igbo (14) and (16), or English (5) and (9), require that agentive verbs in these two languages have their implied agent as a lexical argument, an assumption with little motive in Mandarin. For both Igbo and English, my answer will be a very cautious no.

The chapter unfolds as follows. Section 2 establishes some basic facts about resultatives, as well as the terms I use to describe them. Section 3 reprises the theoretical frame for our discussion, and applies it to the interpretation of objects. I then turn to our two main questions. Section 4 asks how to describe cases like Mandarin (12) and (17), or Igbo (15) and (16), where a resultative with an agentive verb can or cannot inhabit an unaccusative clause. Section 5 concerns such predicates in transitive clauses, such as Mandarin (11), or Igbo (13) and (14). How should we ensure that, in Igbo and English but not Mandarin, the subject then names the agent implied by the verb? I summarize in section 6.

2. Basics of Resultatives

A resultative complex predicate has two parts, a *means predicate* M, and a *result predicate* R. In Mandarin (17) and (18), M contains at least *cai* 'tread on' and R, at least *lan* 'mushy.' In Igbo (19) and (20), M and R contain at least *kụ* 'strike' and *wa* 'split.'

(18) Ta cai   lan   -le   haojige pingguo.
      3s tread mushy -PFV many   apple
      'S/he made a good many apples mushy from treading [on them].'

(19) Ọ kụ   wa -ra   ọba ahụ.
      3sS strike split -FACT gourd that
      'He made that gourd split from striking.' (Hale et al. 1995)

(20) Ọba ahụ kụ   wa -ra   akụwa.
      gourd that strike split -FACT BVC
      'That gourd split from striking.' (Hale et al. 1995)

I take M to be the largest expression containing the predicate head that does not also contain R, or any structure that introduces any part of the meaning associated with the construction. Likewise for R, mutatis mutandis. The smallest constituent containing both M and R, I will call MR.

In surface syntax, resultatives are very similar in Mandarin and Igbo. Both M and R in general house a root that can occur on its own as a verb that exhausts the clausal predicate, as *kụ* 'strike' and *wa* 'split' do in Igbo (21) and (22). In addition, the verbs in M and R are never audibly separated by an adjunct or argument, and suffixes attach to MR as a whole.

(21) Ọ   kụ   -rụ   ọba   ahụ.
      3sS strike -FACT gourd that
      'He struck that gourd.'

(22) Ọba   ahụ wa -ra   awa.
      gourd that split -FACT BVC
      'That gourd split.'

English is different in at least four ways. M and R are separated by the direct object, affixes attach to the verb in M, R may contain adverbial modifiers, and the head of R cannot be a verb or even a deverbal participle.

No audible morphemes signal the meaning of the construction. But a resultative clause entails that there was a change or process that ended with the event of R and was achieved by means of the event described by M. Thus Igbo (19) and (20) entail that there was a change or process that ends with a snap and is achieved with a strike. In general this entails that the M event caused that of R. But there is much more to the semantics than merely causation.[3]

I will assume that any resultative complex predicate, MR, has a meaning with the outlines of (23). Here K is true of $\langle e_1, e_2, e_3 \rangle$ just in case e_1 is a process ending with e_3 and achieved by means of e_2. Thus K can be analyzed as the conjunction of two other relations, say as in (24), but that won't matter in this discussion.

(23) $[\![MR]\!] = \lambda e_1 \exists e_2 \exists e_3 [\ldots K(e_1, e_2, e_3) \& [\![M]\!](\ldots)(e_2) \& [\![R]\!](\ldots)(e_3) \ldots]$

(24) $K(e_1, e_2, e_3) \equiv \text{Means}(e_1, e_2) \& \text{End}(e_1, e_3)$

What will matter greatly is the assumption in (25): an event that satisfies MR need not satisfy M. This implies, contra Parsons (1990), Kratzer (2005), and many others, that the event of MR (e_1) is not identical to that of M (e_2), as allowed by (23).

(25) Third Event Assumption (TEA)
      An event that satisfies MR need not satisfy M, and therefore the two are predicates of different events.

---

[3] If Mo punches Lee, causing Lee to fall, hit his head, and black out, we can say that the punch caused the blackout, just as well as we can say that a rainstorm caused a crop failure. But we cannot say that Mo punched Lee unconscious. For this reason it is common to say that resultatives (Bittner 1999), like single verb causatives (Shibatani 1972; McCawley 1976; Talmy 1976; Wolff 2003), imply "direct" causation. But this is more a name than an analysis (Shibatani 2000; Pietroski 2005).

Adverbs provide one reason for this: an adverb modifying MR need not describe the M event (Rappaport Hovav and Levin 2001). For example, (26a) does not entail (26b). Given that adverbs like *slowly* are predicates of events (Davidson 1967), this would not be possible if satisfiers of MR were always to also satisfy M, much less if the two were predicates of the very same event.[4]

(26)   a.   Al slowly pounded the cutlet flat.

      b.   ⊭Al slowly pounded the cutlet.

In (26a), *slowly* describes the process of flattening the cutlet, the event of MR, e_1 in (23). And in fact it cannot describe the pounding that was done in its service. If it could, we could use (27) to say that the cutlet was slowly flattened by means of quick pounding. But we can't, suggesting that M is inaccessible to direct modification.[5]

(27)   * Al quickly pounded the cutlet flat slowly.
        'Al slowly made the cutlet flat by pounding it quickly.'

Analogous facts hold of Mandarin. An adverb such as *jianjian-de* 'gradually' may describe the MR process without describing its means event, and direct modification of M is arguably impossible, as suggested by (28).

(28)   Leng feng   (#huhu-de)   chui bing -le   ta.
      cold wind   howlingly   blow ill   -PFV   3s
      'A cold wind made him/her ill by blowing (howlingly).'
      (L. Li 1980: 100, translation AW)

I will assume the same for Igbo, and this will be essential for everything to follow in this chapter. Theorists who have not recognized the TEA have also not noticed the challenges we face in this chapter. Without the TEA, many would not arise.

Now turn to the interpretation of the surface subject and object, S and O. These may name participants in the event of M. Interpreting a use of (19), we may take it to concern a striking in which S names the striker, and O names the struck. In addition, a resultative entails that some individual changes, entering a result condition defined by R. The overt phrase that identifies this individual *controls* R. In Mandarin (18) and Igbo (19), it is O that controls R, since the apples wind up mushy and the gourd winds up split. In (17) and (20), however, it is S that controls R. I will refer to resultative clauses in which O controls R as *transitive* and those in which S controls R as *intransitive*. This should not be mixed up with the distributional category, intransitive or transitive, of the verb in M.

---

[4] More obviously, the event of MR is not (or need not be) the event described by the head of R, since an event of pounding flat is not a state of flatness.

[5] Of course, the event of MR may have a certain property *because* its M event has the same. A pounding flat may be loud because its constituent pounding is loud, just like a child may be blonde because its hair is blonde, or illegitimate because its parents are unmarried. But examples like this do not show that an adverb can modify M, any more than *illegitimate blonde child* shows that *child* covertly contains the words *hair* and *parents*, to be modified by the two adjectives (Williams, in press).

My glosses will follow a fixed format, exemplified in the data already given. Transitives are glossed as "S made O R from M'ing," and intransitives as either "S got R from M'ing" or "S R'ed from M'ing." When relevant, I will add an understood subject or object for "M'ing," within square brackets. In the use of *from* with transitives, the result is rarely idiomatic. But the uniformity will avert two unwarranted suggestions. First, that transitive and intransitive resultatives differ in the semantic relation between the events of M and R; second, that S in a transitive must name the agent of its means event, which is not the case in Mandarin, witness (11).

3. A Theory of Resultatives

3.1. OUTSIDE RELATIONS SEMANTICS

In Williams (accepted) I argue that, across languages, resultatives are best analyzed as having an *Outside Relations* (OR) semantics. This says that, in the meaning of a resultative clause, S and O bind thematic relations to the event of MR, besides any relations there might be to the event of M. A transitive has a meaning like (29a), and an intransitive has a meaning like (29b).

(29)   a. $\lambda e[$ Agent$(e, [\![S]\!]) \,\&\,$ Theme$(e, [\![O]\!]) \,\&\, [\![MR]\!](...)(e)]$

       b. $\lambda e[$ Theme$(e, [\![S]\!]) \,\&\, [\![MR]\!](...)(e)]$

S is the surface subject, but I assume that intransitive resultatives are unaccusative clauses. S is an object underlyingly, interpreted as the theme of the clausal event. I defend this explicitly in Williams (accepted); see also Ma (1987: 425–426), Huang (1992: 128–129), and Sybesma (1999: 38–44).

This semantics expresses a familiar idea: in sentences with 'causative' meaning, S and O name the 'causer' and 'causee.' (29) renders these roles as the agent and theme of a process or change. For Mandarin this view is developed in Li (1990, 1995; see also Huang 1992). For English it finds expression in Goldberg and Jackendoff (2004), for example, which develops analogous aspects of Jackendoff (1990) and Goldberg (1995). The OR semantics goes against a common view, however, which would assign (1) a meaning like (30) (Dowty 1979; Parsons 1990; Levin and Rappaport Hovav 1995; Kratzer 2005). Here S and O have thematic relations only to the events of M and R, in disagreement with (29).

(30)   Cause('Lee cut the bone', Become('the bone be open'))

Following Parsons (1990) and Pietroski (2005), I assume that the theme of a change or process is the theme of the event that ends it. This is 'what it means' to undergo a process or change. Using our relation $\mathcal{K}$, we can state this as in (31), echoing Parsons (1990: 119) on "BECOME."[6] Were $\mathcal{K}$ decomposed as in (24), a similar postulate would instead govern the End relation.

---

[6] "The Theme of [BECOME's] event is the same as the Theme of its Target state: BECOME$(e, s) \rightarrow$ [Theme$(e, x) \equiv$ Theme(s, x)]" (Parsons 1990: 119).

(31) $\Box \forall e_1 e_2 e_3 [K(e_1, e_2, e_3) \rightarrow \text{Theme}(e_1, x) \equiv \text{Theme}(e_3, x)]$

Given (31), the phrase that names the theme of the event of MR also controls R as a necessary consequence. Therefore the OR semantics in (29) is alone sufficient to entail that control goes to O in a transitive and to S in an intransitive; it is not necessary to also state a thematic relation to the event of R itself. Presuming as I do that intransitive resultatives are unaccusative, this means in turn that control is always by a direct object underlyingly. Thus given (31), the "direct object restriction" (Simpson 1983; Levin and Rappaport Hovav 1995) is explicitly an instance of the generalization that the theme of a clause's event will be its object, promoted to subject in the absence of an agent (Fillmore 1968; Jackendoff 1972; Perlmutter 1978). In Williams (accepted) I argue that this is the most explanatory derivation of the direct object restriction, and that this, among other facts, argues strongly in favor of the OR semantics. Here I take this for granted.

3.2. VERBS AND ARGUMENTS

Developing ideas in Huang (1992) and Sybesma (1999) in the setting of Carlson (1984) and Kratzer (1996), and in general agreement with Lin (2001), I argue in Williams (2005, 2008) for the *No Argument Theory* of Mandarin and Igbo, or NAT. This is the claim that in these languages, verbs characteristically have no arguments lexically. Semantically I take this to mean that the verb is interpreted simply as a function from events to truth values, like the examples in (32) and (33), from Mandarin and Igbo, respectively.[7] Syntactically, it means that the verb, while it has subcategorial features that may themselves be selected, does not itself express a requirement to combine with a dependent.

(32) a. $[\![\textit{qie} \text{'cut'}]\!] = \lambda e [\text{Cutting}(e)]$

   b. $[\![\textit{cai} \text{'tread on'}]\!] = \lambda e [\text{TreadingOn}(e)]$

(33) a. $[\![\textit{kụ} \text{'strike'}]\!] = \lambda e [\text{Striking}(e)]$

   b. $[\![\textit{gwu} \text{'dig out'}]\!] = \lambda e [\text{DiggingOut}(e)]$

Thematic relations, if not introduced by the verb, are introduced by something in its context. Something other than the verb, either a head (Kratzer 1996; Marantz 1997) or an interpreted syntactic relation (Carlson 1984; Pietroski 2005), imposes an Agent relation on (what surfaces as) S, and a Theme relation on (what surfaces as) O. Here I will say nothing more specific than that, and use (34) and (35) to illustrate the idea as crudely as possible, outlining the underlying verb phrases for transitive and unaccusative clauses, respectively.

---

[7] For speakers of any language, events of cutting or striking involve at least two participants. (32) and (33) say nothing to the contrary. Similarly, to say that $[\![\textit{bicycle}]\!]$ is $\lambda x [\text{Bicycle}(x)]$ is not to deny that bicycles necessarily have two wheels.

(34)

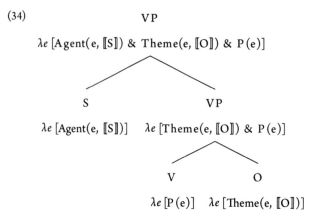

$$\lambda e \,[\text{Agent}(e, [\![S]\!]) \,\&\, \text{Theme}(e, [\![O]\!]) \,\&\, P(e)]$$

S   VP

$$\lambda e \,[\text{Agent}(e, [\![S]\!])] \qquad \lambda e \,[\text{Theme}(e, [\![O]\!]) \,\&\, P(e)]$$

V   O

$$\lambda e \,[P(e)] \qquad \lambda e \,[\text{Theme}(e, [\![O]\!])]$$

(35)

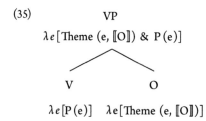

VP

$$\lambda e \,[\text{Theme}(e, [\![O]\!]) \,\&\, P(e)]$$

V   O

$$\lambda e \,[P(e)] \qquad \lambda e \,[\text{Theme}(e, [\![O]\!])]$$

Plugging *cai* 'tread on' from (32b) into (34), we derive (36b) as the meaning for (36a).[8]

(36) a.   Xiao Wei cai   -le   haojige pingguo.
       X.W.   tread on -PFV many   apple
       'Wei tread on a good many apples.'

   b. $\lambda e[\,\text{Agent}(e, \text{Wei}) \,\&\, \text{Theme}(e, \text{apples}) \,\&\, \text{TreadingOn}(e)\,]$

Next I make two assumptions about the structure of resultatives. First, that MR occurs in the same kind of structural context as a simple verb does. For instance, *cai lan* 'tread-on mushy,' *kụ wa* 'strike split,' and *cut open* occur in the same context as do *cai* 'tread on,' *kụ* 'strike,' and *cut* on their own, namely the V slot in (34) or (35). Second, I repeat the standard assumption (Thompson 1973; Lord 1975; Y. Li 1990; Larson 1991; Huang 1992; Ihiọnụ 1992; Hale et al. 1995) that M contains nothing but the verb itself, hence no structure to introduce a thematic relation.

Given the first assumption, plus (34) and (35), S and O will name the agent and theme of the MR event, delivering the OR semantics. Given the second assumption, plus no-argument verb meanings like those in (33), the meaning of a resultative in Mandarin or Igbo will state no relations whatsoever to the event described by M. The Mandarin transitive (37a) will mean (37b), for example, and

---

[8] For clarity I leave the event of the clause bound by a lambda, to distinguish it from any so-called subevents. Eventually this is bound existentially, however.

intransitive (38a) will mean (38b). Here the only stated thematic relations are to the event of MR.

(37) a. Xiao Wei cai   lan   -le   haojige pingguo.
          X.W.   tread on mushy -PFV many   apples
          'Wei made the apples mushy from treading on [them].'

      b. $\lambda e_1 \exists e_2 \exists e_3 [$ Agent(e, Wei) & Theme(e, apples) & $[\mathcal{K}(e_1, e_2, e_3)$ & TreadingOn(e_2) & Mushiness(e_3) $]]$

(38) a. Haojige pingguo cai   lan   -le.
          many   apple   tread on mushy -PFV
          'A good many apples got mushy from treading on [them].'

      b. $\lambda e_1 \exists e_2 \exists e_3 [$ Theme(e, apples) & $[\mathcal{K}(e_1, e_2, e_3)$ & TreadingOn(e_2) & Mushiness(e_3) $]]$

Given the Third Event Assumption in (25), thematic relations to the event of MR do not entail any relations to an event satisfying M. With respect to M, therefore, the meaning of a resultative sentence in Mandarin or Igbo does not itself restrict the interpretation of S and O. Absent any further meaning postulates for $\mathcal{K}$, understood relations to the means event must be pragmatic enrichments meant by the speaker, informed by world knowledge, and consistent with the sentence meaning: S and O are the agent and theme of a process that ends with R and is achieved by means of M. This restriction is substantial, since it entails 'direct causation' and requires that S and O name co-participants in a single event (Pietroski 2005: 188).

For English, on the other hand, I claimed that verbs do characteristically have lexical arguments. Transitive verbs have at least their implied theme as an argument (Kratzer 1996); for example, *strike* and *cut* have meanings with the outlines of (39). Whether they also have their agents as arguments is a question we will turn to next.

(39) a. $[\![$ *strike* $]\!] = \lambda y \dots \lambda e[\dots$ Theme(e, y) & Striking(e) $]$

      b. $[\![$ *cut* $]\!] = \lambda y \dots \lambda e[\dots$ Theme(e, y) & Cutting(e) $]$

Arguments of M are inherited by MR. Thus *cut open* will have a meaning like (40), inheriting the theme argument of *cut* from (39b). All else equal, therefore, this role will come to be bound by a dependent in the resultative clause, specifically O.

(40) $[\![$ *cut open* $]\!] = \lambda y \dots \lambda e_1 \exists e_2 \exists e_3 [\dots \mathcal{K}(e_1, e_2, e_3)$ & $[\dots$ Theme(e, y) & Cutting(e) $]$ & Openness($\dots$)(e_3) $]$

Unlike in Mandarin and Igbo, therefore, interpretation with respect to the M event is restricted in the sentence meaning. The verb in M has arguments and these project to S or O. For details about the derivation, see Williams (2005, 2008).

I will now describe some of the data that these proposals are meant to account for, concerning the interpetation of O relative to the means event.[9]

---

[9] Formally, inheritance of an argument requires an operation like Kratzer's (1996) "Event Identification," which combines function composition with function conjunction. In turn, identifying an argument of MR with an "outside" relation in its context requires an extension of standard conjunction.

3.3. THEMES IN RESULTATIVES

(41) is a familiar kind of example. Here *her throat* controls R, but does not not tell us what Mo sang.

(41)   Mo sang her throat hoarse.

Thus the controller of R does not always name the theme of the means event. In English this possibility is restricted, however. As a rule, it is available only when the verb in M is on its own acceptable in unergative clauses, as *sing* is in (42) (Dowty 1979: 222; Carrier and Randall 1992: 187; Levin and Rappaport Hovav 1995: 39).

(42)   Mo sang.

The verb *cut* is stubbornly transitive, and not generally good in unergative clauses such as (43).[10] Thus O in (44) must name what was cut, and (45) is unacceptable.

(43)   * Lee cut.

(44)   Lee cut the bone open.

(45)   * Lee cut the knife dull.
        'Lee made the knife dull from cutting [with it].'

This is what we expect, given our theory. The transitive verb in M projects its theme argument, deciding the interpretation of O.

For Mandarin the prediction is different. The controller of R should not be restricted relative to M, even when the verb there is transitive. And this is indeed what we find (Lü 1986; Ma 1987; Y. Li 1990; Tan 1991; among others). O need not name the theme of the M event, even when the verb in M is transitive, as in (46).

(46)   a.   Ta hai qie dun -le   nide caidao.
              3s also cut dull -PFV your food knife
              'He also made your cleaver dull from cutting.'
              (adapted from Ma 1987: 428)

        b.   Wo tai   zhong -le   jianbang.
              1s carry swollen -PFV shoulder
              'I made [my] shoulders swollen from carrying.'

This cannot be explained by positing a *pro* object for M, since the sentence cannot accommodate a second object overtly. And in any case, the sentences in (46) may be used felicitously even when the theme of the M event is not topical or salient.

---

[10] There are acceptable unergative uses of *cut*, for example in contexts such as (97), where there is a task under discussion that implies an understood object for the cutting. But this does nothing to change the point.

(97)   We had to prepare the appetizers, first cutting and then arranging the various treats. I cut and Lee arranged.

Igbo lacks object *pro* entirely, and yet shows exactly the same pattern. The verbs *bi* 'cut,' *gwu* 'dig out,' and *tụ* 'throw,' for example, are transitive. On their own they occupy transitive clauses, with direct objects that must name what was cut, dug out, or thrown. They are generally unacceptable in unergative clauses. Yet these same verbs are also natural in (47), where O need not name what was cut, dug out, or thrown. A speaker of (47c), for example, may mean to convey either that Obi has thrown the gourd or that he has thrown something at it.

(47) a. Obi bi kpụ -rụ   mma.
          O. cut dull -FACT knife
          'Obi made the knife dull by cutting [with it].'

      b. Obi gwu ji   -ri   ọgụ.
          O. dig out snap -FACT hoe
          'Obi made his hoe snap by digging out [with it].'

      c. Obi tụ   pu   -ru ọba ahụ.
          O. throw have hole-FACT gourd that
          'Obi made the gourd have a hole in by throwing [something at it].'
          (Igwe 1999)

This pattern is systematic and robust, across transitive verbs. It is even recognized in Igwe 1999, a dictionary that lists common MR combinations. Igwe often glosses these as having several salient readings, differing in the understood relation of O to M. (47c) is one example.

What goes for O in a transitive, moreover, goes equally for S in an intransitive. There the interpretation of S is again unrestricted relative to M. I show this using Igbo in (48).[11] See also the Mandarin examples in (59).

(48) a. Mma ahụ bi kpụ -rụ   ebikpụ.
          knife that cut dull -FACT BVC
          'That knife got dull from cutting [stuff].'

      b. Ọgụ ya gwu ji   -ri   egwuji.
          hoe 3s dig out snap -FACT BVC
          'His hoe got snapped from digging out [stuff].'

      c. Ọba ahụ tụ   pu   -ru atụpu.
          gourd that throw have hole -FACT BVC
          'That gourd got a hole in it by throwing [it/something at it].'

These facts motivate the claim that Mandarin and Igbo verbs do not have implied themes as arguments. The remainder of the chapter, however, concerns the implied agent of the verb in M. And here Igbo differs from both Mandarin and English.

---

[11] The transitivity of clauses is formally clear in Igbo. Were *mma ahụ* 'that knife' to be replaced by a pronoun in (48), the pronoun would have the subject form, not the object form. Moreover, the DP cannot be analyzed as a fronted object, since that would require an overt pronominal clitic to register the subject.

4. Agentive Verbs in Intransitive Resultatives

Igbo *kụ* 'strike' is not an unaccusative verb, witness (49). When it exhausts the predicate in a basic clause, that clause must be transitive, as in (50). There must be a dependent to bind the role of striker.

(49) * Ọba ahụ kụ   -rụ   akụ.
         gourd that strike -FACT BVC
         'That gourd got struck.'

(50) Ọ kụ   -rụ   ọba ahụ.
         3sS strike -FACT gourd that
         'S/he struck that gourd.'

But this is not so when *kụ* 'strike' inhabits M in a resultative, such as *kụ wa* 'strike split.' Then we do find it in unaccusative clauses, with nothing naming the striker (Nwachukwu 1987; Ụwalaka 1988; Hale et al. 1995). (51) has *kụ wa* 'strike split' in a clause that is manifestly intransitive (see note 11).[12] Here *ọba ahụ* 'that gourd' is the subject, and no dependent binds the role of striker.

(51) Ọba ahụ kụ   wa -ra   akụwa.
         gourd that strike split -FACT BVC
         'That gourd split from striking.'   (Hale et al. 1995)

This is not a special case. As suggested by the examples in (48), many transitive verbs can occupy M in an intransitive resultative—though not all, as we will see.

Mandarin is arguably the same, though this is harder to see in a *pro*-drop language with no morphological marking of subjects. Tan (1991) argues that (52), with the resultative predicate *tui fan* 'push over,' has an intransitive parse where *na liang che* 'which car' is the subject, and not a fronted object.[13]

(52) Na   liang che tui fan   -le?
         which CLS car push reverse -PFV
         'Which car was pushed over?'   (adapted from Tan 1991: 79)

Here no argument names the pusher. And yet the verb *tui* 'push' does not on its own occur comfortably in unaccusatives, (53). It is a transitive verb.

(53) ?* Na   liang che tui -le?
          which CLS car push -PFV
          'Which car was pushed?'   (ibid.)

[12] According to Hale, Ihiọnụ, and Manfredi (1995), intransitive resultatives in Igbo are not stative. Were they stative, we could assimilate them to English past participles used predicatively, as in: *The bone is cut.* I believe Hale et al. are correct, since for my consultants intransitive resultatives will accept eventive adverbs, such as *ọsịịsọ* 'quickly,' to describe the pace of the MR process.

[13] In Mandarin, fronting of a *wh*-phrases is generally infelicitous, suggesting that strings like (52) allow an intransitive parse. Tan (1991) gives additional arguments for this conclusion, but see LaPolla (1988) and Li and Thompson (1994) for other views. Certainly there can be no general objection to an intransitive resultative with a transitive verb in M, given the clear data from Igbo.

English, of course, is different. MR can occupy an unaccusative clause, with no agent for the verb in M, only when that verb can do the same on its own. So while *freeze solid* and *slap red* can both occur in transitive resultatives (54), only the former occurs in intransitives (55), since only *freeze* can do the same (56).

(54) a. The January temperatures froze the lake solid.

b. Mo slapped Lee's face red.

(55) a. The lake froze solid.

b. * Lee's face slapped red.

(56) a. The lake froze.

b. * Lee's face slapped.

How should we understand this? The English data suggest that MR inherits its transitivity entirely from M. Applied to Mandarin and Igbo, this would imply that verbs such as Mandarin *tui* 'push' or Igbo *kụ* 'strike' have two lexical entries, one transitive and the other intransitive, to allow for both transitive and intransitive resultatives, respectively, with these verbs in M.[14] But this is unsatisfactory. The intransitive lexical entry would only ever occur inside of a resultative, never on its own. And why should this be? The better view, it seems to me, is that the distribution of MR is determined compositionally, not only by M but also by other parts of the construction. The pattern is simply eclipsed in English, where agentivity is evidently by itself sufficient to exclude a predicate from unaccusative clauses. In other languages the conditions are weaker.

Discussing Mandarin, Tan (1991: 80) suggests that telicity is a relevant factor. The predicate in an unaccusative clause must be telic, she suggests, and *tui fan* 'push over' is telic, while *tui* 'push' on its own is not. This recalls observations in Smith (1978), Van Valin (1990), Dowty (1991), Levin and Rappaport Hovav (1995), and elsewhere. In general, the predicate in an unaccusative clause describes a substantive change or 'activity' in the referent of its subject, where 'activity' includes at least movement and emission of sound or light (Levin and Rappaport Hovav 1995).[15] (58) gives examples.

(57) Theme condition on simple unaccusative clauses
      An unaccusative clause, unless passive or stative or middle,[16] describes its event as involving a substantive change or activity in its theme, the referent of its surface subject.

(58) My phone cracked / vibrated / beeped / glowed.

---

[14] Compare the treatment of examples like *freeze solid* in Levin and Rappaport Hovav (1995).

[15] Even this condition does not hold in every language. In St'at'imcets, for example, nearly every verb can occur in an unaccusative context, including verbs of striking, such as *qamt* 'to hit with a thrown object' (Davis and Matthewson 2009).

[16] Here I use *middle* for a special sort of unaccusative clause, usually modal, with distinctive conditions on its tolerance for otherwise agentive verbs: "The grammatical subject of a middle (if present) must have properties such that it can be understood to be responsible for the action expressed by the predicate" (Ackema and Schoorlemmer 2006). These are not restrictions on the unaccusatives that I discuss here.

For Mandarin, this covers a lot of ground. Almost any telic predicate, and specifically any predicate of change in Mandarin, can occur in unaccusative contexts. A resultative that can be transitive can also be intransitive, no matter what verb is in M. (59) gives a variety of examples that will be relevant later.

(59) a. Na   ba   dao qie dun -le?
        which CLS knife cut dull -PFV
        'Which knife got dull from cutting?'

    b. Ji   ge pingguo cai   lan   -le?
       how many CLS apple   tread on mushy -PFV
       'How many apples got mushy from treading [on them]?'

    c. Na   gen qianbi xie zhe -le?
       which CLS pencil write snap -PFV
       'Which pencil snapped from writing?'   (adapted from Ma 1987: 424)

    d. Sheide shoupa   ku shi -le?
       Whose handkerchief cry wet -PFV
       'Whose handkerchief got wet from crying?'

But (57) is grossly insufficient for English or for Igbo. English *slap red* describes a change, and yet (55b) is ungrammatical. For Igbo, Hale et al. (1995) observe that *kụ* 'strike' in (51) cannot be replaced with *zọ* 'tread on' in (60), in contrast to Mandarin (59b). In these languages, there must be conditions in addition to (57).

(60) *Ọba ahụ zọ   wa -ra   akụwa.
      gourd that tread on split -FACT BVC
      'That gourd split from treading.' (Hale et al. 1995)

In English the further condition seems to be (61). An unaccusative clause, unless passive or middle or stative, must describe its event as conceivably spontaneous, and not necessarily brought about with the involvement external agent (Fillmore 1970; Smith 1978; Van Valin 1990; Levin and Rappaport 1995).

(61) Agent condition on unaccusative clauses in English
      An unaccusative clause, unless passive or middle or stative, describes its event as conceivably spontaneous, not necessarily brought about with the involvement of an external agent.

You cannot get slapped unless somebody slaps you, but at least as we normally view things, a lake can freeze without anything freezing it. (61) therefore allows *freeze* but not *slap* as the predicate in unaccusative clauses. Now consider resultatives. When M entails an agent, MR describes its event as achieved by means of an event with an agent. We can interpret (61) as excluding such a predicate from unaccusative clauses. And if we do, then although *slap red* and *freeze solid* both describe changes, as per (57), only the latter abides by (61) and is therefore permitted in (56). MR will occur in unaccusative clauses only if its M can do the same.

Before returning to Igbo, let me sketch one formalization of these ideas within my general framework. I would like to show how they might be implemented without presuming that agentive verbs ever have their implied agents as arguments—thus preserving the NAT for Igbo, and allowing for the possibility that agents are not arguments of the verb in English either (Schein 1993; Kratzer 1996).

Suppose that the predicate of a clause, pretheoretically its verb phrase, is headed by a functional item of category v (Chomsky 1995; Kratzer 1996; Marantz 1997). We can then stipulate that in unaccusative clauses this v selects a complement with the feature [c] and without the feature [a]. And now let us assume that in all three of our languages, expressions with [c] are all and only those which describe their event as involving "substantive change or activity in its theme." Accordingly, any resultative predicate MR should have the feature [c], contributed by whatever introduces the meaning of the construction; the feature cannot come from M or R, since it may be that neither describes an event with an active or changing theme. The semantic category of predicates with [a], on the other hand, varies by language. In English the predicates with [a] are those that describe their event as having an agent. In Igbo they are some subset of these, including *zọ* 'tread on' but not *kụ* 'strike.' And in Mandarin, where M seems never to keep a resultative from being intransitive, there are perhaps no verbs with [a]. The observed patterns would then follow, provided that MR has [a] whenever its M does.

On this account, we need not say that a verb with [a] itself has an agent as an argument. Its semantic value needn't be a function over agents, and it need not select syntactically for a certain kind of DP. But we do need to say something about headedness. Any complex expression inherits features derivationally from just one of its parts, therefore called its head. But MR seems to have features from more than one source. It has [a] because of M, and [c] because of "whatever introduces the meaning of the construction." Here is a way to resolve this tension. Assume that "whatever introduces the meaning of the construction" is the head of MR, and call this part K. Now let K have either of two syntactic categories: either it has [a] and selects for a complement which itself has [a], or it lacks [a] and selects for a complement without [a]. MR then inherits features from just one of its parts derivationally, but this head happens to echo the category of its complement. This is a familiar kind of solution. It is like saying that *the bone* and *the bones* both have *the* and not *bone(s)* as their head—but the determiner occurs in either of two subcategories. One is marked singular and also selects for a singular complement; the other is marked non-singular and selects for a non-singular complement. The case of finite and nonfinite complementizers is similar.

Back to the Igbo data. In our present terms, the descriptive question is which verbs have [a]. Clearly some verbs have it, unlike in Mandarin. And clearly the category is not defined by (61), as it is in English: strikings involve an agent, and yet Igbo (51) is fine, with *kụ wa* 'strike split' in an unaccusative clause. So then what does make the difference between *kụ wa* 'strike split' and *zọ wa* 'tread split'? The answer is not clear to me, but I would like to venture some observations.

Hale et al. (1995) suggest that it may matter that *zọ* 'tread on' is instrumental, in that treading involves feet. This does not seem likely, however, as verbs like *bi* 'cut with a knife' and *kpọ* 'chop' are fine in intransitives, as are *sọ* 'prick' and *hyi* 'sweep.'

(62) Mma ahụ bi kpụ -rụ   ebikpụ.
      knife that cut dull -FACT BVC
      'That knife got dull from cutting.'

(63) Nkụ   kpọ wa -ra   akpọwa.
      firewood chop split -FACT BVC
      'The firewood got split from chopping.'   (Nwachukwu 1987: 102)

Moreover, there are many unacceptable intransitives that do not involve instrumental verbs, as in (64), for example.[17] Compare these to Mandarin (59) above.

(64) a. *Osisi ahụ b'e   ji   -ri   eb'eji.
          wood that perch on snap -FACT BVC
          'That branch got snapped from perching [on it].'

      b. *Akw'a kpu   wa -ra   ekpuwa.
          egg   brood split -FACT BVC
          'The eggs got split from brooding [them].'

      c. *Tebul ahụ wụ   wa -ra   awụwa.
          table that jump split -FACT BVC
          'That table got split from jumping [on it].'

      d. *Akịsị be de -re   (n'   akwa)   ebede.
          hanky cry wet -FACT (PREP weeping) BVC
          'The hanky got wet from crying [into it].'

      e. *Pensul m   de ji -ri   edeji.
          pencil 1sPOSS write snap -FACT pencil
          'My pencil got snapped from writing [with it].'

The examples in (64) hint that (65) may be a better hypothesis. The predicate of
an unaccusative clause cannot be defined in terms of traits of an animate (or quasi-
animate) creature.

(65) Animacy condition on unaccusative clauses in Igbo
      The meaning of a predicate in an unaccusative clause cannot be defined in terms of the
      traits of an animate creature.

Treading requires mobile feet, and mobile feet are in the first instance a trait of animate creatures. Plausibly, therefore, *zọ wa* 'tread-on split' is defined in terms of an
animate agent, and so is excluded from unaccusative contexts by (65). Likewise it
is animate creatures who perch, brood, jump, and weep.[18] And though we may say
that machines can write, mechanized mark-making counts as writing only relative to

---

[17] Each of these MR combinations is acceptable in a transitive clause.
[18] Only animals can be the agent of *kpu* 'brood,' a transitive verb meaning 'to crouch over (esp.
eggs or infants).' The collocation *kpu wa* 'brood split' is listed in Igwe (1999: 332). The speakers
who judged (64c) all said that *wụ* 'jump' can only describe the jumping of a creature, and not the
bouncing of a ball or a pebble.

intentional conventions of human beings. So in this way (64e) too falls under (65), as I intend it. *Kụ* 'strike,' on the other hand, makes no reference to animates. It simply describes a kind of forceful impact. Thus *kụ wa* 'strike split' complies with (65) and is possible in unaccusative clauses. Similarly for *hịọ pịa* 'rub crushed' in (66): events of rubbing only require two moving surfaces, neither of which needs to be animate.

(66) Anwuta ahụ hịọ pịa   -ra   ahịọpịa.
      Mosquito that rub crushed -FACT BVC
      'That mosquito got crushed from rubbing.'

Unfortunately, there are cases not easily subsumed under (65). Igbo speakers I have consulted do not reject intransitive resultatives with *ta* 'chew' and *bu* 'carry on the head' in M, for example. If there is some sense in which chewing and carrying on the head are not "defined in terms of the traits of animate creatures," it is not clear to me. Further work is needed, therefore, to determine the semantic correlates of being an [a] verb in Igbo.

5. Non-agentive Subjects of Transitive Resultatives

I proposed in section 3.1 that, in both Mandarin and Igbo, a resultative clause has the very spare semantics in (67), where M and R are functions from events to truth values that give the meanings of M and R.

(67) $\lambda e_1 \exists e_2 \exists e_3 [\text{Agent}(e_1, [\![S]\!]) \ \& \ \text{Theme}(e_1, [\![O]\!]) \ \& \ K(e_1, e_2, e_3) \ \& \ M(e_2) \ \& \ R(e_3)]$.

(67) states no thematic relations between the event of M and the referents of either S or O. For O we have seen evidence that this is right; for example, (68) is true whether Chidi dug out his hoe, or dug out other stuff using his hoe.

(68) Chidi gwu   ji   -ri   ọgụ ya.
      C.   dig out snap -FACT hoe 3s
      'Chidi made his hoe snap from digging out.'

But S is a different story. Given just (67), (69) should be acceptable with the given interpretation. This sentence is just like (68), except in how we mean the referent of S to relate to the event of M. Here we mean it to be not the digger but the thing dug out, and this is unacceptable.

(69) *Ji   ahụ gwu ji   -ri   ọgụ ya.
      yam that dig out snap -FACT hoe 3s
      'That yam made his hoe snap from [someone's] digging [with it].'

This represents a categorical fact about Igbo: whenever a transitive resultative has an agentive verb in M, S names the agent of its event. In this way Igbo is like English, where sentences as in (70) are impossible. Both languages accord with (71).

(70) a. * That dough pounded my fist sore.
          'That dough made my fist sore from pounding [it].'

      b. * The intro sang Mo hoarse.
          'The intro made Mo hoarse from singing [it].'

(71) Resultative Agent Observation (RAO)
      When a transitive resultative has an agentive verb in M, S names the agent of its event.

There is a striking contrast with Mandarin, however, where (71) does not apply (Ma 1987; Li 1990, 1995; Tan 1991; Gu 1992; Wang 1995; Ren 2001). Sentences like those in (72) are frequently acceptable.

(72) a. Yifu   xi   lei   -le   jiejie.
          clothes wash tired -PFV elder
          'The clothes made big sister tired by [her] washing [them].'
          (Ren 2001: 326, my translation)

      b. Na   shou gequ chang ya   -le   wo sangzi.
          That CLS song sing hoarse -PFV 1s throat
          'That song made my throat hoarse from [my] singing [it].'

      c. Na   gen gutou qie dun -le   wode caidao.
          that CLS bone cut dull -PFV my   food knife
          'That bone made my knife dull from cutting [it].'

Thus any theory designed to account for the freedom of Mandarin, including the NAT, will not extend to Igbo without elaboration.

What, then, is the best elaboration? Why in Igbo but not Mandarin does S in a transitive resultative name the agent of an agentive verb in M? And how can we describe the difference between Igbo and Mandarin without neglecting what they share? In sections 5.1 and 5.2, I consider how to answer these questions while preserving the OR semantics and the NAT, starting with the answer that I find least unattractive. Then, in section 5.3, I discuss what options are available if we reject the NAT, concluding that they offer no special advantages, whether or not we have an OR semantics. In section 5.4, I observe a problem posed by transitive resultatives in Igbo with apparently *non*-agentive verbs in M, specifically *d'a* 'fall.' Finally, in 5.5, I compare my conclusion with the suggestion that transitive resultatives in Mandarin differ from those of Igbo or English in the thematic interpretation of S.

5.1. THE RESULTATIVE AGENT POSTULATE

The first response to our questions makes no structural distinctions between Igbo and Mandarin. It simply adds a meaning postulate to the one language but not the other, called RAP in (73). We could assume that the RAP holds in English as well.

(73) Resultative Agent Postulate (RAP)
      The agent of the process described by a resultative must be the agent of its reported means event: $\Box \forall e_1 e_2 e_3 [\ K(e_1, e_2, e_3) \rightarrow \text{Agent}(e_1, x) \equiv \text{Agent}(e_2, x)\ ]$

Any such postulate is initially disappointing. It makes no predictions, and follows from nothing else. In particular, contrary to the occasional suggestion that a 'causer' is simply the agent of an event that directly causes something, it does not follow from our normal understanding of changes and processes. When I cut a bone with a saw, the bone may dull my saw. In that case, the bone is the agent of the dulling process, but not of anything else. It simply resists the action of my cutting. The cutting, moreover, surely causes the dullness, and does so quite directly. So (74) does not conflict with how we think about changes or processes. Nor does Igbo (69). The thoughts that these sentences are meant to express are perfectly natural. Indeed, they are thoughts that can be expressed with comparable clauses in Mandarin.

(74)   * The bone cut my saw dull.
         'The bone made my saw dull from cutting.'

So the RAP has no deep motivation. And one cannot say that it expresses some notion of change or causation that is parochial to language, since it does not apply in Mandarin. Perhaps worse, the RAP must apply only to the "reported" means event, the one described by M. For plainly the agent of a process need not be the agent of *every* event by means of which it is achieved. This is an oddly formal restriction for what is supposed to be a meaning postulate.

That said, unexplained restrictions like this seem to be common in the domain of resultatives. Green (1972: 84) judges the sentences in (75) unacceptable, and English speakers generally agree with her. But there is no settled account of why, when the variants in (76) are unobjectionable (though see Goldberg 1995: 195).

(75)   a.   * She shot him lame.

        b.   * He hammered it tubular.

(76)   a.   She shot him dead.

        b.   He hammered it flat.

Similarly, Japanese speakers accept (77a) but reject (77b) (Washio 1997: 9).

(77)   a.   John -wa niku -o   yawaraka -ku   ni -ta.
               J.   -TOP meat -ACC soft   -INFIN boil -PAST
               'John boiled the meat soft.'

        b.   # John -wa niku -o   yawaraka -ku   tatai -ta.
               J.   -TOP meat -ACC soft   -INFIN pound -PAST
               'John pounded the meat soft.'

Washio (1997) subsumes this under the generalization that Japanese only allows "weak resultatives." In a weak resultative, M "strongly implies" a ("tendency toward") a particular result, and R entails a state characteristically associated with that result. According to Washio, boiling "strongly implies" a result correlated with softness, but pounding does not. Despite Washio's insights, however, there is no accepted account of why this restriction should hold in Japanese, or why Japanese should differ in this way from Mandarin, Igbo, and English. In particular it has not been convincingly tied to variation in the structure or logical form of the resultative construction.

Perhaps the Igbo rejection of sentences like (69) has a similar character. Speakers of Igbo and Mandarin share the same basic understanding of change, and the same structure for resultatives, syntactic and semantic. But resultatives just have a slightly narrower meaning in Igbo, which adds a condition that Mandarin does not, the RAP. We can still assume that the Means relation is one of only a few that UG provides to interpret a complex predicate.[19] All the RAP forces us to accept is that languages may add to this in various limited ways, narrowing the constructional meaning. Here is a fictional analogy. Suppose there were several languages where a certain construction is interpreted by disjunction. Should we be distressed if in some other languages the analogous construction has the slightly narrower meaning of exclusive disjunction? Or should such additions be seen as tolerable?

In any case, while the RAP is at first unattractive, the postuate is warranted if making it allows for simplification elsewhere. And as we will now see, without RAP, there will be real complications to the grammar, whether or not we accept the NAT.

5.2. OTHER RESPONSES WITHIN THE NAT

Without the RAP, I see two responses that preserve the NAT. One says that in Igbo but not Mandarin, M includes more than just the verb. It also contains structure that introduces an Agent relation. Suppose with Kratzer (1996) that agents are introduced by a silent morpheme called Ag. Then MR would have a syntax like (78a) and a meaning like (78b). Crucially, (78b) provides an explicit Agent relation for e_2, the means event.

(78) a. $[^{MR}\,[^{M} \ldots Ag\,[V \ldots]\,]\,[^{R}\,V \ldots]\,]$

b. $\ldots \lambda e_1 \exists e_2 \exists e_3 [\,K(e_1, e_2, e_3)\,\&\,[\,Agent(e_2, x)\,\&\,M(e_2) \ldots]\,\&\,[\,R(e_3) \ldots]\,]$

Now suppose we ensure that this agent role for M is bound by S, not O. Technically this is no small matter (Williams 2005), but let us imagine it can be done in an acceptable way. The facts of Igbo will then follow. S will necessarily be interpreted as naming the agent of the M event.

But problems arise when we imagine a transitive verb in M, like *kụ* 'strike' or *gwu* 'dig out.' When such a verb is on its own, it cannot occupy an unergative clause. Thus its immediate context will of necessity include the structure to introduce not only an agent but also a theme—a complete transitive verb phrase. And yet it is necessary that this restriction *not* apply when the verb is in M, since in Igbo there is no requirement that any dependent ever name the theme of the M event. This makes for a puzzle. Why is a transitive verb allowed to occur without a theme dependent exactly and only when it occupies M? Why should the resultative context have exactly this non-local effect on what is licensed inside of its M component? I see no good answer, and therefore reject this first line of thinking.

---

[19] See Bittner (1999) and Rothstein (2004) for relevant discussion.

The second response, still within the framework of the NAT, is to reject the Third Event Assumption in (25). Perhaps in Igbo, MR is a predicate of the very same event as M is, as stated in (79) (Parsons 1990; Kratzer 2005). Here C means something like 'directly causes.' The agent of the event described by MR would then be the agent of the M event. And therefore the subject of a transitive resultative would necessarily name the agent of M, as desired.

(79) $[\![MR]\!] = \lambda e_1 \exists e_2[\ \dots\ C(e_1, e_2)\ \&\ [\![M]\!](e_1)\ \&\ [\![R]\!](e_2)\ \dots\ ]$

But this is otherwise unattractive. The interpretation of adverbs forbids (79), and requires the TEA—a dispositive flaw, in my view. In addition, (79) rules out an OR semantics. We could not assume that O in a resultative is interpreted as the theme of its event, since it would then always name the theme of the M event, contrary to fact. Without an OR semantics, the NAT would lose an important attraction. We could not say that resultative complex predicates occur in the same structural contexts as do simple, one-verb predicates: *kụ* 'strike' would occur in a context where O is interpreted as the theme of its event, but *kụ wa* 'strike split' would not.

5.3. RESPONSES WITHOUT THE NAT

Now consider our options if we reject the NAT. We could then say that Igbo verbs do have at least their agent as a lexical argument. The verb *gwu* 'dig out,' for instance, might then have a meaning with the outlines of (80).

(80) $[\![$ *gwu* 'dig out' $]\!] = \dots \lambda x \lambda e[\ \text{Agent}(e, x)\ \&\ \dots\ \text{DiggingOut}(e)\ ]$

This agent argument is then inherited by any resultative complex predicate in which the verb occurs, so that *gwu ji* 'dig-out snap,' for example, has a meaning like (81).

(81) $[\![$ *gwu ji* 'dig-out snap' $]\!] = \dots \lambda x \lambda e_1 \exists e_2 \exists e_3[\ \kappa(e_1, e_2, e_3)\ \&\ \text{Agent}(e_2, x)\ \&\ \text{DiggingOut}(e_2)$
Snapping$(e_3) \dots]$

The facts of Igbo would then follow if this agent argument is necessarily bound by S, regardless of whether *gwu* occurs on its own, or within a transitive resultative. Let us again ignore technical details, and assume this can be ensured in a natural way, via a Thematic Hierarchy or otherwise. To account for intransitive resultatives where the agent role of M is not assigned, as in (82), we can in turn assume an operation analogous to passive, call it Detrans. Detrans eliminates the agent argument syntactically, and semantically binds its thematic relation with an existential quantifier, as in (83).

(82)   Ọgụ ya gwu   ji   -ri   egwuji.
       hoe 3s dig.out snap -FACT BVC
       'His hoe snapped from digging out [stuff].'

(83)   Detrans($[\![$*gwu ji*$]\!]$) $= \dots \lambda e_1 \exists x \exists e_2 \exists e_3[\ \kappa(e_1, e_2, e_3)\ \&\ \text{Agent}(e_2, x)\ \&\ \text{DiggingOut}(e_2)$
Snapping$(e_3) \dots]$

So far so good. But again problems arise when we consider the entailed theme of the verb. Is this also an argument of the verb? Suppose first that the answer is Yes, so that transitive verbs have not only their agent but also their theme as a lexical argument. This will give *gwu* a meaning like (84).

(84)   ⟦ *gwu* 'dig out' ⟧ = $\lambda y \lambda x \lambda e$[Agent($e, x$) & Theme($e, y$) & DiggingOut($e$)]

But again, in Igbo a transitive verb in M need not realize its theme. So we would have to say that a verb in M, while it must project its agent argument, need not project its theme argument. In effect we would have to stipulate that in M, a transitive verb is antipassivized, optionally or always, and yet never passivized. But why should this be? And why should it be in Igbo but not English? I see no good answer.

I can imagine the following retort: maybe in Igbo, all the arguments of a verb in M are eliminated indiscriminately. Perhaps this is an an effect of 'compounding,' the direct combination of two lexical items, as suggested in McIntyre (2004). This would explain the difference between Igbo and English. And we would be at no disadvantage compared to the NAT, since the result of eliminating arguments is the same as never having any. Whatever the proponent of the NAT says, we could say here. But for three reasons this is less attractive than the NAT. First, there is no reason that compounding should eliminate arguments. Second, there seem to be many languages with resultative 'compounds' that do not behave like Igbo or Mandarin. And third, I argued in Williams (2008) that the Mandarin pattern is exhibited not only in 'compounds,' but whenever the verb combines with something other than a thematic DP (Lin 2001). I discussed the example of V-*de* constructions such as (85).

(85)   Wo (pai   Lao Wei-de mapi,) kua   -de lian ta taitai ye   buhaoyisi.
       1s (smack L.W.'s horse rump,) praise -DE even 3s wife also embarrassed
       '(Flattering Lao Wei,) I praised [him] such that even his wife was embarrassed.'

According to L. Li (1963) and Huang (1992), the verb here forms a constituent, discontinuous on the surface, with the verb phrase to its right. In (85) this is *kua* 'praise' with *ye buhaoyisi* 'also embarrassed.' The two do not form a compound, since the secondary predicate is phrasal. Nonetheless, once again, no argument in the clause containing the complex predicate names the theme of its first verb's event.

So suppose instead that transitive verbs in Igbo do not have their entailed theme as an argument, only their agent. Then *gwu* 'dig out' has a meaning like (86), and *gwu ji* 'dig-out snap' in turn has a meaning like (87), requiring S to name the digger, but not restricting the interpretation of O.

(86)   ⟦ *gwu* 'dig out' ⟧ = $\lambda x \lambda e$[Agent(e, x) & DiggingOut(e)]

(87)   ⟦ *gwu ji* 'dig snap' ⟧ = ... $\lambda x \lambda e_1 \exists e_2 \exists e_3$[$K(e_1, e_2, e_3)$ & [Agent(e_2, x) & DiggingOut(e_2)]
       & [Snapping(e_3) ...]]

Initially this seems odd, since transitive verbs like *gwu* 'dig out' cannot on their own occur in unergative contexts, (88).

(88) *O gwu   -ru   egwu.
3sS dig out -FACT BVC
'S/he dug out [stuff].'

But this oddity does not falsify the hypothesis. We can give transitive verbs a feature, call it [t], that is licit only within a phrase that introduces a theme argument structurally. For concreteness, suppose that such a phrase is headed by a silent morpheme Th of category v, as in (89), where Th means $\lambda x \lambda e$ [Theme(e, x)].

(89) $[_v DP_{th} [_v Th{:}v V[t]]]$

In turn, we could assume that any complex predicate MR whose M has [t] inherits this feature, and must therefore also itself occur in the context of (89). Attractively, this gives us an account of why O in Igbo resultatives need not name the theme of the M event, the very same account afforded by the NAT: with MR in the V slot of (89), the stated theme relation will be to the event of MR, not M.

But still problems remain. Presumably the base position of S, which will have to bind the agent argument that projects from the verb in M, must c-command the base position of O. And given this, it follows that the *gwu* 'dig out' of (86) cannot take its agent argument immediately, as it does in (90), where DP_{ag} and DP_{th} bind the roles of digger and dug out, respectively. It must take its argument only after combining with Th, as in (91).

(90) $* [v DP_{th} [v Th{:}v [_{V[t]} [DP_{ag} gwu]]]]$

(91) $[DP_{ag} ... [v DP_{th} [v Ag{:}v [_{V[t]} gwu]]]]$

This is very odd. Normally we assume that a verb can, or even must, take its lexical arguments immediately, before combining with any other structure. Yet here we need to ensure that this is not even possible. Necessarily, the verb must wait to take its argument.[20] But why should this be, and why just in this one case? Again I see no answer, and without an answer, the proposal holds no interest.

Importantly, the problems observed in this section do not depend in any way on the OR semantics. Suppose we drop that semantics and all explicit thematic relations in a resultative are to the events of M or R. To ensure that S names the agent of the

---

[20] Here is an example of what would be possible were derivations like (91) allowed more generally. Kratzer (1996) proposes structures like (98), where DP_{th} satisfies a lexical argument of *cut*, and DP_{ag} satisfies a lexical argument of Ag. With no change to *cut* or Ag, the proposal we are considering would also allow the alternative derivation in (99), where the lexical argument of *cut* is not satisfied until after V combines with Ag. And this would allow, wrongly, for sentences like (100).

(98) $[v DP_{ag} [v Ag [_v DP_{th} cut]]]$

(99) $[DP_{th} ... [v DP_{ag} [v Ag cut]]]$

(100) * The bone cut Lee.
'Lee cut the bone.'

means event in a transitive, it would then be necessary to have an agent relation projecting from M; it could not be introduced by structure outside M, since it would then relate to the event of MR. And consequently all the same questions posed above would arise anew. Why in Igbo should a transitive verb in M require its usual agent, when it does not require its theme?

5.4. NON-AGENTIVE VERBS IN TRANSITIVE RESULTATIVES

In sum, putting an agent argument inside M, whether by adding syntactic structure or by giving the verb an argument lexically, raises as many questions as it answers. These complications put the RAP in a more favorable light: at least it allows us to keep the grammar simple. Exactly because the RAP is an ad hoc meaning postulate, it does no collateral damage to the mechanics of composition.

But there is a blunt empirical problem for the RAP solution. Igbo speakers accept transitive resultatives with *d'a* 'fall' in M where S names the faller, as in (92).

(92)   Osisi d'a bi   -ri   eriri.
       tree fall in pieces -FACT rope
       'The tree made the rope go to pieces from [the tree] falling [into the rope].'

The RAP requires that S name the agent of the means event. But fallers are usually considered to be themes, at least in unintended fallings. (92) therefore demands one of two responses: either fallers do count as agents in Igbo, but not English, or the RAP does not govern Igbo resultatives.

The first response invokes an unexplained semantic distinction, as does the RAP itself. This is not nice, but what is the alternative? Suppose that fallers are always themes, and consequently that the RAP does not govern Igbo. (69) is then again without an account, and (93) creates a new problem. Most of my consultants reject the meaning in the gloss; for them S must name the faller, so that (93) can only mean that the farmer fell and thereby split the tree.

(93)   *Onye ọlụ ubi d'a ji   -ri   osisi.
       Farmer   fall snap -FACT tree
       'The farmer made the tree snap from [its] falling.'

This fact would follow from the RAP, were fallers to count as agents in Igbo.[21] But how should it be accounted for if they don't? Presumably by giving *d'a* 'fall' the faller as an argument, and requiring that this be bound by the underlying subject. This is already unusual: an unergative verb whose subject is a theme. More important, it does not make the difference between Igbo and English any more natural. English analogues of (92) are unacceptable, as in (94).

---

[21] Likewise, if the RAP governs English, it explains why (101) is unacceptable, even if English, as I am assuming, has an OR semantics.

(101) * The clumsy reporter fell the Jenga tower apart.
      'The reporter made the Jenga tower come apart from [its] falling.'

(94)   * The trees fell my car flat.
     'The trees made my car flat from [their] falling.'

Consequently we would have to say that, while Igbo *d'a* and English *fall* both represent fallers as themes, and both have their implied theme as an argument, the former is unergative and the latter, unaccusative. Is this more attractive than assuming that the languages differ in whether fallers count as agents? The notion of 'agent,' to do the work linguists want it to do, must be extraordinarily vague (Dowty 1991; Baker 1997). Might we not assume that its vagueness is resolved somewhat differently in different languages, with fallers being sorted as agents in Igbo but not English? This seems a reasonable suggestion for cross-linguistic variation in the acceptability of so-called instrumental subjects—in some but not all languages, a wielded knife may count as the agent of a cutting—and perhaps it is also reasonable here.

5.5. MR OR S?

To finish, let me compare the RAP to a more familiar suggestion from the literature on Mandarin. To explain Mandarin examples like (72), it is sometimes suggested that Mandarin differs from English in the interpretation of S, and to English we can add Igbo: in Mandarin but not English or Igbo, S binds the role of "causer," not "agent," at least in cases like (72). Now, given an OR semantics for all three languages, S always binds a relation to the event of MR. So the hypothesis must be that the *content* of this relation differs across languages: it is, let us say, C in Mandarin and A in Igbo or English. The effect of the RAP could then be achieved by instead postulating that, if $K(e_1, e_2, e_3)$, then $A(e_1, x)$ entails that x is the agent of e_2, but $C(e_1, x)$ does not. This locates the variation in the interpretation of S, not MR.

For me this differs from the RAP in one important way. I would like to assume that the semantic context of a resultative predicate, such as *qie dun* 'cut dull,' is the same as that of a simple predicate of action, such as *qie* 'cut.' So if a thematic relation interprets S in a transitive clause with a resultative predicate, it also interprets S in transitive clauses with other predicates. And therefore if Mandarin and Igbo differ in resultative clauses, they should differ this way in all clauses that describe actions. At the moment, however, I have no evidence that this is true. And for this reason I provisionally prefer the RAP, keeping the variation in the meaning of MR.

6. Conclusion

Syntactically, resultatives in Igbo are very like those in Mandarin, with two adjacent verbs followed by O. They also share two notable properties, different from English. First, the interpretation of O is not restricted in relation to M, even when the verb in M is transitive. Second, a resultative predicate MR can occur in an unaccusative clause, even when the M verb is agentive, and so cannot do the same on its own.

Given the common assumption that M contains no more than a verb root, these two facts have a nice account if verbs in Mandarin and Igbo have no arguments lexically. Structure to introduce arguments is then outside M, where it will relate to the event of MR, not the distinct event of M. In addition, the distribution of these arguments must be stated with respect to MR as a whole, and not the root in M. Consequently, since MR may have features from sources other than M, there is no expectation that the two will occur in the same contexts. MR may be licit in an unaccusative clause when M alone is not. This is obscured in English, since unaccusative clauses reject all agentive predicates. But it is visible in Mandarin and Igbo, where the unaccusative frame is more permissive. And this challenges the simplest supposition about English (Levin and Rappaport 1995; Williams 2005), that it forbids agentive verbs in intransitive resultatives because such verbs lexically have their agent as an argument.

Igbo also shares with English, despite their structural differences, two features that distinguish both languages from Mandarin. In Igbo, some agentive verbs cannot occur in intransitive resultatives; and in a transitive resultative with agentive M, S always names the agent of the means event. These contrasts come from no difference in the manifest syntax, since there Igbo looks like Mandarin. Instead, they might be derived by giving agentive verbs in Igbo and English but not Mandarin their implied agent as an argument. But this, I have argued, precipitates quite unattractive complications. It is better to assume that Igbo and English differ, both from Mandarin and from each other, just in which verbs have a syntactic feature [a] that is illicit in unaccusative frames. And perhaps it is also better to stipulate that the constructional meaning of resultatives is slightly narrower in Igbo and English than in Mandarin, entailing that the agent of a process described by a resultative is also the agent of the stated means event. With this difference in content, the logical form is kept as spare in Igbo as it is in Mandarin—for every transitive resultative, it is exactly (95)—and English differs in no more than one small way. A transitive verb in English has its Theme as an argument, and when the verb is M, this is bound by O, as in (96).

(95) $\lambda e_1 \exists e_2 \exists e_3 [\text{ Agent}(e_1, [\![S]\!]) \ \& \ \text{Theme}(e_1, [\![O]\!]) \ \& \ K(e_1, e_2, e_3) \ \& \ M(e_2) \ \& \ R(e_3) \ ]$

(96) $\lambda e_1 \exists e_2 \exists e_3 [\text{ Agent}(e_1, [\![S]\!]) \ \& \ \text{Theme}(e_1, [\![O]\!]) \ \& \ K(e_1, e_2, e_3) \ \& \ M(e_2) \ \& \ \text{Theme}(e_2, [\![O]\!])$ $R(e_3) \ ]$

This seems an attractively minor deviation from the standard set by Mandarin.

References

Ackema, Peter, and Martin Schoorlemmer. 2006. Middles. In *The Blackwell Companion to Syntax*, eds. M. Everaert and H. van Riemsdijk, 131–203. Malden, MA: Blackwell.

Baker, Mark. 1997. Thematic roles and syntactic structure. In *Elements of Grammar*, ed. L. Haegeman, 73–137. Dordrecht: Kluwer.

Bittner, Maria. 1999. Concealed causatives. *Natural Language Semantics* 7(1), 1–78.

Carlson, Greg. 1984. Thematic roles and their role in semantic interpretation. *Linguistics* 22(3), 259–279.

Carrier, Jill, and Janet H. Randall. 1992. The argument structure and syntactic structure of resultatives. *Linguistic Inquiry* 23(2), 173–233.

Chomsky, Noam. 1995. *The Minimalist Program*. Cambridge, MA: MIT Press.

Davidson, Donald. 1967. The logical form of action sentences. In *The Logic of Decision and Action*, ed. N. Asher, 81–95. Pittsburgh: University of Pittsburgh Press.

Davis, Henry, and Lisa Matthewson. 2009. Issues in Salish syntax and semantics. *Language and Linguistics Compass* 3(4), 1097–1166.

Dowty, David. 1979. *Word Meaning and Montague Grammar*. Dordrecht: Reidel.

Dowty, David. 1991. Thematic proto-roles and argument selection. *Language* 67(3), 547–619.

Emenanjǫ, Nolue. 1987. *Elements of Modern Igbo grammar*. Ibadan: University Press Limited.

Fillmore, Charles. 1968. The case for Case. In *Universals in Linguistic Theory*, eds. E. Bach and R. T. Harms, 1–88. New York: Holt, Rinehart and Winston.

Fillmore, Charles. 1970. The grammar of hitting and breaking. In *Readings in English Transformational Grammar*, eds. R. Jacobs and P. Rosenbaum, 120–133. Waltham, MA: Ginn.

Goldberg, Adele. 1995. *Constructions*. Chicago: University of Chicago Press.

Goldberg, Adele, and Ray Jackendoff. 2004. The English resultative as a family of constructions. *Language* 80(3), 532–568.

Gu, Yang. 1992. *The Syntax of Resultative and Causative Compounds in Chinese*. Doctoral dissertation, Cornell University.

Hale, Kenneth, Peter Ihiǫnu, and Victor Manfredi. 1995. Igbo bipositional verbs in a syntactic theory of argument structure. In *Theoretical Approaches to African Linguistics*, ed. A. Akinlabi, 83–107. Trenton: Africa World Press.

Huang, C.-T. James. 1988. *Wo pao de kuai* and Chinese phrase structure. *Language* 64(2), 274–311.

Huang, C.-T. James. 1992. Complex predicates in Control. In *Control and Grammar*, eds. R. K. Larson, S. Iatridou, U. Lahiri, and J. Higginbotham, 109–147. Dordrecht: Kluwer.

Huang, C.-T. James, Audrey Li, and Yafei Li. 2009. *The Syntax of Chinese*. Cambridge: Cambridge University Press.

Ihiǫnu, Peter U. 1992. Verb compounding in Igbo: An overview. In *Proceedings of the Kwa Comparative Syntax Workshop*, eds. C. Collins and V. Manfredi, MITWPL 17, 165–182. Cambridge, MA: MIT Department of Linguistics.

Igwe, G. Egemba. 1999. *Igbo-English Dictionary*. Ibadan: University Press.

Jackendoff, Ray. 1972. *Semantics in Generative Grammar*. Cambridge, MA: MIT Press.

Jackendoff, Ray. 1990. *Semantic Structures*. Cambridge, MA: MIT Press.

Kratzer, Angelika. 1996. Severing the external argument from its verb. In *Phrase Structure and the Lexicon*, eds. J. Rooryk and L. Zaring, 109–137. Dordrecht: Kluwer.

Kratzer, Angelika. 2005. Building resultatives. In *Event Arguments in Syntax, Semantics, and Discourse*, eds. C. Maienborn and A. Wöllstein-Leisten, 89–114. Tübingen: Niemeyer.

LaPolla, Randy J. 1988. Topicalization and the question of the lexical passive in Chinese. In *Proceedings of the Third Annual Conference on Chinese Linguistics*, eds. M. Chan and T. Ernst, 170–188. Bloomington: Indiana University Linguistics Club.

Larson, Richard. 1991. Some issues in verb serialization. In *Serial Verbs*, ed. C. Lefebvre, 185–210. Philadelphia: John Benjamins.

Levin, Beth, and Malka Rappaport Hovav. 1995. *Unaccusativity*. Cambridge, MA: MIT Press.

Li, Charles N., and Sandra A. Thompson. 1994. On 'middle voice' verbs in Mandarin. In *Voice: Form and Function*, eds. B. Fox and P. J. Hopper, 231–246. Philadelphia: John Benjamins.

Li, Linding. 1963. Dai de zi de buyu ju [Sentences with the verb-complement construction]. *Zhongguo Yuwen* 1963(5), 93–103.

Li, Yafei. 1990. On V-V compounds in Chinese. *Natural Language and Linguistic Theory* 8(2), 17–207.

Li, Yafei. 1995. The thematic hierarchy and causativity. *Natural Language and Linguistic Theory* 13(2), 255–282.

Lin, Tzong-hong. 2001. Light verb syntax and the theory of phrase structure. Doctoral dissertation, University of California at Irvine.

Lord, Carol. 1975. Igbo verb compounds and the lexicon. *Studies in African Linguistics* 6(1), 23–48.

Lü, Shuxiang. 1986. Hanyu jufa de linghuoxing [The flexibility of Chinese sentence grammar]. *Zhongguo Yuwen* 1986(1), 1–9.

Ma, Xiwen. 1987. Yu dongjieshi dongci youguan de mou xie juzhi [Some sentence patterns relevant to verbs in the verb-result construction]. *Zhongguo Yuwen* 1987(6), 424–441.

Marantz, Alec. 1997. No escape from syntax. *U. Penn Working Papers in Linguistics* 4(2), 201–226.

McCawley, James. 1976. Remarks on what can cause what. In *Syntax and Semantics 6: The Grammar of Causative Constructions*, ed. M. Shibatani, 117–129. New York: Academic Press.

McIntrye, Andrew. 2004. Event paths, conflation, argument structure and VP shells. *Linguistics* 42(3), 523–571.

Nwachukwu, P. 1987. The argument structure of Igbo verbs. *MIT Lexicon Project Working Papers* 18.

Parsons, Terence. 1990. *Events in the Semantics of English*. Cambridge, MA: MIT Press.

Perlmutter, David. 1978. Impersonal passives and the Unaccusative Hypothesis. *Proceedings of the 4th Annual Meeting of the Berkeley Linguistics Society*, 157–189.

Pietroski, Paul. 2005. *Events and Semantic Architecture*. Oxford: Oxford University Press.

Rappaport Hovav, Malka, and Beth Levin. 2001. An event structure account of English Resultatives. *Language* 77(4), 766–796.

Ren, Ying. 2001. A structural analysis of verbs in the verb-result construction where the subject and object can change positions [Zhu-bin ke huan wei dongjieshi shuyu jiegou fenxi]. *Zhongguo Yuwen* 2001(4), 320–328.

Rothstein, Susan. 2004. *Structuring Events*. Malden, MA: Blackwell.

Schein, Barry. 1993. *Plurals and Events*. Cambridge, MA: MIT Press.

Shibatani, Masayoshi. 1972. Three reasons for not deriving 'kill' from 'cause to die' in Japanese. In *Syntax and Semantics*, Vol. 1, ed. J. Kimball, 125–137. New York: Academic Press.

Shibatani, Masayoshi. 2000. Introduction: Some basic issues in the grammar of causation. In *The Grammar of Causation and Interpersonal Manipulation*, ed. M. Shibatani, 1–22. Philadelphia: John Benjamins.

Simpson, Jane. 1983. Resultatives. In *Papers in Lexical Functional Grammar*, eds. M. Rappaport Hovav, L. Levin, and A. Zaenen, 143–157. Bloomington: Indiana University Linguistics Club.

Smith, Carlotta. 1978. Jespersen's 'move and change' class and causative verbs in English. In *Linguistic and Literary Studies in Honor of Archibald H. Hill*, Vol. 2, *Descriptive Linguistics*, eds. M. A. Jazayery et al., 101–109. The Hague: Mouton.

Sybesma, Rint. 1999. *The Mandarin VP*. Dordrecht: Kluwer.

Talmy, Leonard. 1976. Semantic causative types. In *Syntax and Semantics 6: The Grammar of Causative Constructions*, ed. M. Shibatani, 42–116. New York: Academic Press.

Tan, Fu. 1991. *Notion of Subject in Chinese*. Doctoral dissertation, Stanford University.

Thompson, Sandra A. 1973. Resultative verb compounds in Mandarin Chinese: A case for lexical rules. *Language* 42(2), 361–379.

Uwalaka, Mary Angela A. N. 1998. The Igbo verb: A semantico-syntactic analysis. *Beitrage zur Afrikanistik*, Band 35. Vienna: Institute für Afrikanistik und Ägyptologie der Universität Wien.

Van Valin, Robert. 1990. Semantic parameters of split intransitivity. *Language* 66(2), 221–260.

Wang, Hongqi. 1995. Dongjieshi shubu jiegou peijia yanjiu [Studies on the valence of resultative complement constructions]. In *Xiandai Hanyu Peiji Yufa Yanjiu*, eds. Yang Shen and Ding'ou Zheng, 144–167. Beijing: Beijing University Press.

Williams, Alexander. 2005. *Complex Causatives and Verbal Valence*. Doctoral dissertation, University of Pennsylvania.

Williams, Alexander. 2008. Patients in Igbo and Mandarin. In *Event Structures in Linguistic Form and Interpretation*, eds. J. Dölling, T. Heyde-Zybatow, and M. Shäfer, 3–30. Berlin: Mouton de Gruyter.

Williams, Alexander. 2009. Themes, cumulativity, and resultatives: Comments on Kratzer 2003. *Linguistic Inquiry* 40(4), 686–700.

Williams, Alexander. 2014. Causal VVs in Mandarin. In *The Blackwell Handbook of Chinese Linguistics*, eds. C.-T. J. Huang, A. Li, and A. Simpson, 311–341. Malden, MA: Blackwell.

Williams, Alexander. In press. *Arguments in Syntax and Semantics*. Cambridge University Press.

Williams, Alexander. Accepted. Objects in resultatives. *Natural Language and Linguistic Theory*.

Wolff, Phillip. 2003. Direct causation in the linguistic coding and individuation of causal events. *Cognition* 88(1), 1–48.

12

Verbal Answers to Yes/No Questions, Focus, and Ellipsis

ANDREW SIMPSON

1. Introduction

Law (2006) considers A-not-A questions in Mandarin Chinese and argues convincingly that there is movement of a null operator ("an abstract Q feature") from a low clausal position in the derivation of such questions, building on much previous work on A-not-A questions and locality restrictions (Huang 1982, 1991; Aoun and Li 1989; Ernst 1994). The key novel evidence for such an analysis presented by Law is the patterning of adverbs in A-not-A questions. It is suggested that the frequent unacceptability of adverbials in A-not-A questions is due to the creation of an intervention effect on the output of LF movement of the A-not-A operator from its base position adjoined to VP, bringing it to the C-domain (SpecCP). Law notes that A-not-A questions contrast in this patterning with English yes/no questions, and also with other Mandarin yes/no questions formed with the particle *ma*, which are not ungrammatical when the same kinds of adverbial elements occur that cause unacceptability in A-not-A questions. Law suggests that this naturally leads to the conclusion that there is no operator movement in English yes/no questions and Mandarin *ma* questions, and that in these question forms the interrogative operative is directly base-generated in the C-domain.

Taking Law's interesting work on A-not-A and *ma* questions as its starting point, this chapter develops the claim that movement-related locality effects actually do occur with the use of Mandarin *ma* particle questions, but that these can critically only be detected (and indeed only occur) in the answer-forms to such questions, not in the questions themselves. As in Law's study, the present chapter focuses on the potential occurrence of adverbs of various types in yes-no questions, and shows that the presence of adverbial elements in *ma* questions constrains the ways that such questions can be answered, frequently rendering unacceptable a bare verbal answer-form and requiring instead the use of an alternative answer-form similar to English 'yes' or 'correct.' The potential employment of a bare verb as an affirmative answer-form in Mandarin will be attributed to a process of movement and ellipsis, as argued at length in Holmberg (2001, 2007) for Finnish, this movement being affected by the presence of adverbials in a way similar to, but not identical with, the occurrence of adverbs in A-not-A questions.[1] The common availability of an alternative, non-movement answer strategy—the base-generation of a 'yes'-type particle in the C-domain—will be suggested to avoid and mask the intervention effect that would otherwise arise with movement of the verb in the presence of certain adverbials. In addition to highlighting parallels between Mandarin and Finnish in the way that yes/no questions may be answered, the chapter also uses the conclusions drawn from Mandarin to examine verb-related question-answer patterns in two other East/Southeast Asian languages—Korean and Vietnamese—and shows that insights gained from a consideration of adverbs and focus/background distinctions in Mandarin yes-no questions seem to be mirrored to a considerable extent in other languages of the region, though with certain interesting and revealing variation in the options taken up by these other languages in their affirmative short answer forms.

The structure of the chapter is as follows. Section 2 presents Law's (2006) analysis of the derivation of A-not-A questions as motivated by the patterning of adverbs, and shows how patterns found in *ma* particle questions are different, resulting in a non-movement analysis of *ma* yes-no questions. Section 3 discusses the ways that both types of yes/no questions may be answered in the affirmative in Chinese, via simple repetition of the verb, or by means of a particle approximating English 'yes/correct.' Section 3 also notes the ways that A-not-A and *ma* questions are commonly assumed to differ with regard to the speaker's assumptions about possible answers values— whether a yes-no question is 'open' or the speaker is predisposed to expect an answer of a certain polarity, and how the two common ways of answering yes-no questions may be affected by the speaker's expectations about the type of answer that may be given. Section 4 then outlines two possible approaches to the modeling of affirmative answer forms, which consist in a simple repetition of the verb, a non-movement analysis making use of null subjects and objects, and a verb-movement and constituent/ clausal ellipsis analysis, as argued for Finnish in Holmberg (2001, 2007). It is noted that the two analyses may potentially be distinguished by re-examining *ma* yes-no questions containing adverbs, and how such questions can be answered. Various complications arising from interactions with focus, and differences between broad and narrow focus questions are discussed, which need to carefully be controlled for in any examination of questions containing adverbs. Once this is done, it is argued that the patterns observed support a movement and ellipsis analysis of verbal answers in Chinese, as in Finnish. Section 5 subsequently builds on the investigation of Chinese and extends the coverage of verbal answer forms to Korean and Vietnamese, and shows that there are both strong similarities in the patterning of yes-no questions

---

[1] On the basis of constraints on the use of null subjects in certain polarity conditions, Holmberg (2007) suggests that a range of other languages may also make use of verb movement to create affirmative verbal answers. The patterns presented in this chapter approach this possibility from a different angle, and generally support the view that movement of some kind may be involved in affirmative answers that do not consist simply in a 'yes'-type particle. It remains to be seen whether the set of languages conjectured by Holmberg to be verb-movement languages on the basis of null subject patterns are the same as those for which adverbial patterns support an analysis of verb-movement in answer-forms.

with adverbials, and also interesting differences in the ways such questions may be answered. Certain related patterns in focused answer-forms to yes-no questions English also are presented and are shown to link up in an intriguing way with the general phenomenon under consideration. Section 6 presents the conclusions of the chapter.

2. Law (2006): A-Not-A Questions, *ma* Questions, and Adverbs

Law (2006) notes that A-not-A questions in Chinese show a clear contrast with yes-no questions in English in the ability for adverbs of various types to occur within such questions. Whereas frequency and manner and many other types of adverbs may licitly occur in English yes-no questions, their presence in A-not-A questions results in unacceptability, as illustrated in (1–4):

(1)   Is John attentively reading the book?

(2)   Did John often dance?

(3)   *Zhangsan xiaoxin-de kan-bu-kan   shu?
      Zhangsan carefully   read-not-read book
      Intended: 'Is Zhangsan carefully reading books?'

(4)   *Zhangsan changchang tiao-bu-tiaowu?
      Zhangsan often   dance-not-dance
      Intended: 'Does Zhangsan often dance?'

Law proposes to account for the Chinese-English difference in such patterns with the suggestion that in Chinese A-not-A questions an abstract [+Q] feature is base-generated adjoined to VP, and undergoes movement to SpecCP, whereas in English the +Q feature is base-generated in C. In A-not-A questions, the movement of Q to SpecCP is suggested to give rise to an antecedent-trace relation subject to general locality constraints on variable binding (antecedent-government), which may be blocked by the intervening structural presence of adverbs of a range of types: manner, degree, agent-oriented, subject-oriented, instrumental, aspectual, frequency, epistemic, and modal adverbs.[2] As movement of the Q feature does not need to occur in English, where Q is inserted directly in C, no Relativized Minimality intervention effect occurs when adverbs are present in yes-no questions.

Law also notes that *ma* particle yes-no questions in Mandarin seem to pattern like English yes-no questions and tolerate the presence of adverbs that cause unacceptability in A-not-A questions, as shown in (5–8), which contrast *ma* questions with parallel A-not-A questions:

---

[2] All those adverbial types that cause unacceptability in A-not-A questions are suggested to have tight syntactic or semantic connections with the predicate or proposition. Certain other adverb types, specifically locative, temporal, domain, and speaker/hearer-oriented adverbs, are argued not to have similar connections with the predicate or proposition, and are noted not to cause unacceptability in A-not-A questions (see Law (2006 for further discussion).

(5) ta luan   pao ma?
     he chaotically run Q
     'Did he run all over the place?'

(6) *ta luan   pao-bu-pao?
     he chaotically run-not-run
     Intended: 'Does he run all over the place?'

(7) laoban yanli-de zebei ta   ma?
     boss   sternly   accuse him Q
     'Did the boss sternly accuse him?'

(8) *laoban yanli-de ze-bu-zebei   ta?
     boss   sternly   accuse-not-accuse him
     Intended: 'Does the boss sternly accuse him?'

Law suggests that *ma* is an overt realization of the Q feature and that it is base-generated in C, just as the Q feature in English is argued to be base-generated directly in C. Due to the hypothesized lack of Q-movement in *ma* questions, adverbs of all types are free to occur in such questions and do not give rise to any Relativized Minimality intervention effects.

Law's account of adverbial patterns in A-not-A questions, English yes-no questions, and *ma* particle questions is both coherent and highly plausible, and seems to indicate that operator movement is only to be found in the derivation of A-not-A questions. As noted in the introduction, however, this chapter will argue that a common way of *answering* yes-no questions formed with the *ma* particle also results from a movement strategy and is constrained by focus-related intervention effects. In order to begin considering the potential role of adverbs in the ways that yes-no questions can be answered, section 3 will now provide some relevant background to the ways that yes-no questions in Chinese are regularly answered, and a difference assumed to exist between A-not-A and *ma* particle questions concerning the kind of answer that is anticipated to occur.

3. Answer-Forms to Yes-No Questions in Chinese

Li and Thompson (1989) note that yes-no questions in Chinese formed by the A-not-A strategy and the particle *ma* show a differing sensitivity to the context in which a yes-no question occurs, as described here:

> The A-not-A question is used only in a *neutral context*, whereas the particle-question may be used in a *neutral* or a *non-neutral context*. A neutral context is one in which the questioner has no assumptions concerning the proposition that is being questioned and wishes to know whether it is true. Whenever the questioner brings to the speech situation an assumption about either the truth or the falsity of the proposition s/he is asking about, then that context is non-neutral with respect to that question. (Li and Thompson 1989: 550)

In a neutral context, both A-not-A and *ma* particle questions may consequently be used, as for example in (9):

(9) a. ni   hao   ma?   b. ni   hao-bu-hao?
         you good Q   you good-not-good
         'How are you?'   'How are you?'   (Li and Thompson 1989)

However, in a situation where the speaker has a particular expectation concerning the truth or falsity of the proposition being questioned, only a *ma* particle question can appropriately be used, as illustrated in (10) from Li and Thompson (1989: 553). The context relating to (10) is that the speaker sees that the hearer has returned, and hence expects that the answer to his/her question will be affirmative:

(10) a. ou ni   yijing hui-lai   le   ma?
          oh you already return-come ASP Q
          'Oh, did you get back already?'

      b. #ou ni yijing hui-lai   le   meiyou?
          oh you already return-come ASP not

Turning now to consider the ways that yes-no questions can be answered, both A-not-A and *ma* particle questions can be answered in the affirmative with a simple repetition of the verb, as in (11) and (12):

(11) a. ni   xihuan riben   cai ma?   b. xihuan
          you like   Japanese food Q   like
          'Do you like Japanese food?'   'Yes.'

(12) a. ni   xi-bu-xihuan riben   cai?   b. xihuan
          you like-not-like Japanese food   like
          'Do you like Japanese food?'   'Yes.'

Questions formed with *ma*, but not A-not-A questions, can in principle also be answered in the affirmative with the elements *dui* and *shi-de*, as illustrated in (13) and (14):

(13) a. ni   xi-yan ma?   b. dui/shi-de   c. xi
          you smoke Q   yes   smoke
          'Do you smoke?'   'Yes.'   'Yes.'

(14) a. ta neng Shuo zhongwen ma?   b. dui/shi-de   c. neng
          he can speak Chinese   Q   yes   can
          'Can he speak Chinese?'   'Yes.'   'Yes.'

The particular focus of this chapter will be on attempting to understand how the former, verb-repetition-type answer forms are syntactically derived. In investigating such an answer strategy, we will also compare the availability of verb repetition with the use of *dui* as an answer-form, and consider what differences in the distribution of verbal and *dui* answers may reveal about the underlying syntax of such elements.

With regard to the use of a repeated verb as an affirmative answer to a yes-no question, there are two quite different hypotheses that can be formed as possible modes of analysis, one attributing the phenomenon of verbal answers to the general occurrence of null arguments in Chinese, the other positing an operation of movement and ellipsis, as will be examined in section 4.

4. Investigating the Syntax of Verbal Answers to Yes-No Questions

One quite natural approach to the occurrence of affirmative verbal answers in Chinese and also other East and Southeast Asian languages, such as Korean and Vietnamese, is to suggest that such forms are simply regular sentences in which the subjects and objects of verbs are left phonetically null, as elsewhere in Chinese, Korean, Japanese and other similar languages, under appropriate discourse conditions. Null subjects and objects are common in East and Southeast Asian languages and have been variously analyzed as instances of pro, operator-bound traces, or True Empty Categories/ TEC (e.g., Huang 1984, 1987; Li 2007; Aoun and Li 2008). In such an approach, as illustrated in (15) (with 'ec' being used to represent the null arguments present), the repetition of a verb as an affirmative answer to a yes-no question would not instantiate any different kind of syntactic process or structure from that occurring in regular declarative sentences that are not necessarily answers to yes-no questions. The frequent occurrence of verbal answers in East and Southeast Asian languages would then simply be a function of the general widespread presence of null arguments in languages of this geographical area.

(15) a. ni   mai-le   shu   le   meiyou?
          you buy-ASP book ASP not
          'Did you buy the book?'

      b. ec mai-le ec
              buy-ASP
          'Yes.'

A second potential analysis that may suggest itself for other cross-linguistic reasons, however, is the possibility that verbal answers in Chinese and other East and Southeast Asian languages actually result from a process of verb-movement and ellipsis as has been well-motivated for Finnish by Holmberg (2001, 2007), and also assumed for various other languages such as Welsh and Polish. Example (16) is an illustration of a question-answer pair from Finnish. Holmberg points out that a movement and ellipsis analysis is strongly suggested by two patterns found in such pairs of sentences. First, the verb in Finnish is clearly raised to the initial position of the question and attaches the Q-morpheme, which may be assumed to be in C. This creates a structure in which the clausal complement of C could naturally be elided, deleting the subject and object and resulting in the verbal answer form found in (16b). Second, such an analysis is supported by the observation that third person subjects normally cannot be phonetically null in other environments in Finnish; hence some special process of deletion seems to operate in the answers to yes/no questions in Finnish, allowing for the subject to be missing. Additionally, it can be noted that an alternative answer-form to simple bare repetition of the verb, as in (16b), involves overt repetition of the subject and the object (sometimes pronominalized), and in such sequences the verb still occurs in a clause-initial position, indicating that there is raising of the verb in answer-forms, as in questions, regardless of whether the arguments of the verb are phonetically realized or not.

(16)   a.   Puhuuko Joni ranskaa?   b: Puhuu.
            speaks-Q John French   speaks
            'Does John speak French?'   'Yes.' (Holmberg (2007)

The derivation of verbal answers assumed to occur in Finnish is schematized in (17). First the verb (or possibly a remnant VP containing just the verb) raises to the C-domain, where the Q morpheme –ko is located, and then the constituent containing the subject and object is elided, as represented with strikethrough in (17b):[3]

(17)   a.   verb$_k$-ko [subject ~~verb$_k$~~ object] → b. verb$_k$-ko [~~subject verb$_k$ object~~]

Given the good arguments for such an analysis of verbal answers in Finnish (and also for Welsh), this raises the theoretical possibility that a similar process of movement and ellipsis might perhaps be responsible for the occurrence of verbal answers in Chinese and other East and Southeast Asian languages as well. However, it has to be noted that Finnish and Welsh are languages that very clearly display instances of verb-movement to clause-initial positions in questions and other structures, whereas Chinese and other East and Southeast Asian languages do not independently exhibit clear instances of verb-movement to high clausal positions. It is therefore natural to ask whether there would be any plausible grounds to posit such movement specifically in the answers to yes-no questions?[4]

   While it may not be easy to decide what the correct analysis of verbal answers in Chinese should be when attention is confined to question-answer pairs involving just subjects, verbs, and objects, the two potential approaches outlined above can be argued to make different predictions when other elements are built into question-forms such as adverbials and other adjuncts. An important feature of the verb movement approach to verbal answers is that its derivation involves the ellipsis of a

---

[3] The full mechanics of the movement and deletion process argued by Holmberg (2001, 2007) to occur in Finnish are actually more complex than the representation in (17), and may involve other movements within the constituent following the verb which is ultimately deleted. However, (17) provides a useful approximation of the kind of movement and deletion process that is assumed to underlie verbal answers in Finnish and Welsh.

[4] With head-final languages such as Japanese and Korean, arguments for string vacuous verb-movement to a clause-final C position are hard to construct, but it is also less easy to completely dismiss the possibility that there is overt verb-movement in these languages than in SVO languages such as Chinese, Thai, and Vietnamese, where it is clear that the verb does not raise over subjects to the C-domain in regular questions or declaratives. For a review of issues bearing on verb-movement in Korean and Japanese, see Han, Lidz and Musolino (2007).

constituent containing the subject and the object of the verb, hence hypothetically a TP-level constituent that could also contain various other adverbial elements. It might therefore be expected that it would be possible, at least in principle, for a bare verb to occur as the affirmative answer to a yes-no question in which adverbs and other adjuncts projected within TP are present, and that a bare verbal answer would affirm the full proposition under question, including the content of any adverbs and adjuncts projected in the TP in the question input.

Considering what an alternative non-movement approach to verbal answers might expect in similar circumstances, in order for an element in a yes-no question to be interpreted as part of the answer to the question consisting in simply a repetition of the verb, it has to be assumed to occur as a phonetically null pro/TEC-type equivalent to an overt element in the question. Hence, in such an approach, the subject position in a verbal answer would be occupied by a pro, and the object position by a TEC in Li's (2007) and Aoun and Li's (2008) approach. Were it to be possible for an adverb or other adjunct in a yes-no question to be interpreted as present in a simple verbal answer to such a question, it would need to be assumed that the adverb/adjunct would also be syntactically present in the form of a pro element or TEC. However, the distribution of pro-type elements (and TECs) in syntactic positions is commonly taken to be highly limited and restricted, at most, to just (nominal) arguments of verbs, not other adjuncts, PPs, and adverbial categories. Such a position is argued for at some length in Aoun and Li (2008), and is widely held elsewhere in the literature, following observations in many languages that null pronominal PPs and other adjuncts do not appear to be available in structures that otherwise permit null arguments to occur. For example, a DP in initial topic position can relate to a subject position inside an island structure because a pro can occupy such a position, allowing for the DP to be base-generated in the initial topic position and not occur there as a result of movement, which would cause a violation of Subjacency/the CED and cause ungrammaticality, as illustrated in (18) and (19), from Huang, Li, and Li (2009: 209). However, it is not possible for PPs or other adjuncts to occur in a similar initial topic position and relate to positions within islands, indicating that there are no parallel phonetically null pro-forms available to resume such elements. (20) illustrates a legitimate instance of PP topicalization via movement. (21) shows that a PP cannot be construed as modifying a predicate within an island, because movement of the PP out of the island to topic position would violate Subjacency/the CED, and there is no pro-PP available to serve as a resumptive element within the island, unlike the situation with subject DPs.[5]

(18)   Lisi, [yinwei pro piping-le   Zhangsan], (suoyi)   meiren yao ta.
      Lisi   because   criticize-ASP Zhangsan   therefore nobody want him
      '(As for) Lisi, because (he) criticized Zhangsan, nobody wants him.'

(19)   Zhangsan, [[pro xihuan de] ren]   hen   duo.
      Zhangsan   like   DE person very many
      '(As for) Zhangsan, the people who (he) likes are many.'

---

[5] For similar observations about Japanese, see Saito (1985).

(20) a. Zhangsan qunian   qu Beijing liu-xue.
          Zhangsan last-year go Beijing study-abroad
          'Last year Zhangsan went to Beijing to study.'

      b. Zai Beijing-ne, Lisi shuo Zhangssan pengdao-le yi-ge lao pengyou.
          in Beijing-TOP Lisi say   Zhangsan meet-ASP 1-CL old friend
          'Lisi said [that Zhangsan met an old friend in Beijing].'

(21) a. Zhangsan qunian   qu Beijing liu-xue.
          Zhangsan last-year go Beijing study-abroad
          Last year Zhangsan went to Beijing to study.

      b. Zai Beijing-ne, Zhangsan mai-le   [yi-ben Lu Xun xie   de shu]
          in Beijing-TOP Zhangsan buy-ASP 1-CL   Lu Xun write DE book
          Meaning that is intended but not possible:
          'Zhangsan bought [a book that Lu Xun wrote in Beijing].'
          Only possible meaning:
          'Zhangsan bought [a book that Lu Xun wrote] in Beijing.'

Additionally, Aoun and Li (2008) show that there is an argument/adjunct asymmetry in the so-called Verb Construction illustrated in (22)–(24), which indicates that null adjuncts/adverbs are not available in the way that null arguments are. When the object of the verb and an adjunct/adverbial are omitted in pairs of sentences that differ in the identity of the subject, as in (22)–(24), the object is naturally understood as being present in the second sentence, but the adjunct/adverbial is not. Hence the interpretation of the frequency, duration, and manner adverbials in the first sentences of (22)–(24) is not understood as being present in the follow-on sentences, as captured in the English translations provided. This pattern of behavior is argued to distinguish the Verb Construction from cases of Aux-stranding VP ellipsis and the *shi* construction in Chinese, illustrated with (25)–(27), where the interpretation of similar omitted adverbials is indeed understood, as in English (in addition to that of the missing/elided verb and its object).

(22) a. wo jian-guo ta   san ci   le.   b. tamen ye jian-guo le.
          I   meet-ASP him 3   time ASP   they also meet-ASP ASP
          'I have met him three times.'   'They have met him too.'

(23) a. wo renshi ta   hen jiu le.   b. wo baba ye   renshi.
          I   know him very long ASP   my father also know
          'I have known him for a long time.'   'My father also knows him.'

(24) a. ta (nian) na-ben shu nian-de hen kuai.   b. wo ye nian le
          he read   that-CL book read-DE very quick   I also read ASP
          'He read that book very quickly.'   'I also read it.'

(25) a. wo yao   tanwang ta san-ci. b. tamen ye yao.
          I   want visit   him 3-time   they also want
          'I want to visit him three times.'   'They do too (want to visit him three times).'

(26) a. wo hui renzhende zuo gongke. b. ta ye hui.
          I   will diligently do homework   he also will
          'I will diligently do homework.'   'He also will (diligently do his homework).'

(27) a. wo tanwang ta   san-ci le.   b. tamen ye   shi.
          I   visit   him 3-time ASP   they   also BE
          'I visited him three times.'   'They also did (visited him three times).'

If phonetically null pro-forms for adverbs, PPs, and other adjuncts were available and could be syntactically projected in a way similar to null arguments, it would be expected that they could be interpreted as present in examples such as (22)–(24), but this is not the case. This again indicates that it is just arguments (subjects and objects) that may be licensed to occur as phonetically null base-generated elements, not adverbs or other adjuncts.

Summarizing now the differing predictions of the two approaches to the analysis of verbal answer forms, the hypothesis that verbal answers may result from movement of the verb and deletion of the remnant constituent containing the subject, object, and other TP-internal material creates the expectation that adverbs, PPs, and other adjuncts could be phonetically elided along with other TP-internal material, and could be interpreted as present in the answer form, just as the subject and object of the verb are interpreted as syntactically present and understood in the verbal answer. The analysis of verbal answers as resulting from the use of null subjects and objects (whether pro, topic-bound variable, or TECs) and no movement and deletion strategy does not expect that adverbs and other adjuncts present in a yes-no question input would be interpreted as being syntactically present and understood in a bare verbal answer-form, as phonetically null adverbs and null adjuncts are otherwise not licensed to occur, unlike subject and object arguments of the verb, which may sometimes be licensed to occur as phonetically null elements.

The question that now needs to be answered is whether adverbs and other adjuncts first of all can occur in yes/no question forms that might allow for verbal answer forms, and second, whether such answer forms may be understood as affirming the content of the adjuncts as well as that of the understood subject and object of the verb. In fact, we have already seen and noted in section 2 (examples 5 and 7) that adverbs do seem to be able to occur in *ma* particle yes-no questions, as has been pointed out by Law (2006). We therefore need to verify whether verbal answers may occur with such questions and project the interpretation of the adverb in the question.

So, what are the results of investigating how *ma* particle questions containing adverbs may be answered? Interestingly and intriguingly, they are mixed, and sometimes it is found that a verbal answer may indeed occur and convey the interpretation of the adverb in the input question, but other times it appears that verbal answers are actually not possible as answers responding to questions containing adverbs, where the content of the adverb is also naturally being questioned and in need of confirmation or denial in the answer-form. It will be argued that the variable kinds of patterns found are in fact quite systematic and revealing, pointing to an analysis of focus-sensitive verb-movement and remnant deletion, and that the variability of the answer-form patterns in Chinese is interestingly replicated in other languages in a very similar way, suggesting the generalization of the verb-movement analysis to other languages as well, with certain parametric variation relating to additional options that languages allow for answering yes-no questions containing a narrowly focused constituent.

First, it can be noted that Aoun and Li (2008) do in fact present examples showing that *ma* particle yes-no questions containing adverbs may be answered in the affirmative with a repetition of the verb, and the answer form is understood as containing the referential content of the adverb, as illustrated in (28) and (29). In (28), Aoun and Li note that the verbal-answer is interpreted as confirming that the speaker met the person being referred to three times, hence the frequency adverbial in the question is understood in the answer-form consisting of just a repetition of the verb. In (29), the content of the manner adverbial in the question input is similarly understood as being confirmed in the affirmative verbal answer.

(28) a. ni   jian-guo ta   san-ci ma?   b. jian-guo
         you meet-ASP him   3-time Q   meet-ASP
         'Did you meet him three times?'   'Yes.'

(29) a. ta hen renzhende zuo-le   gongke   ma?   b. zuo-le.
         he very diligently do-ASP   homework Q   do-ASP
         'Did he do the homework very diligently?'   'Yes.'

To such examples, we can add a range of further instances where verbal answers may be used to reply in the affirmative to *ma* particle questions containing adverbial elements and adjunct PPs, and the latter are understood as being confirmed as part of the answer.

Manner

(30)   Context: Asking about a patient in a hospital.
     a. yisheng zixide   kan-le   bingren ma?   b. kan-le.
         doctor Carefully look-ASP   patient Q   look-ASP
         'Did the doctor carefully examine the patient?'   'Yes,'

(31)   Context: A gangster-boss has just found out that one of his gang is a police informant.
     a. heibanlaoda   yongli   da-le   ta   ma?   b. da-le.
         gangster-boss Severely beat-ASP   him Q   beat-ASP
         'Did the gangster-boss severely beat him?'   'Yes.'

Frequency

(32)   Context: Helping someone sort out a problem with a computer.
     a. ni   an-le   liang-ci le   ma?   b. an-le.
         you press-ASP two-time ASP Q   press-ASP
         'Did you click (on the mouse) twice?'   'Yes.'

Duration

(33)   Context: Asking whether someone has prepared food according to the instructions given to him.
     a. ni   (shi-bu-shi) zhao   wo shuo-de rou   yan-le   san-ge-xiaoshi ma?
         you be-not-be   according   I   say DE meat marinate-ASP 3-CL-hour   Q
         'Did you marinate the meat for three hours, as I told you to?'

     b. yan-le.
         marinate-ASP
         'Yes.'

(34)   Context: Doctor asks patient to confirm he has taken medicine as instructed.

    a. ni   zhao   Wo shuo-de yao   chi-le   san tian le   ma?
       You according I   say   DE medicine eat-ASP 3   day ASP Q
       'Did you take the medicine for three days, as I told you to?'

    b. chi-le.
       eat-ASP
       'Yes.'

Location

(35)   Context: At a Christmas party for faculty, staff, and students of USC, the speaker tries to ascertain whether someone he meets is a member of staff, a student, or a member of the faculty.

    a. ni zai USC jiaoshu ma?   b. jiaoshu.
       you in USC teach   Q   teach
       'Do you teach in USC?'   'Yes.'

Agentive

(36)   a. ta guyi   pian-guo ni ma?   b. pian-guo.
       he deliberately cheat-ASP you Q   cheat-ASP
       'Did he deliberately cheat you?'   'Yes.'

Comitative

(37)   Context: The speaker asks the hearer about going to a funeral.

    a. ni zuotian   gen ni   taitai qu canjia Zhangsan-de zangli ma?
       you yesterday with your wife   go attend Zhangsan-DE funeral Q
       'Did you go to Zhangsan's funeral with your wife yesterday?'

    b. qu-le.
       go-ASP
       'Yes.'

Source

(38)   Context: The speaker asks about the scheduled departure of a plane from Los Angeles, which didn't yet arrive at its destination, San Francisco.

    a. feiji   cong luoshanji qifei-le   ma?   b. qifei-le.
       plane from L.A.   take-off-ASP Q   take-off-ASP
       'Did the plane take off from L.A.?'   'Yes.'

Despite the acceptability of (28)–(38), in other instances it is not uncommon to find that speakers reject the possibility of using a verbal answer to a *ma* question containing an adverbial or other adjunct, as illustrated in the following examples, where the attempted use of a verbal answer is felt not to answer the question appropriately, as it merely affirms the content of the verb and its arguments, and not the content of the adverbial present in the question.

Frequency

(39)   a. Zhangsan changchang tiaowu ma?   b. *tiaowu
       Zhangsan often   dance Q   dance
       'Does Zhangsan often dance?'   Intended: 'Yes (he dances often).'

(40) a. ni meitian dou gua huzi ma?   b. *gua (huzi)
          You every   day shave beard Q   shave (beard)
          'Do you shave every day?'   Intended: 'Yes.'

Duration

(41) a. ni deng-le hen jiu le ma?   b. *deng-le
          you wait-ASP very long ASP Q   wait-ASP
          'Have you been waiting for long?'   Intended: 'Yes.'

Manner

(42) a. laoban yanlide zebei ta ma?   b. *zebei.
          boss   severely scold him Q   scold
          'Does his boss scold him severely?'   Intended: 'Yes.'

Location

(43) a. zhei-ge chenshan, ni zai xiaweiyi mai-de ma?
          this-CL shirt   you in Hawaii buy-DE Q
          'Did you buy this shirt in Hawaii?'

      b. *mai-de/-le.
          buy-DE/-ASP
          Intended: 'Yes.'

Source

(44) a. ta cong Beijing lai ma?   b. *lai.
          he from Beijing come Q   come
          'Is he coming from Beijing?'   Intended: 'Yes.'

Means

(45) a. ni zuo huoche lai de ma?   b. *lai-de.
          you by train come DE Q   come-DE
          'Did you come by train?'   Intended: 'Yes.'

Aspectual adverb

(46) a. ta hai xi   yan   ma?   b. *xi.
          he still inhale smoke Q   inhale
          'Does he still smoke?'   Intended: 'Yes.'

So, it is natural to ask what is going on in this apparently contradictory set of patterns. In certain instances it is clearly possible to use a repetition of the verb as an affirmative answer to a *ma* particle yes-no question, whereas in other instances such a strategy is not acceptable. Shortly, it will be argued that there are in fact systematic reasons why certain occurrences of verbal answers are well-formed and others are not acceptable, and that such variation is dictated by the interaction of the underlying syntax of answers to *ma* particle yes-no questions and the particular information structure of the yes-no question that serves as input to the answer form.

First of all, it can be noted and emphasized that the fact that verbal answers may occur as legitimate affirmative responses to yes-no questions containing adverbs or other adjuncts in *any* instances (and convey the interpretation of the adverb/adjunct as part of the affirmed event/state) is quite unexpected for an approach to verbal answers which assumes that these arise simply through the use of the verb accompanied by null subjects and objects, as noted earlier, as null pro-forms of adverbs/adjuncts do not seem to be available cross-linguistically. The interpretation of verbal answers to questions such as those in (28)–(38) is consequently not anticipated to be able to convey the interpretation of the adverbial elements in a base-generated, pro-form approach to bare verb answer forms, contra what is observed. Such interpretations are, however, expected to be at least a theoretical possibility in the verb movement and remnant deletion approach to verbal answers, as this hypothesizes the ellipsis and LF recovery of all material in TP-level constituents that contain the subject and the object, including adverbial elements. The patterns in (28)–(38) thus provide clear and strong support for the latter movement and ellipsis analysis over the pro-form base-generation approach to verbal answers, and it can be suggested that the availability of verbal answers conveying the content of adverbs in the input question arises, wherever possible, as the result of movement of the verb to a higher-clausal position allowing deletion of a lower constituent containing the subject, object, adverbs, and other adjuncts. All such elements being syntactically present but phonetically elided will automatically be interpreted as part of the affirmed answer.

Attempting to account for the challenging, observed variation in the acceptable use of verbal answers to *ma* questions containing adverbs/adjuncts and the fact that bare verbal answers are in many instances not legitimate answer-forms, the adoption of a verb movement and ellipsis analysis of verbal answers would now seem to suggest that some property of yes-no questions such as (39)–(46) has the effect of blocking the hypothesized syntactic derivation of such answer-forms and the movement of the verb necessary to create the remnant clausal ellipsis. The question then is whether it is possible to identify any relevant, shared property in questions such as (39)–(46) that plausibly might interfere with the syntactic creation of bare verbal answer forms? Considering the range of patterns in (39)–(46) and other similar data, it can be suggested that there is indeed such a property, linking up the questions in (39)–(46) and distinguishing them from (28)–(38), and that this relates to a frequent interpretive effect that arises with the use of adverbs and other non-obligatory modifiers in question forms. In many instances, when additional, non-argumental material is explicitly added into questions, it often seems to have the effect of drawing specific attention to that material, with the result that an adverbial element may be naturally interpreted as the narrow focus of a question, in the absence of any other contextual information. Consider the English examples in (47)–(49), as illustrations of this interpretive effect:

(47)   Did you read the book quickly?

(48)   Do you grade the exams carefully?

(49)   Did you buy that shirt in Hawaii?

Presented out of any special context, it is most natural to interpret (47)–(49) as asking specifically for confirmation of the content of the adverb in (47)–(48) and the location PP in (49), and such questions seem appropriate and natural in situations in which the event or habitual action described by the predicate is assumed to have occurred (or to occur regularly), and hence the speaker is not seeking confirmation of the content of the event/habitual occurrence, but of the adverbial modifier. (47) is most naturally uttered in a situation in which the speaker knows that the hearer has read a particular book, and simply wants to know whether this reading event was achieved swiftly. Similarly, (48) is most naturally felicitous in a situation in which the speaker knows that hearer regularly grades exams and wishes to confirm whether the hearer is careful in his/her grading. Example (49) also seems most easily appropriate as a question in a situation where the speaker assumes that the purchase of a shirt present in the discourse situation has taken place, and the speaker is hoping to confirm whether this purchasing act occurred in Hawaii. It would seem that there is frequently a natural tendency for adverbs added into yes-no questions to give rise to interpretations of narrow focus, and cause such questions to effectively be construed and used as constituent questions, assuming the content of the main predicate as given, and requesting confirmation or denial of the interpretative value of the adverb as a modifier of the event being referred to. This property of constituent focus is one that can be argued to be critically present with adverbial elements in questions which do not naturally allow for bare verbal answers, such as those in examples (39)–(46). Here it can be suggested that the speaker is most naturally taken to assume the content of the main predicate to be true, and to be asking specifically for confirmation of whether the action occurs in an adverb-type way. For example, it might seem odd for a speaker to ask (39a) in a situation in which s/he had no idea whether the subject, Zhangsan, went dancing with some frequency; question (40a) naturally comes with an assumption that the hearer shaves with some regularity, and asks whether this is in fact a daily activity; and (41a) will be uttered in a situation where the hearer has evidently waited for some time, and the speaker wishes to confirm whether this was a long time or not. In each case, then, it can be suggested that the adverb/adjunct present in the questions in (39)–(46) is most naturally interpreted as constituting the narrow focus of the question.

Syntactically, it has elsewhere been argued at some length that the occurrence of focused constituents in a structure may prevent the establishment of various other syntactic relations that would link positions structurally above and below the focus—the creation of an 'intervention effect' induced by focus (Beck 2006; Kim 2002, 2006). It can therefore be suggested that the presence of a narrowly focused adverb in *ma* particle questions has the ability to interfere with and block the syntactic mechanism that otherwise results in the production of a verbal answer—movement of the verb to a higher clausal position, followed by ellipsis of the remnant constituent created by evacuation of the verb. The ill-formedness of verbal answers affirming the occurrence of an event carried out in the manner of a focused adverb can thus be attributed to an intervention effect in a way similar to the suggestion in Law (2006) that (the output of) Q-operator movement in A-not-A questions may be blocked by the intervening presence of adverbs of certain types, which interrupt the antecedent-government chain that needs to be established between the Q-operator and its lower extraction-site.[6] Example (50) is a schematization of such an intervention effect in verbal answers, where the structurally intervening presence of a focused adverbial causes the movement of the verb (or perhaps its output chain at LF) to be ungrammatical. Although the remnant XP is elided at PF, the adverbial remains syntactically present in the structure and thus interferes with the movement by the verb from its base position to a position above the subject.

(50)   verb ..[$_{XP}$ ~~subject~~ ~~adverb~~ ~~verb~~ ~~object~~]

Turning to consider the instances where a bare verb is judged to be acceptable as an affirmative answer to a question containing an adverb (as in (28)–(38)), in such cases, contexts and situations were created in which the adverb is part of a broader focus containing the verb and its arguments, and escapes the otherwise frequent tendency to be interpreted as narrowly focused. This incorporation of the adverbial element into a larger focused constituent including the verb was engineered in two ways when judgments of the relevant data were elicited from native speakers. In certain instances, contexts and situations were created in which events described by combinations of an adverbial with a verb and its arguments are expected to occur—hence the medical examination of a patient being carried out carefully (30), the beating of a discovered informant by a gangster being severe (31), and the clicking on a computer mouse being carried out twice (32), and so on. In such situations, hearers are much more easily able to interpret the question as asking for confirmation of whether the whole event described in the question occurred, hence that the whole TP is in broad focus, rather than assuming that the question is more narrowly focused on the content of the adverbial and establishing whether the event may have been carried out in the manner of the adverbial element. In other data presented to native speakers for their judgments of the acceptability of verbal answers, the question contained phrases equivalent to 'following my instructions,' as in (33) and (34), which help establish the content of the adverbial as part of an action that is expected to occur. A question containing such a phrase can again more easily be interpreted as asking for confirmation or denial of the occurrence of a whole event, rather than attracting semi-default narrow focus to the adverbial that is present. In all instances, therefore,

---

[6] The intervention effect caused by adverbials in A-not-A questions may sometimes seem to be stronger than in *ma* particle questions. Investigations with native speakers show that even unfocused adverbs of the types identified in Law (2006) may sometimes cause intervention effects in A-not-A questions. For example, the contexts that allow adverbial elements to be construed as part of a broadly focused TP do not always seem to result in acceptable A-not-A questions, and (i) below remains unacceptable even if the same background context that licenses the *ma* particle question (38) is provided:

(i)   ??feiji   cong L.A. qi-mei-qifei   a?
       plane from L.A. take-off-not-take-off Q
       Intended: 'Did the plane take off from L.A.?'

where hearers find it natural and easy to construe a question as asking whether an entire event may have occurred (broad sentential focus), verbal answers are judged to be acceptable, and indicate affirmation of the event (or situation) as a whole with no special narrow focus. Syntactically, if the verb is part of this broad focus and there is no other narrowly focused element present in the question, movement of the verb to a high clausal position will not be blocked by any intervention effect in the answer-form.

Briefly considering the syntactic derivation of *ma* particle questions (rather than potential answer-forms), because it is evident that narrowly focused adverbial elements may licitly occur in such questions with no impact on their grammaticality, it can be assumed that there is no movement of any type in such questions (for example, null operator movement), unlike in A-not-A questions, as Law (2006) indeed suggests. The question particle *ma* can be assumed to be directly inserted in C, following Law (2006), and the presence of narrowly focused adverbials does not cause any intervention effects. What about the answer-forms to *ma* particle questions that licitly contain narrowly focused elements such as adverbials? As a verbal answer is by hypothesis blocked from occurring due to the interference of the narrow focus and a potential intervention effect, an alternative strategy is regularly made use of to provide an affirmative answer to such questions, which is not the result of any similar movement—the base-generation of the particle *dui* (or *shi-de* in more formal registers) directly in C, just as the question particle *ma* is inserted in this position in the question input. Questions such as those in (39)–(46) containing a narrow focus are consequently given a positive answer with an equivalent to English 'yes,' confirming that the event occurred in the way of the adverbial element.[7]

Interesting, independent support for this view of the derivation of yes-no questions containing focused adverbial elements can be drawn from patterns that are found in Finnish, with its clear, overt-movement strategies in yes-no questions. When narrowly focused adverbials, PPs or arguments DPs occur in yes-no questions in Finnish and undergo raising to SpecCP to attach the Q-morpheme in the initial C-position, as seen in (50)–(52), a verbal answer to such yes-no questions is no longer possible, as in Chinese with the occurrence of focused adverbs in yes-no *ma* questions. In place of repetition of the verb as an affirmative answer-form, which is licensed in the absence of some other narrowly focused element, Holmberg (2001) reports that a Finnish

---

[7] Note that it would not be sufficient to say that *dui/shi-de* are simply required as answer-forms because the speaker has an expectation that the answer will be true/affirmative, as verbal answers *are* indeed used to give an affirmative answer and provide a confirmation of the proposition being true. If yes-no questions contain a focused sub-part of the proposition that is being highlighted, this should still allow for an affirmative answer to be provided with repetition of the verb, confirming that the proposition embedding the focus is true. Furthermore, the occurrence of narrow focus on a constituent in a yes-no question does not imply that the speaker necessarily believes that the reply to the question will be positive (or negative), and simply signals a focused attention on the constituent, frequently in some light contrast to other entities. For example, if a speaker asks 'Did you see Mary at the party?' with narrow focus on 'Mary,' this does not result in or imply any particular expectation about what the answer will be, simply that the speaker is interested in finding out the information asked specifically with regard to Mary.

particle equivalent to 'yes' *kyllä* (or *niin* 'so') is inserted directly into C as a regular answer to such questions, as shown in (50).[8]

(50) a. Houlellisestiko Jussi pesi   auton
          attentively-Q Jussi washed car
          'Was it attentively/carefully that Jussi washed the car?'

      b. */??Pesi.

      c. Niin/kyllä.
          so/yes
          'Yes.'

(51) a. Aamullako Pekka saapui Turkuun?
          in-morning Pekka arrived at-Turku
          'Was it in the morning that Pekka arrived at Turku?' (Karlsson 2007: 71)

      b. ??/*Saapui.
          arrived

      c. Niin/kyllä.
          so/yes
          'Yes.'

(52) a. Pariisissako Matti on käynyt?
          to-Paris-Q Matti has been
          'Is it Paris Matti has been to? (Holmberg 2001: 171)

      b. ??On (käynyt).
          has been

      c. Kyllä.
          yes
          'Yes.'

The unavailability of verb-movement as an answer-strategy in the presence of a focused adverbial (or other focused PP, DP) and its frequent replacement with the base-generation of an equivalent to 'yes' in C thus presents an interesting parallel to what is being described for Chinese and adds support to the hypothesis that focused adverbials create an intervention effect for the use of verb-movement in Chinese as an answer-form, necessitating instead the base-generation of an equivalent to 'yes' (*dui, shi-de*) in C.

Having considered alternating patterns in the ways that Chinese *ma* particle yes-no questions may be answered and having developed an analysis of restrictions on the verbal answer strategy, in section 5 we now turn to consider two other East/Southeast Asian languages, Korean and Vietnamese, and show how similar patterns and restrictions occur in these languages, suggesting that verbal answers in these languages also arise via a strategy of verb-movement that may be blocked by the presence of other focused material. We will also note that there is certain parametric variation in terms of the types of repeated material that may be used to answer yes/no questions that have a constituent focus. Finally, we will examine a previously uncommented-on

---

[8] Many thanks to Elsi Kaiser for very helpful discussion of these patterns in Finnish.

patterning in English that seems to show an interesting similarity to the phenomena seen in answer-forms in Vietnamese and Finnish.

5. Elliptical Answer Forms in Korean and Vietnamese

5.1. KOREAN

Korean allows for the use of verbs as affirmative answers to yes-no questions as in Chinese, as illustrated in (53b). In addition to the use of a repeated verb, yes-no questions in Korean may also regularly be answered with the particle *ne* 'yes,' as seen in the alternate answer-form in (53c).

(53) a. Chayk-ul   sassoyo?   b. Sassoyo   c. Ne.
          book-ACC bought   bought   yes
          'Did (you) buy a/the book?'   'Yes.'   'Yes.'

When adverbial elements occur in yes-no questions in Korean, such questions are fully grammatical, but the use of a verbal answer to such a question is sometimes not available and would not communicate a confirmation of the event in the question, modified by the content of the adverbial. For example, in (54), where a time adverbial *chaknyon* 'last year' occurs, the simple repetition of the verb as an attempted answer form is not perceived to be a legitimate answer to the question, and instead the use of the particle *ne* 'yes' is required to affirm that the buying event occurred in the previous year.

(54)   The speaker comments that the hearer's cell phone looks old and asks:
       a. Chaknyon-e sassoyo?   b. *Sassoyo.   c. Ne.
           last-year-in bought   bought   yes
           'Did you buy (it) last year?'   Intended: 'Yes.'   'Yes.'

However, the unacceptability of a verbal answer to a question containing an adverb is not an across-the-board phenomenon, and in many instances it is possible to use a repetition of the verb to affirm an action modified by an adverbial element as the answer to a question, as seen in (55), where an adjunct PP indicating location occurs.

(55) a. su-up kkus-na-go, tosokwan-eso kongbu haessoyo?
          class finishing   library-in   study   did
          'After class, did you study in the library?'

      b. Haessoyo.
          did
          'Yes.'

In (55), the adjunct PP is easily interpreted as part of the broad focus of the question, as a library is perceived to be an expected, regular location for the act of studying, hence the PP is not perceived as necessarily being in narrow focus. However, when there is no particularly close connection between an event and the place where it occurs, speakers report that it is difficult to accept a verbal answer as a legitimate response to a question with a location adverbial, and the particle *ne* is required instead, as in (56).

(56)   Speaker asks about the purchase of a shirt the hearer is wearing:
    a. Hawaii-e sassoyo?   b. *Sassoyo.   c. Ne.
        Hawaii-in bought   bought   yes
        'Did (you) buy (it) in Hawaii?' Intended: 'Yes.'   'Yes.'

Turning to consider frequency adverbials, a parallel situation is found. When a frequency adverb combines with the verb and its arguments to represent a regular, common activity or event, such as going to school every day, then a verbal answer may be used to confirm the content of the predicate as modified by the adverbial, as in (57).

(57) a. Mae-il   hakkyo-e kayo?   b. Kayo.
          every-day school-to go   go
          'Do you go to school every day?'   'Yes.'

The use of a phrase such as 'following my instructions' can also help speakers readily accept the occurrence of a frequency expression in a yes-no question as part of a broad focus, rather than being in narrow focus, with the result that repetition of the verb is accepted as a legitimate answer, as in (58).

(58) a. Che-ka mal   han kot-chorom,   tu-bon khulik haessoyo?
          I-NOM speech did thing according 2-time click   did
          'Did you click twice, as I told you to?'

      b. Haessoyo.
          did
          'Yes.'

However, in other instances the use of a verbal answer to attempt to affirm that an action is carried out with a certain frequency is not accepted as possible. For example, speakers do not accept the use of a repetition of the verb in (59) to affirm that the speaker watches television every day:

(59) a. TV-rul   chaju pwayo?   b. *Pwayo.   c. Ne.
          TV-ACC often watch   watch   yes
          'Do (you) watch TV often?'   Intended: 'Yes.'   'Yes.'

    With duration adverbials, similar variation in the acceptability of verbal answers is again found. These are noted to be acceptable with events in which the duration is a period of time perceived to regularly occur with a particular activity, for example when it is part of a regularized food preparation activity, as in (60). In such cases, the duration adverbial appears to be easily interpreted as part of a broad predicate focus and does not strike hearers as requiring a narrow focus interpretation:

(60) a. paetchu-rul   han-shigan-tongan choryossoyo?
          cabbage-ACC 1-hour-for   pickled
          'Did you pickle the cabbage for one hour (as you were supposed to)?'

     b. Choryossoyo.
        pickled
        'Yes.'

In other instances, speakers indicate that the attempt to answer a question containing an adverbial of duration is not felicitous and does not communicate the meaning of the adverbial in the question, only the content of the verb and its arguments, as in (61). Here the duration adverbial is strongly perceived to be in narrow focus, and this requires the particle *ne* to occur as an affirmative answer form.

(61)   a. Ku-saram-ul   oraetdongan arassoyo? b. *Arassoyo.   c. Ne.
           this-person-ACC long-time   known   known   yes
           'Have you known him for a long time?'   Intended: 'Yes.'   'Yes.'

Manner and comitative adverbials also show the same kind of variation seen with locative PPs, and frequency and duration adverbs. It is often felt that a manner adverb attracts a narrow focus to the adverb, as in (62), and in such instances a verbal answer is not acceptable, and would not communicate the content of the predicate modified by the manner adverb. However, verbal answers are acceptable in other instances, such as (63), where the manner adverbial is understood to be part of an action that is carried out regularly. Here the adverb is simply interpreted as being part of a broad predicate focus, and this allows for the repetition of the verb as an answer form.

(62)   a. Chelswu-ga   Yongmi-rul   tsege   taeryossoyo?
           Cheslswu-NOM Yongmi-ACC severely beat
           'Did Chelswu beat Yongmi severely?'

       b. *Taeryossoyo.   c. Ne.
          beat   Yes
          Intended: 'Yes.'   'Yes.'

(63)   Army sergeant asks junior soldier:
     a. chubang-ul   ketkutchi tatkan-na   b. Tatkassumnita.
         kitchen-ACC cleanly   polish-Q   polished
         'Did you polish the kitchen cleanly?'   'Yes.

Finally, when a comitative adjunct PP combines with a predicate to convey an activity that can be understood to be a potentially regularized activity which might be asked about, hearers seem able to accept the PP as being part of the broad focus of a question, and find verbal answers to be acceptable answers to such questions, as illustrated in (64).

(64)   a. chu-il-e   nampyon-irang kyohui-e kayo?
           Sunday-on husband-with   church-to go
           'Do you go to church with your husband on Sundays?'

       b. Kayo.
          go
          'Yes.'

However, in other instances where a comitative PP strikes hearers as being the narrow focus of a yes-no question, repetition of the verb cannot be used to convey the meaning of the comitative PP as well as that of the verb and its arguments, as illustrated in (65), and it is reported that *ne* must be used instead:

(65) a. Yongmi-rang baekhwajom-e   kassoyo?
          Yongmi-with department store-to went
          'Did you go to the department store with Yongmi?'

     b. *Kassoyo.   c. Ne.
        went   yes
        Intended: 'Yes.'   'Yes.'

In the way that it makes verbal answers available as legitimate responses to questions containing adverbial elements, Korean thus appears to be very much like Chinese. The fact that adverbs and other adverbial adjuncts can indeed be interpreted as conveyed by a bare verbal answer in various instances cannot be attributed to the occurrence of pro-form adverbs or pro-PPs in Korean, for the same reasons that such elements are generally not assumed to be syntactically available, and the licensing of null pro-forms is restricted to elements projected in argument positions. Such patterns can therefore be argued to support an analysis in which verbal answers to yes-no questions may result from a process of verb-raising and remnant constituent deletion. The additional observation that verbal answers to questions containing adverbs are in other instances clearly restricted and not licensed when the adverbial is understood to be narrowly focused similarly requires an explanation, and can be attributed to a blocking effect caused by the narrowly focused adverbial on the raising of the verb, that is, an intervention effect as suggested to occur in Chinese.

5.2. VIETNAMESE

Vietnamese is a pro-drop SVO language of Southeast Asia, which earlier received much influence from extended contact with Chinese. Verbal answers to yes-no questions also occur in Vietnamese, as illustrated in (66) and (67).

(66) a. Bạn   có thích xem phim không?   b. Thích.
          friend CO like see film NEG   like
          'Do you like watching films?'   'Yes.'

(67) a. Bạn   muốn đi mua sắm   không?   b. Muốn.
          friend want go buy shopping NEG   want
          'Do you want to go shopping?'   'Yes.'

There are three ways that yes-no questions are commonly created. First, the pairing of the element *có* ('to have/be,' similar to Mandarin *you*) and sentence-final negation *không* can occur, frequently bracing the VP as schematized in (68) and seen in (66), (69), and (70). Such questions are 'open' questions in the sense that there is no expectation on behalf of the speaker that the answer will be 'yes' or 'no.' In addition to frequently allowing a verbal answer, *có-không* questions also regularly permit the use of the repetition of *có* as an affirmative answer form, as seen in (69) and (70).

(68)   Subject có VP không?

(69)   a.   Bạn   có   gặp   Nam hôm qua   không?   b. Có.   c. Gặp.
            friend CO meet Nam yesterday NEG   CO   meet
            'Did you see Nam yesterday?'   'Yes.'   'Yes.'

(70)   a.   Bạn   có   học   tiếng   pháp   không?   b. Có.   c. Học.
            friend CO study language France NEG   CO   study
            'Do you study French?'   'Yes.'   'Yes.'

Second, the elements *phải không* (or more informally *hả*) can be placed sentence-finally as schematized in (71), creating a yes-no question that tends to expect an affirmative answer, in certain ways similar to English tag-questions of the form '. . . , is that right?' Such questions can potentially be answered with the particle *ừ* 'correct/ yes' or a verbal answer, as illustrated in (72).

(71)   . . . , phải không?

(72)   a.   Bạn   thích xem ti-vi phải   không?   b. Ừ.   c. Thích.
            friend like see TV correct NEG   yes   like
            'You like to watch TV, is that right?   'Yes.'   'Yes.'

Third, yes-no questions with a perfect tense interpretation can be created with the use of *chưa* 'yet' in sentence-final position, as schematized in (73). Such questions can be answered in the affirmative with a repetition of the verb plus the aspectual morpheme *rồi*, which is similar in meaning to Mandarin sentential *le*, resulting in a verbal answer similar to past time verbal answers in Mandarin of the form V-le seen in examples (29)–(34). *Chưa* yes-no questions may also be answered with the element *rồi* with no accompanying verb, as illustrated in (74c). In this patterning, Vietnamese *rồi* is clearly different from Mandarin *le*, which cannot stand unsupported in a sentence.

(73)   . . . chưa?

(74)   a.   Bạn   có   học   tiếng   pháp   chưa?   b. Học rồi.   c. Rồi.
            friend CO study language France yet   study ASP   ASP
            'Have you studied French yet?'   'Yes.'   'Yes.'

Neither *có-không* questions nor *chưa* yes-no questions can be answered with the particle *ừ*, which is restricted to occurring as an affirmative answer to non-open *phải không* questions.

As in Mandarin and Korean, when adverbs are introduced into yes-no questions, a difference in patterning emerges, relating to whether such elements are understood to be in narrow focus, or part of a broader focus. With *phải không* and *chưa* yes-no questions, when an adverb can be naturally taken to be part of a broader focus, perhaps as part of a frequent action or activity, a verbal answer can be used as an affirmative reply and can convey the meaning of the verb, its arguments, and the accompanying adverb, as illustrated in (75):

(75) a. Bạn nhấn hai lần phải   không/chưa?   b. Nhấn rồi.
          friend click 2 time correct NEG/yet   click ASP
          'You clicked twice, is that right/Did you click twice yet?'   'Yes.'

With *có-không* questions, frequently the element *có* is felt to be required in an affirmative answer, and this may or may not be accompanied by a repetition of the verb. In instances where adverbs or other adjuncts such as PPs are present, the *có* + verb fragment answer may occur when the adverbs/adjuncts are not interpreted as being in narrow focus, as illustrated in (76c), but such a verbal fragment answer is not possible when adverbs/other adjuncts are strongly felt to be the narrow focus of a question, as seen in (77c).

(76) a. Bạn   có đi chùa   với vợ   vào Chủ Nhật không? b. Có.   c. Có đi.
          friend CO go temple with wife on Sunday   NEG   CO   CO go
          'On Sunday, do you go to the temple with your wife?'   'Yes.'   'Yes.'

(77) a. Bạn   có thường xem ti-vi không?   b. Có.   c. */??Có xem.
          friend CO often see TV NEG   CO   CO see
          'Do you often watch TV?'   'Yes.'   Intended: 'yes.'

Such patterns are similar in essence to those found in Mandarin and Korean, with the occurrence of narrow focus on an adverb or other adjunct apparently blocking the use of verbal repetition as an answer-form. Where Vietnamese shows an interesting difference to Mandarin and Korean is in its greater versatility of type of fragment answer forms. In Mandarin and Korean, when the presence of a narrowly focused adverbial in a yes-no question blocks the use of a verbal answer, it requires instead the use of a 'yes' particle, assumed to be base-generated in C. However, in equivalent instances of narrow focus on an adverbial element in Vietnamese, what frequently substitutes for a blocked verbal answer is in fact a repetition of the focused adverbial itself. This is shown in the following set of examples, where the narrowly focused adverbial element which occurs as the fragment answer are, respectively, adverbials of manner (78)–(79), frequency (80)–(81), duration (82), and time (83).

(78) a. Bạn   có học hành chăm chỉ không?
          friend CO study   diligently NEG
          'Did you work <u>hard</u>?'

      b. Chăm chỉ. c. *Học hành. d. Có.
          diligently   study   CO
          'Yes.'   Intended: 'Yes.' 'Yes.'

(79) a. Sếp của Nga đối xử nó tệ   lắm hả?
          boss of Nga treat her meanly very Q
          'Does Nga's boss treat her <u>meanly</u>?'

    b. tệ   lắm.   c. *Đối xử   d. Ừ.
       meanly very   treat   yes
       'Yes.'   Intended: 'Yes.'   'Yes.'

(80) a. Bạn gội đầu mỗi ngày phải   không?
       friend wash hair every day   correct NEG
       'Do you wash your hair <u>every day</u>?'

    b. Mỗi ngày. c. *Gội đầu   d. Ừ.
       every day   wash hair   yes
       'Yes.'   Intended: 'Yes.'   'Yes.'

(81) a. Khi Jean-Louis chào bạn, anh ta có hôn bạn   hai lần phải không?
       when Jean-Louis greet friend he   CO kiss friend 2 time correct NEG
       'When J-L greets you, does he kiss you <u>twice</u>?'

    b. Hai lần. c. *Hôn.   d. Ừ.
       2 time   kiss   yes
       'Yes.'   Intended: 'Yes.'   'Yes.'

(82) a. Trước khi bạn chiên cá, bạn ướp   nó một tiếng phải   không?
       before   friend cook fish friend marinate it 1   hour correct NEG
       'When you cook the fish, do you marinate it <u>for an hour</u>?'

    b. Một tiếng. c. *Ướp.   d. Ừ.
       1   hour   marinade   yes
       'Yes.'   Intended: 'Yes.'   'Yes.'

(83) a. Bạn gặp Nam hôm qua phải   không?
       friend meet Nam yesterday correct NEG
       'Did you see Nam <u>yesterday</u>?'

    b. Hôm qua. c. *Gặp.   d. Ừ.
       yesterday   meet   yes
       'Yes.'   Intended: 'Yes.'   'Yes.'

Such a patterning is not possible in Mandarin and Korean, where only 'yes'-type particles are used when verbal answers are blocked by narrow focus on adverbials. Interestingly, however, they do occur in Finnish, when adverbs are narrowly focused and raised to attach the question morpheme –*ko* in C. Consider example example (50), repeated here as (84). It is pointed out in Holmberg (2001) that such examples containing a raised adverbial may be regularly answered with a particle equivalent to 'yes' *niin/kyllä*, and that repetition of the verb is not possible as an affirmative answers in such instances. However, in addition to the use of *niin/kyllä* 'yes,' it is also possible to use a repetition of the adverb as an answer, without any accompanying *niin/kyllä*, as now shown in answer-form (84d).

(84) a. Houlellisestiko Jussi pesi   auton?
       attentively-Q   Jussi washed car
       'Was it attentively/carefully that Jussi washed the car?'

b. */??Pesi.

c. Niin/kyllä.
    so/yes
    'Yes.'

d. Huolellisesti.
    attentively
    'Yes.'

Although the use of a repeated adverbial as an alternative strategy to the use of a yes-type particle in Finnish is not discussed by Holmberg, the analysis of verbal answers in Finnish developed in Holmberg (2001) in which the verb raises to the C-domain and the clausal complement following this is elided in the answer can be argued to carry over very naturally to the use of adverbial answers. It can be assumed that the focused adverbial also undergoes raising in the answer-form, this being followed by deletion of the remnant clausal constituent to its right, eliding the verb, subject, and object.

If the analysis of verbal arguments in Chinese and Korean that views them as also raising to the C-domain is essentially on the right track, and similar focus-related patterns are found to occur in Vietnamese when adverbials occur, it is natural to suggest that the use of adverbials as fragment answer-forms in Vietnamese is an extension of this patterning, in which the adverbial itself as the narrow focus of the sentence undergoes raising, followed by PF deletion of the remnant constituent created by this movement. Such a movement-and-deletion approach to the use of bare adverbials as answers to yes-no questions would seem to be supported by the observation that this strategy is unavailable when a narrowly focused adverb occurs within an island constituent, and in such instances an alternative way of affirming the answer must be made use of, either the use of *ừ* in a *phải không* question or the repetition of *có* in a *có-không* question.

(85) a. Bạn khen sinh viên ma đọc xong tờ báo nhahn, phải không?
          friend praise student REL read ASP paper quickly correct NEG
          'Did you praise the student who read the paper <u>quickly</u>?'

     b. *Nhahn.   c. Ừ.
         quickly   yes
         Intended: 'Yes.'   'Yes.'

Vietnamese can therefore be argued to show an interesting development of the verbal-answer strategy elsewhere found in Chinese and Korean, allowing various other narrowly focused constituents to undergo raising, similar to the verb in a broad focus question by hypothesis, as an input to the PF deletion of other elements in the answer-form contained in the lower remnant produced by movement. As in Finnish, this strategy regularly exists as an optional alternative to the use of a particle-like element signaling an affirmative answer, *ừ* in a *phải không* question or the repetition of *có* in a *có-không* question, as seen in (78)–(84). It can also be noted that although Vietnamese patterns more like Finnish in this respect and is different from Mandarin and Korean, not all narrowly focused elements appear to be eligible as targets for raising in the attempted creation of affirmative fragment answers, and PPs and DP arguments are regularly unacceptable as isolated, affirmative answers even when interpreted as being in narrow focus. This is illustrated in (86)–(89).

(86) a.   Sau giờ học, bạn   học   trong thư   viện phải không?
           after hour study friend study in   library correct NEG
           'After class, did/do you study <u>in the library</u>?'

      b.   Ừ.   c.   ??Trong thư   viện.
           yes   in   library
           'Yes.'   Intended: 'Yes.'

(87) a.   Bạn   mua cái aó   Này ở Hawaii phải   không?
           friend buy CL shirt that in Hawaii correct NEG
           'Did you buy that shirt <u>in Hawaii</u>?'

      b.   Ừ.   c.   ??Ở Hawaii.
           yes   in Hawaii
           'Yes.'   Intended: 'Yes.'

(88) a.   Bạn   có đi mua sắm   với Nga phải   không?
           friend CO go buy things with Nga correct NEG
           'Did you go shopping <u>with Nga</u>?'

      b.   Ừ.   c.   ??Với Nga.
           yes   with Nga
           'Yes.'   Intended: 'Yes.'

(89) a.   Bạn   có thích Nga phải   không?
           friend CO like Nga correct NEG
           'Do you like <u>Nga</u>?'

      b.   Ừ.   c.   ??Nga.
           yes   Nga
           'Yes.'   Intended: 'Yes.'

In such instances it can be suggested that the relevant (+Affirmative) features that may be generated with verbs and other narrowly focused adverbial elements and that trigger raising of these elements to the C-domain are simply unavailable for combination with PPs and DP arguments, just as they apparently may not be combined with elements other than the verb in Chinese and Korean. Consequently, PPs and DP arguments in Vietnamese may not be attracted to the high clausal polarity position that licenses deletion of its clausal complement in affirmative answer-forms. A consideration of fragment answers to yes-no questions in Vietnamese thus suggests that there is certain parametric variation among East and Southeast Asian languages regarding the range of elements that may participate in such elliptical answer-forms, with the core case being the use of a repetition of the verb in instances of broad focus, and possible use of the repetition of (non-PP) adverbials as affirmative responses to narrow-focus questions in Vietnamese but not Chinese or Korean.

Comparing what is found in Mandarin, Korean, and Vietnamese with Finnish once again, we arrive at an even fuller range of variation relating to possible fragment answer-forms to yes-no questions. Earlier it was noted that when an adverb is narrowly focused and fronted to the clause-initial Q-morpheme –*ko* in Finnish, it may occur naturally as a fragment answer. Now it can be added that Finnish actually extends the range of possible fragment answer constituents further than Vietnamese, and also allows for both PP-like oblique case-marked nominals and DP arguments to occur as elliptical answers when such elements have been fronted in the input questions, as illustrated in (90)–(92) (examples from Karlsson 2007: 70–71):

(90) a. Mäntyniemessäko presidentti assu?
          at.Mäntyniemi.Q president lives
          'Is it at Mäntyniemi that the president lives?'

     b. Mäntyniemessä. c. Niin.
          at.Mäntyniemi   yes
          'Yes.'   'Yes.'

(91) a. Autonko state?
          car.Q   bought
          'Was it a car that you bought?'

     b. Auton c. Niin.
          Car   yes
          'Yes.'   'Yes.'

(92) a. Pekkako saapui Turkuun aamulla?
          Pekka.Q arrived Turku at morning.in
          'Was it Pekka who arrived at Turku in the morning?'

     b. Pekka c. Niin.
          Pekka   yes
          'Yes.'   'Yes.'

This varied distribution of fragment answers to yes-no questions across languages is summarized in the table in (93). As has been noted, the core case of using an element in the question-form to answer a yes-no question where an equivalent to 'yes' is not used is repetition of the verb, and this is common to all four languages considered here. If a language allows verbal answer forms, it may or may not permit other constituents such as adverbials, PPs/locatives, and nominal arguments to also occur as affirmative fragment answers. As it does not seem that the range of elements occurring as fragment answers to yes-no questions can be clearly predicted from other properties of a language (for example, Chinese and Vietnamese are typologically very similar languages, yet differ considerably here in the elements permitted to occur as affirmative answer fragments), the cross-linguistic differences reported in (93) are arguably best described in terms of a purely mechanical, featural way. The direction of argument that has been taken up and pursued in this chapter is to attribute the occurrence of verbal and other fragment answers to a process of movement and ellipsis, resulting in the PF deletion of the clausal constituent from which the fragment answer has been extracted. As such an account critically requires movement of the fragment answer to a clause-initial position and some formal set of features to trigger this movement, the variation in (93) can be ascribed to the ability of different elements to carry the necessary feature in different languages, which can simply be referred to as Aff(irmative) features, signaling an affirmative reply to the question being asked. Hence Aff-features may hypothetically be combined with a full range of elements in Finnish, with elements other than nominal arguments in Vietnamese, and with just verbs in Chinese and Korean, allowing these elements to be attracted to the high clausal polarity head, which functions as the locus of affirmation and negation in answers to yes-no questions.

(93)   Elements potentially occurring as affirmative fragment answers to yes-no questions

	verbs	adverbials	PPs/locatives	nominal arguments
Chinese	✓	*	*	*
Korean	✓	*	*	*
Vietnamese	✓	✓	✓	*
Finnish	✓	✓	✓	✓

5.3. ENGLISH

A final patterning that will be presented here comes from a language that at first sight appears to have no connection with the primary phenomenon of this chapter, that is, the repetition of a verb as an affirmative answer-form. Verbal answers do not occur in English. However, once one starts to consider the potential use of elements other than verbs as affirmative answers to yes-no questions, as in Vietnamese and Finnish, it can be noted that there are patterns in English that actually do seem to exhibit an intriguingly similar use of elements repeated from a yes-no question as fragment answers to such questions. To the best of my knowledge, what will be described here has not been reported on previously and is most certainly restricted to very colloquial, spoken English. In both British and American English, yes-no questions with a narrow focus on an adverbial element or an argument of the verb may be answered with a simple repetition of the narrowly focused constituent under certain circumstances. In all acceptable uses of this strategy, some clear intensification of the repeated element is required. This may be achieved by the addition of an emphatic modifier and/or with the use of special emphatic intonation that involves exaggerated high pitch on the primary stressed syllable of the repeated word, followed by lower pitch on a following syllable. This is initially illustrated in (94) and (95):

(94)   a.   Did you grade the papers <u>quickly</u>?

     b.   <u>VE</u>ry quickly.

     c.   ??Quickly.

(95)   a.   Did you greet <u>everyone</u> who came to the party?

     b.   <u>E</u>veryone!

The responses in (94b) and (95b) are affirmations of the proposition asked about in the question, which also add some additional information about this affirmation. In (94b) the additional information is a simple modification of the degree to which the action was indeed carried out in the manner of the adverb. In (95b), the natural interpretation of the affirmative answer communicated by repetition of the DP object with special high stress on the first syllable is that the speaker did indeed greet every person who came to the party and this is a remarkable achievement, perhaps because there were very many people at the party. (95b) might also naturally occur in a situation in which the speaker wishes to communicate that s/he is exhausted from the chore of having to greet all the many guests at the party. A very similar additional component of meaning occurs in the fragment answer form in (96), which repeats part of the duration adverbial as an affirmation of the content of the question. (96b) might be naturally produced in a situation in which the speaker feels that the period of five years has been an extremely long and perhaps trying time.

(96) a. Have you known this student for <u>five years</u>?

  b. <u>FIVE YE</u>ars!

The importance of a context that is remarkable in some way for the appropriate use of such fragment answer-forms in illustrated further in (97), (98), and (99). The reply to (97a) in (97b) may occur if the speaker feels that it is somehow remarkable and unexpected that she should have attended the party with her husband rather than someone else (perhaps because she and her husband are estranged). (98b) could be used as a reply to a question in which the fact that the speaker made his/her purchase in Hawaii has some additional significance that the person asking the question in (98a) might be expected to understand. Similarly, (99b) may occur naturally in a situation in which the speaker feels that it is remarkable that John would date Mary, and wishes to add this information to the affirmative reply.

(97) a. Did you go to the party <u>with your husband</u>?

  b. With my <u>HUS</u>band...!

(98) a. Did you buy that shirt <u>in Hawaii</u>?

  b. In <u>HAWA</u>ii.

(99) a. Is John now dating <u>Mary</u>?

  b. <u>MA</u>ry!

Syntactically, the use of such emphatic repetitions as affirmative fragment answers seems to be restricted in a way that is island-sensitive and indicative of derivation by movement. As illustrated in (100b) and (101b), it is not possible to repeat fragments that correspond to elements within island constituents in the input yes-no questions.

(100) a. Did John get angry because Mary flirted <u>with Stephen</u>?

  b. ??With <u>STE</u>phen!

(101) a.   Did you know someone who is living <u>in Hawaii</u>?

     b.   ??In <u>HAWA</u>ii.

As with the use of fragment answer to *wh*-questions discussed in Merchant (2004), and the derivation of fragment answers to yes-no questions proposed here for Chinese, Vietnamese, and Korean, and for Finnish and other languages in Holmberg (2001, 2007), it can be suggested that these 'remarkable fragment answers' to yes-no questions in English arise as the result of movement of the repeated constituent to a high clausal position and deletion of the remnant clausal constituent created by this movement. The licensing trigger for this movement can be attributed to the special focal quality of the fragment, and the remarkable, emphatic nature that such answer-forms must have to be acceptable. Formally, it can be suggested that focus-features associated with the fragment constituents make such elements visible for movement to SpecCP and feed the ellipsis of the clausal complement of C.

From a cross-linguistic viewpoint, two final points can be made about this patterning in English and how it relates to what has been documented in the other languages under discussion in this chapter. First, although a wide range of constituents in English seem able to serve as fragment answers to yes-no questions in appropriate 'remarkable' contexts, this possibility does not seem to be open to verbs, even if emphatic intonation is applied and a context in which the content of the verb is focused and remarkable is constructed.

(102) a.   Did you <u>destroy</u> the letter?

     b.   ??*Dest<u>ROY</u>(ed).

(103) a.   <u>Will</u> you go?

     b.   ??*<u>WILL</u>.

English yes-no fragment answers thus seem to show an inverse distribution to Chinese and Korean, where only verbs occur as fragment answers to yes-no questions. Second, it is relevant to point out that the special 'remarkable' focal prominence of fragment answer-forms to yes-no questions in English is not a regular or required property of verbal answer-forms in Chinese, Korean, or Finnish, though a certain amount of speaker emphasis frequently does occur with verbal answers in Vietnamese (yet not signaling any necessary highly remarkable quality of the affirmation, as in English). Furthermore, while the use of adverbials and argument DPs as fragment answers in Finnish requires that these be narrowly focused in the input question, such elements do not necessitate any of the additional 'unexpected' focal quality common in the English data considered here. Finally, it can be noted that an additional feature of the English fragment answer pattern is that there is strong pressure for such answer forms to be accompanied by and supplemented with a simultaneous (slow) nodding of the head as a gestural affirmation of the content of the question. However, no such similar head movements are required for the use of narrowly focused constituents as affirmative answer-forms in (for example) Finnish, which are therefore able to communicate affirmation without any special additional reinforcement. The English use of fragment-answers to yes-no questions is consequently distinguished in certain ways from those found in the other languages investigated here, while also seeming to be best analyzed as the product of movement and clausal ellipsis, as hypothesized for Chinese, Korean, Vietnamese, and Finnish.

6. Summary

Taking as its starting point Law's interesting (2006) paper on adverbs and yes-no questions in Chinese, in which it is convincingly argued that there is some form of operator movement in A-not-A questions but not *ma* particle questions, this chapter has focused its attention on the answer-forms that may occur with the latter type of particle question, and has argued that some kind of movement is in fact associated with *ma* particle questions, not in the questions themselves but in the derivation of verbal answers which consist in a repetition of the verb in the input question. The hypothesized, frequent occurrence of movement of the verb in verbal answers is partially obscured by the fact that there is also an alternative non-movement strategy available to answer many *ma* questions, the use of a particle equivalent to 'yes' (*dui* or *shi-de*) directly inserted into the high C-domain polarity head where interrogativity and affirmation is specified, and this non-movement strategy of answering a *ma* question can be used in instances where movement is by hypothesis not possible; hence there will always be some grammatical way of answering a well-formed *ma* question. The chapter has explored the hypothesis that movement of the verb in answers to *ma* questions is revealed in the restrictions on the availability of the use of a verbal answer form in the presence of adverbs, and in the interpretation verbal answers give rise to when adverbial elements are present in questions. When such elements are part of a broader focus in a *ma* question, the bare repetition of the verb as an affirmative answer also communicates the content of the adverbial element as a modifier of the event/action that is affirmed to have taken place/hold as a situation. It was noted that this 'adverb-inclusive' interpretation is unexpected in an approach to verbal answers that analyzes these as simply resulting from the use of null arguments (pro, TECs) combined with the verb. While null proform-type elements are commonly assumed to be potentially available for subject and object arguments of the verb in many languages, the existence of null adverbials is not supported or assumed to be licensed, and there are patterns which clearly suggest that such elements do not exist. A movement account of verbal answers in which such forms are created by movement of the verb to a high, polarity-related position in the C-domain followed by PF ellipsis of the clausal complement of such a head is straightforwardly able to account for the interpretation of adverbs in answer-forms. These are syntactically projected and present in the answer-form, but phonetically elided as part of a larger clausal constituent, also containing the subject and object, which the verb is extracted from.

Additionally, it was noted that in other instances where an adverbial that is present in a *ma* question is not easily interpreted as being part of a broader predicate/event focus and is instead salient as a narrowly focused constituent, a verbal answer is no longer possible, and it is necessary to use *dui* (or *shi-de*) to answer such a question. This patterning was explained in terms of an intervention effect that the focused adverbial creates, blocking movement of the verb across it (or disrupting the chain formed by this movement and its LF licensing), and requiring a non-movement answer-form—the insertion of *dui* directly in C.

Turning to consider related patterns in four other languages, it was first noted that the distribution of verbal answers in Korean in questions with adverbials bears strong parallels with those in Chinese, and lends itself to a parallel analysis in terms of verb movement and potential intervention effect interference when narrowly focused adverbials occur in the question. In Vietnamese, similar patterns were again found, but with the extra twist that a yes-no question with a narrowly focused adverbial can be answered with a simple repetition of the adverbial itself. Finnish was also shown to allow for this possibility, with movement of narrowly focused adverbials occurring clearly in questions as well. Unlike Vietnamese, however, it was seen that Finnish allows for narrowly focused DP arguments and various PP adjuncts to occur as fragment answers to yes-no questions; hence a range of variation was ultimately discovered with regard to the type of syntactic constituents that different languages allow to occur as fragment answers affirming the content of yes-no questions.

Finally, we considered what appears to be a related phenomenon in English, the use of a range of different elements as fragment answers to yes-no questions, but with the restriction that such fragment answers may only occur when there is a very strong focal-emphasis associated with the affirmation and the speaker implies that the occurrence of the event/action described is somehow remarkable.

Quite generally, it was suggested that the spectrum of variation is best modeled with the assumption that different languages place differing restrictions on the kinds of elements that are permissible hosts for the affirmation-associated features which make such elements legitimate targets for movement in answers to yes-no questions, and that a non-movement approach attributing verbal answers to the simple use of null arguments combined with a verb might not expect such variation to occur and might not be able to model this in a uniform way.

As a very final note, it can be emphasized that taking Chinese as the starting point of an investigation into the phenomenon of verbal answers, the differences found in the patterning of two special types of yes-no question in Chinese (A-not-A and *ma* particle questions) have led on naturally to the discovery of a broader patterning of cross-linguistic variation in the use of fragment answers to yes-no questions, and to the general conclusion that fragment answers occur not only as answers to *wh*-questions, as previously well documented, but also in various languages and forms as answers to yes-no questions. It will now be interesting to attempt to track the use of fragments as answers to yes-no questions further across languages to establish a fuller typology of this understudied phenomenon.

References

Aoun, Joseph, and Audrey Y.-H. Li. 1989. Scope and constituency. *Linguistic Inquiry* 20, 141–172.

Aoun, Joseph and Y.-H. Audrey Li. 2008. Ellipsis and missing objects. In *Foundational Issues in Linguistic Theory*, ed. Robert Freidin, Carlos Otero, and Maria Luisa Zubizarreta, 251–274. Boston: MIT Press.

Beck, Sigrid. 2006. Intervention effects follow from focus interpretation. *Natural Language Semantics* 14(1), 1–56.

Ernst, Thomas. 1994. Conditions on Chinese A-not-A questions. *Journal of Chinese Linguistics* 3, 241–264.

Han, Chung-hye, Jeffrey Lidz, and Julien Musolino. 2007. V-raising and grammar competition in Korean: Evidence from negation and quantifier scope. *Linguistic Inquiry* 38(1), 1–47.

Holmberg, Anders. 2001. The syntax of yes and no in Finnish. *Studia Linguistica* 55,141–174.

Holmberg, Anders. 2007. Null subjects and polarity focus. *Studia Linguistica* 61(3),212–236.

Huang, James C.-T. 1982. *Logical Relations in Chinese and the Theory of Grammar*. Doctoral dissertation, MIT.

Huang, C.-T. James. 1984. On the distribution and reference of empty pronouns. *Linguistic Inquiry* 15, 531–574.

Huang, C.-T. James. 1987. Remarks on empty categories in Chinese. *Linguistic Inquiry* 18, 321–337.

Huang, James C.-T. 1991. Modularity and Chinese A-not-A questions. In *Interdisciplinary Approaches to Languages: Essays in Honor of S.-Y. Kuroda*, ed. Carol Georgepoulous and Robert Ishihara, 305–332. Dordrecht: Kluwer.

Huang, C.-T. James, Y.-H. Audrey Li, and Yafei Li. 2009. *The Syntax of Chinese*. Cambridge: Cambridge University Press.

Karlsson, Fred. 2007. *Finnish: An Essential Grammar*. London: Routledge.

Kim, Shin-Sook. 2002. Intervention effects are focus effects. In *Japanese/Korean Linguistics 10*, ed. Noriko Akatsuka and Susan Strauss, 615–628. Stanford, CA: CSLI.

Kim, Shin-Sook. 2006. More evidence that intervention effects are focus effects. In *Proceedings of the 8th Seoul International Conference on Generative Grammar: Minimalist Views on Language Design*, ed. Changguk Yim, 161–180. Seoul: Hankook.

Law, Paul. 2006. Adverbs in A-not-A questions in Mandarin Chinese. *Journal of East Asian Linguistics* 15(2), 97–136.

Li, Charles, and Sandra Thompson. 1989 *Mandarin Chinese: A Functional Reference Grammar*. Berkeley: University of California Press.

Li, Y.-H Audrey. 2007. Beyond empty categories. *Bulletin of the Chinese Linguistic Society of Japan (Chuugoku Gogaku)* 254, 74–106.

Merchant, Jason. 2004 Fragments and ellipsis. *Linguistics and Philosophy* 27(6), 661–738.

Saito, Mamoru. 1985. *Some Asymmetries in Japanese and Their Theoretical Implications*. Doctoral dissertation, MIT.

13

On the Internal Structure
of Comparative Constructions:

From Chinese and Japanese to English

YANG GU AND JIE GUO

1. Introduction

The similarities and differences between entities and events are obtained through comparison. While individual languages may resort to specific constructions for various kinds of comparison, semantically there is no drastic difference in expressing such comparisons. A comparative construction (CC), or a comparative,[1] following Stassen (1985: 24), is one that "has the semantic function of assigning a graded position on a predicative scale to two objects." The following five major components are commonly identified in constructions using morpho-syntactic means to express comparison: (i) a gradable predicate, mostly a gradable adjective, capable of depicting properties of entities/events that are gradable; (ii) two comparable objects, known respectively as a *comparee* and a *standard* for comparison; (iii) an implicit or explicit comparative marker that sets the order of gradability between the two comparable objects (*-er* in English, for example); (iv) an element introducing the *standard*, such as the Chinese *bi* ('compare'), the English *than*, and the Japanese *yori* ('from'); and (v) a measure expression, which may be present to specify the value of difference between the compared objects. The examples in (1) illustrate prototypical Chinese comparative constructions, where we can find gradable predicates *gao* and *congming*, the comparee *Zhangsan*, the standard *Lisi* introduced by the element *bi*, plus some optional measure phrases.

(1)   a.   Zhangsan bi Lisi gao (liang gongfen).
              Zhangsan BI[2] Lisi tall   two centimeter
              'Zhangsan is (two centimeters) taller than Lisi.'

---

[1] 'Comparative construction' and 'comparative' are used interchangeably in this chapter. Unless specified otherwise, they mainly refer to comparatives of superiority.

[2] Li and Thompson (1981: 564) gloss *bi* in Chinese comparative constructions as *exceed*. But typologically this would wrongly categorize Chinese comparatives as exemplifying 'exceed' comparatives

b. Zhangsan bi Lisi congming (hen duo).
   Zhangsan BI Lisi smart   very much
   'Zhangsan is a lot smarter than Lisi.'

Working within the generative framework, in this chapter we approach the internal structure of comparatives by examining the properties of adjectives used as predicates and relevant properties that manifest functional projections of the adjectives, with an aim to analyze and justify how comparative constructions in Chinese like those in (1) are derived and how the derivation of Chinese comparatives has implications for the analysis of and provides insights into other languages, such as Japanese and English. The chapter is organized as follows. Section 2 starts with a review of early analyses of the derivation of Chinese comparative constructions, along with some discussion of the inadequacies and problems arising from these analyses. Then we discuss how a clarification of the status of *bi* and other elements in comparatives can explicate the internal structure of Chinese comparatives. In section 3, we examine the properties of comparatives of Japanese and discuss the parametric similarities between the two languages in modes of comparison. Section 4 concludes the chapter.

2. Chinese Comparatives

Various attempts have been made to analyze the internal structure of Chinese comparatives, and different accounts for the structural properties of Chinese comparatives have been proposed. In this section, we begin with a brief review of earlier analyses of the derivation of Chinese comparatives and pinpoint the problems arising from the indeterminate status of *bi*. We then adopt Zhang's (2007) analysis of comitatives, and argue that *bi* behaves like a comitative, coordinating the *comparee* and the *standard* in a complex DP structure in the comparative construction. We also demonstrate how the complex DP structure can capture both comparatives of superiority and comparatives of equality in Chinese. Finally, with modification of a recent analysis of Guo (2012), we arrive at a full structural analysis for the Chinese comparatives.

2.1. A COMPLEX STRUCTURE

The earliest formal analysis of the internal structure of Chinese comparative constructions dates back to Yue-Hashimoto (1966) and Fu (1978), who, based on the early generative framework, propose that CCs in Chinese involve a complex structure of two propositions, each of which is a clause with *bi* functioning as a complementizer. For example, Fu proposes that CCs in both English and Chinese (or perhaps cross-linguistically) involve two propositions, each containing a variable quantifier x

(Stassen 1985; Bobaljik 2012). *Bi*, which exhibits strong verbal behavior in constructions other than comparatives (Gu and Guo 2008, 2009), means 'compare' but not 'exceed' nor 'surpass.' Throughout the chapter, we will gloss it as BI. A detailed analysis of *bi* is provided in section 2.3.

or *y* and an abstract gradable predicate with reference to those quantifiers.[3] The element, *than* in English or *bi* in Chinese, is like a complementizer, which does not exist in the underlying structure but is introduced by a transformational rule. Accordingly, a CC is derived from an abstract logical structure consisting of three elements: an abstract comparative predicate and two parallel propositions, each containing a variable quantifier *x* or *y*. The internal structures of a Chinese CC like (2a) and its English equivalent in (2b) are schematically shown in (2a') and (2b'), respectively. The surface structures are derived via several steps of transformational rules.

(2)   a.   Zhangsan bi Lisi gao.
            Zhangsan BI Lisi tall
            'Zhangsan is taller than Lisi.'

       a.' [$_s$ [$_{s1}$ Zhangsan x gao] bi [$_{s2}$ Lisi y gao]] V=BIJIAO]

       b.   John is taller than Mary.

       b.' [$_s$ [$_{s1}$ John x much tall] than [$_{s2}$ Mary y much tall]] V=MORE]

While the structure of (2b') is empirically supported by English subcomparatives, as in (3),[4] where one can find two predicates and a degree gap in the *than*-clause, (2a') is not adequate for Chinese since the Chinese equivalents to (3) are impossible, as shown in (4). This indicates that Chinese CCs do not involve two clauses paired up with two gradable predicates and an abstract predicate like (2b'). For this reason, Fu's analysis has been rejected by other works on CCs in Chinese.

(3)   a.   This table is *wider* [than that shelf is *tall*].

       b.   John bought more candies [than Mary ate cakes].

(4)   a.   *Zhe zhang zhuozi *kuan* bi na   ge shujia *gao*.
            this CL   table   wide BI that CL shelf tall

       b.   *Zhangsan mai le   tang bi Lisi chi le   dangao duo.
            Zhangsan buy ASP candy BI Lisi eat ASP cake   more

2.2. A SIMPLEX STRUCTURE

In more recent studies, comparatives in Chinese are analyzed as involving two phrases with *bi* taken as a functional category and the gradable adjective as the main predicate (Xiang 2005; Erlewine 2007; Xiong 2007; Lin 2009; Gu and Guo 2008, 2009). In these studies, the derivations of comparatives diverge, as the role of *bi* is defined differently.

---

[3] Fu points out that in English, the abstract predicate can be MORE, SAME, or LESS, the choice of which depends on variable quantifiers in comparatives of superiority, equality or inferiority, i.e., whether x > y, or x = y, or x < y. Fu also assumes that in Chinese comparatives of superiority, the abstract predicate is BIJIAO, meaning *compare*.

[4] Sub-comparatives involve multi-perspectival comparisons of the sort encoded in so-called comparative sub-deletion constructions (Kennedy 2009). In these constructions, two propositions containing relevant degrees are being compared or have undergone quantifier raising (Heim 1985; Corver 1993).

Xiang (2005) focuses initially on the sentences in (5).[5]

(5)   a.   Zhangsan gao Lisi liang gongfen.
           Zhangsan tall Lisi two   centimeter
           'Zhangsan is two centimeters taller than Lisi.'
      b.   Zhangsan bi Lisi gao liang gongfen.
           Zhangsan BI Lisi tall two   centimeter
           'Zhangsan is two centimeters taller than Lisi.'

She defines (5a) as involving a three-place predicate, which relates the external argument, the comparee *Zhangsan*, to the two internal degree arguments, the standard
degree argument *Lisi* and the differential degree argument *liang gongfen* ('two centimeters'). To account for the structural position of the three arguments and to derive
the correct surface word order, Xiang proposes, following Larson's shell analysis
(1988, 1991), that there is a phonetically null degree morpheme meaning *exceed*. This
degree morpheme initially merges with the two internal arguments, *Lisi* and *liang
gongfen*, which are projected respectively in the Spec and Complement positions of a
lower DegP. The degree morpheme *exceed* then internally merges with the adjective
in A via head movement. The standard degree argument *Lisi* eventually moves to the
[Spec, AP] to satisfy the EPP feature, yielding a small-clause like structure at the AP
level. Finally, the complex head *exceed-tall* moves to the upper Deg head to introduce
the external argument. The derivation is illustrated in (6a).

Xiang's attempt is to provide a unified analysis for both (5a) and (5b), the derivation of
which is shown in (6a) and (6b). Compared with (5a), (5b) contains an overt morpheme
bi. *Bi* directly merges into the head of the upper DegP, whereas the null degree morpheme
exceed moves to merge with the adjective A but the complex [A-*exceed*] does not move
further into the higher Deg, which is already filled by *bi*. The standard degree argument
Lisi eventually moves to the [Spec, AP] to satisfy the EPP feature.

(6)   a.

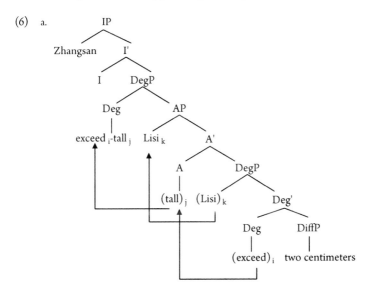

[5] The examples in (5) and their derivations in (6) are adopted from Xiang (2005: 191–192) with
minor modifications.

b.

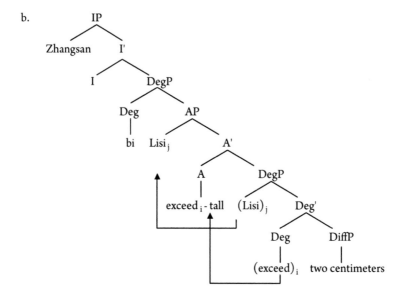

Xiang's analysis treats comparative constructions as involving a three-place predicate and attempts to derivationally relate (5a) and (5b) with the same structure. But the analysis encounters several problems.

The first problem has to do with the proper semantic interpretation of the AP in the structure. As can be observed in (6), AP as a lexical projection is sandwiched between the two functional DegP projections.[6] Under such an analysis, the AP forms a small clause, with *Lisi* as its subject. This would yield an interpretation [AP Lisi exceeds two centimeters], contra to the intended meaning of (5), where *Lisi's* height is actually exceeded by two centimeters by *Zhangsan's* height.

The second problem is related to the structural treatment of the *bi*-phrase. If *bi* in (6b) merges with the whole chunk of AP, as proposed by Xiang, it remains puzzling how the analysis would be able to explain the facts shown in (7b) and (7c), which are replies to (7a) where *bi* and *Lisi* can be extracted as one constituent, leaving the rest of the elements *gao liang gongfen* behind.[7]

(7)   a.   Zhangsan bi shei gao liang gongfen?
           Zhangsan BI who tall two centimeter
           'Who is Zhangsan two centimeters taller than?'

      b.   [Bi Lisi] (gao liang gongfen).
           BI Lisi   tall two   centimeter
           '(Two centimeters taller) than Lisi.'

---

[6] Such an analysis runs counter to current theories of functional projection of lexical items, which assume that functional projections uniformly occur above lexical projections (Abney 1987; Corver 1997; Borer 2005; Bobaljik 2012).

[7] The facts in (7) are initially observed in Liu (1996) and Lin (2009). In (7b) and (7c), the *comparee* 'Zhangsan' has undergone *pro*-drop.

   c. [Bi Lisi], huozhe [bi Wangwu], (gao liang gongfen).
       BI Lisis or   BI Wangwu   tall two centimeter
       '(Two centimeters taller) than Lisi or (two centimeters taller) than Wangwu.'

The third problem concerns the parallel treatment of (5a) and (5b), as presented in (6a) and (6b). The following examples demonstrate that the two sentences do not exhibit systematic parallel structural behavior in the presence of the universal quantifier *dou* ('all'):

(8) a. Tamen *dou* [bi Lisi] gao yi tou.
        they   all   BI Lisi tall one head
        'They are all taller than Lisi by a head.'

     b. Tamen [bi Lisi] *dou* gao yi tou.
        they   BI Lisi all tall one head
        'They are all taller than Lisi by a head.'

     c. Lisi [bi tamen] *dou* gao yi tou.
        Lisi BI they   all tall one head

(9) a. Tamen *dou* gao Lisi yi tou.
        they   all tall Lisi one head
        'They all are taller than Lisi by a head.'

     b. *Tamen [gao Lisi] *dou* yi tou.
        they   tall Lisi all one head

     c. *Lisi [gao tamen] *dou* yi tou.
        Lisi tall they   all one head

A fundamental requirement of *dou* in Chinese is that it can only occur in the preverbal position following the NPs it quantifies over. As shown in (8), *dou* is able to quantify over the NP as long as it is to the left of *dou*. So *dou* can quantify over a plural subject not adjacent to it, as noted by Cheng (1995) and illustrated in (8a), or a plural NP in the *bi*-phrase, as in (8c). Based on Xiang's analysis in (6), the pattern observed in (8) should apply to (9). In (8b, c), *dou* occurs following the *bi*-phrase; however, in the corresponding (9b, c), the sentences are ungrammatical. This questions the accuracy of Xiang's analysis. In other words, (5a) and (5b) involve separate structures.

One more problem has to do with the attempt to draw a parallelism between a three-place predicate and a comparative construction. Xiang parallels the transitive comparative to a three-place predicate, but the argument structure of a three-place predicate like *give* is apparently different from an adjective like *tall*. It has been proposed that gradable adjectives are associated with a degree scale such that the degrees on the scale are ordered by an asymmetric ordering relation (Bierwisch 1989; Kennedy 2006). A well-known property of gradable adjectives that are used predicatively is that the values of the degrees may vary depending on a number of factors such as the properties of the subject, the types of the adjectives, and so forth (Sapir 1944; Cresswell 1976; Klein 1980; Cruse 1986). Examples in (10) illustrate how properties of the subjects affect the interpretation of the adjective.

(10)   a.   Kobe is tall.

    b.   The building is tall.

    c.   The tree is tall.

    d.   The bookshelf is tall.

Apparently, the value of the degrees on the scale of the property of height triggered by the gradable adjective *tall* in each case varies with the referent on which the adjective is predicated. In (8) the interpretation of the gradable property of height characterized by the adjective *tall* is derived from the context, that is, the degree of tallness is measured against a relevant referent or referents, either in the mind of the speaker or in the discourse. However, the context dependency in interpreting (10) does not guarantee that any value of degree is possible given an appropriate context. *Tall* in (10) cannot mean any degree of tallness. As noted by Sapir (1944) and Bresnan (1973), the adjective *tall* in (10) has a positive meaning interpreted as *tall to a high degree*. It is thus assumed that there is a degree argument in the argument structure of adjectives (von Stechow 1984; Kennedy 2006). So the triadic relations involved in a normal three-place predicate and an adjective in a comparative are incomparable.

A final problem has to do with the incorporation in (6). Xiang analyzes *exceed* as an affix realizing the functional head Deg. Being an affix, *exceed* has to incorporate into the nearest head, the lexical head A in the upper level, and then move into another functional head Deg. Such a sequence of movements would be considered illicit in any literature on incorporation, as the movement creates a chain containing mixed heads: the lexical head A is sandwiched by two functional heads, Degs, resulting in a violation of the Head Movement Constraint discussed in Li (1990). Li observes in causative constructions that trigger verb incorporation, head movement cannot take a lexical category and move it through a functional category before attaching it to another lexical category. Li's observation is generalized by Baker (2003: 53) as the Proper Head Movement Generalization, which states that a lexical head A cannot move to a functional head B and then to a lexical head C.

Other works can also be found, such as Erlewine (2007), Xiong (2007), Lin (2009), and Gu and Guo (2008, 2009), which treat *bi* as variants of functional categories. But problems arise for all such accounts. If lexical items are unspecified for all grammatical properties and it is the job of functional heads to specify these grammatical properties (Borer 2005), we expect that the functional heads that support the skeleton of the structure will always have to be present and projected. However, with a clear context, the *bi*-phrase can be omitted in a question-answer pair shown in (11) and (12), where *gao* is still interpreted as a gradable adjective with comparative meaning, due to the context dependency effect, *à la* von Stechow (1984) and Kennedy (2006).

(11)   a.   Zhangsan   he   Lisi, shei gao?
         Zhangshan and Lisi who tall
         'Zhangsan and Lisi, who is taller?'

    b.   Zhangsan gao.
         Zhangsan tall
         'Zhangsan is taller (than Lisi).'

(12) a. Zhangsan he   Lisi, shei gao yi dian?
       Zhangsan and Lisi who tall a bit
       'Zhangsan and Lisi, who is a bit taller?'

    b. Zhangsan gao yi dian.
       Zhangsan tall a bit
       'Zhangsan is a bit taller (than Lisi).'

These examples cast doubts on treating *bi* as a Deg head (Xiang 2005; Xiong 2007), a light verb (Erlewine 2007), a degree operator (Lin 2009), or part of a complex predicate (Gu and Guo 2008, 2009), for they reveal that the presence and absence of the *bi*-phrase do not affect the comparative interpretation of the construction.

The discussion so far shows that past attempts at analyzing Chinese CCs have centered on the treatment of *bi*. In the following we will review a number of relevant discussions of *bi* as a way to probe the structure of the *bi* phrase.

2.3. ON THE ANALYSIS OF *BI*

In many earlier studies, *bi* is viewed as a preposition (Lü et al. 1980; LaPolla 1990; Paul 1993; Liu 1996), but few studies justify its prepositional status, except for Liu's work (1996), which takes *bi* as a preposition assigning case to the *standard*. No substantial discussions have been offered, however, to justify the prepositional status of *bi*.

2.3.1. *The Indeterminacy of* bi

Guo (2012) tackles issues surrounding the grammatical status of *bi* by casting it into the investigation of the syntax and semantics of Chinese CCs. She makes the following observations concerning the structural distribution of *bi*. As reflected in the (b) examples in (13)–(15), evaluative or speaker-oriented adverbs are not restricted to the position preceding *bi*, they can also occur following the *bi* phrase:

(13) a. Zhangsan *kending*   [bi Lisi] gao liang gongfen.
       Zhangsan definitely BI Lisi tall two   centimeter
       'Zhangsan definitely is two centimeters taller than Lisi.'

    b. Zhangsan [bi Lisi] *kending*   gao liang gongfen.
       Zhangsan BI Lisi definitely tall two   centimeter
       'Zhangsan is definitely two centimeters taller than Lisi.'

(14) a. Zhangsan *xianran*   [bi Lisi] gao liang gongfen.
       Zhangsan obviously BI Lisi tall two   centimeter
       'Zhangsan obviously is two centimeters taller than Lisi.'

    b. Zhangsan [bi Lisi] *xianran* gao gao liang gongfen.
       Zhangsan BI Lisi obviously   tall two   centimeter
       'Zhangsan is obviously two centimeters taller than Lisi.'

(15) a. Zhangsan *xingkui*   [bi Lisi] gao liang gongfen.
       Zhangsan fortunately BI Lisi tall two   centimeter
       'Zhangsan fortunately is two centimeters taller than Lisi.'

    b. Zhangsan [bi Lisi] *xingkui*   gao liang gongfen.
       Zhangsan BI Lisi fortunately tall two   centimeter
       'Zhangsan is fortunately two centimeters taller than Lisi.'

These adverbs, which express the speaker's attitudes toward an eventuality, are VP external adjuncts (Alexiadou 1997). According to Cinque (1999), Tenny (2000), and Ernst (2008), speaker-oriented adverbs express the speaker's strong commitment to the proposition conveyed in a sentence, and they occupy a position higher than the core event depicted by the verb phrase. If *bi* heads the *v*P, as argued by Erlewine (2007) and Gu and Guo (2008, 2009), then the *v*P should fall within the core semantic zone of the verb phrase and consistently follow the speaker-oriented adverbs. The fact that they can permute with the *bi*-phrase in the (b) examples of (13)–(15) indicates that the *bi*-phrase actually can fall outside the semantic zone of the core event depicted by the verb phrase. In other words, *bi* is not a functional head contained in the verb phrase.

In addition to its ability to permute with speaker-oriented adverbs, the *bi*-phrase can also occur on either side of the causal *wh*-phrase *zenme*, which is similar to the English 'how come,' as discussed in Tsai and Chang (2003).

(16) a. Zhangsan *zenme hui*   bi Lisi gao liang gongfen?
          Zhangsan how   could BI Lisi tall two   centimeter
          'How come Zhangsan could be two centimeters taller than Lisi?'

      b. Zhangsan bi Lisi *zenme hui*   gao liang gongfen?
          Zhangsan BI Lisi how   could tall two   centimeter
          'How come Zhangsan could be two centimeters taller than Lisi?'

According to Tsai and Chang, the causal *zenme* is in a pre-epistemic modal position. The distribution of the *bi*-phrase in (16) further illustrates its structural flexibility, that is, it is not confined to a verb phrase.

Additional evidence in support of our view that *bi* has a unique status in the structure of CCs can be drawn from the behavior of a set of prepositions known as comitatives. The phrases headed by these comitatives pattern with the *bi*-phrase; they cannot be easily fronted over the *comparee*:[8]

(17) a. *[Bi pingguo] xiangjiao rongyi xiaohua.
          BI apple   banana   easy   digest

----

[8] Recall that in (7b, c) the *bi*-phrase is shown to behave like one constituent. (17a) shows that it cannot be fronted crossing the *comparee*. At first glance, it may appear that the *bi*-phrase in (7b, c) and the ones in (17a) and (18a) exhibit contrastive behavior. We want to point out here that as replies to the question in (7a), repeated here in (i), the *comparee* in (7b, c) is omitted due to *pro*-drop. Recovering the dropped *comparee* will allow us to have complete sentences as in (ii), but not those in (iii). These examples suffice to say that the *bi*-phrase cannot be fronted over the *comparee*. So apparently, the problem of (iii) is identical with that of the (a)-examples in (17)–(21). The *bi*-phrase, as well as the phrases headed by other comitatives, cannot be fronted crossing the *comparee*.

i.   Zhangsan bi shei gao liang gongfen?
      Zhangsan BI who tall two   centimeter
      'Who is Zhangsan two centimeters taller than?'

ii.   a. Zhangsan bi Lisi gao liang gongfen.
          Zhangsan BI Lisi tall two   centimeter
          'Zhangsan is two centimeters taller than Lisi.'

b. Xiangjiao [bi pingguo] rongyi xiaohua.
banana   BI apple   easy   digest
'Bananas are easier to digest than apples.'

(18) a. *[Bi wo] ta gao yi   tou.
BI I   he tall one head

b. Ta [bi wo] gao yi   tou.
he BI I   tall one head
'He is one head taller than me.'

(19) a. *[He   wo] ta shi zhouli.
with me she BE sister-in-law

b. Ta [he wo] shi zhouli.
she with me BI sister-in-law
'She and I are sisters-in-law.'

(20) a. *[Gen wo] ta he-jiao le   yi men ke.
with me she co-teach ASP one CL   course

b. Ta [gen wo] he-jiao le   yi men ke.
she with me co-teach ASP one CL   course
'She cotaught a course with me.'

(21) a. *[Tong yi   dui] jia dui   zhengzai   duilei.
with B team   A team   in progress compete

b. Jia dui [tong yi dui] zhengzai   duilei.
A team   with B team in progress compete
'Team A is competing against Team B.'

b. Zhangsan bi Lisi, huozhe bi Wangwu, gao liang gongfen.
Zhangsan BI Lisi or   BI Wangwu tall two   centimeter
'Zhangsan is two centimeters taller than Lisi or he is two centimeters taller than Wangwu.'

iii. a. *bi Lisi Zhangsan gao liang gongfen.
BI Lisi Zhangsan tall two   centimeter

b. *bi Lisi, huozhe bi Wangwu, Zhangsan gao liang gongfen.
BI Lisi or   BI Wangwu Zhangsan tall two   centimeter

The above behavior of the *bi*-phrase lends support to our ensuing analysis in section 2.3.3 that the *comparee* and the *standard* reside initially in a complex structure headed by *bi*.

Notice that the comitative phrases in (19)–(21) can also appear in an answer with a dropped *comparee*:

iv. a. Zhangsan [he/gen/tong shei] yiyang gao?
Zhangsan with   who same   tall
'Who is Zhangsan as tall as?'

b. [He/gen/tong Lisi] yiyang gao.
with   Lisi same   tall
(Lit.) 'As tall as Lisi.'

We will show that our analysis of the *bi*-phrase can uniformly capture the behavior of all the comitative phrases covered in (19)–(21) and (iv).

A single semantic sense can be attributed to this common behavior observed in the two types of phrases: the noun phrases following *bi* and the comitative prepositions all express a sort of target or a companion. This differentiates them from preposition phrases expressing location, source, or goal, as in (22)–(24), where fronting is possible.

(22) a. Wo [PP zai caochang]   pengdao le   yi ge lao pengyou.
          I   at playground meet   ASP one CL old friend
          'I met an old friend on the playground.'

    b. [PP Zai caochang], wo pengdao le   yi ge lao pengyou.
          at playground I meet   ASP one CL old friend
          'On the playground, I met an old friend.'

(23) a. Ta [PP cong tushuguan] jie   le   henduo shu.
          he from library   borrow ASP many   book
          'He borrowed many books from the library.'

    b. [PP Cong tushuguan], ta jie   le   henduo shu.
          from library   he borrow ASP many   book
          'From the library, he borrowed many books.'

(24) a. Ta [PP gei women xuexiao] juan   le   henduo qian.
          he to we   school donate ASP many   money
          'He donated a lot of money to our school.'

    b. [PP Gei women xuexiao], ta juan   le   henduo qian.
          to we   school he donate ASP many   money
          'To our school, he donated a lot of money.'

If prepositions fall into different semantic subcategories expressing time, location, manner, comitative, comparative, and so on (Li 2001), it is not surprising to see that they behave differently.

It is natural for the *bi*-phrase to pattern with comitative preposition phrases headed by *he* ('with'), *gen* ('with'), *tong* ('with'), and so on. Comitatives express an accompanimental relation between two nominals in the same eventuality. The difference between the comitative phrases and the *bi*-phrases lies in the division of labor. As shown in (25), in canonical comparative constructions, the *comparee* is always accompanied with the target of comparison, the *standard*: with comparatives of superiority, the *standard* is introduced by *bi*; with comparatives of equality, the *standard* is introduced by the comitatives. The complementarity of the two types of *standard*-introducer hence is explained, which provides evidence that *bi* should be treated on a par with the comitatives.

(25) a. Zhangsan *bi* Lisi gao.
          Zhangsan BI Lisi tall
          'Zhangsan is taller than Lisi.'

    b. Zhangsan *he/gen/tong* Lisi yiyang gao.
          Zhangsan with   Lisi same   tall
          'Zhangsan is as tall as Lisi.'

Grouping *bi* with the set of comitatives paves the way to a unified structural analysis of comparatives.

2.3.2. The Structure of Comitatives

Based on Kayne's (1994) analysis of English comitative structures, Zhang (2007) identifies two types of *with* comitatives, the symmetrical comitative as in (26), and the asymmetrical one as in (27), and provides a novel analysis for their respective structures in (28) (Zhang 2007: 152, 156).

(26)   Symmetrical comitative

    a.   John fell in love with Jane.

    b.   Peter compared the beer with the milk.

    c.   John quarreled with his wife.

    d.   Robin combined butter with sugar.

(27)   Asymmetrical comitative

    a.   John baked a cake with Mary.

    b.   John saw the insects with his glasses.

    c.   John will drink beer with Bill by his side.

(28)   a.   b.

The analysis makes the following assumptions. Each of the DPs in (28) is a nominal complex containing two internal DPs, $[_{DP}$ DP$_1$ with DP$_2]$. Adopting Kayne's (1994) analysis for the symmetrical comitative structure in (28a), Zhang further assumes that the head *with* in (28a) is by nature a mixed element. It bears a set of features, categorial feature [D], formal feature [φ $_{plural}$], and Case feature [Case assigning]. With its D feature and number (plural) feature, it is on a par with nominals, and with its Case assigning feature, it is like a preposition. Through feature checking, *with* in D assigns an Accusative Case to DP$_2$, and this eliminates the Case feature of the complex nominal DP. When this DP serves as the external argument of a relevant predicate, it is base-generated in the Spec of the relevant VP. As it has no Case feature left, it cannot move to check the Nominative Case feature in the Spec of TP. Rather, it is DP$_1$ that moves out of the complex DP to check the Nominative Case feature. In the asymmetrical comitative structure (28b), *with* is a regular preposition. It heads a PP that is adjoined to DP$_1$. The preposition *with* has the same Case feature as *with* in (28a), but it has a different set of categorial feature, [-N, -V]. Being the head of an adjunct, the preposition *with* does not determine the categorial feature, or number and Case feature of the complex DP, whose relevant features are determined by the head of DP$_1$.

As shown in (28), it is the dual status of *with* that gives rise to the structural differentiation in relation to the two internal DPs. Although in both structures DP$_2$ is the complement of *with*, there is a clear distinction in the two DP$_2$ with their relation to the respective complex nominal DP regarding the number feature. In (28a), *with* heads the complex DP with DP_1 in the specifier possessing the same property degrees as DP_2 in the complement, so the entire complex DP is necessarily plural, regardless whether DP_1 is plural or singular, thereby accounting for the default plural construal of the complex DP, as observed initially by Kayne (1994). In (28b), *with* is not the head of the complex nominal DP; it heads a PP that is adjoined to DP_1. As DP_2 is inside the adjunct PP, it does not add its property degrees to DP_1 within DP. Accordingly, there is no default plural interpretation for the number feature of the asymmetrical comitative complex DP, and the number feature of DP is solely determined by DP_1.

Zhang (2007) offers an array of syntactic diagnoses to differentiate the two types of comitatives. What is important to us here is her argument that the plural number feature of the symmetrical comitative DP complex is semantically required by a predicate of which the DP is an external argument. Such a predicate is either collective or relational. In other words, (28a) will occur in a predication that brings about an eventuality involving a plural argument or a singular argument accompanied by another argument/other arguments instantiated by DP_2. In contrast, (28b) will occur in a predication that brings about an eventuality where the adjunct *with*-phrase is optional, as DP_2 is only an appurtenant in the relevant eventuality. This structure will apply to arguments selected by verbs or predicates with no plural number requirement on DP_1.

In Zhang's (2010) theory of coordination, the Chinese comitatives such as *he, gen,* and *tong* seen in the (b) examples of (19)–(21) and (25) are not prepositions; they are coordinators projecting a similar structure as the English symmetrical comitatives in (28a). These comitatives also head a nominal DP complex containing DP_1 and DP_2. As argued in Zhang (2007), when such a nominal complex occurs in preverbal position, it has a thematic relation with a collective or relational predicate, which requires its argument to be plural. So if DP_1 is singular, the presence of DP_2 is obligatory, for DP_1 and DP_2 in the nominal DP complex contribute their properties equally in the relevant eventuality. The predicates in (19)–(21), repeated here as (29), exhibit such a behavior—omission of the comitative phrase yields ungrammatical results:

(29) a.   Wo *(he   ta) shi zhouli.
           I   with her BE sister-in-law
           'She *(and I) are sisters-in-law.'

      b.   Ta *(gen wo) he-jiao le   yi men ke.
           she with me co-teach ASP one CL course
           'She co-taught a course *(with me).'

      c.   Jia dui   *(tong yi dui) zhengzai   duilei.
           A Team   with B team in progress compete
           'Team A is competing *(against Team B).'

The same pattern is found in comparatives of equality where the *standard* DP is introduced by the same set of comitatives:

(30) Zhangsan *(he/gen/tong Lisi) yiyang gao.
      Zhangsan with   Lisi same   tall
      'Zhangsan is as tall as Lisi.'

In (30) both the *comparee* 'Zhangsan' and the *standard* 'Lisi' are participants of the single eventuality, hence the obligatory presence of the comitative phrase.

If *he/gen/tong* in (30) are coordinators like the English symmetrical comitatives, they are not prepositions, and they occur in a structure like (28a), a complex nominal containing two DPs, as postulated in Zhang (2007, 2010). As these comitative coordinators introduce the *standard* in comparatives of equality just as *bi* does in comparatives of superiority, their complementary distribution entails that they share the same structural relation with the *standard*. In the following, we will pursue an analysis for *bi* along the same line.

2.3.3. Defining bi

It was pointed out in section 2.2, regarding (11b)–(12b) as an answer to a question, that the omission of the *bi*-phrase does not affect the comparative interpretation of the sentence, and this can be attributed to the positive interpretation of the gradable adjective, a result of context dependency effect of comparativity, that is, the *standard* can be identified in the context. This asserts that a comparative eventuality necessarily involves two participants, that is, plural arguments, a *comparee* and a *standard*. So under normal circumstances, with comparatives of superiority, the presence of the *bi*-phrase is obligatory, just as the case with other comitative phrases seen in (29)–(30). Having equal roles in the same eventuality, the *comparee* and the *standard* bear the same thematic relation with the comparative predicate. This is in line with the argument made in Zhang's (2007: 141, (26)) diagnosis regarding the symmetrical comitative structure that in the following sentence the two DPs in the DP complex bear a single thematic relation with the passivized verb:

(31)   John was killed with Bill (Like John, Bill was the victim of a killer).

The same can be observed in the following comparatives of superiority in (32)–(34), as well as comparatives of equality in (35):

(32)   a.   Zhangsan bi Lisi geng bei jiaolian kanhao.
            Zhangsan bi Lisi even BEI coach   think highly of
            (Lit.) 'Zhangsan is more highly thought of by the coach than Lisi is.'
            (Zhangsan is regarded by the coach to be more promising than Lisi).

       Cf.: Jiaolian hen kanhao   Zhangsan.
             couch   very think   highly of Zhangsan
             'The coach thinks highly of Zhangsan.' (The coach regards Zhangsan to be promising.)

       b.   Zhangsan bi Lisi hai bei dajia   qiaobuqi.
            Zhangsan BI Lisi still BEI everybody despise
            (Lit.) 'Zhangsan is being more despised by everybody than Lisi is.'

       Cf.: Dajia   dou qiaobuqi Zhangsan.
             everybody all despise Zhangsan
             'Everybody despises Zhangsan.'

(33)   a.   Dizhen   bi shuizai hai ke-pa.
            earthquake BI flood   still can-afraid
            'Earthquake is even more terrifying than flood.'

b. Xiao che bi da che rongyi kai.
    small car BI big car easy   drive
    'Small cars drive more easily than big cars.'

(34) a. Taozi bi caomei   hai rongyi lan.
          peach BI strawberry still easy   rotten
          'Peaches go rotten even more easily than strawberries.'

b. Xiao shu bi da shu rongyi duan.
    small tree BI big tree easy   break
    'Small trees break more easily than big trees.'

(35) a. Zhangsan he/gen/tong Lisi yiyang bei dajia   qiaobuqi.
          Zhangsan with   Lisi same   BEI everybody despise
          'Zhangsan is as being despised by everybody as Lisi is.'

b. Dizhen   he/gen/tong shuizai yiyang ke-pa.
    earthquake with   flood   same   can-afraid
    'Earthquake is as terrifying as flood.'

c. Xiao che he/gen/tong da che yiyang rongyi kai.
    small car with   big car same   easy   drive
    'Small cars drive as easily as big cars.'

d. Taozi he/gen/tong caomei   yiyang rongyi lan.
    peach with   strawberry same   easy   rotten
    'Peaches go rotten as easily as strawberries.'

In (32)–(34) the respective *comparees* 'Zhangsan, dizhen, xiao che, taozi' and 'xiao shu' and the corresponding *standards* introduced by *bi* 'Lisi, shuizai, da che, caomei,' and 'da shu' have the same thematic relation with respective predicates, the passives 'kanhao' and 'qiaobuqi' in (32), the middles (Tao 2011) 'ke-pa' and 'kai' in (33), and the unaccusatives 'lan' and 'duan' in (34). (35) shows that the same applies to the *comparee* and the *standard* in comparatives of equality.

So *bi* has the same status as the comitatives *he/gen/tong*. This now allows for a uni-fied account for all the *standard*-introducers in CCs. Such elements occupy the head position of the same complex nominal structure as in (28a) with the *comparee* in DP_1 and the *standard* in DP_2. The head D can be taken by *bi* as well as *gen/he/tong*:

(36)

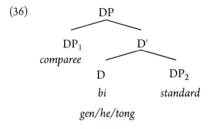

Zhang (2010: 110), following Zhu (1982: 176), points out that DP_1 and DP_2 in the nominal complex can be reversed without affecting the basic meaning of the construction. This is true with the *comparee* and *standard* DPs in comparatives of equality, but not with those in comparatives of superiority:

(37)   a.   [$_{DP}$ [$_{DP1}$ Zhangsan] he/gen/tong [$_{DP2}$ Lisi]] yiyang gao.

       b.   [$_{DP}$ [$_{DP1}$ Lisi] he/gen/tong [$_{DP2}$ Zhangsan]] yiyang gao.

The two sentences in (37) are synonymous, both meaning that the *comparee* and the *standard* are of the same height. It is not the case with the sentences in (38), where the height of the *comparee* exceeds that of the *standard*, so the *comparee* and *standard* cannot reverse order:

(38)   a.   Zhangsan bi Lisi gao.

       b.   Lisi bi Zhangsan gao.

Here the relation between DP_1 and DP_2 is one of subtraction, the former being the *minuend* and the latter the *subtrahend*, and the result is a difference.

2.4. THE INTERNAL STRUCTURE OF CHINESE COMPARATIVES

Having reached an analysis that has determined the structural status of *bi*, we now proceed to the internal structure of Chinese comparatives. We make reference to Guo's (2012) recent analysis of the Chinese comparative predicate structure and incorporate our above account of the nominal complex DP, treating the *comparee* and the *standard* of both comparatives of superiority and equality in a unified way.

Assuming the functional projection of DegP above the lexical item of the adjective (Abney 1987; Corver 1997; Kennedy 1999; Heim 2000) and following den Dikken, Gu, and Guo's (2010) argument that a comparative operator COMP adjoined to DegP is responsible for the comparative reading of the adjective, Guo (2012) makes the following proposal for the syntactic projection of comparative predication. The presence of the COMP operator leads to two exponents of the Deg head in Chinese, realized by a bound morpheme *-chu* ('exceed'/'surpass') and a word *yiyang* ('same') to express comparatives of superiority and of equality, respectively. With the COMP operator responsible for the comparative interpretation of the adjective, a differential phrase (DiffP) occupies the specifier position of DegP to express the difference value computed after comparison. Guo proposes that a gradable adjective projects the partial structure in a comparative construction as illustrated in (39):[9]

---

[9] (39) does not mean a gradable adjective in Chinese expressing positive meaning, i.e., *A to a high degree* analogous to *John is tall* in English, as discussed in Sapir (1944), Bresnan (1973), von Stechow (1984), and Kennedy (2006), has a different structure. Guo (2012) contends that in the absence of the COMP operator, the Deg head is filled by a semantically bleached degree adverb *hen* in Chinese, giving rise to the positive interpretation of the adjective. So *hen* has the function

(39)

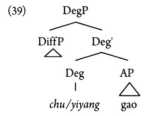

As noted by Guo, the morpheme -*chu* occurs optionally and restrictedly in a comparative involving dimensional adjectives such as *tall, long,* and *wide,* as in (40a–c), but not evaluative adjectives such as those in (40d–f).

(40) a. Zhangsan bi Lisi gao (-*chu*) liang gongfen.
      Zhangsan BI Lisi tall exceed two centimeter
      'Zhangsan is two centimeters taller than Lisi.'

      b. Zhe tiao kuzi bi na tiao kuzi chang (-*chu*) liang gongfen.
      this CL pant BI that CL pant long exceed two centimeter
      'This pair of pants is two centimeters longer than that one.'

      c. Zhe zhang zhuozi bi na zhang zhuozi kuan (-*chu*) shi gongfen.
      this CL   table BI that CL   table wide exceed ten centimeter
      'This table is ten centimeters wider than that one.'

      d. Zhangsan bi Lisi qinfen (*-*chu*) shi bei.
      Zhangsan BI Lisi diligent   exceed ten times
      'Zhangsan is ten times more diligent than Lisi.'

      e. Xiaofang bi Xiaohua piaoliang (*-*chu*) shi bei.
      Xiaofang BI Xiaohua pretty   exceed ten times
      'Xiaofang is ten times prettier than Xiaohua.'

      f. Xiaofang bi Xiaohua congming (*-*chu*) henduo.
      Xiaofang BI Xiaohua smart   exceed a lot
      'Xiaofang is a lot smarter than Xiaohua.'

Guo thus assumes that there is an abstract *CHU* which heads DegP in all cases of comparatives of superiority, though the abstract *CHU* can only have its phonological exponent -*chu* when dimensional adjectives are involved and measure phrases are present.[10] In comparatives of equality as exemplified in (41), *yiyang* realizes the head

analogous to a *standard.* This explains why a degree adverb does not co-occur with an explicit *standard*: * *Zhangsan bi Lisi hen gao* (* Zhangsan is very tall than Lisi'.) In other words, the Deg head has three instantiations: *hen* in the absence of the COMP operator, yielding a positive interpretation; *chu* and *yiyang* in the presence of the COMP operator, responsible respectively for the superiority and equality interpretations.

[10] For a detailed analysis of the grammar of measurement in comparatives, see Grano and Kennedy (2012), and the discussion of Guo (2012) on a different view.

of the DegP and the value of difference after comparison is zero, hence the absence of an explicit measurement in the DiffP.[11]

(41) a. Zhangsan he   Lisi *yiyang* gao.
          Zhangsan with Lisi same   tall
          'Zhangsan is as tall as Lisi.'

      b. Zhangsan gen   Lisi *yiyang* yonggan.
          Zhangsan with Lisi same   brave
          'Zhangsan is as brave as Lisi.'

      c. Zhangsan tong Lisi *yiyang* pang.
          Zhangsan with Lisi same   fat.
          'Zhangsan is as fat as Lisi.'

With a modification of Guo's (2012) analysis[12] of the DegP, we posit that a gradable adjective, when it occurs as a comparative predicate, projects the structure illustrated in (42):

(42)

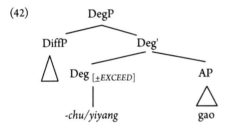

DegP is the functional projection of the lexical item A. It turns the property denoted by A into a degree of the property denoted by A. (42) differs slightly from (39) in that the Deg head in (42) bears a semantic feature *EXCEED* with binary feature values. The [+] value is realized by the affixal -*chu*, either overtly or covertly. When the feature value is [-], it is realized by a free morpheme *yiyang*.

---

[11] Paris (2012) argues that *yiyang* can be decomposed into the numeral *yi* ('one') and the classifier *yang* ('sort'), meaning *one/a single sort* and *yiyang* functions as the degree modifier in a comparative. If this is correct, there is no *prima facie* reason that this modifier cannot be optional. As shown in (i), the absence of *yiyang* renders the sentences ungrammatical. Under the analysis assumed here, *yiyang* heads the functional DegP, hence its obligatory presence.

i.   a.   Zhangsan he Lisi *(yiyang) gao.
      b.   Zhangsan gen Lisi *(yiyang) yonggan.
      c.   Zhangsan tong Lisi *(yiyang) pang.

[12] In Guo (2012: 236), it is assumed that there is a double layer of DegPs projected on top of the AP. The *standard* is merged in Spec of the higher DegP. The *comparee* alone is an argument of the comparative predicate, merged in the Spec of the PredP. Under the analysis proposed here, the *comparee* and the *standard* form one complex DP initially merged in the Spec of PredP, as they are the dual arguments of the comparative predicate. See the structure in (45) and (51) in the ensuing discussion.

The postulation of -*chu* and *yiyang* as exponents of the Deg head is not accidental. It is like a coin with two sides. Conceptually, whenever a comparison takes place in a certain dimension between degrees of relevant properties of two entities, one expects two results: either the degree of property ascribed to one entity exceeds that of the other, or the degree of property ascribed to one entity is the same as that of the other. To be precise, the relation between the *comparee* and the *standard* is either one of the *minuend* versus the *subtrahend* or one of the equal entities, as mentioned in section 2.3.3.

With -*chu* and *yiyang* as two instantiations of the head of DegP in the presence of the COMP operator, DiffP in the structure of (42) expresses the difference value obtained after comparison. Notice that the overt realization of [+EXCEED] by the morpheme -*chu* is confined to dimensional adjectives, as shown in the examples in (40). It can be predicted that when [+EXCEED] is spelled out as -*chu* in (40a–c), the DiffP must be made overt, and when the [+EXCEED] feature does not have overt phonetic realization, DiffP optionally occurs with dimensional adjectives. The prediction is borne out as shown in (43) and (44), respectively. Hence the correlation between the Deg head and the DiffP in its specifier receives a satisfying explanation.

(43) a. Zhangsan bi Lisi gao-chu   *(liang gongfen).
          Zhangsan BI Lisi tall exceed   two centimeter
          'Zhangsan is two centimeters taller than Lisi.'

      b. Zhe tiao kuzi bi na   tiao kuzi chang-chu   *(liang gongfen).
          this CL pant BI that CL pant long exceed   two centimeter
          'This pair of pants is two centimeters longer than that one.'

      c. Zhe zhang zhuozi bi na   zhang zhuozi kuan-chu   *(shi gongfen).
          this CL   table BI that CL   table wide exceed   ten centimeter
          'This table is ten centimeters wider than that one.'

(44) a. Zhangsan bi Lisi gao (liang gongfen).
          Zhangsan BI Lisi tall two centimeter
          'Zhangsan is (two centimenters) taller than Lisi.'

      b. Zhe tiao kuzi bi na   tiao kuzi chang (liang gongfen).
          this CL pant BI that CL pant long   two centimeter
          'This pair of pants (two centimeters) longer than that one.'

      c. Zhe zhang zhuozi bi na   zhang zhuozi kuan (shi gongfen).
          this CL   table BI that CL   table wide ten centimeter
          'This table is (ten centimeters) wider than that one.'

Having established the structure of the *comparee* and the *standard* in (36) and the structure of comparative adjectives in (42), the full structure of comparatives now follows. Following theories of predication (Bowers 1993; Baker 2003), we propose that a functional head Pred whose semantic function is predication merges with DegP, turning the degree of property denoting adjective into a comparative predicate. Since a fundamental semantic requirement of a comparative adjective is that it attributes a degree of a property to an entity (a *comparee* in the present context) against a *standard* of comparison, this is achieved via predication. As discussed in section 2.3.3, a complex DP headed by a comitative coordinator such as *bi* contains two DPs, and the two DPs can accommodate the *comparee* and the *standard*. So structurally, Pred takes the complex DP and projects it in the specifier position, as this is the argument of the comparative predicate. Comparatives in Chinese such as (43a) and (44a) are hence derived as in (45).

(45)

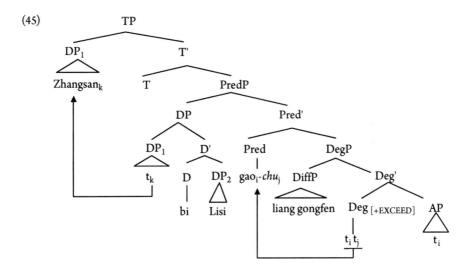

The structure in (45) is motivated on the following grounds. The Deg first merges with AP, and then the DiffP licensed by [+EXCEED] merges with Deg', forming the DegP denoting the property of 'gao-chu liang gongfen' (two centimeters taller). Due to the affixal nature of -*chu*, the adjective 'gao' raises to incorporate into the head of Deg. The complex *gao-chu* moves to Pred via head movement to saturate the argument of the comparative predicate in the Spec of PredP, that is, the *comparee* with relation to the *standard*, in such a way that the property denoted by the DegP is ascribed to the plural entity [DP [DP1 *Zhangsan*] *bi* [DP2 *Lisi*]]. Note that in this instance, the relation between DP₁ the *comparee* and DP₂ the *standard* is one of subtraction held by the head *bi* of the complex DP. In other words, there is a semantic selection between the predicate 'gao-chu' denoting comparative of superiority and the argument 'Zhangsan bi Lisi,' which holds an internal relation of subtraction. Finally, following our discussion in section 2.3.3, since *bi* assigns Case to DP₂, DP₁ must move to Spec of TP to check Nominative Case there. After DP₁ moves out, the rest of the DP cluster [DP [DP1 t_k] *bi* [DP2 *Lisi*]] may move along as an instance of remnant movement (Zhang 2007), or it may remain in the Spec of PredP. This explains the data seen in (13)–(16), where the *comparee* and the *bi*-phrase may be separated by speaker-oriented adverbs and the causal *wh*-phrase, or they may occur next to each other, as recapitulated in (46) and (47), respectively.

(46) a. [DP1 Zhangsan₁] *kending/xianran/xingkui*   [DP [DP1 t₁] bi [DP2 Lisi]] gao
        Zhangsan   definitely/obviously/fortunately   BI   Lisi   tall
      liang gongfen.
      two centimeter
      'Zhangsan definitely/obviously/fortunately is two centimeters taller than Lisi.'

b. $[_{DP1}$ Zhangsan$_i]$ $[_{DP}$ $[_{DP1}$ t$_i]$ bi $[_{DP2}$ Lisi$]]$ *kending/xianran/xingkui*
    Zhangsan   BI   Lisi   definitely/obviously/fortunately
    gao liang gongfen.
    tall two   centimeter
    'Zhangsan is definitely/obviously/fortunately two centimeters taller than Lisi.'

(47) a. Zhangsan *zenme hui*   bi Lisi gao liang gongfen?
          Zhangsan how   could BI Lisi tall two   centimeter
          'How come Zhangsan could be two centimeters taller than Lisi?'

      b. Zhangsan bi Lisi *zenme hui*   gao liang gongfen?
          Zhangsan BI Lisi how   could tall two   centimeter
          'How come Zhangsan could be two centimeters taller than Lisi?'

As for comparatives of equality, they are derived in the same fashion as comparatives of superiority except for the manifestation of the Deg head and the consequences brought about thereby. In comparatives of superiority, the Deg head has the feature [+EXCEED] whose phonological realization can be *–chu* or be null. Since the affixal *-chu* must be supported in order to converge the derivation, the relevant adjective incorporates into the Deg head to host the affix, as seen in the derivation of (45). In contrast, in comparatives of equality, the Deg head has the [-EXCEED] feature, which is realized by a free morpheme *yiyang* ('same'), without triggering adjective incorporation, as evidenced in (48), where the adjective *gao* is attached to *yiyang*, yielding an ungrammatical result.

(48) *Zhangsan he/gen/tong Lisi *gao* yiyang.
       Zhangsan with   Lisi tall same

Meanwhile, as shown by the contrast in (49) and (50), the presence of *yiyang* expresses that the difference value computed after comparison can only be zero. This indicates that the DiffP does not have overt realization.

(49) a. Zhangsan he/gen/tong Lisi yiyang gao.
          Zhangsan with   Lisi same   tall
          'Zhangsan is as tall as Lisi.'

      b. *Zhangsan he/gen/tong Lisi yiyang gao *liang gongfen*.[13]
          Zhangsan with   Lisi same   tall two   centimeter
          'Zhangsan is as tall as Lisi.'

(50) a. Zhangsan he/gen/tong Lisi yiyang congming.
          Zhangsan with   Lisi same   intelligent
          'Zhangsan is as intelligent as Lisi.'

      b. *Zhangsan he/gen/tong Lisi yiyang congming *ji   bei*.
          Zhangsan with   Lisi same   intelligent several times

---

[13] (49b) may have *a transitive comparative* meaning (in the sense of Grano and Kennedy 2012) that Zhangsan and Lisi are both two centimeters tall. This interpretation is not intended here.

Other things being equal, with comparatives of equality, the functional head Pred merges with the whole chunk of DegP in the same way as it does in (45), projecting PredP by saturating an argument in the Spec of PredP. We assume, following Larson's (1991) reanalysis rule, that the Deg' in the structure of comparatives of equality is reanalyzed into a Deg°, which contains a complex [Deg+A], instantiated by [yiyang+A]. Like the complex *gao-chu* in (45), the complex [*yiyang*+A] moves to Pred via head movement to saturate the argument of the comparative predicate in the Spec of PredP, that is, the *comparee* with relation to the *standard*, thereby ascribing the property denoted by the DegP to the plural entity [the *comparee* gen/he/tong the *standard*]. The derivation of (25b), repeated in (49a), is schematically shown in (51).

(51)

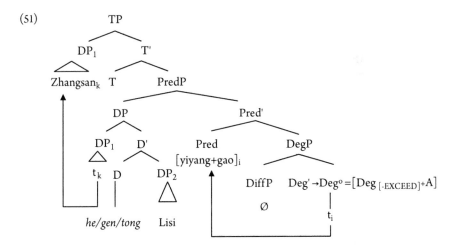

Similar to its counterpart in (45), DP$_1$ in (51) moves to Spec of TP to check Nominative Case, and the rest of the DP cluster [$_{DP}$ [$_{DP1}$ t$_k$] *gen/he/tong* [$_{DP2}$ Lisi]] may move along as an instance of remnant movement or it may remain in the Spec of PredP, as evidenced in the following familiar patterns observed earlier in (46)–(47), which are related to the interactions of the DP cluster with speaker-oriented adverbs and the causal *wh*-phrase, respectively.

(52) a. [$_{DP1}$ Zhangsan$_i$] *kending/xianran/xingkui* [$_{DP}$ [$_{DP1}$ t$_i$] he/gen/tong [$_{DP2}$ Lisi]]
          Zhangsan   definitely/obviously/fortunately   with   Lisi
          yiyang gao.
          same   tall
          'Zhangsan definitely/obviously/fortunately is as tall as Lisi.'

      b. [$_{DP1}$ Zhangsan$_i$] [$_{DP}$ [$_{DP1}$ t$_i$] he/gen/tong [$_{DP2}$ Lisi]]
          Zhangsan   with   Lisi
          kending/xianran/xingkui   yiyang gao.
          definitely/obviously/fortunately   same   tall
          'Zhangsan is definitely/obviously/fortunately as tall as Lisi.'

(53) a. Zhangsan *zenme hui*   he/gen/tong Lisi yiyang gao?
          Zhangsan how   could with   Lisi same   tall
          'How come Zhangsan could be as tall as Lisi?'

b. Zhangsan he/gen/tong Lisi *zenme hui*   yiyang gao?
    Zhangsan with   Lisi how   could same   tall
    'How come Zhangsan could be as tall as Lisi?'

Like the DP cluster [$_{DP}$ [$_{DP1}$ t] *bi* [$_{DP2}$ Lisi]], the DP cluster [$_{DP}$ [$_{DP1}$ t] *he/gen/tong* [$_{DP2}$ Lisi]] may surface as one constituent in answering a question, a phenomenon we have come across in (7) and footnote 8:

(54) a. Zhangsan bi shei gao?
          Zhangsan BI who tall
          'Who is Zhangsan taller than?'

      b. [$_{DP}$ [$_{DP1}$ t] Bi [$_{DP2}$ Lisi]] gao.
          (Lit.) 'Taller than Lisi.'

(55) a. Zhangsan he/gen/tong shei yiyang gao?
          Zhangsan with   who same   tall
          'Who is Zhangsan as tall as?'

      b. [$_{DP}$ [$_{DP1}$ t] He/gen/tong Lisi]] yiyang gao.
          (Lit.) 'As tall as Lisi.'

The DP cluster can also be dropped. This offers an explanation for its absence in (11b)–(12b), as repeated here in (56b) and (57b) with minor modification. The structure involved here is not a superiority comparative, but rather an equality comparative.

(56) a. Zhangsan   he/gen/tong Lisi, shei gao?
          Zhangshan and   Lisi who tall
          'Zhangsan and Lisi, who is taller?'

      b. Zhangsan gao.
          Zhangsan tall
          'Zhangsan is taller (than Lisi).'

(57) a. Zhangsan he Lisi, shei gao yi dian?
          Zhangsan and Lisi who tall a bit
          'Zhangsan and Lisi, who is a bit taller?'

      b. Zhangsan gao yi dian.
          Zhangsan tall a bit
          'Zhangsan is a bit taller (than Lisi).'

2.5. SUMMARY

In a comparative construction, the difference value obtained after comparison between degrees of properties along a relevant dimension possessed by the *comparee* and the *standard* is either *exceeding* or *equal*. It thus provides grounds for us to unify comparatives under one structure. The derivations depicted in (45) and (51) demonstrate that comparatives of both superiority and equality in Chinese share one structure. The distinction between the two types of comparatives is shown to be ascribable to the relevant semantic feature value of the Deg head and the comparative predication relation held between the plural entities under comparison and the relevant predicate. The structural similarities and differences between the two types of comparatives thus receive a unified account. The structures in (45) and (51) also make the right prediction that the English type of subcomparison seen in (3) is not available in Chinese, as reflected in (4), because there is no gradable predicate in the *standard*, and there is only one gradable predicate in the structure, that is, the main predicate predicated on the complex DP in (45) and (51). The structural analysis of Chinese comparatives proposed here nicely depicts the semantic mapping of individual comparison (Kennedy 2005, 2009) onto Chinese syntax. The compared elements are realized as two DPs, coordinated by a comitative.[14]

In the next section, we will proceed to some relevant properties of Japanese comparatives and will discuss the implications of our analysis for the Japanese comparative constructions.

3. Implications

3.1. COMPARATIVE CONSTRUCTIONS IN JAPANESE

The Japanese comparative construction also lacks subcomparatives (Beck et al. 2004). In the following, we will first reflect on the investigation of Japanese comparatives by Beck et al., and then will discuss various issues surrounding subcomparatives.

In a Japanese comparative of superiority construction, the *comparee* normally appears in the topic position marked by *wa*. The *standard* follows the *comparee*. It is introduced by a locative postposition *yori*, literally meaning 'from,' which appears on

---

[14] Our analysis of the *standard* residing in the complex DP makes the right prediction that the English type of object comparison is impossible in Chinese. We thank Paul Law for his comment on this point.

i. a.   John   likes   beer   more than coffee.
    b.   *Zhansan xihuan pijiu duo   bi   kafei.
         Zhangsan like   beer more BI   coffee

Notice that (ia) indicates a bi-clausal structure:

ii.   John likes beer more than he likes coffee.

Such a structure is ruled out in Chinese, as evidenced in (iii). This is predicted by our structural analysis of the *standard* constituent as a DP, which amounts to saying that comparatives in Chinese do not involve a bi-clausal structure.

iii. a.   *Zhangsan xihuan pijiu duo   bi   ta xihuan kafei.
           Zhangsan like   beer more BI   he like   coffee
      b.   *Zhangsan xihuan pijiu bi   ta xihuan kafei   duo.
           Zhangsan like   beer BI   he like   coffee more

the right of the *standard*. A gradable predicate occurs at the end of the sentence. Two illustrative examples are given in (58).

(58) a. [Nihongo-wa] [doitsugo] yori   muzukashi desu.
          Japanese-TOP German   YORI[15] difficult   be
          'Japanese is more difficult than German.'

      b. [[Taroo-ga   kat-ta]   hon-wa] [[Hanako-ga   kat-ta]   no]
          Taroo-NOM buy-PAST book-TOP   Hanako-NOM buy-PAST NO
          yori ooi   desu.[16]
          than many be
          'The books that Taroo bought are more than the ones that Hanako bought.'

In (58a), the *comparee* and the *standard* are realized by two DPs, *nihongo* 'English' and *doitsugo* 'German,' respectively, and they are related by the gradable adjective *muzukashi* 'difficult' plus a linking verb *desu* 'be.' In (58b), they are realized by two complex nominals, where *hon* 'book' and *no*, which is taken here as a nominalizer, are head nouns modified respectively by a relative clause, *Taroo-ga katta* 'Taroo bought' and *Hanako-ga katta* 'Hanako bought.' Word order aside, what (58) shows is that the Japanese *yori* comparatives are quite similar to the Chinese comparatives discussed in section 2 of this chapter. In both constructions, the *comparee* and the *standard* are taken by a nominal constituent.

There is another type of *yori* comparative construction, as illustrated in (59).

(59) a. Mary-wa   John yori   (motto) takusan no ronbun-o   kai-ta.
          Mary-TOP John YORI more   many   NO paper-ACC write-PAST
          'John wrote more papers than Mary.'

      b. Mary-wa [[John-ga   kai-ta]   yori] (motto) takusan no ronbun-o
          Mary-TOP John-NOM write-PAST YORI more   many   NO paper-ACC
          kai-ta.
          write-PAST
          'John wrote more papers than Mary wrote.'

Different from their counterparts in (58), the *comparee* and the *standard* in (59) are not parallel in structure. The *standard,* or the complement of *yori*, is realized either as a single DP, that is, *John* in (59a), or as a clause *John-ga kaita* in (59b). The *comparee* is realized by an element that contains a gradable expression, that is, *takusan no ronbun* in (59b). The main predicate *kaita* appearing in the sentence final position is not a gradable predicate. The only gradable element in the sentence is *takusan* 'many,' which is a modifier of the object *ronbun* 'paper' of the main predicate *kaita* 'wrote.'

On the basis of where the gradable element appears, these two types of comparatives have been labeled respectively as *predicative comparative* and *attributive*

---

[15] We gloss *yori* as capitalized YORI.

[16] The morpheme *no* is a multi-functional element in Japanese, and various terms have been used to identify its different functions, e.g., nominalizer, linker, genitive marker, possessive marker, etc. To avoid confusion, in this chapter, we gloss the morpheme as capitalized NO.

comparative in a recent work of Sudo (to appear). We adopt these labels in the ensuing discussion.

Our concern at this juncture is how comparativity is made in the *attributive comparatives* and whether the sentences in (59) can indeed have an interpretation equivalent to (60).

(60)   John wrote more papers than Mary (did)/wrote.

3.2. PREVIOUS ANALYSES OF JAPANESE COMPARATIVES

The standard semantic analysis of English comparatives, dating back to von Stechow (1984) and Heim (1985, 2000), assumes that sentences like (60) or (61a) have a Logical Form schematized in (61b). Under this assumption, (61b) is treated as the input for compositional interpretation, and the comparative morpheme *–er* is viewed as forming a constituent with the *than*-clause, which is raised to an IP adjoined position. The interpretation thus obtained can be paraphrased in (61c).

(61)   a.   John bought more books than Peter did.
        b.   [[-er [than Peter did (buy d'-many books)]][John bought d-many books]].
        c   The degree d such that John bought d-many books exceeds the degree d' such that Peter bought d'-many books.

Comparatives are then taken as involving a comparison between two degrees, and both the *than*-clause and the main clause of a comparative construction provide a predication of degrees, with the comparative morpheme *–er* denoting a relation between two sets of degrees, and the *than*-clause introducing the *standard* for comparison.

Given the analysis of English comparatives, it is assumed that in the Japanese comparative constructions exemplified in (58) and (59), the complement of *yori* can be treated on a par with the *than*-phrase and *than*-clause in English (Ishii 1991). This may then lead to the assumption that the Japanese attributive comparative constructions like (59) could receive an interpretation in the same way as those in (58), analogous to the English comparatives in (60).

However, the parallelism between the Japanese attributive comparatives in (59) and the English translation in (60) is only deceptive. Beck et al. (2004) challenge the standard analysis derived from English comparatives for interpreting the Japanese comparatives seen in (59). They query the validity of the interpretations of (60) for (59), emphasizing the following three differences between Japanese comparatives and English comparatives.

First, there exists a controversy in the judgment of examples like (62a) and (63a).[17] As reported in Ishii (1991), (63a) is ungrammatical. But to Beck et al., the judgment of (63a) ranges from '?' to '??'.

---

[17] The English translations in (b) (and (c)) are construed based on the standard analysis of English comparatives. Beck et al. (2004) keep them separate from the Japanese examples in (a), as they do not agree with such interpretations.

(62) a. Taroo-wa   [Hanako-ga   kat-ta]   yori   (mo) takusan (no)
        Taroo-TOP Hanako-NOM buy-PAST YORI even many   NO
        kasa-o   kat-ta.
        umbrella-ACC buy-PAST

   b. Taroo bought more umbrellas than Hanako did.

(63) a. ?*Taroo-wa [Hanako-ga   kat-ta]   yori   (mo) nagai kasa-o
         Taroo-TOP   Hanako-NOM buy-PAST YORI even long umbrella-ACC
         kat-ta.
         buy-PAST

   b. Taroo bought a longer umbrella than Hanako did.

Second, Japanese lacks the English type of subcomparatives, as shown in the contrast in (64).

(64) a. *Kono tana-wa   [ano doa-ga   hiroi yori (mo)] (motto) takai.
         Kono shelf-TOP that door-NOM wide YORI even   more   tall

   b. This shelf is taller than that door is wide.

Third, Japanese also lacks English-like negative island effects, as shown by the contrast in (65a) and (65b). (65b) is an unacceptable and incomprehensible sentence in English, but (65a) is well formed and intuitively it means something like (65c).

(65) a. John-wa   [dare-mo kawa-nakat-ta   no] yori   takai   hon-o
         John-TOP anyone   buy-NEG-PAST NO YORI expensive book-ACC
         kat-ta.
         buy-PAST

   b. * John bought a more expensive book than nobody did.

   c. * John bought a book that is more expensive than the book that nobody bought.

The three differences between English and Japanese comparatives pose a challenge to a uniform treatment of English and Japanese comparatives under the standard analysis. If the complement of *yori* in (59) is equivalent to the English *than*-phrase and *than*-clause, the ungrammaticality of (63a) is unexpected, for (63b) is perfectly fine in English. The lack of subcomparatives in Japanese is also unexpected following the standard analysis. As for the negative island effects in English, the standard analysis gives it a natural semantic account. The purported semantics of (65b) is given in (66).

(66) The degree d such that John bought a d-expensive book exceeds the degree d' such that nobody bought a d'-expensive book.

According to Rullmann (1995), the denotation of the *standard* of comparison in (65b) is in fact undefined: there is no maximal degree d' such that nobody bought a d'-expensive book. So (66) is anomalous because comparison of degrees cannot be established. In other words, there does not exist a *standard* for comparison; the d'-expensiveness is nonexistent, as nobody bought a book with such d'-expensiveness. (65b), which exhibits the negative island effects in English, is, therefore, unacceptable because the maximal degree d' does not exist and hence cannot be exceeded by the maximal degree d such that John bought a d-expensive book.

Turn to the Japanese example in (65a). It is grammatical. As mentioned, the intuitive meaning of (65a) is (65c), which entails that there is a particular book that nobody bought. In other words, the price of John's book is comparable with the price of that particular book even though nobody bought it. Yet, under the standard semantic analysis of comparatives, the acceptability of (65a), together with the intuitive interpretation of (65c) associated with it, is unexpected.

With the differences between English and Japanese comparatives illustrated in the preceding examples, Beck et al. (2004) come up with the proposal that the interpretation of the type of Japanese *yori* constructions in (59) is governed to a lesser extent by compositional semantics and to a larger extent by pragmatic strategies than is the case under the standard analysis of English comparatives. The basic idea is that the better English approximation of (67) (= (62a)), is (68), but not (62b), that is, *Taroo bought more umbrellas than Hanako did*, an interpretation assuming the equivalence of Japanese comparatives to English comparatives.

(67) Taroo-wa [Hanako-ga   kat-ta]   yori (mo) takusan (no)
      Taroo-TOP Hanako-NOM buy-PAST YORI even many   NO
      kasa-o   kat-ta.
      umbrella-ACC buy-PAST

(68) a. Compared to what Hanako bought, Taroo bought more umbrellas.

      b. Compared to what Hanako bought, Taroo bought many umbrellas.

The closest translation of (67) as (68) is crucial to such an analysis. By examining the semantics of 'compared to,' Beck et al. made the following claims. First, the complement of *yori* does not pattern with the English comparative *than*- phrase/clause; it is more like the context setting 'compared to' phrase in the paraphrases in (68). The interpretation of the gradable expression in the *yori* constructions is context dependent, and 'compared to' provides such a context, that is, subject to the specific item(s) associated with 'compared to.'

Second, (67) is interpreted as involving either the comparative interpretation of the gradable expression *takusan* 'more (umbrellas)' or the unmodified 'many (umbrellas).' In other words, with *yori* being interpreted as 'compared to,' the two environments *more (umbrellas)* and *many (umbrellas)* can arise and the choice of a particular interpretation is subject to context. As illustrated in (69a, b), both sentences have the same semantic effect, similar to that of a comparative construction in (69c).[18]

(69) a. Compared to Mary, Peter is tall.

      b. Compared to Mary, Peter is taller.

      c. Peter is taller than Mary.

---

[18] See Kennedy (2005) for an analysis of the subtle differences between 'compared to' used with positive forms and with comparative forms of adjectives.

In (67) the constituent *Hanako-ga katta* preceding *yori* is analyzed as a free relative clause, meaning 'what Hanako bought.' This triggers the inference of the *standard* as the number of umbrellas, for in a context of a given set of umbrellas bought, the number of umbrellas becomes very salient.

Given (68) as the closest approximation of (67), Beck et al. offer a pragmatic explanation for the variability in acceptance of (70a) and (71a).To them, the strong '?*' in (63a) is not available, but the slightly odd judgment does exist, as in (71a).

(70) a. Taroo-wa   [Hanako-ga   kat-ta]   yori   (mo) takusan (-no)
          Taroo-TOP Hanako-NOM buy-PAST YORI (even) many   NO
          kasa-o   kat-ta
          umbrella-ACC buy-PAST

      b. Taroo bought more umbrellas than Hanako did.

(71) a. ?(?)Taroo-wa   [Hanako-ga   kat-ta   yori   (mo)]
               Taroo-TOP Hanako-NOM buy-PAST YORI even
          nagai kasa-o   kat-ta.
          long umbrella-ACC buy-PAST

      b. Taroo bought a longer umbrella than Hanako did.

They consider that the appropriate English approximations of (63a) and (70a) should be (72a) and (72b), respectively, instead of (70b) and (71b).

(72) a. Compared to what Hanako bought, Taroo bought a lot of umbrellas.

      b. ? Compared to what Hanako bought, Taroo bought a long umbrella.

It is pointed out that both (71a) in Japanese and (72b) in English are slightly odd because in a set of umbrellas bought, it is more straightforward to infer the maximal number of umbrellas than the maximal size or length of them. In other contexts, for example, if the size or length of the umbrellas becomes salient in a context, (71a) will improve with an interpretation equivalent to (72b).

Third, there is a close connection between relative clauses and *yori* clauses. In Japanese, *yori* marks a nominal complement. Based on the data given by Beck et al., one can arrive at the following patterns: the nominal complement can be a simple noun phrase as in (73a), or a complex nominal containing a relative clause as in (73b), or a free relative clause as in (73c).

(73) a. Mary-wa   [John yori] nagai ronbun-o   kai-ta.
          Mary-TOP John YORI long paper-ACC write-PAST
          'Compared to John, Mary wrote a long paper.'

      b. Mary-wa   [[[John-ga   kai-ta]   ronbun] yori] nagai ronbun-o
          Mary TOP   John NOM write-PAST paper   YORI long   paper-ACC
          kai-ta.
          write-PAST
          'Compared to the paper that John wrote, Mary wrote a long paper.'

c. Mary-wa [[John-ga   kai-ta]   yori] nagai ronbun-o   kai-ta.
   Mary-TOP   John-NOM   write-PAST YORI long paper-ACC write-PAST
   'Compared to what John wrote, Mary wrote a long paper.'

In (73c), the complement of *yori* [John-ga kaita] looks like a plain clause. According to Beck et al., this clause is identical to the relative clause [[John-ga kaita] ronbun] in (73b). The difference lies in the presence and absence of the object *ronbun*. By following Jacobson (1995), Beck et al. assume that without *ronbun*, [John-ga kaita] in (73c) is a free relative clause. This gives rise to the different interpretations of the *standard* in the two sentences, *the paper that John wrote* in (73b) versus *what John wrote* in (73c). It then follows that the complement of *yori* is not a clause; it is a complex nominal with a modifying clause.

Based on these claims, Beck et al. proceed to explaining the lack of subcomparatives in Japanese observed in (64a), which is in contrast with the English subcomparative in (64b). The examples are repeated, respectively, in (74).

(74) a. *Kono tana-wa   [ano doa-ga   hiroi yori   (mo)] (motto) takai.
         Kono shelf-TOP   that door-NOM   wide YORI   even   more   tall

     b. This shelf is taller than that door is wide.

The premise of subcomparatives is the existence of a full clause, which has a gradable predicate independent of the main clause gradable predicate, as in (74b). The comparison is made between two degrees abstracted from two gradable predicates, d-tall and d'-wide, as long as gradability of height and width is along the same dimension.

The situation in (74a) differs from that of (74b) because the clause [ano doa-ga hiroi] is not parallel to the main clause. Based on Beck et al., [ano doa-ga hiroi] is a relative clause in disguise. So what is being compared in (74a) are not two degree predicates. In (74a), *hiroi* 'wide' in [ano doa-ga hiroi] is a predicate of the relative clause; it is not a gradable predicate of the *standard* constituent per se. As a result, no proper structural parallelism can be established for desired sub-comparison.

Beck et al. note that the following sentence in (75) should not be taken as one of subcomparative.

(75) Hanako-wa   [Taroo-ga   ronbun-o   kai-ta   (no) yori]
     Hanako-TOP   Taroo-NOM   paper-ACC write-PAST NO   YORI
     takusan hon-o   kai-ta.
     many   book-ACC write-PAST

The reason is that since the complement of *yori* in (75) is assigned a relative clause-like interpretation, the sentence should be interpreted as (76a), but not (76b).

(76) a. Compared to the papers Taroo wrote, Hanako wrote a lot of books.

     b. Hanako wrote more books than Taroo wrote papers.

The relative clause in (75) does not contain a degree predicate. Its semantics is relative clause-like and *yori* marks an individual as the *standard* of comparison. (75) does not have (76b) as a possible interpretation, and it is not a subcomparative construction. Beck et al. thus conclude that no subcomparatives are available in the Japanese *yori* construction.

Finally, Beck et al. extend the non-degree nature of the *yori* clause to explain the absence of the English-like negative island effects in *yori* constructions as in (77) (= (65a, b)).

(77) a. John-wa   [[[dare mo kawa-naka-tta] no] yori]   takai
          John-TOP [anyone buy-NEG-PAST NO YORI] expensive
          hon-o   kat-ta.
          book-ACC buy-PAST

      b. * John bought a more expensive book than nobody did.

(77a) shows that a *yori* construction equivalent to the English sub-comparative is grammatical. The English comparative in (77b) exhibits a negative island effect. The *standard* 'nobody did' is a clause that contains negation and a covert gradable adjective 'expensive,' that is, 'nobody did' means 'nobody bought an expensive book.' But the Japanese counterpart in (77a) does not. This is because to convey a similar meaning to that expressed in the English subcomparative, Japanese uses nominal scales as in (78) (Kennedy 2009).

(78) Kono tana-no taka-ga-wa   ano doa-no haba yori ookii.
      This shelf-NO height-NOM-TOP that door-NO width YORI great
      'The shelf's height is greater than the door's width.'

(78) is a predicative comparative construction, where *taka* and *haba* are the respective nominal heads of the *camparee* DP and the *standard* DP. So the relevant degree comparison is made between two nominals, height and width, instead of two clauses containing two separate gradable predicates, 'high and wide.' This explains straightforwardly why no negative island effect arises in (77a). Regardless of the fact that (77a) is an attributive comparative construction, the relevant comparison is made between two nominals, that is, two books, one of which, that is, the *standard,* is a nominal head instantiated by *no*, which is modified by a relative clause [dare-mo kawa-naka-tta]. Negation occurs inside the relative clause. The comparative predicate *takai* 'expensive' is outside the relative clause; hence no island effect is invoked.

By resorting to the semantics of 'compared to,' which is geared toward an individual as the standard of comparison, one can arrive at (79b), but not (79a), as the intuitively appropriate interpretation of (77a).

(79) a. * John bought a more expensive book than nobody did.

      b. Compared to the one that nobody bought, John bought an expensive book.

To sum up, Beck et al. propose a semantic analysis of comparative constructions different from the standard semantics of comparatives. According to them, the interpretation of the *yori* constituent is largely determined by pragmatic strategies and the *yori* constituent does not involve degree predicates.

The analysis of Beck et al. captures a number of empirical facts in the attributive *yori* comparatives, offering an account for the lack of sub-comparatives in the construction, which is especially of interest to us. In the following we will take a closer look at some of the data concerned with their analysis and will dwell on further details that may lead us to a better understanding of the construction.

3.3. *TAKUSAN* VERSUS *TAKUSAN NO*

Let us consider the set of complements of *yori* in (80), some of which we have come across in (73).

(80) a. Mary-wa [[John-ga   kai-ta]   yori] nagai ronbun-o   kai-ta.
       Mary-TOP   John-NOM write-PAST YORI long   paper-ACC write-PAST
       'Compared to what John wrote, Mary wrote a long paper.'

   b. Mary-wa [[[John-ga   kai-ta]   no] yori] nagai ronbun-o   kai-ta.
       Mary-TOP   John-NOM write-PAST NO YORI long   paper-ACC write-PAST
       'Compared to the one(s) that John wrote, Mary wrote a long paper.'

   c. Mary-wa [[[John-ga   kai-ta]   ronbun] yori] nagai ronbun-o
       Mary-TOP   John-NOM write-PAST paper   YORI long   paper-ACC
       kai-ta.
       write-PAST
       'Compared to the paper that John wrote, Mary wrote a long paper.'

In (80a), [John-ga kaita] is a free relative clause. It differs from its counterpart in (80b), [John-ga kaita no], which is headed by *no*. We concur with the view (Beck et al. 2004, footnote 11, 341–342) that in the free relative clause, there does not exist an empty nominal pronoun interpreted as 'one' or 'ones,' as suggested by Ishii (1991), Hoji (1998), and Tomioka (2003). If there were an empty nominal head Ø in [John-ga kaita] of (80a), the three complements, Ø in (80a), *no* in (80b), and the overt head noun, *ronbun* in (80c), would differ minimally from each other and they would be in complementary distribution. This being the case, we would expect the sentences in (82), which contrast minimally with (81), to be acceptable. We notice that the acceptability of (82) is conditioned by the presence of the morpheme *no* following *takusan* as in (82a). When *no* is absent, the sentence sounds odd as in (82b).

(81) Taroo-wa [Hanako-ga   kat-ta]   yori (mo) takusan (no) kasa-o
       Taroo-TOP Hanako-NOM buy-PAST YORI even many   NO umbrella-ACC
       kat-ta.
       buy-PAST
       'Compared to what Hanako bought, Taroo bought many umbrellas.'

(82) a. Taroo-wa [[Hanako-ga   kat-ta]   no] yori (mo) takusan no
       Taroo-TOP Hanako-NOM buy-PAST NO YORI even many   NO
       kasa-o   kat-ta.
       umbrella-ACC buy-PAST
       'Compared to the one(s) Hanako bought, Taroo bought many umbrellas.'

b. ??Taroo-wa [[Hanako-ga   kat-ta]   no] yori (mo) takusan
    Taroo-TOP   Hanako-NOM buy-PAST NO YORI even many
    kasa-o   kat-ta.
    umbrella-ACC buy-PAST
    # 'Compared to the one(s) Hanako bought, Taroo bought many umbrellas.'

In (82a), the relative clause [Hanako-ga kat-ta no] refers to umbrellas, as normally the relative nominal head *no* shares denotational meaning with the covert nominal expression under comparison, that is, umbrellas. So one can infer an interpretation that Taroo bought a set of umbrellas that is large or larger in quantity than the one(s) Hanako bought. In (82b), however, this interpretation is not available.

We suspect that the problem of (82) is associated with the status of the bare *takusan* and that of *takusan no*. In other words, whether the sentences in (82) can receive an appropriate interpretation depends on the presence and absence of *no* following *takusan*.

Let us take a closer look at *takusan*. As indicated in the English gloss, both *takusan* in (82) and *ooi* seen in (58b) mean 'many.' Categorially there is a difference between the two. *Ooi* is a predicative adjective, which cannot be used attributively:

(83) a. Nihon-ni-wa   yama-ga   ooi   desu.
      Japan-LOC-TOP mountain-NOM many be
      'There are a lot of mountains in Japan.'

    b. *Nihon-ni-wa   ooi   yama-ga   arimasu.
       Japan-LOC-TOP many mountain-NOM exist

Unlike *ooi*, *takusan* is a numeral quantifier. Although it appears in comparative constructions, it cannot be used as a comparative predicate:

(84) a. *Taroo-ga   kat-ta   hon-wa   Hanako-ga   kat-ta   no
      Taroo-NOM buy-PAST book-TOP Hanako-NOM buy-PAST NO
      yori takusan.
      YORI many

    b. *Taroo-ga   kat-ta   hon-wa   Hanako-ga   kat-ta   no
      Taroo-NOM buy-PAST book-TOP Hanako-NOM buy-PAST NO
      yori takusan desu.
      YORI many   be

Takusan can be used as a modifier of a nominal in (85) or as an adverbial in (86). In the former case, the morpheme *no* must appear following *takusan*.

(85) a. takusan no yama
      many   NO mountains
      'many mountains'

    b. * takusan yama

(86) Taroo-ga   takusan benkyooshimashi-ta.
      Taroo-NOM a lot   study-PAST
      'Taroo studied a lot.'

The sequence of *takusan no* has been analyzed as a determiner (Tanaka 2006). As such, *takusan no* forms a constituent with an NP on its right, that is, in (82a), [takusan no kasa-o] is the object of the main predicate *katta*.

The bare *takusan* in (82b), on the other hand, is an adverbial numeral quantifier (Miyagawa 1989; Bobaljik 1995; among others). So it does not form a constituent with the NP on its right; rather, it quantifies over the VP on its right. The relevant structural difference in (82a) and (82b) is schematized in (87).

(87) a.   ... [$_{DP}$ takusan no   kasa]-o   kat-ta.
              many   NO umbrella-ACC buy-PAST

      b.   ... takusan [$_{VP}$ kasa-o   kat-ta].
              many   umbrella-ACC buy-PAST

The positioning of *takusan* and *takusan no* serves to confirm their distinct status. The adverbial *takusan* can be left behind after the object is stranded, resulting in the following two word orders (Watanabe 2006: (70c), (70d)):

(88) a.   John-wa   hon-o   takusan kat-ta.
           John-TOP book-ACC many   buy-PAST
           'John bought many books.'

      b.   John-wa   takusan hon-o   kat-ta.
           John-TOP many   book-ACC buy-PAST
           'John bought many books.'

With *takuson no*, the constituent NP cannot undergo stranding:

(89) a.   John-wa   takusan no hon-o   kat-ta.
           John-TOP many   NO book-ACC buy-PAST
           'John bought many books.'

      b.   *John-wa   hon-o   takusan no kat-ta.
           John-TOP book-ACC many   NO buy-PAST

In light of the above discussion, it now becomes clear why the two sentences in (82) cannot receive the same interpretation. In (82a), the relevant comparison is between two sets of entities, the many umbrellas Taroo bought versus the ones Hanako bought. In the *comparee* 'umbrellas' there sits a gradable element *takusan*, which attributes (in the sense of Sudo (to appear)) designated gradable property, that is, large amount, to the *comparee*. In (82b), the same kind of comparison cannot be established. The adverbial *takusan* quantifies over the event of 'Taroo buying umbrellas' (assuming some version of the VP Internal Subject Hypothesis), so the main clause means 'As for Taroo, he bought umbrellas a lot.' Strictly speaking, in (82b) gradability of a large amount is not attributed in the same way as that in (82a). While one can infer that many events of umbrella-buying would necessarily result in many umbrellas being bought, it is the precise meaning of *takusan* as an event quantifier that renders (82b) problematic. The complement of *yori* in (82b) contains a relative clause denoting an entity, but the main clause does not have a corresponding entity as a *comparee* with gradable properties. Rather, it has an event-denoting element, *kasa-o katta*, which is modified by the gradable *takusan*.

In a nutshell, *takusan* in (82b) attributes gradability to an event. Thus the sentence depicts a comparison between an entity denoting *standard* and an event denoting *camparee*. It is this lack of parallelism in meaning and structure that renders the sentence problematic.

Note that *takuson no* patterns with normal gradable adjectives in attributive comparatives, as confirmed in (90)–(92).

(90) a. Mary-wa   John-ga   kai-ta   yori   **nagai** ronbun-o   kai-ta.
        Mary-TOP John-NOM write-PAST YORI long   paper-ACC write-PAST
        'Compared to what John wrote, Mary wrote a long paper.'

     b. Mary-wa   John-ga   kai-ta   yori   **takusan no** ronbun-o
        Mary-TOP John-NOM write-PAST YORI many   NO paper-ACC
        kai-ta.
        write-PAST
        'Compared to what John wrote, Mary wrote many papers.'

(91) a. Mary-wa   John-ga   kai-ta   no yori   **nagai** ronbun-o   kai-ta.
        Mary-TOP John-NOM write-PAST NO YORI long   paper-ACC write-PAST
        'Compared to the one(s) that John wrote, Mary wrote a long paper.'

     b. Mary-wa   John-ga   kai-ta   no yori   **takusan no** ronbun-o
        Mary-TOP John-NOM write-PAST NO YORI many   NO paper-ACC
        kai-ta.
        write-PAST
        'Compared to the one(s) that John wrote, Mary wrote many papers.'

(92) a. Mary-wa   John-ga   kai-ta   ronbun yori   **nagai** ronbun-o
        Mary-TOP John-NOM write-PAST paper   YORI long   paper-ACC
        kai-ta.
        write-PAST
        'Compared to the paper that John wrote, Mary wrote a long paper.'

     b. Mary-wa   John-ga   kai-ta   ronbun yori   **takusan no** ronbun-o
        Mary-TOP John-NOM write-PAST paper   YORI many   NO paper-ACC
        kai-ta.
        write-PAST
        'Compared to the paper that John wrote, Mary wrote many papers.'

Conversely, as pointed out in Sudo (to appear), only *takusan,* but not an attributive adjective, can occur in the following comparative construction:[19]

(93) a. *John-wa [Mary-ga   manga-o   yon-da]   yori   omosiroi
          John-TOP Mary-NOM comic-ACC read-PAST YORI interesting
          shoosetu-o yon-da.
          novel-ACC   read-PAST
          *'John read a more interesting novel than Mary read a comic.'

      b. John-wa   [Mary-ga   manga-o   yon-da]   yori   takusan hon-o
          John-TOP Mary-NOM comic-ACC read-PAST YORI many   book-ACC
          yon-da.
          Read-PAST
          'John read more books than Mary read comics.'

This lends support to our earlier analysis: *takusan* is not an attributive adjective.

The attributive comparatives are interesting because the constructions confirm that there exists only one gradable element; hence no degree comparison is available in these constructions.

3.4. PARAMETRIC IMPLICATIONS

The complement of *yori* does not contain a gradable predicate, and there is only one gradable element in the Japanese comparatives, either the main predicate in the *predicative comparatives,* or the modifier in the *attributive comparatives.*

---

[19] The complement clause of *yori* in (93) differs from the relative clauses seen so far. The noun phrase *manga* is inside the clause. Sudo calls sentences like (93a) *attributive sub-comparatives* and (93b) *amount sub-comparatives,* and points out that only the latter is grammatical. But no detailed analysis is given why this is so because sub-comparatives are considered to be unavailable in Japanese. In our view, at least (93) serves to differentiate the adverbial "attributive" *takusan* from regular attributive adjectives.

We suspect that the complement of *yori* in (93a) is analogous to the clause-looking nominal elements in Chinese comparatives (see Gu and Guo (to appear) for detailed discussion). Note that the contrast observed in (93) also arises in Chinese:

(iii) a. Zhansan mai shu bi Lisi mai shu duo.
          Zhangsan buy book BI Lisi buy book more
          'Zhangsan bought books more than Lisi bought books.'

      b. *Zhangsan mai shu bi Lisi mai shu gui.
          Zhangsan buy book BI Lisi buy book expensive
          * 'Zhangsan bought books more expensive than Lisi bought books.'

      b. '*Zhangsan mai shu bi Lisi mai shu hao   kan.
          Zhangsan buy book BI Lisi buy book good-to-read
          *'Zhangsan bought books more interesting than Lisi bought books.'

At this stage, we do not have anything interesting to say about the contrast and will leave the issue for future exploration.

Recall our structure for the Chinese comparatives of superiority in (45). The structure in (45) rules out the possibility of there being a gradable predicate in the *bi*-phrase, which is empirically supported, as our data in (4) show. In both Chinese and Japanese comparatives, there lacks a gradable predicate in the *standard*, that is, the Chinese *bi-phrase* and the Japanese *yori*-phrase/clause. This similarity of the two languages leads to parametric implications regarding modes of comparison in natural languages.

Kennedy (2005, 2009) proposes a semantic parameter in comparatives: individual comparison versus degree comparison. According to him, individual comparison expresses orderings between arbitrary individuals, and degree comparison expresses orderings between individuals and arbitrary degrees, the value of which may be conveyed syntactically by complex degree descriptions. That is to say, individual comparison involves a syntactic *standard* of type *e*, and derives a standard degree by applying the meaning of the gradable adjective to this individual. Degree comparison, on the other hand, concerns a syntactic *standard* that is already type *d*. Given this assumption, the absence of negative island effect and sub-comparatives in Japanese and Chinese follows immediately: in these two languages, comparatives do not involve degree abstraction structures, whereas English comparatives do.[20] Comparatives in Japanese and Chinese are of individual comparison.

As discussed in Beck et al. (2004) and Kennedy (2005, 2009), Japanese comparatives have the following different properties from their English counterparts: (i) they lack specialized comparative morphology comparable to the English *–er*; (ii) they do not allow the English type of sub-comparatives; and (iii) Japanese comparatives do not show English-like 'negative island' effect. Our discussion thus far has witnessed these properties.

Regarding these properties, Chinese is similar to Japanese. It also lacks (i) specialized comparative morphology; (ii) sub-comparatives, as seen in (4); and (iii) 'negative island' effect, as demonstrated in (94).

Like (94), which we have seen in (77a), similar meanings in Chinese are expressed by a relative clause as in (95a), and a non-restrictive relative clause sounds more natural as in (95b).

(94) John-wa   dare-mo kawa-naka-tta   no   yori   takai   hon-o
      John-TOP anyone   buy-NEG-PAST NO YORI expensive book-ACC
      kat-ta.
      buy-PAST
      'Compared to the one that nobody bought, John bought an expensive book.'

(95) a. Zhangsan mai le   yi   ben bi [meiren mai de na ben (shu)] hai gui
          Zhangsan buy ASP one CL BI nobody buy DE that CL   still expensive
          de shu.
          DE book
          'Zhangsan bought a book that is even more expensive than the book that nobody bought.'

---

[20] Degree comparison is not the only option in English comparatives since both degree comparison and individual comparison are empirically evidenced (see Chomsky 1977; Napoli 1983; Corver 1997; Heim 2000; Kennedy 2009).

b. Zhangsan mai le   yi ben shu, bi [meiren mai de na   ben (shu)]
   Zhangsan buy ASP one CL book, BI nobody buy DE that CL book
   hai gui.
   still expensive
   'Zhangsan bought a book, which is more expensive than the one that nobody bought.'

Like Japanese, Chinese also takes nominal scales to convey the meaning of sub-comparatives as in (96) (Fu 1978; Liu 1996; Xiang 2005; Guo 2012).

(96) Zhe ge shujia de gaodu bi na   shan men de kuandu da.
      this CL shelf DE height BI that CL   door DE width   big
      'The shelf's height is greater than the door's width.'

The lack of comparative morphology as well as the absence of sub-comparatives and negative island effect in both Japanese and Chinese can hence be traced back to the parametric nature of comparison: these languages resort to individual comparison where the property of gradability is compared between two nominals instead of two degree predicates.

4. Conclusion

In this chapter, we started from different proposals on the derivation of Chinese comparatives and focused on issues centering around the controversial status of *bi*. Adopting Zhang's (2007, 2010) syntactic analysis of the English symmetrical comitatives and the Chinese comitative coordinators, we arrived at a unified analysis of the structure of the *comparee* and the *standard* in Chinese comparatives. On the basis of Guo's (2012) work, we provided a more refined structural analysis for Chinese comparatives that unifies comparatives of superiority and equality. The unifying analysis captures and accounts for the properties of comparative constructions in Chinese, which serves to illuminate that the language resorts to a coordinate structure to accommodate two nominals as *comparee* and *standard* in executing semantics of comparison, thereby constituting a neat syntax and semantics mapping for Chinese as an individual comparison language.

We also examined the properties of Japanese comparatives, drawing on the work of Beck et al. (2004). By demonstrating that Japanese and Chinese comparative constructions exhibit similar properties in terms of absence of sub-comparatives and lack of negative island effect, we confirmed that no degree comparison is available in these languages.

Our study echos Kennedy's (2005, 2009) proposal of semantic parameters in natural language comparatives. Chinese and Japanese do not involve degree abstraction structures, as do English comparatives. Comparatives in Chinese and Japanese are of individual comparison.

We hope that the discussions in this chapter can pave the way for our future exploration on more parametric properties between comparatives in these languages.

Acknowledgements

We wish to express our sincere thanks to the editors of this volume, Andrew Simpson, Audrey Li, and Dylan Tsai, for their useful comments and suggestions on earlier versions of our analysis, which encouraged us to consider the issues addressed in this chapter from a broader perspective. The part on the internal structure of Chinese comparatives was presented at the 8th Theoretical East Asian Linguistics Workshop (TEAL-8) at National Tsinghua University, Taiwan, 2013. We are grateful to the organizers of the Workshop and the audience there for their helpful feedback. Our special thanks go to Chris Kennedy, James Huang, Paul Law, Jo-wang Lin, Haihua Pan, Niina Zhang and Marcel den Dikken, for their insightful comments on our analysis on various occasions. We are particularly indebted to Li Shen for his helpful confirmation and comments on our discussion about the Japanese data. The remaining errors are ours.

References

Abney, Steven Paul. 1987. *The English Noun Phrase in Its Sentential Aspect*. Doctoral dissertation, MIT.

Alexiadou, Artemis. 1997. *Adverb Placement: A Case Study in Antisymmetric Syntax*. Amsterdam: John Benjamins.

Baker, Mark. 1988. *Incorporation: A Theory of Grammatical Function Changing*. Chicago: University of Chicago Press.

Baker, Mark. 2003. *Lexical Categories: Nouns, Verbs, and Adjectives*. Cambridge: Cambridge University Press.

Beck, Sigrid, Toshiko Oda, and Koji Sugisaki. 2004. Parametric variation in the semantics of comparison: Japanese vs. English. *Journal of East Asian Linguistics* 13, 289–344.

Bierwisch, Manfred. 1989. The semantics of gradation. In *Dimensional Adjectives: Grammatical Structure and Conceptual Interpretation*, ed. Manfred Bierwisch and Ewald Lang, 71–261. Berlin: Springer-Verlag.

Bobaljik, Johnathan. 1995. *Morphosyntax: The Syntax of Verb Inflection*. Doctoral dissertation, MIT.

Bobaljik, Johnathan. 2012. *Universals in Comparative Morphology: Suppletion, Superlatives, and the Structure of Words*. Cambridge, MA: The MIT Press.

Borer, Hagit. 2005. *In Name Only*. New York: Oxford University Press.

Bowers, John. 1993. The syntax of predication. *Linguistic Inquiry* 24, 591–656.

Bresnan, Joan. 1973. Syntax of the comparative clause construction in English. *Linguistic Inquiry* 4, 275–343.

Cheng, Lisa. 1995. On *dou*-quantification. *Journal of East Asian Linguistics* 4, 197–234.

Chomsky, Noam. 1977. On wh-movement. In *Formal Syntax*, ed. Peter Culicover, Tom Wasow, and Adrian Akmajian, 71–132. New York: Academic Press.

Cinque, Guglielmo. 1999. *Adverbs and Functional Heads: A Cross-linguistic Perspective*. Oxford: Oxford University Press.

Corver, Norbert. 1993. A note on subcomparatives. *Linguistic Inquiry* 24, 773–781.

Corver, Nobert. 1997. The internal syntax of the Dutch extended adjectival projection. *Natural Language and Linguistic Theory* 15, 289–368.

Cresswell, Maxwell John. 1976. The semantics of degree. In *Montague Grammar*, ed. Barbara Patee, 261–292. New York: Academic Press.

Cruse, D. Alan. 1986. *Lexical Semantics*. Cambridge: Cambridge University Press.

Dikken, Marcel den, Yang Gu, and Jie Guo. 2010. *Positively Comparative*. Keynote speech presented at the 12th Seoul International Conference on Generative Grammar, Konkuk University, Korea.

Erlewine, Mitcho. 2007. *A New Syntax-Semantics for the Mandarin* bi *Comparative*. Master thesis, University of Chicago.

Ernst, Thomas. 2008. Adverbs and positive polarity in Mandarin Chinese. In *Proceedings of the 20th North American Conference on Chinese Linguistics* (NACCL-20), ed. Marjorie K. M. Chan and Hana Kang, 68–85. Columbus: Ohio State University.

Fu, Yi-Chin. 1978. *Comparative Structures in English and Mandarin Chinese*. Doctoral dissertation, University of Michigan.

Grano, Thomas, and Chris Kennedy. 2012. Mandarin transitive comparatives and the grammar of measurement. *Journal of East Asian Linguistics* 21, 219–266.

Gu, Yang, and Jie Guo. 2008. *The Structure of Comparative Constructions in Mandarin Chinese*. Paper presented at the 12th Symposium on Chinese Contemporary Linguistics, Wuhan, China.

Gu, Yang, and Jie Guo. 2009. *Some Issues of the Chinese Comparatives*. Paper presented at the 5th International Conference on Contemporary Chinese Grammar (ICCCG-5), Hong Kong Polytechnic University.

Gu, Yang, and Jie Guo. (to appear). On the status of the compared elements in Chinese comparatives. In *Peaches and Plums*, ed. James Huang and Feng-his Liu, Monograph in Language and Linguistics, Taiwan.

Guo, Jie. 2012. *Form and Meaning: Chinese Adjectives and Comparative Constructions*. Doctoral dissertation, The Chinese University of Hong Kong.

Heim, Irene. 1985. *Notes on Comparatives and Related Matters*. Ms., University of Texas.

Heim, Irene. 2000. Degree operators and scope. In *SALT X*, ed. Brendan Jackson and Tanya Matthews, 40–64. Ithaca, NY: CLC Publications.

Hoji, Hajime. 1998. Null object and sloppy identity in Japanese. *Linguistic Inquiry* 29, 127–152.

Ishii, Yasuo. 1991. *Operators and Empty Categories in Japanese*. Doctoral dissertation, University of Connecticut.

Jacobson, Pauline. 1995. On the quantificational force of English free relatives. In *Quantification in Natural Languages*, ed. Emmon Bach, Eloise Jelinek, Angelika Kratzer, and Barbara H. Partee (Studies in Linguistics and Philosophy (SLAP) 54), 451–486. Dordrecht: Kluwer.

Kayne, Richard S. 1994. *The Antisymmetry of Syntax*. Cambridge, MA: The MIT Press.

Kennedy, Christopher. 1999. *Projecting the Adjective: The Syntax and Semantics of Gradability and Comparison*. New York: Garland Publishing.

Kennedy, Christopher. 2005. *Parameters of Comparison*. Ms., University of Chicago.

Kennedy, Christopher. 2006. Semantics of comparatives. In *Encyclopedia of language and linguistics* (2nd ed.), ed. Keith Brown, 690–694. Oxford: Elsevier.

Kennedy, Christopher. 2009. Modes of comparison. In *Proceedings from the Main Session of the 43rd Annual Meeting of the Chicago Linguistic Society* 43(1), ed. Malcolm Elliott, James Kirby, Osamu Sawada, Eleni Staraki, and Suwon Yoon, 141–165. Chicago: Chicago Linguistic Society.

Klein, Ewan. 1980. A semantics for positive and comparative adjectives. *Linguistics and Philosophy* 4, 1–45.

LaPolla, Randy. 1990. *Grammatical Relations in Chinese: Synchronic and Diachronic Considerations*. Doctoral dissertation, University of California, Berkeley.

Larson, Richard K. 1988. On the double object construction. *Linguistic Inquiry* 19, 335–391.

Larson, Richard K. 1991. *The Projection of DP and DegP*. Ms., Stony Brook University.

Li, Charles, and Sandra Thompson. 1981. *Mandarin Chinese: A Functional Reference Grammar*. Berkeley: University of California Press.

Li, Yafei. 1990. X°-binding and verb incorporation. *Linguistic Inquiry* 21, 399–426.

Li, Ying-Che. 2001. Aspects of historical-comparative syntax: Functions of prepositions in Taiwanese and Mandarin. In *Sinitic Grammar: Synchronic and Diachronic Perspectives*, ed. Hilary Chappell, 340–368. Oxford: Oxford University Press.

Lin, Jo-wang. 2009. Chinese comparatives and their implicational parameters. *Natural Language Semantics* 17, 1–27.

Liu, Chen-Sheng Luther. 1996. A note on Chinese comparatives. *Studies in the Linguistic Sciences* 26, 217–235.

Lü, Shuxiang, et al. 1980. *Xiandai Hanyu Babai Ci [800 Words in Modern Chinese]*. Beijing: The Commercial Press.

Miyagawa, Shigeru. 1989. Light verbs and the ergative hypothesis. *Linguistic Inquiry* 20, 659–668.

Napoli, Donna Jo. 1983. Comparative ellipsis: A phrasal structural analysis. *Linguistic Inquiry* 14, 675–693.

Paris, Marie-Claude. 2013. Butong 'different' and nominal plurality in Mandarin Chinese. In *Plurality and Classifiers across Languages in China*, ed. Dan Xu, 183–201. Mounton: de Gruyter.

Paul, Waltraud. 1993. A non-deletion account of the comparative construction in Mandarin Chinese. *Cahiers de Linguistique Asie Orientale* 93(1), 9–29.

Rullmann, Hotze. 1995. *Maximality in the Semantics of Wh-Constructions*. Doctoral dissertation, University of Massachusetts, Amherst (URL http://scholarworks.umass.edu/dissertations/AAI9524743/).

Sapir, Edward. 1944. Grading, a study in semantics. *Philosophy of Science* 11, 93–116.

Stassen, Leon. 1985. *Comparison and Universal Grammar*. New York: Basil Blackwell.

Stechow, Arnim von. 1984. Comparing semantic theories of comparison. *Journal of Semantics* 3, 1–77.

Sudo, Yasutada. (to appear). Hidden nominal structures in Japanese clausal comparatives. (*Journal of East Asian Linguistics*).

Tanaka, Takuro. 2006. Lexical decomposition and comparative structures for Japanese determiners. In *SALT XVI*, ed. M. Gibson and J. Howell, 277–294. Ithaca, NY: Cornell University Press.

Tao, Yuan. 2011. *Chinese Middle Constructions: A Case of Disposition Ascription*. Doctoral dissertation, The Hong Kong Polytechnic University.

Tenny, Carol. 2000. Core events and adverbial modification. In *Events as Grammatical Objects: The Converging Perspectives of Lexical Semantics and Syntax*, ed. Carol Tenny and James Pustejovsky, 285–334. Stanford, CA: CSLI publications.

Tomioka, Satoshi. 2003. The semantics of Japanese null pronouns and its cross-linguistic implications. In *The Interfaces: Deriving and Interpreting Omitted Structures*, ed. Kerstin Schwabe and Susanne Winkler, Vol. 61, 321–339. Amsterdam: John Benjamins.

Tsai, Wei-Tien Dylan, and Melody Yayin Chang. 2003. Two types of *wh*-adverbials: A typological study of *how* and *why* in Tsou. In *The Linguistic Variation Yearbook* 3, ed. Pierre Pica, 213–236. Amsterdam: John Benjamins.

Watanabe, Akira. 2006. Functional projections of nominals in Japanese: Syntax of classifiers. *Natural Language and Linguistic Theory* 24, 241–306.

Xiang, Ming. 2005. *Some Topics in Comparative Constructions*. Doctoral dissertation, Michigan State University.

Xiong, Zhongru. 2007. Analyses of the syntactic structure of comparative sentences in Modern Chinese and its dialects. *Language and Linguistics* 8, 1043–1063.

Yue-Hashimoto, Anne. 1966. *Embedding Structures in Mandarin*. Doctoral dissertation, Ohio State University.

Zhang, Niina Ning. 2007. The syntax of English comitatives. *Folia Linguistica* 41, 135–169.

Zhang, Niina Ning. 2010. *Coordination in Syntax*. Cambridge: Cambridge University Press.

Zhu, Dexi. 1982. *Yufa Jiangyi [Lectures on Grammar]*. Beijing: Commercial Press.

14

Root Infinitive Analogues in Chinese and Japanese and the Emergence of Full Syntactic Structure

KEIKO MURASUGI

1. Introduction

Children are born with an innate knowledge of grammar and manifest linguistic competence that is equivalent to the adult speakers of their mother tongue in just a few years. According to Chomsky's hypothesis of Universal Grammar (UG) (e.g., Chomsky 1965, 1995), all human languages are similar when considered from an abstract level, and the hypothesis explains the logical problem of language acquisition, that is, the question of why it is the case that children acquire their first language without being taught, despite that the language system is complex.

There is a lot of evidence indicating that the child knows the grammatical, morphological, and phonological properties of many important elements of his or her mother language at the earliest observable stages. Erbaugh (1992), for example, reports that Chinese-speaking children (1;10–3;10) adhere strictly to canonical SVO word order. The longitudinal study reported there shows that the word order in the target language is acquired very early. Guo, Foley, Chien, Chiang, and Lust (1996) find, based on the experimental study of VP ellipsis in Mandarin Chinese, that Mandarin-speaking children, even at around three years of age, know the ambiguity in the sloppy identity structure, and argue that the binding relation between an operator and a variable is part of the innate language faculty, in accord with a theory of UG.

Generative Grammar makes crucial use of the fact that UG should be powerful enough to enable the child to acquire a first language and at the same time flexible enough to account for all different human languages. Within the Principles and Parameters approach to UG, the process of language acquisition is interpreted as the process of fixing the values of parameters in one of the permissible ways (Chomsky 1995). Generative Grammar suggests that children are equipped with a UG that supports language acquisition by sharply constraining "grammar space." Children innately know this space, reducing their task to one of selecting among a highly limited set of candidate grammars that UG admits, based on their input data. Under this view, the data from child language can (in principle) be quite valuable in evaluating the parameters proposed through the investigations of comparative syntax. In particular, it should be noted that children produce a possible human language that is not the language spoken in their language community at any given time. That is, one might expect to find some "errors" or "ungrammatical strings in the target adult grammar" that caretakers never produce, because children try out other possible values of parameters.

If this expectation is empirically confirmed, it provides strong support for UG. The present study attempts to demonstrate this point through the examination of the development of syntactic structure in child Chinese and Japanese. In particular, we suggest that both Chinese- and Japanese-speaking children (i) go through the Root Infinitive Analogue stage, (ii) produce sentence-final particles earlier than tense/aspect-marked verbs, and argue that this is consistent with the Truncation Hypothesis proposed by Rizzi (1993/1994) for children's early syntactic structure.

2. Grammatical Tense Deficits in Children

2.1. ROOT INFINITIVES

It has been found that in languages with relatively "rich" morphology, such as Dutch, German and French, children are found to optionally use the infinitive forms of inflection (e.g., affix) on the verbs, rather than finite ones, in the root clause.

(1) a. Mama   radio aan doen (Dutch) (2;00)
         mummy radio on to-do
         'Mummy switch on radio.' (Wijnen, Kempen and Gillis 2001)

     b. Thorsten Caesar haben (German) (2;01)
         Thorsten Caesar to-have
         'Thorsten has [the doll] Caesar.' (Poeppel and Wexler 1993)

     c. Voir l'auto papa (French) (2;02)
         to-see the car daddy (Intended meaning: ongoing activity) (Pierce 1992)

In languages that are relatively "poor" in inflectional morphology like English, on the other hand, the bare verb forms appear in finite (root) contexts. In adult English, infinitive forms are generally the bare stems, and English-speaking children produce the bare stems within the age range of 20–36 months, as shown in (2).

(2) a. Papa have it (English) (Eve,1;06)

     b. Cromer wear glasses (English) (Eve, 2;00)

The non-finite verb forms employed by children in finite (root) contexts are termed Root Infinitives (RIs), and their properties have been extensively examined in child language research.

It has been pointed out that RIs/Root Infinitive Analogues (= RIAs) are associated with certain morpho-syntactic and semantic properties (see Deen 2002, among others).

(3)   Properties common among RIs /RIAs

   a.   At the RI stage, no T-related/C-related items are found.

   b.   RIs are produced to describe events in real time, that is, as an ongoing activity in the past, present, or future that the child is involved in.

   c.   RIs occur in modal contexts (Modal Reference Effects).

   d.   RIs are restricted to event-denoting predicates (Eventivity Constraint).

   e.   Head Merger is not available during the RI(A) stage.

As noted in (3a), at the stage where non-finite verbs are used in finite (root) contexts, C-related elements such as *wh*-phrases and complementizers (Haegeman 1995), and T-related elements such as *be*-copula and auxiliaries are not found. In addition, two peculiar types of contextual interpretations have been identified. One type refers to the so-called extensional contexts, whereby RI(A)s are produced to describe events in real time, that is, ongoing activities in the past, present, or future that the child is involved in. For example, the non-finite forms in child French like (1c) are produced to describe an ongoing activity. The other type of interpretation refers to the so-called intentional contexts, whereby RI(A)s are produced to express children's intention, desire, or volition in various "irrealis" modal contexts. This is termed the Modal Reference Effects (MREs) (Hoekstra and Hyams 1998). In addition, RIs, in general, are largely restricted to eventive predicates (Hoekstra and Hyams 1998), and the head merger between V and T is not available during the stage of RI(A)s, as proposed by Phillips (1995, 1996).

Chinese is a heavily isolating language that has commonly been considered not to manifest morphological tense-marking or infinitives. However, one might nevertheless wonder whether there is still any analogue of the RI phenomenon in Chinese and other similar morphologically impoverished languages, given that, for example, case-related phenomena seem to show up in languages that do not exhibit overt morphological case. Before we discuss the RIAs in Chinese in section 2.3, let us briefly discuss the related issues in another argument-drop language, Japanese, in section 2.2.

2.2. SURROGATE VERBS IN CHILD JAPANESE: VERB + *TA* FORM

Like Chinese, Japanese is a language that does not have a specitically infinitive suffix. Japanese is an agglutinating language where bare stems cannot stand alone without, for example, tense or aspect morphemes, as shown in (4). Japanese is, like Italian and Spanish, a [-stem] language whose verbs cannot surface as bare forms.

(4)   a.   *tabe-   (to eat)
      b.   *suwar-   (to sit)

Unlike Italian and Spanish, however, Japanese does not have rich verbal inflection (agreement) that indicates number and gender. Japanese verbs inflect for tense, negation, aspect, and mood.

The conjugations in Japanese are acquired at an early stage, at around the beginning of age two. Murasugi, Fuji, and Hashimoto (2007), Murasugi and Fuji (2008a, b) Murasugi, Nakatani, and Fuji (2010), and Murasugi (2009), based on the corpus analysis of Sumihare (Noji 1973–1977, CHILDES) and the longitudinal study with Yuta (Nakatani and Murasugi 2009), argue that the RI state is found among Japanese-speaking children as well. According to them, some of the typical properties of RIs given in (3) are also observed in Japanese in early non-finite verbal forms: (i) T-related (e.g., Nominative Case, copulative elements, and verbal conjugation) and C-related items (e.g., *to*, the complementizer that heads a Report Phrase (Saito 2009)) are *not* observed with the early non-finite verbs, and tense is underspecified; (ii) the past-tensed adjectives are not produced; (iii) Verb-*ta* forms (past-tensed verb forms) are produced to describe an ongoing activity; (iv) Verb-*ta* forms (past-tensed verb forms) are used in matrix clauses for the irrealis or volition meaning (MRE); (v) Verb-*ta* forms are restricted to event-denoting predicates; and (vi) *no* merger of heads inside the verbal projection are observed at the RIA stages, as Phillips (1995, 1996) proposed.

Sumihare, a Japanese-speaking child, at around 1;06 through 1;11, for example, used the Verb-*ta* form in a different way from adults, semantically denoting the meaning of volition (desire) or request.

(5) a. Atti Atti Atti i-*ta* (1;06) (irrealis/volition) (adult form: ik-u/ik-e)
there there there go-TA
'I want to go there./Go there.'

  b. Tii   si-*ta* (1;07) (irrealis/volition) (adult form: si-ta-i)
onomatopoeia (pee) do-TA
'I want to pee.'

  c. Baba pai-*ta* (1;08) (request) (adult form: pai-si-te)
mud onomatopoeia (throw away)-TA
'Throw (the mud) away.'

Noji (the observer) describes that *i-ta* in (5a)[1] means *ik-u* (go-Pres), and states, "Sumihare uttered *i-ta* as he could not say *ik-u*" (Noji 1973–1977: I: 195). Noji also writes important comments for (5b), which convinces us of the MREs at the early stage of Japanese acquisition: Sumihare used *tii-si-ta* in a volition context when he wanted to pee. As for (5c), Sumihare produced *pai-ta*, attaching -*ta* on the onomatopoeia *pai* (to throw away), in order to ask his mother to remove mud from a potato.

The percentage of V-*ta* forms decreases with age. At 1;06-1;07, he used the V-*ta* form almost 100% of the time. RIAs are not *"optional* infinitives" in Japanese-type languages.

---

[1] The context for (5a) is the following: Sumihare's father (Noji, the observer) went out for a walk with Sumihare on his back. Noji tried to go back home, but Sumihare pointed to a different direction and produced "atti (there)" twice. Frustrated, Sumihare said, "atti i-ta (there go-Past) = (Literal meaning: I went, Intended meaning: I wanna go there)" angrily repeatedly (Noji 1973–1977).

Parallel data are found in a longitudinal study with another Japanese-speaking child, Yuta, as in (6) (Nakatani and Murasugi 2009).

(6) a. Ai-*ta*   Ai-*ta* (1;07.1) (irrealis/volition) (adult form: ake-te)
         open-TA open-TA
         'I want to open this cabinet. / Open this cabinet.'

     b. Hait-*ta*   Hait-*ta* (1;07.16) (volition) (adult form: ire-tai)
         enter-TA enter-TA
         'I want to put this notebook into this bag.'

     c. Oti-*ta*   Otyoto(=Osoto) Oti-*ta* (1;07.13) (progressive)
         drop-TA outside   drop-TA (adult form: otosi-teiru)
         'I am putting this doll outside.'

     d. Oti-*ta* Oti-*ta* Oti-*ta* (1;07.5) (result) (adult form: oti-teiru)
         fall-TA fall-TA fall-TA
         'A container of the videotape is lying there.'

Very young children under two years of age consistently use V-*ta* form to denote intentional meaning as exemplified in (6a) and (6b), and extensional meaning as exemplified in (6c) and (6d). This fact suggests that the verbal conjugation, that is, the merger of V and inflection, is not yet available then. It is the stage where a default morphological form in the target language is used as the first verbal form by a child, and the past-tense form, V-*ta*, which children pick as an RIA, is most unmarked among the possible forms in Japanese.[2]

In adult Japanese, two conjuncts unspecified for tense, for example, are conjoined with -*ta* forms as in (7a, b), and -*ta* forms can be used for future as in (8a, b) and with irrealis meaning as well, as exemplified in (8c).

(7) a. Tabe-**ta** ri non-**da** ri si-yoo/su-ru/si-ta
         eat-TA   drink-TA let's do/do-Pres/do-Past
         'We eat/ate, and we drink/drank.'

     b. It-**ta** ri ki-**ta** ri de taihen   da/dat-ta
         go-TA come-TA for troublesome is /was
         'It is/was troublesome to go back and forth.'

(8) a. Asu-wa   nani-o   suru-no-dat-**ta**-ka-na?
         tomorrow-Top what-Acc do-Nom-Cop-TA-C-Speech Act
         'What am I going to do tomorrow?'

     b. Sooda! Asu-wa   paatii-dat-**ta**!
         so-Cop Tomorrow-Top party-Cop-TA
         'Aha! Tomorrow is a party!'

---

[2] Non-finite verb forms are found in embedded clauses in adult Japanese. The past verbal inflection -*ta* lacks tense interpretation (but it is rather aspectual) in such relative clauses as "*yude-ta tamago*" (boil-past egg, meaning boiled egg (property reading)) in adult Japanese.

c. Mosimo watasi-ga ie-o   tate-ru/-**ta**   nara tiisana
    if   I-Nom   house-Acc build-pres/TA then small
    ie-o   tate-ru/-ta   (deshoo)
    house-Acc build-pres/-TA (would)
    'If I built a house, I would build a tiny one.'

Furthermore, just like infinitives in Italian (Rizzi 1993/1994), V-*ta* forms in adult Japanese can be used as non-finite surrogate forms to express strong imperatives, as shown in (9).

(9) a. Partire immediatamente!
         go   immediately   (Rizzi 1993/1994)

     b. Sassato   Kaet-**ta**!   Kaet-**ta**!
         immediately go back-TA go back-TA
         'Go back immediately.'

Thus, the *ta*-form seems to function as a non-finite form as well as a past-tense form in adult Japanese. Children, without being taught by caretakers, even at one year of age, choose the non-finite V-*ta* form as the surrogate form, attaching a "default" morpheme *ta* to the verb stem, before they fully acquire the conjugation system of the verbs.

Suppose that the unmarked surrogate form in Japanese is the non-finite V-*ta* form in adult Japanese, then agglutinative language-speaking children, even at the age of one year, know the morphological property that verbal stems *cannot* stand *without* tense/aspect morphemes in their target language. And when Tense Phrase is not projected, the unmarked verbal suffix(es) is (are) chosen for the surrogate form(s), that is, the RIA(s).[3]

2.3. IMPERATIVES (BARE VERBS) IN CHILD CHINESE

The discussion so far indicates that if a language L has verbs whose stem cannot stand alone, children speaking L would produce the "surrogate infinitival" forms (e.g., as in Japanese) or infinitival form (e.g., as in Italian). Then, what about an isolating pro-drop, or more precisely, isolating argument-drop language, Chinese?

The history of the research on RI(A) has revealed that the phenomenon is very much related to the imperative. For instance, the bare stem of the verb in English, the Japanese V-*ta*, and infinitives in European languages are generally used as imperatives as well. In fact, there are a lot of cross-linguistic studies reporting that the first non-finite verbal form that children produce is imperative (Salustri and Hyams 2003,

---

[3] Note here that RIAs with the so-called "surrogate infinitives" are found at around age one year, much earlier than RIs are found in European languages, and the non-finite form is not optionally used either. The non-finite form is initially (at around 1;06–1;07) used 100% of the time in a full range of environments, and there is no correlation between null subjects and non-finite verb forms in Japanese, for example, unlike the case of European RIs. As we briefly mention in note 5, the sharp contrast indicates that the so-called "Root Infinitive (Analogue) stage" is actually twofold: tense-truncated stage and tense-unspecified stage (which is termed Optional Infinitives).

2006 for Italian; Bar-Shalom and Snyder 2001 for Russian; Lillo-Martin and Quadros 2009 for ASL). Chinese is not an exception.

Chien (2009), based on the corpus analysis of two children (1;9–3;1, 1;11–3;0) and two adults from Tsing-Hua Mandarin Child Language Corpus, argues that children speaking Mandarin use imperative forms as RIAs. The imperative RIAs are exemplified in (10).

(10)　a.　(ni)　qu chi mian-bao (2;05)
　　　　　(you) go eat bread
　　　　　'You go to eat the bread.'
　　　　　(Context: The child (= speaker) asks the adult to eat the bread.)

　　　b.　(ni)　yong na ge he　cha (2;06)
　　　　　(you) use　that CL drink tea
　　　　　'You use the one to drink tea.'
　　　　　(Context: The child (= speaker) asks the adult to use that cup to drink tea.)

　　　c.　Ni bao ta (2;05)
　　　　　you hold it
　　　　　'You hold it.'
　　　　　(Context: The child (= speaker) asks the adult to hold a toy.)

　　　d.　Ni qian　　ge-ge (2;05)
　　　　　You pull along brother
　　　　　'You pull along my brother.'
　　　　　(Context: The child (= speaker) asks the adult to pull along his/her brother.)

Chien's (2009) finding has striking parallels with Salustri and Hyams's (2003, 2006) proposal that Italian RIAs are imperatives. The evidence is elicited based on the criterion given in (11):

(11)　a.　In null subject languages, imperatives will occur significantly more often in child language than in adult language.
　　　b.　In child language, imperatives will occur significantly more often in the null subject languages than in the RI languages.

(Salustri and Hyams 2003, 2006)

Chien (2009) finds that the frequency of imperatives in child Mandarin is higher than the frequency of imperatives in the adult speech, and argues that the results obtained in her study are consistent with those of Salustri and Hyams (2003, 2006). According to Salustri and Hyams (2003, 2006), Italian-speaking adults use only about 5.6% imperative forms; while Italian-speaking children use about 16.4% to 31.1% imperative forms (and use only 0% to 2.8% infinitive forms). In contrast, in German, a typical RI language, adults use 35.6% imperatives, and children use about 10% imperatives. Chien's (2009) data is basically parallel with those of Salustri and Hyams (2003). For example, according to Chien's (2009) counting, Mandarin-speaking adults use only about 10% imperatives; while a Mandarin-speaking child, at 2;05, uses about 47% imperatives. A closer examination of Chien's (2009) findings indicates that the contrast between child and adult imperatives is much more salient in

Chinese than in the Italian case. For a Mandarin-speaking child at 1;11, her study shows that 60% of the utterances are in imperative form. Thus, just like Salustri and Hyams (2003, 2006), Chien's (2009) finding suggests that there is an RIA stage in Chinese, and the form is imperative in Mandarin Chinese (see also Su 2012).

Given Chien's (2009) finding, then we predict that the very young children producing imperatives as their RIAs would produce the strings that lack tense as well. And there is a piece of evidence that suggests that this prediction is correct.

According to Lin (2008), Mandarin Chinese has TP, and the head T can be finite or nonfinite and the clauses exhibits a finite and non-finite contrast, although there is no specifically morphological tense in the language. According to Lin (2006, 2008), epistemic and obligation modals take a finite TP complement and can only appear in finite contexts. By contrast, future and other types of root modals take a non-finite TP complement and can occur in finite and non-finite clauses.[4] As shown in (12a) and (12b), he argues that epistemic modals always scope over *le* since *le* can be licensed within their finite TP complements. Conversely, root modals always scope under *le* because *le* cannot be licensed within their non-finite TP complements. If *le* is to appear, it must be generated in the matrix Asp and takes the modal verb as its complement. The perfect *le* does not occur inside the scope of the root modals because it does not get licensed by T. This is also true for the preverbal progressive auxiliary *zai* as shown in (12c) and (12d). *Zai* may occur in the TP complement of the epistemic modals, but not in the TP complement of the root modals.

(12) a. Zhangsani Tꜰ [AspP [vp   keneng [TP ti Tꜰ [AspP [vp   qu Taipei] le]]] Ø]
          Zhangsan   likely   go Taipei Prf Stc
          'It is likely that Zhangsan has gone to Taipei.'

      b. Zhangsan Tꜰ [AspP [vp   nenggou [TP PRO Tɴꜰ [AspP [vp   qu Taipei] Ø]]] le]
          Zhangsan   able   go Taipei Stc Prf
          'Zhangsan has (become) able to go to Taipei.'

      c. Zhangsan keneng   [zai   chi hanbao]
          Zhangsan be-likely-to PRG eat burger
          'It is likely that Zhangsan is eating a burger.'

      d. *Zhangsan nenggou [zai   chi hanbao]
          Zhangsan be-able-to PROG eat burger
          'Zhangsan is able to go to be eating a burger.'

What matters for the argument here is the fact that the sentence-final particles *le* (and the progressive aspect marker *zai*) in adult Mandarin distinguishes finite sentences from non-finite ones. Given the adult grammar, the perfect sentence particle *le* (and *zai*) is (are) predicted to be (at least optionally) absent at the stage of RIAs in child Mandarin.

---

[4] As a result, Lin (2006) proposes that modals that take finite TP must precede modals that take a non-finite TP, and Lin thereby sets up the following hierarchy of modals in Mandarin Chinese.

(i)   Necessity > Possibility/Obligation > Future > Ability/Permission/Volition

Crucially, Liu (2009) observes that Mandarin-speaking children do drop the perfective sentence particle *le* at a very early stage of language acquisition. HY (1;09), for example, dropped *le* in the obligatory context as shown in (13). In (13), the child dropped *le* even when repeating what his mother has said to him.

(13)   Mom: Xie huir, lei   le
                 rest a-bit tired LE
                 'Let's rest a bit; you are tired.'
         HY (1;09): Xie huir, lei Ø

A similar example in (14) is found in the production of BB (1;10).

(14)   BB (1;10) : Nainai   qu nar Ø
                        grandma go where
                        'Where does Gramma go?'
                        (Intended meaning: 'Where did Gramma go?')

         Mom: Ta nainai   qu Hangzhou le.
                 his gramma go   LE
                 'His Gramma went to Hangzhou.'

As shown in (15), the achievement verb *po* (to be torn, worn out) should be marked with the perfective marker *le* in adult Mandarin, but a child, LC (1;09), dropped it.

(15)   LC (1;09) : po Ø
                        wear-out
                        'It's worn out.'

Needless to say, we need to confirm that the Mandarin-speaking children using imperatives as RIAs *also* drop *le* at the same time. We also need to examine carefully whether or not the typical RI(A) properties listed in (3) are found in Mandarin Chinese. However, the fact that Mandarin-speaking children dominantly use imperatives (as RIAs) and drop the perfective marker *le* at the age of one year suggests that there is an intermediate stage where the sentence lacks the independent Tense elements, even in the acquisition of a typical argument-drop language, Mandarin Chinese.

To sum up the argument so far, children acquiring Japanese and Chinese, typical pro-drop or argument-drop languages, go through the RI(A) stage. Non-finite verbs in finite (root) contexts are common in very young child production cross-linguistically, and the early verbal forms in child languages reflect the core morphological properties of the adult grammar.

3. The Truncation Model

The findings discussed so far show that the RIAs in Japanese and Chinese are the verbs that very young children produce when (independent) Tense elements are missing.

A potential question, however, still remains unsolved. What does it exactly mean that Tense is missing in the child syntactic structure? What are RI(A)s?[5]

The stage of RIA, in fact, can be explained by the Truncation Hypothesis proposed by Rizzi (1993/1994). The Truncation Hypothesis states that children's structures can be as complex as adult structures, but child grammar allows the choice of optionally truncate structures. To be more concrete, adults build their phrase structure all the way to CP because CP is the root of all clauses, while children might build just a VP or an IP (TP) and stop. According to Rizzi (1993/1994), the axiom that "CP is the root of all clauses" is part of adult grammar. Children also project the phrase structure, but they lack the specific knowledge that every well-formed clause is CP in adult grammar (until the initial stage of RI stage in our term ends). Until children "acquire" the axiom, they hypothesize that phrase structures can only go partway up to CP.

This hypothesis naturally explains why the children's non-finite verbs do not move to I (T): There is no place for them to move to. This would also explain why auxiliary-related items never occur with RIs, if we assume that auxiliary-related items start in I (T). Under the Truncation Hypothesis, we also expect that there are no elements above IP (TP) that are produced by the children at the RI stage. If RIs are missing IP (TP), then they should be missing CP as well, and the hypothesis naturally explains why C-related items are not observed at the stage in question.

The Truncation Hypothesis can also account for the licensing of null subjects in child grammar. RIs are likely to occur with null subjects because the infinitive is a non-finite form, which lacks Tense, and hence it can license null subjects of the type PRO.

Furthermore, we conjecture that the Truncation Hypothesis can also elegantly explain the reason that English-speaking children go through an early stage of acquisition during which subjects are base-generated within VP and may optionally stay in their original position located internal to the predicate (Déprez and Pierce 1993).

---

[5] The RI(A)s found before around the age two years are the default verb forms in the target language, and they are used either when Tense Phrase is not projected, as the Truncation Hypothesis (Rizzi 1993/1994) predicts, or when there are no functional categories, as Radford (1990, 1991) and Galasso (2011) propose. In fact, Galasso (2011) finds that the stage where D is missing (as in *Jim book (= Jim's book)) comes before the Root Infinitive stage where T is optionally morphologically realized and non-nominative subjects appear in the subject position (as in *Her eat it (She eats it.)).

Then, at around the age of two, children speaking Japanese start producing several conjugated verb forms as well as "erroneous" genitive/dative subjects just like English-speaking children do. At this stage, non-nominative subjects optionally appear in the subject position (e.g., *Her eat it (She eats it) in English). Just like English-speaking children, children speaking Japanese, for example, optionally mark the subject of the sentence "erroneously" with genitive or dative (Murasugi and Watanabe 2009; Sawada and Murasugi 2011; Sawada, Murasugi, and Fuji 2010).

The sharp contrast found between the two phases of "RIs" shown above indicates that the so-called "RI(A) stage" actually has two stages. A natural hypothesis for the first stage would be, as we will discuss in this section, to suppose that the sentences in which the (default) verb is not tensed might be those where TP is missing in the child structure as Truncation Hypothesis (Rizzi 1993/1994), for example, predicts. And the RIAs found at a later stage after the age of two would correspond to the so-called Optional Infinitives. Optional Infinitives, or the infinitives optionally used in the matrix clauses, are produced when T is there, but Tense and Agreement features are still "underspecified," as ATOM (Schütze and Wexler 1996) predicts.

It is very well known that English-speaking children, at around the age of two, produce negative sentences in which the negative element occurs to the left of the subject, as shown in (16).

(16)   a.   No mommy doing. David turn. (2;00)

  b.   No lamb have it. No lamb have it. (2;00)

  c.   No Leila have a turn. (2;01)

  d.   Never Mommy touch it. (2;01)

  e.   Not man up here on him head. (2;02)

Déprez and Pierce (1993) argue that the pre-sentential negative element (e.g., *no, never, not*) is an instance of sentential negation. According to Déprez and Pierce (1993), there is a parameter of nominative Case assignment, and young children start producing such examples as (16) based on the assumption that the nominative Case may be assigned under government by Infl (rather than the assumption that the nominative Case is assigned in the Spec-head relation with Infl). Thus, children produce the sentence-initial negative element as sentential negation, as shown in (16). According to Déprez and Pierce's (1993) analysis, the structure children hypothesize for (16a) is (17):

(17)   [$_{IP}$ _____ [$_{NegP}$ no (negative element) [$_{VP}$ mommy doing]]]

Then, why is it the case that subject remains in the VP-internal position in child grammar? In the adult grammar, the arguments of the verb appear within the Verb Phrase, but they may be forced to leave that position by different principles of grammar. If the principles are part of UG, then, we expect that the principles should be applied once the sentence in question (meeting the theta theory) is produced. However, children produce subjects VP-internally without raising it to the Spec of IP (TP).

Given UG, a possible explanation for the acquisition stage of VP-internal subjects in child grammar would be that there is no IP (TP), the position for the subject, to move to. Thus, during the stage where the phrase structure is truncated, children produce such sentences as (16).

This proposal is further supported by the fact that the verbs that children produce exemplified in (16) are bare forms, or RIs. The fact that children producing subjects VP-internally without raising them to the Spec of IP (TP) also produce RIs would support the hypothesis that there is no I (T) projection at the stage.

However, a detailed analysis of child Chinese indicates that the case might not be so simple. As we noted above, if RIAs are missing IP (TP), then they should be missing the syntactic heads above IP (TP) as well. Children, however, do produce sentence-final particles at the earliest observable stage. Lee (2000), for example, using the longitudinal data from a Cantonese-speaking child (MHZ), finds that a very young child (1;7–1;11) productively used sentence-final particles. The child (1;7–1;11) produced 77 utterances with sentence-ending particles out of 553 utterances, and one-third of the child's (2;0–2;8) utterances ended with a final particle (Lee 2000: 11).

How could the three mysteries in child Chinese we have discussed so far—the productive use of imperative forms (RIAs), a stage of missing tense/aspect *le*, and the productive use of sentence-final particles—be explained in acquisition theory? No unifying theoretical explanation has thus far been provided in research on Chinese acquisition.

We cannot fully discern intermediate stages in language acquisition just by looking at one language. However, comparative acquisition studies may perhaps be better positioned to discover solutions to mysteries such as the above. In fact, just like Chinese, Japanese also has rich sentence-ending particles in adult syntax. And interestingly enough, very young Japanese-speaking children produce sentence-ending particles, just as Chinese-speaking children do. Even during the Japanese RIA stage, sentence-final particles, which should reside in the position up above the CP layer in adult grammar, are apparently added on to the "truncated" structure. Observe an example given in (18).

(18)   Buuwa tui-ta   **ne**   **ne** (Sumihare, 1;09)
       candle light-ta Sentence-final particle Sentence-final particle
       Intended meaning: Please light the candle.
       Literal meaning: The candle lit, didn't it?

Example (18) is quite important because the Japanese-speaking child Sumihare produces (i) the intransitive form *tuite* instead of the transitive form *tukete*; (ii) the V-*ta* form (RIA) instead of imperative form V-*te*; and crucially, (iii) the sentence-final particle *ne* following *tuita*, the RIA. In the following section, assuming that sentence-final particles are Speech Act heads, it is argued that the early appearance of sentence-final particles does not constitute a counterexample to the Truncation Hypothesis.

4. The Co-Occurrence of Sentence-Final Particles with RIAs

Just like Chinese, sentence-final particles are in fact produced often at a very early stage of Japanese acquisition. Okubo (1967), based on her longitudinal study with a Japanese-speaking child, finds that sentence-final particles such as *ne* are acquired much earlier than Case particles such as *ga*. Murasugi and Fuji (2008b) report that the Modal Reference Effects of RIAs are often observed with the sentence-final particle *na*, as shown in (19).

(19)   a.   Pan   **naa** (1;05)
            bread Sentence-final particle
            'I want a piece of bread.'

       b.   Sii **si-ta**   **naa** (1;07) (adult: **volition** *si-tai*)
            pee do-TA Sentence-final particle
            '(I) want to pee.'

   c.   Rii   **na**   **na** (1;07)
       go down Sentence-final particle
       'I want to go down.'
       Context: Sumihare is on his father's shoulder. (Murasugi and Fuji 2008b)

Volitional modality in the early stages of acquisition is expressed by the -*ta* form with the sentence-final particle -*na*.

There are languages that have sentence-ending particles which are used to establish discourse relations between the speaker and the hearer. Languages in Asia are particularly well known that they have rich sentence-ending markers such as *nhe* and *nhi* in Vietnamese.

However, it seems that they are not only productively found in the Asian languages. According to Haegeman and Hill (2011), in West Flemish, a dialect of Dutch, for example, there are sentence-initial and sentence-final discourse markers, which encode the speaker's attitude with respect to the (content of the) speech act and/or with respect to the addressee (Haegeman and Hill 2011). The discourse markers are optional in that an utterance remains grammatical even if they are removed, but their deletion results in a change in interpretation. There are some "rules" that sentence-final discourse markers in West Flemish obey.

First, sentence-final discourse markers in West Flemish co-occur only in a specified order. When sentence-final discourse marker *né* and *wè* co-occur, *né* must be to the right of *wè*, as shown in (20a) and (20b).

(20)   a.   Men artikel is gedoan <u>wè</u> <u>né</u>.

       b.   *Men artikel is gedoan <u>né</u> <u>wè</u>.
          My   paper is done
          'My paper is finished.' (Haegeman 2010)

When sentence-final discourse markers *zè* co-occurs with *né* or *wè*, *né* follows *zè*, as shown in (21a, b), but *wè* precedes *zè*, as in (22a, b).

(21)   a.   Men artikel is gedoan <u>zè</u> <u>né</u>.

       b.   *Men artikel is gedoan <u>né</u> <u>zè</u>.

(22)   a.   Men artikel is gedoan <u>wè</u> <u>zè</u>.

       b.   *Men artikel is gedoan <u>zè</u> <u>wè</u>. (Haegeman 2010)

Second, West Flemish has just two positions for discourse markers. Though *né* can co-occur with *zè* as in (21a) and with *wè* as in (20a), and though *wè* can also co-occur with *zè* as in (22a), the three discourse markers cannot co-occur, regardless of the order, as we can see in (23).

(23)   a.   *Men artikel is gedoan <u>wè</u> <u>zè</u> <u>né</u>.

       b.   Men artikel is gedoan <u>wè</u> <u>zè</u>. <u>Né</u>! (Haegeman 2010)

(23b) is acceptable because *né* is clearly set off from the preceding segment.

Sentence-final discourse markers in West Flemish are not clause typers, and they co-occur with clauses that are independently typed. Though some of them are insensitive to clause type, others are sensitive to the type of the sentence. For example, *zè* (and its variant *ghè*) co-occurs mainly with declaratives and with some imperatives. With regard to interrogatives, only rhetorical questions can co-occur with *zè/ghè*.

The properties found in West Flemish are shared by Japanese sentence-final particles. Japanese has sentence-initial and sentence-final discourse markers, such as *ne*, which encode the speaker's attitude with respect to the (content of the) speech act and/or with respect to the addressee. The discourse markers are optional in that an utterance remains grammatical even if they are removed, but their deletion results in a change in interpretation.

There are also "rules" that sentence-final discourse markers in Japanese obey, just as in West Flemish. The sentence-final particles such as *ne*, *na*, and *yo*, among others, are pragmatic markers used to profile the speaker-hearer relationship in Japanese. The particles are involved in the licensing of vocatives. The initial vocative has an "appeal" or attention-seeking function, aiming at establishing a discourse relation; the final vocative consolidates the already established relation of the speaker with an "addressee." Examples are shown in the following:

(24) a. **Nee Nee** Otoosan, torampu siyoo   **yo** (Koko, 8;03)
          NE NE Daddy   card   do-Vocative Sentence-final particle
          'Hey, Daddy, let's play cards.'

     b. Kono kootya-wa oisii   **ne** (Koko, 8;03)
          this tea   -Top yummy-is NE
          'This tea is tasty, isn't it?'

Just like West Flemish, the sentence-final particles display rigid ordering restrictions as shown in (25).

(25) a. Kobe-no   pan-wa   oisii <u>yo ne</u>/<u>yo na</u>.
          Kobe-Gen bread-Top tasty
          'Kobe's bread is tasty.'

     b. *Kobe-no pan-wa oisii <u>ne yo</u>/<u>na yo</u>.

The sequences, *yone* and *yona*, are grammatical, but *neyo* or *nayo* are ungrammatical, as shown in (25b). When sentence-final discourse markers *yo* and *ne* co-occur, *ne* must be to the right of *yo*.

Second, just as in West Flemish, Japanese basically only has two positions for discourse markers. Though *yo* can co-occur with *ne* (26a) and with *na* (26b), the three discourse markers cannot co-occur, regardless of the order, as we can see in (27):

(26) a. Taro-wa mikan -o   taberu <u>yo ne</u>.
          Taro-Top orange-Acc eat

b. Taro-wa mikan -o   taberu <u>yo na</u>.
    Taro-Top orange-Acc eat

(27) *Taro-wa   mikan -o   taberu <u>yo ne na</u>.
      Taro-Top orange-Acc eat
      'Taro eats oranges.'

(27) is only acceptable when *na* is clearly set off from the preceding segment.[6] Just like sentence-final discourse markers in West Flemish, Japanese sentence-final particles are basically not clause-typers either, and they co-occur with clauses that are independently typed. For example, *yo* co-occurs mainly with declaratives and imperatives.

Now, the important question to be addressed here is whether the discourse markers are part of the CP system or not. In fact, it has been pointed out that the property of the right periphery of Japanese parallels with that of left periphery in head-initial languages, such as Italian, in many respects (Saito 2009), and the discourse markers such as *ne, na,* and *yo* all seem to reside outside the CP system.[7]

According to Saito (2009), *to* is the complementizer that heads a Report Phrase, which expresses paraphrases or reports of direct discourse in the sense of Plann (1982); *ka* is a head of Force Phrase (ForceP), for questions. And *no* is the complementizer that heads a Finite Phrase, for propositions. The structure is schematized in the following example.

(28) a. [CP [CP ... [CP ... Finite (*no*)] Force (ka)] Report (to)]

      b. [CP ... [CP ... [CP ... [CP ... Finite (no)] (Topic*)] Force (ka)] Report (to)]

      c. [CP ... [CP ... [CP thematic topic [C'[CP [TP ...] Finite (no)] Topic]] Force (ka)] Report (to)]

And the discourse markers *ne, na,* and *yo* follow *ka*, which is the sentence-typer.

(29) a. [Force[Fin[TP Taroo-wa unagi-o taberu] no] ka]   **ne**
                             -Top eel-Acc eat   Finite Force Sentence-final particle
          'I wonder whether or not Taro eats eels.'

      b. [Force[Fin[TP Taroo-wa unagi-o taberu] no] ka] **na**

      c. [Force[Fin[TP Taroo-wa unagi-o taberu] no] ka] **yo**

ForceP is a sentence typer, and if the sentence is interrogative, *ka* appears in the head of ForceP. As (29a–c) indicate, sentence-final particles follow *ka*, and this shows that the discourse markers are above ForceP at least. And children acquire such discourse markers as *ne* and *na* earlier than *no* or *ka*. Okada and Grinstead (2003), in fact, show

---

[6] Three sentence-final particles are allowed only when *wa* comes first.

(i) Anata Asita   gakko-ni iku <u>wa</u> <u>yo</u> <u>ne</u>.
     You   tomorrow school-Dat go WA YO NE
     'You are going to school tomorrow, aren't you?'

[7] Properties of sentence-ending particles such as *ne, ma, ba,* and *ah* have been examined in detail by Li (2006), and the papers cited therein, for Chinese.

that *ne* appears at 1;11, while *no* and *te* appear later (at 2;02), and *ka* appears even later (at 2;04), based on the corpus analysis of Aki (CHILDES).

Sumihare at 1;06, for example, produces *na* quite clearly when he tries to speak to the addressee, and the observer (Noji) states that it is around then that the social and communicative skills of the child become noticeable. *Ne* is also a discourse marker observed at a very early stage of Japanese acquisition. Sumihare, for example, distinguishes *ne* from *na* just like adults do: he employs *na* when he talks to himself, while he employs *ne* when he talks to the addressee who holds him, as the contrast between (30b) and (30c) indicates:[8]

(30) a. ...**ne** (1;07)
          Sentence-final particle
          'isn't it?' (Sumihare pronounces *ne* clearly.)

      b. Tyun   mien   **naa** (talking to himself) (1;09)
          the plane is-not-visible sentence-final particle
          '(I) cannot see the plane.'

      c. Tyun   mien   **ne** (talking to father, the addressee who holds him)(1;09)
          the plane is-not-visible sentence-final particle
          '(I) cannot see the plane.'

Here, most crucially, as shown in (31), the discourse markers are observed at the RIA Stage, before the full conjugation of the verbs appears in the production. The examples in (31) indicate that the discourse markers follow nominal elements, RIAs, and mimetic/onomatopoeic expressions. Note here that *na* is used in the adult way as a separate item, as shown in (31f) as well (just like *ne* in (30a)).

(31) a. Onbu   **na** (1;08)
          Hold-me-on-your back Sentence-final particle
          'Please hold me on your back.'

      b. Atti   i-ta   **na** (1;07) (volition) (talking to his mother, the addressee)
          over there go-TA Sentence-final particle
          '(I) want to go over there'

      c. Pan   **naa** (1;05)
          bread Sentence-final particle
          'I want a piece of bread.'

      d. Sii   **si-ta**   **naa** (1;07) (adult: **volition** *si-tai*)
          pee   do-TA   Sentence-final particle
          '(I) want to pee.'

---

[8] It has been noted by many researchers that some of the discourse markers are acquired at a very early stage of language acquisition. Shirai, Shirai, and Furuta (1999), for instance, based on the corpus analysis of four Japanese monolingual children's longitudinal data (Aki 1;05–3;00, Ryo 1;03–3;00, Ari 1;0–3;00 and Kok 1;09–3;00 from CHILDES) (MacWhinney 2000) observe that every child began to use sentence-final particles when their MLU (Mean Length of Utterances) was below 1.2.

e. Rii   **na**   **na** (1;07)
go down Sentence-final particle
'I want to go down.'
Context: Sumihare is on his father's shoulder. (Murasugi and Fuji 2008b)

f. ....**na** (talking to his daddy) (Sumihare, 1;05)
    Sentence-final particle

Now, the question is why it is the case that such sentence-final particles as *ne* and *na* follow any syntactic constituent so productively. Crucially, it is intriguing that the sentence-final particles are produced as separate items, that is, *ne* and *na*, follow null phrases (as (30a) and (31f)) in child Japanese.

Here, note that the difference between the discourse markers in adult West Flemish and adult Japanese resides in the fact that the former has them at the sentence-initial or final position only,[9] but the latter allows the discourse markers to be attached basically on any syntactic constituent.

(32)   Neko(-ga)   **ne**, yane-kara **ne**, otita **ne**
       Cat (-Nom)   roof-from   fell
       'The cat fell from the roof.'

Japanese discourse markers can follow NPs, PPs, and VPs, and so on, as far as the structure constitutes a well-formed syntactic constituent. Then, the co-occurrence of RIA with a sentence-final particle in child grammar would indicate that a discourse marker or a Speech Act element can be preceded by the truncated element or a child's syntactic constituent, even if there is no T head, and even if there is no phonetically realized sentence.

If Speech Act elements are acquired earlier than TP and CP, then, as we noted before, we expect that the sentence-final particles are acquired earlier than complementizers. In fact, this predication is borne out. Although it is well known that *no*, the head of FiniteP in the CP layer, is acquired at a very early stage of language acquisition, it appears in child production later than such discourse markers as *na* and *ne*.

(33) a. Nenne ta   **noo** (Sumihare, 1;10)
        sleep   Past NO
        '(I) am sleeping with my daddy.'

     b. Katai   **no** (Sumihare, 1;10)
        is-hard NO
        '(This candy) is (very) hard.'

     c. Katai yo zya **no** (talking to his mother, the addressee) (1;10)
        hard   is   NO
        '(It) is very hard and difficult to take.'

     d. Teen   **no** (talking to his mother, the addressee) (1;10)
        mimetic NO
        (Context: sitting on the Kotatsu)

---

[9] Thanks to Lillian Haegeman (p.c.) for the information.

e. Tantan-wa? Tantan-wa, **no**, **no** (talking to his mother, the addressee) (1;10)
    Tantan-top tantan-top NO NO
    (Context: putting a pencil on the floor near the window)

The observer Noji states that he does not understand the intended meaning of (33d) and (33e). However, the data at least show that *no* indicates the end point of the sentence. And they appear only after 1;10, much later than the stage at which the discourse markers are produced. Furthermore, Sumihare produces such discourse markers as *ne* and *na* earlier than the head of ForceP *ka*, too. Sumihare starts producing *ka* at 2;03, much later than *ne* and *na*, and even after *no*.[10] Interestingly enough, sequences of two discourse markers (or sentence-final particles) such as *yo ne* start to appear a bit before *no* does in the production. Observe examples in (34).

(34) a. Atui yo ne (Sumihare, 1:09)
          hot   YO NE
          'It is hot, isn't it?'

      b. Hairan   yo ne (Sumiare, 1;09)
          doesn't fit YO NE
          '(The feet) do not fit (in the socks).'

      c. Oimo oiti   yo ne. (Sunmiare, 1;10)
          potato delicious YO NE
          'The potatoes (are) delicious, aren't they?'

      d. Toofu kita   yo ne. (Sumihare, 1;11)
          Tofu   came YO NE
          'A man selling Tofu came over, didn't he?'

At around the time children discover the broader adult-like properties of sentence-final particles (e.g., *yo*, *ne*,), that is, that more than one sentence-final particle can be attached to a phrase, the head of FinP and the verbal conjugations start to appear.

Given these descriptive findings, let us come back to our original question. Does the early appearance of sentence-final particles constitute a counterexample to the Truncation Hypothesis because sentence-final particles are the uppermost element above CP? A detailed analysis of child Japanese indicates that it is not the case.

Japanese-speaking children do produce sentence-final particles at the RIA stage, and sentence-final particles look as if they are added on the "truncated" structures, or phases, as shown in (18), repeated in (35):

(35) (= (18)) Buuwa tui-ta   **ne**   **ne** (Sumihare, 1;09)
               candle light-ta Sentence-final particle Sentence-final particle
               Intended meaning: Please light the candle.
               Literal meaning: The candle lit, didn't it?

---

[10] See the parallel finding by Okada and Grinstead (2003) based on the corpus analysis of Aki (CHILDES).

However, given that sentence-final particles follow any syntactic constituent in adult Japanese, and given the fact that child discourse markers not only follow various constituents but also appear as separate items as shown in (30a) and (31f), the child structure of the sentence-final particles following such a truncated phrase as an RIA would be something like (36).

(36) [$_{XP}$ _____] *ne/na*
      X= Syntactic Constituent

XP is a well-formed syntactic constituent, and can be phonetically realized as zero in the argument-drop language Japanese. Children produce truncated sentences or a phonetically null form, followed by a discourse particle that links the speaker and the addressee. Tense Phrase is projected only at around the stage where two particles come to appear in a sequence, as in (34), and several conjugation forms of verbs come to be used.

    The analysis presented here assumes that discourse markers and elements above the CP layer are directly attached to children's RIAs. It should be mentioned here, however, that adult RIAs or tense-less phrases encoding a speech act are somehow difficult to be selected by the discourse markers. In Japanese, the strong imperative -*ta* forms is an RIA for both child grammar and adult grammar. Even in the adult grammar, the strong imperative *ta*-forms such as "*Kaetta! Kaetta!* (Go back! Go back!)" given in (9b), for example, cannot be directly followed by such discourse markers as *ne* and *na*.

(37) a.   Sassato   Kaet-ta!   Kaet-ta!
          immediately go back-TA go back-TA
          'Go back immediately.'

      b. *Sassato   Kaet-ta   **ne/na**!   Kaet-ta **ne/na**!
          immediately go back-TA Sentence-Final Particle
          'Go back immediately.'

It is quite intriguing that children, unlike adults, use sentence-final particles such as *ne* and *na* with RIAs at the age of one year, as shown in (18). Given our analysis so far, the co-occurrence of child RIAs and sentence-final particles would be explained naturally by assuming that children do not yet fully know the (adult) syntactic properties of sentence-final particles at this stage, although they know the pragmatic properties associated with them.

    Now, given the argument so far, let us get back to the acquisition of Chinese to see if the analysis is supported. As we mentioned before, Lee (2000) observes the emergence of discourse markers at a very early stage of Cantonese-speaking children's grammar acquisition. Yang (2010), based on the analysis of BJCELA (Beijing Chinese Early Language Acquisition) corpus, argues that Mandarin-speaking children show that sentence-ending particles such as *ne, ma, ba,* and *a* all emerge very early and well before two years of age. According to Yang (2010), for example, a very young child (1;04) produces the sentence-ending particle *a* in natural contexts even at around the age of one, as shown in (38).

(38) Qui a (1;04)
      ball Discourse-marker
      'It is the ball.'

The fact that discourse markers are produced very early, probably earlier than the RIA (the imperative form) and the tense/aspect marker *le* in Chinese, provides a strong piece of evidence to support the analysis presented in this chapter.[11]

Children's phrase structures are truncated. However, the Truncation Hypothesis does not entail that young children do not know the semantic/pragmatic properties of the uppermost elements in phrase structure. The evidence from Japanese and Chinese indicates that children in fact know the semantic/pragmatic properties of the discourse elements and use them just like adults, even at the age of one year. Just like a jigsaw puzzle, children assemble the border pieces first to get a defined area to work in. Information regarding discourse relations can thus guide the child to identify the missing tense-related items between the Speech Act Phrase and the truncated structure. This leads us to suggest that "discourse bootstrapping" should be probably added to the child's toolkit.

5. Conclusion

In this chapter, we argued that RIs (RIs) and RI Analogues (RIAs) are non-finite (infinitival) verbal forms that children at around one to two years of age use in matrix (root) clauses. We presented evidence for the Truncation Hypothesis proposed by Rizzi (1993/1994) for children's early syntactic structure, based on the analysis of Chinese and Japanese.

Note here that the forms of child RI(A)s per se are not different from those of adults. As we noted earlier, UG constrains "grammar space". As Akmajian (1984) first drew attention to "mad magazine sentences," infinitive constructions are used in matrix contexts in adult English and adult Spanish, for example.

(39)   a.   Me go to that party?! I would never do such a thing! (English)

b.   John go to the movies?! No way, man!

(40)   ¿Yo ir   a esa fiesta? ¡Jamás! (Spanish) (Etxepare and Grohmann 2005)
       I   to-go to that party? Never!
       'Me going to that party? Never!'

Mad magazine sentences, or adult RI(A)s, consist of two overtly expressed parts: the RI proper, orthographically indicated by '?!' (evoking a question-like exclamation), and the Coda (a further exclamation that seems to deny the true value of the mad magazine sentences) (Etxepare and Grohmann 2005). Child Chinese RIAs are in fact imperatives in adult Chinese; child Japanese RIAs are strong imperatives (and past declaratives) in adult Japanese. Child RIAs are possible "well-formed" verbs in the adult grammar.

---

[11] See Murasugi and Nakatani (2005, 2007) and Dejima, Nakatani, and Murasugi (2009) for evidence based on their longitudinal studies that the properties of Speech Act Phrase are found even at the babbling stage in Japanese acquisition.

The very young children's use of non-finite verbs in root contexts can be suggested to be a universal phenomenon. Whether or not the target language is *pro*-drop or argument-drop, children can be suggested to universally go through the very early non-finite verb stage. Yet, there are morphological variations: RI(A)s can be infinitives (e.g., German, Dutch, French, among others), bare verbs (e.g., Chinese, English, among others), or certain (surrogate) full forms (e.g., Japanese, Korean, Turkish, Kuwaiti Arabic, among others). The morphological parameter that determines whether or not the stem can stand by itself is acquired at the very early stage of language acquisition. This finding indicates that even during the stage where the phrase structure is truncated, very young children know the morphological properties of the target language. Without being directly taught by caretakers, children voluntarily express intentional and extensional meanings by picking up their first verbal forms among the possible non-finite forms in their mother tongue. The early emergence of morphological knowledge constitutes further important support for the proposal of inborn grammatical principles, parameters, and UG (Chomsky 1965; Huang 1982).

The difference between child grammar and adult grammar resides in that the child root clause is not CP like adults', but the phrase structure may be truncated, as Rizzi (1993/1994) argues, at a very early stage of grammar acquisition until around age two or so. With regard to the trigger for children to attain the adult axiom that "CP is the root of all clauses," it was suggested in this chapter that acquiring the possible selection of sentence-final particles might bootstrap the children's knowledge of the missing part in their syntactic structure.

The cross-linguistic analysis of child Chinese and Japanese led us to a suggestion for learnability theory. For children to acquire their mother tongue, "discourse bootstrapping" may be employed to acquire the full syntactic structure. Syntactic and semantic bootstrapping would be useful tools for children to acquire language in a bottom-up way, while discourse bootstrapping would be a useful tool for children to acquire the full syntactic structure.

Acknowledgments

I would like to sincerely thank Audrey Li, Andrew Simpson, Dylan Tsai, Chisato Fuji, Tomomi Nakatani, Naoko Sawada, Tomoko Kawamura, Kaede Ito, Tatsuhiko Tanaka, R. Amritavalli, Kamil Deen, K. A. Jayaseelan, Diane Lillo-Martin, Jonah Lin, Luigi Rizzi, Mamoru Saito, Peter Sells, Koji Sugisaki, William Snyder, Ken Wexler, and the anonymous reviewer(s) for the comments and discussions on the topic discussed in this chapter. I would like to take this opportunity to deeply thank Jim and Emily Huang, who have always been our Giving Tree in the hub of the linguistic universe.

The research presented in this chapter was supported in part by the Nanzan University Pache Research Grant I-A 2012-2014, JSPS Grant-in-Aid (C) (# 23520529 and #26370515, Keiko Murasugi), the Japanese Ministry of Education and Science Grant-in-Aid for "Strategic Establishment of Centers for Advanced Research in Private Universities" (Mamoru Saito, Center for Linguistics, Nanzan University), and the National Institute for Japanese Language and Linguistics (NINJAL) Collaborative

Research Project "Linguistic Variations within the Confines of the Language Faculty: A Study in Japanese First Language Acquisition and Parametric Syntax" (Keiko Murasugi, Project Leader, Nanzan University).

References

Akmajian, Adrian. 1984. Sentence types and the form-function fit. *Natural Language and Linguistic Theory* 2, 1–23.

Bar-Shalom, Eva, and William Snyder. 2001. Descriptive imperatives in Child Russian and early correct use of verbal morphology. *Proceedings of the 24th Annual Boston University Conference on Language Development* 25, 94–101.

Chien, Lin-Yu Madelaine. 2009. *Is There a Root Infinitives or Root Infinitive Analogue Stage in Early Mandarin?* Master's thesis, National Tsing-Hua University, Taiwan.

Chomsky, Noam. 1965. *Aspects of the Theory of Syntax*. Cambridge, MA: MIT Press.

Chomsky, Noam. 1995. A minimalist program for linguistic theory. In *The View from Building 20*, ed. Ken Hale and Samuel Jay Keyser, 1–52. Cambridge, MA:MIT Press.

Deen, Kamil Ud. (.2002. *The Omission of Inflectional Prefixes in the Acquisition of Nairobi Swahili*. Doctoral dissertation, University of California, Los Angeles.

Dejima, Mayumi, Tomomi Nakatani, and Keiko Murasugi. 2009. The emergence of speech act phrase: Evidence from a longitudinal study of two Japanese-speaking infants. *Nanzan Linguistics* 5, 17–39.

Déprez, Viviane, and Amy Pierce. 1993. Negation and functional projections in early grammar. *Linguistic Inquiry* 24(1), 25–67.

Erbaugh, Mary S. 1992. The acquisition of Mandarin. In *The Crosslinguistic Study of language Acquisition* 3, ed. Dan Isaac Slobin, 373–455. Hillsdale, NJ: Lawrence Erlbaum Associates.

Etxepare, Ricardo, and Kleanthes K. Grohmann. 2005. Towards a grammar of adult root infinitives. *Proceedings of the 24th West Coast Conference on Formal Linguistics*, 129–137.

Galasso, Joseph. 2011. *Minimum of English Grammar: An Introduction to Feature Theory with a Special Note on the Nature of Early Child Grammars of English*. San Diego, CA: University Readers.

Guo, Fangfang, Claire Foley, Yu-Chin Chien, Chi-Pang Chiang, Barbara Lust. 1996. Operator-variable binding in the initial state: A cross-linguistic study of VP Ellipsis structures in Chinese and English. *Cahiers de Linguistique—Asie Orientale* 25(1), 3–34.

Haegeman, Liliane. 1995. Root infinitives, tense, and truncated structures in Dutch. *Language Acquisition* 4(3), 205–255.

Haegeman, Liliane. 2010. The internal syntax of adverbial clauses." In *Exploring the Left Periphery*, ed. Kleanthes Grohmann and Ianthi Tsimpli, 628–648. Lingua Thematic Issue 120.

Haegeman, Liliane, and Virginia Hill. 2011. *The Syntacticization of Discourse*. Unpublished ms., Ghent University and University of New Brunswick-SJ.

Hoekstra, Teun, and Nina Hyams. 1998. Aspects of root infinitives. *Lingua* 106, 91–112.

Huang, James C.-T. 1982. *Logical Relations in Chinese and the Theory of Grammar*. Doctoral dissertation, MIT.

Lee, Thomas Hun-tak. 2000. Finiteness and null arguments in child Cantonese. *The Tsinghua Journal of Chinese Studies, New Series* 30, 365–393.

Li, Boya. 2006. *Chinese Final Particles and the Syntax of the Periphery*. Doctoral dissertation, Leiden University.

Lillo-Martin, Diane C., and Ronice Müller de Quadros. 2009. Two in one: Evidence for imperatives as the analogue to RIs from ASL and LSB." In *Proceedings of the 33rd Annual Boston University Conference on Language Development* 1, ed. Jane Chandlee, Michelle Franchini, Sandy Lord, and Gudrun-Marion Rheiner, 302–312. Somerville, MA: Cascadilla Press.

Lin, T.-H. Jonah. 2006. Multiple–Modal Constructions in Mandarin Chinese and the Finiteness Properties .Unpublished ms., National Tsing-Hua University, Taiwan.

Lin, T.-H. Jonah. 2008. Finiteness of Clauses and Raising of Arguments in Mandarin Chinese. Unpublished ms., National Tsing-Hua University, Taiwan.

Liu, Haiyong. 2009. The acquisition of Mandarin aspects and modals: Evidence from the acquisition of negation. *Language and Linguistics* 10(1), 133–160.

MacWhinney,m Brian. 2000. *The CHILDES project: Tools for analyzing talk.* Third Edition. Mahwah, NJ: Lawrence Erlbaum Associates.

Murasugi, Keiko. 2009. *What Japanese-speaking Children's Errors Tell Us about Syntax.* Paper presented at the Asian GLOW VII, English and Foreign Languages University, Hyderabad, India, February 28.

Murasugi, Keiko, and Chisato Fuji. 2008a. *Root Infinitives: The Parallel Route That Japanese- and Korean-speaking Children Step In.* Paper presented at *Japanese-Korean Linguistics Conference 18,* City University of New York, November 13. (Appeared in *Japanese and Korean Linguistics* 18, CSLI Publications, Stanford, 3–15, 2011.)

Murasugi, Keiko, and Cchisato Fuji. 2008b. Root infinitives in Japanese and the late acquisition of head-movement. *BUCLD 33 Proceedings Supplement* (http://www.bu.edu/ linguistics/ BUCLD/ supplement33/Murasugi.pdf).

Murasugi, Keiko, Chisato Fuji, and Tomoko Hashimoto. 2007. *What's Acquired Later in an Agglutinative Language.* Paper presented at the Asian GLOW VI, Chinese University of Hong Kong, December 27. (Appeared in *Nanzan Linguistics* 6, 47–78, 2011.)

Murasugi, Keiko, and Tomomi Nakatani. 2005. *The Ontology of Functional Categories.* Paper presented at the Asian GLOW V, New Delhi, India, October 7.

Murasugi, Keiko, and Tomomi Nakatani. 2007. *Very Early Language Acquisition: A View from Japanese.* Paper presented at the workshop on Early Child Phonology, Chinese University of Hong Kong, August 17.

Murasugi, Keiko, Tomomi Nakatani, and Chisato Fuji. 2010. *The Roots of Root Infinitive Analogues: The Surrogate Verb Forms Common in Adult and Child Grammars.* Poster presented at *BUCLD* 34, Boston University, November 7.

Murasugi, Keiko and Eriko Watanabe. 2009. Case errors in child Japanese and the implication for the syntactic theory. *Proceedings of the 3rd Conference on Generative Approaches to Language Acquisition in North America* (GALANA), 153–164.

Nakatani, Tomomi, and Keiko Murasugi. 2009. Gengo Kakutoku ni okeru Shusetsu Futeishi Gensho: Zyudanteki Kansatsuteki Kenkyu [Root Infinitive Analogues as Non-finite Surrogate Forms: A Longitudinal Study of a Japanese-speaking Child]. *Academia* 86, 59–94.

Noji, Junya. 1973–1977. *Yooji no Gengo Seikatu no Jittai* [The Nature of an Infant's Language] I–IV, Bunka Hyoron Shuppan, Hiroshima.

Okada, Keiko, and John Grinstead. 2003. The emergence of CP in child Japanese. In *Proceedings of the 6th Generative Approaches to Second Language Acquisition Conference* (GASLA 2002), ed. Juana M. Liceras, Helmut Zobl, and Helen Goodluck, 213–218. Somerville, MA: Cascadilla Proceedings Project.

Okubo, Ai. 1967. *Youji Gengo no Hattatu* [The Development of Child Language]. Tokyo: Tokyodou Shuppan.

Phillips, Colin. 1995. Syntax at age two: Cross-linguistic differences. In *Papers on Language Processing and Acquisition,* ed. Carson T. Schütze, Jennifer B. Ganger, and Kevin Broihier, 325–382. MIT Working Papers in Linguistics 26.

Phillips, Colin. 1996. Root infinitives are finite. *BUCLD* 20, 588–599.

Pierce, Amy E. 1992. *Language Acquisition and Syntactic Theory: A Comparative Analysis of French and English Child Grammars.* Dordrecht: Kluwer.

Plann, Susan. 1982. "Indirect questions in Spanish. *Linguistic Inquiry* 13, 297–312.

Poeppel, David, and Ken Wexler. 1993. The full competence hypothesis of clause structure in Early German. *Language* 69(1), 1–33.

Radford, Andrew. 1990. *Syntactic Theory and the Acquisition of English Syntax: The Nature of Early Child Grammars of English.* Oxford: Blackwell.

Radford, Andrew. 1991. The acquisition of morphosyntax of finite verbs in English. In *The Acquisition of Verb Placement: Functional Categories and V2 Phenomena in Language Acquisition*, ed. Jürgen M. Meisel, 23–62. Dordrecht: Kluwer.

Rizzi, Luigi. 1993/1994. Some notes on linguistic theory and language development: The case of root infinitives. *Language Acquisition* 3, 371–393.

Saito, Mamoru. 2009. *Selection and Clause Types in Japanese*. Paper presented at the International Conference on Sentence Types: Ten Years After, Universität Frankfurt am Main, June 27.

Salustri, Monala, and Nina Hyams. 2003. Is there an analogue to the RI stage in the null subject languages? *BUCLD* 27, 692–703.

Salustri, Monala, and Nina Hyams. 2006. Looking for the universal core of the RI stage. In *The Acquisition of Syntax in Romance Languages*, ed. Vincent Torrens and Linda Escobar, 159–182. Amsterdam: John Benjamins.

Su, Yi-chin. 2012. Modal reference effects as the analogue to root infinitives in child Mandarin. *IACL* 20. August 29.

Sawada, Naoko, and Keiko Murasugi. 2011. A cross-linguistic approach to the 'erroneous' genitive subjects: Underspecification of tense in child grammar revisited. *Selected Proceedings of the 4th Conference on Generative Approaches to Language Acquisition in North America* (GALANA), 209–226. Somerville, MA: Cascadilla Proceedings Project.

Sawada, Naoko, Keiko Murasugi, and Chisato Fuji. 2010. A theoretical account for the 'erroneous' genitive subjects in child Japanese and the specification of tense. *BUCLD 34 Proceedings Supplement*. (http://www.bu.edu/linguistics/BUCLD/Supp34/Sawada Naoko.pdf).

Schütze, Carson and Kenneth Wexler. 1996. Subject case licensing and English root infinitives. In *Proceedings of the 20th Annual Boston University Conference on Language Development 2*, ed. Andy Stringfellow, Dalia Cahana-Amitay, Elizabeth Hughes, and Andrea Zukowski, 670–681. Somerville, MA: Cascadilla Press.

Shirai, Junko, Hidetoshi Shirai and Yoshiteru Furuta. 1999. On the acquisition of sentence-final particles in Japanese. In *New Directions in Language Development and Disorders*, ed. Michael Perkins and Sara Howard, 243–250. New York: Plenum.

Wijnen, Frank, Masja Kempen, and Steven Gillis. 2001. Root infinitives in Dutch early child language: An effect of input? *Journal of Child Language* 28, 629–660.

Yang, Xiaolu. 2010. *CP and the Left Periphery in Early Child Mandarin Chinese: The Case of Sentence Final Particles*. Poster presented at the Asian GLOW VIII, Beijing Language and Culture University, August 13.

Part Three

THE C-DOMAIN

15

Wh-adjuncts, Left Periphery, and Wh-in-situ

MASAO OCHI

1. Introduction

Since Huang's (1982) seminal work on Chinese syntax, Chinese has played a key role in the development of the Principles and Parameters Theory. Among many other things, Huang's detailed analysis of syntactic dependencies involving *weishenme* 'why' had a huge impact on our conception of displacement and locality. Against this theoretical background, this chapter investigates several species of reason and causal *wh*-adjuncts with respect to their underlying positions. Some recent studies have argued that *why* in a variety of languages is always externally merged into the CP-periphery (see Rizzi 1990, 2001; Ko 2005; Stepanov and Tsai 2008; among others). According to this view, a local construal of *why* in examples such as (1) arises when *why* is externally merged into the domain of an interrogative C (that is, the matrix C), whereas a long-distance construal arises when *why* is merged into the domain of a non-interrogative C (i.e., the embedded C) and undergoes movement to the higher CP.

(1)   Why do you think that Peter is upset?

One of the goals of this study is to argue against this restrictive hypothesis of the base position of *whys*. In particular, I will argue for the following points:

(2)   Reason *wh*-adjuncts (e.g., *why, weishenme, naze*) are base-generated in the CP-periphery (interrogative or non-interrogative) or elsewhere (i.e., within T').

(3)   Causal *wh*-adjuncts fall into the following two groups:
      a.   Many of them (e.g., *how come, why the hell* in English, *zenme* in Chinese, and so on) are always base generated in the left periphery of an interrogative CP.

      b.   A species of causal *wh*-adjunct in Chinese and Japanese is a V'-level adjunct.

This chapter is organized as follows. In section 2, I will discuss the points summarized in (2) and (3a) by reviewing Ochi's (2004) analysis of several causal *wh*-adjuncts that do not behave like reason *whys*. Chomsky's (1973) observation plays an important role in this section. In section 3, I will discuss two further issues arising from the discussion in the previous section. Section 4 focuses on (3b). I will discuss the base position of a causal *wh*-adjunct in Chinese and Japanese, arguing that it is a V'-level adjunct in the two languages. Section 5 concludes the discussion.

2. "Uniformity" in Multiple *Wh*-Questions

I will begin this section with a discussion of the following descriptive generalization, due originally to Chomsky (1973).

(4)   Uniformity Condition on Multiple *Wh*-questions[1]
      A *wh*-element externally merged into the specifier of the interrogative CP cannot participate in multiple *wh*-questions.

Chomsky's (1973) original idea is that the interpretation of multiple *wh*-phrases must be *uniform* in terms of trace (or variable) binding: each and every *wh*-phrase interpreted by the same interrogative C must bind a trace (or a variable).

(5)   *$[_{CP} wh_1 C [_{TP} .... wh_2 .....]]$
      $[+Q]$
                  (where wh_1 is externally merged into the periphery of an interrogative CP)

Let us consider (6). According to Chomsky (1973), (6a) satisfies (4), assuming that *what* moves to the specifier of the interrogative C in covert syntax, leaving behind a trace, as illustrated in (7a). On the other hand, assuming that *whether* is directly merged with the interrogative C (or *whether* itself is a C head), (6b) fails to satisfy (4), as shown in (7b).

(6)   a.   I wonder who bought what.

      b.   *I wonder whether John bought what.

(7)   a.   I wonder [who$_i$, what$_j$ C [t$_i$ bought t$_j$]]

      b.   *I wonder [whether, what$_j$ C [John ate t$_j$]]

One word of caution is in order here, as there is evidence from Chinese that the ungrammaticality of (6b) is actually not due to (4). As the ungrammaticality of (8) shows, an A-not-A constituent and another *wh*-phrase cannot form a multiple *wh*-question in Chinese, although, unlike *whether* in English, the

---

[1] Chomsky's (1973: 282) original formulation:

(i)   Assign a *wh*-phrase not in COMP to some higher structure $[_{COMP} +wh]$ and interpret as in (248) where *the interpretation is uniform in this COMP node* (note: (248) is a rule that interprets *wh*-quantifiers that bind a trace/variable).

A-not-A constituent in Chinese is standardly analyzed as undergoing (covert) movement (see Huang 1991).[2]

(8) *wo xiang-zhidao Lisi xihuan bu xihuan na-zhong jiu.
    I wonder Lisi like not like which-kind wine
    '(lit.) I wonder whether Lisi likes which kind of wine.'

Therefore, the empirical validity of (4) needs to be checked in light of paradigms other than those involving *whether*.

Now let us list a few instances of causal *wh*-adjuncts falling under (4), following Ochi (2004). First, based on several facts about *how come* (in contrast to *why*), including its lack of a long-distance construal (as shown in the following), Collins (1991) argues that *how come* never undergoes movement, which means that the surface position of *how come* directly corresponds to its merging site (see also Shlonsky and Soare 2011).

(9) a. **Why** did John say Mary left?   (ambiguous)

   b. **How come** John said Mary left?   (matrix only)

As pointed out by Collins, *how come* fails to participate in multiple *wh*-questions, unlike *why*. I follow Collins (1991) and attribute the ungrammaticality of (10b) to the uniformity condition under discussion.

(10) a. **Why** did John buy what?

    b. *****How come** John bought what?

Second, *why the hell* in English also fails to participate in multiple *wh*-questions.

(11) a. **Why** did you buy what?

    b. *****Why the hell** did you buy what?

In fact, *why the hell* does not allow a non-local reading for the speakers with whom I consulted.

(12) a. **Why** did John say that Peter is upset?   (ambiguous)

    b. **Why the hell** did John say that Peter is upset?   (matrix only)

Given these similarities between *how come* and *why the hell*, we can analyze the two *wh*-items in the same fashion: *why the hell* must also be base-generated in the periphery of an interrogative CP and no movement is involved in deriving *wh*-questions with *why the hell*.[3]

---

[2] Thanks to Thomas Lee (p.c.) and Mamoru Saito (p.c.) for drawing my attention to this particular point.

[3] In Ochi (2004), I proposed an analysis of this property of *how come* and other causal *wh*-adjuncts based on the virus theory of feature strength (Chomsky 1995). The theoretical tools that I employed in that account are no longer available, although I believe that the basic idea behind it is not off the mark.

Third, a peculiar type of *what*-question found in several *wh*-fronting languages also conforms to (4). As discussed by Ochi (1999, 2004), this type of *wh*-adjunct is found in a number of languages: in several *wh*-fronting languages (e.g., Bulgarian, Hebrew, Serbo-Croatian, and Hungarian) and in two *wh*-in-situ languages (Chinese and Japanese). In this section, I will mainly focus on German as a representative of the *wh*-fronting group, but it should be noted that the discussion of the German data equally applies to the rest of the *wh*-fronting group (see Ochi 1999). I will discuss Chinese and Japanese in section 4.

Let us start with the observation that *was* 'what' in German can be used to question reasons/causes, as illustrated by the examples below. To distinguish this peculiar use of *what* from its ordinary usage, I will refer to the former as WHAT.

(13) a. **Was**   schläfst du so lange?
          WHAT sleeps   you so long
          'Why (the hell) are you sleeping for so long?'

      b. **Was**   tadeln Sie Hans denn?
          WHAT blame you Hans
          'Why (the hell) are you blaming Hans?'

The use of WHAT is most natural in contexts in which emotions such as annoyance, impatience, surprises, and so on are expressed. In this sense, it is similar to a *wh-the-hell* phrase discussed earlier.[4, 5]

Ochi (1999) argues that WHAT in German (and the other members of the *wh*-fronting group) behaves just like *how come* and *why the hell*. WHAT-questions in German do not allow a long-distance construal, as shown by the contrast between *warum* 'why' in (14a) and WHAT in (14b).

(14) a. **Warum** glaubst du dass er so lange schläft?
          why   believe you that he so long   sleeps
          'Why do you believe that he sleeps so long?'   (ambiguous)

      b. **Was**   glaubst du dass er so langue schläft?
          WHAT believe you that he so long   sleeps
          'Why (the hell) do you believe that he sleeps so long?'   (matrix reading only)

---

[4] This remark also applies to WHAT in Chinese and Japanese. See section 4.

[5] In all the languages possessing WHAT, this *wh*-adjunct occurs within the complement of a verb selecting an interrogative clause, which clearly demonstrates the interrogative nature of this *wh*-adjunct (see Ochi 1999). Furthermore, WHAT does not easily occur in the complement clause of a factive-type predicate, as shown in (i). In this sense, too, WHAT is akin to *wh-the-hell*, as shown in (ii) (see den Dikken and Giannakidou 2002).

(i) a. Ich frage mich/weiss nicht/*weiss, **was**   Hans so gestresst ist.
         I   ask   myself/know not/know **WHAT** Hans that stressed is
         'I wonder/don't know/*know why (the hell) Hans is so stressed.'   (German)

     b. Boku-wa Taro-ga **nani**-o   hashitteiru (no) ka tazuneta/sir-anai/*sitteiru.
         I-Top   Taro-Nom **what**-Acc running   (no) Q asked/know-not/know
         'I asked/don't know/*know why (the hell) Taro is running.'   (Japanese)

(ii) I wonder/don't know/*know why the hell he is avoiding me.

The lack of an embedded reading in (14b) immediately follows if we suppose that WHAT in German, like *how come* and *why the hell* in English, must be directly inserted into the specifier of an interrogative CP and, consequently, no *wh*-movement is involved in this construction.

Crucially, WHAT in German (and its counterparts in the other *wh*-fronting languages) fails to occur in multiple *wh*-questions. As (15a) and (16a) show, *warum* 'why' occurs in multiple *wh*-questions under certain circumstances. I will tentatively attribute the contrast between (15a) and (15b) to superiority effects involving an adjunct *wh*-phrase in German (although it is often assumed that no superiority effect is observed in this language).[6] In contrast, WHAT is not allowed in multiple *wh*-questions, regardless of the word order, as shown in (15c, d) and (16b) (thanks to Klaus Abels (p.c.) for the data).

(15) a. Wer   schläft **warum** so lange?
          who.Nom sleeps **why**   so long
          'Who is sleeping why so long?'

      b. ??/***Warum** schläft wer   so lange?
          why   sleeps who.nom so long
          'Who is sleeping why so long?'

      c. *Wer   schläft **was** so lange?
          who.Nom sleeps **WHAT** so long
          'Who sleeps why (the hell) so long?'

      d. ***Was**   schläft wer   so lange?
          WHAT sleeps who.Nom so long
          'Who sleeps why (the hell) so long?'

(16) a. **Warum** tadeln Sie wen?
          why   blame you who.Acc
          'Why are you blaming who?'

---

[6] Haider (2000) claims that *wh*-adjuncts cannot stay in situ in German, which seems to indicate that there is some variation among speakers concerning this point. One source of this variation may be related to intonation patterns. According to Wiltschko (1997), intonation patterns (which Wiltschko relates to the issue of D-linking) affect the acceptability of adjunct *wh*-in-situ. There are two possible intonation patterns for morphologically complex *wh*-words like *warum* 'why.' Either the *wh*-part is stressed (indicated below as WARum), or the preposition part is stressed (waRUM). When *warum* is in the spec of CP, either stress pattern is allowed as shown in (i).

(i)   WARum/waRUM hat Peter was   getrunken?
      why   has Peter what drunk?
      'Why did Peter drink what?'

When *warum* is in situ, however, only the pattern in which the *wh*-part is stressed is acceptable, as shown in (ii).

(ii) Was hat Peter WARum/?*waRUM getrunken?
      what has Peter why   drunk
      'What did Peter drink why?'

b. *Was   tadeln Sie wen?
WHAT blame you who.Acc
'Why (the hell) are you blaming who?'

Example (15c) does not conform to our earlier assumption that WHAT in German must be inserted into the specifier of an interrogative CP. Further, (15d) may be ruled out for the same reason as (15b), possibly as a superiority violation. Now, the crucial example is (16b). Nothing other than the uniformity requirement (4) would rule out this example.

Before proceeding further, let us note that the *wh*-adjuncts discussed above all seem to yield causal rather than reason questions. Tsai (2008) teases apart the two readings by using a stative predicate. Consider the following.

(17) a. How come the sky is blue?

b. Why the hell is the sky blue?

c. Why is the sky blue?

As Tsai (2008) notes, the question in (17a) presupposes that the sky is blue and furthermore that something caused the sky to be blue. From this presupposition, we could derive the fact that such a causal question is often accompanied by a counter-expectation on the part of the speaker, for example, "the sky should not be blue." Exactly the same point applies to *why the hell* questions, with *the hell* expressing the counter-expectation. As noted above, WHAT-questions in languages like German also share this pragmatic aspect of the causal question. On the other hand, (17c) merely presupposes that the sky is blue and the speaker in this case may not expect any particular event to be responsible for the sky being blue.

Returning to the main discussion, the content of the uniformity requirement in (4) follows rather naturally from the probe-goal system as currently conceived in the minimalist literature (see Ochi (2004)). Let us assume the following:

(18) a. Probe and Goal must both be active for Agree/Move to apply.

b. Each and every *wh*-phrase bears an uF.[7]

Before discussing how the generalization in (4) follows from the probe-goal system, we should consider several types of *wh*-questions, starting with a single *wh*-question such as (*I wonder*) *what John bought*. At the point of a derivation at which the interrogative C is introduced into the structure (shown in (19a)), Agree holds of

(19) a.   C   [$_{TP}$ John bought what]
       [uQ]   [uWh]
       [EPP]

b. [$_{CP}$ what$_i$ C   [$_{TP}$..........t_i]]
       [~~uWh~~] [~~uQ~~]
              [~~EPP~~]

[7] Contrary to Bošković (2007).

C and *what*. The latter also moves and remerges with the C head to satisfy the EPP property of C (whatever this property turns out to be), as illustrated in (19b).

As for multiple *wh*-questions (such as *who bought what?*), I adopt the proposals of Chomsky (2004), Frampton et al. (2000), and Hiraiwa (2001) to the effect that the probe P can agree with multiple goals in a simultaneous fashion, which means that intervention effects are evaded insofar as an intervening element is rendered as inactive by P. Assuming that the interrogative C simultaneously agrees with each and every *wh*-phrase which it interprets, C in (20a) establishes an Agree relation with both *who* and *what*.

(20) a. C [$_{TP}$ who   bought what]
          [uQ] [uWh]   [uWh]
          [EPP]

      b. [$_{CP}$ who $_i$ C   [$_{TP}$ t_i bought what]]
          [~~uWh~~] [~~uQ~~]   [~~uWh~~]
                  [~~EPP~~]

Since English requires just one *wh*-phrase to move, the higher *wh*-phrase, *who*, remerges with the interrogative C, as illustrated in (20b).

Now let us turn to the multiple *wh*-questions involving a *wh*-adjunct. We saw in the previous section that causal *wh*-adjuncts (e.g., *how come* and *why the hell* in English and WHAT in languages like German) must be externally merged in the spec of an interrogative CP. Crucially, their distribution is different from that of reason *wh*-adjuncts (e.g., *why* in English and *warum* in German). For the sake of convenience, I will use the term WHY to refer to both types of *wh*-adjuncts. Let us start with the situation in which WHY is merged somewhere in the complement domain of the C head, an option available for some but not all instances of WHYs. In this case, WHY is probed by C along with other *wh*s.

(21) C ..... *wh* ..... WHY   (order irrelevant)
          └──────↑────────↑

Turning to the situation in which WHY is merged into the spec of an interrogative CP (which is in fact the only merging option for causal *wh*-adjuncts such as *how come*, *why the hell*, and WHAT), I assume that WHY in this case acts as a probe, taking care of the *u*Q-feature as well as the EPP-feature of the interrogative C (see Ko 2005).

(22) [$_{CP}$ WHY   C   [$_{TP}$ .....]]
          [~~uWh~~] [~~uQ~~]
              └─[~~EPP~~]────↑

Now let us examine the following crucial configuration, exemplifying (4).

(23) *[$_{CP}$ WHY C [$_{TP}$ ... *wh* ...]]   (WHY is merged into its surface position)

Let us focus on a point in the derivation at which the interrogative C is merged with TP, with WHY still in the numeration and ready to be introduced into the derivation.

(24)   C   [$_{TP}$...wh...] N = { WHY }
    [EPP]   [uWh]   [uWh]
    [uQ]

Two different derivational paths are available: (i) Agree holds of C and *wh* or (ii) WHY is merged into the specifier of the interrogative CP.[8] Let us consider the former option. As shown in (25a), the *u*Fs of the C head and the *wh*-phrase are taken care of. The next derivational step would be to have WHY merged into the spec of CP. However, the *u*F of WHY remains, as shown in (25b).

(25)   a.   C   [$_{TP}$ ... *wh* ...]
        [EPP]   [~~uWh~~]
        [~~uQ~~]

    b.   WHY   C   [$_{TP}$...*wh*...]
        [uWh] [~~EPP~~]   [~~uWh~~]
             [~~uQ~~]

Suppose instead that WHY is merged into the structure immediately after the derivational point shown in (24) is reached. As discussed above, I assume that WHY acts as a probe in this configuration. Although this Agree relation could take care of the relevant features of WHY and the C head, the *u*F of the *wh*-phrase in situ remains, as shown in (26).

(26)   WHY   C   [$_{TP}$... *wh* ...]
      [~~uWh~~] [~~EPP~~]   [u**Wh**]
          [~~uQ~~]

In short, once the configuration shown in (24) is constructed, the derivation is bound to crash in one way or another. One immediate implication of this analysis is that probes (and presumably goals as well) become inactive the moment their *u*Fs are taken care of (see, for example, Epstein and Seely 2002). If the *u*Q of the C head in (25) or (26) were active for a short while after the checking/valuation is executed (e.g., until the completion of a phase domain), we would lose an account of the uniformity requirement.

Let us now discuss two issues in connection with this analysis. First, to the extent that the behavior of causal *wh*-adjuncts such as *how come*, *why the hell*, WHAT in German, and so on is captured by our analysis in terms of the uniformity requirement in (4), it would argue, in one way or another, against the cartographic approach to the CP periphery, since what is crucial for our analysis is that causal *wh*-adjuncts

---

[8] Chomsky (2000) proposes that external Merge preempts Move, whereas Shima (2000) argues to the contrary. But we have a competition of Agree and external Merge here.

and other *wh*-phrases are licensed by the same interrogative head. The analysis entertained here would immediately lose its force if *wh*-phrases such as *who* and *what* are licensed by Foc, while causal/reason *wh*-adjuncts are licensed by the Interrogative head, as proposed by Rizzi (2001).

Second, Stepanov and Tsai's (2008) discussion of multiple *wh*-questions featuring *why*s in a variety of languages, including Russian and Chinese, is highly relevant to the material presented in this section, so it is worth discussing it here. Although they draw a parallel between Russian and Chinese in the formation of *wh*-questions, I will focus on Chinese here. They report that *weishenme* does not occur in multiple *wh*-questions (see also Tsai 2008):

(27) a. *nimen, shei weishenme hui likai?
         you guys who why (reason) will leave
         'You guys, who will leave why?'

     b. *nimen, weishenme shei hui likai?
         you guys why (reason) who will leave
         'You guys, who will leave why?'

They argue that *weishenme* is not phrasal but is an interrogative C head. With this hypothesis, they propose that the word order in (27a) is never generated, assuming that a *wh*-phrase such as *shei* 'who' does not topicalize into the CP-periphery. As for the ungrammaticality of (27b), they claim that the *wh*-subject *shei* 'who' is not licensed in this case via unselective binding, since the C-slot normally occupied by the Q-operator is taken up by *weishenme*. However, their hypothesis about *weishenme* being a C head is problematic in light of the well-known fact that *weishenme* allows a long-distance construal: they would need to devise a long-distance head movement to accommodate the relevant fact.

(28) Ni   renwei Lisi weishenme pao?
      you think Lisi why   run
      'Why do you think that Lisi is running?'

Let us see what our analysis can say about (27). Assuming that *weishenme* in (27b) is base-generated in the spec of an interrogative CP, the unacceptability of this example would fall out as a violation of the uniformity requirement in (4). But our analysis has nothing to say about the unacceptability of (27a). Let me stress, however, that some speakers do accept Chinese multiple *wh*-questions in which *shei* precedes *weishenme* (see Ochi 2004). How to account for this variation among speakers is an issue that I need to set aside for another occasion.

Although Stepanov and Tsai's analysis of *weishenme* as a C head may be problematic for the reason given earlier, their proposal may be directly relevant for the distribution of the causal *wh*-adjuncts discussed in this section. If these *wh*-elements were in fact interrogative complementizers, we could adopt Stepanov and Tsai's logic to explain why they cannot occur in multiple *wh*-questions, and no recourse to the uniformity requirement in (4) would be necessary. Of the three types of *wh*-items, we could perhaps safely say that *why the hell* is not a C head: after all, it consists of *why* (which acts as a phrasal element) and *the hell* (see Huang and Ochi 2004). How about the other two *wh*-adjuncts? In fact, Collins regards *how come* as an interrogative C-head. However, there is a piece of evidence for the phrasal status of *how come*: it licenses sluicing (see Ochi 2004; Shlonsky and Soare 2011), which is normally assumed to require a spec-head agreement (see Lobeck 1995).

(29) A: I'd like to leave.

B: [$_{CP}$ With whom/Why/How come [$_{C'}$ C [$_{TP}$ ~~you would like to leave~~]]]?

What about WHAT-questions in German? Could this *wh*-element be an interrogative C head? The answer seems to be negative. As discussed by Ochi (2004), the *wh*-question featuring WHAT exhibits verb-second (V_2) effects; see (13). Given the standard view about V_2 (i.e., a verb occupies the C-slot and whatever precedes the verb is located in the specifier of CP), we should conclude that WHAT sits in the spec of an interrogative CP. In short, we need (4) to explain the fact that these *wh*-items fail to occur in multiple *wh*-questions.

3. Merging Sites of Reason *Wh*-Adjuncts

Let us now turn to the merging site(s) of reason *wh*-adjuncts such as *why*. Given that they can be construed non-locally, the first thing to note is that they must have the option of being externally merged into a non-interrogative clause, unlike causal *wh*-adjuncts like *how come, why the hell*, and WHAT in languages like German. Moreover, our discussion in the previous section shows that reason *wh*-adjuncts may be base-generated in a position below the CP periphery. Suppose that they were always externally merged into the left periphery of a clause (interrogative or declarative). Then, examples like (10a) and (16a), where we have a single interrogative clause, would be expected to be unacceptable, contrary to the fact. Of course, our discussion up to this point does not exclude the possibility that reason *wh*-adjuncts have the option of being merged into the left periphery. In what follows, I would like to explore the hypothesis that reason *wh*-adjuncts may be either merged into the left periphery of a clause (interrogative or non-interrogative) or merged elsewhere, possibly as TP-level adjuncts (or even below TP). Our position, which is less restrictive than the view endorsed by Rizzi (1999, 2001), Ko (2005), and Stepanov and Tsai (2008), is in line with Collins (1991), Aoun and Li (1993), and Tsai (2008), among others. Next, I would like to discuss two issues in relation to these two competing hypotheses about the merging sites of *why*.

3.1. MULTIPLE *WH*-QUESTIONS IN SPANISH AND THE UNIFORMITY CONDITION

I believe that the behavior of Spanish reason *wh*-adjuncts offers a nice confirmation of the "weaker" position. Let us start with the observation that subject-verb inversion is normally obligatory in Spanish *wh*-questions, as shown in (30), whereas it is optional with *por qué* as shown in (31).

(30)　a.　*Qué Juan vio?
　　　　　what Juan saw
　　　　　'What did Juan see?'

　　　b.　Qué vio Juan?
　　　　　what saw Juan
　　　　　'What did Juan see?'

(31)　a.　**Por qué** vio Juan a Maria?
　　　　　why　　 saw Juan A Maria
　　　　　'Why did Juan see Maria?'

　　　b.　**Por qué** Juan vio a Maria?
　　　　　why　　 Juan saw A Maria
　　　　　'Why did Juan see Maria?'

Now consider (32) (see Uriagereka 1988; Boeckx 2008). While (32a) is ambiguous with respect to the modification domain of *por qué*, the example in (32b), where inversion does not apply, lacks the embedded reading of *por qué*. We can take this fact to be an indication that inversion is in fact obligatory when *por qué* undergoes movement, short- or long-distance. This in turn shows that *por qué* has more than one merging site. It may be merged somewhere below CP and moved to the spec of CP, as in (31a). Or it may be directly merged into the spec of CP as in (31b) (and CP in this case happens to be an interrogative CP); in such cases, no inversion takes place.

(32)　a.　**Por qué** pensaste tú　que Juan vio a Maria?　(ambiguous)
　　　　　why　　 thought you that Juan saw A Maria
　　　　　'Why did you think that Juan saw Maria?'

　　　b.　**Por qué** tú　pensaste que Juan vio a Maria?　(*embedded reading)
　　　　　why　　 you thought that Juan saw A Maria
　　　　　'Why did you think that Juan saw Maria?'

Interestingly, the lack of inversion affects multiple *wh*-questions with *por qué* in a subtle but important way. The example in (33b), which lacks subject-verb inversion, does not yield the ordinary pair-list reading.[9]

(33)　a.　**Por qué razon** hizo Juan qué　cosa?　(pair-list answer possible)
　　　　　why　　 reason did　Juan what thing
　　　　　'Why did Juan do what thing?'

　　　b.　**Por qué razon** Juan hizo qué　cosa?　(single pair answer only)
　　　　　why　　 reason Juan did　what thing
　　　　　'Why did Juan do what thing?'

This fact could be attributed to (4). When *por qué* is base-generated in the spec of an interrogative CP, it disrupts the formation of a full-fledged multiple *wh*-question, with the single pair reading somehow surviving. How a single pair reading is obtained in (33b) remains unclear. Nevertheless, there seems to be a general consensus in the

---

[9] Thanks to Juan Uriagereka (p.c.) for the data and discussion.

literature that the loss of an otherwise available (or a default) pair-list reading occurs when some syntactic constraint is violated. Such violations include (potential) superiority violations (Barss 2000), intervention effects (Pesetsky 2000), and *wh*-in-situ within an island (Dayal 2002). In a similar vein, we can tie the lack of the pair-list reading in (33b) to a violation of the uniformity condition (4), whose effect, as we argued earlier, follows from the syntax of the probe-goal system.

3.2. *WH*-QP INTERACTIONS AND THE LEFT PERIPHERY OF A CLAUSE

I would like to turn now to scope interactions between *why*s and the subject QP from the perspective of the stronger and weaker views mentioned above. Let us examine the following contrast, noted by Collins (1991) (see also Shlonsky and Soare 2011).

(34) a. **Why** did everyone leave?   (*every > wh; wh > every*)

 b. **How come** everyone left?   (**every > wh; wh > every*)

Below, I would like to defend Collins's proposal that the ambiguity of (34a) is due to the movement of *why*. Assuming that the subject QP in English is located in the spec of TP, let us suppose that *why* in this case is base-generated somewhere inside T', as shown in (35a). On the other hand, (34b) is unambiguous because *how come* does not undergo movement at all (as shown in (35b)) and accordingly *how come* never falls within the scope of the subject QP.

(35) a. [$_{CP}$ Why$_i$ did [$_{TP}$ everyone [$_{T'}$ leave t_i]]]

 b. [$_{CP}$ How come C [$_{TP}$ everyone left]]

Essentially the same account could cover Chinese data such as (36), taken from Aoun and Li (1993). I assume that, like *why* in English, *weishenme* can be base-generated in the CP-periphery or below the surface position of the subject. Let us further assume that there is no overt movement of *weishenme*, which means that the surface position of *weishenme* corresponds to its base position. According to this view, the ambiguity of (36a) is on par with that of (34a): *weishenme* undergoes covert *wh*-movement across the subject QP. And (36b) is on par with (34b): base-generated in the CP-periphery, the adjunct *wh*-phrase remains outside the scope of the subject QP throughout the derivation.

(36) a. Meigeren dou **weishenme** da ta?   (*every > wh; wh > every*)
  everyone all **why**   hit him
  'Why did everyone hit him?'

 b. **Weishenme** meigeren dou da ta?   (**every > wh; wh > every*)
  why   everyone all hit him
  'Why did everyone hit him?'

We should now consider whether or not this kind of contrast can be accommodated under the hypothesis that the reason *wh*-adjunct is always merged as the spec of CP. Fitzpatrick (2005) in fact provides an interesting analysis of the contrast between *why* and *how come* along this line. He first argues that *how come* is exceptional among English *wh*-phrases (including *why*) in that it is a factive *wh*-phrase, a point also noted by Collins (1991). This point is demonstrated by the contrast in (37). *Why*-questions in this type of context have the flavor of a rhetorical question, as the speaker in this context expects a negative answer (e.g., *He would not leave.*). According to Fitzpatrick, a *wh*-question employing *how come* is strange in such contexts because of the conflict between the negative bias mentioned above and the factive/presuppositional nature of *how come*, as summarized in (38). According to Fitzpatrick, such conflicts do not arise with *why* because it is not a factive *wh*-phrase.

(37) Speaker A : Did John leave?

Speaker B : No. Why would he leave?/*How come he would leave?

(38) a. Factive presupposition: He would leave.

b. Negative bias: He would not leave.

Fitzpatrick goes on to analyze the ambiguity of (34a) in terms of the covert movement of the subject QP over *why*, as illustrated in (39a). Further, he suggests that the same covert movement of the subject QP is not available in the presence of *how come*, and this is where the factive nature of *how come* becomes crucial for Fitzpatrick. His idea is that this property renders the TP complement of *how come* a factive island, barring the (covert) movement of the subject *wh*-phrase over *how come*, as shown in (39b).

(39) a. everyone$_i$ [why [$_{TP}$ t_i left]]

b. [how come [$_{island}$ everyone left]]

As for the Chinese data in (36), one could follow Ko (2005) and claim that (36a) is derived from (36b) via the movement of *meigeren* across *weishenme* 'why' in Chinese. The ambiguity of (36a) could then be treated on a par with that of (34a), the only difference between the two being the timing of the movement of the subject QP (i.e., overt in Chinese and covert in English). It would thus appear that the contrast that we see in examples such as (34) and (36) can be accommodated under the stronger hypothesis that *why* is always merged into the spec of CP (as well as under our weaker position).

However, there are empirical reasons to question this line of analysis. First, according to Tsai (2008), causal *zenme* 'how come' in Chinese is always base-generated in the edge of an interrogative CP. In particular, causal *zenme* does not allow a non-local construal, as shown by the ungrammaticality of (40) taken from Tsai (2008: 102) (see also Chou 2012: 5). This *wh*-element is similar to *how come* in this respect (see (10b)).

(40) *Akiu renwei [Xiaodi **zenme** hui chiuli   zhe-jian shi]?
     Akiu think   Xiaodi how   will handle this-CL matter
     'How come Akiu thinks [Xiaodi will handle this matter *t*]?'

Now, according to Tsai (2008: 104), causal *zenme* fails to occur in multiple *wh*-questions, regardless of the word order among the *wh*-phrases and regardless of whether the *wh*-phrase occurring with *zenme* is a subject as in (41), or an object as in (42). This fact is quite expected from the perspective of the generalization in (4).

(41) a. *(nimen,) shei **zenme** hui chuli   zhe-jian shi?
         you guys who **how**   will handle this-Cl matter
         '*How come who will handle this matter?'

     b. *(nimen,) **zenme** shei hui chuli   zhe-jian shi?
         you guys **how**   who will handle this-Cl matter
         '*How come who will handle this matter?'   (Tsai 2008: 104)

(42) a. *ni **zenme** hui he   na-zhong jiu?
         you **how**   will drink which-kind wine
         '*How come you will drink which kind of wine?'

     b. ***zenme** ni hui he   na-zhong jiu?
         how   you will drink which-kind wine   (Tsai 2008: 104)
         '*How come you will drink which kind of wine?'

Crucially, Tsai (2008) reports that the order of *zenme* and the subject QP does not affect scope. In particular, (43b) lacks the wide scope reading of *meigeren* 'everyone.'

(43) a. (nimen,) **zenme**   meigeren hui dai   yi-ben shu?
         you guys **how come** everyone will bring one-Cl book
         'How come everyone will bring one book?'   (*wh* > *every*; **every* > *wh*)

     b. (nimen,) meigeren **zenme**   hui dai   yi-ben shu?
         you guys everyone **how come** will bring one-Cl book
         'How come everyone will bring one book?'   (*wh* > *every*; **every* > *wh*)

This shows that movement of the subject QP across a causal *wh*-adjunct located in CP is in fact possible (contrary to Fitzpatrick's claim), but it does not establish a new scope relation (for whatever reasons). This casts doubt on the explanation of the ambiguity seen in (36a) in terms of the movement of the subject QP.[10]

Second, recall our earlier discussion that *why the hell* in English, like *how come*, is always merged into the spec of an interrogative CP. Crucially, *why the hell* is not factive in Fitzpatrick's (2005) sense, since it is fine in the kind of context discussed earlier:

(44) Speaker A: Did John leave?

     Speaker B: No. Why the hell would he leave?

---

[10] Tsai (2008) assumes that causal *zenme* is an interrogative C head, but it should not make a difference for the purpose of scope calculations whether a *wh*-element involved in *wh*-QP configurations is a phrase or a head.

And yet, it behaves on par with *how come* in disallowing the subject QP to take scope over it.[11]

(45) **Why the hell** did everyone leave?   (*wh* > *every*; **every* > *wh*)

In summary, the ambiguity of (34a) and (36a) should not be tied to the movement of the subject QP. Rather, it arises via overt movement of *why* and covert movement of *weishenme*, assuming that they can be base-generated within T'.

4. Causal *Wh*-Adjuncts in *Wh*-in-Situ Languages

So far, I have proposed that reason *whys* are not always base-generated in the left periphery of CP (interrogative or declarative), whereas some causal *wh*-adjuncts are always merged into the periphery of an interrogative CP. Focusing on Chinese and Japanese, I will argue in this section that a species of causal *wh*-adjuncts occurs fairly low in the structure.

As discussed by Kurafuji (1996, 1997), Ochi (1999, 2004), Nakao and Obata (2009), and Iida (2011), among others, Japanese, like German and other *wh*-fronting languages, allows *nani-o* 'what-Acc' to be interpreted very much like 'why (the hell).'

(46) Kimi-wa nani-o   manga-o   yon-deiru no?[12]
       you-Top **WHAT**-Acc cartoon-Acc read-Prog Q
       'Why (the hell) are you reading such a thing as a cartoon?'

And, as discussed by Ochi (1999), Chinese also allows *shenme* 'what' to be interpreted as 'why (the hell)': this is shown in (48a). Note that *pao* 'run' does not take the direct object, as shown in (48b).

(47) a. Lisi **weishenme** pao?
          Lisi **why**   run
          'Why is John running?'

      b. Lisi wei-le zhege yuanyin pao.
          Lisi for   this reason run
          'Lisi is running for this reason.'

(48) a. Lisi pao **shenme**?
          Lisi run **WHAT**
          'Why (the hell) is John running?'

---

[11] According to den Dikken and Giannakidou (2002), even the argument *wh-the-hell* fails to yield scope ambiguity in examples like *what the hell did everyone buy?* But my informants report that if we use *each* instead of *every*, the wide scope reading of the subject QP becomes salient.

(i)   What the hell did each girl buy?

[12] This example is slightly degraded due to the double-*o* constraint (see Harada 1973) operating in Japanese. I will abstract away from this point, since it is also known that double-*o* is tolerated when one of the -*o* phrases is an adjunct (see Kuroda 1992: chapter 6).

b. *John pao jiankang / zhege yuanying.
    John run health /   this   reason
    'John is running for health/this reason.'

The Chinese data are particularly enlightening, since they show that *weishenme* 'why' in (47a) and *shenme* 'what' in (48a) occupy distinct positions. I will return to this point shortly.

Now recall our earlier discussion that WHAT in languages like German yields a causal question. As Dylan Tsai (p.c.) observes, this point also holds for WHAT in Chinese (and Japanese). As briefly discussed in section 2, Tsai (2008) teases apart causal and reason questions by using a stative predicate. The following are the Chinese counterparts of the English data in (17a) and (17c).

(49) a. Tiankong **zenme** shi lande?
          sky   **how**   be blue
          'How come the sky is blue?'

      b. Tiankong **weishenme** shi lande?
          sky   **why**   be blue
          'Why is the sky blue?'

Just like (17a), (49a) presupposes that (i) the sky is blue and (ii) something caused the sky to be blue. Because of this second presupposition, this example has the counter-expectation of the sort that we discussed in connection with (17a) and (17b). On the other hand, (49b), like the *why*-question in (17c), does not presuppose (ii). Now, if we put WHAT in this context, the sentence necessairly has the causal interpretation (Dylan Tsai (p.c.)).

(50) Tiankong zai lan **shenme**?
      sky   Prog blue WHAT
      'Why the hell is the sky is blue?'

With respect to this, WHAT in Chinese is akin to the causal *zenme* 'how' in Chinese, rather than the reason *weishenme* 'why.'

Note that WHAT in Japanese does not easily occur with a stative predicate, as originally observed by Kurafuji (1997).

(51) Sora-ga **naze/*nani-o**   aoi no?
      sky-Nom why/WHAT-Acc blue Q
      'Why is the sky is blue?'

One way to make (51) more natural is to use a progressive (or perfective) aspect, as shown in the following example.[13]

(52) Sora-ga **naze/?nani-o**   aoku nat-teiru   no?
      sky-Nom why/WHAT-Acc blue become-Prog Q
      'Why (the hell) is the sky being blue?'

[13] In general, WHAT-questions in Japanese sound degraded without the use of the progressive aspect (see Kurafuji 1997). Note that the Chinese example in (50) is also in the progressive form.

To the extent that this example is acceptable with *nani-o,* it has the counter-expectation, "the sky should not be blue."

Returning to the main discussion, WHAT in Japanese allows long-distance dependencies, as noted by Kurafuji (1997).

(53) Kimi-wa [hanako-ga   **nani**-o   hashit-teiru to]   omoimasu ka?
      you-Top Hanako-Nom **WHAT**-Acc run-Prog   that think   Q
      'Why (the hell) do you think [that Hanako is running *t*]?'

And this is true of WHAT-questions in Chinese.[14]

(54) Ni   renwei Lisi pao **sheme?**
      you think Lisi run what
      'Why (the hell) do you think [that Lisi is running *t*]?'

Now, as discussed by Ochi (1999), WHAT in these two languages is fine in multiple *wh*-questions.[15,16] We can conclude from this fact that unlike their counterparts

----

[14] Dylan Tsai (p.c.) finds an example such as (54) to be unnatural. According to him, the example improves with the use of a counterfactual predicate such as *yiwei* 'thought' under some negative mood.

(i)   buran,   ni yiwei Lisi zai pao shenme?!
      otherwise you thought Lisi Prg run WHAT
      'Otherwise, what the hell did you think Lisi was running for?!'

It seems that WHAT in Japanese shows the same effect. (ii) sounds more natural than (53).

(ii) Kimi-wa [hanako-ga   **nani**-o   hashit-teiru to]   omotteita   no?
      you-Top Hanako-Nom **WHAT**-Acc run-Prog   that was thinking Q
      'Why (the hell) were you thinking [that Hanako was running *t*]?'

As Dylan Tsai (p.c.) suggests, some special illocutionary force seems to be needed to license causal WHAT. If translated into cartographic terms, this could mean that causal WHAT-questions require some functional element in the Force domain, but I need to leave an investigation of this issue for another occasion.

[15] Daiko Takahashi (p.c.) observes that examples such as (55a) do not allow a pair-list reading. While I concur with this judgment, the same observation holds of *naze* 'why' in the same configuration (see Nishigauchi 1999 for a very relevant discussion).

(i)   Dare-ga   naze sawai-deiru no?
      who-Nom why clamor-Prog Q
      'Who is clamoring why?'

Nevertheless, I believe that both *naze* and *nani-o* can yield a pair-list reading when an appropriate context is provided. For example, (ii) easily yields a pair-list reading in a context where residents in several dorm rooms are each clamoring.

(ii) Dono   heya-no   jyuunin-ga   naze/nani-o   sawai-deiru no ka
      which   room-Gen resident-Nom why/WHAT-Acc clamor-Prog   Q
      subete sirabete kite kudasai.
      thoroughly check   please
      'Please go and check thoroughly which room's resident is clamoring why.'

[16] Some Chinese speakers do not accept this type of multiple *wh*-question with causal *shenme.* Although I have no explanation for this variation, it is worth noting here that we seem to find some

in German and other languages with overt *wh*-movement, Chinese and Japanese WHAT are not (always) merged into the left periphery of an interrogative CP.

(55) a. Dare-ga **nani-o**   sawai-deiru no?
          who-Nom **WHAT**-Acc clamor-Prog Q
          'Who is clamoring why (the hell)?'

      b. Shei shui **shenme?**
          who sleep **WHAT**
          'Who is sleeping why (the hell)?

This point is important in another respect. Although causal WHAT does not occur in multiple *wh*-questions in languages like German, the data in (55) shows that there is no intrinsic property of WHAT that renders it incompatible with other *wh*-phrases in multiple *wh*-questions: It occurs in multiple *wh*-questions, provided that it is merged in a position other than the left periphery of an interrogative CP. In the following sections, I explicate the base position of WHAT in Chinese and Japanese.

4.1 ON THE MERGING SITE OF WHAT-IN-SITU

In this subsection, I provide evidence that WHAT in these *wh*-in-situ languages can never be base-generated in the left periphery of a clause, interrogative or non-interrogative. To be more specific, WHAT in Chinese and Japanese will be shown to be a V'-level adjunct.

Let us start with Kurafuji's (1997) important observation about inner island effects in Japanese: the causal *wh*-adjunct *nani-o*, unlike *naze* 'why,' cannot occur with clause-mate negation, as shown in (56). This contrast follows if *naze* 'why' can be base-generated in a position higher than negation, while WHAT is always base-generated in a position lower than negation.

(56) a. Taro-wa **naze** awatetei-nai no?
          Taro-Top **why** panic-not   Q
          'Why is Taro not panicking?'

      b. *Taro-wa **nani-o**   awatetei-nai no?
          Taro-Top **WHAT**-Acc panic-not   Q
          'Why is Taro not panicking?'   (Japanese)

Kurafuji's observation regarding Japanese is directly mirrored by the following contrast in Chinese.

(57) a. Lisi **weishenme** bu huang-zhang?
          Lisi why   not hurry
          'Why isn't Lisi hurrying?'

      b. *Lisi bu huang-zhang **shenme?**
          Lisi not hurry   **WHAT**
          'Why isn't Lisi hurrying?'

variation in judgment among speakers with respect to multiple *wh*-questions involving reason *weishenme* as well (as briefly mentioned in section 2). I need to leave a detailed investigation of this issue for another occasion.

Although we can conclude from the above discussion that WHAT in these languages is never base-generated in the CP-periphery, one may nevertheless try to find a connection between this causal *wh*-adjunct in Chinese/Japanese and the left periphery. Specifically, given that causal WHAT in languages like German is always base-generated in the left periphery of an interrogative CP, and given that its counterpart in Chinese and Japanese is always base-generated below negation, could it be that the latter is base-generated in the left periphery of *v*P, which constitutes another phase domain?[17] For example, Stepanov and Tsai (2008) propose that while *why* in English is base-generated in the CP-periphery, *warum* in German is base-generated in the *v*P-domain. Although they do not pinpoint the exact base position of *warum*, we could interpret their conclusion to mean that *warum* is base-generated in the *v*P-periphery. Their reasoning for this contrast between English and German is as follows. Reason *whys* in languages like English are always merged into the CP-periphery because (i) they select a proposition as their sole argument, and (ii) TP is the domain in which all arguments are saturated, with the subject located in the spec of TP. But German is arguably different from English in that the external argument may be licensed within *v*P in this language, and hence all the arguments are saturated in *v*P, enabling *v*P to serve as a propositional argument for *warum*. Applying the same logic to Japanese (see Lasnik and Saito 1992, among others), one could propose that WHAT in Japanese (and possibly in Chinese, too) is base-generated in the *v*P-periphery. Although theoretical feasible, I will provide evidence against this possibility.

Let us pinpoint the location of WHAT, starting with Chinese. As already shown in (48), WHAT in Chinese occurs postverbally, unlike *weishenme* 'why.' In transitive constructions, this causal *wh*-adjunct occurs between a verb and the direct object, as shown in (58a).

(58) a. Lisi qiao **shenme** men?
       Lisi knock **what** door
       'Why is Lisi knocking on the door?'

     b. ?Lisi qiao men qiao **shenme**?
        Lisi knock door knock WHAT
        'Why is Lisi knocking on the door?'

Assuming with Huang (1994) and Huang et al. (2009) that Chinese main verbs raise within *v*P but do not raise out of *v*P, WHAT must occur (deeply) inside *v*P, a conclusion consistent with the ungrammaticality of (57b).

[17] See Tsai (2011) for a proposal that WHAT-questions in Chinese involve a light verb construction. Note that Stepanov and Tsai (2008) propose that the purpose *why*, in contrast to the reason *why*, is base-generated in the *v*P-domain. Crucially, WHAT discussed in this chapter is not an instance of the purpose *why*, as evidenced by the fact that it easily occurs with predicates such as *awateru* 'panic.'

(i) kimi-wa nani-o   awate-teiru no?
     you-Top WHAT-Acc panic-Prog Q
     'Why the hell are you panicking?'

In fact, the distribution of *shenme* 'what' is parallel to that of nominal frequency adverbs:

(59)　a.　Lisi qiao-le　　san-ci　　　men.
　　　　　Lisi knock-ASP three-times door
　　　　　'Lisi knocked on the door three times.'

　　　b.　Lisi qiao　men qiao-le　　san-ci.
　　　　　Lisi knock door knock-Asp three-times
　　　　　'Lisi knocked on the door three times.'

Huang et al. (2009) argue that such frequency/duration phrases (FPs) occur as V'-level adjuncts. I thus would like to pursue the hypothesis that WHAT in Chinese is also a V'-level adjunct.

(60)　$[_{vP} NP_1 [_{v'} v [_{VP} NP_2 [_{V'} FP [_{V'} V NP_3]]]]]$

Predicate-fronting data support the hypothesis that WHAT is always base-generated within VP in Japanese as well. As shown in (61b, c), there is an asymmetry between subjects and objects in this construction: subjects can be stranded, whereas objects cannot. Following Yatsushiro (1997), I attribute the ill-formedness of (61c) to a violation of the Proper Binding Condition (PBC), as illustrated in (62). (61b) does not violate the PBC, assuming that what is fronted is a VP and the subject is base-generated in the domain of *v*P.

(61)　a.　Taro-ga　　hon-o　　　uri-sae　shita.
　　　　　taro-Nom book-Acc sell-even did
　　　　　'Taro even sold books.'

　　　b.　Hon-o　　uri-sae　taro-ga　shita.
　　　　　book-Acc sell-even taro-Nom did

　　　c.　*Taro-ga　　uri-sae　hon-o　　shita.
　　　　　 taro-Nom sell-even book-Acc did

(62)　$[_{VP} t_i \text{ sell}]_j$ taro book$_i$ t_j did

Now let us apply this type of predicate fronting to the examples containing *naze* and WHAT. In (63) and (64), the (a)-examples serve as the baseline data for the (b)-examples. (63b) involves a predicate fronting that strands *naze* 'why,' and is grammatical. In contrast, (64b), which strands WHAT, is ungrammatical. Note that the (c)-examples may be structurally ambiguous: *naze/nani-o* may or may not be included in the fronted constituent.

(63)　a.　Taro-wa　**naze** kodomo-ni tsuraku-atari-sae shi-teiru no?
　　　　　taro-Top why child-Dat badly-treat-even do-Prog Q
　　　　　'Why is Taro even treating his child badly?'

　　　b.　Kodomo-ni tsuraku-atari-sae taro-wa　**naze** shi-teiru no?
　　　　　child-Dat badly-treat-even taro-Top why do-Prog Q
　　　　　'[Even treating his child badly]$_j$, why is Taro doing t_i?'

c. **Naze** kodomo-ni tsuraku-atari-sae taro-wa shi-teiru no?
why   child-Dat   treat badly-even taro-Top do-Prog Q

(64) a. Taro-wa **nani-o**   kodomo-ni tsuraku-atari-sae shi-teiru no?
taro-Top WHAT-Acc child-Dat   badly-treat-even do-Prog Q
'Why is Taro even treating his child badly?'

b. *Kodomo-ni tsuraku-atari-sae taro-wa **nani-o**   shi-teiru no?
child-Dat   badly-treat-even taro-Top WHAT-Acc do-Prog Q
'[Even treating his child badly]$_i$, why is Taro doing t_i?'

c. **Nani-o**   kodomo-ni tsuraku-atari-sae taro-wa shi-teiru no?
WHAT-Acc child-Dat   treat badly-even taro-Top do-Prog Q

I assume that (64b) is excluded for the same reason as (61c): a violation of the PBC. It then follows that WHAT in Japanese originates in VP, lower than the base position of the subject. This is consistent with our conclusion about position of WHAT in Chinese (i.e., the location of FP in (60)).

Let us zoom in a little closer. Since FP in (60) is located in a position sandwiched between two NPs within VP (i.e., NP$_2$ and NP$_3$), we may expect that this is also true of WHAT in Japanese. In fact, there is evidence for this conjecture. As Iida (2011) observes, the word order between causal WHAT and the direct object is fixed: the former must precede the latter, as indicated by the unacceptability of (65c). No such restriction applies to the word order between WHAT and the subject, as (65a) and (65b) show. (66) illustrates the same point with a dative object.

(65) a. **Nani-o**   kare-wa henna uta-o   utat-teiru no?
WHAT-Acc he-Top funny song-Acc sing-Prog Q
'Why is he singing a funny song?'

b. Kare-wa **nani-o**   henna uta-o   utat-teiru no?
he-Top   WHAT-Acc funny song-Acc sing-Prog Q
'Why is he singing a funny song?'

c. *Kare-wa henna uta-o   **nani-o**   utat-teiru no?
he-Top   funny song-Acc WHAT-Acc sing-Prog Q
'Why is he singing a funny song?'

(66) a. **Nani-o**   kimi-wa hanako-ni at-teiru   no?
WHAT-Acc you-Top hanako-Dat meet-Prog Q
'Why the hell are you seeing Hanako?'

b. Kimi-wa **nani-o**   hanako-ni at-teiru   no?
you-Top WHAT-Acc hanako-Dat meet-Prog Q
'Why the hell are you seeing Hanako?'

c. ??Kimi-wa hanako-ni **nani-o**   at-teiru   no?
you-Top hanako-Dat WHAT-Acc meet-Prog Q
'Why the hell are you seeing Hanako?'

Let us assume for the sake of discussion that causal WHAT constitutes a barrier for extraction (for whatever reasons): the object cannot be fronted in (65c) because it is base-generated in a position lower than *nani-o*.[18] (65b), on the other hand, is fine, because the subject originates in a position higher than the base-position of *nani-o*. Now, let us consider the distribution of *naze* 'why' and WHAT in a double object construction.

(67) a. Kimi-wa **naze/nani-o**   hanako-ni   tegami-o okut-teiru no?
         you-Top **why/WHAT-Acc** hanako-Dat letter-Acc send-Prog Q
         'Why are you sending a letter to Hanako?'

     b. Kimi-wa hanako-ni   **naze/(?)nani-o**   tegami-o okut-teiru no?
         you-Top hanako-Dat **why/WHAT-Acc** letter-Acc send-Prog Q
         'Why are you sending a letter to Hanako?'

     c. Kimi-wa hanako-ni   tegami-o **naze/*nani-o**   okut-teiru no?
         you-Top hanako-Dat letter-Acc **why/WHAT-Acc** send-Prog Q
         'Why are you sending a letter to Hanako?'

(67a, b) show that the relative order between WHAT and the indirect object is free. The fact that the indirect object patterns with the subject, and not with the direct object, with respect to the relative order against causal WHAT tells us that the base position of the indirect object is higher than that of WHAT. Thus, the base position of WHAT appears to correspond to FP in (60). In short, the base position of WHAT seems to be constant within the two *wh*-in-situ languages.

Note that this conclusion is reinforced by Yatsushiro's (1997) discussion of ditransitive constructions and VP-fronting. As she points out, the indirect and the direct object behave differently when VP is fronted. In particular, the former is a good remnant in VP-preposing contexts, while the latter is not. This again shows that the direct object and WHAT are structurally lower than the indirect object.

(68) a. Taro-ga   jiro-ni   hanako-o   syookaishi-sae shita.
         taro-Nom jiro-Dat hanako-Acc introduce-even did
         'Taro even introduced Hanako to Jiro.'

     b. Hanako-o   syookaishi-sae taro-ga   jiro-ni   shita.
         hanako-Acc introduce-even taro-Nom jiro-Dat did
         'Even introduce Hanako, Taro did to Jiro.'

     c. *Jiro-ni   syookaishi-sae taro-ga   hanako-o   shita.
         jiro-Dat introduce-even taro-Nom hanako-Acc did
         'Even introduce Hanako, Taro did to Jiro.'

On the basis of these considerations, I propose the following base structure for *v*P in Japanese when causal WHAT appears:[19]

(69) [$_{vP}$ SUBJ [$_{v'}$ [$_{VP}$ IO [$_{v'}$ WHAT [$_{v'}$ DO V]]] *v*]]

---

[18] See Iida (2011) for an analysis of this subject–object asymmetry in terms of Fox and Pesetsky's (2004) cyclic linearization model.

[19] Given that the indirect object can be stranded, as shown in (68b), and the general idea that an X'-element cannot be affected by a movement operation (see Chomsky 1995), we may have to adopt a VP-shell structure rather than the one in (69). See Yatsushiro (1997).

As a variety of causal wh-adjuncts (e.g., *how come* and *why the hell* in English, causal WHAT in languages such as German, and causal *zenme* in Chinese) are always merged in the left periphery of an interrogative CP, causal WHAT in Chinese and Japanese appear to be an exception, and I have no proposal to offer regarding why its base position is so low. Nevertheless, the proposal that causal WHAT in Chinese and Japanese is base-generated as a V'-adjunct is interesting in the following theoretical sense. It seems that Chinese and Japanese causal WHAT need to be introduced into the structure "as early as possible": they must be merged with V as soon as the derivation unfolds. On the other hand, the majority of causal wh-adjuncts are introduced into the structure "as late as possible," so much so that they cannot undergo movement: the only option for them is to be directly merged into their 'final destination.' Reason wh-adjuncts seem to lie halfway between the two types of causal wh-adjuncts. They are sometimes base-generated in the TP domain, and although they are sometimes base-generated as the spec of CP, this CP is not restricted to an interrogative CP.

4.2 ARGUMENT VERSUS ADJUNCT ASYMMETRY

Let me end this chapter with one important theoretical implication brought out by causal WHAT in Chinese and Japanese. As Kurafuji (1997) points out, WHAT in Japanese shows the same locality as *naze* 'why': it can be construed non-locally, as long as it is not within an island, as shown in (70).

(70) a. Kimi-wa taro-ga   nani-o   awate-teiru to   omoi-masu ka?
        you-Top taro-Nom WHAT-Acc panic-Prog that think   Q
        'Why$_i$ do you think [that Taro is panicking t_i]?'

     b. *Kimi-wa [[**nani-o**   awate-teiru] hito]-o   shikatta no?
        You-Top   WHAT-Acc panic-Prog person-Acc scolded Q
        '*Why$_i$ did you scold [a person [who was panicking t_i]]?'

The following data shows the same point for WHAT in Chinese.[20]

(71) a. (?)Ni renwei Lisi qiao   shenme men?
         you think Lisi knock what   door
        'Why$_i$ do you think [Lisi is knocking on the door t_i]?'

     b. *Ni taoyen [[qiao **shenme** men]-de ren]?
        you hate   knock what   door-De person
        '*Why$_i$ do you hate [the person who is knocking on the door t_i]?'

This fact has an important theoretical implication for the nature of wh-in-situ, as Nobuhiro Miyoshi (p.c.) points out (see also Ochi 1999).

Tsai (1994), Reinhart (1998), Stepanov and Tsai (2008), and Fujii et al. (2010) propose that the traditional argument/adjunct asymmetry in the realm of wh-in-situ should be recast in terms of an asymmetry between a nominal and a non-nominal element: typical argument wh-phrases such as *who* and *what* are nominal elements, whereas typical adjunct wh-phrases such as *why* and *how* are adverbial. These authors

---

[20] (71a) is slightly degraded, presumably for the reason discussed in footnote 14.

argue that nominal *wh*-phrases are licensed in situ by unselective binding, an option not available for adverbial *wh*-phrases in situ. As a technical implementation of this idea, Reinhart (1998) sets up the semantics of unselective binding in such a way that only function variables (in the D-position) that bind N-variables (in N) can be unselectively bound (via choice function), which is not available for *wh*-adverbs. Hence, nonnominal *wh*-phrases must move to the spec of an interrogative CP for interpretation.

Reinhart (1998) provides empirical evidence for this hypothesis. As shown in (72), the argument/nominal *wh*-phrase can occur in situ. Now consider (73). Given that *how* and *what way* are synonymous, the contrast in grammaticality could be due to the categorial difference between the two *wh*-phrases: *what way* is an NP, whereas *how* is not. Hence only *what way* in (73b) can be interpreted by unselective binding, according to Reinhart.

(72) Who kissed whom?

(73) a.   *Who kissed Mary how?

      b.   Who kissed Mary what way?

However, recall that causal WHAT in Chinese and Japanese patterns with *weishenme/naze* in terms of locality, despite its nominal status. This fact tells us that the nominal status of an in-situ *wh*-phrase is not sufficient (or is simply irrelevant) for the purpose of unselective binding. I therefore propose that the correct distinction is the one between arguments and adjuncts, as originally proposed by Huang (1982: chapter 7).

Given this discussion, we need to reconsider (73). For Reinhart, *what way* in (73b) can be licensed in situ due to its nominal status. But this is not conclusive, since this example may contain a null preposition in the sense of Huang (1982).[21] Under his analysis, *what way* is an argument of this preposition, while *how* is not. In short, the island sensitive property of causal WHAT leads us to adopt the structures in (75) and not those in (74).

(74) a.   *Who kissed Mary [$_{AdvP}$ how]

      b.   Who kissed Mary [$_{NP}$ what way]

(75) a.   *Who kissed Mary [$_{AdvP}$ how]

      b.   Who kissed Mary [$_{PP}$ (in) [$_{NP}$ what way]]

A similar comment can be made about Fujii et al.'s (2010) recent discussion of *wh*-in-situ in Chinese and especially Japanese. Building on Tsai's (1994) analysis of *weishenme* 'why' versus *wei(-le)shenme* 'for what' in Chinese, Fujii et al. (2010) provide an analysis of the *wh*-adjunct *nande* in Japanese, which typically yields two readings in many (but not in all) contexts: reason and instrumental. Fujii et al. use several tests to demonstrate that these two readings in fact come from two types of *nande* that

---

[21] Causal WHAT in Japanese is always accompanied by *-o*, which shows that there is no null postposition accompanying this *wh*-phrase.

are morpho-syntactically distinct from one another: The reason interpretation arises when *nande* is a *wh*-adverb, as shown in (76a), and the instrumental reading arises when *nande* is PP, as shown in (76b), consisting of the *wh*-nominal *nan(i)* 'what' and the postposition *-de* 'with,' thus yielding the meaning 'with what.'

(76) a.
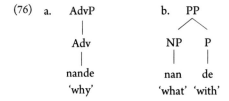

Crucially, they observe that the instrumental *nande* is licensed in situ across an island boundary, which is not the case with the reason *nande*. They take this observation as an additional piece of evidence that a *wh*-nominal can be licensed in situ via unselective binding, while a non-nominal *wh*-element cannot (and hence it needs to resort to movement to be licensed). But this observation can also be accommodated under the view defended here, which takes the crucial distinction to be the one between arguments and adjuncts. The nominal *wh*-element *nan(i)* in (76b) is an argument of the postposition *-de,* whereas *nande* in (76a) is an adjunct in its own right.

5. Conclusion

In the first half of this chapter, I argued that reason *whys* are not always merged into the CP-periphery. The discussion capitalized on the differences between reason *wh*-adjuncts and causal *wh*-adjuncts (*how come, why the hell,* and causal WHAT in languages like German). On the theoretical side, I argued that the substance of Chomsky's (1973) uniformity requirement on multiple *wh*-questions follows from the way in which the probe-goal system operates. To the extent that this analysis is tenable, we obtain the following theoretical conclusions. First, the analysis supports the idea that probes and goals have *u*Fs in *wh*-dependencies as well as in φ-agreement dependencies. Second, it supports the idea of multiple feature-checking as a simultaneous operation. Third, it shows that probes and goals become inactive the moment their *u*Fs are taken care of.

In the second half of the chapter, I focused on causal WHAT in Chinese and Japanese, arguing that it is a V'-adjunct and thus its underlying position has nothing to do with the left periphery of CP or *v*P. The locality of WHAT in Chinese and Japanese provides a strong piece of evidence that argument *wh*-phrases can be licensed in situ, whereas adjunct *wh*-phrases cannot, as originally proposed by Huang (1982).

Acknowledgement

It is a great pleasure for me to contribute this chapter for a volume in honor of Jim Huang. I thank Jim for giving me opportunities to do collaborative work with him over the years.

Parts of the material included here were presented at the 3rd Kansai Annual Meeting of the English Literary Society of Japan (October 2008), Nanzan University (March 2011), Chinese University of Hong Kong (April 2011), and TEAL8 workshop (June 2013). I would like to thank the audiences at those events for their useful comments. My sincere thanks also go to the editors of this book, especially Dylan Tsai, for very useful comments on an earlier version of this chapter. This research is financially supported by the Grant-in-Aid for Scientific Research (C) (No. 25370431), the Ministry of Education, Culture, Sports, Science, and Technology of Japan.

References

Aoun, Joseph, and Y.-H. Audrey Li. 1993. *Syntax of Scope*. Cambridge, MA: MIT Press.

Barss, Andrew. 2000. Minimalism and asymmetric *wh*-interpretation. In *Step by Step: Essays on Minimalism in Honor of Howard Lasnik*, ed. R. Martin, D. Michaels, and J. Uriagereka, 31–52, Cambridge, MA: MIT Press.

Boeckx, Cedric. 2008. *Bare Syntax*. Oxford: Oxford University Press.

Bošković, Željko. 2007. On the locality and motivation of Move and Agree: An even more minimal theory. *Linguistic Inquiry* 38, 589–644.

Chomsky, Noam. 1973. Conditions on transformations. In *A Festschrift for Morris Halle*, ed. S. Anderson and P. Kiparsky, 232–286. New York: Holt, Rinehart and Winston.

Chomsky, Noam. 1995. *The Minimalist Program*. Cambridge, MA: MIT Press.

Chomsky, Noam. 2000. Minimalist inquiries: the framework. In *Step by Step: Essays on Minimalism in Honor of Howard Lasnik*, ed. R. Martin, D. Michaels, and J. Uriagereka, 89–155, Cambridge, MA: MIT Press.

Chomsky, Noam. 2004. Beyond explanatory adequacy. In *Structures and Beyond: The Cartography of Syntactic Structures*, ed. A. Belletti, Vol. 3, 104–131. Oxford: Oxford University Press.

Chou, Chao-Ting Tim. 2012. Syntax-pragmatics interface: Mandarin Chinese *wh-the-hell* and point-of-view operator. *Syntax* 15, 1–24.

Collins, Chris. 1991. *Why* and *how come*. *MIT Working Papers in Linguistics* 15, 31–45.

Dayal, Veneeta. 2002. Single-pair versus multiple-pair answers: *Wh*-in-situ and scope. *Linguistic Inquiry* 33, 512–520.

Dikken, Marcel den, and Anastasia Giannakidou. 2002. From *hell* to polarity: "Aggressively non-D-linked" *wh*-phrases as polarity items. *Linguistic Inquiry* 33, 31–61.

Epstein, Samuel, and Daniel Seely. 2002. Rule applications as cycles in a level-free syntax. In *Derivation and Explanation in the Minimalist Program*, ed. S. Epstein and D. Seely, 65–89. Malden, MA: Blackwell.

Fitzpatrick, Justin. 2005. The whys and how comes of presupposition and NPI licensing in questions. In *Proceedings of the 24th West Coast Conference on Formal Linguistics*, 138–145. Somerville, MA: Cascadilla Press.

Fox, Danny, and David Pesetsky. 2004. Cyclic linearization of syntactic structure. *Theoretical Linguistics* 31, 1–46.

Frampton, John, Sam Gutmann, Julie Legate, and Charles Yang. 2000. Remarks on "Derivation by Phase": Feature valuation, agreement, and intervention. Ms., Northeastern University and MIT.

Fujii, Tomohiro, Kensuke Takita, Barry C.-Y. Yang, and W.-T. Dylan Tsai. 2012. Comparative remarks on *wh*-adverbials in-situ in Japanese and Chinese. Ms., Yokohama National University, Tohoku University, National United University, and National Tsing Hua University.

Haider, Hubert. 2000. Towards a superior account of superiority. In *Wh-Scope Marking*, ed. U. Lutz, G. Müller, and A. von Stechow, 231–248. Amsterdam; Philadelphia: John Benjamins.

Harada, Shin-Ichi. 1973. Counter equi NP deletion. *Annual Bulletin of the Research Institute of Logopedics and Phoniatrics* 7, 113–147.

Hiraiwa, Ken. 2001. Multiple agree and the defective intervention constraint in Japanese. In *MIT Working Papers in Linguistics* 40, 67–80, MITWPL.

Huang, C.-T. James. 1982. *Logical Relations in Chinese and the Theory of Grammar.* Doctoral dissertation, MIT.

Huang, C.-T. James. 1991. Modularity and Chinese A-not-A questions. In *Interdisciplinary approaches to language: Essays in honor of S.-Y. Kuroda,* ed. C. Georgopoulos and R. Ishihara, 305–332. Dordrecht: Kluwer Academic Publishers.

Huang, C.-T. James. 1994. Verb movement and some syntax-semantics mismatches. *Chinese Languages and Linguistics* 2, 587–613. Taipei: Academia Sinica.

Huang, C.-T. James, and Masao Ochi. 2004. Syntax of the hell: Two types of dependencies. In *Proceedings of NELS* 34, 279–294. Amherst, MA: GLSA Publications.

Huang, C.-T. James, Y.-H. Audrey Li, and Yafei Li. 2009. *The Syntax of Chinese.* Cambridge: Cambridge University Press.

Iida, Yasuhiro. 2011. On the adjunction-based licensing of the accusative *wh*-adjunct *nani-o.* In *The Proceedings of the Twelfth Tokyo Conference on Psycholinguistics,* ed. Y. Otsu, 93–112. Tokyo: Hitsuji Shobo.

Ko, Heejeong. 2005. Syntax of *why-in-situ:* Merge into [Spec, CP] in the overt syntax. *Natural Language and Linguistic Theory* 23, 867–916.

Kurafuji, Takeo. 1996. Unambiguous checking. In *MIT Working Papers in Linguistics 24: Formal Approaches to Japanese Linguistics* 2, 81–96, MITWPL.

Kurafuji, Takeo. 1997. Case checking of accusative *wh*-adjuncts. In *MIT Working Papers in Linguistics 31: Papers from the Eighth Student Conference in Linguistics,* 253–271, MITWPL.

Kuroda, S.-Y. 1992. *Japanese Syntax and Semantics.* Dordrecht: Kluwer Academic Publishers.

Lasnik, Howard, and Mamoru Saito. 1992. *Move α.* Cambridge, MA: MIT Press.

Lobeck, Anne. 1995. *Ellipsis: Functional Heads, Licensing, and Identification.* New York: Oxford University Press.

Nishigauchi, Taisuke. 1999. *Ronrikouzo to Bunpoo Riron: Nitieigo no Wh Genshyoo* [*Logical Structures and the Theory of Grammar: Wh Phenomena in English and Japanese*]. Tokyo: Kuroshio Publishers.

Nakao, Chizuru, and Miki Obata. 2009. When 'what' means 'why': On accusative *wh*-adjuncts in Japanese. In *University of Pennsylvania Working Papers in Linguistics* 15, 153–161.

Ochi, Masao. 1999. *Constraints on Feature Checking.* Doctoral dissertation, University of Connecticut.

Ochi, Masao. 2004. *How come* and other adjunct *wh*-phrases: A cross-linguistic perspective. *Language and Linguistics* 5(1), 29–57.

Pesetsky, David. 2000. *Phrasal Movement and Its Kin.* Cambridge, MA: MIT Press.

Reinhart, Tanya. 1998. *Wh*-in situ in the framework of the minimalist program. *Natural Language Semantics* 6, 29–56.

Rizzi, Luigi. 1990. *Relativized Minimality.* Cambridge, MA: MIT Press.

Rizzi, Luigi. 2001. On the position 'Int(errogative)' in the left periphery of the clause. In *Current Studies in Italian Syntax: Essays Offered to Lorenzo Renzi,* ed. Guglielmo Cinque and Giampaolo Salvi, 267–296. Amsterdam: Elsevier.

Shima, Etsuro. 2000. A preference for Move over Merge. *Linguistic Inquiry* 31, 375–385.

Shlonsky, Ur, and Gabriela Soare. 2011. Where's *'why'?. Linguistic Inquiry* 42, 651–669.

Stepanov, Arthur, and W.-T. Dylan Tsai. 2008. Cartography and licensing of *wh*-adjuncts: A cross-linguistic perspective. *Natural Language and Linguistic Theory* 26, 589–638.

Tsai, W.-T. Dylan. 1994. *On Economizing the Theory of A-bar Dependencies.* Doctoral dissertation, MIT.

Tsai, W.-T. Dylan. 2008. Left periphery and *how-why* alternations. *Journal of East Asian Linguistics* 17, 83–115.

Tsai, W.-T. Dylan. 2011. Bunpoo to goyoo-no intaafeisu kara mita tyuugokugo gimonshi-no hitenkeiteki yohoo [Non-typical usages of Chinese interrogatives from the perspective of the grammar-pragmatics interface]. In *The New Deployment of Theoretical Linguistics of Japanese and Chinese 1: Syntactic Structures*, ed. Taro Kageyama and Riki Shin, 127–147. Tokyo: Kuroshio Publishers.

Uriagereka, Juan. 1988. *On Government*. Doctoral dissertation, University of Connecticut.

Wiltschko, Martina. 1997. D-linking, scrambling and superiority in German. *Groninger Arbeiten zur germanistischen Linguistik* 41, 107–142.

Yatsushiro, Kazuko. 1997. VP-scrambling in Japanese. In *UConn Working Papers in Linguistics* 8, 325–338, MITWPL.

16

Cartographic Syntax of Pragmatic Projections

SZE-WING TANG

1. Pragmatic Projections: Evidence from Comparative Data

Austin (1962: 32) makes an interesting claim that the imperatives in English, such as (1), can be rephrased as sentences with an explicit performative, such as (2), and notes that "we should say cheerfully in either case, describing subsequently what someone did, that he ordered me to go."

(1) Go!

(2) I order you to go.

Based on Austin's (1962) speculation, Ross (1970: 224) proposes an abstract representation for declarative sentences and argues that declarative sentences, such as (3), are analyzed as implicit performatives and are derived from a deep structure that contains an explicit performative verb, as represented in the simplified structure in (4). Ross (1970: 262 note 13) points out that the highest verb in this structure dominates a bundle of syntactic features [+V, +performative, +communication, +linguistic, + declarative] which may appear in the lexical representation of such actually existing verbs as *assert, declare, say, state, tell*, and so on, in English. To derive sentences like (3) on the surface, Ross (1970: 249) proposes a rule of performative deletion, according to which the speaker *I*, the bundle of syntactic features under the performative verb, and the addressee *you* in (4) will be deleted. Although the pragmatic layer cannot be seen on the surface, it does exist as an underlying element.

(3) Prices slumped.

(4) $[_S [_{NP} I] [V [_{NP} you][_S prices slumped]]]$

The performative hypothesis can be supported by Arabic. In Arabic, there are three complementizers, namely *ʔan*, which is used after verbs denoting expectation, command, or request; *ʔinna*, which is used only after the verb *ʔaquulu* '(I) say'; and *ʔanna*, which is used after all other verbs. Given that (5) and (6) are synonymous and in free variation in Arabic, Ross (1970: 245) argues that the performative verb ²aquulu '(I) say' must be in the deep structure and is deleted by the rule of performative deletion, deriving (6) with the complementizer ²inna on the surface.

(5)   ²aquulu   ²inna lwalada   qad   taraka lbayta.
      I say (indic.) that the boy (acc.) (past) leave the house (acc.)
      'The boy left the house.'

(6)   ²inna lwalada   qad   taraka lbayta.
      that the boy (acc.) (past) leave the house (acc.)
      'The boy left the house.'

Data from Thai further support the performative hypothesis. Sentences in Thai end with either the particle *khráp* or the particle *kâ*, as shown in (7). The first particle signifies that the speaker of the sentence is a male; the second, that the speaker is a female. Ross (1970: 260) proposes that *khráp* and *kâ* are morphemes that agree in semantic gender with the superordinate *I*, which are placed at the right end of the sentence before the rule of performative deletion applies. If his analysis of the utterance particles *khráp* and *kâ* is correct, (7) should have an underlying structure similar to (4), in which there are a syntactic position for the speaker, with which the utterance particles agree, and a performative verb.

(7)   Khaw maa   khráp/kâ.
      he   come Part
      'He is coming.'

The insights of Ross's performative hypothesis (1970) have been revived in works under the cartographic approach (Rizzi 1997, 2004; Cinque 1999; among many others), particularly in recent work by Speas (2004), Tenny (2006), and Hill (2007), according to which a fine-grained syntactic structure of left periphery is proposed, based on typological studies of a number of languages, to capture the grammatical as well as pragmatic properties of speech act and evidentiality.

Speas (2004) points out that evidential features, which express the means by which the speaker acquired the information that he or she is conveying and reflect an evaluation of the source of evidence, interact closely with inflectional features that are syntactically projected in a number of languages. Following Culy's (1994) study of logophoricity and Cinque's (1999) cartographic analysis, Speas (2004) proposes the following hierarchical structure in syntax.

(8)   SAP > EvalP > EvidP > EpisP

According to Speas (2004), Speech Act Phrase (SAP) is associated with speech acts, as are the hearsay and speech-verb categories (e.g., *say*). Evaluative Phrase (EvalP) is associated with an assessment of the value of the event or situation, just as inferences from indirect evidence have to do with an assessment of data relating to the event or situation, and verbs of thought predicate (e.g., *think*). Evidential Phrase (EvidP) is parallel to the direct evidence category, and verbs of knowledge (e.g., *know*). Epistemological Phrase (EpisP) is associated with the speaker's degree of certainty, and personal experience and direct perception are the most reliable types of evidence (e.g., *perceive*).

Speas (2004) further proposes that each functional category is associated with an implicit argument that bears a pragmatic role, namely: Speaker, the utterer of the sentence (i.e., the subject of SAP); Evaluator, the one responsible for judgments of quality or value of the situation (i.e., the subject of EvalP); Witness, the one who has the evidence regarding the truth of the proposition (i.e., the subject of EvidP); and Perceiver, the one whose degree of experience with the event determines how likely the proposition is to be true (i.e., the subject of EpisP). These implicit arguments, as represented by *pro* in (9), are subject to binding, and there are four possible binding configurations. In (9a), Speaker is Evaluator, Witness, and Perceiver. In (9b), Speaker is Evaluator and Witness, but someone else is Perceiver. In (9c), Speaker is Evaluator, but someone else is Witness and Perceiver. In (9d), someone other than Speaker is Evaluator, Witness, and Perceiver.

(9) a. $[_{SAP}$ ***pro***$_i$ $[_{EvalP}$ ***pro***$_i$ $[_{EvidP}$ ***pro***$_i$ $[_{EpisP}$ ***pro***$_i$ ...   (personal experience)
     b. $[_{SAP}$ ***pro***$_i$ $[_{EvalP}$ ***pro***$_i$ $[_{EvidP}$ ***pro***$_i$ $[_{EpisP}$ *pro*$_j$ ...   (direct evidence)
     c. $[_{SAP}$ ***pro***$_i$ $[_{EvalP}$ ***pro***$_i$ $[_{EvidP}$ *pro*$_j$ $[_{EpisP}$ *pro*$_j$ ...   (indirect evidence)
     d. $[_{SAP}$ ***pro***$_i$ $[_{EvalP}$ *pro*$_j$ $[_{EvidP}$ *pro*$_j$ $[_{EpisP}$ *pro*$_j$ ...   (hearsay)

The proposed hierarchical structures in (9a–d) offer a formal analysis of pragmatic notions like evidentiality cross-linguistically and can be used to provide analyses of a range of patterns relating to evidentiality. Three examples of potential instantiations of (9) can be given from Tibetan, Maricopa, and Akha. First in Tibetan (Standard Tibetan), DeLancey (1986: 205) claims that the difference between *yod* and *'dug* is associated with evidentiality, particularly related to the "relative novelty or the degree to which it has been integrated into the speaker's overall scheme of knowledge of the world." In the minimal pair in (10) and (11) given by DeLancy (1986: 204–205), (10) could be used to describe what the speaker knows of the distribution of yaks in Tibet through daily experience (for example, a Tibetan), or by hearsay (for example, someone who has known the fact for years). Example (11), however, might be the response of someone who was fascinated with yaks but knew nothing of where they existed until visiting Tibet and encountering one. According to the hierarchical structures schematized in (9), I suggest that the speaker of sentences with *yod* is the evaluator, witness, and perceiver, while the perceiver of sentences with *'dug* is not the speaker. What *'dug* signals is the speaker's uncertainty. In other words, *yod* is the head of EpisP, as an instantiation of (9a), and *'dug* is the head of EvidP, as an instantiation of (9b).

(10) Bod la   gyag yod.
      Tibet LOC yak   exist
      'There are yaks in Tibet.'

(11) Bod la   gyag 'dug.
      Tibet LOC yak   exist
      'There are yaks in Tibet.' (without experience)

Second, in Maricopa, a Yuman language of the River branch spoken by the Native American Maricopa tribe (Gordon 1986), Speas (2004) argues that the –*k* morpheme is an evidential morpheme that marks the fact that Speaker, Evaluator, Witness, and Perceiver are the same person. Examples (12) and (13) are cited from Gordon (1986: 78, 87). In (12), -*k* indicates that "the speaker presents the information as fact, not as possibility, inference or preference, and with no hint as to its source or any doubt as to its veracity" (Gordon 1986: 78). On the other hand, the presence of –*k* in (13) entails that the speech act roles are assigned to a higher subject, that is, being linked to the speaker and evaluator of the proposition (and also possibly the witness and perceiver), although the subjects of *chuy* 'marry' and *uu'ish* 'they-say' are not the same (Speas 2004: 273). I suggest that –*k* is the head of EpisP and the sentences with –*k* are again instantiations of (9a).

(12) 'iipaa-ny-sh   puy-k
      Man-DEM-SJ die-ASP
      'The man died/The man is dead.'

(13) Bonnie-sh chuy-k uu'ish-k
      Bonnie-SJ marry-k say = PL-ASP
      'They say Bonnie got married.'

Third, in Akha, a language spoken in the Yunnan Province in southern China, there is a morpheme -*e* (nonpast -*é* and past -*è*) on the verb, which marks the first person subject in statements, as in (14), but the second person subject in questions, as in (15) (Thurgood 1986: 219–220). This morpheme is a nonexpected nonsenorial particle, which does not indicate the source of evidence for a statement and appears to have represented a "speculative" future (Thurgood 1986: 221). It has been argued that the morpheme -*e* marks the source of information or authority associated with the evaluator, that is, the speaker in a statement and the hearer in a question (Speas 2004). Given that the speaker of sentences with -*e* is the evaluator but someone else is the witness and the perceiver, I suggest that -*e* is the head of EvalP and examples (14) and (15) are instances of the pattern in (9c).

(14) ŋá nɔ̀-áŋ   dì-è
      I you-OBJ beat-è
      'I beat you.'

(15) nɔ̀ ŋà-áŋ dì-é-ló
      You I-OBJ beat = è = Q
      'Will you beat me?'

Evidentiality is central in some semantic and pragmatic studies, yet it has been largely ignored in syntactic approaches. Ross (1970) is a pioneering attempt to scrutinize the performatives at the periphery of sentences where the syntax--semantics interface is located. In recent works under the cartographic approach, the fine-grained syntactic structure of the periphery, such as the one in (8), seems to be reminiscent of the performative hypothesis in Ross (1970) and is supported by cross-linguistic data.

2. Evidentiality in Cantonese

We now turn to issues of evidentiality in Cantonese, focusing specifically on a set of morphemes in Cantonese that occur as utterance particles (or are known as sentence final particles). I will try to show how these utterance particles are related to evidentiality. We will see that the cartographic structuring of evidentiality proposed in (8) can further be supported by utterance particles in Cantonese.

There is an utterance particle *wo5* with the low rising tone in Cantonese,[1] as in (16), which is analyzed in the literature as a hearsay evidential particle that is used in reported speech (Cheung 1972; Kwok 1984; Leung 2005; Ding 2006; Matthews and Yip 2011). Example (16) shows that *wo5* is an implicit hearsay evidential. In (17), although the complement of the verb of saying *waa* 'say' seems to be the explicit quotation, it is also possible that *wo5* in this sentence may also implicitly introduce hearsay information, which means "Someone said that he said he will go."

(16)   Keoi wui heoi wo5.
       he   will go   WO
       'It is said that he will go.'

(17)   Keoi waa keoi wui heoi wo5.
       he   say he   will go   WO
       '(It is said) he said he will go.'

The particle *wo5* can be used in declaratives, as in (16), and imperatives, as in (18), and is incompatible with interrogatives, as in (19), and exclamatives, as in (20).

(18)   Mgoi nei heoi wo5.
       please you go   WO
       'It is said that you are requested to go.'

(19)   *Bingo wui heoi wo5?
        who   will go   WO
       '(*It is said) who will go?'

---

[1] The Romanization system for Cantonese used in this chapter is the Linguistic Society of Hong Kong Cantonese Romanization Scheme known as *Jyutping*. Tones are represented as follows: 1: high level, 2: high rising, 3: mid-level, 4: low falling, 5: low rising, and 6: low level, which will be marked when necessary.

(20) *Keoi gei lek   wo5.
       he   how clever WO
       '(*It is said) how clever he is!'

The scope of *wh*-words plays a role in sentences with *wo5*. The *wh*-word *bingo* 'who' in (21), which is in an embedded clause selected by the verb *soengzidou* 'wonder,' has narrow interpretive scope. Although *bingo* 'who' in (22) is also in an embedded clause, the embedded clause is the complement of *waa* 'say,' and the *wh*-word has wide interpretive scope (cf. Huang 1982), incompatible with *wo5*.

(21) Keoi soengzidou bingo wui heoi wo5.
       he   wonder   who will go   WO
       '(It is said) he wondered who will go.'

(22) *Keoi waa bingo wui heoi wo5?
       he   say who will go   WO
       '(*It is said) who did he say will go?'

The following examples show that *wo5* cannot occur in relative clauses, as in (23), and subordinate clauses, as in (24), exhibiting root/non-root distinction.

(23) *gin [keoi zungji sik wo5] ge   daangou
       Cl   he   like   eat WO Mod cake
       'the cake that (*it is said) he likes to eat'

(24) *[Jyugwo keoi wui heoi wo5], ngo zau m   gouhing.
       if   he   will go   WO I   then not happy
       'If (*it is said) he will go, I will not be happy.'

Adding the verb of saying to these contexts does not help.

(25) *gin [keoi waa keoi zungji sik wo5] ge   daangou
       Cl   he   say he   like   eat WO Mod cake
       'the cake that he said that he likes to eat'

(26) *[Jyugwo keoi waa keoi wui heoi wo5], ngo zau m   gouhing.
       If   he   say he   will go   WO I   then not happy
       'If he said that he will go, I will not be happy.'

Given the constraints on clause types and the root phenomena, it is highly likely that the evidential particle *wo5* should be in a very high peripheral position in the syntactic structure.

3. Cartographic Analysis of Evidentiality

It is noted in the literature that *wo5* is an evidential marker in Cantonese, expressing reported information without guarantee of its truth and accuracy (Leung 2005; Ding 2006). In sentences with *wo5*, the speaker may have heard someone's speech indirectly and may not express a reliable situation. For example, in (16), as repeated in (27), the speaker does not know whether the information that is reported is true, as the speaker does not have any direct evidence for it. In such a context, the speaker is not the evaluator, the witness, or the perceiver. Someone other than the speaker, normally the third person, should be the evaluator, the witness, and the perceiver.

(27)   Keoi wui heoi woS.
        he   will go WO
        'It is said that he will go.'

On the contrary, (28) may sound deviant because the speaker, the evaluator, the witness, and the perceiver are normally expected to be the same person. If (28) was originally uttered by someone other than the speaker, and what the speaker did is to report what he or she heard without guarantee of its truth, the judgment of (28) improves. In this context, the evaluator, the witness, and the perceiver should be someone else, not the speaker, similar to the situation in (27), and (28) becomes more natural.

(28)   (??)Ngo waa ngo wui heoi woS.
        I   say I   will go WO
        '(It is said) I said that I will go.'

If it is assumed that pragmatic projections in the C-domain are decomposed into SAP, EvalP, EvidP, and EpisP, along the lines in Speas (2004), (27) should be analyzed as an instance of (9d), as repeated in (29), in which the subjects of EvalP, EvidP, and EpisP are not bound by the speaker, that is, the subject of SAP. I suggest that *woS* is an overt realization of the head of head-final SAP and signals the "independent" characteristic of the subject of SAP, deriving the function of hearsay of *woS*.

(29) $[_{SAP}$ **pro**$_i$ $[_{EvalP}$ **pro**$_j$ $[_{EvidP}$ **pro**$_j$ $[_{EpisP}$ **pro**$_j$ ...

Matthews (1998) notices that some pre-verbal expressions, such as *tenggong* 'hear-say' in (30), can explicitly mark the hearsay source. I suggest that *tenggong* 'hear-say' and the evidential particle *woS* form a "discontinuous construction" syntactically, along the lines in Tang (2009),[2] located within the SAP domain, and that

---

[2] In Cantonese, some pre-verbal modifiers (such as adverbs) and post-verbal elements (such as affixes and particles) appear to be "redundant" not only semantically but also functionally, as they have a similar meaning and can jointly modify the predicate. It is claimed that they form a discontinuous unit in an underlying manner (Tang 2009). For example, the post-verbal element *gamzai* 'almost' in (i) is linked to the adverb *caa'mdo* 'almost,' forming a discontinuous construction. Syntactically, the post-verbal element is analyzed as the head of a functional projection, whereas its pre-verbal counterpart is normally regarded as an adjunct.

(i)   Ngo caa'mdo gong-jyun   gamzai.
       I   almost speak-finish almost
       'I almost finished talking.'

tenggong 'hear-say' occurs structurally in the position shown in (31).[3] The intervention of *tenggong* 'hear-say' in the configuration in (31) explicitly blocks the binding relation between the speaker, that is, the subject of SAP, and the rest of the implicit arguments.

(30) Tenggong keoi wui heoi wo5.
      hear-say he   will go   WO
      'It is said that he will come.'

(31) [$_{SAP}$ ***pro***$_i$ [*tenggong* [$_{EvalP}$ ***pro***$_j$ [$_{EvidP}$ ***pro***$_j$ [$_{EpisP}$ ***pro***$_j$ ...

It has been noted in the literature that there is another utterance particle *wo4* with the low falling tone, as in (32), that expresses unexpected and perhaps newly discovered information, which is regarded as a variant of *wo5* (Cheung 1972; Kwok 1984; Leung 2005).

(32) Keoi wui heoi wo4.
      he   will go   WO
      'Unexpectedly he will go.'

Unlike *wo5*, the speaker of sentences with *wo4* should have evidence regarding the truth of the proposition, though he or she may or may not be the perceiver, depending on the degree of experience that determines how likely the proposition is to be true. I suggest that *wo4* is an overt realization of the head of head-final EvidP in (9b), as repeated in (33), in which the subject of EpisP, that is, perceiver, is not necessarily bound by the higher subjects.

(33) [$_{SAP}$ ***pro***$_i$ [$_{EvalP}$ ***pro***$_i$ [$_{EvidP}$ ***pro***$_i$ [$_{EpisP}$ ***pro***$_j$ ...

The meaning of the unexpectedness of *wo4* can be contrasted with another utterance particle *lo1*, as in (34), which is analyzed in the literature as an obviousness particle that conveys what is taken to be evident fact to the speaker, something unquestionable that does not require explanation (Luke 1990; Lee and Law 2001; Leung 2005; Matthews and Yip 2011).

(34) Keoi wui heoi lo1.
      he   will go   LO
      'He (obviously/definitely) will go (needless to say).'

The obviousness particle *lo1* indicates the speaker's degree of certainty. I suggest that *lo1* is the head of head-final EpisP, which requires that the subject of

---

[3] In (30), the head of SAP is overtly realized as *wo5* and is head-final. Assuming that the *pro* subject that refers to the speaker is the specifier of SAP, I claim that *tenggong* 'hear-say' is adjoined to SA.'

EpisP (in the specifier of EpisP) be bound by the witness (and consequently by the evaluator and the speaker), having the structure in (9b), as repeated in (35).

(35) $[_{SAP}\ \textbf{\textit{pro}}_i\ [_{EvalP}\ \textbf{\textit{pro}}_i\ [_{EvidP}\ \textbf{\textit{pro}}_i\ [_{EpisP}\ \textbf{\textit{pro}}_i\ \ldots$

The contrast between the unexpectedness particle *wo4* in (32) and the obviousness particle *lol* in (34) is reminiscent of the minimal pair of Tibetan *yod* and *'dug*. As pointed out by DeLancy (1986: 212) in another couple of examples, in (36) the cat is presumed to be the speaker's or one that for some reason the speaker expects to find in his or her house, while in (37) the speaker has no reason to expect there to be a cat in his or her house and unexpectedly finds a strange cat wandering about.

(36)   ŋa'i   k'aŋ   la   si-mi yod.
         I-GEN house LOC cat   exist
         'There's a cat in my house.'

(37)   ŋa'i   k'aŋ   la   si-mi 'dug.
         I-GEN house LOC cat   exist
         'There's a cat in my house (unexpectedly).'

Interestingly, these two Tibetan examples could be translated into Cantonese by using *lol* and *wo4* to convey the obviousness and unexpectedness, respectively.

(38)   Ukkei jau   zek maau lol.
         home have Cl cat   LO
         'There's a cat in my house.'

(39)   Ukkei jau   zek maau wo4.
         home have Cl cat   WO
         'There's a cat in my house (unexpectedly).'

If our discussion is on the right track, it can be suggested that the major difference between *wo5* and *wo4* can be captured by means of the hierarchical configuration proposed in Speas (2004) given in (8): "SAP > EvalP > EvidP > EpisP." It can be suggested that *wo5* is the head of SAP, whereas *wo4* is the head of EvidP, responsible for different roles of evidentiality. The obviousness particle *lol* is the head of EpisP, similar to *yod* in Tibetan.

4. Grammaticalization

Diachronic evidence suggests that the evidential particle *wo5* (and its variants) in Cantonese underwent grammaticalization from the verb of saying *waa6* 'say' (or *huà* 'say, words' in Mandarin).

Chao (1947: 121, note 22) speculates that *wo5* was derived from the Cantonese verb *waa* 'say' plus an utterance particle *o* by segment reduction and syllable fusion, deriving the meaning of "so he says, so they say, as the saying goes." The particle *o* is said to indicate "noteworthiness" (Sybesma and Li 2007: 1764). Evidential *waa* was attested in the nineteenth century. Leung (2006: 66) cites the following example with the utterance particle *waa1* with the high-level tone in early Cantonese from Ball (1888) and argues that *waa1* had a similar function as the evidential particle *wo5* in contemporary Cantonese. Diachronic evidence suggests that *wo5* may have emerged as a result of grammaticalization of the verb of saying *waa6* 'say' plus the meaning of noteworthiness contributed by *o*.

(40)   Keoi daa ngo waa1.
       he   beat I   WAA
       'He said he would strike me.'

Interestingly, while the verb of saying *waa6* 'say' has developed into the evidential particle *waa1* in the nineteenth century and *wo5* in contemporary Cantonese, it also developed a second use as an interrogative particle *waa2* involving tone change from the low level tone to the high rising tone, which is used to mark echo questions in Cantonese (Tang 1998: 62), as illustrated in (41).

(41)   Nei sik-zo   matje waa2?
       you eat-Perf what Q
       'You ate WHAT?'

The major difference between the evidential particle *wo5* and the interrogative particle *waa2* is the identity of the evaluator, which is the third person in sentences with *wo5* and the hearer in echo questions with *waa2*. I suggest that both *wo5* and *waa2* are overt instantiations of the head of SAP, having the same structure in (29),[4] and that these two particles are in complementary distribution, as evidenced by the different clause types they are compatible with, for example, the ungrammatical interrogative with *wo5* in (19) and the ungrammatical declarative with *waa2* in (42).

(42)   *Keoi wui heoi waa2.
        he   will go   Q
        'It is said that he will come.'

In our previous discussion of (30), I argued that *tenggong* 'hear-say' is located in the SAP domain and forms a discontinuous construction with *wo5*, the head of SAP. Notice that in (43) *tenggong* 'hear-say' can co-occur with *waa2*. If *tenggong* 'hear-say' and *waa2* also form a discontinuous construction, both of them should be in the SAP domain and *waa2* should be analyzed as an evidential particle, that is, the head of SAP, in a parallel fashion.

[4] To determine the identity of the implicit subject of EvalP, one possibility is to assume that the head of SAP may trigger an operator that binds the subject of EvalP. Another possibility is to assume with Tenny (2006) that switching a declarative to an interrogative involves a simple flip of the role with respect to the discourse participants by a kind of "passivization" from (i) to (ii), on a par with dative shift in the Larsonian shell.

(i)   [speaker [utterance [**addressee**]]]   (declarative)
(ii) [speaker [**addressee** [utterance]]]   (interrogative)

(43)   Tenggong bingo wui heoi waa2?
       hear-say   who   will   go   Q
       'It is said that WHO will come?'

   To sum up this section, a cartographic analysis of pragmatic projections allows us to have a better understanding of the *waa/wo* family in Cantonese. Their properties of evidentiality can be systematically captured under the hierarchy proposed in (8), that is, *wo5* (hearsay) and *waa2* (interrogative) in the SAP domain associated with the speaker and *wo4* (unexpectedness) in the EvidP domain that blocks the binding relation between the witness and the perceiver. Sentence initial expressions like *tenggong* 'hear-say' may form a discontinuous construction with *wo5* and *waa2* and can be suggested to be in the highest SAP domain of the clause.

5. Concluding Remarks

In his seminal work on performatives, Ross (1970) argued for the existence of an additional pragmatic layer in the syntactic structure by making use of cross-linguistic data, such as evidence from the complementizers in Arabic and utterance particles in Thai, that is, morphemes in the periphery of the clause. Insights of the performative hypothesis have recently been revived under the cartographic approach. In this chapter, I have examined the grammatical properties of the utterance particles *wo5*, *wo4*, *waa2*, and *lo1* in Cantonese and have shown that their similarities and variations with respect to evidentiality can be systematically captured by the syntactic hierarchy in (8) proposed by Speas (2004). Considering the facts from Cantonese and other languages, namely Akha, Maricopa, and Tibetan, and their relation with various syntactic categories, the phenomena we have examined are summarized in the table in (44), presenting a complete picture of the discussion.

(44)   Typology of the hierarchy of pragmatic projections

	Languages	Examples
SAP (speech act)	Cantonese *wo5* (hearsay)	(16), (17)
	Cantonese *waa2* (interrogative)	(41)
EvalP (evaluative)	Akha *-e*	(14), (15)
EvidP (evidential)	Tibetan *'dug*	(11), (37)
	Cantonese *wo4* (unexpectedness)	(32)
EpisP (epistemological)	Tibetan *yod*	(10), (36)
	Maricopa *-k*	(12), (13)
	Cantonese *lo1* (obviousness)	(34)

   By considering evidential morphemes to involve the relation of the witness to the speaker and other pragmatic roles (cf. indexing of *pro* in (9)), Speas (2004: 266) conjectures that consistent indexing, that is, all the four empty subjects referring to the same person (speaker), is the unmarked case, and each indexing disjoint from speaker would be regarded as marked.[5] If her conjecture is correct, *yod* in Tibetan, *-k* in Maricopa, and *lo1* in Cantonese can be considered to be instances of unmarked cases, while *wo5* and *waa2* in Cantonese would be marked. This is then a conclusion that could be investigated further. Quite generally, it can be said that the hypothesis of markedness of evidentiality opens up a new way to study evidential morphemes in a formal approach as well as in a typological approach. Needless to say, a comprehensive study of evidentiality along these lines is beyond the scope of this chapter and I will leave it for my future research, awaiting further consequences.

Acknowledgments

I would like to dedicate this chapter to my beloved supervisor and mentor Prof. Jim Huang to express my deep gratitude for all the years of guidance and support. Earlier versions of this paper were presented at Moving Forward— International Symposium on Chinese Linguistics and Philology (The Chinese University of Hong Kong, December 2012), Seminar of the Department of Chinese Language Studies (Hong Kong Institute of Education, January 2013), and the Eighth International Workshop on Theoretical East Asian Linguistics (National Tsing Hua University, June 2013). I would like to collectively thank the participants at those presentations for helpful comments and questions. I am particularly indebted to Audrey Li, Andrew Simpson, and Dylan Tsai for their friendly encouragement, endless patience, and detailed comments through the revising process. Needless to say, all errors remain my own. This work has been supported in part by funding from the project "On the Discontinuous Constructions in Cantonese," funded by the General Research Fund (GRF), Research Grants Council, Hong Kong Special Administrative Region (CUHK 5493/10H), to which I am grateful. The following abbreviations are used in giving glosses for Cantonese examples: Cl: classifier, Mod: modifier marker, Perf: perfective aspect marker, and Q: question particle.

References

Austin, J. L. 1962. *How to Do Things with Words*. Oxford: Oxford University Press.
Ball, J. D. 1888. *Cantonese Made Easy* (2nd ed.). Hong Kong: The China Mail Office.
Chao, Yuen Ren. 1947. *Cantonese Primer*. New York: Greenwood Press.
Cheung, Samuel Hung-nin. 1972. *Xianggang Yueyu Yufa de Yanjiu* [Cantonese as Spoken in Hong Kong]. Hong Kong: The Chinese University of Hong Kong.
Cinque, Guglielmo. 1999. *Adverbs and Functional Heads*. New York and Oxford: Oxford University Press.
Culy, Christopher. 1994. Aspects of logophoric marking. *Linguistics* 32, 1055–1094.
DeLancey, Scott. 1986. Evidentiality and volitionality in Tibetan. In *Evidentiality: The Linguistic Encoding of Epistemology*, ed. Wallace L. Chafe, and Johanna Nichols, 203–213. Norwood, NJ: Ablex Publishing.

---

[5] Using Speas's (2004) own words, each indexing disjoint from the speaker would have an "additional cost."

Ding, Picus Sizhi. 2006. Yueyu de "juyou" zhuci chutan [a preliminary study on evidential markers of Cantonese]. *Journal of Macao Polytechnic Institute* 4, 105–113.

Gordon, Lynn. 1986. The development of evidentials in Maricopa. In *Evidentiality: The Linguistic Encoding of Epistemology*, ed. Wallace L. Chafe and Johanna Nichols, 75–88. Norwood, NJ: Ablex Publishing.

Hill, Virginia. 2007. Vocatives and the pragmatics: Syntax interface. *Lingua* 117, 2077–2105.

Huang, C.-T. James. 1982. Logical relations in Chinese and the theory of grammar. Doctoral dissertation, MIT.

Jacobsen, William H. 1986. The heterogeneity of evidentials in Makah. In *Evidentiality: The Linguistic Encoding of Epistemology*, ed. Wallace L. Chafe and Johanna Nichols, 3–28. Norwood, NJ: Ablex Publishing.

Kwok, Helen. 1984. *Sentence Particles in Cantonese*. Hong Kong: Centre of Asian Studies, The University of Hong Kong.

Lee, Thomas Hun-tak, and Ann Law. 2000. Evidential final particles in child Cantonese. In *The Proceedings of the Thirtieth Annual Child Language Research Forum*, ed. E. V. Clark, 131–138. Stanford: Center for the Study of Language and Information.

Leung, Chung-sum. 2005. *Dangdai Xianggang Yueyu Yuzhuci de Yanjiu* [A Study of the Utterance Particle in Cantonese as Spoken in Hong Kong]. Hong Kong: Language Information Sciences Research Centre, City University of Hong Kong.

Leung, Wai-mun. 2006. On the synchrony and diachrony of sentence-final particles. Doctoral dissertation, The University of Hong Kong.

Luke, Kang Kwong. 1990. *Utterance Particles in Cantonese Conversation*. Amsterdam: John Benjamins.

Matthews, Stephen. 1998. Evidentiality and mirativity in Cantonese: wo3, wo4, wo5! Paper presented at the Sixth International Symposium on Chinese Languages and Linguistics, Academia Sinica.

Matthews, Stephen, and Virginia Yip. 2011. *Cantonese: A Comprehensive Grammar* (2nd ed.). London and New York: Routledge.

Rizzi, Luigi. 1997. The fine structure of the left periphery. In *Elements of Grammar*, ed. Liliane Haegeman, 281–337. Dordrecht: Kluwer Academic Publishers.

Rizzi, Luigi. 2004. Locality and the left periphery. In *Structures and Beyond: The Cartography of Syntactic Structures*, ed. Adriana Belletti, Vol. 3, 223–251. New York and Oxford: Oxford University Press.

Ross, John Robert. 1970. On declarative sentences. In *Readings in English Transformational Grammar*, ed. Roderick A. Jacobs and Peter S. Rosenbaum, 222–272. Waltham, MA: Ginn and Company.

Speas, Margaret. 2004. Evidentiality, logophoricity and the syntactic representation of pragmatic features. *Lingua* 114, 255–276.

Sybesma, Rint, and Boya Li. 2007. The dissection and structural mapping of Cantonese sentence final particles. *Lingua* 117, 1739–1783.

Tang, Sze-Wing. 1998. Parametrization of features in syntax. Doctoral dissertation, University of California, Irvine.

Tang, Sze-Wing. 2009. The syntax of two approximatives in Cantonese: Discontinuous constructions formed with zai6. *Journal of Chinese Linguistics* 37(2), 227–256.

Tenny, Carol L. 2006. Evidentiality, experiencers, and the syntax of sentience in Japanese. *Journal of East Asian Linguistics* 15, 245–288.

Thurgood, Graham. 1986. The nature and origins of the Akha evidential system. In *Evidentiality: The Linguistic Encoding of Epistemology*, ed. Wallace L. Chafe and Johanna Nichols, 214–222. Norwood, NJ: Ablex Publishing.

Index

Note: Letter 'n' followed by the locators refer to notes.

CPSIA information can be obtained at www.ICGtesting.com
Printed in the USA
BVOW05s1131101014

370290BV00002B/4/P